P9-CKN-223

ACADEMIC ADVISING

ACADEMIC ADVISING

A Comprehensive Handbook

Second Edition

Virginia N. Gordon, Wesley R. Habley,
Thomas J. Grites, and Associates

JOSSEY-BASS
A Wiley Imprint
www.josseybass.com

Copyright © 2008 by John Wiley & Sons, Inc. All rights reserved.

Published by Jossey-Bass
A Wiley Imprint
989 Market Street, San Francisco, CA 94103-1741—www.josseybass.com

No part of this publication may be reproduced, stored in a retrieval system, or
transmitted in any form or by any means, electronic, mechanical, photocopying,
recording, scanning, or otherwise, except as permitted under Section 107 or 108 of
the 1976 United States Copyright Act, without either the prior written permission
of the publisher, or authorization through payment of the appropriate per-copy fee
to the Copyright Clearance Center, Inc., 222 Rosewood Drive, Danvers, MA 01923,
978-750-8400, fax 978-646-8600, or on the Web at www.copyright.com. Requests to
the publisher for permission should be addressed to the Permissions Department,
John Wiley & Sons, Inc., 111 River Street, Hoboken, NJ 07030, 201-748-6011,
fax 201-748-6008, or online at www.wiley.com/go/permissions.
Readers should be aware that Internet Web sites offered as citations and/or sources
for further information may have changed or disappeared between the time this
was written and when it is read.

Limit of Liability/Disclaimer of Warranty: While the publisher and author have
used their best efforts in preparing this book, they make no representations or
warranties with respect to the accuracy or completeness of the contents of this book
and specifically disclaim any implied warranties of merchantability or fitness for a
particular purpose. No warranty may be created or extended by sales representatives
or written sales materials. The advice and strategies contained herein may not be
suitable for your situation. You should consult with a professional where appropriate.
Neither the publisher nor author shall be liable for any loss of profit or any other
commercial damages, including but not limited to special, incidental, consequential,
or other damages.

Jossey-Bass books and products are available through most bookstores. To
contact Jossey-Bass directly call our Customer Care Department within the U.S.
at 800-956-7739, outside the U.S. at 317-572-3986, or fax 317-572-4002.
Jossey-Bass also publishes its books in a variety of electronic formats. Some content
that appears in print may not be available in electronic books.

Library of Congress Cataloging-in-Publication Data

Academic advising : a comprehensive handbook / Virginia N. Gordon, Wesley R.
Habley, Thomas J. Grites, and associates.—2nd ed.
  p. cm.
Includes index.
ISBN 978-0-470-37170-1 (alk. paper)
  1. Counseling in higher education—United States—Handbooks, manuals, etc.
2. Faculty advisors—United States—Handbooks, manuals, etc. I. Gordon, Virginia
N. II. Habley, Wesley R. III. Grites, Thomas J. (Thomas Joseph), (date–)
LB2343.A29 2008
378.1'94—dc22
                                                        2008026275

Printed in the United States of America
SECOND EDITION
HB Printing   10 9 8 7 6 5 4 3 2 1

CONTENTS

First, we dedicate this book to all the academic advisors who have committed their professional lives to students and have contributed more than they know to the realization of innumerable goals and dreams. In addition, we recognize individuals too numerous to mention who, for more than three decades, have advanced the field of academic advising through research, publications, presentations, and untiring advocacy and affirmation.

VNG/WRH/TJG—2/15/08

PREFACE

The students who are matriculating in our colleges and universities today are the last of the thirteenth generation of Americans (born 1977 to 1997) to attend college since the first students entered the colonial colleges when the nation was born. Yale, Brown, and other early colleges were cognizant of their students' academic and personal concerns, and academic advising became the natural process for attending to those individual students' needs. Since then, academic advising has continued to play an important role in the lives of students. True, it has experienced many cycles of reemphasis and renewal, and the advising process itself has been defined and redefined in many forms, but its acceptance as an integral part of higher education has never been stronger than it is today.

As the size of institutions increased over the years to accommodate growing numbers of students and as curricula proliferated and became more complex, advising took on new and sometimes expanded responsibilities. Community colleges have played a predominant role in advising's latest rebirth because they are the portal of entry for many new students, such as older adults, minority students, part-time students, and those with limited financial resources.

In the late 1960s and 1970s, students were demanding more personalized attention in their academic planning. It is no accident that this was when Crookston's (1972) and O'Banion's (1972) models for a more humane and developmental approach to advising students appeared. Later, many institutions began to realize the importance of advising in the retention of students, especially during their initial enrollment. This brought about a major examination of how advising was delivered on some campuses, and as a result, reorganization took place at many institutions. The advising center was introduced on some campuses as a vehicle for offering a more visible and centralized location that students could use in place of or in addition to their regular faculty advising system.

The advent of technology has had a profound effect on how advisors interact with students and how administrative advising tasks function. Many advisors believe that technology will continue to revolutionize advising, teaching, and learning. Rather than depersonalize contact between advisor and student, it is hoped that technology will encourage more meaningful and frequent contact.

In this new, exciting milieu, it seems appropriate to once again update and document the current status of academic advising in a detailed way. The need to learn from its past and project its role into the future has never been stronger. The second edition of *Academic Advising: A Comprehensive Handbook* has been updated to accomplish just that. As in the first edition, this volume is intended to be a handy reference for professional advisors—those who spend their day working with students who have a variety of academic, vocational, and personal needs. Faculty advisors will find much helpful information about students, resources, and advising techniques in these pages. Administrators can review the many approaches to advising that are described and perhaps find new ways of thinking about how their delivery system might become more student-responsive. The many elements of the advising process described in this book can open new vistas for everyone involved in the advising enterprise.

It is obvious that academic advising is not an isolated function but an integral part of the mission of higher education. This book will help those involved in advising either directly or indirectly and at every level not only to appreciate the importance for good advising in students' lives but also to understand how it can contribute to the purpose of higher education. This handbook contains five sections representing important facets of academic advising, and the chapters in each part are authored by experts who are well equipped to share their expertise. The sixth section contains descriptions of current advising programs that demonstrate how some of the ideas and concepts presented by the authors can be put into advising practice.

The authors would like to acknowledge the assistance of Marsha Miller, Assistant Director, Resources and Services, NACADA's publications liaison, for her outstanding work in coordinating the various collection stages of the manuscript. We would also like to thank the many NACADA members who acted as Section reviewers. Their suggestions have greatly improved the quality of the book's content.

Virginia N. Gordon
The Ohio State University

Wesley R. Habley
ACT, Inc.

Thomas J. Grites
Richard Stockton College, New Jersey
August 2008

FOREWORD

As Executive Director of the National Academic Advising Association (NACADA), let me be the first to congratulate you on your very wise decision to pick up this book. Short of saying it will change your life, I can honestly say it has the potential to change your professional practice and dramatically change the lives of the students on your campus. The editors and authors have truly created the pivotal resource for academic advising and student success in higher education.

As you read this Second Edition of the *Academic Advising: A Comprehensive Handbook,* you will find a foundation of theory and research that grounds what you do on a daily basis with your students. The strategies and practices you learn from this book will help you to have a more positive impact on the success of your students.

NACADA is pleased to publish this text in partnership with Jossey-Bass. Just as NACADA's Concept of Academic Advising defines academic advising as "integral to fulfilling the teaching and learning mission of higher education," NACADA is integral to higher education's goal of providing the highest-quality academic advising and student success initiatives. NACADA, with nearly 11,000 members internationally, is the leader within the global education community for the theory, delivery, application, and advancement of academic advising that enhances student learning and development. For thirty years, NACADA has been recognized for providing quality programming, publications, and networking opportunities that support the work of professional advisors, faculty, administrators, and graduate students who create the academic advising experiences that support student learning and success.

As you read, you will derive the most from this text by using the following questions as your guide:

- What are the key concepts that will make me a better advisor?
- What are the key concepts that will enhance the academic advising experiences of my students?
- How can I use the strategies I have learned to impact our advising program?
- What have I learned that I can use in working with my colleagues and administrators on my campus to affect change in our advising program?
- What have I learned that triggers my own thoughts for research and publication within the field?

The answers to these questions will ensure that this text will become for you what was intended by the editors and authors—a living and working resource that you will repeatedly use to change your professional life and your students' lives for many years to come!

Charlie L. Nutt
Executive Director
National Academic Advising Association

THE AUTHORS

Susan Ames is director of first-year and transition programs at Le Moyne College and is a member of the College's Academic Advisement Center, whose staff works closely with faculty and student affairs to assist new students in their transition to Le Moyne and also coordinates activities related to undergraduate academic advising, study abroad, academic support and tutoring, and disabilities support. Previously, as Le Moyne's coordinator of academic initiatives, Ames was responsible for working with both academic affairs and student affairs in planning and implementing the College's residential learning communities. Ames holds an M.S. in higher education administration from Syracuse University and a B.A. in English and magazine journalism from SU's S. I. Newhouse School of Public Communications.

Drew C. Appleby received his B.A. in psychology from Simpson College in 1969 and his M.S. (1971) and Ph.D. (1972) in experimental psychology from Iowa State University. After teaching at Marian College for twenty-seven years—and chairing its Psychology Department for the last twenty-one of those years—he assumed the position of Director of Undergraduate Studies in the Indiana University-Purdue University Indianapolis (IUPUI) Psychology Department in 1999, where he is a tenured full professor in charge of advising, assessment, enrollment management, and community-building. He is the author of *The Savvy Psychology Major,* has over eighty professional publications, and has made over 400 presentations to a wide variety of professional and nonprofessional audiences. He was elected to Fellow status of Division Two of the American Psychological Association (The Society for the Teaching of Psychology [STP]) in 1992 and to Division One (The Society for General Psychology) in 2002. Appleby received STP's Outstanding Psychology Teacher Award in a Four-Year College or University in 1993, Marian College's Award for Teaching Excellence in 1993, IUPUI's Chancellor's Award for Excellence in Teaching in 2003, and the IUPUI School of Science Teacher of the Year Award in 2007. He was also chosen by the American Psychological Association (APA) to present its G. Stanley Hall Teaching Lecture in 1998 and by Psi Chi (the national honor society in psychology) to present its Distinguished Lecture during the 2008 APA convention. Appleby was recognized for his advising skills by NACADA when he received the Outstanding Advisor Award of its Great Lakes Region in 1988, by the IUPUI School of Science when he received their Advisor of the Year Award in 2002, and by the IUPUI Psychology Department when he received their Advisor of the Year Award in 2002, 2003, and 2006. He was recognized for his mentoring skills by being the charter recipient of Marian's Mentor of the Year Award in 1996, IUPUI's Psychology Department's Mentor of the Year in 2000, and IUPUI's Alvin Bynum Mentor of the Year award in 2007. He created STP's Project Syllabus, directs STP's Mentoring Service, and has served as a consultant to other psychology departments.

Jennifer L. Bloom is a Clinical Associate Professor and Director of the master's degree program in the Higher Education and Student Affairs Program housed in the Department of Educational Leadership and Policies at the University of South Carolina. Prior to her appointment at the University of South Carolina in August 2007, she served as the Associate Dean for Student Affairs and the Medical Scholars Program at the University of Illinois College of Medicine at Urbana-Champaign. She earned her doctorate in Higher Education Administration from the University of Illinois at Urbana-Champaign in 1995.

Dr. Bloom was elected President of the National Academic Advising Association (NACADA) for the 2007–2008 term. She serves on the Board of Directors of NACADA (2005–2008) and previously chaired the Advising Graduate and Professional Students Commission and the Member Career Services Committee. She received the NACADA Outstanding Advising Administrator Award in 2005 and the University of Illinois' Campus Academic Professional Excellence Award in 2007. Her research interests include appreciative advising, academic advising in general, career paths in higher education administration, leadership, and change management.

Thomas Brown served as an academic and student affairs educator for twenty-seven years, most recently as the Dean of Advising Services/Special Programs at Saint Mary's College of California. Tom developed and administered Saint Mary's nationally recognized faculty-based academic advising program. He was also responsible for new student and family orientation programs, Academic Support and Achievement (e.g., tutoring, services for students with disabilities), pre-law advising, and the Offices of Asian Pacific American, Black, Latino, and International Student Programs. Brown developed the College's High Potential Program, which provides access and support to first-generation students from historically underrepresented backgrounds. When he left Saint Mary's in 1998, the students and faculty instituted the *Dean Thomas Brown Award,* which is presented annually to an outstanding academic advisor.

Brown has held numerous leadership positions in the National Academic Advising Association (NACADA) and served as Chair of the Pre-law Advisors National Council. For twenty years, he facilitated the plenary session on Advisor Development at the annual NACADA Summer Institutes on Academic Advising. He has earned awards and recognition for his leadership and service in the US and abroad.

Brown is Managing Principal of Thomas Brown & Associates, a consulting group that has served more than 300 colleges and universities related to assessment, program design and implementation, and faculty and staff development. He has published and presented extensively on academic advising, student retention, and promoting the achievement and success of multicultural and at-risk students.

James E. Bultman became the eleventh president of Hope College on July, 1, 1999. Dr. Bultman was previously president of Northwestern College in Orange City, Iowa, where he served with distinction from 1985 to 1999. Prior to assuming the presidency at Northwestern, Dr. Bultman was a faculty member at Hope College, chaired the department of education from 1976 to 1982, and was dean for the social sciences from 1982 to 1985. He was also Hope's baseball coach from 1971 to 1985 and an assistant football coach from 1970 to 1984.

Dr. Bultman received his A.B. degree in chemistry from Hope College in 1963 and the M.A. and Ed.D. degrees in education from Western Michigan University in 1966 and 1971, respectively. He holds an honorary degree from Keiwa College, Shibata City, Japan (L.H.D.), and an honorary degree from Hope College (Litt.D.). In October 2001, he was awarded the "Distinguished Alumni Award" from Western Michigan University. A similar award was presented to Dr. Bultman from Hope College in 1995.

Dr. Bultman has been an active leader in higher education circles. He served as chair of the board of directors of the Council for Christian Colleges and Universities, was a member of the Council of Presidents of the National Association of Intercollegiate Athletics (NAIA), and was chair of the Iowa College Foundation, the Iowa Association of Independent Colleges and Universities, and the Commission on Campus Concerns for the National Association of Independent Colleges and Universities. Present memberships include the Michigan Colleges Foundation (MCF) Board Chair; Great Lakes Colleges Association (GLCA) Board Vice Chair; Association of Independent Colleges and Universities of Michigan (AICUM) Board Chair; Michigan Intercollegiate Athletic Association (MIAA) Board of Control; National Collegiate Athletic Association (NCAA), where he serves on the President's Advisory Council; National Association of Independent Colleges and Universities (NAICU), where he serves on the Board of Directors and is Chair of the Student Financial Aid Committee; Annapolis Group; Holland

Area Chamber of Commerce Board of Directors; Economic Club of Grand Rapids Board of Directors; Van Andel Institute Board of Governors; and the Holland Rotary Club. He also serves on the Board of Directors for The Bank of Holland.

Susan M. Campbell earned her undergraduate degree in speech and theatre from Ball State University, her M.S. in adult education from the University of Southern Maine, and her Ed.D. in higher education administration from the University of Massachusetts at Amherst. Since arriving at the University of Southern Maine in 1977, Dr. Campbell has held a number of administrative positions in student and academic affairs. She became the Director of Advising Services in 1993 and was promoted in 2001 to Executive Director of the Division of Advising and Academic Resources and in 2005 to Associate Vice-President for Academic Affairs. Dr. Campbell holds an adjunct appointment as associate professor in USM's College of Education and Human Development and coordinates the student affairs concentration in the Masters in Adult Education program.

Dr. Campbell served as the 2006–2007 President of NACADA and has worked on committees at both the national and regional level. She is the recipient of the 2004 Service to NACADA Award and the 2005 Virginia N. Gordon Award for Excellence in Academic Advising. Dr. Campbell's publications include coauthoring the NACADA *Guide to Assessment in Academic Advising* (2005), coediting the 2005 NACADA Monograph, *Peer Advising: Intentional Connections to Support Student Learning,* and being a contributing author to *The Distance Learner's Guide* (1999 and 2004) published by Prentice-Hall. Dr. Campbell also participated in the 2005 American Association of State Colleges and Universities (AASCU) Graduation Rate Outcomes Study and served on the Engagement Task Force for the Voluntary System of Accountability Project sponsored by AASCU and the National Association of State Universities and Land-Grant Colleges (NASULGC).

Philip D. Christman has been at Malone University in Canton, Ohio, since 1985 and currently serves as a consultant in advising and testing. Prior to that, he was the Director of Advising and Testing (1990–2007) and Director of Admissions (1985–1990). During his twenty-eight years in higher education, he has worked in admissions, financial aid, records, and athletics, and has also been an adjunct faculty member. Some of his publications and research interests include *Narrative Advising,* the role of family in college persistence leading to graduation, Q Methodology, and Appreciative Advising. He earned is B.A. (1976) in psychology from Bloomsburg State University, and his M.Ed. (1997) and Ph.D. (2004) in community counseling from Kent State University in Ohio.

Evette Castillo Clark is the Executive Administrator for Initiatives and Divisional Planning at Tulane University. Her role entails strategic planning, new initiatives, assessment and research, and staff development for the Division of Student Affairs. She is adjunct faculty at Tulane University and teaches graduate students in the College of Education and Human Development at the University of New Orleans. She was formerly the Assistant Dean of Students at San Diego State University and adjunct faculty in the College of Education. Dr. Clark is a past National Co-Chair of the Asian and Pacific Islander Knowledge Community of the National Association of Student Personnel Administrators (NASPA) and Board Member of the National Academic Advising Association (NACADA). Dr. Clark received her B.A. in sociology from the University of California, Irvine; her M.A. in student personnel administration in higher education from New York University; and completed her D.Ed. in the area of international and multicultural education at the University of San Francisco. Her areas of research concern college students of color, creating a pipeline of undergraduate students to careers in student affairs, and leadership in higher education.

Joe Cuseo holds a doctoral degree in educational psychology and assessment from the University of Iowa. Currently, he is a Professor of Psychology at Marymount College (California), where for twenty-five years he has directed the first-year seminar, a course required of all new students. He has been a member of the Advisory Board for the National Resource Center for The First-Year Experience & Students in Transition, and has received the Center's "outstanding first-year advocate award." He is also a thirteen-time recipient of the "faculty member of the year award" on his home campus, a student-driven award based on effective teaching and academic advising. Joe has authored articles on the relationship between academic advisement and student retention, and on advising strategies for students who are undecided and "in transition" between majors, and has delivered conference presentations and keynote addresses on the power of advising for promoting student success. He has also authored numerous articles on the first-year experience, a textbook for first-year seminar, titled, *Thriving in College and Beyond: Research-Based Strategies for Academic Success & Personal Development,* and is currently completing a monograph on the first-year seminar, titled, *The First-Year Seminar: Research-Based Guidelines for Course Design, Delivery, & Assessment.*

Kathy Davis has been Director of the Academic Advisement Center at Missouri State University since 1993. Earlier in her career, she worked in residence life at Stephens College and directed new student orientation at Wichita State University. She was a member of the Board of Directors of the National Orientation Directors Association for five years, edited *The Orientation Review,* and hosted the National Orientation Directors Association national conference in 1992. She wrote a chapter for the 2003 National Academic Advising Association (NACADA) monograph: *Advisor Training: Exemplary Practices in the Development of Advisor Skills.* Davis was Commission Chair for the NACADA Advisor Training and Development Commission from 2005 to 2007. Davis was recognized as Missouri's "Outstanding Advising Administrator" in 2003 and as a NACADA "Outstanding Advising Administrator" in 2004. She has enjoyed serving as an advisor training consultant and workshop leader on numerous campuses.

Jayne K. Drake, who earned her Ph.D. in English at Penn State, is an Associate Professor of English, Vice Dean for Academic Affairs, and Director of the Master of Liberal Arts Program in the College of Liberal Arts at Temple University in Philadelphia. Dr. Drake is passionate about her students and has been publicly acknowledged for outstanding teaching, with awards including the College of Liberal Arts Excellence in Teaching Award and the 2008 Temple University Faculty Advisor of the Year Award. Her scholarly and publication interests are in pre-twentieth-century American literature and the history of American print culture.

She served on the National Academic Advising Association's (NACADA's) Board of Directors, chairs the Video Advisory Board charged with revamping the Faculty Advising Training Video, and serves as a mentor in NACADA's Emerging Leaders Program. Drake does extensive consulting and speaking at colleges and universities on assessment of campus-wide advising programs, faculty advising, rewards and recognition for advising, and advising as teaching.

Pat Folsom is Assistant Provost for Enrollment Services and Director of the Academic Advising Center at the University of Iowa. She has worked in academic advising for twenty-seven years in the University's large, centralized professional advising center, both as an academic advisor and as an advising administrator. During this time, Folsom has overseen the implementation of an advisor-development program that was selected as an exemplary practice for the National Academic Advising Association (NACADA) *Advisor Training and Development* monograph. Folsom also has focused on program development for first-year students at the University, including IowaLink, a first-year program for at-risk students; The College Transition, a first-year seminar program; and College Success Seminar, a course for first-year students who are placed on probation. Her recent advising-related work has focused on advisor development: she has offered a preconference workshop designed for advisors new to the profession for several national conferences and was the editor of *The New Advisor Guidebook: Mastering the Art of Advising Through the First Year and Beyond*. She is active in NACADA, where she is currently Chair of the Commission on Advisor Training and Development and a member of other commissions and boards as well. Folsom earned a B.A. in 1969 from Ohio Wesleyan University and an M.L.S. from the State University of New York at Geneseo in 1973.

Rusty Fox serves as Vice President for Student Development Services at Tarrant County College Southeast Campus, that campus's Chief Student Affairs Officer. Active in his profession, he presents at national and regional conferences and serves as a member of the National Academic Advising Association (NACADA) Consultant's Bureau. He has worked for the past several years as faculty at the American College Testing (ACT)/NACADA Summer Advising Institute and has served at the Administrator's Institute as well. As a past board member, he served twice as the association's national commission chair for Two-Year Colleges.

Likewise, Fox is involved in community and educational organizations, currently serving on the board for the Martin Luther King Jr. Celebration Committee for the city of Arlington, a board that coordinates one of the largest series of MLK events in the nation.

Fox served as Dean of Student Development and Director of Counseling/ Advising at Oklahoma City Community College, and Coordinator of Academic Advising at Brookhaven College, Dallas. He holds a B.A. in Speech Communications from Texas A&M University and an M.S. in counseling from Texas A&M—Commerce, where he was named an *Outstanding Alumnus*. He is currently a Ph.D. candidate in higher education at Capella University.

Virginia N. Gordon is assistant dean emeritus and adjunct associate professor at The Ohio State University. She has extensive experience in teaching, administration, advising, and counseling in higher education settings. Her bibliography includes many books, monographs, book chapters, and journal articles on advising administration, career counseling, working with undecided students, and advisor training. Her most recent publications include *The Undecided College Students* (2007), *Foundations—A Reader for New College Students* (2007), and *Career Advising—An Academic Advisors' Guide* (2006). She is past president of the National Academic Advising Association (NACADA) and the founder and first director of the National Clearinghouse on Academic Advising. Gordon has received national acclaim and numerous awards for her contributions to the field, the most fitting of which is NACADA's naming of its award for outstanding contributions to the field of academic advising the Virginia N. Gordon Award.

Paul A. Gore is an Associate Professor of Educational Psychology and Student Success Special Projects Coordinator at the University of Utah. Dr. Gore consults in the United States and abroad with high schools and postsecondary institutions on the development of student success programs. He is the editor of *Facilitating the Career Development of Students in Transition,* a monograph published by the National Resource Center for the First-Year Experience and Students in Transition, and was recently featured in a teleconference titled *Academic and Career Advising: Keys to Student Success.* Dr. Gore conducts research on factors influencing high school and college students' career and academic success, and has published over forty book chapters and research articles in this area. Dr. Gore serves on the editorial boards of *Career Development Quarterly* and *Journal of Career Assessment* and is the Chair of the Society for Vocational Psychology, a section of the Division of Counseling Psychology of the American Psychological Association.

Thomas J. Grites is assistant to the provost at The Richard Stockton College of New Jersey. He has been directly involved in and a student of the academic advising process in higher education for over thirty years. Information and materials from his presentations at national conferences and from his publications have been used by advisors in a variety of institutions. He has served as a consultant and faculty development workshop leader to over 100 different campuses, and he has addressed numerous high school and community groups in his home state. He was instrumental in forming the National Academic Advising Association and served as its second president for two terms.

His research and writing have linked the importance of academic advising to such seemingly diverse areas as admissions, general education, high school counseling, economic profits, ethics, collective bargaining, and faculty development. His landmark publication, *Academic Advising: Getting Us through the Eighties,* served as a basis for the review of campus advising programs for many years. *Developmental Academic Advising,* of which he is a coauthor, was used as the "standard text" for advising programs and advisor training programs for many years. He has authored more than fifty journal articles, position statements, book chapters, and consultant reports, and he has delivered over seventy conference presentations. He recently completed an orientation and textbook for transfer students.

In addition to his work in academic advising, he has worked in college housing programs on three campuses; he regularly taught a general methods course in teacher education; he has also taught a Freshman Seminar course, a Basic Skills course in Critical Thinking, a graduate course on "Developmental Academic Advising" at Teacher's College, Columbia University, and most recently a "transfer student seminar" that is modeled on the freshman seminar concept. He has also served on his local Board of Education for over twenty years.

He is a native of Danville, Illinois, and earned his bachelor's and master's degrees from Illinois State University. His doctoral work was completed at the University of Maryland. Both these institutions have awarded him their Distinguished Alumni Award; most recently he was inducted into the College of Education Hall of Fame at Illinois State during its 150th anniversary celebration.

Wesley R. Habley is a Principal Associate and Coordinator of American College Testing's (ACT's) Office of State Organizations. He received his B.S. in music education and his M.Ed. in student personnel from the University of Illinois-Urbana/Champaign, and his Ed.D. in educational administration from Illinois State University. Prior to joining ACT, Habley directed advising programs at Illinois State University and the University of Wisconsin-Eau Claire.

Habley's recent publications include two chapters in *Fostering Student Success in the College Community* and *What Works in Student Retention?* a series of four research reports on college retention practices. He is coeditor of *Academic Advising: A Comprehensive Handbook* and the author of monographs on four of ACT's National Surveys of Academic Advising. He contributed chapters to *Developmental Academic Advising, Foundations: A College Reader* and *Faculty Advising Examined,* as well as numerous journal articles and chapters in monographs published by Jossey-Bass, the Center for the First Year Experience, and the National Academic Advising Association (NACADA).

Habley is a charter member of NACADA and has served the association in numerous roles, including president and treasurer. He originated the NACADA Summer Institute on Academic Advising in 1987, and in 2006 the NACADA Summer Institute Scholarship was named in his honor. He is also the recipient of NACADA's awards for Outstanding Contributions to the Field of Academic Advising and Service to NACADA.

Habley has served as a consultant, speaker, and workshop leader at more than 125 colleges in the United States, the Middle East, and Canada.

Peter L. Hagen serves as Director of the Center for Academic Advising at the Richard Stockton College of New Jersey. He was the founding Chair of the National Academic Advising Association (NACADA) Theory and Philosophy of Academic Advising Commission, served as Guest Editor of the *NACADA Journal* for its Fall 2005 issue, and was a member of the task force that wrote "The Concept of Academic Advising." For NACADA he currently serves on the *Journal's* Editorial Board, the Publications Review Board, and the Research Committee. He won the 2007 Virginia Gordon Award for Service to the Field of Advising.

Blane Harding currently serves as the Director of Advising, Recruitment and Retention for the College of Liberal Arts and as an adjunct faculty member for the Center for Applied Studies in American Ethnicity at Colorado State University. Harding is the former coordinator of the Black Studies program at CSU and has taught courses in African American history and Ethnic Studies for the past eighteen years. He received his B.A. in interdisciplinary communication from the State University of New York at Brockport and his M.A. in nineteenth-century American history from Colorado State University. He has also served as a retention faculty member with the Council for Opportunity in Education which oversees the national TRIO programs and is on the Advisory Board for the National Academic Advising Association Summer Institutes. Harding is a multicultural consultant for the National Academic Advising Association and is involved in a variety of workshops and multicultural training sessions for schools and organizations. He is the recipient of several honors and awards, including CSU Minority Distinguished Service Award, College of Liberal Arts Excellence in Teaching Award, CSU Alumni Association "Six Best" Teacher Award, History Department Phi Alpha Theta Outstanding Professor Award, the Provost's Jack E. Cermak Advising Award, and most recently the Provost Oliver P. Pennock Distinguished Service Award from CSU.

Jocelyn Y. Harney is currently the Vice President of Enrollment and Student Affairs, having formerly served as the Dean of Students at College of DuPage, Associate Dean of Counseling, Transfer and Advising, and as Counseling Faculty. As Vice President of Student Affairs, she is responsible for counseling, career services, co-op, special services for students with disabilities, and new-student orientation, along with general, international, multicultural, developmental education advising. She is also responsible for student judicial,

Admissions, Athletics, Financial Aid, Records, Registration, and Student Activities. She has provided institutional leadership for a three-year Academic Quality Improvement Program (AQIP) project to improve advising as a part of institutional accreditation and continues to lead advising improvement and enrollment management efforts campus-wide. She received recognition for the dissertation of the year award from the National Council on Student Development upon receipt of a Ph.D. degree from the University of Illinois in Education with a focus on special education and transition leadership. She also secured a M.S. degree in rehabilitation counseling from the University of Illinois and a B.S. in rehabilitation education from Wright State University. Harney has appeared in a national teleconference for the National Resource Center for the First-Year Experience and Students in Transition and serves on the Board. She continues to serve on various special interest boards and is faculty for the National Association of Academic Advising. She has a number of previous teaching and conference presentations to her credit.

Martha (Marti) Hemwall received her B.A. from Lawrence University, and her M.A. and Ph.D. in anthropology from Brown University. She served as the Dean of Student Academic Services and Associate Professor of Anthropology (adjunct) at Lawrence University in Appleton, Wisconsin, from 1995 to 2007. In addition to teaching in anthropology, she helped to create curricular programs in both Gender Studies and Ethnic Studies. In her administrative position, she was responsible for student academic affairs, including the faculty advising system, academic support services, disability accommodations, the academic honor code, academic regulations, and the academic standing system. In addition, she supervised the Center for Teaching and Learning.

Hemwall has been active in the National Academic Advising Association (NACADA) since 1986, and helped to create the Commission on Small Colleges and Universities, chairing that group from its inception until 1996. She went on to coedit a NACADA monograph, *Advising and Learning: Academic Advising from the Perspective of Small Colleges and Universities* (2003), and has contributed articles to the *NACADA Journal* focused on the decline of the developmental paradigm in academic advising, and the emergence of an alternative paradigm based on learning and teaching (1999, 2005). She has presented at numerous conferences in higher education, conducted faculty workshops on effective advising, given presentations on rethinking the nature of academic advising, and done numerous program evaluations.

Mary Stuart Hunter is the Assistant Vice-Provost and Executive Director of University 101 and The National Resource Center for The First-Year Experience & Students in Transition at the University of South Carolina. Her work centers on providing educators with resources to develop personal and professional skills while creating and refining innovative programs to increase undergraduate student learning and success. Her recent publications include coediting *Academic Advising: New Insights for Teaching and Learning in the First Year* (2007), "The First-Year Experience: An Analysis of Issues and Resources" in the Association of American Colleges and Universities' (AAC & U's) *Peer Review* (2006), "Could Fixing Academic Advising Fix Higher Education" in *About Campus* (2004), "The Second-Year Experience: Turning Attention to the Academy's Middle Children" in *About Campus* (2006), and "New Frontiers for Student Affairs Professionals: Teaching and the First-Year Experience" in *New Directions for Student Services* (2007). She serves on national advisory boards of the National Society of Collegiate Scholars, Policy Center on the First Year of College, The Network Addressing Collegiate Alcohol and Other Drug Issues, serves on the editorial board for the *Journal of Learning Communities Research,* and is an elder at Forest Lake Presbyterian Church.

Jennifer Crissman Ishler is an assistant professor of Human Development and Family Studies and an affiliate assistant professor of counselor education at The Pennsylvania State University. She holds a B.S. degree in elementary education from Millersville University, an M.S. degree in counseling and college student personnel from Shippensburg University, and a D.Ed. in higher education from The Pennsylvania State University. Her student affairs experience includes residence life, academic advising, and new student programs. Her undergraduate teaching experience includes first-year seminars, human development and family studies courses, and graduate courses in student affairs and counseling. Her research interests include the first-year experiences, assessment in student affairs, and the concept of "friendsickness" and female college students.

Peggy Jordan is a Professor of Psychology at Oklahoma City Community College, where she teaches Developmental Psychology and Introduction to Psychology. She was awarded the National Academic Advising Association's (NACADA's) 2007 Outstanding Advising Award in the Faculty Advising category and previously served as NACADA's Two-Year Colleges Commission Chair. Dr. Jordan authored a chapter, "Building Effective Communication Through Listening, Interviewing and Referral" in the NACADA monograph, "The New Advisor Guidebook: Mastering the Art of Academic Advising through the First Year and Beyond" (2007). She was also coeditor for the NACADA monograph on "Advising Special Student Populations" (2007). She has a "Voice of Experience" and an "Exemplary Practices: Oklahoma City Community College" section in the 2003 NACADA Monograph, "Advisor Training." Her article, "Advising College Students in the 21st Century" was published in the *NACADA Journal* in Fall 2000. She has served as a faculty member for NACADA's Faculty Seminar and Summer Institute as well as presented numerous workshops for NACADA regional and national conferences.

Dr. Jordan earned her Ph.D. in counseling psychology from Oklahoma State University. For the first twenty years of her professional career, she worked in various state agencies and a private practice. After years of teaching clients coping skills and strategies to enhance motivation and feelings of worth, Dr. Jordan returned to the college campus, with a strong belief that teaching and advising students offers them the greatest opportunities for empowerment.

Jane Kalionzes is the Associate Director at the International Student Center at San Diego State University. She holds a B.A. degree (1976) in liberal studies and a K-12 Multiple Subjects California Teaching Credential from San Diego State University. She has been an international student advisor for over twenty-five years, specializing in cross-cultural and immigration-related advising. Kalionzes has held many leadership positions in NAFSA: Association of International Educators, is a charter member of the NAFSA Trainer Corps, and was the recipient of the NAFSA Region XII Service Award in 1998 and the national NAFSA Service Award in 2007. She is a founding member and past chair of the San Diego Professional International Educators Roundtable and was a member of Phi Beta Delta from 1988 to 2005. She was a recipient of a Senior Fulbright Fellowship, Seminar for International Educators in the Federal Republic of Germany in 1990 and was the recipient of a U.S. Department of State/NAFSA Professional Development grant in Brazil in 1999. Kalionzes has chaired and presented on numerous panels at NAFSA conferences and Projects for International Education and Research (PIER) workshops.

Leah Kendall is a master's student in the Higher Education and Student Affairs program at the University of South Carolina. She currently serves as a graduate assistant for the National Resource Center for the First-Year Experience & Students in Transition. She earned her undergraduate degree in Communication Studies with an emphasis in Public Relations from the University of North Carolina at Charlotte.

Kirsten Kennedy is associate director of residential life for housing operations and an adjunct faculty in the department of Educational Leadership and Policy Analysis at the University of Missouri, Columbia. She formerly worked in residential programs at Bloomsburg University and taught basic business courses at the Pennsylvania College of Technology. Kennedy received her B.S./B.A. degree in management and her M.B.A. degree from Bloomsburg University of Pennsylvania. She earned her Ph.D. in Educational Leadership and Policy Analysis at the University of Missouri, Columbia. She was selected for the National Association of Student Personnel Administrators (NASPA) Alice Manicur Symposium for women aspiring to be senior student affairs officers and is a graduate of the University of Missouri System Administrative Leadership Development Program. Kennedy has published on topics such as faculty participation in learning communities and assessing cost-effectiveness in student affairs. Other research interests include parental influence on college student development, the history of higher education, and the financial management of higher education and student affairs.

Margaret C. (Peggy) King is Associate Dean for Student Development at Schenectady County Community College in Schenectady, New York, where she provides leadership for the Division of Student Affairs as one of a team of three associate deans reporting directly to the president. In her position, she directs the Academic Advisement Center and supervises Counseling and Career and Employment Services. She received her B.A. in history from Ursinus College (Pennsylvania) and her M.S. in student personnel and Ed.D. from the University at Albany (New York). Prior to her work at SCCC, King was Assistant Director of Counseling at Ocean County College (New Jersey).

A founding member of the National Academic Advising Association (NACADA), King was president from 1991 to 1993. She has been a faculty member for the Summer Institute on Academic Advising since its inception in 1987, served on the faculty of the first Advising Administrators Institute, and serves as a consultant on academic advising and student affairs for both two- and four-year colleges and universities. In her consulting role, Peggy has delivered numerous keynote speeches, facilitated many workshops, and spent several days at institutions helping to assess and revise services for students.

King was editor of the New Directions for Community Colleges publication, *Academic Advising: Organizing and Delivering Services for Student Success* (1993). In addition, she has authored numerous chapters and articles on academic advising in the two-year college, on advisor training, and on organizational models and delivery systems for advising. She is a recipient of the State University of New York Chancellor's Award for Excellence in Professional Service, the NACADA Award for Service to the organization, and the NACADA Virginia N. Gordon Award for Excellence in the Field of Advising.

Dr. Nancy S. King is Vice President for Student Success and Enrollment Services and Professor of English at Kennesaw State University in Kennesaw, Georgia. Dr. King holds a B.A. in English and Psychology from Mercer University and an M.A. and a Ph.D. in English from Georgia State University.

Dr. King served as president for the National Academic Advising Association (NACADA) from 1997 to 1999. She has published in the field of academic advising and freshmen seminar programs and serves frequently as a consultant to colleges and universities in the area of advising, freshmen-year-experience programs, and student success. Dr. King has made presentations on these topics at state, regional, national, and international conferences. She has also published and presented on the topic of collaboration between student affairs and academic affairs. Dr. King has been a fellow in the American Association of State Colleges and Universities' Academic Leadership Academy and is listed in *Who's Who in American Education.*

Dr. King has received numerous national awards. In 1998 she was awarded the first-ever Outstanding Advisor of the Year award at the Golden Key International Conference; in 1999 she received the Outstanding First-Year Student Advocate award from the National Resource Center for the First-Year Experience & Students in Transition at the University of South Carolina and the Houghton Mifflin Company; in 2000 she received the Virginia N. Gordon Award for Excellence in the Field of Advising from the National Academic Advising Association (NACADA); and in 2001 she received the Service to NACADA Award.

George D. Kuh is Chancellor's Professor of Higher Education at Indiana University Bloomington, where he directs the Center for Postsecondary Research. Founding director of the National Survey of Student Engagement and related initiatives, Kuh has published about 300 items, made several hundred presentations on topics related to student engagement, assessment, institutional improvement, and collegiate cultures and consulted with more than 200 educational institutions and agencies in the United States and abroad. Past president of the Association for the Study of Higher Education, Kuh has received awards from several organizations, including the Academic Leadership Award from the Council of Independent Colleges, the Virginia B. Smith Award for Innovative Leadership from the National Center for Public Policy in Higher Education, the Lifetime Achievement Award from the American College Personnel Association (ACPA), the Outstanding Contribution to Higher Education Award from the National Association of Student Personnel Administrators (NASPA), and four honorary degrees. In 2001 he received Indiana University's prestigious Tracy Sonneborn Award for a distinguished record of scholarship and teaching.

Terry Kuhn was Professor of Music and Vice Provost for Undergraduate Studies at Kent State University when he retired in 2003. His professional life began as a teacher of band, chorus, and general music in Oregon public schools for six years. After earning a Ph.D. at Florida State University in 1972, he was assistant professor of music at the College Park campus of the University of Maryland for five years and associate professor and professor of music at Kent State University for twenty-five years. During his professorial years he routinely had an assigned advising load that averaged thirty undergraduate and graduate students. Dr. Kuhn has edited two music journals, coauthored three books, written chapters or articles for five books, and published twelve adjudicated research articles in seven journals. He is currently in his second term as coeditor of the *NACADA Journal*.

Michael J. Leonard is the assistant director of Penn State's Division of Undergraduate Studies. He received a master's degree in educational psychology from Penn State and has worked in the field of academic advising since 1979. He is a past chair of the National Academic Advising Association's (NACADA's) Technology in Advising Commission, a recipient of its Service to Commission Award, and a current member of the commission's steering committee and the selection committee for Advising Technology Innovation Awards. He has presented numerous sessions and workshops at professional conferences, including a First-Year Experience conference and national and regional NACADA conferences. He has provided consulting services to higher education institutions on the topic of technology in advising and is the author or coauthor of multiple articles and book chapters about technology in advising. He is managing editor of *The Mentor: An Academic Advising Journal*, an award-winning electronic publication, and a charter member of the team that developed eLion, Penn State's interactive advising system.

Marc Lowenstein is Dean of Professional Studies at The Richard Stockton College of New Jersey, where he has served in a variety of teaching and administrative positions since 1976. In his current role he oversees a number of undergraduate and graduate degree programs; past responsibilities have included managing Stockton's Liberal Studies program, a student-self-designed major, and supervising the academic component of orientation. Dr. Lowenstein earned his bachelor's degree in philosophy at Colgate University, and master's and doctorate degrees in the same subject at the University of Rochester.

Dr. Lowenstein has published articles on ethics in academic advising and on the theory and philosophy of advising and has made numerous presentations on these topics at national and regional conferences.

Among other community activities, Dr. Lowenstein served for ten years on the ethics committee of the Atlantic City Medical Center.

Melinda McDonald is Associate Director for Honors in the Fisher College of Business at The Ohio State University, where her work focuses on directing honors programming and advising. Her prior positions include program coordinator for the Alternatives Advising program in University College at Ohio State and program administrator specialist for the Ohio Board of Regents. She completed a B.A. degree in Spanish education and an M.A. in counselor education from Rollins College, and a Ph.D. degree in counselor education from Ohio State. Her research interests include advisor training, advising high-ability students, and career development and decision-making with undecided and major-changing students.

A. J. Metz is a Visiting Assistant Professor in the Department of Educational Psychology at the University of Utah. For over ten years, Dr. Metz has investigated factors related to career and academic success in diverse student populations. This research has resulted in journal articles, book chapters, electronic media, national conference presentations, and faculty in-service training. Dr. Metz's consulting activities include work with advisors to integrate career and academic advising and the creation and implementation of a career-counseling component to supplement placement activities in a college of business. Dr. Metz has taught career planning and academic success courses. She has administered and interpreted career assessments and has provided individual and group career counseling.

Mary M. Richard graduated from Central College in Pella, Iowa, where in her senior year she served as a student advisor assisting first-year students with their initial enrollments. At The University of Iowa, she completed her M.A. in education, with a focus in student development in postsecondary education. At the UI, for eleven years she coordinated services for students with learning disabilities. During that time she also served as national secretary, vice-president, president and past-president of CHADD (Children and Adults with Attention Deficit Disorders), served on a committee of the National Academy of Sciences Institute of Medicine, and gave congressional testimony in regard to disability and education issues. Ms. Richard has authored several articles in peer-reviewed journals, and has contributed book chapters on various topics related to postsecondary education and disabilities. Ms. Richard has given a number of presentations at state and national conferences, including the national meetings of the American College Personnel Association, Learning Disabilities Association, and CHADD. In 2002, Ms. Richard entered The University of Iowa College of Law. Since graduation, she has been admitted to practice in the state of Iowa and the U.S. Federal District Court for the Southern District of Iowa, and is engaged in the general practice of law, including, but not limited to, the areas of litigation and education law.

John H. Schuh is distinguished professor of educational leadership at Iowa State University. Previously he held administrative and faculty assignments at Wichita State University, Indiana University—Bloomington, and Arizona State University. He earned his B.A. in history from the University of Wisconsin-OshKosh, and he received an M.S. in counseling and a Ph.D. in counseling from Arizona State. He is the author, coauthor, or editor of more than 24 books and monographs, 60 book chapters, and 100 journal articles. Most recently, he was a contributing author to *Fostering Student Success in the Campus Community* (2007), and *One Size Does Not Fit All: Traditional and Innovative Models of Student Affairs Practice* (2006). Currently, he is editor-in-chief of the *New Directions for Students Services* series and is associate editor of the *Journal of College Student Development*. John Schuh has made more than 240 presentations and speeches to campus-based regional and national meetings. He is a member of the Evaluator Corps and the Accreditation Review Council of the North Central Association of Colleges and Schools. He received a Fulbright award in 1994 to study higher education in Germany.

Casey Self serves as the Executive Director for the University College Center for Academic Advising at Arizona State University. His current responsibilities at Arizona State include oversight of academic advising centers on four ASU campuses serving over 4,000 exploratory and undeclared majors.

Self became a member of the National Academic Advising Association (NACADA) in 1994. He has served as the chair for the NACADA LGBTA Concerns Commission, the NACADA Diversity committee, and the NACADA Membership Committee, and was elected to become the first Commission and Interest Group Division Representative. Self was elected to the NACADA Board of Directors for the 2006–2009 term, as vice president for 2007–2008, and as president of NACADA for 2009. He also recently authored a chapter addressing Lesbian, Gay, Bisexual, Transgender, Queer/Questioning (LGBTQ) Issues in the NACADA/First-Year Experience Monograph, "Academic Advising: New Insights for Teaching and Learning in the First Year."

Self is a Colorado native and earned his bachelor's in speech communication at the University of Northern Colorado in Greeley in 1986, then completed his M.S. in college student personnel administration at Western Illinois University in Macomb in 1990.

A scientist by training, **John Smarrelli, Jr.** became interim president of Le Moyne College in Syracuse, New York, in May 2007. He is the first alumnus and layman ever to lead the Jesuit College.

Dr. Smarrelli came to Le Moyne as academic vice president and a professor of biology in 2001 and was named provost in 2005. Prior to that, Dr. Smarrelli served as the dean of the College of Arts and Sciences and chair of the Biology Department at Loyola University Chicago; he was also the chair of the Advanced Placement Biology Program at Loyola.

As provost, Dr. Smarrelli was responsible for articulating the College's academic vision—one that was rigorous and balanced and in which students were truly engaged. He successfully guided the College through the reaccreditation process, oversaw its planning committee, and headed the senior leadership team.

He also has been involved in the largest capital campaign in the College's sixty-year history—helping to set priorities for the campaign and meeting with benefactors and other supporters. One of his keen interests has been in the construction of a new science building that will help the College attract the most talented students and prepare them to make meaningful professional contributions to their communities.

Dr. Smarrelli earned doctoral and master's degrees from the State University of New York College of Environmental Science and Forestry and a bachelor's degree from Le Moyne. He also conducted postdoctoral work in biology at the University of Virginia in Charlottesville.

George E. Steele is director for educational access at The Ohio Learning Network (OLN). OLN is a consortium of two- and four-year public and independent colleges and universities in Ohio working together to improve learning through the use of technology. He coordinates and manages the student services and advising issues for OLN and coordinates OhioLearns!, an online catalog of distance-offered content. Steele has been a member of the National Academic Advising Association for over twenty years and has held a variety of offices and responsibilities, including a term on the Board of Directors. He has written on topics such as advising undecided and major-changing students and the use of technology in academic advising. He also received the 2008 Service to the NACADA Award.

Wendy G. Troxel is an Assistant Professor in the Department of Educational Administration and Foundations, teaching research methods courses in both quantitative and qualitative methods, program evaluation and assessment, and the American college student. Her research interests are in the area of teaching and learning in the first year of college, the impact of formative assessment techniques in the classroom, faculty and staff roles in the program-assessment process, and the identification of teaching skills in precollege students.

She most recently served as the Director of the University Assessment Office at Illinois State University, coordinating student learning outcomes research on campus and assisting faculty and staff with the development, implementation, and use of assessment activities to improve learning and development. She earned her doctorate in educational leadership at the University of Alabama at Birmingham (UAB), with special emphases in both educational research and education law. She also served as Director of Undergraduate Admissions at UAB.

Dr. Troxel serves on the editorial board of *Planning and Changing Journal* and is a member of the Board of Directors for The Hoenny Center for Research and Development in Teaching. She is a frequent presenter and workshop facilitator at national and international conferences and special events on a wide range of topics related to the assessment of student learning.

Dick Vallandingham's educational background includes a bachelor's degree in speech and hearing science from Oklahoma State University, a master's degree in audiology from the University of Tulsa, and a doctorate in rehabilitation counseling from the University of Arizona. His community college career began almost twenty years ago at Johnson County Community College in Overland Park, Kansas. First working with students with disabilities, he later became a counselor and academic advisor, director of the counseling center, and director of student development. He left JCCC to become vice president for student development at Coastal Georgia Community College, where he initiated an integrated advising program using an interactive student success center. He is now serving as dean of students at Black Hawk College in Moline, Illinois. He continues to be directly involved in the development of advising programs that emphasize student engagement and involvement.

Vallandingham was coeditor of the NACADA monograph "Advising Students with Disabilities." His other publications include "Advising First Year Students with Disabilities" in *Advising the First Year Student,* "Student Success Based on Student Development: An Integrated Student Services Approach," and "Student Development Model as the Core to Student Success."

Faye Vowell currently serves as Provost and Vice President of Western New Mexico University. WNMU is a four-year, comprehensive university with campuses in Silver City, Deming, Truth or Consequences, and Gallup. It serves a primarily first-generation, nontraditional, majority minority student body. She is a long-time member of the National Academic Advising Association (NACADA), presenting at national and regional conferences. Her areas of advising interest include faculty advising, advising with technology, and multicultural advising issues. She has received both the Service to NACADA and Virginia Gordon Awards.

ACADEMIC ADVISING

PART ONE

FOUNDATIONS OF ACADEMIC ADVISING

Thomas J. Grites

INTRODUCTION

The opening section of the second edition of *Academic Advising* somewhat parallels the initial edition in its overall content. However, new authors have identified and described new approaches, new information, new circumstances, and some new topics since the initial edition. These topics enrich the ever-growing thinking, research, and practices that provide the foundations for academic advising in higher education.

In Chapter One Terry Kuhn traces the evolution of three advising eras in American higher education and how they developed according to the purposes for which our various types of institutions originated. He also describes the personnel responsible for these advising environments as this evolution occurred, and he suggests that faculty and advisors collaborate in developing future theory and research in academic advising.

Peter Hagen and Peggy Jordan expand our theoretical foundations for academic advising in Chapter Two. They reinforce the developmental foundation that has guided the field for many years by examining several types of theories; they reflect on the new theoretical approaches that have stimulated various modes of thinking about and performing academic advising; and they challenge those in the field to continue this expansion.

Marc Lowenstein uses practical examples of dilemmas that advisors have likely faced in his analysis of the ethical foundations for academic advising in Chapter Three. The ideals and principles he describes provide a basis for advisors to understand their dilemmas better when trying to resolve them. He concludes with a set of supplemental statements to the NACADA Core Values.

Conversely, in Chapter Four Mary Richard cautions advisors about attempting to apply the law to individual situations without expert opinion. Her thorough review of the many aspects of the law that might directly or indirectly affect academic advisors in their roles provides a solid foundation for the areas about which advisors need to be aware when practicing their role.

The next three chapters in this section provide the foundation for what academic advising seeks to achieve—student success through teaching and learning that results in productive career and life planning. In Chapter Five George Kuh demonstrates the importance of quality academic advising through results acquired through the National Survey of Student Engagement. His descriptions of specific programs provide examples for review and potential application of certain elements of these programs in many institutions, and his review of five principles for effective advising provide a template for achieving this success.

Drew Appleby anchors the "advising as teaching" principle practiced by most contemporary academic advisors in Chapter Six. His comparison of the syllabus used in traditional classroom teaching to an advising syllabus provides the relevance, rationale, and utility of this academic advising tool and strategy.

In Chapter Seven Paul Gore and A. J. Metz examine the current theories and research in career development as they relate to academic advising. Their sample worksheet also provides advisors with a starting point in this process for use with their advisees.

Having read this section, academic advisors will have the complete foundation to enable themselves and their advisees to share the most rewarding and productive advising experience they can create and develop.

CHAPTER ONE

Historical Foundations of Academic Advising

Terry L. Kuhn

For the purposes of this chapter, *academic advising* will refer to situations in which an institutional representative gives insight or direction to a college student about an academic, social, or personal matter. The nature of this direction might be to inform, suggest, counsel, discipline, coach, mentor, or even teach. Such activities have occurred throughout the history of academic advising in higher education, and this chapter will briefly summarize the historical development of academic advising, characterize academic advising as it occurs in different institutional types, and discuss how to achieve advising as an examined activity by amalgamating theory, practice, and research.

Readers are urged to examine the chapter by Susan H. Frost on "Historical and Philosophical Foundations for Academic Advising" that appeared in the first edition of this book (Frost, 2000). This current chapter intends to complement Frost's chapter.

ERAS OF ACADEMIC ADVISING

The First Advising Era

Advisors in a designated separate role were not an aspect of American higher education at its inception. In 1636, the founders of Harvard College cast the mold for the liberal arts college in what was to become the United States of America. They created a four-year residential institution whose Puritan classical curriculum was designed to produce well-educated ministers, lawyers, and doctors for an emerging society. This institution would create "a society of scholars, where teachers and students lived in the same building under common discipline, associating not only in lecture rooms but at meals, in chambers, at prayers, and in recreation" (Morison, 1946, p. 12). Writing about his travels in the United States and Canada in 1818, John Duncan (1823) said that at Princeton "a President, two Professors, and two Tutors, form the whole corporation" (p. 169).

From 1636 until about 1870, the period that Frost (2000) identified as "Higher Education Before Academic Advising Was Defined," all students took the same courses, and no electives were available. In this era, the college ideal was "a large family, sleeping, eating, studying, and worshiping together under one roof" (Rudolph, 1962, p. 88). The mind was viewed as a tool to be sharpened, and subjects like Latin, Greek, and mathematics were favored sharpening stones. Religion was included in the curriculum to ensure appropriate moral training. During this period "a president, two professors, and one or two tutors perform the whole duty of instruction and government" (Brown, 1862, p. 10). These small colleges had no student service professionals, administrators, secretaries, or custodial staff. The president and faculty served *in loco parentis* and assumed responsibility not only for students' intellectual and academic lives, but also for their moral training and extracurricular activities. Getting everything done comprised their bundle of responsibilities.

Tutors supplemented the instructional staff of these small colleges. "A typical tutor was a young man in his early twenties who had himself only recently graduated from the institution where he was employed . . . [and] his chief duties were to hear student recitations and act as a disciplinarian and overseer of students under his charge." Professors typically received appointments at their alma maters after having served in some nonacademic occupation, usually a pastorate. The "conditions precluded a professor from specializing: it was not at all unusual to find the same person teaching geography, mathematics, and natural philosophy; or Latin and Greek literature, plus history, ethics, and moral philosophy" (Lucas, 2006, p. 124).

By the 1870s, the general social climate had become very formal and rigid, and students were kept in line by an inflexible system of rules, regulations, and punishments. "No longer was it considered appropriate for faculty to speak with students on a personal basis; neither was it considered proper for students to approach faculty members" (Bush, 1969, p. 599). Students thought of faculty as a "necessary evil" and faculty treated students as an "unavoidable nuisance" (Veysey, 1965, p. 295). For many years there was disorderly conduct in the classrooms, chapels, commons, and dormitories that ranged from throwing spitballs at the professors, drinking, throwing food and utensils during meals, barring doors shut, cursing, and threatening to burn the president's house (Morison, 1946). Rebellions often were directed at "bad food in the dining commons to restrictions on student activities and autonomy. Presidents, assisted by tutors, were constant disciplinarians" (Thelin, 2004, p. 21). This restrictive control widened an increasing gulf that divided students from tutors and faculty and continued until the elective system provided: (1) more choices to students, (2) better faculty interaction that softened relations with students, and (3) increasing use of seminars and laboratories ("the seminar and the laboratory lent themselves to a more intrinsically democratic relationship between student and professor than had the lecture method alone" (Bush, 1969, p. 605).

The introduction of curricular electives in the 1870s initiated the need for advisors to guide students in the successful pursuit of their chosen paths. Also, the broader curriculum required faculty specialization, which brought the pansophic approach of faculty to an end. As institutions grew in size and complexity, and as more was demanded of faculty members in the way of research and service, traditional faculty responsibilities gradually unbundled, spawning new roles and positions, one of which was the academic advisor. The need for academic advisors was recognized by President David Bates Douglass at Kenyon College. President Douglass's action was described by Rutherford B. Hayes, 19th President of the United States, then a junior at Kenyon College, in a June 1841 letter written to his mother. In that letter he said:

> A new rule has been established that each student shall choose from among the faculty some one who is to be his adviser and friend in all matters in which assistance is desired and is to be the medium of communication between the student and faculty. This I like very much. My patron is a tutor in the Grammar School who has graduated since I came here. (Hayes, 1841, p. 54)

Hayes' enthusiasm for the new practice may have been spurred by his ability to choose his "patron."

The Second Advising Era

Frost (2000) called the era from 1870 through about 1970 "Academic Advising as a Defined and Unexamined Activity." Beginning in the 1870s, American higher education institutions began to include more practical courses as alternatives to Greek, Latin, and other traditional courses. As more courses were offered in this new elective system, students could have choices. Instituting an elective system was controversial for those who wanted to preserve the classical curriculum. Developing an academic advising process was one answer to those critics, who feared that the elective system used unwisely by students would result in a less focused education. For example, the elective system that President Eliot instituted at Harvard in 1872 (Thelin, 2004) was later defended on the basis of Harvard's having a Board of Freshman Advisers, who helped students make appropriate choices among elective subjects (Rudolph, 1962). In 1877, Johns Hopkins had a system in which students could choose from seven groups of courses, each group being similar to today's "major." Hopkins also had faculty advisors (Hawkins, 1960) in "recognition that size and the elective curriculum required some closer attention to undergraduate guidance than was possible with an increasingly professionally oriented faculty" (Rudolph, 1962, p. 460).

President Daniel Coit Gilman at Johns Hopkins University, whose initiatives helped to usher in this second advising era, not only used the word "adviser" to refer to someone who gave direction to a student concerning an academic, social, or personal matter, but stated the responsibilities required of the role. In 1886, Gilman showed keen understanding of the undergraduate advising role when he wrote that:

> The adviser's relation to the student is like that of a lawyer to his client or of a physician to one who seeks his counsel. The office is not that of an inspector, nor of a proctor, nor of a recipient of excuses, nor of a distant and unapproachable embodiment of the authority of the Faculty. It is the adviser's business to listen to difficulties which the student assigned to him may bring to his notice; to act as his representative if any collective action is necessary on the part of the board of instruction; to see that every part of his course of studies has received the proper attention. (p. 565)

Gilman appears to have had an idealistic view of the advisor-advisee relationship. In reality the advisor system "degenerated into a perfunctory affair involving only brief, impersonal interviews" (Veysey, 1965, p. 297). For instance, Morison (1946, p. 403) states that the Board of Freshman Advisers at Harvard "did little except address the entering class *en masse,* approve study cards, and invite the advisee to a pallid luncheon at the Colonial Club." While these systems were designed partially to help students choose among electives, they were also intended to diminish a growing gulf between students and faculty (Veysey, 1965). Thus, institutions like Harvard and Johns Hopkins identified "advisors" with specified expectations, but they paid little attention to the relative success of their advising processes. Although the concept of advising was beginning to be defined, it remained an unexamined activity.

By the 1920s, "most colleges and universities were busy perfecting various systems of freshman counseling, freshman week, faculty advisers, and before long the campus psychologist as well as the college chaplain would join these many agencies in giving organized expression to a purpose that had once been served most simply by a dedicated faculty" (Rudolph, 1962, p. 460). Rudolph lists examples of such advising systems at Wesleyan University, the University of Minnesota, the University of Oregon, Iowa State University, Columbia University, Emory University, Denison University, University of Miami, Stanford University, Ohio State University, and Marietta College.

As student support systems proliferated during the 1930s and 1940s, a more student-centered philosophy within higher education emerged. This philosophy was described in the 1949 *Student Personnel Point of View (SPPOV)* issued by the American Council on Education,

> The student personnel point of view encompasses the student as a whole. The concept of education is broadened to include attention to the student's well-rounded development—physically, socially, emotionally, and spiritually—as well as intellectually. The student is thought of as a responsible participant in his own development and not as a passive recipient of an imprinted economic, political, or religious doctrine, or vocation skill. (American Council on Education, 1949, pp. 17–18)

The *SPPOV* went on to define the key elements of a student personnel program that included "the service to the student of trained, sympathetic counselors to assist him in thinking through his educational, vocational, and personal adjustment problems." More than anything else, the *SPPOV* established the legitimacy of academic counseling along with personal, vocational, and job placement counseling in higher education. This heritage still held true in the early 1970s (Morrison and Ferrante, 1973) and extends to the modern day.

The Third Advising Era

Frost (2000) characterized the third era, from the 1970s to the present, as "Academic Advising as a Defined and Examined Activity." In contrast to the second era, during which advising was primarily assisting students with course scheduling and registration, academic advising became an examined activity.

Academic advising became an examined activity when those doing advising began to compare how they conducted advising to how it was being conducted at other institutions. The first formal instance of such comparison occurred when over 300 people attended a national meeting on academic advising in October 1977 in Burlington, Vermont. Over the next two years the National Academic Advising Association (NACADA), an adjudicated journal, a professional staff, and annual national and regional conferences were established (Beatty, 1991). Other seminal influences on the development of "advising as an examined activity" were the publication of research articles by Crookston (1972), O'Banion (1972), and others who conceptualized notions of what it meant to "advise" a student with terms such as *prescriptive advising* and *developmental advising.*

While *prescriptive* and *developmental* refer to the act of advising itself, Habley (1983) examined the administrative structure of advising using several different organizational models. While the nuances of advising practices cannot be categorized with precision, the advising models first identified by Habley provide useful constructs for the description and analysis of advising programs. He later (2004) described the models as follows:

Faculty-Only Model. All students are assigned to an instructional faculty member for advising. There is no advising office.

Supplementary Model. All students are assigned to an instructional faculty member for advising. There is an advising office that provides general academic information and referrals for students, but all advising transactions must be approved by the student's faculty advisor.

Split Model. A specific group(s) of students (e.g., undecided, underprepared, etc.) are advised in an advising office. All other students are assigned to academic units or faculty advisors.

Dual Model. Each student has two advisors. A member of the instructional faculty advises the student on matters related to the major. An advisor in an advising office advises the student on general requirements, procedures, and policies.

Total Intake Model. Staff members of an administrative unit are responsible for advising all students for a specified period of time or until some specific requirements have been met. After meeting these requirements, students are assigned to an academic subunit or member of the instructional faculty for advising.

Satellite Model. Each school, college, or division within the institution has established its own approach to advising.

Self-Contained Model. Advising for all students from the point of enrollment to the point of departure is done by staff in a centralized unit.

The models are used in the next section to characterize how advising is conducted in different types of institutions.

DEVELOPMENT OF INSTITUTIONAL TYPES

In 2005 the United States had a plethora of 4,387 higher education institutions that differed in type and auspices, in the purposes they held sacrosanct, in the instructional programs they offered, and in the students they served (2005 Carnegie Classification, 2006). Among the types of institutions were small and large, two-year and four-year, undergraduate and graduate, public and private, religious and secular, and nonprofit and for-profit. The institutions themselves were varied in these qualities, and their student bodies displayed a diversity of gender, age, and race. Most institutions offered an extensive array of programs, while some had but a single curricular focus. Within that array of institutions was a dualism of purpose seeking an appropriate balance between liberal and practical education. This chapter continues with descriptions, in relative historical order, of the predominant types of existing institutions and their respective approaches to academic advising.

Liberal Arts Colleges

Liberal arts colleges have a distinctly undergraduate focus, and the popularity and proliferation of small private colleges is ample testament to the success of this ideal. The early colleges were "shaped by aristocratic traditions and they served the aristocratic elements of colonial society." Indeed, only elite white males attended. The people who established the first colleges had an idealistic desire "to advance learning and perpetuate it to posterity" (New England's First Fruits, 1640, ¶ 1). While the high importance given to learning and education was a fundamental element of the social philosophy of the time, it was also the case that this aristocratic order was giving way to the dynamics of mobility "such that Benjamin Franklin, [who] had no more than a few years of elementary schooling" would become a "symbol of the self-made man in social and economic terms" (Rudolph, 1962, pp. 18–19).

The venerable liberal arts college was the bastion of the Faculty-Only model, and because of their long history, typically small size, and intimate character, liberal arts colleges remain the primary exemplar of advising by instructional faculty. The Faculty-Only model was and remains the model most able to provide holistic integration of major, general education, vocational, and extracurricular aspects of the undergraduate college experience (Habley, 2004).

Normal Schools

"The first publicly funded Normal School opened in Massachusetts . . . and . . . provided only a two-year, post eighth grade education to prepare teachers to teach in the primary grades" (The Normal Schools, nd, ¶ 1). Normal schools were created to provide prospective teachers with a laboratory for learning, using model classrooms as a place to practice their new skills (Cheek, nd, ¶ 3, 8). In that respect, the meaning of "Normal" was "in the sense of setting an excellent model—or "norm"—for other schools" (Hilton, nd, ¶ 3).

Many Normal Schools evolved into four-year teachers colleges, liberal arts colleges, and then universities. In those latter stages, teacher training was only one aspect of a broader curricular mission. The change from Michigan State Normal School (1852), to Michigan State Normal College (1899), to Eastern Michigan College (1956), and then to Eastern Michigan University (1959) illustrates this metamorphosis (Eastern Michigan University, nd).

There was formal advising by the president and faculty. It appears that the singular purpose of this advising was to help students enroll for classes, and that help was provided through the Faculty-Only advising model. In illustration of this point, the Kirksville Missouri's 1912 Normal School Bulletin stated that "All members of the Faculty are to be at the President's Office from 8 to 12 A.M. and from 2 to 5 P.M., Tuesday, September 10th, for the purpose of assisting students in making programs" (1912 Normal School Bulletin, 1912, p. 10 ¶ 4).

Historically Black Colleges and Universities

Quakers founded the Institute for Colored Youth in Philadelphia as a teacher training college in 1837. This Institute was the first of the Historically Black Colleges and Universities (HBCU) (Historically Black Colleges, nd, ¶ 1). The establishment of this institute was important because educating blacks was prohibited by public policy in the South before the Civil War, and as a result, higher education for black students was virtually nonexistent (Thelin, 2004).

"As the Civil War was raging, the Morrill Land-Grant Act of 1862 gave federal lands to the states for the purpose of opening colleges and universities that would train Americans in the applied sciences, agriculture, and engineering— quite a departure from the classical curriculum of the early colleges" (HBCU, nd, ¶ 2). However, after twenty-eight years of intransigence throughout the country, Senator Morrill created the second Land Grant Act of 1890 which specified that States could ". . . either make their schools open to both blacks and whites or allocate money for segregated black colleges to serve as an alternative to white schools" (Rudolph, 1962, 253–254). In that year, funds from the Second Land Grant served as impetus to establish sixteen exclusively black institutions (HBCU, nd, ¶ 2).

The second Land-Grant Act was worded the way it was because of the "separate but equal" doctrine. That doctrine was formulated into law by the Supreme Court in 1896 when Homer Plessy, a thirty-year-old Creole of African descent whose light skin allowed him to "pass," challenged the state of Louisiana's Separate Car Act, arguing that requiring blacks to ride in separate railroad cars violated the thirteenth and fourteenth Amendments. The 1896 U.S. Supreme Court upheld the Louisiana law requiring separate railroad cars for blacks and whites and made the "separate but equal" doctrine a legal precedent for other segregation laws, including separate but equal education (Brown, 1896, ¶ 1–2).

In relation to Habley's categories, academic advising administrative structures in HBCU's are diverse both within and across institutions, making them reflective of advising in all of higher education. For example, J. P. Reidy, associate provost at Howard University, stated that Howard does not have a university-wide advising center, but that its Educational Advisory Center in the College of Arts and Sciences comes close to filling that function. Staff advisors (rather than faculty) provide the advising to all first- and second-year students. In contrast, Howard's College of Engineering, Architecture and Computer Sciences, uses an assistant dean (staff, not faculty) to provide much of the advising regarding general education requirements, with some assistance from faculty members in the respective departments. Reidy further indicated that there are differences among HBCU's based on program differences, institution and program size, and local customs and that these approaches change over time to serve changing student demographics (J. P. Reidy, personal communication, December 28, 2007).

Community Colleges

Since the founding of Joliet Community College in 1901, there has been a dramatic growth to 1,821 community colleges in the year 2006. About 39 percent of higher education students attend community colleges (Chronicle Almanac, 2006). Depending on their mission and funding source, community colleges have been called junior colleges, technical colleges, county colleges, and city colleges (Community College, nd, ¶ 1).

In defining a community college, Bogue (1950) amplified the 1922 definition developed for the American Association of Junior Colleges, "an institution offering two years of instruction of strictly collegiate grade" to include "General education and vocation training make the soundest and most stable progress toward personal competence when they are thoroughly integrated" (p. 22). Thus, community colleges offer two-year associate degrees that can either be weighted heavily in liberal arts (Associate of Arts) as a precursor to a four-year baccalaureate degree, or focused on the development of workplace skills and immediate job placement (Associate of Science, Associate of Applied Science, or Associate of Technical Studies). Today's community colleges also offer baccalaureate-degree opportunities, usually through partnerships with colleges and universities.

The three most common organizational structures for academic advising at community colleges are the Self-Contained, Split, and Faculty-Only models. A noticeable trend away from the Faculty-Only model was noted in two-year public colleges (Habley, 2004). This finding has been supported by King, who wrote that:

> The one model that is more unique to community colleges is the Self-Contained model because that model grew out of the guidance office concept common in public schools at the time many community colleges were being created. That

model is where all advising takes place in a centralized unit, typically an advising or counseling center, and advising often reports through the Dean or Vice President of Student Affairs. (King, nd, ¶ 1)

Research Universities

Research universities are large, complex institutions that can include campuses, colleges, departments, centers, and programs, as well as ancillary business operations. Even though research universities have a preponderance of undergraduate students, they have a distinctly graduate focus in their mission and programs. Criteria for faculty promotion and tenure at research universities are usually weighted heavily on the faculty member's productivity in grantsmanship and scholarship in adjudicated journals and books, with relatively less emphasis given to teaching, institutional service, and advising undergraduate students.

The underpinning of the research component in the teaching–research–service mission of today's institutions was in good part due to the influence of German universities. Indeed, Benjamin Franklin, who was instrumental in the establishment of what was to become the University of Pennsylvania, visited Gottingen in 1766, and urged "American students to go to Germany rather than to England or to Scotland" to study (Thwing, 1928, p. 12). During the 1800s and early 1900s, thousands of American students attended German universities and hundreds of German teachers were hired in American universities (Thwing, 1928). One of the primary elements in the German ideal was reflected in the desire by presidents of American institutions, such as Daniel Coit Gilman, president at Johns Hopkins University from 1876 to 1901, to appoint "professors who had shown their ability as investigators, whose duties as teachers would not be so burdensome as to interfere with the prosecution of their [scientific] researches, whose students should be so advanced as to stimulate them to their best work, and the fruit of whose labors in the advancement of science and learning should be continually manifest in the shape of published results" (Franklin, 1910, p. 196). In these words can be seen the template for faculty expectations in the contemporary research university.

The Morrill Act in 1862 gave prominence to agriculture and engineering as high-profile purposes for higher education. In the late 1800s there was need for research to make food grow, to build machinery and factories, and to find out how things worked so that society could be improved and protected. Over time this research agenda has imprinted itself within the missions of most institutions of higher education, and, in particular, on what are known as research universities (Veysey, 1965, pp. 174–179).

In public four-year colleges the Split model is the most popular. In private four-year colleges Faculty-Only is the predominant model. In a large complex research university, the advising unit might be within a single program, a major, a department, a college, a campus, or a university-wide center. Because some of these sub-administrative units can be quite large, several advising models can coexist: a small department with a single major might use the Faculty-Only model, or one college might use the Split model, while another college might reflect the Satellite model (Habley, 2004).

For-Profit Institutions

In an era when our economy is becoming increasingly knowledge-based, the number of people seeking postsecondary education is increasing, and the personal computer and Internet are providing unprecedented access to information and educational opportunities, the growth of for-profit institutions has found fertile soil. The University of Phoenix, a for-profit institution, enrolled 115,794 students in the fall of 2004 (Campuses, 2006). This number more than doubled the number enrolled in either Miami Dade College or Ohio State University's main campus. Ruch (2001) contrasted nonprofit with for-profit institutions. He described nonprofit institutions as being tax-exempt, having donors and stakeholders, using shared governance, and cultivating knowledge within academic disciplines. He contrasted for-profit institutions as being tax-paying, having investors and stockholders, using traditional top-down management style, and applying learning to market-driven problems. For-profit institutions typically emphasize student learning to the exclusion of faculty research, offer degree programs that reflect market demand, and deliver courses at convenient locations and times for students.

While online learning has amalgamated itself into the teaching/learning environments at all types of institutions, it has been mostly for-profit institutions that have built their facilitating infrastructures and identities with the Internet rather than bricks and mortar. Moreover, online learning is transforming higher education because it is shifting accountability from institutional inputs to student outcomes, changing expectations for faculty employment and ownership of curricular material, shifting credit hours from the time students spend in class to their acquisition of knowledge and skills, altering the nature of attending classes for students, and rendering meaningless the concept of "geographical service area."

Out of concern for students, and in response to guidelines from the eight regional accreditation associations that distance learners must be provided appropriate student support services, online programs are giving careful consideration to how they provide academic advising as well as other support services (Best Practices, nd). For instance, the Ohio Learning Network (OLN) is a statewide effort to coordinate information about online offerings from eighty-one of Ohio's higher education institutions. It employs Regional Coordinators, whose responsibility is to help current and potential students find information about online learning opportunities in Ohio. OLN also provides a free orientation course for distance learners, and it maintains a Web page on how students can obtain available support that includes names, e-mail addresses, addresses, and telephone numbers of academic advisors at each participating institution offering online courses (Ohio Learns, nd). Likewise, Capella University provides academic advisors, career counselors, disability services, enrollment counselors, financial aid assistance, and tech support. In addition to the personal support from these individuals by e-mail and telephone, Capella has many online resources (Capella, nd). According to the Director for Educational Access of OLN, the majority of advising for distant students takes place through e-mail correspondence and telephone conversations, although there is experimentation with other formats such as wikis, podcasts, and blogs (G. Steele, personal communication, July 27, 2007). In Habley's (2004) schema, these online advising efforts tend to reflect the Self-Contained model.

LOOKING TO THE FUTURE

From its inception as one form of counseling within student personnel services, academic advising emerged as an independent field within higher education. Manifestations of academic advising as a separate field include the growth in number of staff advisors, the development of a professional advising literature, establishment of centers for undecided and undeclared students, and the identification of multiple administrative structures for advising. Advancing the place of academic advising in the university community will require inquiry that integrates theory, practice, and research. This integration will depend on collaborative inquiry being conducted by practicing advisors and faculty researchers. Working together, they could expand the body of scholarly literature as they form a praxis of academic advising—a profession in which theory unites the dichotomy of practice and research into a continuum.

Several programs and efforts have helped to make academic advising an examined activity. Some of these include the assessment and accountability movements; advisors sharing their expertise in public conference presentations; the use of Council for the Advancement of Standards in Higher Education (CAS) standards; the American College Testing (ACT) Survey of Academic Advising to evaluate academic advising programs; and awards programs to recognize and publicize exemplary advisors and programs. Another example of advising as an examined activity was the publication of *NACADA Journal* issue 25(2), which focused on several new and unique theories of advising.

The works of Habley, Crookston, O'Banion, and many others have contributed to the vocabulary used in the field of academic advising. Terms like *advising, prescriptive, developmental, intrusive,* and *faculty-only* have been constructed to permit discussion of ideas about what advising is and how it is conducted. When such ideas are coined, they are described as constructs. Constructs are the ideas that we treat as things to study in this field. The future of advising as an examined activity will depend on how well advising theory, practice, and research can define and study advising constructs.

A *theory* is an explanation of how something works. Theories allow someone to describe a process and to predict future events under given circumstances. Some examples of famous scientific theories include evolution (biology), big-bang (astronomy), global climate change (climatology), plate tectonics (geology), probability (mathematics), and relativity (physics). Advising theories have been identified as friendship, strengths-based, Socratic self-examination, conflict resolution, teaching, educating, prescriptive, and developmental.

Advising practice is the interaction between an institutional representative and a student that is intended to give the student insight or direction about an academic, social, or personal matter.

Research is inquiry that uses formal methods, such as qualitative, quantitative, or historical, to answer a question based on a theory.

Constructs are ideas that can be only indirectly observed, such as intelligence, bravery, and prescriptive advising. Things such as chairs, cars, or trees, on the other hand, can be directly observed and measured.

Assumptions are beliefs accepted without proof within the context of an inquiry based on theory. Within a theory, assumptions are neither true nor false, since there is no way of proving them to be either. For instance, as a starting point in developing the theory of relativity, Einstein assumed that the speed of light was a constant.

As an illustration, consider a study of undecided exploratory honors students as they choose a major. The *theory* supporting this inquiry will be a condensation of William Perry's "Scheme of Intellectual and Ethical Development" (Perry, 1970). It is assumed that Perry's nine positions can be meaningfully compressed into four stages, including dualism, multiplicity, relativism, and commitment. The purpose of this fictitious inquiry sketch is to determine whether these four stages are evident in a sample of thirty exploratory majors as they enter college and choose a major. These students are all advised in a student advising center by staff advisors; they are expected to declare a degree-granting major by the time they achieve between forty-five and sixty-four semester hours. *Practice* includes what advisors routinely do to assist students in choosing a major. The research, using qualitative methods of interviews, examination of student records for GPA, course selection and other facts, as well as advisors' notes and documentation, attempt to determine whether Perry's four stages are evident. The assumptions about this study include: (1) multiple influences exist on student choice, including family members, academic advisors, friends, interest in different majors, and physical and intellectual capabilities; (2) students with high intellectual prowess will find it easier to choose a major; and (3) stages parallel to Perry's can be identified in the process of students choosing a major. While this illustration is brief, it does show that a research inquiry in academic advising can address theory, practice, research methodology, and assumptions. While the theory in this example is a formal published theory, any explanation of how a process works can sufficiently address the theory dimension.

Collaboration between academic advisors and faculty researchers has the potential to increase the effectiveness of academic advising (Padak et. al., 2004). By collaborating, advisors could identify problems in need of investigation while researchers could provide the methodological expertise. Such collaborations could make advising a more thoroughly explored field. Together advisors and researchers can investigate problems that are important to the field using respectable and accepted research methods. Academic advising must be examined for its effectiveness in the lives of students. The future history of academic advising will lie in its ability to create and use theory, apply findings in practice, and assess effectiveness through research.

References

1912 Normal School Bulletin Kirksville, Missouri. Retrieved July 16, 2007, from http://www.rootsweb.com/~moadair/NormalSchool/2-Normal_School.htm

2005 Carnegie Classification of Institutions of Higher Education. (2006, August 25). *The Chronicle of Higher Education, LIII* (1).

American Council on Education. (1949). *The student personnel point of view* (rev. ed.). American Council on Education Studies, series 6, no. 13. Washington, DC: American Council on Education.

Beatty, J. D. (1991, Spring). The National Academic Advising Association: A brief narrative history. *NACADA Journal, 11* (1), 5–25.

Best Practices For Electronically Offered Degree and Certificate Programs. (n.d.). Chicago: The Higher Learning Commission. Retrieved July 27, 2007, from http://www.ncahlc.org/index.php?option = com_content&task = view&id = 37&Itemid = 116

Bogue, J. P. (1950). *The community college.* New York: McGraw-Hill.

Brown, H. B. (1896). *Landmark Supreme Court cases, Plessy v Ferguson (1896).* Retrieved May 28, 2007, http://www.landmarkcases.org/plessy/background3.html

Brown, S. G. (1862). *The works of Rufus Choate with a memoir of his life.* Boston: Little, Brown.

Bush, N. B. (1969). The student and his professor: Colonial times to twentieth century. *Journal of Higher Education, 40* (8), 593–609.

Campuses with the largest enrollments, fall 2004. (2006, August 25). *The Chronicle Almanac, 2004–5: The Chronicle of Higher Education, LIII* (1).

Capella University Distance Learning Resources. (n.d.). Retrieved July 26, 2007, from http://www.capella.edu/online_learning/support_services.aspx

Cheek, K. (n.d.). *The Normal School.* Retrieved May 25, 2007, from http://www.nd.edu/~rbarger/www7/normal.html

The Chronicle Almanac, 2006–7: 2005 Carnegie Classification of Institutions of Higher Education. (2006). *The Chronicle of Higher Education, LIII* (1), 35.

Community College. (n.d.). *Wikipedia.* Retrieved May 24, 2007, from http://en.wikipedia.org/wiki/Community_college

Crookston, B. B. (1972). A developmental view of academic advising as teaching. *Journal of College Student Personnel, 13,* 12–17.

Duncan, J. M. (1823). *Travels through part of the United States and Canada in 1818 and 1819.* Glasgow: Printed at the University Press, for Hurst, Robinson, & Company, London.

Eastern Michigan University. (n.d.). *EMU style guide.* Retrieved September 8, 2007, from http://www.emich.edu/styleguide/timeline.htm

Franklin, F. (1910). *The life of Daniel Coit Gilman.* New York: Dodd, Mead.

Frost, S. H. (2000). Historical and philosophical foundations for academic advising. In V. N. Gordon, W. R. Habley, et al. (Eds.), *Academic advising: A comprehensive handbook.* San Francisco: Jossey-Bass.

Habley, W. R. (1983). Organizational structures in academic advising: Models and implications. *Journal of College Student Personnel, 26* (4), 535–539.

Habley, W. R. (2004). *The status of academic advising: Findings from the ACT Sixth National Survey.* (NACADA Monograph Series, no. 10.) Manhattan, KS: National Academic Advising Association.

Hawkins, H. (1960). *Pioneer: A history of the Johns Hopkins University, 1874–1889.* Ithaca, NY: Cornell University Press.

Hayes, R. B. (1841). At Kenyon College, 1840–1841. In *Diary and letters of Rutherford B. Hayes* (Vol. I). Retrieved August 24, 2007, from http://www.ohiohistory.org/onlinedoc/hayes/volume01.html

HBCU Historically Black Colleges & Universities. (n.d.). Indiana State University College View. Retrieved May 28, 2007, from http://www.collegeview.com/articles/CV/hbcu/hbcu_history.html

Hilton, F. (n.d.). *James Madison University: What's a Normal School?* Retrieved May 25, 2007, from http://www.jmu.edu/centennialcelebration/normalschool.shtml

King, M. C. (n.d.). *Community college advising.* Retrieved December 8, 2007, from http://www.nacada.ksu.edu/Clearinghouse/AdvisingIssues/comcollege.htm

Lucas, C. J. (2006). *American higher education: A history.* New York: Palgrave MacMillan.

Morison, S. E. (1946). *Three centuries of Harvard: 1636—1936.* Cambridge, MA: Harvard University Press.

Morrison, J. L., & Ferrante, R. (1973, February). The public two-year college and the culturally different. Presented at the annual meeting of the American Educational Research Association, New Orleans.

New England's First Fruits 1640: The history of the founding of Harvard College. From Collections of the Massachusetts Historical Society, 1792 (Vol. 1, pp. 242–248). Retrieved September 8, 2007, from http://www.constitution.org/primarysources/firstfruits.html

The Normal Schools (n.d.). Retrieved May 25, 2007, from http://www.lib.virginia.edu/fine-arts/guides/brown-normal.html

O'Banion, T. (1972). An academic advising model. *Junior College Journal, 42* (6), 62–69.

Ohio Learns! Student Services Get support. (n.d.). Retrieved July 26, 2007, from http://www.ohiolearns.org/get_support/displayinst.php

Padak, G., Kuhn, T., Gordon, V., Steele, G., & Robbins, R. (2004). Voices from the field: Building a research agenda for academic advising. *NACADA Journal, 25*(1).

Perry, W. G., Jr. (1970). *Forms of intellectual and ethical development in the college years: A scheme.* New York: Holt, Rinehart, & Winston.

Ruch, R. S. (2001). *Higher Ed, Inc.: The rise of the for-profit university.* Baltimore: Johns Hopkins University Press.

Rudolph, F. (1962). *The American college and university: A history.* New York: Knopf.

Thelin, J. R. (2004). *A history of American higher education.* Baltimore: Johns Hopkins University Press.

Thwing, C. F. (1928). *The American and the German University: One-hundred years of history.* New York: MacMillan.

Veysey, L. R. (1965). *The emergence of the American university.* Chicago: University of Chicago Press.

CHAPTER TWO

Theoretical Foundations of Academic Advising

Peter L. Hagen and Peggy Jordan

Hands off: neither the whole of truth nor the whole of good is revealed to any single observer, although each observer gains a partial superiority of insight from the peculiar position in which he stands. . . . It is enough to ask of each of us that he should be faithful to his own opportunities and make the most of his own blessings, without presuming to regulate the rest of the vast field.
—William James, "On a Certain Blindness in Human Beings," 1910

The pressure to ennoble academic advising and align it with other academic pursuits has been in the literature of academic advising from the start. On the first page of the inaugural issue of the *NACADA Journal*, John H. Borgard (1981, p. 1) prophesied that "we need something more if academic advising is to become a truly educative function rather than an adjunct to teaching, research, and service." That "something more" was theory. The passion for enhancing the legitimacy of the field remains today. Some have sought for that legitimacy in an overarching theory to explain and guide all of academic advising. We wish to cite the admonishment of William James and state from the outset that there is no such thing. Instead, the authors welcome an array of theories, and will attempt to present the most important and useful ones in this chapter. Any one theory alone may have its limitations; but the use of an array of theories will lead to an understanding of this broadly complicated phenomenon known as academic advising and will tend to vouchsafe its rightful place among teaching, research, and service.

In recent years, the National Academic Advising Association (NACADA) has focused on the ways in which academic advising is linked to other academic activities, especially teaching, learning, and theory-building. The NACADA leadership rightly surmises that strengthening ties to the other central processes in academe will enhance the way advising is viewed by academic decision-makers and by those in other fields of practice and inquiry, such as teaching, medicine, and law. The connection between advising and teaching has been made manifest in "The Concept of Academic Advising" (NACADA, 2006). But advisors cannot afford to forget their connections to the other activities that constitute academic life: learning, research, theorizing, and publication. Academic advisors are and should be *academics*. This is true whether one is a staff advisor or a faculty member who advises. All advisors are "professors" who profess the same thing: that they are academics worthy of being consulted as advisors.

THE ROLE OF THEORY IN ACADEMIC ADVISING

Theory-building provides lenses through which academic advising can be seen more clearly. In the optometrist's office, one must try out a few lenses before finding one that gives the clearest picture of what one wishes to see. As with vision, so with theory: one lens doesn't last a lifetime because both the observer and the observed change over time. One lens will not serve to clarify the whole of advising for all time. The lens of developmental theory has served quite well for several decades, and it continues to be a powerful theory. But a growing number of academic advising researchers and practitioners feel that developmental advising doesn't tell the whole story, that there can and should be not one lens, but many, through which to scrutinize academic advising.

Academic advising is a unique field. Practitioners, whether faculty or staff, come from a wide array of academic backgrounds. Colleges generally do not require a specific degree in order to practice advising. The same is true in research and scholarly inquiry in academic advising. One can be taken as seriously engaging in scholarly inquiry in academic advising without possessing a specific degree or background. Traditionally, the field has used theory that was available—developmental and others taken from the fields of career development, student personnel, and counseling—in order to understand itself as a field and to avoid perceptions of being an ancillary or adjunct field. Given the wide array of backgrounds of practitioners and researchers in both faculty and staff roles, it is time to strike out in new directions, engaging in theory-building using other fields in the arts, humanities, and social sciences without losing the rich explanatory power of developmental theory. Researchers and practitioners in the field have *license* to do this because of the wide spectrum of their collective scholarly backgrounds and the *obligation* to search far and wide for theories because of the rich complexity of academic advising. No one theory is likely to explain the whole of academic advising; just as no one theory could explain the whole of teaching, medicine, or law.

Academic advising has long been recognized as a field of practitioners; certainly, the main purpose of this *Handbook* is to provide guidance as one engages in the practice of academic advising. In recent years, academic advising has gained recognition as a field of scholarly inquiry and is taking its rightful place in the history of scholarly inquiry. These two aspects of academic advising—as a field of practice on the one hand and as a field of scholarly inquiry on the other—are not antithetical. Practice points to fruitful avenues for scholarly inquiry and published scholarly inquiry improves practice. Theory is necessary for both aspects. Academic advising cannot be performed or studied without theory.

In the first edition of this *Handbook,* Creamer (2000, p. 31) asserted that "no theories of academic advising are currently available." But there are really tens of thousands of theories of academic advising: one for every practicing academic advisor. It may be true that there is no grand unified theory of advising, just as there is no master theoretical perspective that informs practice and research in the other professions. Such an all-embracing perspective is neither possible nor desirable. Multiple theories can exist at the same time, as is the case in all other fields of scholarly inquiry and in all other fields of practice. It may even be the case that practitioners *should* have a broad palette of theories to meet the diverse needs of the students seen on a single day.

It is useful to use metatheoretical terms to make sense of the array of theories now available (Hagen, 2005). *Analogic* theories are basically metaphorical, seeing one thing (advising, the tenor of the metaphor) in terms of another (the vehicle of the metaphor). This means borrowing theory and ideas from other fields and applying them to advising. *Normative* theories exhort advisors to advise in a certain way. They construct an ideal toward which advising should tend. This dichotomy will be used to structure the remainder of this chapter and categorize the variety of theories.

TRADITIONAL NORMATIVE APPROACHES TO ACADEMIC ADVISING

Crookston (1972/1994), an early proponent of developmental advising said "Developmental advising is concerned not only with a specific personal or vocational decision but also with facilitating the student's rational processes, environmental and interpersonal interactions, behavioral awareness, and problem-solving, decision-making, and evaluating skills" (p. 5). King (2005) describes it as both a process and an orientation, with a holistic focus and a dedication to student growth and development. O'Banion (1972/1994) described five dimensions of academic advising: "(1) exploration of life goals, (2) exploration of vocational goals, (3) program choice, (4) course choice, and (5) scheduling courses" (p. 10). Chickering (2006) agreed with the holistic function of advising and found that faculty members who are committed to student success are concerned with those students' total personal development, including academic, personal, intellectual, and social development. Crookston (1994) viewed the relationship between student and advisor as the crucial element in student growth. The goal is "toward openness, acceptance, trust, sharing of data, and collaborative problem-solving, decision-making, and evaluation" (p. 9).

Developmental advising does not require advisors to discuss issues that go beyond the individual advisor's scope of knowledge or comfort. In fact, Crookston recommended making decisions about limits and responsibility and negotiating central issues as part of the establishment of the relationship between advisor and student. Even prescriptive advising has its place in the developmental model because there are times when a simple answer to a question is the only reasonable response. Developmental advising focuses on the needs of the student in determining how the advising interaction shall transpire. Seen from Crookston's perspective, there can be no schism between the personal and the academic development of students because education is seen as transforming individuals not only intellectually, but personally.

Theories of student development can be placed into one of three categories: psychosocial-identity formation, cognitive-developmental structures, and personal preference or types (Strange, 2004; King, 2000).

Psychosocial-Identity Formation Theories

Psychosocial-identity formation theories look at different periods or stages in people's lives and the issues faced during these stages. The focus is on developmental tasks, transitions, and identity formation.

Erikson (1963) described eight stages (or crises) of development over the life span. A positive or negative resolution is possible at each stage. Healthy resolutions allow for positive consequences of the crisis to be incorporated into the person's future development. Negative resolutions lead to breaks or discontinuities in development, which are carried over into subsequent stages. Negative resolutions stemming from childhood crises can remain with the person into adulthood. There continue to be opportunities, however, for individuals to mend these breaks through more positive resolutions of later developmental stages. For example, a person who never learned to trust authority figures can, through a trusting relationship cultivated by a teacher, mentor, advisor, or friend, learn to trust.

Table 2.1 offers a summary of Erikson's eight stages and offers descriptions of potential student behaviors that might have resulted from a prior negative resolution in each of Erikson's stages. The table is not intended to be diagnostic: one cannot draw the conclusion that if the behavior is present a student has necessarily had a negative resolution. It is a tool to show what negative resolution of a stage may look like, rather than a yardstick to measure gaps in development.

Chickering and Reisser (1993) based their work on Erikson's theory of identity formation. Their model demonstrates how college students change psychosocially through stages they called "vectors." Student growth along these vectors can occur at different rates and can interact with movement of other vectors. Students of traditional ages are thought to explore the first three vectors in their initial college years and to deal with the fourth, fifth, and maybe the sixth vectors as upper-class students. Throughout life individuals may work through the last three vectors. Table 2.2 displays college experiences that may be associated or learned at each of the seven vectors. Chickering and Reisser (1993) promote high student–faculty contact and define student development professionals as educators, collaborating with faculty in the application of student development theory.

Table 2.1. Behavioral Description of Negative Resolution of Erikson's Eight Stages.

Stage	Developmental Crisis	Possible Display of Negative Resolution
1	Trust vs. Mistrust	Student does not trust word of professional advisor—wants everything in writing.
		Student confrontational with faculty members—complains of lack of fairness of grading policy, exams, etc.
2	Autonomy vs. Shame and Doubt	Student has difficulty making decisions—wants everything spelled out or done for him/her.
3	Initiative vs. Guilt	Student does not take responsibility for enrollment, course work, etc., but then feels anxious or guilty about lack of progress.
4	Industry vs. Inferiority	Student feels inadequate even when experiencing success—cannot seem to believe success is a result of own effort or ability.
5	Identity vs. Role Confusion	Student models self almost totally after someone else (parent, friend, etc.) or has no idea what his or her identity is.
6	Intimacy vs. Isolation	Student is isolated, does not seem to have any friends, is very self-absorbed.
7	Generativity vs. Stagnation	By middle adulthood, this student may be frustrated with career and/or relationships—feels stuck or at a dead end.
8	Ego Integrity vs. Despair	Mature adult—if he/she is attending college it is in an attempt to make up for lost time, lost chances, try to obtain what might have been.

Seligman and Csikszentmihalyi (2000) are leaders of the positive psychology movement, which looks at how normal individuals flourish under ordinary conditions. Positive psychology runs counter to what they call a "disease framework" (p. 7)—that is, approaches that focus on what is wrong or diseased in working with people. Seligman and Csikszentmihalyi (2000) wrote about raising children, but their work also applies to college students. "Raising children is more than fixing what is wrong with them. It is about identifying and nurturing their strongest qualities, what they own and are best at, and helping them find niches in which they can best live out these strengths" (p. 6). Clifton and Anderson (2004) also champion the focus on student strengths rather than student deficits. They have developed an approach called "strengths-based advising," which allows students to be who they are and develop the strengths they possess to manage a variety of tasks. This is counter to many advisors' focus on deficits, particularly with underprepared students. Clifton and Anderson (2004) suggest that advisors talk with

Table 2.2. Chickering's Vectors of Development.

Vector	Vector Description	College Experience	Advisor Interactions
Developing Competence	Intellectual competence, physical and manual skills, and interpersonal communication	Precollege reading, math courses, participation in a club—any activity that increases the feeling of personal accomplishment	Advisor gives accurate placement and course sequencing information.
Managing Emotions	Delaying impulses, managing physical expression of emotions—at highest level is a deep awareness of one's authentic emotions and acceptance of the emotions	Effectively dealing with and appropriately expressing strong emotions such as anger, depression, or romantic feelings for another	Advisor offers resources and referral for dealing with anxiety, depression, motivational issues, etc.
Moving through Autonomy to Interdependence	Self-sufficiency and interconnectedness	Maintaining positive relationships with family members, while moving away and establishing independence	Advisor encourages and reinforces students' independent decision-making.
Developing Mature Interpersonal Relationships	Acceptance and understanding of diverse groups of people (different ethnicities, cultures, races, and sexual orientations) and tolerance for individual idiosyncrasies	Developing intimate relationship with another person Tolerance and appreciation for personal and cultural differences	Advisor models acceptance and appreciation for personal and cultural differences.
Establishing Identity	Requires mastery of previous four vectors; requires developing positive self-regard, confidence in oneself, optimism about the future, positive body image, and clear sexual identification.	Positive self-image and knowledge of one's self	Advisor expands students' knowledge of self through interview questions and reflects positive view of students' personal characteristics, including gender, social and cultural heritage, and sexual orientation.
Developing Purpose	Focus is on vocational and lifestyle goals and involves personal interests and intentional decisions about family.	Vocational plans and personal interests related to a meaningful lifestyle	Advisor uses interview and assessments to assist students' career exploration.
Developing Integrity	Involves humanizing values, such as issues of faith or other belief systems that are considered throughout the lifespan.	Humanize and personalize values; develop congruence between beliefs and actions	Advisor listens attentively to students' conflicting values and beliefs, offering clarifying questions that aid students' move toward congruence.

underprepared students about their strengths—what got them this far, what they enjoy, what they believe they can do well. By using their assets, underprepared students may be able to build their skills in other areas. Schreiner and Anderson (2005) offer further applications of this approach to advising: "Strengths-based advising is predicated on students' natural talents and is used to build their confidence while motivating them to acquire the knowledge base and skills necessary for college-level achievement" (p. 22). While strengths-based advising is a holistic approach like developmental advising, it differs in that it is based on student motivation, rather than on needs assessment; it focuses on possibilities, rather than on problems; and it focuses on talents and skills and on how those strengths lead to success.

With strengths-based advising, students feel understood at a deeper level, express higher motivation, greater self-confidence, and report higher satisfaction with advising. Focusing on student deficits is "focusing on the student who is not there" (p. 22).

Vygotsky developed a sociocultural theory of development, which stressed the social context of cognitive development (Berk, 2007). He saw cognitive development as a "socially mediated process" (Berk, 2007, p. 23) that required support from adults and more mature peers as individuals attempt new tasks. One of the keystones of his theory is the "zone of proximal development," which he defined as "the distance between the actual developmental level as determined by independent problem solving and the level of potential development as determined through problem solving under adult guidance or in collaboration with more capable peers" (Vygotsky, 1978, p. 86). For example, a first-year student may lack the critical-thinking skills required to progress to more advanced classes. The professor, through explanations, modeling, demonstrations, and opportunities to discuss concepts assists the student in shifting from his or her actual developmental level to a potential level of development. According to Harland (2003), Vygotsky argued that learning and development differ and that learning not only leads development, but that learning creates a zone of proximal development. A concept related to Vygotsky's theory is "scaffolding," which Harland defines as "the process of providing higher levels of initial support for students as they entered the zone of proximal development with the gradual dismantling of the support structure as students progressed towards independence" (p. 268). According to Vygotsky (1978), "What is the zone of proximal development today will be the actual developmental level tomorrow" (p. 87). Using Vygotsky's constructs, advisors focus on the potential of all students by taking into account where they are developmentally, providing support to learn what is needed, then allowing students' independence to flourish. By knowing students' levels of development, advisors can offer them information that is a little above their understanding but within their ability to comprehend.

Cognitive-Development Theories

Cognitive-development theories refer to how individuals perceive and interpret their life experiences. The stages of Kohlberg's (1969) theory of moral development, shown in Table 2.3, focus on the way a person reasons about moral dilemmas rather than the content of a person's verbal response to such dilemmas. The first two stages are typical of children through elementary school. By early adolescence Stage 3 develops, and by mid to late adolescence Stage 4 is in place. Few people progress higher than Stage 4 (Berk, 2007).

Table 2.3. Kohlberg's Stages of Moral Development.

Stage	Level	Sublevel	Description
	Preconventional Level		Morality is externally controlled. Individual accepts rules of authority figures. Behavior that is rewarded is seen as good; behavior that is punished is seen as bad.
1		The Punishment and Obedience Orientation	The focus is on fear of authority and avoidance of punishment in deciding morality of issues.
2		The Instrumental Purpose Orientation	Concrete understanding of issues. The focus is on self-interest and mutual reciprocity.
	Conventional Level		Conformity to social rules is important, but at this level the purpose of conformity is to maintain societal order and positive relationships.
3		The "Good boy–Good girl" Orientation	The motivation for conforming is to maintain affection and approval from significant others.
4		The Social-Order-Maintaining Orientation	A larger perspective is taken into account. Societal laws should be enforced to ensure order and cooperation between individuals.
	Postconventional Level		Morality is defined in abstract terms that uphold principles and values applying to all societies.
5		The Social Contract Orientation	Rules and laws are viewed as flexible and should uphold individual rights as well as promoting good for the majority.
6		The Universal Ethical Principle Orientation	Behavioral decisions are based on ethical principles that are seen as good for all people, regardless of laws.

According to Dawson (2002), however, attending college increases the likelihood that an individual will progress beyond Kohlberg's Stage 4. This increase is due to wider exposure to social and cultural issues outside the student's immediate environment, and is enhanced when students are exposed to open discussions of diverse opinions.

William Perry's (1970) research on how college students interpret and make meaning of their college experiences formed the basis of his model of intellectual and ethical development. He proposed nine *positions,* as opposed to stages of development, because he considered them to be an individual's worldview, rather than discrete linear stages of development. Perry's nine positions are: (1) Basic Duality, (2) Multiplicity Prelegitimate, (3) Multiplicity Legitimate but Subordinate, (4a.) Multiplicity Coordinate, (4b) Relativism Subordinate, (5) Relativism, (6) Commitment Foreseen, and (7–9) Evolving Commitments.

Dualism is a view of the world as a dichotomy of right or wrong, good or bad. It is oriented toward authority and consists of doing what one is told and responding with correct answers. Multiplicity is a position that begins with cognitive dissonance, the discomfort one feels when the knowledge one has conflicts with new knowledge. In this position, the individual acknowledges that there may be no right answers to certain questions and accepts diverse opinions as equally valid. Analytical thinking improves during this time. Relativism is stimulated by the need for logical support for the diverse opinions that multiplistic thinkers simply accepted as possibly valid. Supporting arguments and logical explanations are needed for opinions to be considered useful, and opinions without support are recognized as being inferior. Commitment "refers to an act, or ongoing activity relating a person as agent and chooser to aspects of his life in which he invests his energies, his care and his identity" (Perry, 1970, p. 135). These commitments may be decisions about relationships, major, career, religion or other areas of one's life.

Current student development theories may not adequately describe all groups of students. Kodama, McEwen, Liang, and Lee (2002), focusing on Asian American students, suggest that it is inappropriate to continue using traditional student development theories to explain the development of diverse populations. "Knowing and taking into account students' familial and cultural contexts and helping them draw on their strengths and values, rather than viewing them as deficient in relation to dominant society ideals, will assist Asian American students in greater and more meaningful psychosocial development" (p. 56).

Cross (1995) developed a Model of Black Identity Formation. As their personal black identity develops, individuals go through five stages: (1) Pre-encounter, in which identity is Eurocentric and the individual is trying to assimilate into the dominant, white culture; (2) Encounter, which involves some experience that triggers a reinterpretation of previous beliefs; (3) Immersion-Emersion, which has two phases; first, the person totally immerses himself or herself in blackness, withdrawing from other groups, especially whites, whereas the second phase involves internalization of the new identity; (4) Internalization, which occurs as the person develops self-assurance about being black; and (5) Internalization-Commitment, where the individual has a positive plan for participation in improvement of the black community.

Cass (1979) developed a theory of homosexual identity development that integrates psychological and social aspects of development. It incorporates both individuals' views of themselves and how they feel about others' perceptions of them. D'Augelli (1994) produced a life span model of lesbian, gay, and bisexual identity development. He identified six interactive processes, rather than stages of development. He maintained in his model that in addition to reacting to one's environment, individuals also shape their environments. His six processes are: (1) exiting heterosexual identity; (2) developing a personal lesbian/gay/bisexual identity; (3) developing a social identity of lesbian/gay/bisexual; (4) becoming a lesbian/gay/bisexual offspring; (5) developing a lesbian/gay/bisexual intimacy; and (6) entering a lesbian/gay/bisexual community.

Personal Preference or Type Theories

Personal preference or type theories focus on differences that are more preferential, on personality differences, and on how students approach their learning environment as well as the world at large. These factors are relatively stable over the students' development, and they influence other developmental areas. Personal types are nonevaluative. They offer information about how an individual tends to respond to environmental stimuli and what sources of support they tend to use. The Myers-Briggs theory of personality type (Myers & McCauley, 1985) and Kolb's theory of learning styles (1984) are noted contributors to personal type theories.

The Myers-Briggs Type Indicator is based on Carl Jung's (1960) theory of personality types. It emphasizes how people gather information and how they use that information to make decisions. Preferences are organized in four dyads: Extroversion-Introversion, Sensing-Intuition, Thinking-Feeling, and Judging-Perceiving. (Evans, Forney, & Guido-DiBrito, 1998). Extroverts are more comfortable in group settings, while introverts are more likely to choose solitary work. Sensing individuals like objective data and routines, while Intuitives perceive information based on imagination, connections, and impressions, and may feel stifled by routine. In making decisions, Thinkers prefer logical analyses of facts and logic. Those dominant on the Feeling dyad make decisions based on likes, dislikes, and subjective values. The Judging-Perceiving dyad displays an individual's orientation to the outer world. Judging types gather information quickly and make decisions to lead an orderly life. Perceivers seem to take more time observing and gathering information. They prefer a more spontaneous life (King, 2000). Crockett and Crawford (1989) found the developmental model of advising, focusing on a close working relationship with their advisor, and dealing broadly with their goals and experiences, were preferred by more feeling students and intuitive students. Sensing students appeared to prefer advising focusing on practical details of course registration and academic planning.

Kolb (1984) identified four learning styles, which people habitually use to perceive information and process experiences. They are convergers, divergers, assimilators, and accommodators. Convergers tend to be good problem-solvers and decision-makers. They are good at applying information to practical situations and are best when they must identify one right answer to a question. Divergers are imaginative and aware of meaning and values. They see a variety of perspectives and are good at coming up with alternatives. They are feeling-oriented and are interested in people. Assimilators are good at inductive reasoning and have the ability to create theories through the integration of seemingly disparate ideas. They value ideas because of their logic rather than their practical value. Accommodators implement plans. They are doers. They complete tasks, are open to new experiences, willing to take risks, adaptive to changing conditions, and prefer trial-and-error methods of problem-solving rather than analytical ability. Accommodators are also comfortable with people (Evans et al., 1998).

The implications of learning styles for advisors include the academic disciplines with which people with certain learning styles are comfortable. It may be that convergers more frequently study the physical sciences and engineering, divergers study the humanities and liberal arts, assimilators study the basic sciences and mathematics, and accommodators study practical fields like business (Evans et al., 1998). Kolb (1984) found a tendency for academic disciplines to have within their majors students with certain learning styles. While this should not be used to stereotype students, learning may be more difficult for students with differing learning styles. Learning styles are also important in how advisors approach students with academic, career, and personal information. Table 2.4 offers examples of majors and advising approaches that may be more useful with each learning style.

Table 2.4. Kolb's Learning Styles.

Learning Style	Typical Major	Advising Approach
Convergers	Engineering, technological, and specialist careers	May prefer initially accessing information on computer and getting answers to specific questions from advisor.
Divergers	English, arts, entertainment, and service	May prefer reading printed information with time to reflect and follow-up with personal contact with an advisor.
Assimilators	Math, information careers, and science	May prefer direct contact with an advisor who will give information verbally, with opportunities for student to bring up questions as they develop.
Accommodators	Education, business, and organizational careers	These students may appreciate personal contact with an advisor and get specific information in person.

PARADIGM EXPANSION: NORMATIVE THEORIES

Since 1999, theoretical perspectives that seek to provide alternatives to developmental theory have emerged. These new normative approaches have tended to focus on advising in the context of the learning process and have paved the way for the "Concept of Advising" (NACADA, 2006) and the widespread endorsement of "advising is teaching" as a guiding metaphor within NACADA.

Hemwall and Trachte (1999) sought to align academic advising more closely with academic affairs. They argued that "the model of developmental academic advising should be abandoned and replaced by alternative theoretical traditions" (p. 5) because, in their view, developmental theory is less concerned than it should be with learning, the life of the mind, and the curriculum—indeed with the central missions and purposes of higher education—in its effort to bring about the development of the whole person. While no one, including Hemwall and Trachte, would argue that the self-actualizing movement through developmental stages is not a worthy goal, they argue that the curriculum of higher education is not necessary for the attainment of that goal. Moreover, Hemwall and Trachte assert that developmental advising theory tends to alienate academic faculty, who see their primary mission as educating, not seeing to the personal growth of the individual student. When learning is placed at the core of faculty-centered advising, Hemwall and Trachte argue, that advising supports "the centrality of the academic curriculum" (p. 7).

Hemwall and Trachte (2003) suggest that the centrality of teaching and learning in the advising process may be more easily found at smaller colleges and universities because at such locations advising is more likely to be done by faculty members. "Advisors need to think about advising as if they were teachers. Curricular goals must be identified and effective pedagogies must be developed if advisors hope that advisees will learn the values and goals educators set as the main purpose of college education" (p. 9). This is not to say that faculty are the only or the best advisors; rather, they are first and foremost "teachers, and typically they view their roles as advisors as part of the learning and teaching process and not as a means to facilitate student development" (p. 9). If advising is teaching, then it can be said to have a curriculum and a pedagogy.

Hemwall and Trachte (2005) flesh out the notions of a *curriculum* ("what should students learn through advising" [p. 75]) and a *pedagogy* ("how might the learning take place" [p. 75]) of academic advising seen through the lens of the learning paradigm. The basic curriculum of academic advising should facilitate student learning: (1) about the mission of the college, (2) of both lower- and higher-order thinking skills, and (3) about how to achieve the goals imbedded in the mission statement of the college Hemwall and Trachte (2005). The "curriculum" of advising-as-teaching is thus the curriculum itself; or more broadly, it is to teach according to the mission of the college that brought forth that curriculum. Advising-as-teaching is advising that has become aligned with the central missions of higher education.

As to the pedagogy of advising-as-teaching, Hemwall and Trachte (2005) put forth seven principles:

1. Students must actively construct their learning of the institutional mission and the mission of liberal learning.
2. Advisors should incorporate knowledge of different learning styles into their practice of academic advising.
3. Advisors must be able to take into account how the social context of the student may affect her or his understanding of the meaning of education.
4. The student's preexisting knowledge and background concepts affect her or his possibilities for learning.
5. Advisees must be allowed an equal part in the dialogue, with the freedom and the obligation to express, justify, and discuss their goals and ideas.
6. Advisors must guide, not goad, leading and attracting the learner to higher and more sophisticated understandings of the goals of liberal learning.
7. Advisors should guide students to benefit from anomalies, disequilibria, and apparent contradictions. (Adapted from Hemwall and Trachte, 2005, pp. 77–81.)

Lowenstein (1999) also argued for more academically centered advising and regarded the notion of "prescriptive advising" as not altogether deleterious, as is suggested by some proponents of developmental advising. He argues that developmental advising is not the true opposite of prescriptive advising and that those who claim that they are opposite make a category mistake: developmental advising is a theory of advising, prescriptive advising is a style of advising.

Lowenstein (2000, 2005) has provided the most complete account of what has become known as "the learning-centered paradigm" of academic advising. He provides an answer to the implied question raised by the master metaphor of advising as teaching/learning, "So, if advisors are teachers, then what do they teach?" The answer to this question has far-reaching implications for the future of advising as a profession and as an activity carried out by faculty members. If advising is teaching and the partaking of advising is learning, then it clearly behooves staff academic advisors to become more like faculty and it clearly behooves faculty advisors to conduct advising in ways that are parallel to classroom teaching. The answer to the question, according to Lowenstein, is that advisors teach the curriculum itself, its intrarelations, its relevance to the life of the mind, and its power as a pathway to lifelong learning. In short, advisors teach the "logic" of the curriculum:

> Learning transpires when a student makes sense of his or her overall curriculum just as it does when a person understands an individual course, and the former is every bit as important as the latter. In fact, learning in each individual course is enhanced by the learning of the curriculum, and thus may continue long after the course has been completed. Finally, whereas the individual course is the

domain of the professor, the overall curriculum is most often the domain of the academic advisor, and the excellent advisor coaches the student through the process of learning the curriculum. (2005, p. 69)

This is advising transformed and situated squarely in academic affairs. Advisors are academics, and "the advisor is arguably the most important person in the student's educational world" (Lowenstein, 2005, p. 72). Lowenstein recognizes that this has far-reaching implications for the hiring and training of advisors and for NACADA itself. If advising is teaching, and the result is learning, then the advisor must be a good teacher, not narrowly trained but instead the recipient of a liberal education preferably in the liberal arts, because "they have been trained to take a broad view, to integrate ideas synthetically" (p. 72). Training should focus on educative processes like assessment of learning outcomes of a learning-centered advising.

The phrase *educative advising*, introduced by Borgard (1981), was resurrected by Melander (2005) to cover the same general semantic territory as was intended by Hemwall and Trachte's (2000) "learning at the core," and Lowenstein's "academically centered advising" (2000) and "learning-centered advising" (2005). "Educative advising" can easily serve to set aside any confusion that may come from using the phrase "advising as teaching," which does not necessarily imply the partaking of advising as learning. Melander (2005) rightly calls for educative advising that is in accordance with "generally accepted, research-based principles of how students learn" (p. 88).

PARADIGM EXPANSION: ANALOGICAL THEORIES

The "Concept of Advising" (NACADA, 2006) is itself a fleshing out of the metaphor "advising is teaching," but this is not the only way in which a metaphor or an analogy can shed light on advising. Other analogies or cognates to advising can provide rich theoretical pathways into the explanation and elucidation of the concept of advising. They can do this without dislodging other theoretical perspectives. For example, consider *The Presentation of Self in Everyday Life*, a sociological study by Goffman (1959) that starts from the theoretical stance that human interactions can be seen as dramas that are played out on a stage. Not even Goffman would argue that sociology can only be done by adopting this metaphor as the single relevant perspective. But the sociological study of human interaction is advanced by regarding it, at least in some contexts, as drama. By viewing a less-well-known concept, human interaction, as an analog to a better-understood concept, drama, the lesser-known is illuminated by the better-known.

The field of advising is wide open to other illuminating metaphors (analogs) from other fields. Theory is translatable from one field to another. Academic advising could, for example, be fruitfully examined from the perspective of narrative theory, on the assumption that advising is really all about storytelling. If this metaphor is adopted, then everything known about both literature and about ethnography can be used to examine academic advising.

Narrative therapy developed in psychology in the 1980s; it came from the field of family therapy and has much to offer to the field of advising (Hester, 2004). It proposes that individuals construct stories to make sense of their own lives and is a social constructive view of reality. People are selective in the stories they recall, which leads to the person's identity, or sense of who they are, being based on the stories they tell about themselves and that others tell of them. Themes such as inadequacy, powerlessness, depression, and perfectionism are examples that permeate personal narratives (Daigneault, 1999). The role of the therapist is to coconstruct a new story that is more positive and leads to a more satisfying and adaptive outcome. Narrative therapy has also been used in multicultural counseling to develop strategies for reversing negative identity development based on negative cultural messages (Semmler and Williams, 2000). Narrative advising has been described as "The structured application of metaphors to the advising setting whereby the advisor helps students access past experiences in order to find solutions to create successful and lasting change" (Christman, 2005). Using narrative techniques in advising, Christman (2003) suggests borrowing tools from narrative therapy and challenging students' belief structures and assisting them in creating new stories about themselves. Advisors can assist students to use their education as an avenue to write a new chapter, if not a whole new story, in their development. Advisors can also use narrative approaches when discussing what keeps students from reaching their goals, what interferes with their commitment to career decisions, what contributes to their success, and what they can do to overcome obstacles and adversity.

Narrative advising is not the only theoretical perspective that draws analogically from other fields. Hagen (1994) views academic advising as a form of Socratic dialectic comprised of two equal participants, the advisor and the advisee. This approach was expanded by Kuhtmann (2005), who carefully examines Socratic method and its shortcomings before concluding that it may be useful in most, but not necessarily all, advising situations. Beck (1999) looks at how chaos theory can possibly inform the practice of advising undecided students.

Several articles examining the possibility of theories analogous to academic advising appeared in the Fall 2005 issue of the *NACADA Journal* and provide examples of how one could theorize about academic advising. Jackson (2005) looks at the ways in which the academic pursuit of philosophy can inform both the practice and the theory of academic advising. Demetriou (2005) adapted developmental advising theory by showing how a lesser-known aspect of that theory, social norms theory, can be directly applied to academic advising. McClellan (2005) shows how knowledge of conflict theory, and even the neuroanatomy of conflict, can suggest strategies for advising practice. Finally, Rawlins and Rawlins (2005) provide the clearest example of how one field can be used to shed light on another. Taking what has already been established in friendship studies, a field that incorporates communication studies and sociology, they show how friendship theory can help advisors better negotiate the advising relationship. Like friendships, "advising relationships are not static;

they are subject to numerous contingencies, dialectical tensions, and concrete limitations of time and energy on the parts of both participants" (p. 18), and so what is known about friendships can increase knowledge of advising.

FUTURE THEORETICAL TRADITIONS IN ACADEMIC ADVISING

It would be foolish to speculate on the future direction of academic advising theory. Predictions have a way of biting back at those who make them. Still, it seems reasonable to suppose that the current groundswell of theory-building based on advising-as-teaching has not yet reached its peak. It is reasonable to expect to see major works that build upon the groundwork laid by Hemwall, Trachte, Lowenstein, and others. At the same time, it is reasonable to expect that developmental theory will continue to engage and inform practice and research in academic advising for many years to come.

Rather than engage in predictions, the authors wish instead to suggest some possible avenues for future theorizing. Where *can* the field go? Here is where analogical theory-building can come to the fore and truly magnify what is known about academic advising. No list can be final. But the following possibilities might be heuristic and may spark the imagination of some future theorist: narrative theory, systems theory, hermeneutics, postmodern theory, method acting, games theory, and cubism. Perhaps something like these new directions will be seen in future editions of this chapter, drawing upon what is already known in some aspect of the arts, humanities, social sciences, education, sciences, business, and the other professions, and applying it to advising.

Advisors have *license* to draw upon a wide array of theoretical perspectives because they have come to advising not from one field, but from many; they have the *obligation* to resist adopting only one theoretical perspective because the phenomenon of academic advising is so very complex.

References

Beck, A. (1999). Advising undecided students: Lessons from chaos theory. *NACADA Journal, 19* (1), 45–49.

Berk, L. E. (2007). *Development through the lifespan* (4th ed.). New York: Pearson Education.

Borgard, J. H. (1981). Toward a pragmatic philosophy of academic advising. *NACADA Journal, 1* (1), 1–6.

Cass, V.C. (1979). Homosexual identity formation: A theoretical model. *Journal of Homosexuality, 4,* 219–235.

Chickering, A. W. (2006). Every student can learn-If. . . . *About Campus, 11* (2), 9–15.

Chickering, A. W., & Reisser, L. (1993). *Education and identity.* San Francisco: Jossey-Bass.

Christman, P. (2003). Narrative advising: Guiding students to better academic decisions. In M. K. Hemwall and K. Trachte (Eds.), *Advising and learning: Academic advising from the perspective of small colleges and universities* (pp. 37–42), (NACADA Monograph Series, No. 8.) Manhattan, KS: National Academic Advising Association.

Christman, P. (2005). Narrative advising: A hands on approach to effective change. Presented at the national conference of the National Academic Advising Association, Las Vegas, NV.

Clifton, D. O., & Anderson, E. (2004). *StrengthsQuest: Discover and develop your strengths in academics, career and beyond.* Washington, DC: The Gallup Organization.

Creamer, D. G. (2000). Use of theory in academic advising. In V. N. Gordon, W. R. Habley, and Associates (Eds.), *Academic advising: A comprehensive handbook* (pp. 18–34). San Francisco: Jossey-Bass.

Creamer, D. G., & Creamer, E. G. (1994). Practicing developmental advising: Theoretical contents and functional application. *NACADA Journal, 14* (2), 17–24.

Crockett, J. B., & Crawford, R. L. (1989). The relationship between Myers-Briggs Type Indicator (MBTI) scale scores and advising style preferences of college freshmen. *Journal of College Student Development, 30*, 154–161.

Crookston, B. B. (1972). A developmental view of academic advising as teaching. *Journal of College Student Personnel, 13*, 12–17.

Cross, W. E., Jr. (1995). The psychology of nigrescence: Revising the cross model. In J. G. Ponterotto, J. M. Casas, L. A. Suzuki, & C. M. Alexander (Eds.), *Handbook of multicultural counseling*. Thousand Oaks, CA: Sage.

Daigneault, S. D. (1999). Narrative means to Adlerian ends: An illustrated comparison of narrative therapy and Adlerian play therapy. *Journal of Individual Psychology, 55* (3), 298–315.

D'Augelli, A. R. (1994). Identity development and sexual orientation: Toward a model of lesbian, gay, and bisexual development. In E. J. Trickett, R. J. Watts, and D. Birman (Eds.), *Human diversity: Perspectives on people in context*. San Francisco: Jossey-Bass.

Dawson, T. L. (2002). New tools, new insights: Kohlberg's moral judgment stages revisited. *International Journal of Behavioral Development, 26* (1), 154–166.

Demetriou, C. (2005). Potential applications of social norms theory to academic advising. *NACADA Journal, 25* (2), 49–57.

Erikson, E. H. (1963). *Childhood and society* (2nd ed.). New York: Norton.

Evans, N. J., Forney, D. S., & Guido-DiBrito, F. (1998). *Student development in college.* San Francisco: Jossey-Bass.

Goffman, E. (1959). *The presentation of self in everyday life.* New York: Doubleday.

Hagen, P. L. (1994) Academic advising as dialectic. *NACADA Journal, 14* (2), 85–88.

Hagen, P. L. (2005). Theory building in academic advising. *NACADA Journal, 25* (2), 3–8.

Harland, T. (2003). Vygotsky's zone of proximal development and problem-based learning: Linking a theoretical concept with practice through action research. *Teaching in Higher Education, 8* (2), 263–272.

Hemwall, M. K., & Trachte, K. (1999). Learning at the core: Toward a new understanding of academic advising. *NACADA Journal, 19* (1), 5–11.

Hemwall, M. K., & Trachte, K. (2003). Learning at the core: Theory and practice of academic advising in small colleges and universities. In M. K. Hemwall and K. Trachte (Eds.), *Advising and learning: Academic advising from the perspective of small colleges and universities* (pp. 5–11). (NACADA Monograph Series, No. 8.) Manhattan, KS: National Academic Advising Association.

Hemwall, M. K., & Trachte, K. (2005). Academic advising as learning: 10 organizing principles. *NACADA Journal, 25* (2), 74–83.

Hester, R. L. (2004). Early memory and narrative therapy. *Journal of Individual Psychology, 60* (4), 338–347.

Jackson, R. L. (2005). Academic advising and philosophy. *NACADA Journal, 25* (2), 30–36.

Jung, C. G. (1960). *The structure and dynamics of the psyche.* New York: Bollingen Foundation.

King, M. C. (2005). Developmental academic advising. Retrieved July 30, 2007, from *NACADA Clearinghouse of Academic Advising Resources* Web site: http://www.nacada.ksu.edu/Clearinghouse/AdvisingIssues/dev_adv.htm

King, P. (2000). Using student development theory to inform institutional research. *New Directions for Institutional Research, 108,* 19–36.

Kodama, C. M., McEwen, M. K., Liang, C. T. H., & Lee, S. (2002). An Asian American perspective on psychosocial student development theory. *New Directions for Student Services, 97,* 45–60.

Kohlberg, L. (1969). Stage and sequence: The cognitive-developmental approach to socialization. In D. A. Goslin (Ed.), *Handbook of socialization: Theory in research.* Boston: Houghton-Mifflin.

Kolb, D. A. (1984). *Experiential learning: Experience as the source of learning and development.* Englewood Cliffs, NJ: Prentice Hall.

Kuhtmann, M. S. (2005) Socratic self-examination and its application to academic advising. *NACADA Journal, 25* (2), 37–48.

Lowenstein, M. (1999). An alternative to the developmental theory of advising. *The Mentor,* November 22, 1999. Retrieved August 10, 2007, from http://www.psu.edu/dus/mentor

Lowenstein, M. (2000). Academic advising and the "logic" of the curriculum. *The Mentor,* April 14, 2000. Retrieved August 10, 2007, from http://www.psu.edu/dus/mentor

Lowenstein, M. (2005). If advising is teaching, what do advisors teach? *NACADA Journal, 25* (2), 65–73.

McClellan, J. (2005). Increasing advisor effectiveness by understanding conflict and conflict resolution. *NACADA Journal, 25* (2), 57–64.

Melander, E. R. (2005). Advising as educating: A framework for organizing advising. *NACADA Journal, 25* (2), 84–91.

Myers, I. B., & McCaulley, M. H. (1985). *Manual: A guide to the development and use of the Myers-Briggs Type Indicator.* Palo Alto, CA: Consulting Psychologists Press.

National Academic Advising Association. (2006). *NACADA concept of academic advising.* Retrieved August 7, 2007 from http://www.nacada.ksu.edu/Clearinghouse/AdvisingIssues/Concept-Advising.htm

O'Banion, T. (1972). An academic advising model. *Junior College Journal, 42(6),* 62–69. Reprinted (1994). *NACADA Journal, 14* (2), 10–16.

Perry, W. (1970). *Forms of intellectual and ethical development in the college years.* New York: Holt, Rinehart & Winston.

Rawlins, W. K., & Rawlins, S. P. (2005). Academic advising as friendship. *NACADA Journal*, *25* (2), 10–19.

Schreiner, L. A., & Anderson, E. (2005). Strengths-based advising. *NACADA Journal*, *25* (2), 20–29.

Seligman, M., & Csikszentmihalyi, M. (2000). Positive psychology: An introduction. *American Psychologist*, *55* (1), 5–14.

Semmler, P. L., & Williams, C. B. (2000). Narrative therapy: A storied context for multicultural counseling. *Journal of Multicultural Counseling & Development*, *28* (1), 51–60.

Strange, C. (2004). Constructions of student development across the generations. *New Directions for Student Services*, *106*, 47–57.

Vygotsky, L. S. (1978). *Mind in society: The development of higher psychological processes*. M. Cole, V. John-Steiner, S. Scribner, & E. Souberman (Eds.). Cambridge, MA: MIT Press.

CHAPTER THREE

Ethical Foundations of Academic Advising

Marc Lowenstein

A my Trueheart, a senior and a candidate for graduation, comes to see her advisor, Sophia Wyse.

"Hi, I haven't seen you for a while. How are things going?"

"Right, well, I felt that I pretty much knew the requirements so I've been picking my own courses. Got a problem right now though."

"Well sometimes it seems that's what I'm here for. What is it?"

"I'm getting ready to graduate, and in fact I have a job offer that's only valid if I have my degree—but now it turns out I'm short a math course."

"But you thought you knew the requirements?"

"I did. I thought I took enough math at one of my other schools."

"Hmm. One of your other schools? Your file only shows you went to one other school."

"I guess I only sent in the one transcript—didn't do very well at the other places so I didn't bother. I knew I wouldn't get any credits accepted because my grades weren't high enough."

"You know, when you applied for admission you signed a statement that you were including all relevant information. Maybe if Admissions had known about your weak performance at other schools you would not have been accepted."

"Maybe. Seriously, I wasn't really trying to trick anyone, just figured I wasn't going to get any credits anyway, so I saved myself the $5 an official transcript would have cost. You aren't going to tell them, are you?"

The problem of Amy's graduation requirement will be addressed later. The initial focus will be upon her last remark to Sophia: What indeed should Sophia do with the new information? Should she inform the Admissions

Office about Amy's dishonesty on her application? This question belongs to the domain of *ethics*.

WHAT IS ETHICS?

Briefly put, *ethics* is the attempt to think critically about what is right and what is wrong, what is good and what is bad, in human conduct. Put another way, how should people act? Students of ethics are usually interested in how these questions apply to life in general, but it is also important to discuss how ethics applies to particular areas of life and work—for example in medical ethics, which deals with some of the notoriously difficult questions about the end of life. Ethical issues apply to academic advising as well, and while these are less momentous in some ways, they are certainly important to practitioners. Advisors have the potential to do much good for their students and also for their institutions, but the potential to do much harm exists as well. So they would like to know how to maximize the good and minimize the harm.

Ethics asks not only "What is the right thing to do?" but also "How does one *know* what is the right thing to do?" Anyone can provide a list of rules or principles and announce that they are binding on everyone, but how does one know these are the right rules? This chapter will present some principles that advisors can use to act ethically, and will provide at least some grounds for believing they constitute a good set of rules for advisors to follow. The chapter will explain why, even if there is a great set of rules, dilemmas will nonetheless arise in advisors' practice and will also provide some advice about resolving these dilemmas. Finally, the chapter will explore the advantages and disadvantages of promoting a code of ethics for advisors and reflect upon the National Academic Advising Association (NACADA, 2004) Core Values.

One thing that makes ethics difficult is that it does not study what one person or one group considers to be right and wrong. That is an interesting enough topic, but advisors do not just want to know what someone *considers* to be right, they are interested in what *is* right. The distinction is that "Boy Scouts consider it wrong to lie" is a descriptive statement about Boy Scouts but does not indicate whether lying is really wrong. The latter question is not about the mores of any culture, including our own. A concise way of representing the difference is to say that the principles of ethics are "prescriptive" rather than "descriptive" statements.

ETHICS AND RELATED STUDIES

Two areas of human activity—religion and law—are sometimes closely related to ethics, and it is important to be aware of how they are related and how they are different.

Ethics and Religion

In many persons' lives ethics and religion are tightly connected. For many of these individuals, religion provides ethical principles to follow, and it also provides the reason or foundation for following them—because they have been decreed by a supreme being, perhaps in a sacred text. This is such a common state of affairs that it is widely believed that ethics and religion are inseparable. But there are many people whose ethical principles do not rest on such religious foundations. Moreover, different religious traditions sometimes embrace somewhat different ethical principles, so one person's religious foundation for ethics may not be at all convincing to another person. If the answer to "How do we know what is right?" is "God commands it," then the skeptic's next question may be "How do we know what God commands?" Rather than become entangled in such issues, the ideas presented in this chapter will not be explicitly based on a religious foundation.

Ethics and Law

Law is similar to ethics in being prescriptive since it dictates what to do and what not to do. Moreover, what is ethical and what is legal will often coincide. But they are not guaranteed to do so. There are such things as unjust laws, more perhaps in some places than in others. What is legal is determined by the actions of specific people, such as legislators, public officials, and judges, and these people can change their minds from time to time. But what is right or wrong is independent of such whims. Finally, the ethical problems advisors need to resolve are often entirely unrelated to the law; in deciding how best to advise a particular student, in most cases the main alternatives are all equally legal, so the law does not help one to choose.

That is not to say that legal matters are unimportant to advising, quite the contrary. They are quite important and are discussed in the next chapter.

KEY ETHICAL IDEALS

This section will examine five ethical ideals or fundamental statements of what makes actions right or wrong that can apply to all areas of life. The concepts in this section are discussed in somewhat more detail in Lowenstein and Grites (1993). The next section will show how these ideals apply specifically to academic advising.

A Brief Note on Ethical Theories

If the goal is not only to have rules about what is right but also to have reason to think these rules are sound, then an ethical theory is needed—that is, a statement that offers a complete and accurate but concise account of right and wrong. For many centuries philosophers have been trying to devise an overall account of right and wrong and debating the pros and cons of many theories. There is not space here to consider this abstract subject at length. Instead, some time-tested ideas will be borrowed from a variety of sources that most philosophers would agree tell at least part of the story. Rachels and Rachels (2006) provide a comprehensive overview of ethical concepts and a guide to some of the historical sources of the philosophical ideas described here that will be helpful to advisors who wish to explore this area further. One important concept drawn from the philosophers' tradition will be important in looking at concrete ethical problems. Some ethical ideas focus on the consequences of actions and some do not. For example, if an advisor does not take time to look up a student's record and as a result gives bad information to the student, resulting in the student's graduation being delayed, that negative consequence contributes to marking the advisor's conduct as wrong. On the other hand, suppose an advisor misleads a student about an option that is open to him because she thinks the student might choose that option and it would be a big mistake. Here perhaps harm is actually avoided, but the advisor's decision is dishonest and, at least in that regard, wrong.

Ethical theories have tended either to focus on consequences, and hold that actions are right or wrong primarily because of the good or bad that they bring about, or to argue that some things (for example, dishonesty) are right or wrong irrespective of their consequences. The principles laid out in the next section may be classified according to those that focus on consequences and those that do not.

Basic Ethical Ideals

Following are the key ideals that will serve as the foundations for ethics in advising. They are not original, but stem from a variety of traditional ethical theories. Readers will easily see how some of them may apply to the advising context, and the next section will derive some more specific ethical principles for advising that are based on these ideals.

Beneficence. Always bring about as much well-being as you can among all of the people who will be affected by your actions, both directly and indirectly and in both the short and long term.

Non-Maleficence. Always avoid or minimize the harm caused by your actions to all of the people who will be affected by them, both directly and indirectly and in both the short and long term.

Beneficence and non-maleficence both concentrate on consequences. Following these principles conscientiously obliges people to think very carefully about exactly what the consequences of their actions will be. Getting this right can sometimes be difficult, and advisors can all think of times that they or someone they know failed to calculate correctly what would happen as a result of a decision. But the thinkers who most strongly argue for these two principles, who are often termed "utilitarians," hold that this is indeed what one needs to do if one wants to be ethical.

Justice. Treat all individuals fairly or equitably, granting no one any special rights or privileges that are not open to all. "Equitably" does not have to mean "the same"; it just means that differences must not create inequalities, and should have a defensible basis.

Respect for Persons. Treat individuals as ends in themselves, never solely as means to your own ends. Treat them as rational, autonomous agents, not as things that can be manipulated. The hypothetical advisor mentioned previously who withheld information from a student was failing to observe this ideal.

Fidelity. Live up to all the commitments you have made, whether explicitly or implicitly. An explicit commitment is a stated promise, like a wedding vow, but what is an *implicit* commitment? It is a commitment that is built into a role one has taken on even if one did not realize it; for example, not everyone who becomes a parent has considered all of the commitments that come with that role.

Unlike beneficence and non-maleficence, the latter three ideals are not focused on the consequences of actions; they all hold that certain things are wrong whether they have bad consequences or not. For example, the obligation to keep promises is not based on the outcome of the promise-keeping. Similarly, many would hold that at least normally it is wrong to lie, even to accomplish a desirable outcome. In medicine it is now generally considered wrong to lie to patients about their condition in order to spare them the pain of knowing the gravity of their prognosis.

As mentioned earlier, these ideals come from a variety of sources; they have been chosen for inclusion here because they have been used effectively by writers about ethics over a long period of time and have proved themselves useful in guiding people to behave ethically.

Ethical action is not a simple matter of observing these ideals, however, and the reason is quickly apparent. There could be occasions when lying might seem to be the best way to bring about a desirable outcome, or occasions when one can keep a promise only if one ignores the harm that will result. The ethical ideals, in other words, can conflict with each other. When this happens, deciding what to do appears to be a matter of choosing one ideal over another. Such a situation is called an ethical *dilemma.*

Dilemmas arise because of an important and easily overlooked feature of the ethical ideals, which will also be true of the ethical principles for advising described below. The ideals are *prima facie* reasons for choosing a course of action; they are not absolute, hard-and-fast commandments that are figuratively "carved in stone." They are reasons for acting a certain way that can, under the right circumstances, be superseded by better reasons for acting a different way. Ethical dilemmas are discussed below. First it is necessary to look more specifically at what these ethical ideals have to do with academic advising.

ETHICAL PRINCIPLES FOR ADVISING

The ethical ideals provide guidance for ethical actions whether at work, at home, or driving on the highway, but it may take considerable thought to see how they apply to advising. To make the relevance of the ideals clearer, following is a series of ethical principles that refer directly to advising and that are derived from the ideals.

1. Seek to enhance the student's learning whenever possible. This principle applies the ideals of beneficence and non-maleficence to the advising setting. If these values hold that advisors should maximize the student's well-being and minimize harm to him or her, and the advisor's particular province is the student's education, or more specifically, learning, then the implication is that the advisor's ethical duty is to maximize that learning. An advisor who recommends taking two courses in a particular order, or who helps a student accept the rationale for a particular general education requirement, is following this principle. In the chapter's initial example, this principle may incline Sophia to want Amy to take her missing math course.

2. Treat students equitably. This principle applies the ideal of justice or fairness to advising. It mandates that advisors not play favorites among students, exerting more effort on behalf of those whom they like more, or whose values they find compatible with their own. All students are equally entitled to advising services. Of course, treating students equitably does not mean treating them the same. Students are all different and so are their needs. One student may need more time than another, for example. Applying the principle of equity is tricky because it is not always obvious which differences among students justify differences in treatment. Does a student with a higher GPA deserve more help? Probably not. Does a student who habitually misses appointments deserve a lower priority the next time the advisor has too many issues and too little time? Perhaps so. One way in which equity applies to Amy's case is that it is wrong for her to receive favors that are not available to all students.

3. Enhance the student's ability to make autonomous decisions. This principle is derived from the ideal of respect for persons because it develops individual autonomy, and thus is part of treating the student as an independent agent, an end in himself or herself. You violate this principle if you make decisions for the student or pressure the student to do what you think he or she should do. Notice that the reason for doing these things might be to follow the first principle, to enhance the student's education. In other words, there may very well be a conflict between the two principles. Sophia may have her own opinion about what is best for Amy educationally, but Principle 3 says she should support Amy in making the decision.

4. Advocate for the student. Even though advisors should build students' autonomy, it is a fact of life at most institutions that students will not get all the services or benefits they need without a little help. There may be an office where heavily burdened staff do not always go out of their way for students without a bit of prompting; there may be a faculty member who always tells students he will not add anyone to a full class but who in fact will do so when a fellow professional gives him a good reason; there may be a dean who is reluctant to grant an exception to a policy or a requirement until the advisor makes the case more cogently than the student can. In such an environment, advisor advocacy is an application of the ethical ideal of fidelity. It is part of the commitment you make to your students. Not to serve as an advocate when you can readily do so with modest effort is to fail to do your best for the student. Conversely, to go the extra mile in this regard may be exemplary advising behavior.

If Amy admits her earlier deception to the Admissions office, Sophia may support her request for leniency based on this principle.

5. Tell the truth. Telling the truth is the paramount expression of respect for persons because autonomous decision makers need to have the truth in order to make their decisions. There are two parts to this, however, as described below.

> **Tell the truth to your advisees.** You cannot treat a student as a developing decision-maker and withhold the information he or she needs to make decisions. This may seem obvious, but some of its implications are not so straightforward. For example, some of the information you are obliged to give may be information the student might be better off without. Perhaps the student has two options, one of which the advisor believes is educationally far superior to the other; it is dishonest to fail to disclose the entire picture, however. In this way, truth-telling may conflict with the principle of maximizing educational benefit.

> **Tell the truth to others.** Faculty, staff, and administrators may be making decisions that affect the advisee, and they may ask the advisor for information. They, like the advisee, are entitled to accurate information on which to base their decisions. This is the case even though providing the information may compromise one's ability to advocate for the student. Perhaps it may also interfere with efforts to maximize the student's educational benefit— for example, by causing the student to be denied an exception to a policy or admission to a class.

> Both parts of this principle apply to Sophia's problem with Amy. Sophia may be obliged to tell Amy all that she knows about the possibilities of having her math requirement waived. She may also be obliged to inform Admissions of the deception in Amy's application.

6. Respect the confidentiality of communication with the student. Advisors are not therapists, clergy, or physicians, and legally they do not have the same traditional assurance that their interactions with their students can be maintained as confidential. Fidelity, however, dictates that you have an obligation to keep your commitment to maintain the confidentiality of these interactions, at least where the student has reason to believe you will do so. If the advisor is told something in confidence, it should be kept that way. This obligation is no sooner mentioned, however, than you can see that it may conflict with the obligation to tell the truth to offices and individuals at the institution. Such a conflict can give rise to an agonizing dilemma. In some cases the dilemma can be avoided by not making the promise of confidentiality in the first place, but this could result in a less-productive advising session. Both sides of this discussion clearly apply to Sophia's awareness of the omissions in Amy's application, as Amy notes by asking whether Sophia intends to reveal the secret.

7. Support the institution's educational philosophy and policies. This is another implication of the ideal of fidelity. By accepting employment with an institution you undertake a commitment (usually an implicit one) to abide by and to respect its rules. That means, for example, that it is wrong to tell a student that you disagree with the graduation requirements or that you do not believe in the honor code.

Does this conflict with academic freedom? This matter is clarified by noting the following distinction. It is entirely appropriate to argue your views about institutional policies within the forums that exist for that purpose, for example, in curriculum committees, in faculty senates, in advising staff meetings. But if you have not prevailed in those forums, you need to concede, and in dealing with students, support the position of the institution. Advisors who think conscientiously about educational issues may find this principle a bit hard to swallow, but it does "come with the territory."

This principle provides one of the reasons why Sophia will be reluctant to encourage Amy to try to circumvent the math requirement.

8. Maintain the credibility of the advising program. This is another instance of fidelity, similar to the previous principle. To be part of the program is to embrace a commitment to its integrity. Beneficence and non-maleficence play a role here as well, because any behavior that undercuts the credibility of the advising program runs a risk of harming students' education, since they may make worse decisions if they do not respect advice they receive from advisors, or may even cease consulting advisors at all. If students' overall success at the institution suffers from this development, the impact on the institution could be considerable. Sophia needs to concern herself with this principle if she contemplates intervening on Amy's behalf, since advocating for a weak appeal could make her office appear uninterested in curricular integrity.

9. Accord colleagues appropriate professional courtesy and respect. This is not merely an exhortation to observe good manners, but an admonition not to express to students any negative opinions you may harbor about faculty or staff at the institution. More is at stake here, from the perspective of non-maleficence, than hurt feelings if the behavior becomes known. Students are often eager for advice about which instructor to take for a particular course, or for confirmation about gossip they have heard about a particular individual. Advisors may also have opinions of their own about the people in question, but they should not contribute to a culture of character assassination and backstabbing that will only harm the institution in the long run.

This line of reasoning may appear to contradict at least two other ethical principles. If you know a reason why a student would better succeed by not taking a class with a particular instructor but do not inform the student, is this not a failure to tell the truth (Principle 5)? And if you fail to counsel the student away from a less-than-optimal educational experience have you not also violated Principle 1? Many advisors have found ways to navigate these waters without telling untruths. Steering the student to a different class section by emphasizing the positive qualities of its instructor is at least a partial solution, since it supports the educational benefit goal and at the same time says nothing at all about the other instructor. The latter means that you have not told the whole truth, to be sure, but that appears to be the lesser evil in this case.

ETHICAL PRINCIPLES AND ETHICAL DILEMMAS

The ethical ideals on which the ethical principles for advising are based are *prima facie* guidelines, which can under certain circumstances conflict with each other, so that those seeking to make ethical decisions seemingly need to choose among them. The same is true for the ethical principles for advisors, for example, in the tension between telling a student the truth and affording respect to colleagues as just described, or between enhancing the student's educational experience and encouraging her to make her own decisions as mentioned earlier. Other examples can readily be found.

For instance, you should advocate for your students. But what if advocacy for the advisee results in his obtaining an unearned advantage over another student, which would appear to violate the principle of equitable treatment? Since you are obliged to support the institution's educational policies, including the math requirement, and to maximize the student's learning, should you tell her the truth when she asks whether it is worth seeking an exception from a dean who you know will probably grant it?

If the ethical principles for advising are supposed to help advisors with ethical decision-making, and yet dilemmas arise when advisors try to use them for this purpose, some questions are brought to mind: Are these really the right principles? Wouldn't better principles help advisors avoid dilemmas rather than create them? Are these principles worth following? Are advisors any better off with these principles than they were without them? Advisors who are looking for practical help in making ethical decisions are entitled to answers to these questions.

The most important point in reply to these questions is that ethical ambiguity—the impossibility of simple, unqualified answers to all the issues people encounter—is a fact of life. This is true even though everyone might wish it were otherwise. If advisors are seeking a simple formula to avoid ambiguity and always know the right answer, they will be disappointed. In fact it is precisely because advisors do such important work and touch crucial areas of their students' lives that they face difficult ethical dilemmas. It is not a flaw in the ethical principles that they cannot prevent this.

As to the last part of the previous question, advisors *are* better off for having ethical principles. For one thing, not every decision they make involves a dilemma, and most of the time the principles do provide good guidance, as indicated by the illustrations that helped to introduce them. Second, it is possible to supplement the principles with tools that can provide some assistance in resolving dilemmas. Another look at the Amy Trueheart dilemma will help illustrate these tools. This time the focus will not be on the dishonesty question but on Amy's missing math requirement.

Amy is an art history major. Although the math requirement is university-wide, individual deans have discretionary authority over students' graduation cases. In this case, the advisor knows that the dean with jurisdiction over Amy happens to think the math requirement is excessive for students in the humanities, a position with which Sophia disagrees. If Amy were to appeal to the dean, she may very well be granted an exception and be permitted to graduate. So Sophia confronts another dilemma, whether to advise Amy of the availability of the appeal option.

Doing so seems to follow the principle of telling the truth, so withholding the information seems dishonest (Principle 5). Moreover, it would also mean missing an opportunity to enhance Amy's ability to make decisions (Principle 3). On the other hand, the advisor believes that not taking the required math course would be detrimental to Amy's education, so doing anything that helps her "escape" it seems to be a violation of Principle 1. There is also a danger of failing to treat all students equitably (Principle 2), since other students are fulfilling the requirement. And finally, doing so also seems to violate Principle 7 by failing to support the institution's policies. As with regard to the dishonesty-disclosure issue that Amy's situation raises, the advisor seems to have powerful reasons pushing in opposite directions—a dilemma.

There is a course of action the advisor can follow to make the best of this situation, and it illustrates a strategy that can be recommended in general for advisors facing dilemmas. The advisor should broach the idea of an appeal to Amy, but for the purpose of engaging her in a serious discussion of the pros and cons of the matter. For example, the advisor would help Amy think about the fact that she cannot predict her future or what skills she may need. This observes the obligation to tell the truth and enhance decision-making, and it has at least some chance of causing Amy to consider her education with a longer view in mind. Arguably, this strategy also meets the advisor's obligation to support institutional policies, and perhaps also that of equitable treatment, since it is an advising practice that the advisor could follow for everyone.

Thus, the advisor, in following this strategy, does at least a fair job of meeting all of her ethical obligations as expressed in the principles. To be sure, it is not a perfect solution, and it is likely that in the end Amy will choose to appeal, which will leave the advisor dissatisfied with the outcome. But advisors never have full control of students' choices. This strategy is probably as good as could have been found. Summarized as concisely as possible, it can be stated this way: *"When confronted with conflicting principles, do the best you can to follow all of them to the extent possible."*

Now it is time to return to the other dilemma facing Sophia, whether to turn Amy in for making a false statement on her application for admission. It will be helpful to focus on Amy's statement that the reason for her omission was that she did not expect to have any of her other transfer credits accepted. Suppose Sophia believes this to be sincere. That may be ethically relevant. If it were otherwise—that is, if Sophia believes there was an intent to deceive—she may feel that the imperatives of equity, truth-telling, and institutional integrity outweigh those of confidentiality and advocacy. But taking that hypothetical factor out of the picture may seem to tip the balance the other way. Sophia might alert Amy to the seriousness of her predicament and work with her to craft an approach to Admissions, acknowledging her error but seeking forgiveness on the grounds that at this point it is better for both her and the institution to let her complete her education. This may or may not be successful. For the present purpose, the key point lies in the method of addressing the advisor's dilemma, which was a type of thought experiment that sought an element in the situation that was ethically crucial. In this case the crucial element was Amy's lack of intent to deceive. This was identified by imagining a similar situation with only that element changed. The second strategy for resolving dilemmas may then be stated this way: *"Compare the situation to similar, real or hypothetical, situations to see whether any element in it is crucial to evaluating it."*

A third strategy will emerge from considering the following case:

Douglas Wright, an ROTC cadet, has come to see his advisor complaining that the instructor in his required course on world issues is pursuing themes critical of the American military and U.S. foreign policy, which are making him very uncomfortable. The advisor explains that part of the purpose of this distribution requirement is to make sure that students are engaged in structured discussions of controversial issues, but Douglas says he comes from a family with a strong tradition of patriotism and military service, and he cannot tolerate the leftist antimilitary bias that he is experiencing.

Douglas's advisor feels obliged to encourage him to stick with this class, believing that this encounter with challenging ideas will be beneficial for Douglas. She also knows that there are other classes that meet the same requirement and would have a slightly different emphasis, enabling Douglas to avoid the problem he is encountering. Should she tell him this? She believes that doing so will reduce the educational benefit Douglas can obtain from the course, and she also feels that it would compromise her obligation to support the institution's educational philosophy. At the same time, not to tell Douglas would be to withhold the truth from him, and also would fail to support his autonomy in decision-making. So she faces a dilemma.

Here the key point may be that even if Douglas remains in his current class, he says he is determined to avoid opening his mind to the ideas he despises. If that is the case, perhaps the advisor should inform him of his other options, thus living up to the truth-telling and autonomy principles. She would be risking violation of the other principles, but her judgment might be that she has no hope of implementing these *effectively* in any case. Thus, her chosen course of action seems to be the lesser of the evils.

The advisor's ethical strategy in this case might be stated this way: *"In considering two solutions, each of which would violate an ethical principle, try to identify the choice that leads to a less substantial violation."*

There is no guarantee that the three strategies described above will always yield a satisfactory resolution of an ethical dilemma, but they will very often do so, and thus help to support the usefulness of the ethical principles for advising.

CODES OF ETHICS AND CORE VALUES

Many professions have codes of ethics to which their practitioners are obliged to adhere. Typically, such professions have a single professional organization that has the authority to implement a code of ethics and to insist on adherence to it. Although many advisors are members of the National Academic Advising Association (NACADA), others are not, and no one is proposing that advisors be required to join in order to obtain a "license" to advise. Unlike other professional associations, NACADA probably would not wish, nor would it be able, to enforce sanctions on people who violated such a code. Accordingly, it would be presumptuous for NACADA to bring forward a code of ethics.

Moreover, it is not clear that a code would be desirable. Codes of ethics, where they exist, seem to promise a guarantee of certainty, which the principles offered here do not. As the preceding discussion illustrates, navigating difficult ethical passages is more art than science, and there is no claim that following the ethical principles for advising guarantees ethical practice.

Rather than propose a code of ethics, NACADA (2004) has created a "Statement of Core Values." The examination of ethical foundations for academic advising will conclude by reviewing how this Statement compares to the system of ethical principles described earlier. Mindful of the diversity of NACADA membership, the Statement refrains from specifying what advisors should and should not do. The values are not articulated in the form of principles that prescribe how advisors should behave, but in the form of "responsibility" statements, enumerating what advisors are "responsible to" and "responsible for," for example "Core Value 1: Advisors are responsible to the individuals they advise."

At first glance these statements look quite different from ethical principles, but when the detailed expositions are examined, much of the same content is present. For example, part of the "Exposition" of Core Value 1 is that advisors help students "become more responsible and accountable," which reflects Principle 3 on autonomy; under the same heading is the statement that advisors "respect student confidentiality rights," similar to Principle 6. "Core Value 3: Advisors are responsible to their institutions" includes the statement that "Advisors . . . abide by the specific policies, procedures, and values of the department and institution in which they work" (Principle 7), and that they "remain neutral when students make comments or express opinions about other faculty or staff" (Principle 9).

Numerous other examples can also be found, and identifying these may be a useful activity for the reader, since there is not space for it here. Interestingly, there does not seem to be a clear articulation of Principle 2, equitable treatment; though there are multiple acknowledgments of student diversity, this is not exactly the same thing.

The Statement includes other material, some of which may not be purely ethical but rather, describes the *means* that advisors may use to pursue their ethical ends. For example, "Academic advisors must develop relationships with personnel critical to student success . . . ," which is certainly useful advice for advisors, but not a proposition that they will use to distinguish ethical from unethical conduct. Other statements may be more about law than about ethics, such as a reference to the Family Educational Rights and Privacy Act (FERPA). A number of statements focus more on effective advising practice than on professional ethics, such as "Advisors understand the intricacies of transfer between institutions and make appropriate referrals to enable students to achieve their goals."

Thus, the NACADA Statement includes much material that reinforces the specific ethical Principles laid out in this chapter, but does so in the context of a number of other priorities as well. It is an excellent resource for a new advisor who would like an introduction to the profession's priorities, though it is not organized in such a way as to serve as a reference for ethical problem-solving, nor does it attempt to do so. Accordingly, the discussion in this chapter serves as a useful supplement to the Statement.

The Ethical Foundations of Academic Advising, then, consist of at least the following:

- recognition of how ethics differs from other areas of thought,
- acceptance of a set of basic ethical ideals, which most people will find valid and that apply to human relationships in general, including academic advising,
- derivation of a set of Ethical Principles for Advising from the ethical ideals, and knowing how to apply them specifically to advising situations, and
- awareness of why ethical dilemmas arise, even though our principles are valid, and knowledge of some strategies for dealing with them.

These foundations may best be considered a set of tools to be used for finding ethical solutions to situations that advisors encounter. Advisors have a wide variety of other tools, such as theories and models of advising, technical skills, networking skills, and knowledge of student development. This chapter has focused on the tools that specifically support ethical decision-making.

Going beyond the foundations is a matter of identifying ethical problems when they appear, recognizing which tools can apply to them, and honing one's skills at using the tools to find solutions to the problems, including resolving dilemmas when they occur. This chapter has described and explained the tools, but ultimately your understanding of them will grow and develop more from repeated experience in applying them to real situations than from any further exposition here.

References

Lowenstein, M., & Grites, T.J. (1993). Ethics in academic advising. *NACADA Journal*, *13* (1), 53–61.

NACADA. (2004). NACADA statement of core values of academic advising. Retrieved October 14, 2007, from the *NACADA Clearinghouse of Academic Advising Resources* Web site: http://www.nacada.ksu.edu/Clearinghouse/AdvisingIssues/Core-Values.htm

Rachels, J., & Rachels, S. (2006). *The elements of moral philosophy* (5th ed.). New York: McGraw-Hill.

CHAPTER FOUR

Legal Foundations of Academic Advising

Mary M. Richard

Robinson (2004) and Gordon and Habley (2004) have recognized advisor awareness of current legal issues in postsecondary education among the competencies of an advising skill set. The Statement of Core Values of the National Academic Advising Association (NACADA, 2004) and the Council for the Advancement of Standards (CAS) Standards and Guidelines for Academic Advising (2005) also support this position. Bickel and Lake (1999) have noted that court applications of legal doctrines describing the relationship of students and postsecondary institutions continue to change, in part as a response to changes in the policies and procedures of postsecondary institutions. Acknowledging that the law of postsecondary education is not static, the following sections are intended to provide a broad discussion of a variety of laws and legal theories that currently define and describe the relationships between students, academic advisors, and their postsecondary institutions.

WHAT LAWS AND COURT DECISIONS APPLY?

Whether or not a particular law or court decision will directly affect the work of an academic advisor employed by a specific institution is related to whether the law or court decision has authority over conflicting laws or decisions in the

---

This chapter is intended to inform, but not advise readers about legal issues in academic advising. No one should ever construe its contents as legal advice for a specific situation. Likewise, no one should ever attempt to interpret or apply any law or court opinion without the aid of an attorney who is competent to practice in the relevant area of law and licensed in the state where the law would be interpreted or applied.

advisor's state and federal jurisdictions. The following information is intended to provide an overview of the relevant legal hierarchies.

The Supremacy Clause (U.S. Constitution, Article VI, clause 2) establishes that the Constitution, federal statutes, and U.S. treaties are the supreme law of the land (*Marbury v. Madison*, 1803, p. 180). As the highest form of law, lower federal courts and all state courts are required to uphold the Constitution at all times. When the U.S. Supreme Court has not ruled on the constitutionality of a law, its interpretation is governed separately in each federal appellate jurisdiction by the highest federal court in that territory that has ruled on it. As used here, *jurisdiction* refers both to actual geographic territories and to the authority of state courts within their respective states and the federal courts within their multistate federal territories. Federal courts can consider opinions of courts in other circuits, although they are not required to follow them; state courts may also consider rulings of courts in other states, but are not bound by their decisions. As a result, laws, legal standards, and interpretations of laws may vary from state to state and federal circuit to circuit.

When Congress enacts federal legislation under its constitutional powers to legislate exclusively, the resulting federal laws and implementing regulations trump conflicting state laws. However, advisors should be aware that when Congress enacts laws in areas where the Constitution does not grant it power to legislate exclusively, then these laws do not prevail unless the states agree to comply with them, which is commonly a condition of receiving related federal funding. These laws include many of the federal laws through which postsecondary institutions receive funding through the U.S. Department of Education.

LEGAL DOCTRINES AND THEORIES

Courts apply a variety of legal doctrines based on the principles and theories of specific bodies of law in deciding cases involving student claims against postsecondary institutions. The bodies of law commonly involved are briefly described as follows:

1. *Agency law* is the law of principal-agent relationships. The statements or conduct of an agent may obligate the principal to act or refrain from acting in a certain way.

2. *Fiduciary law* applies to relationships in which the person who is a "fiduciary" owes to another person certain duties, including those of good faith, trust, confidence, and candor.

3. *Constitutional law* refers to the law set forth in the federal and state constitutions, which state the powers of and limitations on the powers of government, and the rights guaranteed to people.

4. *Tort law* is the body of law that applies to judicial determination of whether a civil wrong has occurred for which one of the parties may be held liable.

5. *Contract law* is concerned with interpreting agreements, setting out the parties' rights and obligations, and providing remedies for breaches of contractual obligations.

The Law of Agency

Academic advisors are "agents" of their employing institutions. NACADA's Statement of Core Values (2004) and the CAS Standards and Guidelines for Academic Advising (2005) each recognize this status. As agents, their statements and acts may be construed as promises that obligate the institution to act or refrain from acting in a certain way. If a perceived promise is broken and a student claims that he or she has suffered harm, the institution may be liable to fulfill the terms of the promise. Buck, Moore, Schwartz, and Supon (2001) have counseled that when advisors speak about any aspect of their employing institutions, their statements should accurately represent the institution's goals, services, facilities, programs, and policies.

The Law of Fiduciary Relationships

While agency law focuses on the advisor's relationship to the institution, fiduciary law focuses on the advisor's relationship to students. A fiduciary is a person who is in a position of trust with respect to another person. Black's Law Dictionary (Garner, 2004) defines a fiduciary as "One who owes to another the duties of good faith, trust, confidence and candor." These duties are among those stated and implied in values that NACADA (2004) expects advisors to reflect in their daily interactions.

While many people associate fiduciary duties with the statutory duties of a trustee or board member, fiduciary relationships arise in a variety of other situations in which a person entrusts a special confidence in another person, who becomes bound to act in good faith and with due regard to the interests of the person entrusting the confidence. Historically, the relationship between educators and students was considered to be of a fiduciary nature (Seavy, 1957). More recently, Weeks and Haglund (2002) noted that schools may owe fiduciary duties to students arising from both academic services and other nonacademic matters. In *Schneider v. Plymouth State College* (1999), the New Hampshire Supreme Court ruled that in regard to the harassment of a student by a faculty member, the relationship between a postsecondary institution and its students is a fiduciary one (p. 462). In *United States v. Frost* (1997), the U.S. Supreme Court held that faculty members owe a fiduciary duty to protect the property of their employing institutions, not just with respect to the use of funds, but with respect to their own duty to provide to the institution their "honest services" (p. 364).

Due Process

Section 1. All persons born or naturalized in the United States and subject to the jurisdiction thereof, are citizens of the United States and of the State wherein they reside. No State shall make or enforce any law which shall abridge the

*privileges or immunities of citizens of the United States; nor shall any State deprive
any person of life, liberty, or property, without due process of law; nor deny to any
person within its jurisdiction the equal protection of the laws.*
—U.S. Constitution, Amendment XIV, § 1

The Fourteenth Amendment protects people against state action that
would deprive them of life, liberty, or property without due process of law.
Substantive due process protects students from actions of public institutions
that would deprive them of their liberty interests. Procedural due process protects students from actions of public institutions to deprive them of their property rights without providing fair procedures.

In order for a student to claim that a postsecondary institution has not provided due process, the student's life, liberty, or property must actually be at
stake. As the Seventh Circuit Court of Appeals explained, "A procedural due
process claim requires two principal inquiries: first, whether the plaintiff was
deprived of a protected property or liberty interest, and second, whether the
plaintiff was deprived of that interest without sufficient procedural protec-
tions" (*Galdikas v. Fagan*, 2003, p. 691). If the court finds that the institution
offered fair decision-making processes, then it will generally find that procedural due process has been provided (*Gauder v. Leckrone*, 2005, p. 789).

When an advisor at a public institution participates in any decision or process related to a student's discipline or dismissal, he or she should assume
that the student has liberty and property interests at stake (see for example,
Hillman v. Elliott, 1977, p. 817). Academic advisors employed at state postsecondary institutions are required to comply with the Constitution's requirements for substantive and procedural due process because as state employees,
they are "state actors," and their acts are "state action."

Liberty Interests. Liberty interests arise from the Constitution and, unless
there is a compelling interest, government cannot infringe upon them no
matter how fair or how many procedures it provides. Advisors should be
aware that some institutional policies or the manner in which they might
be applied have the potential to run afoul of students' liberty interests. Among
these interests are rights named in the Bill of Rights: establishment of religion
(*Everson v. Board of Education*, 1947), free exercise of religion (*Cantwell v.
Connecticut*, 1940), freedom of speech (*Gitlow v. New York*, 1925), freedom of
the press (*Near v. Minnesota*, 1931), freedom of assembly (*DeJonge v. Oregon*,
1937), freedom of association (*NAACP v. Alabama ex rel. Patterson*, 1958),
and freedom against unreasonable search and seizure (*Wolf v. Colorado*,
1949). Furthermore, the Supreme Court has also used substantive due process to protect rights called "fundamental interests" that are not named in the
Constitution. In *Washington v. Glucksberg* (1997), these interests are described
as "deeply rooted in this Nation's history and tradition" (p. 702). They include
interstate travel (*Mitchell v. United States*, 1941), marriage (*Loving v. Virginia*,
1967), contraception (*Griswold v. Connecticut*, 1965), procreation (*Eisenstadt v.
Baird*, 1972), abortion (*Roe v. Wade*, 1973), family relationships (*Moore v. East*

Cleveland, 1977), and child-raising (*Pierce v. Society of Sisters,* 1925). While the Court did not hold that sexual relationships between consenting adults are fundamental interests protected by the Constitution, in *Lawrence v. Texas* (2003), it noted that after *Griswold,* it had recognized that the right to make certain decisions regarding sexual conduct extends beyond the marital relationship (p. 565), and that the Court had never held that "moral disapproval was a sufficient rationale under the Equal Protection Clause to justify a law that discriminates among groups of persons" (p. 582).

Property Interests. The U.S. Supreme Court has found that property interests are not created by the Constitution. In *Board of Regents v. Roth* (1972) the Court explained that property interests are created by existing rules or understandings governed by another source, such as state law (p. 577). In *Logan v. Zimmerman Brush Co.* (1982), the Court further explained that property interests include entitlements created by the state that cannot be denied except for cause (p. 430).

Advisors are especially likely to encounter property interests in regard to students who have gained property rights as the result of the receipt of scholarships or financial aid, or admission to special programs. Whenever a public institution takes any action that will have the effect of taking such property away, due process is required (*Morrissey v. Brewer,* 1972, p. 480). In general, the more significant the interest of the student that is at stake, the more formal the procedures that will be required to pass legal muster for due process. In *Mathews v. Eldridge* (1976), the U.S. Supreme Court explained that whenever the state acts to deprive a person of a property interest, it must provide him with "the opportunity to be heard at a meaningful time and in a meaningful manner" (p. 333). The Court further explained that to determine the procedures that due process requires in a specific situation, the governmental entity must consider three factors: (1) the nature of the private interest that will be affected by the official action; (2) the risk of an erroneous deprivation of the interest through the procedures used, and the probable value, if any, of additional or different procedures; and (3) the government's interest, including the function involved and the fiscal and administrative burdens that the additional or substitute procedures would require (p. 335).

Due Process and Academic Dismissal. In *Board of Curators of University of Missouri v. Horowitz* (1978), the U.S. Supreme Court ruled that postsecondary institutions are not required to provide hearings to students who have been academically dismissed (p. 86). In *Schuler v. University of Minnesota* (1986), the Eighth Circuit Court of Appeals followed *Horowitz,* indicating that the student had received adequate notice, because, prior to her dismissal, she had been made aware of the faculty dissatisfaction with her performance (p. 514).

Due Process and Nonacademic Discipline and Dismissal. It is well established in law that due process requires public institutions to provide more formal procedures in regard to nonacademic dismissal and discipline decisions than are required for academic dismissals. In *Dixon v. Alabama State Board of*

Education (1961), the U.S. Supreme Court decided that due process required notice and some opportunity for a hearing before students could be expelled for nonacademic reasons (p. 150). Later, in *Goss v. Lopez* (1975), it found that students have a liberty interest in their reputations because of the hindrances of having an academic record of disciplinary action or expulsion (p. 575). The Court stated that a student who has been suspended for disciplinary reasons must be given oral or written notice of the charges against him and, if the student denies them, an explanation of the evidence the authorities have and an opportunity to present his side of the story, noting that it would be "a strange disciplinary system in an educational institution if no communication was sought by the disciplinarian with the student in an effort to inform him of his dereliction and to let him tell his side of the story in order to make sure that an injustice is not done" (pp. 583–584).

The Law of Torts and Contracts

While academic advisors have a relatively low risk of becoming involved in a tort or contract action brought by a student, they may be aware of cases in which students have claimed that poor advising was responsible for the loss of a scholarship or athletic eligibility. *Byrd v. Lamar* (2002) and *Hendricks v. Clemson University* (2003) contain examples of contract and torts claims asserted in state laws. In *Byrd* (2002), the court allowed a postsecondary student to go forward with claims against his advisor and the vice president of academic affairs. The student had selected the institution on the basis of the music media program described in its catalog. After enrolling he was assured by advisors, faculty, and administrators that the courses for this major would be available. In his fourth year, he was finally informed that the program never existed, and he sued the institution for fraud. In *Hendricks* (2003), the student filed tort and contract claims, when, after transferring to a Division I school to play baseball during his final year of eligibility, he learned that his academic advisor had not informed him that he had not completed the courses required for eligibility.

Tort Actions. A *tort* may be defined as a civil wrong caused by the negligent or intentional act or omission of another person or entity that is not a breach of contract, for which the court may impose liability and award relief to the injured party. A student who files a lawsuit alleging harm from an advisor's negligence will generally be required to prove all of the following four elements: (1) that the institution owed the student a certain duty of care in advising him or her with respect to advising acts or failures to act that could foreseeably result in harm to the student, (2) that the institution failed to uphold that duty, (3) that its negligence was the cause of the harm that occurred to the student, and (4) that the student suffered actual injury.

Governmental Immunity. At times, courts refuse to hold postsecondary institutions liable for their torts, even when a student has presented credible evidence to support each tort claim element. In cases like *Hendricks* (2003), courts have found that state-supported institutions are protected by "sovereign" or governmental immunity. The doctrine of sovereign immunity originated in the medieval concept that since the king ruled by divine right, he could do no wrong (see, for example, *McMahon v. United States,* 1951). Until 1946, when Congress, passed the Federal Tort Claims Act (FTCA), governmental immunity prohibited individuals from bringing civil suits against the federal government for actions arising out of the negligent acts of their employees. After Congress passed the FTCA, the fifty states enacted their own state tort claims acts, based more or less on the federal model. Following the FTCA, these laws permit an individual to sue the state for property loss, injury, or death caused by the negligent or wrongful act or omission of a state employee, that occurred while the employee was acting within the scope of his or her office or employment, if under the same circumstances a private employer or employee would be found liable. State-supported institutions are generally not protected against liability if the institution or its employee is found to have engaged in harmful conduct willfully, maliciously, fraudulently, in bad faith, beyond the scope of authority, or under a mistaken interpretation of the law or they have violated a student's rights under a federal civil rights law. However, state-supported institutions often remain protected by governmental immunity if the allegedly harmful conduct falls into the "discretionary function" exception, in which a state entity is immune from liability if the challenged act, omission, or decision involved the good faith exercise of policy discretion rather than policy implementation.

Some courts have raised questions about how much longer states will continue to immunize state-supported institutions when their harmful conduct, while not "willful, malicious, or fraudulent," is seriously negligent. In *Scott v. Savers Property & Casualty Insurance Company* (2003), a student alleged that he lost a scholarship as a result of inaccurate academic advising. While the court found that the institution was immune from liability, one of the reviewing justices wrote that the result was unjust, stating:

> Here, Scott did nothing wrong. In fact, he did everything right. Scott sought out the appropriate individual to assist him in choosing courses to fulfill the requirements for his NCAA scholarship. Scott relied on the advice of his high school guidance counselor, the school official who was privy to the information Scott requested; regrettably, it was to his detriment. (p. 63)

Courts have generally followed *Ross v. Creighton University* (1992) in rejecting educational malpractice claims that would require the court to inquire into educational theories and processes, or to oversee day-to-day school operations and policy formulation. In *Ross,* the Court noted that courts do not favor the theory of educational malpractice because: (1) courts do not have a standard of care by which to evaluate an educator's conduct; (2) it is difficult for courts to determine the actual cause and nature of a student's damages; (3) allowing educational malpractice suits to proceed in court could open the floodgates for lawsuits against schools; and (4) litigating educational malpractice cases might entangle courts in supervising day-to-day school operations. However, with respect to the first point, in *Sain v. Cedar Rapids Community*

School District (2001), the Iowa Supreme Court suggested that in a future case it might decide to apply a legally enforceable duty of care to course advising. Mr. Sain was a student who, after accepting a full scholarship to play college basketball, found out just prior to enrollment that he lacked the required number of English credits needed to participate in intercollegiate athletics. Although the court ultimately rejected his claims, it stated:

> The tort of negligent misrepresentation is broad enough to include a duty for a high school guidance counselor to use reasonable care in providing specific information to a student when the guidance counselor has knowledge of the specific need for the information and provides the information to the student in the course of a counselor-student relationship, and a student reasonably relies upon the information under circumstances in which the counselor knows or should know that the student is relying upon the information. (p. 129)

In contrast to the reluctance of courts to adjudicate educational malpractice tort claims, they have often been willing to adjudicate student claims involving allegations of misrepresentation and fraud. In *Pell v. Trustees of Columbia University* (1998), the court explained that when there is a contract between a student and a postsecondary institution, the law implies that the institution must act in good faith in its dealings with that student (p. 63). In *Alsides v. Brown Institute, Ltd.* (1999), the court explained that it was better prepared to adjudicate claims of misrepresentation and fraud because it could objectively assess whether an institution had made a good faith effort to make good on its promise. As a result, it adopted the rule that a student may bring an action against an educational institution for breach of contract, fraud, or misrepresentation, if the student alleges that the institution failed to perform on specific promises it made to the student (p. 473).

Contract Actions. Commentators are fond of quoting *Zumbrun v. University of Southern California* (1972), in which the court stated that the basic relationship between students and their educational institutions is "contractual in nature" (p. 10). Contract law may be distinguished from tort law in that it is based on "obligations imposed by bargain, and allows parties to protect themselves through bargaining" (*Mackenzie v. Miller Brewing Company*, 2001).

Indeed, a contract is a legally enforceable written or oral agreement in which the parties each agree to perform or refrain from performing certain acts. A student and a postsecondary institution generally form a contract when the institution makes an offer of admission to the student, and the student accepts it, agrees to pay tuition, and enrolls at the institution. In *Cloud v. Trustees of Boston University* (1983) the First Circuit Court of Appeals found that a portion of terms of a contract between student and institution were contained in the institutional guidelines, rules, policies, procedures, and other materials that the institution had distributed to the student. The court will give the meaning to the contract terms that it thinks a student will give to those terms. In other words, if a procedure states that each semester a particular service will be offered "frequently," if it was offered only once, it is unlikely that the court will agree that this was "frequent."

A student may be able to assert a breach of contract action against an institution if the student is damaged as a result of the institution's breach of a term of the contract between them. However, the student cannot simply protest that the institution has breached the contract by complaining generally that he has not received a quality education. Instead, he or she must present evidence to support each of the elements of a breach of contract claim, which generally include: (1) the existence of a valid and binding contract between the student and the institution; (2) the terms of that contract; (3) that the student complied with the contract's terms; (4) that the institution breached a specific duty or promise imposed on it by the contract; and (5) that as a result of the breach, actual damages occurred to the student. In regard to the fourth item, the student must identify the specific contractual promise that he or she claims the institution failed to honor. A student may be able to demonstrate the first two elements by submitting materials published by the institution provided to him or her by the institution.

The student in *Byrd* (2002) based his claims on the institution's failure to offer courses listed in its catalog of courses. In *Zumbrun* (1972), the student asserted a breach of contract action after her instructor failed to deliver the number of lectures listed for the course in the institution's catalog. In *Alsides* (1999), the court found that the student had not been provided the instruction and computer equipment that had been promised in its publications.

Some terms of the contract between students and institutions are implied by law. In *Ikpeazu v. University of Nebraska* (1985), the Eighth Circuit Court of Appeals found that the institution's published appeal procedure implied a term that students would not be graded capriciously. In *Branum v. Clark* (1991), the Second Circuit found that the contract between a student and a postsecondary institution contains implied terms requiring the institution to "act in good faith in its dealing with students" (p. 705). In *Carr v. St. John's University* (1962), the court found that when a student is admitted into a degree program, there is an implied contract that if the student complies with the terms set out by the institution, the student will obtain the degree (p. 633).

The law implies good faith and fair dealing as terms of every contract between a student and a postsecondary institution. This protection is particularly important for students enrolled in private postsecondary institutions that are not subject to constitutional requirements for due process. Courts have used good faith and fair dealing principles to hear a variety of student claims. For example, in *Sylvester v. Texas S. University* (1997), the court found that the requirements of good faith and fair dealing provided a vehicle for protecting students against arbitrary and capricious treatment by their institutions. In *CenCor, Inc. v. Tolman* (1994), the court held that students have a cause of action when an institution fails to provide the equipment and qualified faculty promised in its catalog. In *Lesure v. State* (1990), the court found that a postsecondary institution was liable for damages when it misrepresented that its respiratory therapy school was accredited.

Claims Related to Discipline and Dismissal. Courts generally defer to postsecondary institutions with respect to academic dismissal decisions. In *Horowitz*

(1978), the U.S. Supreme Court explained that courts are not well equipped to evaluate a student's academic performance. However, courts are more likely to look into cases in which a student has alleged that the academic dismissal was arbitrary, capricious, or in bad faith. Nonetheless, such a student must first carry the heavy burden of proof required to sustain such allegations. In *Regents of University of Michigan v. Ewing* (1985), the Supreme Court explained that a court may not set aside an academic decision unless the institution's actions depart so far from accepted academic norms that they demonstrate the failure of the institution's representatives to exercise professional judgment (p. 225).

Courts are much less deferential to the decisions of academic institutions in regard to student claims involving discipline or dismissal for nonacademic reasons. For example, in *Okafor v. Yale University* (2004), the court held that contracts between a student and an institution contain an implied term that the student will not be arbitrarily dismissed from the institution (p. 15).

In regard to students' nonacademic contractual obligations, students must submit themselves to reasonable rules and regulations, which, if broken, may subject them to discipline or dismissal. If a student at a public institution breaks such a rule, then the Constitution requires the institution to offer procedural due process. However, a private institution's obligation to provide fair procedures arises out of its contractual duties. If it fails to provide adequate process, a court could find that the discipline or dismissal was arbitrary, and therefore improper (see, for example, *Schaer v. Brandeis University*, 1999).

THE FAMILY EDUCATIONAL RIGHTS AND PRIVACY ACT

Congress enacted the Family Educational Rights and Privacy Act (FERPA) during the 1974 reauthorization of the Elementary and Secondary Education Amendments of 1965. FERPA applies to all schools that receive federal funds, and its provisions state that compliance with FERPA is a condition of receiving those funds. The U.S. Department of Education enforces FERPA, and students alleging violations may file complaints with its Family Policy Compliance Office.

> FERPA protects against disclosure the personally identifiable information for each student that is contained in the education records maintained by the institution or a party acting for the institution. This includes records maintained in any format, including, but not limited to class schedules and rosters, transcripts, academic progress reports, grade reports, college placement test scores, photographs, advising notes, and most disciplinary records.

While students cannot sue a postsecondary institution for violating FERPA, the statute provides them certain rights, including the right to: (1) access their educational records held by postsecondary institutions; (2) provide written consent before the institution discloses personally identifiable information, subject to exceptions in which FERPA can make disclosures without student consent; (3) inspect and review the student's education records within 45 days of the date the school receives a written request from the student for access; (4) request the amendment of the education records that the student believes are inaccurate, misleading, or otherwise violate the student's privacy rights under FERPA; (5) the right to file a complaint with the Department of Education alleging that the institution has violated their rights under FERPA; and (6) if the records that the student is seeking are not maintained by the school official to whom the request is sent, the right to be informed of the official in control of the records. Furthermore, with certain exceptions, institutions must record the names of all third parties who request access or are allowed access to a student's records in the record file, and a third party who is allowed to access a student's records is prohibited from disclosing that information further without the student's written consent. While FERPA conditions the receipt of federal education funding on institutional compliance with the statute and its regulations, at this time, I have not found any record of a matter in which such funds have been withheld as the result of a FERPA violation.

FERPA and Campus Safety

In April 2007, the media spotlight focused on FERPA after the shooting deaths of thirty-two individuals on a Virginia campus by a student who then shot himself to death. This tragedy spurred discussions in which some commentators suggested that problems with FERPA contribute to risk and harm on postsecondary campuses. Subsequently, in June 2007, the director of the Department of Education Family Policy Compliance Office issued a statement on the disclosure of information to parents of students enrolled in postsecondary education. This statement makes it clear that nothing in FERPA prohibits postsecondary faculty, staff, and administrators from notifying parents or law enforcement of suspicious activity or behavior they have personally observed. Furthermore, nothing in FERPA prevents postsecondary staff, faculty, and administrators from encouraging a student to contact his or her parents.

FERPA Exceptions

In general, FERPA restricts institutional disclosure of information contained in student records unless the student has consented to its release, or the record for which disclosure is sought falls within a statutory exception that includes: disclosure pursuant to educational audits as required by Internal Revenue Service regulations; compliance with court subpoenas in connection with disciplinary matters in which safety issues have arisen; and disclosure of campus crime statistics. If a student is under twenty-one years of age, a postsecondary institution may inform his or her parents about the student's use or possession of alcohol or a controlled substance.

FERPA also permits disclosure of information to a student's parents without the student's consent if the student is a dependent for tax purposes. In addition, postsecondary institutions may disclose student information to appropriate parties when necessary to protect the health or safety of the student or other individuals. This health and safety exception permits, but does not require information disclosure. Courts among the jurisdictions have not consistently ruled on the matter of whether or not postsecondary institutions have a duty to contact parents in such an emergency. For example, in *Jain v. Iowa* (2000), the court held that the institution had no duty to prevent a student's suicide because there was no legally defined special relationship. However, in *Schieszler v. Ferrum College* (2002), the court held that a special relationship can exist between a student and a postsecondary institution that gives rise to a duty to protect the student when harm is foreseeable.

In regard to FERPA's health and safety exception, Rooker (2005) provided the following guidance to the president of a private university:

> [A]n educational agency or institution may disclose personally identifiable, non-directory information from education records under the "health or safety emergency" exception only if it has determined, on a case-by-case basis, that a *specific situation* presents *imminent danger* or *threat* to students or other members of the community, or requires an *immediate need* for information in order to avert or diffuse serious threats to the safety or health of a student or other individuals. Any release must be *narrowly tailored* considering the immediacy and magnitude of the emergency and must be made only to parties who can address the specific emergency in question. This exception is temporally limited to the period of the emergency and generally does not allow a blanket release of personally identifiable information from a student's education records to comply with general requirements under State law.

These statements appear to require institutions to make an initial determination of whether a disclosure is necessary to protect the health or safety of the student or other individuals. They narrowly limit its application to specific situations that present a threat of imminent danger to students or other members of the community, or require the immediate provision of information in order to avert or diffuse a serious threat to the safety or health of a student or other individuals.

FERPA and the Patriot Act

Each time advisors enter something in writing in a student's record, they should consider whether it might be susceptible to misinterpretation if reviewed by a governmental agency in the course of a terrorism investigation. As amended by the Section 508 of the Patriot Act of 2001, FERPA permits disclosure of personally identifiable information from education records without student consent to the U.S. Attorney General for the purpose of investigating and prosecuting certain terrorism crimes. In a 2002 letter to educational institutions, Rooker explained that when a court issues an order to compel such disclosures without notice to the student, then the institution is not required to make a record of this in the student's file.

FREEDOM OF SPEECH AND EMPLOYMENT

The First Amendment to the U.S. Constitution establishes the freedom of speech against intrusion by the federal government and is applied to the states through the Fourteenth Amendment. It prohibits governmental, not private, interference with speech and expression. The U.S. Supreme Court ruled in *Pickering v. Board of Education* (1968) and *Rankin v. McPherson* (1987) that employees are protected against discrimination, harassment, and termination on the basis of their political views. However, legally and practically speaking, the free speech rights of public and private employees are limited.

Free Speech and State Postsecondary Institutions

Academic advisors should keep in mind that while a state-supported postsecondary institution cannot prevent them from writing a letter to a newspaper, it may discipline or terminate them on the basis of its contents unless the court finds that the advisor's expression qualifies as a matter of public concern. Even when the expression involves a matter of public concern, the court will weigh the employee's interest in commenting on that concern against the employer's interest in promoting the efficiency of public services (see, for example, *Siebert v. University of Oklahoma Health Sciences Center,* 1989; *Pickering v. Board of Education,* 1968; *Connick v. Myers,* 1983). Finally, if the employee's expression is false or made for the purpose of venting personal feelings, it is unlikely that a court will afford it First Amendment protection.

Free Speech and Private Postsecondary Institutions

The First Amendment does not restrict private postsecondary institutions from regulating employee speech. However, other federal laws, such as Title VII of the Civil Rights Act of 1964, prohibit speech that constitutes sexual harassment, and state laws generally prohibit private employers from censoring speech altogether. Nonetheless, the bottom line is that no state or federal law completely protects persons employed by private institutions from being terminated on the basis of their speech or expression.

If an advisor does not have an employment agreement that states otherwise, in most states, he or she is an at-will employee. An at-will employee can be terminated, subject to public policy limitations, with or without good cause. Public policy reasons do not include the right to free speech. As a result, a private postsecondary institution may be legally able to discipline or terminate an advisor for what he or she says at lunch, in e-mail messages, in a blog, or on social networking Web sites. Although an at-will employee may be terminated for no reason, or for an arbitrary or irrational reason, private employers do not have the right to impose termination for an unlawful reason, such as an employee's refusal to commit a crime, or for a purpose that is contrary to public policy, an employee's refusal to exercise or waive constitutional rights, or for alleging in good faith that the employer has violated a law of public importance.

CIVIL RIGHTS LAW

Federal Antidiscrimination Laws

Title VI of the Civil Rights Act of 1964 prohibits discrimination on the basis of race, color, and national origin in federally funded programs and activities. The U.S. Department of Education is responsible for its enforcement against postsecondary institutions receiving funding through that agency. In addition, state laws generally place limitations on state action involving differential treatment of people on the basis of race, color, or national origin.

Title IX of the Education Amendments of 1972 provides that no person can be excluded from participation in, be denied the benefits of, or be subjected to discrimination on the basis of sex, by an education program or activity receiving federal funding. While Title IX is frequently known for its impact in promoting gender equity in athletics, it covers educational activities in all areas of academic life.

Section 504 of the Rehabilitation Act of 1973 prohibits discrimination against students with disabilities enrolled in postsecondary institutions that receive federal funds. It served as the model for Title II of the Americans with Disabilities Act of 1990 (ADA), which extended Section 504's prohibitions against discrimination on the basis of disability. Despite recent cases in which courts have refused to award monetary damages in connection with Title II violations, the ADA and Section 504 remain good laws.

Both Section 504 and the ADA prohibit postsecondary institutions from establishing eligibility criteria that screen out or tend to screen out people with disabilities, unless such criteria are necessary to meet program objectives. They also prohibit institutions from providing separate or different benefits, services, or programs to people with disabilities, unless this is necessary to ensure that the benefits and services received are equally effective. The affirmative provisions of Section 504 and the ADA state that postsecondary institutions must: (1) provide services and programs to students with disabilities in the most integrated setting appropriate to their needs; (2) make reasonable modifications in their policies, practices, and procedures to avoid discrimination on the basis of disability, unless it would result in a fundamental alteration in their program or activity; (3) ensure that buildings are accessible; and (4) provide auxiliary aids to individuals with disabilities, at no additional cost, where necessary to ensure effective communication with individuals with hearing, vision, or speech impairments.

Section 508 of the Rehabilitation Act of 1973 applies to each of the fifty states as a condition of their receipt of federal funding under the Assistive Technology Act of 2004. It requires that when state entities purchase new computer hardware or software or other electronic equipment for their employees or for use by students, they must ensure that these new acquisitions work with existing assistive technologies such as screen-reading software and Braille display units. Section 508 further requires that students and members of the public seeking information or services from a state entity must have access to and use of information and data that are comparable to that provided to members of the public who do not have disabilities, unless this would impose an undue burden on the federal agency.

Acts of discrimination prohibited by the federal laws described above include institutional action or inaction that: (1) denies any service, financial aid, or other benefit provided under the program; (2) provides any service, financial aid, or other benefit to an individual that is different, or provides it in a manner that is different from that in which it is provided to others; (3) subjects an individual to segregation or separate treatment in any matter related to his or her receipt of any service, financial aid, or other benefit under the program; (4) restricts an individual in any way in the enjoyment of any advantage or privilege enjoyed by others receiving any service, financial aid, or other benefit under the program; (5) treats an individual differently from others in determining whether he or she satisfies any admission, enrollment, quota, eligibility, membership, or other requirement or condition that individuals must meet in order to be provided any service, financial aid, or other benefit provided under the program; (6) denies an individual an opportunity to participate in the program through the provision of services or otherwise afford him or her an opportunity to do so that is different from that afforded others under the program; or (7) denies a person the opportunity to participate as a member of a planning or advisory body that is an integral part of the program.

Academic advisors clearly need to be aware of these laws and simply use common sense in order to refrain from potential and unintended violations in their daily interactions with students.

Civil Rights Issues in Recruitment and Retention Programs

A number of academic advisors play significant roles in postsecondary recruitment and retention programs that consider race and ethnicity among their eligibility factors. Absent the necessary conditions, such programs have the potential to violate Title VI of the Civil Rights Act of 1964. However, under some circumstances, Title VI permits, but does not require, institutions to consider race and ethnicity.

Guidance concerning the application of Title VI to recruitment and retention programs may be inferred from Supreme Court cases that have involved the consideration of race and ethnic background in postsecondary admissions. In *Regents of University of California v. Bakke* (1978), the U.S. Supreme Court found that an institution could use race and ethnic background for its particular purpose of furthering its attainment of a diverse student body. More recently, in *Grutter v. Bollinger* (2003), the Supreme Court again stated its view that the attainment of student-body diversity is a compelling state interest that can justify the use of race in university admissions. The Court found that the institution considered race only as a "plus" factor with respect to individual applicants as a part of a narrowly tailored approach that: (1) provided for individualized consideration of each applicant; (2) conducted a good faith consideration of race-neutral alternatives; (3) did not impose an undue burden on nonminority applicants; and (4) provided for periodic reviews to evaluate whether racial diversity had been achieved, such that the preference-based approach might be discontinued at some point. While the Supreme Court's decisions in these cases do not address the consideration of race and ethnicity in private school admissions, it stated in *Grutter* (2003) that it would use these standards in reviewing other Title VI claims. In view of this, private institutions should review their own admissions policies in the context of that decision.

In *Bakke* (1978), the Court observed that race is only one of the elements that a postsecondary institution may consider in attaining a diverse student body.

Other factors may include economic disadvantage, graduation from rural or inner-city schools, graduation from schools that have been historically underrepresented in the institution's student body, intellectual, athletic, and artistic skill, experience living and working in diverse environments or with people in historically underserved or underprivileged populations, graduation from a historically black institution, first generation to attend college or graduate school, and demonstrated success in overcoming substantial educational or economic obstacles.

CONCLUSION

This chapter has briefly described a portion of the formidable body of law and legal theories that are variously applied to the relationships between students, academic advisors, and their institutions. World and national events will continue to bring about changes, such as the amendments to FERPA, that affect students, academic advisors, and postsecondary education in general. These changes will continue to challenge advisors in their work to enhance the learning and development of individual students and in strengthening what NACADA described in 2004 as the "importance, dignity, potential, and unique nature of each individual within the academic setting."

References

Alsides v. Brown Institute, Ltd., 592 N.W.2d 468, 473 (Minn. Ct. App. 1999).

Americans with Disabilities Act of 1990, 42 USCS §§ 12101 et seq.

Assistive Technology Act of 2004, 29 USCS §§ 3001 et seq.

Bickel, R. D., & Lake, P. F. (1999). *The rights and responsibilities of the modern university: Who assumes the risks of college life?* Durham, NC: Carolina Academic Press.

Board of Curators of University of Missouri v. Horowitz, 435 U.S. 78, 86 (U.S. 1978).

Board of Regents v. Roth, 408 U.S. 564, 577 (U.S. 1972).

Branum v. Clark, 927 F.2d 698, 705 (2d Cir. 1991).

Buck, J., Moore, J., Schwartz, M., & Supon, S. (2001). *What is ethical behavior for an academic adviser?* Retrieved August 1, 2007, from http://www.psu.edu/dus/mentor

Byrd v. Lamar, 846 S.2d 334 (Ala. 2002).

Cantwell v. Connecticut, 310 U.S. 296 (1940).

Carr v. St. John's University, 17 A.D.2d 632, 633 (N.Y. App. Div. 1962).

CenCor, Inc. v. Tolman, 868 P.2d 396, 399 (Colo. 1994).

Civil Rights Act of 1964, 42 U.S.C. § 2000d et seq.

Cloud v. Trustees of Boston University, 720 F.2d 721, 724 (1st Cir. 1983).

Connick v. Myers, 461 U.S. 138, 146 (1983).

Council for the Advancement of Standards (CAS). (2005). *CAS Standards and Guidelines for Academic Advising.* Retrieved August 22, 2007, from http://www.nacada.ksu.edu/Clearinghouse/Research_Related/CASStandardsForAdvising.pdf

DeJonge v. Oregon, 299 U.S. 353 (1937).

Dixon v. Alabama State Board of Education, 294 F.2d 150 (5th Cir. 1961).

Education Amendments of 1972, 20 U.S.C. §§ 1681–1688.

Eisenstadt v. Baird, 405 U.S. 438 (1972).

Everson v. Board of Education, 330 U.S. 1 (1947).

Family Educational Rights and Privacy Act of 1974, 20 USCS § 1232g.

Federal Tort Claims Act of 1946, 28 USCS §§ 2671 et seq.

Galdikas v. Fagan, 342 F.3d 684, 691 (7th Cir. 2003).

Garner, B. A. (Ed.). (2004). *Black's law dictionary.* (8th ed.) Eagan, MN: Thomson West.

Gauder v. Leckrone, 366 F. Supp. 2d 780, 789 (D. Wis. 2005).

Gitlow v. New York, 268 U.S. 652 (1925).

Gordon, V. N.& Habley, W. R. (2000). *Academic advising: A comprehensive handbook.* San Francisco: Jossey-Bass.

Goss v. Lopez, 419 U.S. 565, 575 (1975).

Griswold v. Connecticut, 381 U.S. 479; 85 S. Ct. 1678 (U.S. 1965).

Grutter v. Bollinger, 539 U.S. 306, 325 (U.S. 2003).

Hendricks v. Clemson Univ., 578 S.E.2d 711 (S.C. 2003).

Hillman v. Elliott, 436 F. Supp. 812, 817 (D. Va. 1977).

Ikpeazu v. University of Nebraska, 775 F.2d 250 (8th Cir. 1985).

Jain v. Iowa, 617 N.W. 2d 293, 299–300 (2000).

Lawrence v. Texas, 539 U.S. 558, 565 (2003).

Lesure v. State, 1990 Tenn. App. LEXIS 355 (Tenn. Ct. App. 1990).

Logan v. Zimmerman Brush Co., 455 U.S. 422, 430 (U.S. 1982).

Loving v. Virginia, 388 U.S. 1 (1967).

Mackenzie v. Miller Brewing Co., 2001 WI 23 (Wis. 2001).

Marbury v. Madison, 5 U.S. 137, 180 (U.S. 1803).

Mathews v. Eldridge, 424 U.S. 319, 333 (1976).

McMahon v. United States, 342 U.S. 25, 27 (1951).

Mitchell v. United States, 313 U.S. 80 (1941).

Moore v. East Cleveland, 431 U.S. 494 (1977).

Morrissey v. Brewer, 408 U.S. 471, 480 (1972).

NAACP v. Alabama ex rel. Patterson, 357 U.S. 449 (1958).

NACADA. (2004). *NACADA statement of core values of academic advising.* NACADA Clearinghouse of Academic Advising Resources Web site. Retrieved August 22, 2007, from http://www.nacada.ksu.edu/Clearinghouse/AdvisingIssues/Core-Values.htm

Near v. Minnesota, 283 U.S. 697 (1931).

Okafor v. Yale University, 2004 Conn. Super. LEXIS 1657 (Conn. Super. Ct. 2004).

Pell v. Trustees of Columbia Univ., 1998 U.S. Dist. LEXIS 407 (D.N.Y. 1998).

Pickering v. Board of Education, 391 U.S. 563 (1968).

Pierce v. Society of Sisters, 268 U.S. 510 (1925).

Rankin v. McPherson, 483 U.S. 378 (1987).

Regents of University of California v. Bakke 438 U.S. 265 (1978).

Regents of University of Michigan v. Ewing, 474 U.S. 214, 225 (U.S. 1985).

Rehabilitation Act of 1973, 29 USCS §§ 701 et seq.

Robinson, S. (2004). *Legal issues for advisors: A primer.* NACADA Clearinghouse of Academic Advising Resources Web site. Retrieved July 24, 2007, from http://www .nacada.ksu.edu/Clearinghouse/AdvisingIssues/legal.htm

Roe v. Wade, 410 U.S. 959 (1973).

Rooker, L. (2002). Letter from Director of the Family Compliance Office Statement of LeRoy Rooker, Director, Family Policy Compliance Office, U.S. Department of Education. (April 12, 2002). Letter to the President of Strayer University. Retrieved on July 19, 2007, from http://www.ed.gov/policy/gen/guid/fpco/pdf/htterrorism.pdf

Rooker, L. (2005). Letter from Director of the Family Compliance Office Statement of LeRoy Rooker, Director, Family Policy Compliance Office, U.S. Department of Education. (March 11, 2005). Letter to the President of Strayer University. Retrieved on July 19, 2007, from http://www.ed.gov/policy/gen/guid/fpco/ferpa/library/ strayer031105.html

Ross v. Creighton University, 957 F.2d 410, 412, 417 (7th Cir. 1992).

Sain v. Cedar Rapids Community School District, 626 N.W.2d 115, 129 (Iowa 2001).

Schaer v. Brandeis University, 48 Mass. App. Ct. 23, 716 N.E.2d 1055 (Mass.App. 1999).

Schieszler v. Ferrum College, 236 F. Supp. 2d 602, 609 (W.D. Va. 2002).

Schneider v. Plymouth State College, 144 N.H. 458, 462 (N.H. 1999).

Schuler v. University of Minnesota, 788 F.2d 510, 514 (8th Cir. 1986).

Scott v. Savers Property & Casualty Insurance Co., 262 Wis. 2d 127, 159–160 (Wis. 2003).

Seavy, W. (1957). Dismissal of students: Due process. *70 Harv. L. Rev. 1406, 1407 n. 3.*

Siebert v. University of Oklahoma Health Sciences Center, 867 F.2d 591 (10th Cir. 1989).

Sylvester v. Texas S. University, 957 F. Supp. 944, 947 (D. Tex. 1997).

U.S. Constitution, Amendments I through X (The Bill of Rights).

U.S. Constitution, Amendment XIV, § 1.

U.S. Constitution, Art. VI, cl. 2.

United States v. Frost, 125 F.3d 346, 367 (6th Cir. 1997).

Washington v. Glucksberg, 521 U.S. 702 (1997).

Weeks, K.& Haglund, R. (2002). Fiduciary duties of college and university faculty and administrators, 29 J.C. & U.L. 153, 154–55, 156, 173.

Wolf v. Colorado, 338 U.S. 25 (1949).

Zumbrun v. University of Southern California, 25 Cal. App. 3d 1, 10 (Cal. Ct. App. 1972).

CHAPTER FIVE

Advising for Student Success

George D. Kuh

Helping more students prepare for and graduate from college is a priority for institutional leaders and policy makers at every educational level. Broadly defined, student success represents academic achievement, engagement in educationally purposeful activities, satisfaction, acquisition of desired knowledge, skills, and competencies, persistence, and attainment of educational objectives (Kuh, Kinzie, Buckley, Bridges, & Hayek, 2007).

Certain institutional conditions have been linked with student success, such as supportive peers, faculty, and staff members who set high expectations for student performance, and academic programs and experiences that actively engage students and foster academic and social integration (Kuh, Kinzie, Schuh, & Whitt, 2005b). Among the latter are well-designed and well-implemented precollege and ongoing orientation programs, first-year seminars, and other new student advising and study group experiences (Muraskin & Wilner, 2004; Reason, Terenzini, & Domingo, 2006; Upcraft, Gardner, & Barefoot, 2005; Upcraft, Mullendore, Barefoot, & Fidler, 1993). In fact, persistence and graduation rates are, in part, a function of the average amount of time it takes students to earn a degree. This suggests that low graduation rates may be related to institutional conditions that impede academic progress, including course availability, scheduling, and problems with advising (Blose, 1999). Without effective academic advising in the first year and beyond, these programs and practices will almost certainly have less than optimal impact.

National studies of student satisfaction indicate that advising is an aspect of college with which students are the least satisfied (Low, 2000). Even so, academic advisors can play an integral role in promoting student success by assisting students in ways that encourage them to engage in the right kinds of activities, inside and outside the classroom. Advisors are especially important because they are among the first people new students encounter and are the people with whom students often have frequent interaction throughout the first year.

This chapter summarizes some of the key findings from the literature on academic advising and dimensions of student success such as persistence, achievement, personal development, and student engagement. Five principles are offered for effective advising, drawing on advising policies and promising practices at high-performing colleges.

WHAT ADVISORS NEED TO KNOW ABOUT STUDENT SUCCESS IN COLLEGE

To be effective, academic advisors must be familiar with the research on students and their success. The following list highlights eight major risk factors that threaten college persistence and graduation (Berkner, Cuccaro-Alamin, & McCormick, 1996; Carroll, 1989; Horn & Premo, 1995; McCormick & Horn, 1996). Students with two or more of these characteristics are more likely to drop out than their peers (Choy, 2001; Muraskin & Lee, with Wilner & Swail, 2004; State Higher Education Executive Officers, 2005; Swail with Redd & Perna, 2003).

Risk Factors:
- Being academically underprepared for college-level work;
- Not entering college directly after high school;
- Attending college part-time;
- Being a single parent;
- Being financially independent (i.e., students who rely on their own income or savings and whose parents are not sources of income for meeting college costs);
- Caring for children at home;
- Working more than thirty hours per week; and
- Being a first-generation college student.

The conditions associated with premature departure from college partially explain the low baccalaureate-attainment rates of certain groups of students, including community college students and many ethnic minorities (Adelman, 2006). For example, almost 50 percent of all first-time community college students (and in some settings significantly more) are assessed as underprepared for the academic demands of college-level work. This is another major reason that approximately half of community college students do not return to college for their second year of studies (Community College Survey of Student Engagement, 2005). Just over half of Latino students attended postsecondary institutions part-time (52 percent), compared with 37 percent of white students. Although nearly two-thirds (64 percent) of whites attended postsecondary institutions continuously, only two-fifths of Latinos attended postsecondary institutions without stopping out (Swail, Cabrera, Lee, & Williams, 2005). Latinos were more likely to delay enrollment in postsecondary education, as about 5 percent fewer than whites (77 percent and 82 percent, respectively) entered postsecondary education within seven months of graduating from high school. In addition, African American and Latino community college students are less likely to earn baccalaureate degrees because they are overrepresented in certificate programs (Bailey, Jenkins & Leinbach, 2005). Attending a tribal college seems to have a positive impact on encouraging Native American community college graduates to pursue baccalaureate degrees (American Indian Higher Education Consortium, Institute for Higher Education Policy, Sallie Mae Education Institute, 2000). Academic advisors should be knowledgeable about these persistence and graduation statistics when working with students from different backgrounds.

Structured academic advising can help students successfully make their way through postsecondary education (Cohen & Brawer, 1996; Kramer & Associates, 2003). Advising is thought to be most effective in terms of promoting student growth, learning, and success when it is integrated into academic support services and when it is sensitive to the developmental needs of diverse students (Kramer & Associates, 2003). Advisors are particularly important in helping students plan an educational program appropriate to their educational and vocational goals and raising questions about the coherence and sequencing of the educational program. These issues are essential to consider as more students attend multiple institutions on the way to a baccalaureate degree (McCormick, 2003).

Advising takes many forms, making it difficult to tease out the effects of advising by staff advisors or faculty members. Research that does not control for student characteristics typically produces mixed results in terms of the quality of advising (Aitken, 1982; Brigman, Kuh, & Stager, 1982; Kowalski, 1977). Some studies that do control for factors such as entering students' academic ability show that institutions that provided the most extensive orientation and advising programs had higher graduation rates (Dunphy, Miller, Woodruff, & Nelson, 1987; Forrest, 1985; Fidler & Hunter, 1989). Tinto (2004) found that advising positively affects retention and graduation when advisors focused on the needs of undecided students, those who decide to change their major, and first-generation students who may not have the knowledge of how to successfully navigate higher education. Like orientation, the quality of academic advising may also have an indirect effect on persistence when factors such as high school grades, gender, and age are taken into account (Metzner, 1989).

What Students Say About Advising

The vast majority of students (88 percent) say they take advantage of academic advising at some point during the first year of college (National Survey of Student Engagement [NSSE], 2005). About half of both first-year and senior students say that their primary source of academic guidance is their advisor. However, more than a quarter (27 percent) of first-year students turns to family or friends as their main source of academic advising (Figure 5.1). It is

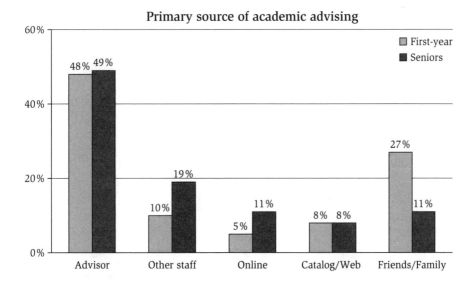

Figure 5.1. Primary Source of Academic Advising.

impossible for advisors to foster student success if they do not interact with their advisees, which is the case for about one in ten students (7 percent of first-year students, 11 percent of seniors) who *never* met with their advisor in the current academic year; part-time, female, and Caucasian students were less likely than full-time, male, and students of color to meet with their advisor (NSSE, 2007). Students who met with their advisor more frequently were more satisfied with advising and also were generally more satisfied with their institution. NSSE results also indicate that four-fifths of both first-year and senior students agree that they received accurate information from their advisor (Figure 5.2) (NSSE, 2005).

Meeting with one's academic advisor is important because students who met with their academic advisor at least twice during the current academic year tended to engage more frequently in the range of educationally purposeful activities measured by the five benchmarks used by the National Survey of Student Engagement (2007). In addition, more frequent contact with the advisor also was related to greater self-reported gains in personal and social development, practical competence, and general education, and more frequent use of deep approaches to learning (NSSE, 2007).

Fortunately, most students are reasonably satisfied with the quality of their academic advising. Only 6 percent of first-year students described it as "poor." Seniors are somewhat less satisfied, with 11 percent saying their advising was poor. Satisfaction with advising does not vary in any appreciable way between men and women (Figure 5.3) or between students from different racial and ethnic groups (Figure 5.4). While four-fifths of full-time students rate their advising as either good or excellent, only two-thirds of part-time, first-year students rate their advising this highly (NSSE, 2005). In fact, almost twice as many part-time students say advising is poor (11 percent, compared

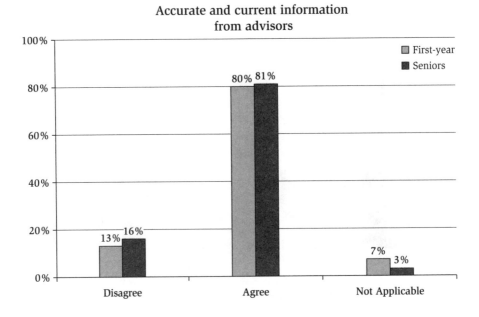

Figure 5.2. Accurate and Current Information from Advisors.

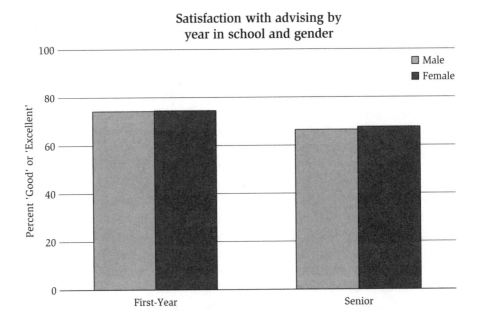

Figure 5.3. Satisfaction with Advising by Year in School and Gender.

with 6 percent of full-time students). This is perhaps due to the time limitations of part-time students, who have less time to meet with an advisor. Part-time students are also twice as likely to be undecided in terms of major, which may require different types of advising skills, such as less information dispensing and more career exploration. Student athletes (both high-profile

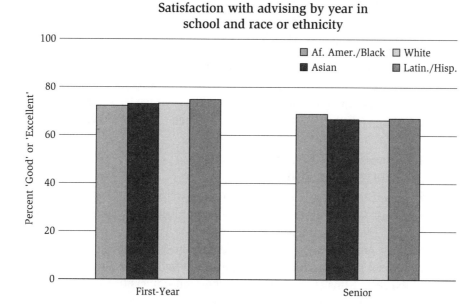

Figure 5.4. Satisfaction with Advising by Year in School and Race or Ethnic Group.

and other sports) at Division I institutions are more satisfied with the quality of their academic advising than are their nonathlete peers, which may likely reflect a successful approach by established athletic department academic advising programs for providing more extensive assistance to student athletes (Broughton & Neyer, 2001).

Satisfaction with advising is important because NSSE (2005) data indicate that students who rate their advising as good or excellent:

- Are more likely to interact with faculty in various ways,
- Perceive the institution's environment to be more supportive overall,
- Are more satisfied with their overall college experience, and
- Gain more from college in most areas.

Indeed, the quality of academic advising is the single most powerful predictor of satisfaction with the campus environment for students at four-year schools (NSSE, 2005).

Advising can be improved, since two-fifths of students (37 percent of first-year students, 44 percent of seniors) said that their advisor did not inform them of academic support services, such as tutoring (NSSE, 2007). Two-fifths of students (35 percent first-year students, 42 percent seniors) said that their advisor did not provide information about various educational options such as study abroad or national and international exchange programs. Advisors were rated significantly lower by seniors than by first-year students in the quality of career support and information about educational support services (NSSE, 2007).

All in all, it is fair to say that most students are generally satisfied with the quality of the academic advising they receive and believe the information they receive is accurate. At the same time, academic advising is about more than dispensing information. The nature of the relationship between advisors and advisees, how institutions organize and deliver advising, and the contributions of advisors to creating a student-centered institutional culture are also important. We can better understand these contributions by seeing what academic advising looks like at strong-performing colleges and universities.

Lessons for Academic Advisors from Strong-Performing Institutions

Student Success in College: Creating Conditions That Matter (Kuh, Kinzie, Schuh, & Whitt, 2005b) describes the factors and conditions shared by twenty very different four-year colleges and universities. These schools had higher-than-predicted graduation rates and scores on the NSSE, given their student and institutional characteristics, such as institutional size, location, and selectivity. In the rest of this chapter these colleges and universities will be referred to as DEEP schools, using the acronym of the research project—Documenting Effective Educational Practices (DEEP).

DEEP Participating Institutions

Alverno College

California State University, Monterey Bay

The Evergreen State College

Fayetteville State University

George Mason University

Gonzaga University

Longwood University

Macalester College

Miami University (Ohio)

Sewanee: The University of the South

Sweet Briar College

University of Kansas

University of Maine, Farmington

University of Michigan

University of Texas at El Paso

Ursinus College

Wabash College

Wheaton College (Massachusetts)

Winston-Salem State University

Wofford College

DEEP institutions used a variety of academic advising models and approaches. At the University of Kansas and Miami University, for example, first-year student advising programs are staffed by full-time professional advisors; faculty serve as academic advisors once students are accepted into a major. For example, at Alverno College, a women's college, professional support staff members are aided by peer advisors who work with new students during orientation. The advisor typically works with advisees for the first two years, a period during which the curriculum is fairly well prescribed. Once the student selects her major, a faculty advisor from that area takes over. Throughout the student's time at Alverno, the professional advising staff works closely with the faculty to support an ethic of collaborative learning, which is a key to succeeding at the college. Similarly, at George Mason University, academic advising center staff members work closely with department faculty, the career center, orientation, and other offices to make sure students get the necessary information to make good decisions. One of the main vehicles is the midterm progress grade report. Faculty members receive reports on the students they are advising and the Academic Advising office receives grades for undeclared students. Students are contacted if their grades are low and asked to visit the respective resource.

To the extent possible, most DEEP institutions attempt to connect students with faculty members in their major department early in their college career and create innovative advising structures for student-faculty interaction. Longwood University assigns a faculty advisor who may work with the student in that role throughout the student's undergraduate program. Some schools embed the advising function in the first-year experience. Macalester College, Wofford College, and Sewanee: The University of the South, connect students to their advisor via the first-year seminar course in which the faculty member serves as students' academic advisor until students declare their major and are assigned a departmental advisor. Wheaton College created an advising team composed of a faculty member, peer mentor, librarian, and administrator assigned to instruct the first-year seminar.

While advising approaches varied across DEEP institutions, the common thread was that of a network of competent, skilled people who provide good, timely information buttressed by an ethic of support. In addition, advisors generally enjoy good working relations with one another and with their advisees. Preceptors, peer mentoring, and tutoring programs are common, with student affairs generally providing the space and infrastructure for such services and faculty members selecting and supervising peer mentors.

Principles for Effective Academic Advising

DEEP schools generally adhered to five principles (De Sousa, 2005).

1. Advising is grounded in a talent-development philosophy. Faculty members and advisors are duty bound to work with the students they have, not those they wish they had. This sentiment has been a popular refrain at Fayetteville State University and other institutions, and is the philosophical underpinning of a talent-development perspective on education. That is, advisors, faculty members, and others subscribe to the belief that students can learn anything the institution teaches, provided the right conditions are established, including optimal portions of challenge and support. Advisors enact this belief by meeting students where they are—academically, socially, and psychologically. These faculty and staff advisors share a cool passion for student learning. They exhibit an unwavering enthusiasm for the task at hand, with the unrelenting flame of innovation burning steadily.

In addition, advisors at high-performing institutions are well informed about their students. They know their students' demographics, preferred learning styles, individual talents, and when and where they need help. They also establish high but attainable expectations for students, making explicit what students need to know and do to be successful. Advisors challenge, implore, cajole, and support students to go beyond the level of effort they typically invest in their studies. When accompanied by copious amounts of timely feedback, they help students cultivate the habits of the mind that become the foundation for pursuing excellence.

At the University of Texas at El Paso, faculty members along with peer leaders gain a deeper awareness of the talents and abilities of students enrolled in their first-year seminar (UNIV 1301: Seminar in Critical Inquiry) by meeting one-on-one with each student twice during the fall semester. The individual sessions deliberately focus on students' academic progress during their first semester, with attention to connecting students to the institution's multiple support services. Faculty members are encouraged to keep abreast of their students' progress even after the seminar has ended.

All new Macalester first-year students take a discipline-based First Year Seminar (FYS) in their first semester. Sections are limited to only 16 students, and the seminar instructor serves as the advisor to FYS students for the first two years or until the student declares a major. A peer "writing preceptor" works with students on their written work. A series of workshops throughout the academic year prepare faculty to deal with the needs of the current first-year student cohort. Because of the FYS instructor's dual role—seminar leader and advisor—faculty learn a good deal firsthand about their advisees' intellectual interests and relative strengths and weaknesses. Moreover, they see their advisees several times a week in class, which provides regular opportunities for informal conversation about various matters as well as to monitor students' academic and social adjustment. As a result, Macalester students have at least one faculty member who knows them very well by the end of the first term and is in a position to know whether students seem to be struggling and if so, to make appropriate referrals.

At Sewanee: The University of the South, the faculty member teaching a student's First-Year Program (FYP) course also is the student's primary advisor. As with similar models elsewhere, faculty members get to know their advisees academically and personally. Some FYP instructors send letters to their students before they arrive on campus, which helps connect new students to Sewanee. As one first-year student put it, "I get to know my advisor much better because I see him in class."

2. Advising is a tag team activity. Given the array of academic and social issues that students must manage during the transition from high school to college, a cookie-cutter approach to advising students from increasingly diverse backgrounds will not be sufficient. Faculty and staff members at high-performing colleges and universities accept their fair share of responsibility for student success by adopting a "tag team" approach to advising students, incorporating a wide spectrum of people and expertise and multiple perspectives in the advising process.

Staffing the First Year Seminars (FYS) at Wheaton are a faculty member, administrator mentor, librarian, and two preceptors who are junior- or senior-level students. All serve as advisors to FYS students. The faculty member is the student's academic advisor throughout her or his first year, or until the student selects an academic major. Faculty members receive special training to deal with the needs of first-year students, including a series of workshops throughout the academic year. Preceptors assist the faculty in a peer mentoring role. Throughout orientation, new students meet daily with their preceptors either individually or in their advising teams. After orientation and throughout the student's first year, the preceptors work with the faculty advisor and administrative mentor to help students obtain the academic and life skills they need. In addition, one of the two preceptors lives in the residence hall with the students to maintain frequent contact. Preceptors are trained as study-skills tutors and offer workshops focusing on test taking, study strategies, time management, and note taking. Team members regularly meet to discuss the progress of the class and individual students. Some students call this carefully designed support network the "freshman family."

Almost all first-year students at Fayetteville State University enroll in the University College, an administrative unit that coordinates programs designed to facilitate transition to college. Because every student is assigned a faculty advisor who also teaches the freshman seminar course, students are in contact with their advisors several times a week. This regular contact opens up frequent opportunities to talk about academic, career, and personal matters that might affect the student's academic performance. Also, because advisors are seminar instructors, they have firsthand knowledge of what students are learning in class.

At Ursinus College, residence life staff contributes to academic advising by providing feedback to faculty and staff advisors. Residence life staff receive "academic warning" slips for students experiencing academic problems. Staff members compare this information with feedback from Resident Advisors to identify issues associated with the students' difficulties, including out-of-class life and other personal factors that might contribute to a student's poor academic performance. Communication also goes in the other direction: faculty advisors are notified if students are subject to significant disciplinary action for out-of-class indiscretions. The goal of all these interactions is to provide effective "safety nets" for students at risk.

Administered by the offices of the Dean of Students and Minority Affairs (OMA), Sewanee's Faculty Minority Mentor Program was founded in 1989 to augment its existing advising system. Several dozen faculty mentors meet with students throughout the school year. Meetings may be social in nature, with faculty and students attending concerts together in a nearby city or dining together using funds provided by OMA. Most important, perhaps, is that the faculty mentors are available to "provide guidance about life" and assist with the various trials and tribulations associated with adjusting to college.

These team approaches to advising make certain that students do not fall through the cracks. Students get the information they need to take full advantage of the opportunities and resources for learning their school provides for their academic achievement and social needs.

3. Students are expected to map out a path to success. The road to success in college can be full of challenges, surprises, and disappointments. Advisors, faculty, and staff at DEEP institutions know this and go to great lengths to make certain students know what to expect even before they matriculate, either as a first-time first-year or as a transfer student. To keep students on track, advisors should regularly convey what students need to do to be successful. Central to the task is working with students to plot a course of action for their educational success. For instance, advising sessions can be used to teach newcomers about campus culture—the traditions, rituals, and practices that communicate how and why things are done at the school (Kuh & Whitt, 1988).

Some schools, such as Fayetteville State University, University of Texas at El Paso, University of Maine, Farmington, and Winston-Salem State University, attract large numbers of first-generation students who, because of inadequate academic preparation and lack of knowledge about college, need explicit directions about how to make the best use of institutional resources and support services. To be sure that students take advantage of resources, these institutions require students to take part in activities, such as summer advising, orientation, and fall welcome week, and follow up with advising opportunities to monitor students' progress over the course of the first year.

George Mason University monitors students' performance to ensure that they do not slip through the cracks. In addition to the midterm grade report, mentioned earlier, the University 100 orientation course uses a series of assessments as student performance indicators. After reviewing this information, students with low grades are contacted. George Mason also offers online mentoring and advising, "virtually" pairing first-year students considering, for example, psychology as a major with a current psychology major. Undeclared students can learn about departmental expectations and requirements, workload, and potential career choices in the field by e-mailing their mentor. As an incentive for their time and support, mentors are offered one credit of course work. In addition, the Academic Support and Advising Center provides an "Ask an Advisor" Web site for students who are undeclared, pre-med, or changing their major.

At Ursinus, many instructors in the College's required first-year Common Intellectual Experience course serve as the academic advisor for the students in their section. Thus, through regular and ongoing contact, advisors provide advisees with a good sense of their academic performance and overall adjustment to college life.

Miami University emphasizes advising by requiring new first-year students to live in residence halls with a live-in academic advisor. The first-year advisor serves as the academic advisor and as the residence hall director to students living in residence halls ranging in size from 75 to 360 students. In some specialized academic programs, such as the schools of Fine Arts, Engineering and Applied Science, and Teacher Education, an additional advisor is assigned to first-year students. First-year students are expected to have a thirty-minute conference with their first-year advisor and about 90 percent of them actually do so.

The University of Kansas established its Freshman-Sophomore Advising Center in response to lower-than-desired levels of student satisfaction with academic advising. Its "Graduate in Four" advising notebook, distributed at orientation, provides students with information about how to make the most of their undergraduate years and what they need to do to complete their degree program in a timely manner. In the welcome letter at the front of the notebook, the university encourages students to "plan out-of-classroom activities such as organizations and internships that develop your skills and experiences, broaden you as a person, and enhance your opportunities for employment or graduate or professional school." The notebook then includes a section for each of the four undergraduate years along with a "checklist" that students can use to ensure that they are making appropriate choices. The notebooks also help students monitor whether they are, in fact, making progress toward the completion of their degree.

4. Every advising contact is a precious opportunity for meaningful interaction. Another feature that stands out at DEEP institutions is the frequency and quality of interactions students have with their advisors, teachers, and peers. These relationships are critical to helping students adjust to college life. Students also benefit from their interactions with faculty members who advise department clubs or organizations. Finally, getting involved *early* with students is essential to establishing meaningful advisor-advisee interactions. Advisors, along with faculty members, department chairs, student affairs professionals, and other staff at DEEP institutions, do this principally through first-year orientation programs and experiences.

Occasionally needed is intrusive advising—making plain to students what they need to do to attain their educational objectives. For example, when starting college, the vast majority of students (87 percent) say they will at least "occasionally" use campus academic support services such as writing skills centers. Yet by the end of the first year almost half (46 percent) had *not* done so (NSSE, 2005). This is troublesome because students who do use such services tend to perform better in college. For example, at Indiana University, Bloomington, students who used skill centers for mathematics and writing improvement were much more likely to persist to the second year and get higher grades than peers who did not, even though they are similar in most background characteristics, including academic ability (Hossler, Kuh, & Olsen, 2001). Academic advisors can play a key role by continually reminding and encouraging students to use these services, perhaps even entering into a contract or some other arrangement.

Timely interventions are essential. Waiting until midterm examinations is often too late to give students an idea of how well they are performing. Advisors do some of their most important work by paying attention to student class attendance patterns, drop and add information, early semester and midterm grades, and preregistration information. Some institutions, such as Brigham Young University, Norfolk State University, Southern Connecticut State University, and Truman State University, have used the individualized advising profile based on information College Student Expectations Questionnaire (CSEQ) or the Beginning College Student Survey of Student Engagement (BCSSE). Advisors use this information to talk with their advisees about their participation in educationally purposeful in-class and out-of-class activities such as studying, talking with faculty members about various matters, and participating in cocurricular activities.

Finally, advisors can do their students and institutions a great service by encouraging their advisees to engage in educationally purposeful activities. Even though some students may benefit more than others from exposure to certain of these practices (Kuh, Cruce, Shoup, Kinzie, & Gonyea, in press), it behooves faculty and staff to create opportunities for all students to participate in what research from NSSE and other quarters indicate are "high-impact" practices (Association of American Colleges and Universities, 2007; NSSE, 2007). These include learning communities, student-faculty research, service learning, internships, study abroad, and capstone seminars or other culminating experiences. These practices tend to have greater effects in engagement and student learning because they require students to take responsibility for activities that require daily decisions and tasks; as a result, students become more invested in the activity and more committed to the college and their studies. Academic advisors could use some of their time with students explaining the advantages of engagement and encouraging them to become involved with peers in campus events and organizations and invest effort in educational activities known to promote student learning and development (Braxton & McClendon, 2001–2002; Kuh, Kinzie, Schuh, & Whitt, 2005b; Kuh, Kinzie, Buckley, Bridges, & Hayek, 2007). If faculty and staff used these and other effective educational practices more frequently throughout the institution, and advisors routinely implored students to take advantage of one or more of these opportunities, colleges and universities could more effectively help ameliorate the shortcomings in students' academic preparation and create a culture that fosters student success (Allen, 1992; Fleming, 1984).

Also, simply offering programs based on promising practices does not guarantee student success; institutional programs and practices must be of high quality, customized to meet the needs of students they are intended to reach, and firmly rooted in a student success-oriented campus culture (Kuh et al., 2005a). Therefore, colleges and universities must ensure that interconnected learning support networks, early warning systems, and safety nets are in place and working as intended. As evidenced by DEEP institutions, using a multi-faceted approach to student success is essential.

5. Recognize that advising is a cultural and culture-bound activity. Efforts to enhance student success often falter because too little attention is given to understanding the properties of the institution's culture that reinforce the status quo and perpetuate everyday actions—"the way we do things here" (Kuh & Whitt, 1988). As with other aspects of institutional performance, creating a campus culture that supports student success is ultimately about the right people doing the right things. The DEEP schools featured in this chapter became successful in promoting student success by virtue of having cultivated an improvement-oriented ethos—a deeply rooted belief of the power of being in a perpetual learning mode focusing on where they are, what they are doing, and where they want to go.

In this light, the following questions are starting points to help advisors and campus administrators determine the extent to which their institution's culture and advising approaches are organized to foster student success.

> To what extent does your institutional culture promote and support a talent-development philosophy of teaching, learning, and advising?
>
> How well does your advising system work? How do you know?
>
> Are advising resources arranged to maximize students' potential?
>
> To what degree do the advising system and the efforts of individual advisors complement other institutional student success initiatives?
>
> To what extent do advisors challenge students to go beyond what they are expected to do in college?
>
> In what ways do academic advisors interact with students? Does the interaction appear meaningful?
>
> To what extent do advisors contribute to programs and activities that socialize first-year students to the academic expectations of the institution?
>
> To what extent do advisors encourage students to take advantage of curricular and cocurricular diversity experiences to enhance the quality of students' learning?
>
> What are you not doing with your advising program that you should?

Assessing Conditions to Enhance Educational Effectiveness: The Inventory for Student Engagement and Success. (Kuh et al., 2005a) also provides a template for institutions to use to identify areas of advising and other institutional functions that can be improved to promote student success.

CONCLUSION

Academic advisors are essential to promoting student development and success. Effective academic advisors are available to students and responsive to their educational needs and career interests. They also can help students develop as independent thinkers and problem-solvers and teach them how to navigate the institutional culture.

Certainly there is more to learn about the design and delivery of educationally effective advising and related services that foster the success of different types of learners in different types of settings. The results of such inquiries can help to establish realistic performance frameworks that policymakers, funding agencies, and institutional leaders can use for purposes of accountability and institutional improvement. In the meantime, we can learn some valuable lessons by looking to strong performing colleges and universities for some ideas to emulate and adapt.

References

Adelman, C. (2006, February). *The toolbox revisited: Paths to degree completion from high school through college.* Washington, DC: Office of Vocational and Adult Education.

Aitken, N. D. (1982). College student performance, satisfaction, and retention: Specification and estimation of structural equation model. *Journal of Higher Education, 53,* 32–50.

Allen, W. R. (1992). The color of success: African-American college student outcomes at predominantly white and historically black public colleges and universities. *Harvard Educational Review, 62* (1), 26–44.

American Indian Higher Education Consortium (AIHEC), The Institute for Higher Education Policy (IHEP), & Sallie Mae Education Institute. (2000, May). *Creating role models for change: A survey of tribal college graduates.* Alexandria, VA: Author.

Association of American Colleges and Universities. (2007). *College learning for the new global century.* Washington, DC: Author.

Bailey, T., Jenkins, D., & Leinbach, T. (2005). *Graduation rates, student goals, and measuring community college effectiveness* (CCRC Brief Number 28). New York: Columbia University Community College Research Center.

Berkner, L., Cuccaro-Alamin, S., & McCormick, A. (1996). *Descriptive summary of 1989–90 beginning postsecondary students: Five years later* (NCES 96–155). Washington, DC: National Center for Education Statistics.

Blose, G. (1999). Modeled retention and graduation rates: Calculating expected retention and graduation rates for multicampus university systems. *New Directions for Higher Education, 27* (4), 69–86.

Braxton, J. M., & McClendon, S. A. (2001–2002). The fostering of social integration and retention through institutional practice. *Journal of College Student Retention: Research, Theory & Practice, 3* (1), 57–71.

Brigman, S., Kuh, G. D., & Stager, S. (1982). Those who choose to leave: Why students voluntarily withdraw from college. *Journal of the National Association of Women Deans, Administrators, and Counselors, 45* (3), 3–8.

Broughton, E.& Neyer, M. (2001). Advising and counseling student athletes. *New Directions for Student Services, 93,* 47–53.

Carroll, D. (1989). *College persistence and degree attainment for the 1980 high school graduates: Hazards for transfers, stopouts, and part-timers* (NCES 89-302). Washington, DC: National Center for Education Statistics.

Choy, S. P. (2001). *Students whose parents did not go to college: Postsecondary access, persistence, and attainment.* (NCES 2001-126). Washington, DC: National Center for Education Statistics.

Cohen, A. M., & Brawer, F. B. (1996). *Policies and programs that affect transfer.* Washington, DC: American Council on Education.

Community College Survey of Student Engagement (CCSSE). (2005). *Engaging students, challenging the odds: 2005 findings.* Austin, TX: Author.

De Sousa, D. J. (2005). *Promoting student success: What advisors can do* (Occasional Paper No. 11). Bloomington: Indiana University Center for Postsecondary Research.

Dunphy, L., Miller, T., Woodruff, T., & Nelson, J. (1987). Exemplary retention strategies for the freshman year. *New Directions in Higher Education, 15* (4), 39–60.

Fidler, P., & Hunter, M. (1989). How seminars enhance student success. In M. Upcraft, J. Gardner, & Associates (Eds.), *The freshman year experience: Helping students survive and succeed in colle* (pp. 216–237). San Francisco: Jossey-Bass.

Fleming, J. (1984). *Blacks in college.* San Francisco: Jossey-Bass.

Forrest, A. (1985). Creating conditions for student and institutional success. In L. Noel, R. S. Levitz, D. Saluri, & Associates (Eds.), *Increasing student retention: Effective programs and practices for reducing dropout rate.* San Francisco: Jossey-Bass.

Horn, L. J., & Premo, M. (1995). *Profile of undergraduates in U.S. postsecondary institutions: 1992–93* (NCES 96-237). Washington, DC: National Center for Education Statistics.

Hossler, D., Kuh, G. D., & Olsen, D. (2001). Finding fruit on the vines: Using higher educational research and institutional research to guide institutional policies and strategies. Part II. *Research in Higher Education, 42* (2), 223–235.

Kowalski, C. (1977). *The impact of college on persisting and nonpersisting students.* New York: Philosophical Library.

Kramer G. L., & Associates (2003). *Student academic services: An integrated approach.* San Francisco: Jossey-Bass.

Kuh, G. D., Cruce, T., Shoup, R., Kinzie, J., & Gonyea, R.M. (in press). Unmasking the effects of student engagement on college grades and persistence. *Journal of Higher Education.*

Kuh, G. D., Kinzie, J., Buckley, J., Bridges, B., & Hayek, J. C. (2007). Piecing together the student success puzzle: Research, propositions, and recommendations. *ASHE Higher Education Report, 32* (5).

Kuh, G. D., Kinzie, J., Schuh, J. H., & Whitt, E. J. (2005a). *Assessing conditions to enhance educational effectiveness: The Inventory for Student Engagement and Success.* San Francisco: Jossey-Bass.

Kuh, G. D., Kinzie, J., Schuh, J. H., & Whitt, E. J. (2005b). *Student success in college: Creating conditions that matter.* San Francisco: Jossey-Bass.

Kuh, G. D., & Whitt, E. J. (1988). *The invisible tapestry: Culture in American colleges and universities.* (ASHE-ERIC Higher Education Report no. 1). Washington, DC: The George Washington University School of Education and Human Development.

Low, L. (2000). *Are college students satisfied? A national analysis of changing expectations.* Indianapolis: USA Group (now Lumina Foundation).

McCormick, A. C. (2003). Swirling and double-dipping: New patterns of student attendance and their implications for higher education. *New Directions for Higher Education, 121,* 13–24.

McCormick, A. C., & Horn, L. J. (1996). *A descriptive summary of 1992–93 bachelor's degree recipients: 1 year later* (NCES 96-158). Washington, DC: National Center for Education Statistics.

Metzner, B. (1989). Perceived quality of academic advising: The effect on freshman attrition. *American Educational Research Journal, 26,* 422–442.

Muraskin, L., & Lee, J. (with Wilner, A., & Swail, W. S.). (2004, December). *Raising the graduation rates of low-income college students.* Washington, DC: The Pell Institute for the Study of Opportunity in Higher Education.

Muraskin, L., & Wilner, A. (2004). *What we know about institutional influences on retention.* Washington, DC: JBL Associates.

National Survey of Student Engagement (NSSE). (2005). *Student engagement: Exploring different dimensions of student engagement.* Bloomington: Indiana University Center for Postsecondary Research.

National Survey of Student Engagement. (2007). *Experiences that matter: Enhancing student learning and success.* Bloomington: Indiana University Center for Postsecondary Research.

Reason, R. D., Terenzini, P. T., & Domingo, R. J. (2006). First things first: Developing academic competence in the first year of college. *Research in Higher Education, 47,* 149–175.

State Higher Education Executive Officers. (2005). Accountability for better results—a national imperative for higher education. *Network News, 24,* 1–4.

Swail, W. S. (with Redd, K. E., & Perna, L. W.). (2003). *Retaining minority students in higher education: A framework for success.* (ASHE-ERIC Higher Education Report no. 2). Washington, DC: The George Washington University School of Education and Human Development.

Swail, W. S., Cabrera, A. F., Lee, C., & Williams, A. (2005). *Latino students and the educational pipelines: A three-part series. Part III: Pathways to the bachelor's degree for Latino students.* Stafford, VA: Education Policy Institute.

Tinto, V. (2004). *Student retention and graduation: Facing the truth, living with the consequences.* (Occasional Paper 1). Washington, DC: The Pell Institution for the Study of Opportunity in Higher Education.

Upcraft, M. L., Gardner, J. N., & Barefoot, B. O. (2005). *Challenging and supporting the first-year student: A handbook for improving the first year of college.* San Francisco: Jossey-Bass.

Upcraft, M. L., Mullendore, R. H., Barefoot, B. O., & Fidler, D. S. (1993). *Designing successful transitions: A guide for orienting students to college* (Monograph No. 13). Columbia: University of South Carolina, National Resource Center for the Freshman Year Experience, National Orientation Directors Association.

CHAPTER SIX

Advising as Teaching and Learning

Drew C. Appleby

"**A**dvising is teaching" is the guiding principle of the National Academic Advising Association. The source of this compelling axiom was a pioneering article by Crookston (originally published in 1972 and reprinted in 1994) titled *A Developmental View of Academic Advising as Teaching*. Since then many theories and approaches to academic advising have evolved, as described by Hagen and Jordan in Chapter Two.

Crookston's (1972) approach established the groundwork for examining this principle of "advising as teaching." He introduced the term *developmental advising* by contrasting it with *prescriptive advising* with the following medical analogy. Patients (advisees) seek the advice of doctors (advisors) when they realize they have medical (academic) problems, and doctors are the authorities who prescribe treatments to cure patients' problems. According to Crookston (1994), a prescriptive advisor assumes that "once advice is given, his responsibility is largely fulfilled; now it is up to the student to fulfill his responsibility to do what is prescribed" (p. 6).

The prescriptive style of advising is not without its merits. Research indicates that students whose cultures stress "hierarchical patterns of interaction and deference to authority" prefer its more directive style (Brown & Rivas, 1994, p. 109). Fielstein (1994, p. 78) reminds us that prescriptive advising can provide a successful foundation for advising because students have the right to expect their advisors to provide them with "precise information regarding curriculum choices, major requirements, and graduation requirements." However, the prescriptive style fails to engage students actively in their education and does not help them develop a sense of responsibility for their academic choices. This lack of academic responsibility is diametrically opposed to the principles of active learning as described by Mathie, Beins, Benjamin, Ewing, Hall, Henderson, McAdam, & Smith (1993), one of which is to empower students by helping them understand that they can make choices in the classroom and that the consequences of these choices can have profound effects on their postbaccalaureate aspirations.

Many students are unaccustomed to this type of freedom because parents or school counselors have chosen their past educational experiences for them. A developmental advisor is in a perfect position to introduce advisees to their new freedom in a gradual manner that motivates them to exercise their educational choices with enthusiasm. Appleby (2001a) contrasted prescriptive and developmental advising, using ten dimensions from Crookston's 1994 article and nineteen more he identified during his teaching and advising career. The major theme that unites these differences is that developmental advisors gradually shift the responsibility of the relationship to their advisees by helping them develop problem-solving and decision-making skills, challenging them to develop higher-order thought processes, and enabling them to gain clearer insights into their own goals as well as the goals of higher education.

Crookston (1994) clearly equated advising with teaching when he argued that developmental advising is "concerned not only with a specific personal or vocational decision but also with facilitating the student's . . . problem-solving, decision-making, and evaluation skills. Not only are these *advising* functions but, deriving from the above assumption, they are essentially *teaching* functions as well" (p. 5) ". . . Based on a negotiated agreement between the student and the teacher in which varying degrees of learning by both parties to the transaction are the product" (p. 9). Habley (1981, p. 46) stated that when advising is performed as a teaching function, it can "enable students to clarify their educational goals and relate those goals to academic offerings on the campus." Kramer (1983) argued that advising is a specific teaching activity during which an advisor should question and challenge a student's educational choices. Eble (1988) stated that faculty should consider advising as an extension of their teaching role in which they can demonstrate genuine concern for their students' welfare by being available and approachable outside the classroom.

Another source that provides strong support for the connection between teaching and advising is *Roget's Thesaurus,* which reflects a richly reciprocal relationship between the words *teacher* and *advisor.* Roget provides the words *mentor, guide, confidant, consultant,* and *advisor* as synonyms for the word *teacher* and *mentor, guide, confidant, consultant,* and *teacher* for the word *advisor.* It appears that, at least within a lexical context, *teaching* and *advising* are words with similar meanings, but is this similarity also perceived in higher education? Reflecting upon his experiences during hundreds of advising workshops, Grites (1994) reported his disappointment at having asked thousands of faculty to "Write down your synonym(s) for academic advising . . . and never (not once!) receiving teaching as a response" (p. 82).

In her presidential address to the National Academic Advising Association titled *Advising as Teaching,* Ryan (1992) explored the parallels between teaching and advising, and she encouraged faculty to regard advising as an integral part of their teaching role. Ryan reported the results of a comprehensive search of the *ERIC* database to identify the shared characteristics of effective teachers and advisors (see Table 6.1). Appleby (2001b) added seven more similarities between

Table 6.1. A Comparison of Effective Teachers and Advisors.

Knowledge, Skills, and Characteristics of Effective Teachers	Knowledge, Skills, and Characteristics of Effective Advisors
Master their subject matter.	Possess accurate information about the policies, procedures, resources, and programs of their departments and institutions.
Plan, organize, and prepare materials for classroom presentation.	Are well prepared for advising sessions.
Engage students actively in the learning process.	Enable advisees to participate actively in the advising process by challenging them with new, more demanding learning tasks involving alternative ideas or choices and encouraging them to ask questions to clarify these ideas and explore these choices.
Provide regular feedback, reinforcement, and encouragement to students.	Provide timely feedback, reinforce learning that has taken place, and applaud student successes.
Create an environment conducive to learning.	Create a good learning climate within advising sessions.
Stimulate student interest in their subject by teaching it enthusiastically.	Project enthusiasm for their area of academic expertise and their advisory duties.
Help students learn independently.	Encourage advisees to become self-directed learners.
Teach students how to evaluate information.	Help advisees evaluate and reevaluate their progress toward personal, educational, and career goals.
Teach students how to express ideas clearly.	Use questioning techniques that will encourage shy advisees to express themselves.
Act as co-learners during the learning process.	Set performance goals for themselves and their advisees.
Serve as a resource to students.	Provide materials to advisees and refer them to others when referral is an appropriate response.

(Continued)

Table 6.1. (Continued).

Knowledge, Skills, and Characteristics of Effective Teachers	Knowledge, Skills, and Characteristics of Effective Advisors
Relate course content to students' experiences.	Assist students in the consideration of their life goals by helping them relate their experiences, interests, skills, and values to career paths and the nature and purpose of higher education.
Provide problem-solving tasks to students.	Provide tasks to be completed before the next advising meeting that will require the advisee to use information-gathering, decision-making, and problem-solving skills.
Personalize the learning process.	Help students gain self-understanding and self-acceptance.
Deliver information clearly and understandably.	Communicate in a clear and unambiguous manner with advisees.
Exhibit good questioning skills.	Serve as catalysts by asking questions and initiating discussions.
Exhibit good listening skills.	Listen carefully and constructively to advisees' messages.
Exhibit positive regard, concern, and respect for students.	Provide a caring and personal relationship by exhibiting a positive attitude toward students, their goals, and their ability to learn.
Are approachable and available outside the classroom.	Provide accessible and responsive advising services.
Present themselves to students in an open and genuine manner.	Provide a climate of trust in which advisees feel free to ask questions, express concerns, revise ideas, make decisions, and share personal experiences and knowledge.
Serve as role models who can help students understand the mission, values, and expectations of the institution.	Model the tenets of the university, and demonstrate enthusiasm and knowledge about the goals and purposes of higher education.
"Promote effective learning climates that are supportive of diversity" (Puente, 1993, p. 82).	Respect diverse points of view by demonstrating sensitivity to differences in culture and gender.
Use outcomes assessment to "make data-based suggestions for improving teaching and learning" (Halpern, 1993, p. 44).	Make changes or add to advising knowledge and skills by assessing the advising process.

Knowledge, Skills, and Characteristics of Effective Teachers	Knowledge, Skills, and Characteristics of Effective Advisors
"Stimulate learning at higher cognitive levels" (Mathie et al., 1993, p. 185).	Help students move beyond rote memorization or recall (Grites, 1994), help advisees test the validity of their ideas (Hagen, 1994), and "challenge students to confront their attitudes, beliefs, and assumptions" (Laff, 1994, p. 47).
Engage in the "lifelong learning they espouse for their students" (Fretz, 1993, p. 95).	"Participate in training and learn about educational issues that influence advising and about students served" (Frost, 1991, p. 74).
Help students "choose careers that best suit their aptitudes and interests" (Brewer, 1993, p. 171).	Help students explore career goals and choose programs, courses, and cocurricular activities that support these goals.
Use professional networks to share ideas, solve problems, provide support, and develop collegiality (Weiten, 1993).	"Learn from each other, share enthusiasm for their duties, and discuss mutual problems" (Frost, 1991, p. 65).
Utilize interactive computer software that promotes active learning (Mathie et al., 1993).	Use institutional technology (e.g., degree audit reports) to augment advising, recommend interactive software (e.g., SIGI PLUS) that can help advisees clarify goals and identify career options (Rooney, 1994), and communicate with advisees via e-mail.

Note: All the information in this table has been summarized from Ryan (1992) unless another reference is provided.

teachers and advisors gleaned from a more recent review of the teaching and advising literature.

These similarities between teaching and advising accurately reflect the trend in American higher education *away* from what Barr and Tagg (1995) called the instructional paradigm and *toward* what they called the learning paradigm. Describing the learning paradigm, Diamond (1997, p. viii) wrote, "This new perspective calls for a shift in the faculty role from disseminator of knowledge to facilitator of learning. This shift calls for changes in how we think about the courses we teach, how we design students' learning experiences, and how we articulate our expectations of our students and ourselves." It appears that the teaching community had to wait until 1995 before Barr and Tagg made it aware of what Crookston had shared with the advising community twenty-five years earlier.

The similarities between the instructional paradigm and prescriptive advising and between the learning paradigm and developmental advising are clear. The teaching paradigmatic teacher delivers expert lectures, and the prescriptive advisor dispenses expert advice. The learning paradigmatic teacher interacts dynamically with students to create opportunities for them to actively discover, evaluate, and synthesize knowledge. The developmental advisor views advising "as a teaching function based on a negotiated agreement between the student and the teacher in which varying degrees of learning by both parties to the transaction are the product" (Crookston, 1972/1994, p. 9).

Advisors can learn about their advisees' "strengths, weaknesses, and academic and career goals, as well as personal information (family obligations, work schedule, etc.)" (Kelly, 2006, p. 1). They can also discover from students about "what is really working in classrooms" (Miller & Alberts, 1994, p. 44) so they can guide students into classes that will provide successful learning experiences. In essence, the learning paradigm and developmental advising both adhere to the second sentence of the ancient Chinese proverb, "Give a man a fish and you feed him for a day. Teach him how to fish and you feed him for a lifetime."

By now, the meaning of the "advising is teaching" guiding principle of the National Academic Advising Association (NACADA) should be clear. However, regardless of how clear this principle is to advisors, it would be unwise to assume that advisees are also aware of its meaning and the implications this meaning has for the advising process. "Too often both parties launch into a relationship assuming both have the same idea of what role of each is to be in the advisor-student relationship. The result is often counterproductive, if not total disaster. Taking time to discuss and agree upon interpersonal and working relationships and conditions can help avoid the conflict that is inevitable from untested, disparate assumptions" (Crookston, 1972/1994, p. 7). Thirty-four years after Crookston's original article was published, Lowenstein (2006, p. 1) captured the essence of Crookston's message in his statement "An excellent advisor does for students' entire education what the excellent teacher does for a course: helps them order the pieces, put them together to make a coherent whole, so that a student experiences the curriculum not as a checklist of discrete, isolated pieces but instead as a unity, a composition of interrelated parts with multiple connections and relationships."

One strategy to accomplish these lofty goals is the advising syllabus (Trabant, 2006, McKamey, 2007). Teaching faculty use course syllabi to: (a) plan and clarify their courses, (b) introduce themselves to their students, (c) set the tone for their courses, (d) provide a rationale for why students should take their courses, (e) describe how students will change as a result of successfully completing their courses, (f) identify the various aspects of a course, (g) communicate a course's nature and content to other faculty and administrators, and (h) provide a documented record of their teaching careers. Effective advisors should also engage in these activities, and they can use an advising syllabus to: (a) plan and clarify the advising process, (b) introduce themselves to their advisees, (c) set a positive tone for advising, (d) provide a rationale for why students should seek their advice, (e) help their advisees understand how they will change as a result of engaging in advising, (f) identify the various components of the advising process, (g) communicate the nature and content of advising to faculty and administrators, and (h) create a documented record of their advising careers. When advisors create and use syllabi to accomplish these goals, they are telling their advisees that advising is much more than simply scheduling classes that fulfill graduation requirements, and they are announcing to faculty and administrators that they are serious about their intention to treat advising as a teaching process.

THE ADVISING SYLLABUS

A course syllabus enables teachers to make their courses clear to their students. An advising syllabus can produce the same results for advisors by providing them with a tool that helps advisees understand the nature, purpose, and chronology of the advising process; comprehend the advisor-advisee relationship; and become aware of the positive changes they can experience during the advising process. The advising syllabus is an important step toward the perception of academic advising as a legitimate educational process that can support the mission of an advisor's institution. Most advisors have never been required to write a syllabus, so it is necessary to provide them with a clear set of analogies between the purposes and components of teaching and advising syllabi.

Purposes of a Syllabus

Rubin (1985) identified the basic purposes of a course syllabus, which serve not only students, but also those who teach them. These purposes also have clear applications for advisees and advisors when viewed within the context of academic advising as a teaching process.

To Help Teachers Plan and Clarify Their Courses. Writing a well-constructed syllabus requires teachers to clarify, organize, and communicate their thoughts about how their courses will operate. Gabbenesch (1992) called the results of such a thoughtful process an "enriched syllabus" because it compels instructors to reveal their private assumptions in a public manner. This purpose can also serve academic advisors by providing them with the opportunity to identify and to clarify the assumptions they make about themselves, their advisees, and the advising process. Reflecting on the answers to questions about the advisor-advisee relationship such as "who takes the initiative, who takes responsibility, who supplies knowledge and skills and how are they obtained and applied" (Crookston, 1994, p. 6) can help advisors write syllabi that facilitate advisees' understanding of what they can expect during the advising process. Statements in an advising syllabus such as "My primary goal is to provide you with accurate advice that will enable you to graduate in the most time- and cost-effective manner" or "My primary goal is to provide a collaborative atmosphere in which we work together to create a plan for your undergraduate education that will prepare you to accomplish your career and life goals" can clarify the purpose of the advising process for advisees very successfully.

To Introduce Teachers to Their Students and Set the Tone for a Course. The syllabus provides teachers with the opportunity to share their pedagogical philosophy with students, reveal how their course is structured, and create an initial emotional tone for their course. D'Antonio (2007) described what she learned from an assignment that required her to read hundreds of syllabi written by the faculty of a large, Mid-Atlantic university. "As I reviewed the syllabi, I began to see patterns and symbols. Suddenly I realized I had a unique window into academe. The project allowed me to get to know professors in the college without ever having to meet them or attend their classes. There was no need to do either to figure out what kind of a faculty member they were. Their syllabi said it all" (para. 3).

Some of these syllabi failed to include the basic components her university requires, such as the teacher's name, contact information, office hours, grading and attendance policies, course objectives, assignment schedules, and required texts and materials. One syllabus simply paired each week of the semester with each chapter in the textbook for all fifteen weeks of the semester on one page, "with no test dates, no contact information, nothing" (para. 9). A student could infer several things from such a meager syllabus—for example, that the teacher obviously feels no need to follow campus rules, does not wish to be contacted, lacks respect for busy students who need a schedule of assignments and tests to plan their lives, and believes "he has the power to add whatever he chooses to the syllabus because it was never in writing in the first place" (para. 16).

The inclusion of appropriate information in a clear, complete, and considerate manner provides a compelling message to students that their teacher will be a good communicator, a competent instructor, and a caring human being. "Professors, as critical thinkers themselves, should be aware that their syllabi are alive, symbolic, and vocal. A syllabus really can talk, and it's saying a lot more than we think" (para. 35). Just substitute the word *advisors* for the word *professors* in the previous quote, and it becomes obvious that even before the first advising meeting, advisees have already formed an opinion of their advisors if they have been supplied with an advising syllabus. A clear, carefully written advising syllabus in a caring and supportive tone can set the stage for a successful and productive advisor-advisee relationship.

To Explain Why Students Should Take a Course and How They Will Change as a Result of Completing It Successfully. After students read a course syllabus, they should know why they are taking the course on at least two levels. On a purely prescriptive level, Crookston (1994) argues they should be aware of the answers to the following questions: Is this course a specific degree requirement and, if it is not, will it count as credit toward my degree? The answers to these questions provide students with external justification. However, the most important reason for enrolling in a course is to use it as a developmental opportunity to accomplish student learning outcomes—that is, the knowledge, skills, and values that enable students to create themselves in the image of what they want their undergraduate education to help them become, such as successful applicants to the graduate program or job of their choice or informed citizens of a progressive community (Crookston, 1994). Advisors can use their syllabi to communicate the same type of information to their advisees about the advising process. Many students are initially more interested in the requirement-fulfilling characteristics of courses, and are often reluctant to enroll in courses that do not allow them to put check marks on a programmatic checklist of required courses.

As students mature and their advisors help them to understand that successful entrance into the careers to which they aspire will require more than simple proof of graduation, they become more conscious of and interested in the student learning outcomes they can develop in their courses. Advisors can then begin to help advisees understand that electives should not be selected because they are easy, occur at a convenient time, or are taught by entertaining professors. They should be chosen because they can enable advisees to develop the skills their future careers and lives will require them to possess and use.

Finally, advisors can also use the syllabus as an opportunity to make advisees aware of what they can learn during the advising process. According to Martin (2007, p. 1), the student learning outcomes of the advising process should answer the question "what should students learn through academic advising? Specifically, what should advisees learn to do as a result of academic advising; what information should they be able to articulate; and what skills should they be able to demonstrate?"

To Explain the Various Aspects of a Course. A course syllabus should be explicit about assignments, methods of evaluation, and the level of participation required. Will papers be graded on content, style, or both? Will tests be objective or essay? Will students listen passively to lectures or will they participate in challenging discussions requiring advance preparation? If a course requires students to exhibit specific skills (e.g., writing in APA style or using SPSS), will they learn these skills in the course, or is it assumed they have already acquired these skills in prerequisite courses? As Rubin (1985, p. 56) observed, "We seem to assume that our colleagues and our students will intuitively be able to reconstruct the creature we see in our mind's eye from the few bones we give them in the syllabus."

Students are not mind readers, and neither are advisees. If faculty members fail to describe the fundamental aspects of their courses clearly, they cannot expect their students to be successful partners in the teaching-learning process. Worse yet, they may find that some students feel as if they have been treated unfairly, perhaps even betrayed, because their expectations of what it takes to earn a good grade do not match their instructors' grading criteria. According to Grunert (1997, p. 19), the syllabus serves as a learning contract, which defines "mutual obligations between instructor and students." These obligations take the form of a set of reciprocal responsibilities dealing with issues such as grading, attendance, and academic integrity. For example, instructors should include a final grade distribution in their syllabi that clearly communicates to students how their final grades will be determined. Communicating these expectations clearly and unambiguously not only promotes student understanding of what is required in a course, but also enables instructors to defend their grading decisions if they are challenged.

Although advisors do not grade advisees, the advising process has various aspects that must be clarified. Two of the most important of these aspects are expectations and assignments. How should an advisee prepare for an advising appointment? Crookston's (1994) purely prescriptive advisor may simply expect an advisee to show up for the appointment, express a need for assistance, pay attention to the advice given, and then carry out that advice. A developmental advisor may expect an advisee to explore several options prior to an advising session, come to the session ready to discuss the pros and cons of these options, and accept an assignment from the advisor to locate further information before reaching a final decision. Creating a section in an advising syllabus that identifies the level of preparedness expected and explains the nature and purpose of advising assignments can bring the expectations of advisors and advisees into more accurate alignment.

To Communicate a Course's Nature and Content to Other Faculty and Administrators and Provide a Documented Record of a Teacher's Career. Syllabi are a faculty member's teaching legacy. A well-written syllabus provides a record of a course for those who may teach it later. A chronology of syllabi represents an evolving record of an instructor's teaching philosophy, commitment to teaching, and pedagogical innovations. "When job hunting, syllabi are also integral components of the application portfolio. They can also serve as salary, promotion, and tenure documents that evaluation committees request when assessing teaching ability" (Appleby, 1999, p. 21). Syllabi are also documents that can facilitate departmental and institutional planning and assist outside agencies that assess programmatic goals and effectiveness during program reviews and accreditation visits. Syllabi can also serve these purposes for advisors who seek new positions, apply for promotions, train their replacements, or participate in programmatic assessment.

Essential Components of a Syllabus

The functions of an advising syllabus manifest themselves in the component parts of that document. Altman (1989) and Grunert (1997) have described the essential components for course syllabi, and Trabant (2006), McKamey (2007), and Erickson and Strommer (1991) have provided similar descriptions of the components of an advising syllabus. It is crucial to heed Trabant's advice about these components so that the advising syllabus can be perceived as a legitimate teaching document: "The advising syllabus should adhere to the course syllabus guidelines used by campus faculty. It is important to use the tool in a recognizable and consistent format for students and campus stakeholders" (p. 1). The following components of an advising syllabus are introduced by analogous components of a course syllabus.

Title Page Containing Basic Identifying Information. A course syllabus should begin by informing its reader of the institution (Idaho State University), the time period for which it is in effect (fall semester, 2008), and the course title and identifying code (W131 Elementary Composition). An advising syllabus should contain the first two parts of this information and clearly identify itself as an advising syllabus. Grunert (1997) suggests that this identifying information should be displayed as a formal title page so it can be clearly identified as an official teaching document from its author's institution. The legitimacy of an advising syllabus can be established in a similar manner.

Table of Contents. According to Grunert (1997), a syllabus should contain a table of contents to help students understand its organizational structure and navigate its contents. An advising syllabus can benefit from a table of contents for the same reasons, especially for first-year advisees who may be encountering syllabi for the first time. A simple listing of syllabus section headings and the page numbers of these sections are all that is necessary.

Advisor's Name and Contact Information. A course syllabus should contain the name and title of its instructor and information that will allow a student to contact the instructor in person, including the office location and hours, telephone number(s), and/or e-mail address. An advising syllabus should contain the same basic contact information, but may give the name and location of an office if it is the product of an advising unit rather than an individual advisor.

Letter to Advisees. Grunert (1997, p. 28) recommends that "Including a letter to the student in the syllabus enhances the personal nature of the course, can help to relieve student discomfort, and can set a dialogic tone for your course." Although this section is not mentioned in any published source describing an advising syllabus, it makes perfect sense. What better way for an advisor to begin developing rapport with advisees than to write them a letter that welcomes them to the advising process, helps them understand the process and benefits of advising, and perhaps most importantly, provides them with written evidence that their advisor cares about them as unique and worthy individuals?

Definition of Advising. An essential section of a course syllabus is the course description, which includes the major topics covered in the course; the knowledge, skills, and attitudes acquired during the course; and any special opportunities the course provides. As Thurmond and Nutt (2006, p. 12) state, "Just as any academic syllabus clearly defines the course (course description), the academic advising syllabus must clearly define academic advising." This is an especially crucial section for an advising syllabus because it compels advisors to reflect carefully on their underlying assumptions about the advising services they provide so they can clearly communicate the type of advising their advisees will receive. Rubin (1985, p. 56) said "We keep forgetting that what we know—about our disciplines, our goals, about our teaching—is not known or agreed upon by everyone." Although the course syllabus was the subject of Rubin's quote, it is remarkably compatible with NACADA's (2006) Concept of Academic Advising as teaching, which includes curriculum (what advisors teach), pedagogy (how advisors teach), and student learning outcomes (how advisees change as a result of what and how their advisors teach them). The insightful work of Lowenstein (1999), which uses the concepts of style and content to compare and contrast four different approaches to advising (prescriptive, developmental, collaborative, and academically centered), should be mandatory reading for all advisors who plan to create a personalized definition of advising for their syllabi. Advisors should examine Lowenstein's work to identify: (1) the *curriculum* of their advising (graduation requirements, course sequencing, and registration procedures or strategies to choose curricular and cocurricular activities that will enable students to accomplish their postbaccalaureate aspirations); (2) the *pedagogy* of their advising (information flowing in a hierarchical fashion from the active advisor to the passive advisee or the advisee as an active participant in a dialogue with the advisor composed of questions and answers from both parties); and (3) the *student learning outcomes* of advising (graduation in a timely and efficient manner, facilitation of the advisee's personal growth and development, or a steady increase in advisees' ability to understand how to use their curricular and cocurricular activities to identify and accomplish their postbaccalaureate aspirations).

Once advisors have carefully contemplated and clearly explicated the curricula, pedagogies, and student learning outcomes of their advising approaches, and ensured that these are in alignment with the mission and goals of their institutions, they will have created the definitions of advising that should appear in their syllabi.

Advising Resources. The purpose of this section in a course syllabus is to direct students to sources of instruction in the course other than the instructor. These can be printed materials (the textbook), electronic sources (Web sites), human resources (the teaching assistant), and locations (the library). Advisors also use resources other than themselves to teach their advisees. The college catalog or an advising handbook can serve the same purpose for an advisor that the textbook does for a teacher. Advisors also provide advisees with sources of instruction that are electronic (the university Web page), human (counselors in the Career Center), and locational (the computer lab). It is also important to provide advisees with the information necessary to access these resources, such as campus and Web addresses.

Expectations and Responsibilities of Advisors and Advisees. Well-written course syllabi contain a section that describes what teachers expect or require their students to do in the course, such as take tests, write papers, and give oral presentations. Some even contain sections that describe what students can expect from their teachers, such as maintain regular office hours. This section is particularly important in an advising syllabus because a match between what an advisor expects from an advisee and vice versa is crucial to the success of the advising process. For example, a strongly prescriptive advisor expects advisees to arrive for advising sessions with nothing more than the need to be advised, the willingness to listen carefully, and the motivation to carry out the advice provided (Crookston, 1994). On the other hand, collaborative advisors view advisors and advisees as equal partners in the advising process and prefer a question-and-answer format to which advisees have brought options to be discussed (Lowenstein, 1999).

A mismatch between an advisor's and an advisee's expectations of what should take place before, during, and after an advising session can be frustrating for both parties. This is why it is crucial for advisors to include a section in their syllabi that clearly identifies the expectations they have for their advisees and what their advisees can expect of them. Habley (1981) supported the necessity of this strategy when he said that academic advising provides "assistance in the mediation of dissonance between student expectations and the actualities of the educational environment" (p. 46). Because academic advising is an integral component of the academic environment, advisors should lead by example by including crystal-clear expectations in their syllabi. If an advisor wants advisees to prepare for advising sessions by constructing a list of questions, then that should be stated clearly in the advising syllabus. Some advisors may even give their advisees information-gathering assignments to complete outside the advising session (McKamey, 2007), which may also include reporting the results back to the advisor so that the advisor becomes more knowledgeable and the advisee develops a genuine understanding of the advisor-advisee partnership in which valuable information can flow in both directions.

Student Learning Outcomes of the Advising Process. The section of an academic syllabus that describes the objectives of the course is of particular importance because of the current national emphasis on accountability and the subsequent emphasis on the assessment of student learning in higher education. The assessment movement has necessitated a shift in the course syllabus from a description of what an instructor teaches to a precise explanation of what a student learns by successfully completing the course. A clear set of instructional objectives provides direction for teaching methods, yields guidelines for testing, communicates instructional intent to students, and creates a foundation for assessment. If advising is to be considered a teaching process, then advisors must also clearly articulate what their advisees will learn as a result of the advising process.

Student learning outcomes can be cognitive: the knowledge an advisee learns, such as university and program graduation requirements; behavioral: the skills an advisee develops, such as the ability to use the university's Web-based registration process; or affective: the values or appreciation an advisee acquires, such as a willingness to enroll in classes to acquire knowledge and skills rather than merely to accumulate credit hours toward graduation. These outcomes will vary from institution to institution and from advisor to advisor, so it is crucial to heed Martin's (2007, p. 2) advice that, "Learning objectives need to be tailored to fit the needs of the university, college, or departmental environment in which students function. They also must be shaped to fit the academic advising model in use and, of course, they must be tailored to the needs of the students being advised."

Because outcomes are an essential part of the assessment process, it is imperative that the advisors who create them must also be able to measure them in valid ways so that the efficacy of these outcomes can be evaluated and, when necessary, improved. "This on-going cycle of outcome development and student learning assessment should be used to visibly connect academic advising to institutional expectations regarding student learning. In this way, academic advising is firmly attached to the institution's central teaching and learning process, further affirming academic advising as a form of teaching" (Cunningham, 2006, p. 23).

Before leaving this crucial component of an advising syllabus, it is essential to emphasize the necessity of creating outcomes that can be measured in meaningful ways. An examination of fifty online advising syllabi by Appleby (2007) revealed that twenty-seven contained student learning outcomes, but that these student learning outcomes varied significantly in their measurability. Some were stated in concrete, measurable ways that would enable advisors to gather and present solid evidence of the effectiveness of their work, such as identify a career goal, create an educational plan to successfully achieve stated goals, and work in an internship connected to one's major. Others, described as ineffable by Ewell (1991), focused on the acquisition of broad, abstract concepts that, while highly desirable, would be difficult to measure, such as understand the nature and purposes of higher education. One solution to this dilemma is the advising portfolio, which was described in a few syllabi. This portfolio could contain the results of advising assignments—for example, an essay in which advisees explain their views of the nature and purposes of higher education, which could be qualitatively assessed.

The bottom line of this challenging situation is accountability. Advisors are now being asked to state the intended outcomes of their advising activities and to provide evidence that these outcomes are being attained successfully. Their ability to accomplish these two tasks will have profound effects upon their individual advising careers and upon the willingness of the higher education community to accept advising as a legitimate teaching activity. Gronlund (2004) provides detailed instructions on how to write learning outcomes.

Advising Calendar. A course syllabus should contain a calendar that includes "topics or activities planned for each class meeting, assignment due dates, and special occasions or events" (Grunert, 1997, p. 45). To provide maximum benefit to advisees, an advising syllabus should contain an advising calendar that includes not only important dates for advising-related events during the current semester, such as drop, add, and registration dates, but also the sequence of advising-related events or deadlines students will encounter during their college careers. Examples include career fairs, when majors must be declared, and when students must indicate their intent to graduate. The purpose of this section of an advising syllabus is to keep advisees on track in terms of their temporal responsibilities.

How to Prepare for an Advising Session. Grunert (1997) recommends that course syllabi contain a section that provides strategies used by prior students who have been successful in the course, such as how to prepare for class sessions, take notes, read the textbook, write papers, collaborate with class-mates, and study for tests. Although advisors do not require advisees to write papers or take tests, they may expect advisees to come prepared to appoint-ments by familiarizing themselves with printed or online materials and to take notes during advising sessions so they can successfully retain and use the advice they are given. Many advisors are frustrated when advisees simply appear for appointments, expect their advisors to tell them what to do, and assume they will remember their advisor's advice simply because they heard it. From the student's perspective McKamey (2007, p. 2) indicates that "Much of students' dissatisfaction with advising may come from not knowing what to expect from, or what to do to prepare for, an advising appointment. Most students' first experiences with an academic advisor are based on their experi-ences in high school, where they may not have had any real responsibilities."

Caveats. Syllabi are written contracts between teachers and students, so each syllabus should end with a caveat to protect its author and its author's institu-tion if changes in the syllabus are made once the course is underway. Altman (1989, p. 2) suggests that all syllabi should end with the following sentence: "The above schedule and procedures in this course are subject to change in the event of extenuating circumstances." While advisors need not concern themselves with students challenging the legitimacy of final grades, they must be concerned about advisees who may accuse them of providing inaccurate advice that resulted in lost time or money.

Although none of the online syllabi examined by Appleby (2007) contained a statement to protect against such claims, several advising Web sites contain cave-ats that would be appropriate final statements in an advising syllabus. A compos-ite of these statement that advisors could include on their syllabus might be:

> Please understand that I will not make decisions for you during our advising
> sessions. I will provide you with the most accurate information available to me,
> and we will work together to create a realistic plan to accomplish your educational
> and career goals. However, the educational choices you make are yours and the
> responsibility for knowing and fulfilling degree requirements rests with you.

Statements such as this in advising syllabi will not only protect advisors, but will also help advisees realize their role as responsible partners in the teaching-learning partnership of advising.

Sample Advising Syllabi

Examples of advising syllabi can be downloaded from the NACADA Web site at http://www.nacada.ksu.edu/Clearinghouse/Links/syllabi.htm.

CONCLUSION

The publication of this book marks the thirty-sixth anniversary of Crookston's (1972) contention that advising is a form of teaching. Advisor-scholars have used this time to identify, examine, and debate many crucial issues produced by this teaching-advising amalgamation. The consensus of these scholars is that effective advisors are also effective teachers. Lowenstein (2006, p. 1) captured the essence of this consensus when he said, "An excellent advisor does for students' entire education what the excellent teacher does for a course." Twelve years prior to Lowenstein's statement, Ramos (1994, p. 90–91) provided perhaps the most compelling piece of advice about teaching to advisors when he stated they should, "Think of academic advising as a course offered to your advisees. You are the instructor or facilitator; the student is a learner; your office is the classroom; [and] facilitating growth along several dimensions is the curriculum." If I could add one more line to Ramos's quote, it would be "*. . . and the advising syllabus is the teaching tool that will enable your advisees to understand, value, and participate successfully in the advising process.*" Even if advisors choose not to include all the sections of a syllabus described in this chapter, the process of reflecting upon the contents of these sections can have a deeply transformative effect upon their way of thinking about advising.

References

Altman, H. (1989). Syllabus shares what the teacher wants. *The Teaching Professor, 3* (5), 1–2.

Appleby, D. C. (1999). How to improve your teaching with the course syllabus. In B. Perlman, L. I. McCann, & S. H. McFadden (Eds.), *Lessons learned: Practical advice for the teaching of psychology* (pp. 19–24). Washington, DC: American Psychological Society.

Appleby, D. C. (2001a, February 26). The teaching-advising connection: Part II. *The Mentor: An Academic Advising Journal.* Retrieved August 17, 2007, from http:// www.psu.edu/dus/mentor/appleby2.htm

Appleby, D. C. (2001b, March 19). The teaching-advising connection: Part III. *The Mentor: An Academic Advising Journal.* Retrieved August 17, 2007, from http:// www.psu.edu/dus/mentor/appleby3.htm

Appleby, D. C. (2007). [The contents of online advising syllabi]. Unpublished raw data.

Barr, R. B., & Tagg, J. (1995, November/December). From teaching to learning—A new paradigm for undergraduate education. *Change,* 13–25.

Brewer, C. L. (1993). Curriculum. In T. V. McGovern (Ed.), *Handbook for enhancing undergraduate education in psychology* (pp. 161–182). Washington, DC: American Psychological Association.

Brown, T., & Rivas, M. (1994). The prescriptive relationship in academic advising as an appropriate developmental intervention with multicultural populations. *National Academic Advising Association Journal, 14* (2), 108–111.

Crookston, B. B. (1972). A developmental view of academic advising as teaching" *Journal of College Student Personnel, 13*, 12–17.

Crookston, B. B. (1994). A developmental view of academic advising as teaching. *National Academic Advising Association Journal, 14* (2), 5–9. (Reprinted from *Journal of College Student Personnel, 13*, 12–17, 1972.)

Cunningham, L. (2006). *What is academic advising?* Manhattan, KS: National Academic Advising Association.

D'Antonio, M. (2007, July). If your syllabus could talk. [Electronic version]. *The Chronicle of Higher Education: Chronicle Careers.* Retrieved August 14, 2007, from http://www.chronicle.com/jobs/news/2007/07/2007071901c/printable.html

Diamond, R. (1997). Foreword. In J. Grunert, *The course syllabus: A learning-centered approach.* Bolton, MA: Anker.

Eble, K. E. (1988). *The craft of teaching: A guide to mastering the professor's art.* San Francisco: Jossey-Bass.

Erickson, B. L., & Strommer, D. W. (1991). *Teaching college freshmen.* San Francisco, CA: Jossey-Bass.

Ewell, P. T. (1991). To capture the ineffable: New forms of assessment in higher education. In G. Grant (Ed.), *Review of research in education, 17* (pp. 75–125). Washington, DC: American Educational Research Association.

Fielstein, L. L. (1994). Developmental versus prescriptive advising: Must it be one or the other? *National Academic Advising Association Journal, 14* (2), 76–79.

Fretz, B. R. (1993). The compleat scholar: Faculty development for those who teach psychology. In T. V. McGovern (Ed.), *Handbook for enhancing undergraduate education in psychology* (pp. 93–122). Washington, DC: American Psychological Association.

Frost, S. H. (1991). Fostering the critical thinking of college women through academic advising and faculty contact. *Journal of College Student Development, 32,* 356–359.

Gabennesch, H. (1992). The enriched syllabus: To convey a larger vision. *The National Teaching and Learning Forum, 1* (4), 4–5.

Grites, T. J. (1994). From principle to practice: Pain or gain? *National Academic Advising Association Journal, 14* (2), 80–84.

Gronlund, N. E. (2004). *Writing instructional objectives for teaching and assessment* (7th ed.). Upper Saddle River, NJ: Pearson.

Grunert, J. (1997). *The course syllabus: A learning-centered approach.* Bolton, MA: Anker.

Habley, W. R. (1981). Academic advisement: The critical link in student retention. *National Association of Student Personnel Administrators (NASPA) Journal, 18* (4), 45–50.

Hagen, P. L. (1994). Academic advising as dialectic. *National Academic Advising Association Journal, 14* (2), 85–88.

Halpern, D. F. (1993). Targeting outcomes: Covering your assessment concerns and needs. In T. V. McGovern (Ed.), *Handbook for enhancing undergraduate education in psychology* (pp. 23–46). Washington, DC: American Psychological Association.

Kelly, S. (2006). Advisors teach students to become mobile. *The Mentor: An Academic Advising Journal, 8* (2). Retrieved September 1, 2007, from http://www.psu.edu/dus/mentor/060613sk.htm

Kramer, H. C. (1983). Advising: Implications for faculty development. *National Academic Advising Association Journal, 3* (2), 25–31.

Laff, N. S. (1994). Reconsidering the developmental view of advising: Have we come a long way? *National Academic Advising Association Journal, 14* (2), 46–49.

Lowenstein, M. (1999). An alternative to the developmental theory of advising. *The Mentor: An Academic Advising Journal, 1* (3). Retrieved July 29, 2007, from http://www.psu.edu/dus/mentor/991122ml.htm

Lowenstein, M. (2006). A learning-centered view of teaching as advising. *The Mentor: An Academic Advising Journal, 8* (2). Retrieved September 5, 2007, from http://www.psu.edu/dus/mentor/proc01ml.htm

Martin, H. (2007). *Constructing learning objectives for academic advising.* Retrieved July 26, 2007, from the NACADA Clearinghouse of Academic Advising Resources. http://www.nacada.ksu.edu/Clearinghouse/AdvisingIssues/Learning-outcomes.htm

Mathie, V. A., Beins, B., Benjamin, L. T., Ewing, M. M., Hall, C. C. I., Henderson, B., McAdam, D. W., & Smith, R. A. (1993). Promoting active learning in psychology classes. In T. V. McGovern (Ed.), *Handbook for enhancing undergraduate education in psychology* (pp. 183–214). Washington, DC: American Psychological Association.

McKamey, J. N. (2007). An advising syllabus: A tool to increase advising effectiveness. *The Mentor: An Academic Advising Journal, 9* (1). Retrieved July 29, 2007, from http://www.psu.edu/dus/mentor/070321jm.htm

Miller, M. A., & Alberts, B. (1994). Developmental advising: Where teaching and learning intersect. *National Academic Advising Association Journal, 14* (2), 43–45.

National Academic Advising Association. (2006). *NACADA concept of academic advising.* Retrieved August 6, 2007, from http://www.nacada.ksu.edu/Clearinghouse/AdvisingIssues/Concept-Advising.htm

Puente, A. E. (1993). Toward a psychology of variance: Increasing the presence and understanding of ethnic minorities in psychology. In T. V. McGovern (Ed.), *Handbook for enhancing undergraduate education in psychology* (pp. 71–92). Washington, DC: American Psychological Association.

Ramos, B. (1994). O'Banion revisited: Now more than ever. *National Academic Advising Association Journal, 14* (2), 89–91.

Rooney, M. (1994). Back to the future: Crookston and O'Banion revisited. *National Academic Advising Association Journal, 14* (2), 35–38.

Rubin, S. (1985, August 7). Professors, students, and the syllabus. *The Chronicle of Higher Education,* 56.

Ryan, C. C. (1992). Advising as teaching. *National Academic Advising Association Journal, 12,* 4–8.

Thurmond, K., & Nutt, C. (2007). *Academic advising syllabus: Advising as teaching in action.* Manhattan, KS: National Academic Advising Association.

Trabant, T. M. (2006). *Advising syllabus 101.* NACADA Clearinghouse of Academic Advising Resources. Retrieved July 30, 2007, from http://www.nacada.ksu.edu/Clearinghouse/AdvisingIssues/syllabus101.htm

Weiten, W. (1993). From isolation to community: Increasing communication and collegiality among psychology teachers. In T. V. McGovern (Ed.), *Handbook for enhancing undergraduate education in psychology* (pp. 123–159). Washington, DC: American Psychological Association.

CHAPTER SEVEN

Advising for Career and Life Planning

Paul A. Gore, Jr., and A. J. Metz

College students today have exceedingly high academic and career aspirations and very practical expectations for their education. An increasing number of students report attending college to obtain higher pay and more prestigious jobs (Astin, 2007). Unfortunately, students often lack realistic plans for achieving their academic, career, and life goals. Students who lack a clear plan may remain in school longer than necessary, fail to take advantage of curricular and cocurricular activities that would prepare them for work, or may drop out of school altogether. As students leave college they face employers with equally high and practical expectations.

Academic advisors are uniquely situated to help students establish cohesive educational and occupational goals. Academic advisors may help students understand how educational experiences prepare them to be competitive in the workforce and to achieve their life goals. Academic advisors are better prepared to work effectively with their students if they are familiar with career theory, models of career advising, academic and career planning resources, and recent advances in career and academic advising interventions. The goals of this chapter are to: (a) provide advisors with an understanding of current career development theory and how theory informs practice, (b) briefly describe a model of career-advising and review resources available to support the use of that model, (c) discuss recent advances in understanding and working with decided, undecided, and indecisive students, and (d) describe recent research on effective career advising interventions and factors that promote student academic and career success. This chapter will not provide a comprehensive review of any of these topics, nor should it be considered a primer for career advising. Rather, this chapter will highlight critical elements of the theory and practice of career advising and provide advisors with a snapshot of recent advances in the field.

CAREER ADVISING VERSUS CAREER COUNSELING

Gordon (2006) offers an excellent discussion of the similarities and differences between career advisors and career counselors and describes the larger domain of career services and career planning. Career advising may be offered by professional advisors, faculty advisors, student services personnel, or peer advisors. Career advising differs from career counseling in that the former does not generally involve formal psychological assessment of career-related variables. Career counseling is recommended when students have strong emotional issues related to their academic or career choices, or when they appear to have more entrenched difficulties with the career decision-making process. Career advising is offered in an effort to help students understand the often complex relationships that exist between academic experiences and career fields. Career advising promotes self-exploration, the acquisition of academic and career information, and decision-making.

For the purposes of this chapter, the term *advisor* will refer to the full range of academic and career advisors currently employed in postsecondary environments. Although clearly the roles and responsibilities of faculty advisors, staff advisors, and student service professionals differ across and within campuses, the concepts described in this chapter apply to all those individuals who strive to promote the academic and career planning of their students. For some advisors, the information in this chapter will be a sufficient review to alert them to the kinds of issues faced by some of their students. For other advisors, training and information beyond the scope of this book may be necessary in order to provide comprehensive career advising services to students. Finally, advisors are encouraged to consult with career services colleagues in an effort to coordinate career services on campus in a way that benefits all students.

CAREER-DEVELOPMENT THEORY AND PRACTICE

Career-development theories provide a framework for integrating academic and career advising. Specifically, career-development theories highlight important characteristics related to career choice and implementation and suggest possible strategies for working with students (Gordon, 2006). There are many career-development theories in use today. Three prominent theories are included in this chapter based on their appropriateness when applied to the academic and career transitions of college students, and on the strength of the research supporting their hypotheses. For a more comprehensive review of current career theories, readers are referred to Brown (2002) and Swanson and Gore (2000).

John Holland's (1997) theory of career choice is by far the most widely used career theory today. Holland suggests that individuals develop academic and career interests over time as a result of learning experiences and opportunities. He suggests that interests, as well as academic and work environments, can be described along six dimensions: Realistic (working with animals or things, outdoors), Investigative (working with ideas, science), Artistic (creative/expressive work), Social (helping, training, guiding), Enterprising (leading, persuading, managing others), and Conventional (ordered and structured work, often with data and files). By the time students reach college, their interests have begun to stabilize (Low, Yoon, Roberts, & Rounds, 2005) and they will probably have more clearly defined interests in one or two of these dimensions.

Although most academic and career advisors will not engage in formal assessment of students' interests, they can make use of Holland's taxonomy for the purpose of helping students understand and articulate their interests and find academic and career paths that might be congruent with those interests. Students pursuing educational paths that are incongruent with their interests may report lack of satisfaction or frustration or they may present an expressed desire to change their college major. Alternatively, their lack of motivation to pursue an academic path may result in less-than-optimal performance. Research punctuates the important relations between the congruence of student interest and choice of college major with intended outcomes (Tracey & Robbins, 2006; Leuwerke, Robbins, Sawyer, & Hovland, 2004).

There are many resources available to advisors to promote students' understanding of their interests and how those interests fit with college majors, occupations, and even avocations. Advisors can collaborate with students in the use of "self-directed" and online exploratory tools such as the Self-Directed Search and related support materials such as the College Majors Finder and the Occupations Finder (for review of these materials see Reardon and Lenz, 1998), the O*NET Online (2007) and associated career inventories, or comprehensive computer-assisted career guidance programs such as DISCOVER (ACT, 2007a) or Choices (Bridges, 2007). Pope and Minor (2000) have provided an excellent resource for advisors working with students in small groups or classrooms.

Advocates of the social cognitive career theory (Lent, 2005) highlight the importance of variables such as self-efficacy and outcome expectations in promoting the development of interests and, ultimately, career and academic choice and performance. According to this theory, students' academic and career interests may be negatively influenced by prior failure experiences or the lack of realistic expectations. For example, a student with a history of poor performance in math is much less likely to express interest in math than a student with a neutral or strong performance history. Alternatively, students' interests may be shaped by very unrealistic expectations related to their future career choice (e.g., the student who aspires to criminal science based solely on their viewing of the television show *CSI*). On the other hand, students' interests and career choices are bolstered and strengthened through the development of strong positive self-efficacy beliefs that result from their personal accomplishments and their accurate and desirable expectations about probable outcomes.

This theory emphasizes the importance of helping students develop realistic educational and career expectations. One way to accomplish this is to make sure students have access to reliable and up-to-date information. A wealth of information is available describing the world of work. Free information is available through the U.S. Department of Labor's Occupational Outlook Handbook (2007) and the Occupational Information Network Online (O*NET, 2007). Most university academic departments and career advising, counseling, or placement centers will also house up-to-date information related to college majors.

The social cognitive career theory also highlights the importance of self-referent thought in the development and implementation of an academic or career choice. It is not enough to know whether a student got an A or an F on an assignment; career advisors should consider discussing how that performance was interpreted, the attributions made by the student (e.g., "I didn't study hard enough" vs. "I am just no good at science"), and how those attributions served to shape subsequent choices. Advisors can help students explore their self-efficacy beliefs for various academic subjects and for the academic endeavor itself. Further, advisors can discuss students' efficacy for making a career decision. Students with confidence in their ability to gather career information, to explore their interests and values, and to make decisions are more likely to engage in the process and find satisfaction with the result.

Finally, Super (1990) described a life-stage model of career development that is relevant to the academic and career choices of college students. Super suggests that people's career choices are expressions of their vocational self-concept. A vocational self-concept is formed through stages that include growth, exploration, establishment, maintenance, and disengagement. Many college students find themselves in the exploration and early establishment stages of career development. It is during these stages that students' self-concepts begin to solidify (e.g., they develop a better understanding of their interests, values, and skills) and they begin to express tentative career goals. As students move toward the establishment stage, they develop a strong connection with their chosen field of study and begin the socialization process that marks the transition into a career field.

Advisors are perfectly positioned to facilitate this process. They can encourage students to explore their tentative academic or career choice by interviewing a faculty member or job incumbent; by promoting participation in academic or career-related professional organizations, honor societies, or service organizations; or by informing students of relevant internships, practicum opportunities, or service learning experiences.

Super also recognized that vocational self-concept was only part of an individual's total self-concept. He introduced the notion of life roles to highlight the importance of the many roles that individuals play over the course of a life (e.g., child, student, citizen, worker, and caretaker) and to describe how those roles can complement, coexist, or conflict with one another. For example, Senecal, Julien, and Guay (2003) found that academic procrastination is partly a function of the conflict between students' motivations toward academic and social-interpersonal activities. Such role conflict is virtually unavoidable given the complex lives experienced by most college students today. Advisors can be alert to the possible conflicting roles confronting a student and can help students identify other concurrent roles that might complement their role as a student and facilitate their educational and career success.

Helping Students Make Educational and Career Decisions

In an effort to help advisors promote the academic and career decision-making of their students, Gordon (2006) described the 3-I model of career advising (Inquire, Inform, Integrate). During the Inquire phase, advisors help students to articulate their academic and career needs or concerns and provide responses in an effort to move students toward the information-gathering stage of career advising. It is during this stage that advisors might come to some tentative conclusions about which course of action is most appropriate for which student. For example, advisors would probably treat a student who had decision-making deficits but adequate career information differently from a student with decision-making confidence and a lack of information. During the Inform stage of this model students are encouraged to gather information about themselves (e.g., interests, values, and skills) and their educational and career opportunities. Finally, Gordon suggests that the Integration stage is where the student and advisors face the challenge of organizing the information and deriving meaning from it with respect to the student's needs and plans. Advisors adopting this model should be familiar with self-assessment strategies, sources of educational and occupational information, and decision-making difficulties that may arise during the Integration stage of career advising.

Self-Assessment. One of the first steps in career planning is self-exploration and discovery. Students enter college with varying levels of self-knowledge. Some will be able to clearly articulate their interests, skills, values and personality; others will provide blank stares in response to the statement "Tell me about yourself." An accurate understanding of the self is important not only for making a good career decision, but also for entering the job market. Employers want to hire individuals whose skills, interests, and values are consistent with occupational and organizational characteristics and who have an engaging personality. At the same time, an individual will want to evaluate a job offer based on which of their values will be reinforced and which may have to be sacrificed. It is important to explain to students that the process of self-exploration and discovery may require time and effort, but ultimately it is worthwhile.

Depending upon the needs of a student, self-information can be gained formally or informally. Most colleges offer formal strategies for assessing students' academic and career-related interests, values, skills, and personality characteristics. For example, there are standardized career assessments such as the Strong Interest Inventory, the Minnesota Importance Questionnaire, and the Myers-Briggs Type Indicator. Other career measures are bundled or administered within a larger inventory or computer-based career planning program. Formal career assessment may be administered and interpreted individually, or group-administered within a classroom or workshop setting. At many institutions, formal career assessment may be the purview of career counselors. Advisors unfamiliar with career assessment and interpretation should seek additional training or make appropriate referrals.

Advisors can use informal career-assessment procedures to help students gather self-information. In a classroom or workshop setting, activities such as Holland's Party Exercise (Metz, 2005), Sophie's Choice (Niles, 2000), and the SkillScan Cardsort (2007) are fun and creative ways to explore interests, values, and skills and discuss their application to college majors and careers. Alternatively, students can be guided through the self-exploration process during advising sessions or through the use of written homework assignments. Advisors might use questions to elicit interests such as what are your favorite and least favorite school subjects, hobbies, previous jobs and volunteer experiences, early career aspirations, current career aspirations, and occupational daydreams. Students typically respond very favorably to experiential self-exploration activities. For more information on formal and informal career instruments and activities used to promote self-exploration and discovery in college students, readers are directed to Metz (2005).

Career Exploration. Prior to making a career decision, it is important for students to have accurate information about the world of work. The availability and volume of educational and occupational information can be daunting. Advisors are strongly encouraged to evaluate critically all sources they recommend to their students (Hitch & Gore, 2005). The U.S. Department of Labor maintains two separate Web sites providing comprehensive and detailed information about occupations and the workforce. The O*NET (2007) allows students to browse occupations using key words, job titles, job families, and high-growth industries. O*NET provides information about specific occupations, including work activities, context, wages, and job outlook, as well as information about the worker, such as general knowledge, basic skills, education, training, abilities, work styles, interests, and values. The Occupational Outlook Handbook (U.S. Department of Labor, 2007) also provides accurate and detailed information about the nature of work, working conditions, the number and distribution of workers, training and education requirements, average earnings, and employment projections. For a more comprehensive account of occupational information resources and occupational classification systems, the reader is directed to Hitch and Gore (2005).

Informational interviewing is one of the best sources for helping students gain information about an occupation or an industry. Talking to people who currently work in the field of interest can yield valuable up-to-date career information. This strategy can also help students clarify career goals, discover possible internship and employment opportunities, expand their professional networks, build confidence for job interviews, and identify professional strengths and weaknesses. For suggested questions to ask during an information interview, advisors are directed to a page maintained by the University of Texas—Austin (2008).

Job shadowing, or spending time observing a person on the job, can be even more informative. Some colleges offer formal job shadowing experiences with alumni. Although time-consuming, using these sources of occupational information can help students confirm their career choice. For additional occupational information, students can enroll in an introductory course in their field of interest, speak to a professor in the field, visit the career center, do research in the library, read professional trade journals, attend career fairs, explore company Web sites, or join professional organizations.

Decision-Making. Choosing a major and a career can be an anxiety-provoking process for students. It may be helpful to normalize this process by informing students that many students entering college experience indecision related to their career choice. Even students who have declared a major admit various levels of uncertainty or indecisiveness.

Peterson, Sampson, Reardon, and Lenz (1996) provided a framework for understanding differences in decision-making. They categorized individuals as decided, undecided, or indecisive. Individuals in the decided category have made some type of commitment to an occupation or major. However, these authors suggested that decided students may still need career advising. For example, a student may need to confirm a tentative decision or clarify the appropriateness of their choice by comparing and contrasting with other possibilities. Alternatively, a decided student may require help implementing a career choice. As an example, this student may want to be a lawyer but may not know which majors would be appropriate for this career path. Finally, a decided student may have committed to a career path prematurely to reduce stress or avoid conflict with significant others. Peterson et al. (1996) indicated that these students may need guidance similar to that for undecided or indecisive students.

Students who have not made a career decision because they lack specific knowledge are categorized as undecided. Peterson et al. (1996) further subdivided this dimension to include the undecided-deferred, undecided-developmental, and undecided-multipotential. For some students it may be appropriate to be undecided-deferred. An example is a first-year college student taking general education classes and exploring career interests. A student who is undecided-developmental is unable to commit to an occupational or major choice because of a lack of self-information, occupational information, or career decision-making skills. These students may benefit from clarifying their interests, values, skills, and personality or may need additional career or educational information. These students may also need help analyzing and synthesizing information they have gathered and sorting this information according to their value system. These are activities described by Gordon (2006) as occurring during the Integration stage of career advising. The worksheet included as an Appendix to this chapter was developed with the help of academic and career advisors at Salt Lake Community College to aid students in this process. Finally, the undecided-multipotential category characterizes undecided students who feel overwhelmed, given their numerous and diverse interests, skills, and opportunities. In addition to helping these students narrow their potential occupational choices and compare them to their interests, values, skills, and personality, it may be important to help them clarify what is complicating the decision. For example, it may be that pressure from family, low self-efficacy beliefs, lack of resources, multiple role conflicts, skill deficits, or a number of other obstacles are preventing a student from deciding on a career or major.

The final category of decision-making is the indecisive student. The indecisive student is similar to the undecided student but has a dysfunctional level of anxiety and a maladaptive approach to problem-solving (Peterson et al., 1996; Chartrand, Martin, Robbins, McAuliffe, Pickering, & Calliotte, 1994). An advisor can help such a student by providing support and reassurance and by helping the student identify resources in his or her environment that may be of assistance in the decision-making process. Often, such students are appropriate candidates for a more formal program of career development such as a career-development course, a first-year experience seminar, or individual career counseling.

Critical Ingredients in Career Advising Interventions

Advisors use many methods and strategies when working with students engaged in career decision-making. Advisors may ask students about their likes and dislikes or which general education courses they find particularly appealing, or they may rely on a more formal assessment of students' interests. Whether a student is trying to decide on an academic major or is discussing possible career alternatives, research suggests that some strategies for helping students make important career choices are more successful than others.

Brown and his colleagues (Brown and Krane, 2000; Brown, Krane, Brecheisen, Castelino, Budisin, Miller, & Edens, 2003) reanalyzed data from studies on the effectiveness of career-choice activities. Of the many strategies that career advisors and counselors use, these authors identified five that were routinely associated with the most beneficial student outcomes. These "critical ingredients" include the use of written exercises, individualized one-on-one sessions, use of information about the world of work, role-modeling, and efforts to help students develop their support network.

Advisors might consider how they can incorporate these critical ingredients into their individual and group sessions, their workshops and credit-bearing courses, and Web sites. For example, advisors might consider building upon the elements included in the Appendix as a way to promote written documentation of an academic or career plan. They might encourage students to identify resources such as other advisors, faculty mentors, peers, family, or professional organizations that could help them implement a tentative academic or career decision. Students who have established a tentative choice should be encouraged to document short- and long-term goals and specific actions steps and timelines to achieve those goals. Many advisors already encourage students to create a written academic plan that includes timelines for advising, declaration of a major, specific course sequences, and other elements. In fact, some institutions now build this process into their advising syllabi, which were described in Chapter Six. Other examples are available on the Web site of the National Academic Advising Association (NACADA, 2008).

Brown and his colleagues (2000, 2003) noticed that career guidance efforts were more effective if opportunities for individualized one-on-one advising were available to students, regardless of their primary mode of delivery. This is not to discount the effectiveness of group or classroom-based career advising but rather to emphasize how those efforts should include mechanisms for students to meet with advisors personally at some point to discuss their academic and career plans.

In addition to written exercises and individualized attention, advisors should refer students to reliable and current sources of academic and occupational information. As described above, there are a growing number of reliable public and private sources for occupational information—many of them available via the Internet. Based on results from his 2003 study, Brown suggests that introducing students to reliable and current educational and occupational information may be the most important of the five critical ingredients. He encourages advisors to take the time to introduce students to complex sources of information in an advising session to ensure that students develop confidence in their ability to use the system.

The critical ingredient of modeling refers to the process of exposing students to individuals who can share their experiences for the purposes of advancing the career development of the student. Csikszentmihalyi and Schneider (2000) argue that adolescents and young adults are relatively isolated from meaningful adult role models or are exposed only to adult role models who are athletes, entertainers, or celebrities. There are many applications of role models in the advising relationship. Many advising offices have developed peer advising programs to capitalize on the benefits of using age-related peers to help students identify potential educational and career directions. Advisors themselves might serve as models for the career-decision-making process by sharing lessons from their own career-decision process. By encouraging students to engage in service learning opportunities, internships, externships, and academic clubs and societies, advisors are likely increasing the number of relevant adult models to whom a student will be exposed.

Finally, helping students to build their support network will go a long way toward preparing them for a successful transition into their major and the world of work. A support network might include resources such as the O*NET for occupational information, an alumni association, friends, family, advisors, and professors. Whereas some students might be naturally gifted in identifying and strengthening their support network, others will require some guidance and support as they develop theirs. Engaging in curricular and cocurricular activities on campus, seeking campus employment or other part-time work opportunities, and taking advantage of career services functions such as on-campus interviewing, employer presentations, or internships are also excellent ways of strengthening a support network. Advisors can increase the probability that a student will feel confident in his or her ability to develop and use a support network if this topic is explicitly discussed during advising sessions.

SUCCESS FACTORS

The alarming rates of postsecondary attrition (ACT, 2007b) and the profound personal and societal ramifications of this phenomenon (Pascarella & Terenzini, 2005; Baum & Payea, 2004) continue to fuel efforts by educational and psychological researchers to understand and predict postsecondary success and persistence (Astin, 1999; Daugherty & Lane, 1999; Pascarella & Terenzini, 2005). These efforts have identified student attitudes, characteristics, and behaviors associated with positive academic outcomes.

Robbins, Lauver, Le, Davis, Langley, and Carlstrom (2004) described nine factors that routinely predict student academic performance and retention: academic motivation, academic goals, institutional commitment, perceived social support, social involvement, academic self-efficacy, general self-concept, academic-related skills, and contextual influences. Subsequently, these authors developed a measure of these factors (Student Readiness Inventory [SRI], Le, Casillas, Robbins, & Langley, 2005) in an effort to help institutions identify students that might be at risk for academic failure and to help academic and student support units fine-tune their services based on knowledge of their incoming students.

Cole, Saltonstall, and Gore (in press) describe how the SRI can be used by academic and career advising units to identify students' specific strengths and needs even before students arrive on campus. By doing so, advisors are able to prepare early outreach interventions for at-risk students or to align their programs and services to the specific needs and talents of incoming students. Research evidence suggests that these early outreach and referral programs are beneficial to students' academic performance and persistence. Results described by Robbins, Allen, Casillas, Akamigbo, Saltonstall, Cole, Mahoney, and Gore (submitted) suggest that academic and career advising efforts driven by SRI scores result in significant advantages in student performance and persistence.

Gore & Keller (2007) have described the conceptual overlaps between these student academic success factors and characteristics employers seek in their employees (see Table 7.1). In essence, by promoting the development of these student success factors, advisors are simultaneously preparing their students for future workplace success. Many leading student success textbooks (e.g., *From Master Student to Master Employee* [Ellis, in press], and *Your College Experience: Strategies for Success* [Gardner, Jewler, & Barefoot, 2006]) explicitly acknowledge the relationships between academic and workplace success factors.

Advisors can provide valuable guidance to students with or without student SRI scores. For example, the construct of commitment to college is a critical one that permeates most advising functions. Students who ask themselves the question "Why am I here" may be in need of career advising or counseling services. By helping students identify life or career goals and connecting those goals to success in college, advisors can help students create a stronger sense

Table 7.1. A Comparison of Academic and Workforce Success Factors.

Academic Success Factors	Workforce Success Factors
Academic discipline	Work ethic*
Goal striving	Motivation/initiative*
Commitment to college	Organizational commitment
Social activity	Interpersonal skills*
Social connection	Adaptability*
Academic self-efficacy	Self-confidence*
General determination	Integrity/dependability*
Study skills	Job related skills
Communication skills	Communication skills*
Emotional control	Well mannered/polite*

*NACE Job Outlook (2006).

of belonging and commitment to the institution and to the concept of completing college. Alternatively, students with particularly strong tendencies toward social activity and social connection with the institution might be encouraged to get involved in student government or in leadership positions in student organizations or academic clubs or societies. These individuals might be recruited by student support services to assume peer leadership roles. By getting involved, students are simultaneously contributing to the strength of the institution and strengthening their own portfolio in preparation for transition to the workforce.

CONCLUSION

College students today have very high expectations for their future. Unfortunately, they don't always have clearly established plans for how to get there. Complicating this scenario is the fact that current trends in the economy and the workforce demand that college graduates be active managers of their own career. Advisors serve a critical function in helping students establish educational and occupational plans, identify the link between college major and career, and take advantage of curricular and cocurricular opportunities that will promote their future success. By providing career advising interventions that draw on theory, are developmentally and contextually appropriate, make use of evidence-based techniques, and promote the acquisition or development of academic and workplace success skills, attitudes, and behaviors, advisors are promoting the long-term academic and career success of their students.

References

ACT. (2007a). *Discover.* Retrieved December 1, 2007, from http://www.act.org/discover

ACT. (2007b). *2007 Retention/Completion Summary Tables.* Retrieved November 18, 2007, from http://www.act.org/path/policy/pdf/retain_trends.pdf

Astin, A. W. (1999). Student involvement: A developmental theory for higher education. *Journal of College Student Development, 40,* 518–529.

Astin, A. W. (2007). *The American freshman: National norms for Fall 2006.* Los Angeles: Higher Education Research Institute.

Baum, S., & Payea, K. (2004). *Education pays 2004: The benefits of higher education for individuals and society.* Washington, DC: The College Board.

Bridges. (2007). *Choices.* Retrieved December 15, 2007, from https://access.bridges.com

Brown, D. (2002). *Career choice and development* (4th ed). San Francisco: Jossey-Bass.

Brown, S. D., & Krane, N.E.R. (2000). Four (or five) sessions and a cloud of dust: Old assumptions and new observations about career counseling. In S. D. Brown & R. W. Lent (Eds.), *Handbook of counseling psychology* (3rd ed., pp. 740–766). New York: Wiley.

Brown, S., Krane, N. R., Brecheisen, J., Castelino, P., Budisin, I., Miller, M., & Edens, L. (2003). Critical ingredients of career choice interventions: More analyses and new hypotheses. *Journal of Vocational Behavior, 62,* 411–428.

Chartrand, J. M., Martin, W. F., Robbins, S. B., McAuliffe, G. J., Pickering, J. W., & Calliotte, A. A. (1994). Testing a level versus an interactional view of career indecision. *Journal of Career Assessment, 2,* 55–69.

Cole, R. P., Saltonstall, M., & Gore, P. A., Jr. (in press). Assessing student readiness to promote student success: A campus collaboration. *Exploring the Evidence: Institutional Initiatives to Promote Student Success* (Monograph No. 47). Columbia: University of South Carolina, National Resource Center for the First-Year Experience and Students in Transition.

Csikszentmihalyi, M., & Schneider, B. (2000). *Becoming adult: How teenagers prepare for the world of work.* New York: Basic Books.

Daugherty, T. K., & Lane, E. J. (1999). A longitudinal study of academic and social predictors of college attrition. *Social Behavior & Personality, 27,* 355–362.

Ellis, D. (in press). *From master student to master employee* (2nd ed.). New York: Houghton Mifflin.

Gardner, J. N., Jewler, A. J., & Barefoot, B. (2006). *Your college experience: Strategies for success* (7th ed.). Belmont CA: Wadsworth.

Gordon, V. N. (2006). *Career advising: An academic advisor's guide.* San Francisco: Jossey-Bass.

Gore, P. A., Jr., & Keller, B. (2007, July). *Promoting academic and career success: Critical concepts and strategies.* Professional Development Institute presented at the annual meeting of the National Career Development Association, Seattle, WA.

Hitch, J. L., & Gore, P. A., Jr. (2005). Living in an information age: Occupational classification systems and sources of occupational information. In P. A. Gore, Jr. (Ed.), *Facilitating the career development of students in transition* (Monograph No. 43, pp. 61–86). Columbia: University of South Carolina, National Resource Center for the First-Year Experience and Students in Transition.

Holland, J. L. (1997). *Making vocational choices: A theory of vocational personalities and work environments* (3rd ed.). Odessa, FL: Psychological Assessment Resources.

Le, H., Casillas, A., Robbins, S. B., & Langley, R. (2005). Motivational and skills, social, and self-management predictors of college outcomes: Constructing the Student Readiness Inventory. *Educational and Psychological Measurement, 65*, 482–508.

Lent, R. W. (2005). A social cognitive view of career development and counseling. In S. D. Brown & R. W. Lent (Eds.), *Career development and counseling: Putting theory and research to work* (pp. 101–130). New York: John Wiley and Sons.

Leuwerke, W., Robbins, S., Sawyer, R., & Hovland, M. (2004). Predicting engineering major status from mathematics achievement and interest congruence. *Journal of Career Assessment, 12*, 135–149.

Low, K. S. D., Yoon, M., Roberts, R. W., & Rounds, J. (2005). Stability of vocational interests from early adolescence to adulthood: A quantitative review of longitudinal studies. *Psychological Bulletin, 131*, 713–737.

Metz, A. J. (2005). Selecting instruments and exercises to facilitate the career development of students in transition. In P. A. Gore, Jr. (Ed.), *Facilitating the career development of students in transition* (Monograph No. 43, pp. 27–43). Columbia, SC: University of South Carolina, National Resource Center for The First-Year Experience and Students in Transition.

NACE. (2006). *Jobs outlook report.* Retrieved February 2, 2007, from https://store. naceweb.org

National Academic Advising Association. (2008). *Advising issues and resources.* Retrieved January 12, 2008, from http://www.nacada.ksu.edu/Clearinghouse/ AdvisingIssues/index.htm

Niles, S. (2000). Sophie's Choice: A values sorting activity. In M. Pope & C.W. Minor (Eds.). *Experiential activities for teaching career counseling classes and for facilitating career groups.* Columbus, OH: National Career Development Association.

O*NET Online. (2007). Retrieved December 1, 2007, from http://online.onetcenter.org

Pascarella, E. T., & Terenzini, P. T. (2005). *How college affects students: A third decade of research.* San Francisco: Jossey-Bass.

Peterson, G., Sampson, J., Reardon, R., & Lenz, J. (1996). A cognitive information processing approach to career problem solving and decision making. In D. Brown, L. Brooks, & Associates (Eds.), *Career choice and development* (2nd ed.). San Francisco: Jossey-Bass.

Pope, M., & Minor, C. W. (2000). *Experiential activities for teaching career counseling classes and for facilitating career groups.* Columbus, OH: National Career Development Association.

Reardon, R. C., & Lenz, J. G. (1998). *The Self-Directed Search and related Holland materials: A practitioner's guide.* Odessa, FL: Psychological Assessment Resources.

Robbins, S., Allen, J., Casillas, A., Akamigbo, A., Saltonstall, M., Cole, R., Mahoney, E., & Gore, P. A., Jr. (submitted). Associations of resource and service utilization, risk level, and college outcomes.

Robbins, S. B., Lauver, K., Le, H., Davis, D., Langley, R., & Carlstrom, A. (2004). Do psychosocial and study skills factors predict college outcomes? A meta-analysis. *Psychological Bulletin, 130*, 261–288.

Senecal, C., Julien, E., & Guay, F. (2003). Role conflict and academic procrastination: A self-determination perspective. *European Journal of Social Psychology, 33*, 135–145.

SkillScan Cardsort. (2007). Retrieved December 23, 2007, from http://www.skillscan.net

Super, D. E. (1990). A life-span, life-space approach to career development. In D. Brown, L. Brooks, & Associates (Eds.), *Career choice and development* (2nd ed.). San Francisco: Jossey-Bass.

Swanson, J. L., & Gore, P. A. (2000). Advances in vocational psychology theory and research. In S. D. Brown & R. W. Lent (Eds.), *Handbook of counseling psychology* (3rd ed., pp. 233–269). New York: Wiley.

Tracey, T. J. G., & Robbins, S. (2006). The interest-major congruence and college success relation: A longitudinal study. *Journal of Vocational behavior, 69,* 64–89.

U.S. Department of Labor. (2007). *Occupational outlook handbook.* Retrieved September 8, 2007, from http://www.bls.gov/oco

University of Texas—Austin. (2008). Career exploration center: Services for students. Retrieved January 12, 2008, from http://www.utexas.edu/student/careercenter/services

APPENDIX

Career Decision-Making Worksheet

Directions: Write the names of three occupations you have been considering in the occupation boxes below. Read about each occupation using the O*NET Online (http://online.onetcenter.org) or the Occupational Outlook Handbook (http://www.bls.gov/oco). If the occupation matches an important characteristic, place an X in the appropriate box. If you are unsure, place a "?" in that box.

Important Characteristics	*Sample: Zookeeper*	*Occupation #1*	*Occupation #2*	*Occupation #3*
Would enjoy nature of work/tasks	X			
Would enjoy work context/ conditions	X			
Already have necessary skills				
Desire to develop necessary skills	X			
Seems to fit my personality	X			
Industry expected to grow	?			
Years of education acceptable	X			
Opportunity for advancement	?			
Potential income is desirable	X			
Matches my top five work values*(List work values below)				
1.				
2.				
3.				
4.				
5.				

*Complete the work values inventory: http://www.du.edu/career/handouts/Values.pdf.

Interpreting the Table

1. Looking at the question marks in the table, what information do you still need?

2. Looking at the Xs in the table, does one occupation seem to meet your needs better than another? What do you consider to be the benefits and drawbacks of each occupation?

3. Are there additional occupations that interest you? You may want to complete another table using additional occupations.

4. To help you narrow your career options, consider doing one or more of the following:

   _____ Share your list with family, friends, and/or your advisor.

   _____ Make an appointment with a career counselor (especially if you feel very anxious about choosing a major or career path).

   _____ Create a pro and con list for each occupation of interest.

   _____ Take an introductory course in the subject(s) of interest.

   _____ Speak to a faculty member who teaches the subject(s) of interest.

   _____ Interview a professional with the occupation(s) of interest.

   _____ Job shadow a professional with the occupation(s) of interest.

   _____ Attend a workshop or seminar related to exploring majors or careers.

PART TWO

STUDENT DIVERSITY AND STUDENT NEEDS

Virginia N. Gordon

Chapter One of this volume outlines significant historical changes that have had an impact on the status of higher education and academic advising. The characteristics and number of students who have been advised over the years have changed just as dramatically. Section Two addresses the heart and focus of advising—the individual student. To its credit, academic advising in American colleges has been student-centered over most of its history. Although the characteristics of students have changed, the basic purpose of advising—that is, to assist them with their academic and personal experiences, has not. This section focuses on today's diverse student populations and the unique advising challenges they present.

Kirsten Kennedy and Jennifer Crissman Ishler introduce in Chapter Eight a general profile of the students who are enrolled in our colleges and universities today. They describe how advising needs are influenced by student age, enrollment patterns, place of residence, gender, sexual orientation, race and ethnic group, disabilities, and online learning. Also discussed are the educational experiences of students prior to enrollment, including their level of academic preparation for college course work. The chapter concludes with a review of the changing attitudes and values of today's college students, including political views, social issues, family issues, mental and physical well-being, accessing, affording, and financing higher education, and the impact that technology has had on students.

Chapters Nine, Ten, and Eleven describe the transitions students experience as they move into, through, and on from college. Chapter Nine focuses on the needs of students who are entering college for the first time and on students who are transferring out of or into other colleges. Mary Stuart Hunter and Leah Kendall address many of the issues that students encounter as they make the transition *into* college, including preenrollment and the first contact they have with new freedoms, routines, and academic challenges. In keeping with the changing demographics of students entering college today, the authors describe the perceptions of different types of students, including the millennials, returning adults, international and transfer students, and students with disabilities and mental health concerns. Parent expectations influence many students' perceptions of college, and as these authors contend, advisors must understand that "recruiting a student often means recruiting a family." Learning the culture of higher education and their particular institution is a challenge for students of all backgrounds, abilities, and interests. Many suggestions are offered for how academic advisors can help students successfully assimilate into their new environment and culture.

George Steele and Melinda McDonald discuss the transitions of specific groups of students *during* the college years in Chapter Ten. These include students who make the transition from indecision to decision about academic and vocational choices, from one major to another, and into developmental or remedial education. Students are also faced with transitions that are institutionally based (e.g., allowed to enter undecided about a major, controlled enrollment or exclusion from a major, availability of remedial course work). The authors use a framework of an advisor-counselor continuum of responsibilities to suggest ways that advisors can assist students who are experiencing these challenging transitions during their college years.

Chapter Eleven addresses the last phase of the college experience by examining the pivotal role advisors play in helping student *move from* college to meaningful postcollege experiences. Jennifer Bloom writes about not only the transition into the workplace, but transitions to further educational experiences (graduate or professional schools), and transitions into public service (Peace Corps, Teach for America, and nonprofit organizations). She suggests that advisors use the four stages of Appreciative Advising (Discover, Dream, Design, and Deliver) to help students plan for their future. She outlines a "7-Step Self-Authored Moving On" model to demonstrate how advisors can help students deal with the "moving on" transition from college.

Blane Harding writes about other groups of students who have specific advising needs. In Chapter Twelve he focuses on high-ability students, student athletes, students with disabling conditions, first-generation students, adult students, and gay-lesbian-bisexual or transgender students. Although it is impossible to place students into one group since they often incorporate several of the above types, this chapter describes the additional needs of these students and suggests specific advising techniques, including coalition-building, acquiring cultural competence, and relationship-building. The author emphasizes that advisors must understand that students want to be treated as individuals and not always as members of a special group with special needs.

In Chapter Thirteen, Evette Castillo Clark and Jane Kalionzes focus on college students of color, including African Americans, Asian Pacific Islander Americans, Latino/as, Native Americans, and Multiracial and Biracial students. Although international students confront many of the same issues as American students, they also face additional challenges that require advisors to approach them with special academic and institutional knowledge and advising skills. More and more college students are coming from very diverse ethnic and cultural backgrounds, and many of the concerns they present need special attention. This chapter describes the different ways these students perceive the advising process and provides specific advising strategies.

The chapters in Section Two offer a comprehensive portrait of today's college students and their astonishingly diverse backgrounds, needs, and concerns. The authors outline many helpful suggestions not only to help advisors acquire a deeper understanding of the students they advise, but also to help them sensitively tailor their approaches to take into account students' unique academic, personal, and social needs that continuously challenge advising practices.

CHAPTER EIGHT

The Changing College Student

Kirsten Kennedy and Jennifer Crissman Ishler

T
o advise students effectively, academic advisors should be familiar with changing student demographics, characteristics, and experiences. The demographic profile of today's college student is different from that of thirty years ago. It is no longer true that college students are mostly eighteen-year-old, middle-class, white, heterosexual males who recently graduated from high school and plan to attend college full-time and graduate in four years. This chapter reviews current national data about the many ways students have changed and the implications of these changes for academic advising.

CHANGING DEMOGRAPHICS

This section reviews how college students have changed over time in age, enrollment status, place of residence, gender, sexual orientation, race and ethnic group, international students, and students with disabilities.

Age

In 2005, 27 percent of undergraduate students were younger than twenty-four years old. Of the total college enrollment in 2005 (including graduate and professional students), 37 percent were twenty-five years of age or older (*Almanac*, 2007). Adult students are more likely to: (1) delay enrollment into postsecondary education beyond the first year after high school graduation, (2) attend part-time, (3) be financially independent from their parents, (4) work full-time, (5) have dependents other than a spouse, (6) be a single parent, and (7) have a general equivalency diploma (GED) in lieu of a high school diploma (National Center for Education Statistics [NCES], 2002). For the past ten years, the age of undergraduate students enrolled in college has remained fairly constant, and the U.S. Department of Education's projections of annual growth in postsecondary students assumes a slower growth rate for students over age twenty-five in college credential programs than for traditional eighteen- to twenty-one-year-olds during 2005–2010 (NCES, 2004).

Adult students tend to have lower college completion rates than traditional students. Berker, Horn, and Carroll (2003) found that six years after beginning postsecondary studies, 62 percent of adult students had not completed a degree or certificate and were no longer enrolled. In part, this lack of persistence can be attributed to the barriers adult students face as they attempt to complete their degrees. Silva, Calahan, and Lacireno-Paquet (1998) found four barriers common to nontraditional students: lack of time to pursue their education, family responsibilities, scheduling of course time and place, and the cost of educational courses.

Adult students may present some additional academic problems, as compared with traditional students. Their academic schedules are likely to be influenced by their commitments outside their student life. For example, those with families and children may need help in balancing their lives. They may have to rely more on e-mail contacts rather than on face-to-face interactions and use online academic services more frequently. Advisors should consider providing services after 5 P.M. and on weekends, when adult students are more available. Adult students may also feel out of place in classrooms in which the majority are traditional students, and they may need remedial services if they have been away from education for a while.

Enrollment Status

Student enrollment patterns have changed drastically from the days of attending one college full-time for four years at a four-year institution. Today's students can choose from many options. They can attend full- or part-time; choose among public, private, for-profit, and online institutions; attend two-year or four-year institutions; transfer among institutions; and even attend multiple institutions simultaneously, a phenomenon known as "swirling."

For example, in 1995, 57 percent of students were enrolled full-time for all or part of the academic year (*Almanac*, 1995), compared with 41 percent in 2004 (*Almanac*, 2007). The majority of part-time students were twenty-two to thirty-nine years old and attended two-year institutions (*Almanac*, 2007). In 1993, 21 percent of students were enrolled in public four-year institutions, while 19 percent were enrolled in four-year private institutions (*Almanac*, 1995). By contrast, in 2004, 30 percent of students were enrolled in public four-year institutions and 13 percent were enrolled in private four-year institutions. Public two-year institutions also saw an increase from 37 percent in 1993 (*Almanac*, 1995) to 40 percent in 2004 (*Almanac*, 2007), and private two-year institutions saw an increase from 2 percent in 1993 (*Almanac*, 1995) to 7 percent in 2004 (*Almanac*, 2007). Eight percent of students enrolled were listed as attending private for-profit institutions (*Almanac*, 2007).

Nearly 3.2 million students took at least one online course during the fall 2005 term, a substantial increase over the 2.3 million reported the previous year (Allen & Seaman, 2006, p. 1). Over 80 percent of students taking online courses are studying at the undergraduate level, with only 14 percent taking graduate-level online courses (Allen & Seaman, 2006). According to the National Study on Student Engagement (NSSE), online and distance learners were slightly older than average undergraduates. The median age of first-year distance learners was twenty-five; the median age of seniors was thirty-two. The median age for students attending college in person was eighteen for first-year students and twenty-two for seniors (NSSE, 2006).

Transfer students comprise a significant portion of student enrollment, particularly those coming from community colleges. In 2001, students under the age of twenty-two constituted 42 percent of all credit-seeking students in community colleges, and those under the age of twenty-four comprised nearly three-fourths of first-time community college students (Adelman, 2005). The NSSE (2006) found that 55 percent of transfer students took the majority of their courses at vocational-technical schools or at community or junior colleges.

A growing number of undergraduates are engaged in the complex enrollment pattern of "swirling," which refers to students who transfer between several community colleges, public universities, and private colleges, perhaps taking courses from different institutions in the same semester (Rab, 2007). Swirling students must juggle travel between institutions, navigate complicated financial aid issues, and figure out which courses transfer to which institutions (Smith Bailey, 2003). Another concern is "whether students who piece together their own education are getting the big picture" (Smith Bailey, 2003, p. 38). As advisors, it is critical to identify swirling students and to stay informed of the courses students are taking and where they are taking them to help students select courses that can be transferred for credit. Discussing where the student will ultimately be granted a degree is important, and established transfer and articulation agreements with other institutions will assist in that process.

Students with different enrollment patterns require different kinds of advising. Those studying part-time may have more difficulty in scheduling classes than full-time students and may be ineligible for many student services. Transfers will need help in assessing the best "next" institution. Different advising mechanisms using online technologies may be necessary for online learners to get them oriented, enrolled, and advised.

Residence

In colonial higher education, students at Harvard and Yale lived in residential colleges. College presidents of that time were convinced that good housing accommodations were essential in contributing to academic success and that securing proper housing was as important as securing good classroom instruction (Brubacher & Rudy, 1999). While there is ample evidence that today's students benefit academically and socially simply by living on campus (Pascarella & Terenzini, 2005), these benefits' effects are magnified when students participate in residentially based learning communities, defined as "a residential education unit . . . that is organized on the basis of an academic theme or approach and is intended to integrate academic learning and community living" (The Residential Learning Communities International Clearinghouse, 2006, p. 1). These benefits include increased faculty-student interaction, enhanced cognitive development, increased academic achievement and retention, increased involvement, and increased interaction with peers (Pascarella & Terenzini, 2005).

However, because only 15 percent of today's college students live on campus—25 percent live with their families and 60 percent live off campus (*Almanac, 2007*)—the benefits of learning communities do not apply to the vast majority of students, who must seek other ways of acquiring these benefits. Some of these include becoming an off-campus affiliate of an on-campus learning community and involving themselves in other campus activities and interactions.

Gender

In Colonial United States, the privilege of attending and completing college belonged only to white, Anglo-Saxon men. Women were allowed the opportunity of higher education in 1833, when Oberlin opened as the first coeducational school, and in 1865, when Vassar was founded as an all women's school (Geiger, 1992). Since that time, women's enrollment has grown. The number of women attending college equaled that of male students for the first time in 1979 (Woodard, Love & Komives, 2000). Currently, women represent 55 percent of enrollment in higher education. Limited research exists on gender identity among "transgender" college students (Carter, 2000; Connolly, 2000; Rankin & Beemyn, 2008; Wilson, 1996). (See Chapter Twelve for more information on these students.)

Advisors must understand that, although women are in the majority in higher education, they can still be subject to gender discrimination, sexual assault, gender-based stereotyping, and other unequal treatment, both in and out of the classroom, by faculty, administrators, and other students. For example, women in fields traditionally dominated by men may need help in interpreting their classroom and peer experiences. Advisors must be sensitive to the unique needs of female students and should use campus resources to assist them with their needs.

Sexual Orientation

Sexual orientation refers to the degree to which a person experiences same-sex attractions and romantic relationships on a continuum ranging from exclusively heterosexual to exclusively homosexual (Balsam & Mohr, 2007).

The percentage of people who consider themselves lesbian, gay, bisexual, or transgender is difficult to estimate because many choose to keep their sexual orientation to themselves, but some estimates are as high as 7 percent (Eyermann & Sanlo, 2002).

Lesbian, gay, bisexual, transgender, queer, and questioning (LGBTQQ) students are the sexual minority on college campuses. In a study of 1,700 self-identified lesbian, gay, bisexual, and transgendered faculty, students, and staff from across the country, Rankin (2003) reported they find the college campus is not an empowering and affirming environment and that they are often the victims of intolerance and harassment.

In a sense, a student's sexual orientation is really none of an academic advisor's business. On the other hand, LGBTQQ students may experience academic difficulty because of their sexual orientation or confusion, and that should be a legitimate concern of academic advisors. They should have some knowledge and awareness of sexual orientation issues and be aware of campus services that can help educate and counsel LGBTQQ students. Participating in safe-space training and posting such a designation in a place where students can easily view it is an affirming action advisors can take.

Race and Ethnic Group

Minority enrollment is certainly increasing (*Almanac,* 2007). Total minority enrollment rose from 23.4 percent in 1995 to 30.1 percent in 2005. The current minority enrollment in higher education mirrors the U.S. population; as in the 2000 Census, 29.9 percent identified as minority (U.S. Census Bureau, 2001). In higher education specifically, Native American enrollment increased 34.3 percent from 1995 to 2005 and accounted for 1 percent of total college enrollment in the United States. According to the 2000 Census, 0.9 percent of the population in the United States was Native American. Asian enrollment increased 42.3 percent and made up 6.5 percent of college enrollment in 2005. Asian Americans made up 3.6 percent of the U.S. population in 2000. Black (non-Hispanic) enrollment increased 50.3 percent, accounting for 12.7 percent of the enrollment in 2005. This percentage is consistent with the overall U.S. population, in which blacks make up 12.3 percent of the population. Hispanic enrollment increased 72.1 percent, making up 10.8 percent in 2005, compared with 6 percent of the population in the United States in 2000. White, non-Hispanic enrollment increased 11.5 percent, but white enrollment declined as a portion of total enrollment, from 72.3 percent in 1995 to 65.7 percent of total enrollment in 2005. In 2000, whites made up 69.1 percent of the population. The following states had the highest minority percentage enrollment in 2005: Hawaii (66.0 percent), New Mexico (54.8 percent), California (53.8 percent), Washington, DC (45.8 percent), Texas (44.1 percent), and Mississippi (41.1 percent). Two-year colleges have the highest percentages of enrolled minority students (47.3 percent at private two-year schools and 36.4 percent at public two-year schools), while minorities make up just over a quarter of four-year college enrollment (27.2 percent at private four-year schools and 27.5 at public four-year schools).

Differences within minority groups, however, may be as great as differences among them (Crissman Ishler, 2005). For example, within Hispanic, Asian, Native American, and African American minorities, there may be different histories, traditions, and cultures. This means that reaching conclusions about students based on gross categorizations of race and ethnic group may do more harm than good. The growing number of racially mixed students complicates these categorizations even further.

Academic advisors are required to treat all students equally and with dignity and respect, regardless of their race or ethnic group. However, advisors should understand that the college experience of minorities is likely to be different, and perhaps even more difficult, than that of majority students. Minority students may have unique issues to resolve. Advisors should be aware of these issues and deal with them directly or refer these students to appropriate campus resources.

International Students

The number of international students enrolled at the graduate, professional, and undergraduate levels has grown, increasing from 3.2 percent in 1995 to 3.3 percent of enrolled students in 2005, but representing an overall increase of 28.7 percent in the international population (*Almanac*, 2007). However, international student enrollment from 2002 to 2005 actually decreased by 1.0 percent, presumably due to the tightening of federal regulations after 9/11. International-student enrollment from India, China, South Korea, and Japan accounts for over 45 percent of the international enrollment in the United States.

Both legal and illegal immigrant students must also be considered. There are an estimated 50,000 undocumented students in college today. An undocumented student is "a foreign national who: (1) entered the United States without inspection or with fraudulent documents; or (2) entered legally as a nonimmigrant but then violated the terms of his or her status and remained in the United States without authorization" (Badger & Yale-Loehr, 2006, p. 5).

The implications for higher education are enormous. For example, legislative debates have focused on whether or not illegal immigrant children should be entitled to a college education at in-state rates at public institutions (Field, 2006a, 2006b; Hebel, 2006, 2007; Keller, 2007). The influx of immigrants, particularly those whose first language is Spanish, will likely necessitate an increase of English as a Second Language (ESL) courses in college to prepare them for course work taught in English.

Academic advisors must be aware of the unique barriers, including language, cultural differences, and lack of social support, faced by undocumented students (Field, 2006). Isolation and loneliness surface when undocumented students' families remain in the homeland and the student cannot make return visits. Other illegal immigrants worry about how they will pay their tuition and what kind of work they will get after they complete their degree. Deportation is always a possibility. Despite defeat of the Senate's immigration bill in 2007, some education leaders are advocating for illegal immigrant students to gain legal status and in-state college tuition rates (Dervarics, 2007). However, others are less willing to accommodate illegal immigrants. Arizonans "voted to bar students who are not legal residents of the United States from being offered in-state tuition or state student aid" (*Almanac*, 2007, p. 3). The governor of Connecticut "vetoed a bill to offer in-state tuition to illegal immigrants who had graduated from one of the state's high schools" (*Almanac*, 2007, p. 3).

Advisors must be prepared to help immigrants, both legal and undocumented, because they may seek out advisors for all kinds of problems, from financial aid to visa issues to career counseling to emotional support. Advisors must be well versed on these issues and know what campus and community resources are available to these students.

Students with Disabilities

Merriam-Webster defines disability as "1 a. the condition of being disabled b: inability to pursue an occupation because of a physical or mental impairment; *also:* a program providing financial support to one affected by disability < went on *disability* after the injury > 2: lack of legal qualification to do something 3: a disqualification, restriction, or disadvantage" (Merriam-Webster, 2007). In fact, students with disabilities can have visual, hearing, speech, or orthopedic problems; specific learning disabilities; attention deficit disorder (ADD) or attention deficit-hyperactivity disorder (ADHD); mental illness; health impairments or problems; or other medical conditions.

Data about students with disabilities have been scattered and inconsistent, but overall, the number of students who report a disability appears to be increasing. In the fall of 1995, 6 percent of enrolled undergraduates reported having a disability (NCES, 1999). Of the 6 percent reporting a disability, 20 percent reported a learning disability, 23 percent an orthopedic disability, 16 percent a hearing disability, 16 percent a visual disability, 3 percent a speech disability, and 21 percent some other disability. In 2003–2004, 11.3 percent of enrolled students identified as having some type of disability (*Almanac,* 2007), as defined and outlined by the 1973 Rehabilitation Act and the 1991 Americans with Disabilities Act (ADA). The ADA mandated that institutions provide "reasonable accommodations" when students supply substantiating documentation of their disability.

Traditionally, disabilities have been assumed to be physical and easily identifiable, but some disabilities are hidden, such as ADD, ADHD, and other specific learning disabilities. The percentage of students with hidden disabilities in college increased from 3 percent in 1978 to 9 percent in 1998 (Foster, 2001), perhaps because of better awareness and more specific criteria for diagnosis in the Diagnostic and Statistical Manual of Mental Disorders, fourth edition (DSM-IV). Advisors may not be aware of the hidden disabilities students have unless the student chooses to disclose that information. Because of confidentiality language in the ADA, campus disability services staff may not be able to legally disclose student disability information to advisors. Appropriate academic accommodations will likely be defined by the campus disability services office and relayed directly to faculty.

One study suggests that students with disabilities are less likely to persist to graduation (NCES, 1999). Students with disabilities were "more likely to have attributes associated with lower rates of persistence and degree attainment" (NCES, 1999, p. vi). Some of those attributes included passing the GED test to qualify for college, being older, and having dependents other than a spouse. Students with disabilities who graduate from college tend to have similar chances at landing a job or being admitted to graduate school as their nondisabled counterparts.

Advisors must first recognize that reasonable accommodations for students with disabilities are not only desirable but legally required. Advisors must know and understand what constitutes reasonable accommodations and be prepared to help these students when accommodation issues arise, both in and out of the classroom. Advisors must also be thoroughly familiar with campus services designed to help students with disabilities. Advisors should also be aware that some students with disabilities may not want to be identified, and their privacy must be respected.

CHANGING CHARACTERISTICS

Demographics are not the only changes seen in college students: their attitudes and values, family issues, mental and physical health, academic preparation, academic misconduct, and financial states are different, as well.

Attitude and Values

Students are becoming more polarized in their political views; moderates are in decline, and more students are labeling themselves as either liberal or conservative. For example, 28.4 percent of students consider themselves liberal, while 23.9 percent consider themselves conservative (Hurtado & Pryor, 2006). These 2006 percentages are the highest since 1975, and represent a 1.3 percent increase (for both liberals and conservatives) from 2005. Students labeling themselves as middle of the road comprised 43.4 percent of students, the lowest percentage since 1970, and a decrease of 1.7 percent from 2005 to 2006.

Students have strong opinions on social issues. According to the 2007 *Almanac*, 74 percent of students wanted more gun control from the federal government; 78 percent of students believed the federal government should do more to control environmental pollution; 73 percent of students thought that a national health care plan is needed to cover everyone's medical costs; and 61 percent of students believed that same-sex couples should have the right to legal marital status. When asked about their priorities in life, 76 percent of students rated raising a family as their first priority, and "being well" rated as the second priority for 74 percent. Helping others was the third priority for 67 percent, which is the highest this attitude had been rated in the past ten years (*Almanac*, 2007).

While these changes in attitude may not have direct implications for academic advisors, they do constitute a context within which the advising relationship is established.

Family Issues

The definition of the American family has undergone significant change; gone is the assumption that every home has a mother, a father, and one or two children. Instead, families are now defined in more inclusive terms, encompassing single-parent families, stepparents, stepsiblings and half-siblings, grandparents, and families with two mothers or two fathers.

The term *helicopter parent* was coined in the early 1990s (Zeman, 1991) but has recently received attention in the national media (Lipka, 2005;

White, 2005). Helicopter parents are defined as those "who hover over their college-age children and challenge administrative decisions" (Lipka, 2005, p. A22). While administrators may view helicopter parents as having a negative affect on students' development toward independence, the parents view their role as ensuring their student's success and happiness. According to the College Board, helicopter parents have intervened in roommate conflicts, registered their children in classes, sat in on career-counseling appointments, and disputed professors' grades (*How Not to be a Helicopter Parent*, n.d.). The Family Educational Rights and Privacy Act (FERPA) has further complicated the institution-parent relationship, as the act protects the student's record from being revealed to anyone, including parents, without the student's consent. There are provisions in FERPA that permit, but do not require, institutions to share student records with parents.

Parents may want to be included in advising sessions to influence what courses their student takes. Because parents of traditional-age students are likely financing their student's education, they may feel they have a right to these discussions. Setting up expectations during orientation of the institution-parent relationship may be helpful in preventing conflict. While traditional-age students are dealing with helicopter parents, nontraditional, older students may be dealing with aging parents, a divorce, or being a single parent. Balancing the demands of academic work with tending to elderly parents, a spouse, or children is challenging. Financial problems and finding affordable, reliable, quality day care are other issues that compete with academic work (Lipka, 2005).

After the student rights advances of the 1970s and legislation protecting students' privacy, many academic advisors assumed that cooperating with family and parents was inappropriate and illegal. The reality is that family and parents are significant influences on their student, and to ignore that relationship is to ignore the possible assistance they can provide. However, this must be done in the best interest of students and with their concurrence. At the same time, there will be instances when "helicopter parents" will be overly intrusive; advisors should seek clarity on how to deal with them within institutional policies and the law.

Mental Health

The mental and physical well-being of students has an impact on their ability to focus on learning while at college (Pascarella & Terenzini, 2005). Robert Gallagher annually conducts the National Survey of Counseling Center Directors (2006) and reports that 92 percent of directors "believe that the increase of students with more serious problems is a growing concern in their centers, 77 percent believe it is a growing concern for the administration, 67 percent for faculty and 81.5 percent for residence life staff" (p. 5). According to the survey results, the counseling center directors report that, on average, their staff sees 9 percent of enrolled students. About a quarter of those only see a counselor for one session (Gallagher, 2006, p. 4).

Gallagher's 2006 study reports counselors spent nearly 80 percent of their time counseling students with personal problems, 6 percent in career counseling, and

8 percent on academic counseling. College students can feel overwhelmed, as evidenced by the American College Health Association's report that more than 75 percent of college students feel that way and that 35.5 percent were sometimes unable to function because they felt so depressed (ACHA, 2007). The University of California, Los Angeles (UCLA) found that since 1985, freshmen reporting less-than-average emotional health has been on the rise (2002). Other relevant facts include:

- 15.9 percent of college women and 8.5 percent of college men reported being diagnosed with depression at some time (Ross, 2004);

- 11 percent of college students reported that they had considered suicide within the previous year (Ross, 2004); and

- 77 percent of juniors reported feeling depressed "frequently" or "occasionally" during the past year, while 61 percent reported those feelings when they first entered college (Higher Education Research Institute, 2004).

Students who do not have fully developed coping mechanisms or who do not access mental health professionals may manifest their stress through alcohol abuse, drug abuse, prescription drug abuse, self-injury, or eating disorders, among others. Alcohol and drug abuse (both illegal and prescription drugs) have negative effects on students, including hangovers and blackouts, driving under the influence, high-risk sexual behavior, assault, and death (Wood, Sher, & Rutledge, 2007). Some students may find temporary relief through self-injury, in which persons attempt to physically harm themselves without intending to cause death (Roberts-Dobie & Donatelle, 2007). Approximately 1 percent of adults and 12 percent of adolescents engage in self-injurious behavior (Roberts-Dobie & Donatelle, 2007), and engaging in this behavior is a way to cope with strong emotions, intense pressure, or upsetting relationships. Some students, particularly women, may cope through bulimia and anorexia. Bulimia is characterized by recurrent binge eating followed by compulsory purging and affects approximately 1 to 2 percent of the population (Wilson, Grilo & Vitousek, 2007). Anorexia is the "successful pursuit of thinness through dietary restriction and other measures" (Wilson, Grilo, & Vitousek, 2007, p. 199). While both bulimia and anorexia are rooted in mental health issues, they both have serious medical consequences. Students with mental health problems should be referred to a mental health professional.

Because there is some evidence that students who experience psychological problems are more likely to experience academic difficulties or drop out (Wilson, Mason, & Ewing 1997) and because there is evidence that troubled students will seek out advisors for help (Winston, 1996), it is especially important that academic and staff advisors be alert to troubled students and make appropriate referrals.

Physical Health

Traditional-age college students may experiment with alcohol and drugs, possibly as a coping mechanism for emotional and mental-health issues. The Core

Alcohol and Drug Survey was administered to first-year students in 1999, 2000, and 2001 at 438 institutions (Meilman & Presley, 2005). The results were staggering, in that first-year students are consuming alcohol in excess, even though they cannot legally purchase alcohol. On average, women consumed 3.9 drinks per week, males 8.6 drinks per week. According to Meiman & Presley, one in four first-year students "report consuming ten or more drinks per week on average" (p. 450). The effects of excessive drinking include having a hangover, driving a car under the influence, vomiting, and memory loss. Students who participated in the Core Survey said they drank to enhance social activity, to break the ice, to give them something to do, and to allow them to have more fun.

Traditional-age college students also may engage in sexually risky behavior and can, therefore, be the recipients of sexually transmitted infections (STIs). The rate of STIs is most prevalent among traditional-age college students (Afifi & Weiner, 2006). Approximately nineteen million new infections are diagnosed each year, with almost half of them diagnosed in people ages sixteen to twenty-four (Centers for Disease Control and Prevention [CDC], 2006). According to Afifi and Weiner, possible outcomes of STIs include cancer, neurological syndromes, pelvic inflammatory diseases, infertility, ectopic pregnancy, and preterm delivery. Students who engage in risky sexual behavior may also contract the human immunodeficiency virus (HIV) and the acquired immunodeficiency syndrome (AIDS). According to the CDC, approximately 40,000 new cases of HIV and AIDS are identified each year.

All of these physical health issues lead to emotional, psychological, and economic concerns for students. Institutions with on-campus health services can accept referrals for students who need medical assistance or counseling services. Advisors at institutions without health or counseling services must know about community medical facilities that can treat students with physical health problems.

Academic Preparation

"The hard truth is that success in college is strongly related to precollege academic preparation and achievement" (Kuh, 2007, p. 4). The majority of high school seniors say they intend to go on to postsecondary education, but many do not engage in educational activities that will prepare them to do well in college (McCarthy & Kuh, 2006). According to the 2004 Community College Survey of Student Engagement (CCSSE), almost half (47 percent) of the respondents study only three or fewer hours per week, well below the average of thirteen to fourteen hours per week of first-year students at four-year colleges. The CCSSE also found that two-thirds of high school students who study three or fewer hours a week reported earning mostly A and B grades.

The retooled Scholastic Aptitude Test (SAT) was administered for the first time in March 2005. Compared to the previous version, which included only verbal and math tests, the new version added a writing test. The average SAT scores had slowly increased over the past decade, but they slightly decreased with the implementation of the new format. According to the College Board's

Vice President of Research, Wayne Camara, "The College Board has conducted a substantial amount of research that shows no evidence that changes to the test contribute to the small score differential between this year's and last year's mean scores" (Camara, 2006).

The average SAT score for all students in 1986–1987 was 507 for verbal and 501 for math (NCES, 2005). During the last year of the older version of the SAT, the average verbal score was 508, and the average math score was 520. With the new version of the SAT, the mean critical reading scored decreased five points to 503 in 2006; the mean SAT math score decreased two points to 518. Scores in all categories remained unchanged from 2005 to 2006.

Some students fall outside the norm of the institution's admitted class. Developmental courses may be required for students who are not well prepared for the academic rigors of college. These courses are often defined by the state, with some states providing a placement test to determine placement in appropriate college courses (Jenkins & Boswell, 2002). The number of entering students requiring remedial courses in community colleges ranges from 10.4 percent in Alabama to 70.9 percent in Tennessee (Jenkins & Boswell, 2002). For four-year colleges, the number of entering students requiring remedial courses ranges from 5.5 percent in Connecticut to 50 percent in Indiana. While some students are not prepared for the vicissitudes of college, some require additional challenge in their academic work. For institutions that cannot raise their admission selectivity criteria, honors programs may be created to attract high-achieving students (Seifert, Pascarella, Colangelo, & Assouline, 2007).

Most professional advisors are well versed in the issue of students being underprepared and are typically able to assist students in this regard. However, faculty who are academic advisors may not be fully prepared to deal with these students and may need assistance in deciding how to help them. Fortunately, most institutions offer developmental courses and counseling to create a level playing field for underprepared students.

Academic Misconduct

Student academic misconduct, such as cheating and plagiarism, has increased in recent decades (McCabe, Trevino, & Butterfield, 2001). McCabe and Trevino's 1997 study of 6,000 students at thirty-one selective colleges and universities found that 70 percent of students acknowledged cheating on exams, 84 percent confessed to cheating on written assignments, and nearly half admitted to inappropriately collaborating with others on assignments. Cheating practices appear to be equally distributed among race and social class (Cochoran, Chamlin, Wood, & Sellers, 1999; Tang & Zuo, 1997). A relationship seems to exist between gender and academic dishonesty (Crown & Spiller, 1998; McCabe & Trevino, 1997; Whitley, 1998), in that male students were slightly more likely to cheat than their female counterparts (Storch & Storch, 2002; Tang & Zuo 1997; Tibbetts, 1999).

Academic dishonesty is never easy for advisors to deal with. Virtually all institutions have academic dishonesty policies, but their interpretation is often unclear and their application uneven. Advisors may also find themselves between the accusing faculty member and the accused student, particularly if the student denies the allegation. It is incumbent on advisors to know institutional academic dishonesty policies, seek help in their application and interpretation, and apply them fairly to both faculty and students. It is also helpful if advisors are skilled in conflict management and resolution.

Accessing, Affording, and Financing Education

The cost of attending college is increasing. According to the *Almanac,* tuition increased 98.1 percent at four-year public institutions from 1995 to 2004, by 65.8 percent at two-year public institutions, and by 71.3 percent at four-year private institutions. During that same time, state appropriations nationwide increased 55.6 percent, but inflation increased only 24 percent (Bureau of Labor Statistics, 2007). Need-based financial aid increased 120.7 percent during the same period, and 50 percent of full-time enrolled students had loans as part of their financial aid packages, while 25 percent of part-time students had loans (*Almanac,* 1995, 2004). Both part-time and full-time students at private four-year colleges had the largest percentages (43 percent and 66 percent, respectively) of their financial aid packages comprised of loans, compared with part-time and full-time students at public four-year institutions (35 percent and 51 percent, respectively).

Rising tuition and increasing student loan debt affects who can access higher education and influences the majors students choose. In 1999–2000, the average amount of debt for students from four-year colleges was $16,928, compared with $9,188 in 1992–1993 (U.S. PIRG, 2006). According to this report, sometimes student loan debt is so burdensome that college graduates default on their loans, ruining their credit. Other times, college graduates find that the debt prevents them from making major purchases, such as cars and homes. Ultimately, the report asserted, students may choose their major based upon the return they will receive on their educational investment, leaving majors in the humanities and liberal arts on the decline. For some potential students, the fear of debt is paralyzing and has kept them from applying to college (U.S. PIRG, 2006). Most academic advisors have little expertise in student financial aid, so it is probably best to refer students with financial problems to appropriate campus resources.

TECHNOLOGY AND TODAY'S STUDENTS

Undoubtedly, no trend in the past twenty years has changed student and campus life more than technology. For example, in 1985, 23.8 percent of entering students had used a computer, compared with 85.8 percent in 2005 (Hurtado & Pryor, 2006). Students use computers for personal written communication (e-mail, text messaging, and instant messaging), social networking (Facebook, MySpace, and YouTube), access to information (Google and Wikipedia), online degrees and courses (University of Phoenix and other institutions), personal digital assistants (Blackberry, Bluetooth, and Treo), oral communication (cell phones) and many others technologies (O'Hanlon, 2007). Students can apply for admission, gain acceptance, qualify for financial aid, pay tuition, access academic advising information, register for courses, take online courses or degrees, and track progress toward a degree without much human contact. Technology is used—and is sometimes required—to participate in the classroom and communicate with faculty. Most recently, institutions have been exploring the use of technology to inform students and parents of campus crises; this was primarily prompted by the Virginia Tech shootings. The amount of time students spend using technology may be as high as twenty hours per week (Morgan & Cotton, 2003).

The question is whether or not student use of these technologies is a good thing. Junco and Mastrodicasa (2007) reviewed the current literature on this issue and concluded that, in general, technology has a positive impact on students' academic experiences (faculty-student interactions, cooperation among students, active learning, reported learning gains), social interactions (social skills, psychological well-being, self-esteem), and improved communication with parents. The impact of technology on psychological development was mixed.

On the other hand, technology has resulted in several "digital divides" on college campuses. For example, in 2007, Junco and Mastrodicasa found differences in technological skills and access to technology related to race, gender, class, and academic background, with women, minority groups, students from lower socioeconomic levels, and students with academic deficiencies at the greatest disadvantage. There is also a digital divide between the overall technological skills of faculty and students (Junco, 2005).

The implications for academic advisors are enormous. First and foremost are the various digital divides. As institutions move toward more reliance on technology to support academic advising, they must be sure that students who have less access and are less skillful have an equal opportunity to receive quality advising and academic information. Also, advisors may have to assume a stronger role in helping students become more computer literate, particularly if the academic advising they receive is heavily dependent upon computer technologies. Advisors should consider ways in which academic advising might be enhanced through the use of technology. Although students may access academic information electronically, they may also need direct, face-to-face help in understanding and interpreting this information. Because technology plays such a prominent role in students' lives, advisors themselves must be at least on a par with students in understanding and using technology. (See Chapter Nineteen for more on technology in advising.)

IMPLICATIONS FOR ADVISORS

In addition to the implications already reviewed, there are additional overall consequences of today's changing student for academic advisors. First, not all national trends translate to every campus. Keeping abreast of recent national trends is important, but academic advisors must know how to access campus-specific demographic information and use it to inform policy and practice.

Second, *within* student groups differences may be just as dramatic as those *between* groups. For example, not all women experience discrimination in the classroom. Not all adult students lack academic skills. Not all students are computer illiterate. Reaching conclusions about students based on gross categorizations and stereotypes may do more harm than good.

Third, locally developed demographic student profiles can be of help in reconsidering academic advising policies and practices, making them more responsive to student needs. Such profiles can be useful in advisor orientation and training programs. This information can also be shared with other campus student services in order to strengthen advising referral resources.

Finally, because of the changing characteristics of today's students, academic advisors face new and difficult challenges. Successfully meeting these challenges will improve students' ability to achieve their educational goals and will enhance the quality of education offered to our increasingly diverse students.

References

Adelman, C. (2005). Moving into town—and moving on: The community college in the lives of traditional-age students. Washington, DC: Department of Education.

Afifi, W. A., & Weiner, J. L. (2006). Seeking information about sexual health: Applying the theory of motivated information management. Human Communication Research, 32 (1), 35–57.

Allen, I. E., & Seaman, J. (2006). Making the grade. Online education in the United States, 2006. Needham, MA: Sloan Center.

Almanac. (1995). Chronicle of Higher Education, 42 (1).

Almanac. (2004). Chronicle of Higher Education, 51 (1).

Almanac. (2007). Chronicle of Higher Education, 54 (1).

American College Health Association. (2007). American College Health Association—National College Health Assessment: Reference Group Executive Summary Fall 2006. Baltimore: Author.

Badger, E., & Yale-Loehr, S. (2006). They can't go home again: Undocumented aliens and access to U.S. Higher Education. Bender's Immigration Bulletin, 15, 5.

Balsam, K. F. & Mohr, J. J. (2007). Adaptation to sexual orientation stigma: A comparison of bisexual and lesbian/gay students. Journal of Counseling Psychology, 54 (3), 306–319.

Berker, A., Horn, L., & Carroll, C. (2003). Work first, study second: Adult undergraduates who combine employment and postsecondary enrollment. Washington, DC: Department of Education, National Center for Education Statistics.

Brubacher, J. S., & Rudy, W. (1999). Higher education in transition: A history of American colleges and universities (4th ed.). New Brunswick, NJ: Transaction.

Bureau of Labor Statistics. (2007). Inflation calculator. Retrieved September 2, 2007, from http://www.bls.gov

Camara, W. J. (2006, September 7). Letter from College Board's Vice President of Research. Retrieved September 14, 2007, from http://www.collegeboard.com/satscores/letter.html

Carter. K. A. (2000). Transgenderism and college students: Issues of gender identity and its role on our campuses. In V. A. Wall & N. J. Evans (Eds.) Toward acceptance: Sexual orientation issues on campus (pp. 261–282). Lanham, MD: University Press of America.

Centers for Disease Control and Prevention. (2006). Sexually transmitted disease surveillance, 2005. Atlanta: Department of Health and Human Services.

Cochoran, J., Chamlin, M., Wood, P., & Sellers, C. (1999). Shame, embarrassment and formal sanction threats: Extending the deterrence-rational choice model to academic dishonesty. Sociological Inquiry, 69 (1), 91–105.

Community College Survey of Student Engagement (CCSSE). (2004). Engagement by design. Austin: University of Texas Community College Leadership Program.

Connolly, M. (2000). Issues for lesbian, gay, and bisexual students in traditional college classrooms. In V. A. Wall & N. J. Evans (Eds.), Toward acceptance: Sexual orientation issues on campus (pp. 109–130). Lanham, MD: American College Personnel Association.

Crissman Ishler, J. (2005). Today's first year students. In M. L. Upcraft, J. N. Gardner, & B. O. Barefoot (Eds.), Challenging and supporting the first-year student: A handbook of improving the first year of college (pp. 13–26). San Francisco: Jossey-Bass.

Crown, D., & Spiller, S. (1998). Learning from the literature on collegiate cheating. Journal of Business Ethics, 17, 687–700.

Dervarics, C. (2007, July 5). Immigration bill dead, but not DREAM Act. Diverse Issues in Higher Education. Retrieved September 14, 2007, from http://www.diverseeducation.com/artman/publish/article_8017.shtml

Diagnostic and Statistical Manual of Mental Disorders, Fourth Edition (DSM-IV). (1994). Arlington, VA: American Psychiatric Association.

Eyermann, T., & Sanlo, R. (2002). Documenting their existence: Lesbian, gay, bisexual and transgender students on campus. In R. Sanlo, S. Rankin, & R. Schoenberg (Eds.), Our place on campus: Lesbian, gay, bisexual, and transgender services and programs in higher education. Westport, CT: Greenwood.

Fay, R. E., Turner, C. F., Klassen, A. D., & Gagnon, J. H. (1989). Prevalence and patterns of same gender sexual contact among men. Science, 243, 338–348.

Field, K. (2006a, June 2). Resident hopes: Illegal immigrants at American colleges carry big dreams into an uncertain future. Chronicle of Higher Education, 52 (39), A30.

Field, K. (2006b, June 23). Measure reinforces immigrant-tuition law. Chronicle of Higher Education, 52 (42), A26.

Foster, A.L. (2001, January 26). Colleges focus on making web sites work for people with disabilities. Chronicle of Higher Education, 47 (21), A30.

Gallagher, R. P. (2006). National Survey of Counseling Center Directors. (Monograph Series no. 8P.) Pittsburgh: International Association of Counseling Services.

Geiger, R. (1992). The historical matrix of American higher education. History of Higher Education Annual, 12, 7–28.

Gonsierek, J. (1993). Foreword. In G. M. Herek & B. Greene (Eds.), Lesbian and gay psychology: Theory, research and clinical applications. Psychological perspectives on lesbian and gay issues, Volume 1 (vii-ix). Thousand Oaks, CA: Sage.

Hebel, S. (2006, January 6). California law suit opposes immigrant-tuition law. Chronicle of Higher Education, 52 (18), A39.

Hebel, S. (2007, June 1). Senate plan offers help to illegal aliens. Chronicle of Higher Education, 53 (39), 20.

Higher Education Research Institute. (2004). The spiritual life of college students: A national study of college students' search for meaning and purpose. Los Angeles: Higher Education Research Institute at University of California, Los Angeles.

How not to be a helicopter parent. (n.d.). Retrieved September 14, 2007, from http://www.collegeboard.com/parents/plan/getting-ready/50129.html

Hurtado, S., & Pryor, J. H. (2006, April). Looking at the past, shaping the future: Getting to know our students for the past 40 years. Presented at the annual meeting of the National Association of Student Personnel Administrators and the American College Personnel Association, Orlando, FL.

Jenkins, D., & Boswell, K. (2002). State policies on community college remedial education: Findings from a national survey. Denver: Center for Community College Policy.

Junco, R. (2005). Technology and today's first-year students. In M. L. Upcraft, J. N. Gardner, & B. O. Barefoot (Eds.), Challenging and supporting the first-year student: A handbook of improving the first year of college. (pp. 221–38). San Francisco: Jossey-Bass.

Junco, R., & Mastrodicasa, J. (2007). Connecting to the Net generation: What higher education professionals need to know about today's college students. Washington, DC: National Association of Student Personnel Administrators.

Keller, J. (2007, April 13). State legislatures debate tuition for illegal immigrants. Chronicle of Higher Education, 53 (32), A28.

Kuh, G. D. (2007, Winter). What student engagement data tell us about college readiness. Peer Review, 4–8.

Laumann, E. O., Gagnon, J. H., Michael, R. T., & Michaels, S. (1994). The social organization of sexuality: Sexual practice in the United States. Chicago: University of Chicago Press.

Lipka, S. (2005, December 16). State legislators as co-pilots: Some "helicopter parents" play politics to protect their children's interests on campus. Chronicle of Higher Education, 57 (17), A22.

McCabe, D., & Trevino, L. (1997). Individual and contextual influences on academic dishonesty: A multi-campus investigation. Research in Higher Education, 38, 379–396.

McCabe, D. L., Trevino, L. K., & Butterfield, K. D. (2001). Cheating in academic institutions: A decade of research. Ethics and Behavior, 11, 219–232.

McCarthy, M. M., & Kuh, G. D. (2006). Are students ready for college? What student engagement data say. Phi Delta Kappan, 87, 664–669.

Meilman, P.W., & Presley, C.A. (2005). The first-year experience and alcohol use. In M. L. Upcraft, G. N. Gardner, & B. O. Barefoot (Eds.), Challenging and supporting the first-year student: A handbook of improving the first year of college. (pp. 445–466). San Francisco: Jossey-Bass.

Merriam-Webster (2007). Retrieved September 14, 2007, from http://www.m-w.com/dictionary/Disability

Morgan, C., & Cotton, S.R. (2003). The relationship between Internet activities and learning. Research in Higher Education, 42 (1), 87–102.

National Center for Education Statistics. (1999). Students with disabilities in post-secondary education: A profile of preparation, participation, and outcomes. Washington, DC: Department of Education.

National Center for Education Statistics. (2002). Nontraditional graduates: Digest of educational statistics. Washington, DC: Department of Education.

National Center for Education Statistics. (2004). Digest of educational statistics. Washington, DC: Department of Education.

National Center for Education Statistics. (2005). Digest of educational statistics: 2005. Washington, DC: Department of Education. Retrieved September 14, 2007, from http://nces.ed.gov/programs/digest/d05/tables/dt05_126.asp

National Survey of Student Engagement (NSSE). (2006). Engaged learning: Fostering success for all students. Bloomington, IN: Indiana University Center for Postsecondary Research.

O'Hanlon, C. (2007). If you can't beat 'em, join 'em. Technical Horizons in Education, 42 (44), 39–40.

Pascarella, E. T., & Terenzini, P. T. (2005). How college affects students: Volume 2, a third decade of research. San Francisco: Jossey-Bass.

Rab, S. (2007). Understanding the "swirling" undergraduate attendance pattern: The role of student background characteristics and college behaviors. Presented at the annual meeting of the American Sociological Association, Atlanta, GA.

Rankin, S. (2003). Campus climate for sexual minorities: A national perspective. New York: National Gay and Lesbian Task Force Policy Institute.

Rankin, S., & Beemyn, B. (2008). The lives of transgender people. New York: Columbia Press.

Roberts-Dobie, S., & Donatelle, R. J. (2007). School counselors and self-injury. Journal of School Health, 77 (5), 257–264.

Ross, V. (2004). Depression, anxiety, and alcohol or other drug use among college students. Newton, MA: The Higher Education Center for Alcohol and Other Drug Prevention.

Seifert, T. A., Pascarella, E. T., Colangelo, N., & Assouline, S. (2007). The effect of honors program participation on experiences of good practices and learning outcomes. Journal of College Student Development, 48 (1), 57–74.

Silva, T., Calahan, M., & Lacireno-Paquet, N. (1998). Adult education participation decisions and barriers. Review of conceptual frameworks and empirical studies. Washington, DC: Department of Education.

Smith Bailey, D. (2003). "Swirling" changes to the traditional path. Monitor on Psychology, 34, 36–38.

Storch, E., & Storch, J. (2002). Fraternities, sororities and academic dishonesty. College Student Journal, 36, 247–253.

Tang, S., & Zuo, Z. (1997). Profile of college examination cheaters. College Student Journal, 31, 340–347.

The Residential Learning Communities International Clearinghouse. (2006). Retrieved November 4, 2007, from http://pcc.bgsu.edu/rlcch/index.php

Tibbetts, S. (1999). Differences between men and women regarding decisions to commit test cheating. Research in Higher Education, 40, 323–341.

U.S. Census Bureau. (2001). Overview of race and Hispanic origin 2000: Census 2000 Brief. Retrieved October 27, 2007, from http://www.census .gov/prod/2001pubs/c2kbr01–1.pdf

U.S. PIRG. (2006). Paying back, not giving back: Student debt's negative impact on public service career opportunities. Retrieved October 27, 2007, from http://www .pirg.org/highered/payingback.pdf

UCLA. (2002). Mental health association facts. Retrieved November 11, 2007, from http://www.mentalhealthconnection.org/facts_stats.php

White, W. (2005, December 16). Students, parents, colleges: Drawing the lines. Chronicle of Higher Education, 52 (17), B16.

Whitley, B. (1998). Factors associated with cheating among college students. Research in Higher Education, 39, 235–274.

Wilson, A. (1996). How we find ourselves: Identity development and two-spirit people. Harvard Educational Review, 66 (2), 303–317.

Wilson, G. T., Grilo, C. M., & Vitousek, K. M. (2007). Psychological treatment of eating disorders. American Psychologist, 62 (3), 199–216.

Wilson, S. B., Mason, T. W., & Ewing, M. J. M. (1997). Evaluating the impact of receiving university-based counseling services on student retention. Journal of Counseling Psychology, 44 (3), 315–320.

Winston, Jr., R. B. (1996). Counseling and advising. In S. R. Komives, D. B. Woodard, Jr., & Associates (Eds.). Student services: A handbook for the profession (3rd ed., pp. 335–360). San Francisco: Jossey-Bass.

Wood, P. K., Sher, K. J., & Rutledge, P. C. (2007). College student alcohol consumption, day of the week, and class schedule. Alcoholism: Clinical and Experimental Research, 31 (7), 1195–1207.

Woodard, D. B., Love, P., & Komives, S. R. (2000). Leadership and management issues for a new century. San Francisco: Jossey-Bass.

Zeman, N. (1991, September 9). Buzzwords. Newsweek, 9.

CHAPTER NINE

Moving into College

Mary Stuart Hunter and Leah Kendall

A s students have changed in recent decades, so has the role of academic advisors. Prior to the late 1800s, students and faculty with widely varying interests and motivations coexisted in academic settings. According to Kuhn in Chapter one, one early attempt at academic advising took place at Johns Hopkins University in 1889. This effort to connect students and faculty is considered by some to be the birth of academic advising. Over the intervening years, academic advising has evolved into a well-developed and highly valued aspect of undergraduate education. As the advising profession developed, staff advisors were hired, and one of their many important roles was to assist students between the times of their admissions acceptance to an institution and their eventual matriculation and enrollment. A typical advisor might have spent an hour with a student helping him or her line up a class schedule and select a major. There was no demand for advisors to be a driving force in the student's learning outside of the classroom. Thankfully, their roles have changed.

In a review of the literature, Appleby (2001) notes that the role of advising is defined as a developmental process: "The facilitation of learning is the duty of both teachers and advisers and . . . both of these roles involve working with students to improve their problem-solving and decision-making skills"(p. 1). O'Banion's ground-breaking proposal in 1972 for an integrated approach to academic advising took center stage. He claimed the role of the academic advisor was to help students begin the journey of reaching their highest potential by first identifying their programs of study. As part of this process, O'Banion (1972) identified five hierarchical steps to the advising process: (a) exploration of life goals, (b) exploration of vocational goals, (c) program choice, (d) course choice, and (e) scheduling options.

The idea that developmental advising is essentially a form of teaching emerged, and Kramer (1983) claimed that the quality of education a student receives is directly related to the student's involvement with his or her academic experience. For the relationship between an academic advisor and student to be successful, interactions must be student-centered. Advisors must be responsive to student needs and intentional in their efforts to support student growth and development. An important role of the advisor is to encourage self-authorship. Magolda and King (2004) define self-authorship as the "capacity to internally define a coherent belief system and identity that coordinates mutual relations with others" (p. 8). Advisors should work alongside students as they develop cognitive maturity, integrated identity, and mature relationships to become effective citizens (Magolda & King, 2004). In doing so, students are encouraged to participate in the advising process by asking strong questions to clarify ideas and develop self-identity through the advising process. As stated by Kramer (1983), "a quality shared-advising effort leads to students' persistence to gradation, motivation to succeed in college, involvement in the institution, interaction with faculty, satisfaction with college, academic and career connections, personal and academic success, and cognitive development"(p. 85). The role of the advisor now includes efforts to facilitate discussions, which include students' thought patterns, relationships with their environment and peers, self-awareness, critical-thinking and decision-making skills, and evaluation techniques (Darling and Woodside, 2007).

Effective academic advising is critical as students prepare to establish themselves as college students. The experiences students encounter during the advising process and their reactions to these experiences follow a predictable pattern. Understanding these predictable stages can assist advisors as they work with students to plan developmentally effective interventions, programs, and initiatives. To ensure the most successful advising relationship possible, advisors must also understand the characteristics and the developmental needs of today's diverse college populations—millennial students, returning adult students, international students, transfer students, students with disabilities, and students with mental health concerns. This chapter will: (a) bring to light the characteristics and predictable experiences of students as they move into college, (b) address specific characteristics and needs of diverse populations, and (c) offer suggestions for strategies that advisors can use in their important work with first-year students and their parents.

THE NEW STUDENT EXPERIENCE

Preenrollment

The official letter of acceptance has been mailed. For some students, bags are packed and caravans are headed to residence halls where housing check-in staff awaits. For others, the morning commute to school takes a different direction, and while streets are familiar, new routines create a new anxiety.

For additional students, plane tickets have been purchased and families are saying their final goodbyes. For still other students, discussions are held with children about the fact that mom or dad will be going back to school and doing homework just like them. Regardless of the exact scenario, every student experiences strong emotions, which may include anxiety, nervousness, eagerness, and fear. They are on the brink of moving into college. At no time in a new college student's experience are connections with an academic advisor more significant and imperative than before and during the first semester. Apprehensive of the experience ahead, students arrive on campus vulnerable, impressionable, and in need of a guide. By recognizing this susceptible time, advisors can channel students' mixed emotions toward a positive advising and mentoring relationship and toward a journey of personal self-discovery and development.

Advisors have a tremendous opportunity during the pre-enrollment phase to positively influence students, so meeting the needs of students at this time is especially important. Kramer (2000) identified a taxonomy of student services and identified themes by students' academic levels. He suggested that, during the pre-enrollment phase, students acquire expectations and spend time preparing for their early college experiences and that they concentrate on the following developmental tasks: (a) preparing for entry into an academic discipline; (b) becoming familiar with college requirements, course contents, and course terminology; (c) completing initial registration; (d) learning to adjust to the class schedule before the semester begins; and (e) learning about financial aid and scholarship options. These educational tasks have implications for academic advisors as they plan their communications, interventions, programs, and interactions with students moving into college.

It is imperative that advisors know as much as possible about incoming students as they prepare to work with them in an advising relationship. Researchers recognize that a "student's pre-enrollment characteristics such as their cultural background, prior academic experience, gender, and socioeconomic status may have a greater impact on college success than the campus environment and the educational experience" (Black, 2007, p. 87).

TRANSITION AND ESTABLISHMENT

Early in their time on campus, students experience new freedoms, set new behavior patterns and routines, and face the academic challenges of college. As traditional students settle in, the newness of college wears off, and they begin to balance newly found freedoms with the responsibilities of their lives as college students (Hunter and Gahagan, 2003). For nontraditional students, new routines can create increased anxiety and added stress to their already hectic schedules. Advisors have the opportunity to engage students in a positive advising program and to help students know how to take the initial steps toward academic success. The advisor's role is an essential one during this period. In these first few weeks on campus, it is important for advisors to help students deconstruct their behavior as it relates to academic success. What worked in high school may not work at the collegiate level. It is therefore critical for advisors to encourage students to reassess study skills, time management and priorities, and other academic success components during these initial weeks.

It is during this transition and establishment phase that peer advising can be especially powerful. As new college students look to older and more experienced students for guidance and role-modeling, structuring a process for peer advising to occur can be helpful to advisors and new students alike. Such mentoring efforts can take place in a variety of settings, including the advising office, first-year seminars, residence halls, and existing programs for commuter students. When face-to-face peer education is not possible or feasible, testimonials, materials written or produced by upper-level students, electronic resources that are attractive to students, and blogs can be considered as possible interventions.

Attention to these transition issues through the advising process can have significant influence on student behavior and success if harnessed at developmentally appropriate times. If the opportunity to critically assess student habits and skills is missed, it is often more difficult for students to develop effective student success habits later when their behavior patterns are firmly set.

TODAY'S STUDENTS

Students change as society changes. The "traditional" student no longer exists. The latest picture of the American college setting today may look something like this: three students (two women, one man) sitting in a wireless coffee shop on campus. One Latina student is using her PDA to research gay marriage on the online encyclopedia, Wikipedia, for a sociology paper due in one hour. The male student, who is Asian American, sits next to her, shuffling through the latest music downloads on his iPod, trying to drown out the student behind him who is talking to her teenage son on her cell phone.

Today's students have specific characteristics and needs that present to advisors and educators unique challenges and opportunities. Understanding these needs can inform better academic advising practice. Advisors must test assumptions they make about their students. For example, are students enrolled at only one campus? Are they moving from campus to campus from semester to semester? More students today are "swirling" than ever before, and such mobile behaviors have an impact on academic advising. Being familiar with the data on specific populations is important, but ultimately, it is key for advisors to make an extra effort to understand the values, goals, and priorities of each individual student especially as they move into to college.

Millennial Students

Born between 1977 and 1997, this generation has always had computers and cell phones in their world. A generation familiar with hyperlinks and on-demand options, millennials have short attention spans and insist on quick answers to academic questions (Rockler-Gladen, 2006). They live in a culture of immediacy, expecting rapid turnaround on admissions decisions, financial aid awards, transfer credit evaluations, and advising assignments (Black, 2007). And, according to the National Center for Education Statistics (2006), millennial students make up nearly 56 percent of total fall enrollment in degree-granting institutions.

According to the Cooperative Institutional Research Program data (Institutional Assessment and Compliance, 2007), incoming students today are the most financially well-off cohort in the past thirty-five years, with median family incomes 60 percent above the national average. When asked about their priorities, "being well-off" ranked second only to raising a family, while "helping others" was ranked third (U.S. Department of Education, 2007). The priorities of students today have implications for academic advisors as they work with students. Again, advisors must test assumptions made about today's students. Staying current with research about students and being aware of campus-specific data on students is imperative for effective advising, especially during the first year.

Finally, millennial students, influenced by the tragic events of 9/11, have little trust in government or other authority figures (Rockler-Gladen, 2006). As a result, advisors may be more challenged in attempting to develop mentoring relationships with millennial students than with earlier generations of students. But overcoming the challenge is a necessity for cultivating an optimal advising relationship.

Returning Adult Students

Greater numbers of adults are seeking college degrees than in years past. In light of recent activity with the Iraq war, many campuses are seeing returning veterans as a new micropopulation. These adult students bring nontraditional characteristics—part-time enrollment, full-time employment, financial independence, and parental responsibilities—and create needs and priorities that differ from traditional students (Council for Adult and Experiential Learning, 2000).

According to the National Digest of Education Statistics (2007), 18.9 percent of students are twenty-four years or older, 36.9 percent of undergraduate students are older than twenty-four years old. Most students in this group are born between 1965 and 1980 and are commonly referred to as Generation X. They have different needs and expectations from their millennial counterparts. Many times, adult students are in the midst of personal transitions: changing careers, seeking job security, facing life challenges such as divorce, loss of a loved one, or an empty nest (Skorupa, 2002; Black, 2007). Some students in this phase of life are eager to share experiences with an advisor and readily accept guidance. Others, however, view pre-enrollment advising as a nuisance, feeling as though they have more pressing demands on their time.

When engaging adult students, it is important to remember that many of them view education as a service they have purchased. They bring with them significant work experience and demand prompt and reliable service (Lindsey, 2003). Since these students usually have multiple demands on their time, they want their orientation and advising to be accomplished as efficiently as possible.

Most adults are commuting students and spend a limited amount of time on campus, making face-to-face contact with academic advisors difficult (Kuh, 2007). Establishing trust and mutual levels of respect and providing a less formal environment are all ways for advisors to establish positive relationships with adult students. From there, advisors must find creative ways to engage students in their limited time on campus.

The Council for Adult and Experiential Learning (2000), in its report "Educational Principles That Work for Adults Who Work," suggests that academic advisors should help adult learners: (a) overcome barriers of time, place, and tradition; (b) create lifelong access; (c) address their career and life goals; (d) assess skills acquired through the curriculum and experience; (e) enhance their capabilities to be self-directed learners; (f) access information technology to enhance the learning [advising] experience; and (g) engage in strategic relationships and collaborations with employers and other organizations (Skorupa, 2002).

Most adult students were raised in a learning environment in which "the authority figure took responsibility for nearly every aspect of the process, what was done, how it was done, and how it was evaluated" (Taylor, Marienau, & Fiddler, 2000, p. 1). While this environment is the one with which they are most familiar, most adult students want the freedom to learn in a cooperative and interactive environment (Skorupa, 2002).

International Students

In the past decade, the number of international students attending colleges and universities in the United States has increased significantly. In 2005, an estimated 600,000 international students studied in American institutions (Kantrowitz, 2007). Students arrive excited about their new opportunities and expect to enjoy an enriching educational experience. Unfortunately, many institutions do not adequately plan for the special needs of international students. It is often assumed that they will be similar to American students, when, in reality, they have special and increased transition needs, especially as they adjust to a new academic culture.

According to Lamont (2005), "International students are actively recruited—indeed enticed—to study in America. However, agencies and institutions sometimes fail to study the long-term implications of their efforts" (p. 1). As a result, students find themselves on the doorsteps of institutions ill equipped to handle their often vulnerable situations.

Understandably, one of the most pressing demands on academic advisors today, especially as they work with international students, is the need to develop multicultural competency skills. Before we can welcome international students to American institutions, we must first prepare for their arrival. In a review of the literature, Priest and McPhee (2000) state that international students present an array of issues, including:

- Clashes between international students' native cultures and the culture of the United States
- Feelings of homesickness and alienation

- Legal and financial concerns of negotiating contractual obligations (i.e., housing rental leases or automobile purchase agreements)
- Language communication difficulties

Advisors must work with academic partners in international programs to identify and understand the specific needs of different ethnic groups. Once these needs are identified, advisors should engage international students prior to enrollment by sending overview materials regarding the advising process long before they board the plane. When international students arrive on campus, advisors must immediately reach out to them. Advisors must clearly communicate their role, as "many international students are not accustomed to planning their own courses of study and are not familiar with the practice of academic advising" (Upcraft & Stephens, 2000, p. 76). Often, offering a listening ear or serving as a referral to other campus resources may be just what a student needs to find their niche.

During their initial days on campus, international students have many of the same first-day experiences as their American counterparts—dining in a cafeteria, walking to and from class, attending sporting events, and talking to friends—experiences they have had before, but now in a different, unfamiliar culture. In this time of transition, students seek even the slightest level of familiarity or comfort. According to Priest and McPhee (2000), "it is not unusual for international students to seek out their academic advisor 'just to talk' because that is the person to whom they feel the closest" (p. 113).

Advisors must be cognizant of the biases, attitudes, and values they bring to the advisor-advisee relationship. "A crucial aspect of advisor knowledge," Lamont (2005) suggests "is the extent to which advisors are able to understand advisees rather than attempt to force them into an over-generalized advising paradigm" (p. 112). Advisors who embrace human and cultural diversity will better serve students from diverse cultures. (See Chapter Thirteen for more on international students.)

Transfer Students

Research suggests that transfer students may be at risk in terms of adjustment, performance, and retention (Brit & Hirt, 1999; Glass & Harrington, 2002; Hoyt, 1999; McCormick, 2003; Woosley, 2005). While many transfer students believe they already know what to expect, they actually may experience "transfer shock." Hills (1965) coined the term *transfer shock* to refer to the temporary dip in grade point average during the first or second semester at the new institution. Advisors must recognize this shock and develop ways to help transfer students in their transition.

An important first step in embracing transfer students "involves taking time to assess a student's prior non-academic experiences" (Holaday, 2005, p. 1). When discussing the needs of transfer students, advisors often forget to look beyond their course work. While course work is at the core of the transfer experience, advisors must look at the contrasts between the student's prior institution and his or her new one. In most cases, students will experience significant differences in the areas of institutional environment, college policies and procedures advising structures, terminology, and faculty and academic expectations (Grites, 2004).

Thurmond (2003) suggests that some students make "unplanned transfers" for various reasons—"forced relocation by reason of employment . . . , academic failure at a first choice institution, failed relationships, or other circumstances, including some over which the student has little control" (p. 2). Students who transfer unexpectedly need individual attention and guidance, which is best received through academic advising. Welcome week events, group orientation sessions, and first-year seminar classes designed for this population may or may not attract their interest without intervention from an academic advisor.

Developing key intervention strategies will provide transfer students with their best chance of minimizing transfer shock. One response is a post-orientation program, such as an interest group or for-credit course, specifically designed to help transfer students adapt to their new environment. Many campuses already have post-orientation programs that help first-year students forge connections to their new campus but do not supply these same services to transfer students (Holaday, 2005).

Another strategy is to strengthen articulation agreements. According to Grites (2004), "The real value of articulation agreements has somewhat eroded as a result of recent trends toward legislated statewide mandates, common course numbering systems, and other seemingly well-intended guarantees for transfer students"(p. 1). Most of these well-intended efforts have little value if they are not clearly stated within the student's major academic program of study (Grites, 2004). In the end, clear communication and articulated expectations between university departments better serve the transfer student and both institutions.

As transfer students become increasingly familiar and even dependent on technology resources, academic advisors must use this to their advantage. Grites (2004) suggests using "on-line admissions applications, course equivalency determinations, electronic transcript submission and retrieval, and advance registration capabilities" (p. 1) to readily improve the transfer process. While many of these efforts are ongoing and others have yet to be discovered, academic advisors should maximize institutionally specific opportunities and capabilities to serve transfer students more effectively.

Students with Disabilities

Students with disabilities bring with them additional questions of how the institution will accommodate their unique needs and how these needs will impact their learning and success. In addition to the challenges faced by all students, students with disabilities also face challenges related to limitations created by their disability. The "standard struggles with class schedules, roommates, and sexual and social freedom are complicated by decisions about if or when to use campus counseling services, whether or not to take medication and whether to disclose an illness to friends or professors" (Clemetson, 2006).

According to the Profile of Undergraduates in U.S. Postsecondary Institutions (Horn, Peter, Rooney, & Malizio, 2002), 9 percent of undergraduates report having some type of disability, a significant increase from previous years (Vallandingham, 2007). Epstein (2005) cites a similar report by the American Council on Education, which shows that the number of full-time first-year students with learning disabilities—dyslexia and attention-deficit/hyperactive disorder among the most common—more than doubled to 27,000 in the decade leading up to 2000.

Whether this increase is due to more diagnoses or an actual increase in disabilities is immaterial. Rather, it is imperative that advisors educate themselves about the various types of disabilities. Hemphill (2002) suggests several key ways to do this: (a) become familiar with the difficulties imposed by a particular disability; (b) determine whether the college poses structural, educational, or bureaucratic barriers for a student; (c) learn something about the teaching style of various instructors, and be prepared to enroll students with disabilities accordingly; and (d) develop collaborative relationships with faculty, financial aid, counseling, and other organizations within the college.

Advisors must also understand the provisions for higher education under the Americans with Disabilities Act. They also should know their institution's policies and procedures and be willing to listen to students as they share their unique experiences. Hemphill (2002) suggests that advisors maintain a thorough understanding of the student's educational, personal and career goals, their disability (i.e., limitations, side effects, treatments), the barriers the institution may have inadvertently created, and the resources the college provides that can be used to assist the student in pursuing his or her educational aspirations. Advisors should also establish successful working relationships with their counterparts in disability services.

Students with Mental Health Concerns

For the increasing number of students who arrive on campus with serious mental disorders, the transition to college can be even more challenging. The April 2007 attack at Virginia Tech in which student Cho Seung-Hui, who was later deemed to have a mental illness, killed thirty-two people and then himself in a shooting rampage on campus, has brought new attention to institutional responsibilities in dealing with students with mental illnesses. Academic advisors are in a key position to identify and assist students who exhibit questionable or troubling behaviors. Knowing when and how to intervene is often our greatest obstacle.

College counseling centers across the country report an increased frequency and severity of students' mental health concerns. Two major studies document these observations. At Kansas State University, counseling center staff conducted a retrospective analysis of client problems over thirteen years. The analysis found a significant increase in student psychopathology in fourteen of nineteen areas, including depression, suicidal thoughts, sexual assaults, and personality disorders (Benton, Robertson, Wen-Chih, Newton, & Benton, 2003). Kitzrow (2003) reported a survey showing that from 1996 to 2001, 85 percent of directors of college counseling centers said they saw more severe psychological problems. In addition, the survey respondents described more cases of learning disabilities, self-injury incidents, eating disorders, alcohol and drug use, warnings to third parties, and stalking.

Clearly linked to retention and academic performance, Backels and Wheeler (2001) suggest that mental health issues interfere with college students' success more than ever before. Academic advisors have an increasingly important responsibility to recognize and refer students who face these problems. In a time of such rapid increases in mental health issues, it is important that academic advisors know when and how to report these issues. According to Harper and Peterson (2005), academic advisors should first be aware of the following signals of distress: (a) excessive procrastination, (b) decrease in the quality of work, (c) too frequent office visits (dependency), (d) listlessness, (e) sleeping in class, (f) marked changes in personal hygiene, (g) impaired speech or disjointed thoughts, (h) threats regarding self or others, and (i) marked changes in behavior.

Once advisors recognize signs of distress, they should not directly attempt to provide therapy to students unless they are qualified to do so. Referring students to a campus mental health counselor is the best response. Behavioral intervention teams (including representatives from judicial, counseling, and academic offices) have been designed on many campuses to help campus administrators respond to students' behavior. Communication with your behavioral intervention team, faculty members, or residence life staff about your concerns is encouraged as long as advisors respect a student's privacy and adhere to confidentiality requirements. General comments regarding a student's sudden change in mood, motivation, or behaviors, for example, can be shared with a hall staff member, while specific information about grades cannot be shared because of FERPA (Family Educational Rights and Privacy Act) privacy guidelines (Harper & Peterson, 2005). Keeping a psychiatric disorder under control in an environment often fueled by all-night cram sessions, junk food, and heavy drinking is a challenge for even the most motivated student. In addition, the normal separation that goes along with college requires new roles and boundaries with parents, the people who best know the history and contours of the student's illness (Clemetson, 2006).

As institutions develop standard operating procedures for dealing with such students in the wake of the Virginia Tech tragedy, academic advisors must involve themselves with the institutional responses to policy development and implementation. In addition, advising leadership on campuses should address these topics in comprehensive advisor training programs.

Parents and Families

Traditional-aged millennial students rely heavily on their parents and families for support. In fact, the term, *helicopter parents* has become a common descriptor for these parents because of their tendency to hover over their child's every move during their collegiate experience. Helicopter parents have implications for advisors as well.

Today's traditional-aged college students are not entering the doors of higher education institutions alone. The March 2006 National Survey of College Parent Preparation and Expectations conducted by College Parents of America (CPA,

2006) clearly shows how ignoring parents is not an option. Of the 525 parents surveyed:

- 88 percent expect to go on campus visits
- 85 percent have helped or expect to help their child decide to which schools he or she will apply
- 77 percent expect to be heavily involved in their child's selection of a college
- 69 percent have helped or expect to help draft their child's college applications
- 49 percent have arranged or expect to arrange for a SAT/ACT preparation course or tutoring for their child before the SAT/ACT test

These results send a clear message to advisors across the country: "Recruiting a student really means recruiting a family" (CPA, 2006). As students move into college, advisors must partner with specific offices to come alongside parents as their students develop a new sense of autonomy. Collaborating with offices of admissions, financial aid and scholarships, and new student orientation to send significant and consistent messages to parents can provide academic advisors with vehicles to educate parents about the goals, objectives, and processes of academic advising long before students arrive on campus.

Academic advisors, within FERPA guidelines, can create partnerships with parents, including them in their student's personal, social, and academic development. Through these partnerships, parents encourage students to discuss their experiences with their advisors and take advantage of campus resources. Stack (2003) offers the following advice when communicating with parents: (a) provide parents (whether in person or by mail) written information they can refer to when curious about academic advising services, (b) be sympathetic but not apologetic—students must take responsibility for their actions, (c) clearly outline the student's options, (d) do not get in the middle of family situations, and (e) remember that parents always have their children's best interests at heart.

As part of their commitment to parents, advisors should partner with their campus parents programs office, if available. These offices, designed to create a positive relationship between parents, students, and the institution, can provide many unique outlets for advisors to be heard. Parent program offices frequently publish handbooks, calendars, and newsletters and sponsor parents' weekends and other events during welcome week activities. Such resources can be helpful to advisors and can provide opportunities to communicate with parents concerning advising expectations, processes, and policies.

CONCLUSION

Moving into college—the months from acceptance through the end of the first year—is a time of significant transition for new students. Learning the culture of higher education and a particular institution can be a challenge for students of all backgrounds, abilities, and interests. Academic advisors can play a critical role as students successfully assimilate into the new environment and culture. But to do so, they must first understand students of today and their experiences during the period of transition and then explore options available within the advising relationship for helping new students succeed.

Understanding students is not a simple task that is accomplished early in a career in the way that a credential or degree is attained. Understanding students is an ongoing process that continues throughout an entire advising career. Students change as our society changes. Advances in the field of academic advising encourage institutional leaders and advising professionals to enhance their skill development and knowledge acquisition, and to expand advising services to better meet the needs of new students. Doing so will better serve both students and institutions. There are no students for whom this is more important than for those who are moving into college.

References

Appleby, D. (2001). The teaching-advising connection. In *The Mentor.* Center for Excellence in Academic Advising. Retrieved September 7, 2007, from http://www .psu.edu/dus/mentor

Backels, K., & Wheeler I. (2001). Faculty perceptions of mental health issues among college students. *Journal of College Student Development, 42* (2), 173–176.

Benton, S. A., Robertson, J. M., Wen-Chih, T., Newton, F. B., & Benton, S. L. (2003). Changes in counseling center client problems across 13 years. *Professional Psychology: Research and Practice, 34* (1), 66–72.

Black, J. (2007). Advising first-year students before enrollment. In M. S. Hunter, B. McCalla-Wriggins, & E. R. White (Eds.), *Academic advising: New insights for teaching and learning in the first year* (Monograph No. 46 [National Resource Center]; Monograph 14 [National Academic Advising Association]; pp. 87–97). Columbia: University of South Carolina, National Resource Center for the First-Year Experience and Students in Transition.

Britt, L. W., & Hirt, J. B. (1999). Student experiences and institutional practices affecting spring semester transfer students. *NASPA Journal, 36,* 198–209.

Clemetson, L. (2006, December 6). Troubled children: Off to college alone, shadowed by mental illness. *New York Times.* Retrieved March 26, 2008, from http://www.nytimes.com/2006/12/08/health/08Kids.html?ex = 1323234000&en = 0ed888f81e5aa10e&ei = 5088&partner = rssnyt&emc = rss

College Parents of America (CPA). (2006). National survey shows strong parent-student connection in college preparation, search and selection activity. Retrieved September 7, 2007, from http://www.collegeparents.org/cpa/about-press .html?n = 1310

Council for Adult and Experiential Learning. (2000). Serving adult learners in higher education: Principles of effectiveness. In K. Skorupa (Ed.) *Adult learners as consumers.* Chicago: Council for Adult and Experiential Learning. http://www.acel.org

Darling, R., & Woodside, M. (2007). The academic advisor as teacher: First-year transitions. In M. S. Hunter, B. McCalla-Wriggins, & E. R. While (Eds.), *Academic advising: New insights for teaching and learning in the first year* (Monograph No. 46 [National Resource Center]; Monograph No. 14 [National Academic Advising

Association]; (pp. 5–17). Columbia: University of South Carolina, National Resource Center for The First-Year Experience and Students in Transition.

Epstein, D. (2005). Reaching students with learning disabilties. *Inside Higher Education News.* Retrieved September 7, 2007, from http://insidehighered .com/news/2005/10/25/landmark

Glass, J. C., & Harrington, A. R. (2002). Academic performance of community college transfer student and "native" students at a large state university. *Journal of Research and Practice, 26,* 415–430.

Grites, T. (2004) Advising transfer students: Issues and strategies from academic advising today. *Quarterly Newsletter, 27* (3). NACADA Clearinghouse of Academic Advising Resources Web site. Retrieved September 6, 2007, from http://www .nacada.ksu.edu/AAT/NW27_3.htm#16

Harper, R., & Peterson, M. (2005). Mental health issues and college students. NACADA Clearinghouse of Academic Advising Resources. Retrieved August 20, 2007, http:// www.nacada.ksu.edu/Clearinghouse/AdvisingIssues/Mental-Health.htm

Hemphill, L. L. (2002). Advising students with disabilities. *The Academic Advising News, 25* (3). NACADA Clearinghouse of Academic Advising Resources Web site. Retrieved August 30, 2007, from http://www.nacada.ksu.edu/Clearinghouse/ AdvisingIssues/disability.htm

Hills, J. (1965) Transfer shock: The academic performance of the transfer student. *The Journal of Experimental Education, 33*(3). (ERIC Document Reproduction Service No. ED 010 740.)

Holaday, T. (2005). Diversity in transfer. *Advising Today—Quarterly Newsletter, 28* (1). *NACADA Clearinghouse of Academic Advising Resources* Web site. Retrieved September 5, 2007, from http://www.nacada.ksu.edu/AAT/NW28_1.htm#5

Horn, L., Peter, K., Rooney, K., & Malizio, A. (2002). *Profile of undergraduates in U.S. postsecondary institutions: 1999–2000.* (NCES2002–168.) Washington, DC: Government Printing Office.

Hoyt, J. E. (1999). Promoting student transfer success: Curriculum evaluation and student academic preparation. *Journal of Applied Research in the Community College, 6* (2), 73–79.

Hunter, M.S., & Gahagan, J. (2003) It takes a year: The transition to college doesn't happen in just a few weeks. *About Campus, 8*(4), 31–32.

Institutional Assessment and Compliance (2007). *CIRP data.* University of South Carolina. Retrieved September 12, 2007, http://www.ipr.sc.edu

Kantrowitz, M. (2007). College admissions: Number of international students. FinAid Page. Retrieved September 6, 2007, from http://www.edupass.org/admissions/ numstud.phtml

Kitzrow, M. A. (2003). The mental health needs of today's college students: Challenges and recommendations. *NASPA Journal, 41* (1), 165–179.

Kramer, G. (2000). Advising students at different educational Levels. In V. N. Gordon, W. R. Habley, et al. (Eds.), *Academic advising: A comprehensive handbook* (pp. 84–104). San Francisco: Jossey-Bass.

Kramer, H. C. (1983). Advising: Implications for faculty development. *National Academic Advising Association Journal, 3,* 25–31.

Kuh, G. (2007). How to help students achieve. *The Chronicle Review, 53* (41), B12. http://chronicle.com. Retrieved September 5, 2007, from pallas2.tcl.sc.edu/weekly/v53/i41/41b01201.htm

Lamont, B. J. (2005). East meets west—Bridging the academic advising divide. NACADA Clearinghouse of Academic Advising Resources Web site. Retrieved August 31, 2007, from http://www.nacada.ksu.edu/Clearinghouse/AdvisingIssues/East-Meets-West.htm

Lindsey, P. (2003). Needs and expectations of Gen-Xers. In J. Black (Ed.), *Gen-Xers return to college: Enrollment strategies for a maturing population* (pp. 53–67). Washington, DC: American Association of Collegiate Registrars and Admissions Officers.

Magolda, B., & King, P. (2004). *Learning partnerships: Theory and models of practice to educate for self-authorship.* Sterling, VA: Stylus.

McCormick, A. C. (2003). Swirling and double-dipping: New patterns of student attendance and their implications for higher education. *New Directions for Higher Education, 121,* 13–24.

National Center for Education Statistics. (2006). Enrollment in postsecondary education, by student level, type of institution, age, and major field of study: 2003–2004. Table 216. http://nces.ed.gov/programs/digest/d06/tables/dt06_216.asp. Retrieved September 12, 2007.

National Digest of Education Statistics. (2007). Percentage of population 3 to 34 years old enrolled in school, by age group: Selected years, 1940 through 2006. National Center for Educational Statistics Web site. Retrieved March 26, 2008, from http://nces.ed.gov/programs/digest/d07/tables.xls/tabn007.xls

O'Banion, T. (1972). An academic advising model. *Junior College Journal, 42* (6), 62–69.

Priest, R., & McPhee, S. A. (2000). Advising multicultural students: The reality of diversity. In V. N. Gordon, W. R. Habley, et al. (Eds.). *Academic advising: A comprehensive handbook* (pp. 105–115). San Francisco: Jossey-Bass.

Rockler-Gladen, N. (2006). Generation Y college students: Who are these young, cynical down-to-business college students who inhabit today's college campuses? Suite 101. Retrieved September 5, 2007, from http://college university.suite101.com

Skorupa, K. (2002, December). Adult learners as consumers. *Academic Advising News, 25*(3). Retrieved March 17, 2008, from http://www.nacada.ksu.edu/Clearinghouse/AdvisingIssues/adultlearners.htm

Stack, C. (2003). Talking with the parents of advisees. *The Mentor: An Academic Advising Journal.* Retrieved February 28, 2005, from http://www.psu.edu/dus/mentor/030714cs.htm

Taylor, K., Marienau, C., & Fiddler, M. (2000). *Developing adult learners.* San Francisco: Jossey-Bass.

Thurmond, K. (2003). Transfer shock: Why is a term forty years old still relevant? NACADA Clearinghouse of Academic Advising Resources Web site. Retrieved September 7, 2007, from http://www.nacada.ksu.edu/Clearinghouse/AdvisingIssues/Transfer-Shock.htm

U.S. Department of Education. (2007). Six-year graduation rates of 1999–2000 freshmen at 4-year institutions. *The Chronicle of Higher Education Online Almanac.*

Retrieved September 7, 2007, from http://chronicle.com.pallas2.tcl.sc.edu/weekly/almanac/2007/nation/0101404.htm

U.S. Department of Education, National Center for Education Statistics. (2006). *Digest of education statistics, 2005* (NCES 2006–030), Table 205. Washington, DC: Department of Education.

Upcraft, M. L., & Stephens, P. S. (2000). Academic advising and today's changing students. In V. N. Gordon, W. R. Habley, et al. (Eds.), *Academic advising: A comprehensive handbook* (pp. 73–82). San Francisco: Jossey-Bass.

Vallandingham, D. (2007). Advising first-year students with disabilities. In M. S. Hunter, B. McCalla-Wriggins, & E. R. White (Eds.), *Academic advising: New insights for teaching and learning in the first year* (Monograph No. 46 [National Resource Center]; Monograph 14 [National Academic Advising Association]; pp.157–172). Columbia: University of South Carolina, National Resource Center for the First-Year Experience and Students in Transition.

Woosley, S. (2005). Making a successful transfer: Transfer student expectations and experiences. the National Resource Center for the First Year Experience and Students in Transition Web Site. Retrieved September 5, 2007, from http://www.sc.edu/fye/resources/assessment/newessay/author/woosley.html

CHAPTER TEN

Moving through College

George E. Steele and Melinda L. McDonald

The college years are a time of significant change for students enrolled in institutions of higher education. Some of these students have charted a realistic plan from matriculation to graduation and are able to glide smoothly and successfully through the college experience. Other students face hurdles along the way that impede progress in attaining academic and career goals. Whether a student sails smoothly through college or has a rocky experience, each will encounter transitions along the way that provide opportunities for personal growth and learning.

Laanan (2006) states, "Understanding students in transition is not an easy task. It requires that we have an understanding of what students bring to the college experience; that is, prior academic preparation or training, life experiences, and cultural experiences" (p. 2). Spending time getting to know our students not only in terms of their academic and career interests, but also in terms of their backgrounds and personal experiences is a key component to working with students as they move through the college experience. This task, however, becomes increasingly challenging as the college student population continues to grow in size and in diversity. Currently there are close to fifteen million students enrolled in two-year and four-year colleges and universities in the United States alone. By 2015, this number is projected to be over sixteen million (Chronicle of Higher Education, 2007). Students who enroll in higher educational institutions are diverse in background (race, religion, socioeconomic origin, gender, gender identity, sexual orientation, age, generation, students with disabilities, and international students) and situation (full- or part-time enrollment, working, different degree objectives, residential or commuter, intermittent or transfer students, students with multiple enrollments, type of institution, and online student) (El-Khawas, 2003). Advising a diverse population of students as they move through college and face multiple transitions requires an understanding of the transition process and a framework for conceptualizing how advisors can help students experience change.

In this chapter we will describe the types of transitions (Schlossberg, 1989) that undecided, major-changing, and underprepared students may encounter during the college years. In addition, we will use Kuhn, Gordon, and Webber's (2006) advising-counseling responsibility continuum as a way for advisors to structure the advising process with these students. A list of triggers for determining the need for advising and/or counseling services is included for each population.

TYPES OF TRANSITIONS

In the first section of Schlossberg's three-part model for understanding individuals in transition (1989), she describes three types of transitions: anticipated transitions, unanticipated transitions, and non-event transitions (Schlossberg, 1989). Anticipated transitions are expected, predictable life events that may include choosing a major, graduating from college, and securing a job upon graduation. Since these events are common for most individuals and occur at similar times in the life span, most individuals move through these transitions with little to moderate levels of stress. Unanticipated transitions are unexpected events and are not tied to a particular time frame. Examples of unanticipated transitions are an untimely death of a close friend, parents' divorce, or winning the lottery. Because of the unpredictable nature of these events, these types of transitions can be highly stressful or, at the extreme, result in crisis. Non-event transitions are those events that were expected but did not occur. A dream of being a doctor dashed because of poor performance on the MCAT, membership in a fraternity or sorority that never occurred, and the high school superstar who could not compete at the college level are all non-event transitions. Similar to unanticipated transitions, non-event transitions often result in anxiety for individuals who are not able to accomplish their desired goals. In addition, some individuals experience loss when the one thing they have set their sights on does not happen. Students who are not able to perform well in pre-medicine course work and who come from families in which there is a long line of physicians may feel a sense of loss in not being able to carry on the family tradition.

The concepts of relativity, context, and impact must also be taken into consideration when working with individuals in transition (Schlossberg, Waters, & Goodman, 1995). *Relativity* refers to how each individual interprets or perceives the change. Depending on the individual, the same change could be seen as positive, negative, or neutral. For some students, the process of changing majors may result in relief and an opportunity to take classes that they enjoy and in which they excel, while others may feel uncertain about the change and that they are settling for something "less." Advisors need to carefully assess the meaning that students attach to changes and to keep in mind that the same events will have different meanings for different students. The *context of the event* refers to the relationship that the individual has to the event or non-event. The context could be personal or interpersonal, it could start with the individual or with another person, or it could involve the public or the community. Perhaps most important is the type of impact the event has on the individual. After a parent has been diagnosed with cancer, is the student able to continue attending classes and go about her day-to-day activities, or has the event had a significant impact, causing her to withdraw from school?

THE ADVISING-COUNSELING CONTINUUM OF RESPONSIBILITIES

Challenging and supporting students through their transitions as they pursue academic success is the nature of the work all advisors do. As Kuhn, Gordon, and Webber (2006) observed, "Advisors are the institutional front line for such support" (p. 26). Not all full-time advisors, faculty advisors, and administrators, or for that matter students and parents, agree as to what that level of support should be. These authors provide greater insight into this issue by defining, on a continuum, the roles and responsibilities of two different groups: advisors and counselors. Their continuum provides a framework for identifying different types of student transitional issues and how advisors and counselors can work together and individually to help students as they move through their college years.

Often terms such as *advisor* and *counselor,* or *advising* and *counseling* are used interchangeably. This can lead to confusion. For Kuhn, Gordon, and Webber, *advising* and *advisors* refer to "academic advising and academic advisors," while *counselors* and *counseling* refer to "those who are trained in a graduate-level program to provide personal counseling and related services."

Table 10.1. The Advising-Counseling Responsibility Continuum.

	Informational	*Explanatory*	*Developmental*	*Mentoring*	*Counseling*
Purpose	Informational	Clarification	Insights	Growth	Pinpoint problem
Content	Information	Procedures	Opinions and values	Values	Devise resolution
Focus	The information	The institution	The student	The person	Modification of student's behavior
Length of contact	5–15 minutes	15–30 minutes	30–60 minutes	Varies; many contacts are made	Determined by severity of problem

Source: Kuhn, T., Gordon, V.N., and Webber, J. (2006). The advising and counseling continuum: Triggers for referral. NACADA Journal, 26(1): 25

The critical point they state is that advisors are not trained to be counselors—that is, to help students with psychological concerns; likewise counselors rarely have the institutional knowledge about curriculum, academic resources, and services that advisors have. Yet both advisors and counselors "help students set goals so they can improve their personal functioning, identify barriers that may impact successful accomplishment of their goals, develop strategies to accomplish these goals, and assess whether or not the strategies are successful" (p. 26).

The advising-counseling continuum developed by Kuhn, Gordon, and Webber (Table 10.1) identifies five different levels of involvement: informational, explanatory, developmental, mentoring, and counseling. Each of these levels has implications for the advising or counseling session in terms of purpose, content, focus, and length of contact. The least complex level of advising is informational advising, which anchors one end of the continuum while personal counseling anchors the other end. Because of the nature of the continuum, the authors state that the "severity of the issue and the student's coping abilities should be factors in deciding whether the problem is best handled by an advisor or referred to a counselor" (p. 26). This does not mean that the columns identifying levels of involvement on the table should be interpreted as self-contained "silos." In addition to roles and responsibilities, the continuum also provides a means for interpreting advisors' level of comfort in addressing issues or problems students present to them in an advising session.

Using the advisor-counselor responsibility continuum, Kuhn, Gordon, and Webber propose a way of categorizing issues students might bring to a session. They identify three areas of primary responsibilities: (1) Advisor, (2) Either or (Advisor or Counselor), and (3) Counselor. Examples of primary "advisor responsibility" issues are course selection, registering for classes, and procedures. Issues advisor and counselors might share include death in the family, time management, and decision-making. Examples of issues that are clearly counselor responsibilities include substance abuse, physical and emotional abuse, and sexual harassment (p. 27).

By implication, advisors who see their roles as predominantly "informational" and "explanatory," might not believe it is their responsibility or feel comfortable addressing the issues that could be shared with a counselor. Many of these issues, however, are normal student developmental transitional issues. Advisors who see their roles as "developmental" or "mentoring" might well feel the need to help students with these transitional issues in the shared category with counselors, called "Either or." Many of the issues in this category are predominantly focused on students' personal or social concerns. For example, a student may be doing poorly in a course and the lack of progress could have certain curricular implications. This issue could be the primary focus of the advising session. Or, an advisor might probe and discuss what might be causing the difficulty. After listening to the student and reviewing his record, an advisor might determine that the issue is related to transitional issues such as not being able to adapt academically to the new college environment. Perhaps the student did not have a strong precollege academic preparation or has not considered his academic or vocational goals. If the student did not anticipate such academic difficulty, he might be experiencing an unanticipated transition.

Academic advisors will hold different opinions about their roles, responsibilities, and level of comfort when addressing students' transitional issues. These views can be greatly affected by institutional expectations, rules, and culture. Kuhn, Gordon, and Webber also state that "the severity of the issue and the student's coping abilities should be factors when deciding whether the problem is best handled by the advisor or if the student should be referred to a counselor"(p. 26). To help advisors determine when it may be appropriate to refer a student to counseling, Kuhn, Gordon, and Webber (2006, p. 29) suggest considering observable behaviors, emotions, or thinking patterns. They term these collectively as *triggers*. Some examples of triggers that may prompt an advisor to refer a student to a counselor are listed below:

- Depressed junior has no commitment to any major
- First-year student's grades drop after death of father
- First-year student cannot communicate with domineering parent

When advisors experience a trigger moment with a student, they must first confirm and define it. This requires interaction with students and reference to their record. Depending on the nature of the transitional issues, the advisor may assist the student or refer the student to other campus resources or to the counseling center.

The Kuhn, Gordon, and Webber framework of advisor roles and responsibilities and their use of triggers are a useful means of organizing advising issues and approaches when working with undecided, major-changing, or underprepared students. It is important to note that implicit in Kuhn, Gordon, and Webber's continuum are the type and nature of advising goals that should be pursued. If advisors work at an institution that believes the role of the advisor is predominantly informational or explanatory, their advising goals would be significantly different from those working at an institution that perceives advisor roles as developmental or mentoring. As we consider the advising needs of those selected students in transition in this chapter, it becomes quite obvious that their needs cannot be met through only an informational or explanatory perspective or philosophy. To serve these students in transition, advising goals need to be student-centered, rather than institutionally centered. That is not to say that informational or explanatory advising tasks are not necessary. These are indeed critical, but they are not sufficient to address these students' transitional needs. While a much more in-depth presentation of how advising goals relate to advising as teaching is presented elsewhere in this book, it is important to note this relationship here. For without this perspective, attempts to align advising goals to reflect students at different levels (Kramer, 2000) or writing an advising syllabus (Trabant, 2006) would be inadequate.

ADVISING UNDECIDED AND INDECISIVE STUDENTS

Background

In the research literature, there is a clear distinction between the use of the terms *undecided* and *indecisive* when describing college students. This is an important consideration when defining the roles and responsibilities of advisors and counselors as well. Gordon (2007, p. x) defined *undecided students* as those students who were "unwilling, unable, or unready to make educational and/or vocational decisions." A student who has difficulty making *any* decision, however, may be considered indecisive (Appel, Haak, & Witzke, 1970; Goodstein, 1965). Gordon (2007) described an indecisive student as having characteristics deriving from the "result of unsatisfactory habits of thinking that permeates the individual's total life" (p. 11). The important distinction between these two definitions is that advisors, working within the framework of either the developmental or mentoring role as defined by Kuhn, Gordon, and Webber (2006), should be prepared to not only work with undecided students but to have the capability to detect characteristics of indecisive students so that they may refer them for personal counseling.

The transitions undecided students go through vary greatly and truly reflect issues most students must address during their progression through college. After reviewing the literature on undecided students, Lewallen (1993) concluded that the research was "conflicting, contradictory, and confusing." Other researchers have determined that undecided students are a heterogeneous group with few similarities (Baird, 1967; Hagstrom, Skovholt, & Rivers, 1997; Holland & Holland, 1977). Perhaps the key to understanding this phenomenon is that many early studies attempted to compare "undecided" students with those who were "decided." During the 1990s, much of the research was focused on investigating undecided student characteristics by defining subtypes of undecided and decided students (Newman, Fuqua, & Minger, 1990; Savickas & Jorgourna, 1991). These studies suggested ways of grouping decided and undecided students so that specifically designed interventions, based upon their personality characteristics and decision-making abilities, could be created.

Gordon (1998) took on the task of comparing these studies on decided and undecided students. She reviewed fifteen studies and proposed seven subtypes: (a) very decided, (b) somewhat decided, (c) unstable decided, (d) tentatively undecided, (e) developmentally undecided, (f) seriously undecided, and (g) chronically indecisive. Gordon identified the similarities and differences among these subtypes and proposed interventions and advising strategies. A critical element in her proposed synthesis of subtypes is that the states of decidedness and undecidedness lie on a continuum rather than exist as separate entities. This perspective is critical for all advisors, in that it clearly suggests that more than just those first-year students who have declared themselves as decided could benefit from learning and using techniques to assist them with active educational and vocational decision-making or exploration.

Transition Issues

Undecided students clearly experience a number of transitional issues. As Gordon (2007) noted, "the developmental approach views undecided students not as persons searching for an academic or career niche but as individuals continually engaged in a series of developmental tasks that ultimately enables them to adapt and change in a pluralistic world" (p. 56). Some may go through anticipated transitions, such as accepting that it is all right to enter college as undecided on the assumption that the "right" major or occupation will "happen" to them eventually. Some may not anticipate any difficulty in pursuing a general direction such as health-related careers and the course work needed to achieve their goals. Some may believe that a particular major leads to only one career field or that a particular occupation can be accessed only through one academic path. Success and disappointment in fulfilling these anticipated transitions can lead to unanticipated transitions when students find they must engage in new or renewed exploration. This occurs in many ways, as when students need to reconsider their abilities for an academic area or recognize that the relationship between academic preparation and occupations is multidimensional.

General non-event transitions that could affect undecided students can involve many personal or social issues. Not receiving anticipated financial support to attend the college of their choice may influence a student who was decided to become undecided about choice of major. Attending college and developing a new peer group with different expectations can also affect students' initial ideas about the goals they want to pursue. The dynamics of the interactions students experience prior to and during college can create a multiplicity of potential anticipated and unanticipated transitions.

The Advising-Counseling Continuum and Triggers

Considering all the social and personal developmental issues college students address during their first year, helping them focus on academic and vocational decision-making is difficult but necessary. There are a host of decision-making models advisors can use to help students make satisfying decisions. Gordon (1992) proposed an integrated academic and career-planning model that relies on a student-centered approach that seeks to integrate self-knowledge, occupational knowledge, educational knowledge, and decision-making knowledge. Schein and Laff (1997) proposed a student-centered approach in which students answer questions about their likes and dislikes, strengths and weaknesses, and hopes for the future. This engages them in a process of designing a field of study rather than selecting an established major. Beck (1999) used chaos theory as a metaphor to articulate several key guides for advising undecided students. Bertram (1996) offered a model that advocated a less rational approach to working with undecided students by contrasting it with the rational decision-making model used by many advisors. Steele (2003) reviewed and summarized common characterizes found in all four models.

For advisors encountering students who are more certain about their academic major but less certain about their vocational goals, two authors offer models and guidance for integrating career development techniques and goal-setting into their advising. Gordon's 3-I process (Inquire, Inform, and Integrate) (2006) describes the advisor's role in the decision-making process, which includes a questioning period during which students' needs and concerns are explored, a period when many types of information essential to decision-making are gathered, and finally a period of integration when the process is internalized and action is taken. In a similar manner, McCalla-Wriggins (2000) reviews career theories and elements of career planning and offers suggestions for integrating these with academic advising.

These proposals, models, and theories share the characteristic of addressing in various ways the common needs of undecided students that Gordon (2007) describes (i.e., information deficits, developmental-skills deficits, and personal and social concerns). All these models assume that undecided students will demonstrate different levels of readiness to explore. As Gordon (2007) notes, "The programs and services offered undecided students must reflect many levels of ability to differentiate and integrate aspects of the decision-making process" (p. 58).

Since the exploration process is part of the transition most college students go through, advisors can help them develop the skills and habits necessary for setting academic and vocational goals and decision-making. Once these skills are acquired, they may carry over into how students address similar unanticipated transitions and non-event transitions in their future.

Students graduating from college for the past several decades have faced a world of work in which career change is the constant. There are no economic projections for the future that suggest that lifetime employment with one employer will once again become the norm. Social customs and global economic disruptions such as divorce and outsourcing of jobs can create dramatic and unanticipated changes at the personal level. As students struggle with academic and career decision-making, advisors can have a lasting impact when they recognize and take advantage of important "advisable moments."

As advisors confront the issues surrounding decided and undecided college students, they are clearly working in the middle of Kuhn, Gordon, and Webber's (2006) advisor-counselor responsibility continuum as Explanatory, Developmental, or Mentoring advisors, since the focus of the advising session is centered on the student, or the person. The issues and the need to address them are centered on students' concerns and the task of clarifying personal, social, educational, and vocational goals. Using the triggers identified by Kuhn, Gordon, and Webber, there are several observable behaviors, emotions, and modes of thinking that should suggest that a student may need a referral to a counselor. The research on undecided students provides us with a grounded basis for identifying these triggers. Some triggers that characterize students needing help in decision-making include anxiety about occupational choice (Appel, Haak, & Witzke, 1970; Fuqua, Seaworth, & Newman, 1987; Kimes & Troth, 1974; Mau, 1995), fear of commitment (Serling & Betz, 1990; Zytowski, 1965), poor self-efficacy (Luzzo & Andrews, 1999; Srsis & Walsh,

2001; Taylor & Betz, 1983), ego-identity status (Gordon & Kline, 1989), identity and vocational immaturity (Holland & Holland, 1977), lack of persistence and academic success (Foote, 1980), gender and sex-role stereotyping (Gianakos & Subich, 1986; Harren, Kass, Tinley, & Moreland, 1978; Orlofsky, 1978; Rose & Elton, 1971), and learning disabilities and reasoning weakness (Layton & Lock, 2003). Examples of how these could be manifested as observable behaviors, emotions, or modes of thinking are listed below.

Examples of Triggers for Undecided or Exploring Students

1. Student "declares" a different major at each advising session.
2. Student registers for course work that does not correspond to her "declared" major.
3. Student declares a popular major without any explanation.
4. There is a serious disconnect between student's academic abilities and skills and declared major.
5. Student informs advisor that her choice of major is due to parental or peer pressure or expectations.
6. A male student decides not to pursue nursing as a major despite his interests and abilities because of the perception that it is a career field for women.
7. A student with high math ability fears committing to an engineering degree because the course work might adversely affect her grade point average.
8. A student will not commit to a major in history because he does not want to teach.
9. Student is unaware of curricular and career information available through the advising office.
10. A student admits he is undecided, but would rather discuss issues related to his problems adapting to the campus social environment.

Indecisive students often experience similar developmental and decision-making problems, but at much higher levels of anxiety and intensity that are often combined with other social or psychological problems (Gaffner & Hazler, 2002; Salamone, 1982; Van Matre & Cooper, 1984). Indecisive students, in general, have difficulty taking a particular course of action, since the inability to make a commitment permeates most areas of their lives. While very few students manifest extreme characteristics, those who do should be referred for more in-depth counseling (Heppner & Hendricks, 1995). Steele (2003) makes the following suggestions for when advisors refer indecisive students to counselors: "(advisors) should focus on whether a student has a general inability to make any type of decision. They should also pay attention to other signs of social or psychological problems. If these problems are detected, the advisor then must show great empathy and consideration when referring the student to counseling services" (p. 13).

ADVISING MAJOR-CHANGING STUDENTS

Background

Major-changers are defined as "students who enter college ostensibly decided about a major, but change their minds during the college years" (Gordon, 2007, p. 86). While difficult to capture, it has been estimated that the number of students who go through a process of re-deciding during their college years is approximately 50 to 75 percent (Foote, 1980; Noel, 1985; Steele, 1994; Titley & Titley, 1980).

Students who change their academic direction do so for a variety of reasons. The most frequently cited reason for changing majors is lack of information (Kramer, Higley, & Olsen, 1994). Major-changers tend to have done little to explore different majors, gather information about curricular requirements, or learn about career opportunities related to majors. Many of these students have not been exposed to the variety of academic options that are available at the college level, nor are they aware of the number and type of occupations that exist. Some students may not have been given the opportunity to go through a formal career-decision-making process during high school (Lewallen, 1993). Similarly, these students have not examined their interests, abilities, and values and how that information relates to major and career choices. As a result, once these students begin to acquire information about the requirements for their major, take premajor or major course work, and learn about related career alternatives, they see the need to change direction and examine other academic possibilities. Other students may discover that the course work for their initial major is too challenging academically and realize they need to find a major in which they can succeed. One common example is students who are encouraged to pursue engineering or medicine but find that the mathematics and science requirements for these academic programs are beyond their reach.

Some students may feel pressured by family members or friends and enter college majoring in something that someone else has decided for them (Berrios-Allison, 2005; Gordon & Polson, 1985; Pearson & Dellman-Jenkins, 1997). Other students may avoid or delay engaging in the exploration process since they are not ready or motivated. Some are preoccupied with other developmental issues.

Perhaps the most challenging group of major-changers to advise are the students who are denied access to their intended program of study (e.g., business, nursing) because of selective or oversubscribed majors. Some of these students may have entered college underprepared for the rigors of college-level academics while others may not have devoted the time and energy to what is required to compete in certain academic fields. Others hold on to the belief that they will get into their major despite concrete evidence to the contrary. This mind-set can be frustrating for advisors who want to help these students move beyond this initial setback by examining alternative majors that could include some of the desirable characteristics of their original choices. Some students avoid seeing advisors since they know they will be told what they do not want to hear.

Gordon (2007) describes six different types of major changers. The *Drifters* are those students who realize early in their college career that their initial choice of major is not a good fit but delay engaging in the exploration process. Some of these students may be faced with multiple demands on their time and have not made selecting a major a priority. Others do not feel pressured to explore alternative majors until the system forces them to make a choice. Students who change their majors without informing others and without making contact with their academic advisor are referred to as *Closet Changers.* Some of these students may be concerned with how others will judge them if they change, particularly if they are defying the wishes of a parent. The *Externals* are very comfortable with changing majors and seem to prefer being constantly in a "change mode." These students tend to be concerned about making a wrong choice or missing a major that may be "better" than their previous one. They do not engage in a systematic exploration process, and prefer to gather information about majors from those in their social network or anyone who else who has an opinion. The *Up-Tighters* are those major-changers who are not able to attain their initial choice of major. These students may have been denied admission to selective majors and may have unrealistic expectations of their skills and abilities. Some of these students are not open to examining alternative majors and are often anxious and upset about their inability to pursue their initial choice. The *Experts* operate "as if" they have gone through a thorough exploration process and made a well-informed decision about a major. They appear knowledgeable and tend not to seek help. Frequently these students have made unrealistic choices but are determined to continue in the major despite performing poorly. Advisors enjoy working with *Systematic* major-changers, since these students accept the need to change and are open to exploring new alternatives. They seek out academic and career advising services and actively participate in the decision-making process.

Transition Issues

Many students who enter college with a declared major but change it later may be identified as experiencing an unanticipated transition. While most unanticipated events can be very stressful, the impact of this change will vary greatly depending on how invested students were in their original choice. Some students may have known at the outset of declaring the major that they really did not have an interest in it but just wanted to make a choice. For these students the transition may not be a difficult one, and in fact, may be welcome and positive. Some students may be concerned about letting others down (e.g., parents) by changing their major. For example, a student whose parent encouraged her to study business so that she could take over the family business may find changing majors highly stressful and therefore may tend to delay or avoid following through with the change process. Other students may experience some level of stress with changing majors because the process entails concentrated work—researching major and careers, exploring self-information, and talking to an advisor about options.

Students whose initial choice of major was blocked because of enrollment limits may experience a non-event transition. For students who decided early that they wanted to major in business and are not admitted to that major, the results can be anywhere from annoying to traumatic. Some students, while disappointed that they cannot pursue their initial choice of major, are able to move on and explore alternative majors. Other students have difficulty accepting the fact that they will not be able to pursue their major of choice. For these students this academic field may have been a lifelong dream. Schlossberg and Robinson (1996) describe the "Dream-Reshaping Process" as a way to help individuals cope with nonevents. (Steele and McDonald (2000) discuss how this process can be applied to the advising process in the first edition of *Academic Advising: A Comprehensive Handbook.*) Whether the transition is the result of an unanticipated event or a non-event, there are a number of possible triggers an advisor should be alerted to in order to detect a major-changing student.

Examples of triggers for major-changing students

1. Student is not making academic progress in current major.
2. Student is no longer interested in initial choice of major.
3. Student has unrealistic expectations about gaining entrance into her current major.
4. Parents or significant others are pressuring student against his wishes to remain in current major.
5. Student frequently changes majors.
6. Entrance requirements for a particular selective major become more competitive.
7. Student has not examined interests, abilities, and values in relation to major choice.
8. Student has limited knowledge of career opportunities for current major.
9. Student continues to register for premajor courses despite poor performance.
10. Sophomore student informs advisor that he wants to change his major after a conversation with his uncle despite the fact that the student has not completed any premajor courses.

The Advising-Counseling Continuum and Triggers

Advisors working with students who are changing their majors will use the first three levels of involvement on the advising-counseling continuum—informational, explanatory, and developmental. The starting point on the continuum will depend on how students present their initial concerns.

Some students may begin the advising session with a request for information about one or more majors. The Informational level of responsibility is an appropriate way to respond to the student. Once this information has been provided, the level of the student's concern about the current major may warrant a move to the Explanatory or Developmental level. Some major-changing students may need to understand the requirements to enter a particular major and an explanation for why capacity limits are in place. Explanatory advising is used with these students to help them understand entrance requirements and whether they meet the requirements to compete for admittance to the major. This discussion may lead to the Developmental level in helping students examine information about themselves in relation to alternative majors. Some major-changers may not know what to do now that they are no longer interested (or no longer competitive) for a certain major. Advisors might begin with a developmental approach that involves not only an explanation of the exploration process but also takes into consideration the students' personal needs, interests, abilities, and values.

Major-changing students who refuse to look at themselves and their circumstances realistically despite multiple advising sessions may be good candidates for personal counseling. Not gaining admission to a particular major for some students may be viewed as a personal defeat. Some students may feel shame because they are not able to meet the expectations set by parents or significant others. These students may be anxious or depressed, and personal issues need to be addressed before the student can engage in productive exploration. For some students, changing majors is merely a symptom of underlying problems that may be longstanding. These students should be referred to a professional counselor so that the focus can be on personal concerns.

Clearly, major-changing students need advisors who have a good *general* knowledge of academic requirements and the career opportunities related to majors. These advisors need to know entrance requirements and how to help students put together a realistic plan for success that incorporates both academic and career goals. Academic advisors and career advisors who are cross-trained and knowledgeable about both majors and related occupational opportunities have an advantage when working with these students.

Advisors who work with major-changers need to be patient and have a thorough understanding of the developing college student. Readiness to engage in the major- and career-decision-making process varies from student to student. Forcing this process on a student who is not ready can have negative outcomes. Similarly, advisors need to feel comfortable when students express emotions. Most importantly, advisors need a positive attitude in working with these students, and strong communication skills are often required. Students need to hear that it is perfectly normal to change their major and to know that they will be supported through the change process (Gordon, 2007).

UNDERPREPARED STUDENTS

Background

Attending college is a widely and strongly anticipated transition. In one survey, 83 percent of the high school students in the United States stated that they expected to attend college (High School Survey on Student Engagement [NCES], 2005, p. 3). Yet, of those students who enter the ninth grade, only 70% will graduate from high school and only *half* are academically prepared for postsecondary education (Green & Winters, 2006). In addition to traditional-aged students, many adults who never entered or did not complete college also believe in the dream of going to college. Motivation for adult students vary, but the desire to remain competitive in the global job market and for personal growth and satisfaction remain strong incentives. The adult population who do not have degrees is reported to be fifty-four million adults, with thirty-four million having no college experience (Lumina Foundation, 2007). Regardless of whether the transition is from high school to college, returning to college, or beginning college after a long absence from formal education, this is often a difficult transition for many learners. To be successful in college, many of these students need help and support with academic preparedness. Consideration should be given to the multiplicity of social, psychological, economic, and cultural factors in play.

The term *underpreparedness* carries with it strong negative connotations. Often overlooked when considering the term, is that it is heavily dependent on context. For Ender and Wilkie (2000) *underpreparedness* is a term "referring to a student's ability to compete academically with other students attending the same institution" (p. 133). This is not a new phenomenon. Courses designed to raise the levels of underprepared students' academic skills were offered as far back as the nineteenth century (Cross, 1976; Brier, 1984). During the later quarter of the twentieth century, many educators recognized that although remedial courses were valuable, they were not sufficient (Maxwell, 1985). For these educators, academic underpreparedness was related to a host of other psychological, social, economic, and cultural factors. These related issues must be addressed in a holistic manner if underprepared students are to succeed in college (Enright, 1994). These ideas helped to establish the basis for Developmental Education. As Boylan (1995) noted:

> Students fail to do well in college for a variety of reasons, and only one of them is lack of academic preparedness. Factors such as personal autonomy, self-confidence, ability to deal with racism, study behaviors, or social competency have as much to do with grades, retention, and graduation than how well a student writes or how competent a student is in mathematics. (p. 1)

Just because students are not performing well academically in college does not mean they are not academically capable. Many students who enter college are naïve about the academic challenges they will encounter. The need to serve all students is rooted both in our history of encouraging access to higher education for as many citizens as possible and in institutional necessity. Providing access to higher education is a core value in a democratic culture and rooted in what Lincoln, in his first inaugural address in 1861, might have called an example of following "the better angels of our nature." Correspondingly, this motivation guides elements of our educational policies and does create a reality in which some learners enter college academically underprepared. If assistance were not provided to these students, however, institutions would have to either "fail large numbers of students or lower their academic standards to accommodate student deficiencies" (Boylan, 1995, p. 4). Still, this does not come cheap. It has been estimated that the cost of remediation for colleges, students, families, employers, and taxpayers is $3.7 billion a year (Alliance for Excellent Education, 2006).

Considering the advantages of having learners graduate from college rather than just gaining access to it creates other benefits. As Tinto (2004) points out, people with college degrees are much more likely to participate in public issues, perform community service, consume fewer public services, have lower levels of unemployment, and commit fewer crimes. Individuals completing a bachelor's degree "stand to earn $1 million more over their working career than do people with only a high school diploma" (Tinto, 2004, p. 7). In helping students achieve their dreams and rewards of a college education, advisors will encounter many anticipated and unanticipated transitions as they work with those students who are academically underprepared.

Transition Issues

Underprepared students may or may not be ready for the academic challenges that they will encounter in their transition to college. What often becomes the critical unanticipated transition is the scope of the difference between high school and college-level work in terms of pace, amount, and expectations. A host of unanticipated transitional issues may center on this point. A student may believe her study, time-management, and organizational skills, as well as her academic preparations, are equal to the task at hand. The complexity of the advising issue is how to address these in a holistic manner and how to approach other unanticipated issues that may arise. A student may need to reconsider his academic major or vocational direction while concurrently working on academic preparation issues. Unanticipated additional course work may need to be taken. This may be particularly pertinent to returning adult students who have been away from formal education for a number of years. Like other students, those non-event transitions that affect underprepared students may center on any combination of personal or social issues. As highlighted in the Kuhn, Gordon, and Webber (2006) advising continuum, advisors can work in conjunction with a counselor on many of these issues or refer the student to a counselor when indicated.

The Advising-Counseling Continuum and Triggers

Students who enter college underprepared for the academic challenges they will face are less likely to graduate than students who do not need remediation (Wirt, Choy, Rooney, Provasnik, Sen and Tobins, 2004). These students share several characteristics. Underprepared students tend to come from lower-income socioeconomic backgrounds, be first-generation college students, and have ethnic backgrounds other than white European. What often holds these students back from graduating from college are inadequate high school academic preparation, social and cultural barriers that do not support successful academic behaviors, and unmet needs, such as financial aid (Tinto, 2004).

The critical focus for advising these students is helping them make the anticipated and unanticipated transitions while in college. Ender and Wilkie (2000) propose that a developmental advising relationship be followed that focuses on three major themes: academic competence, personal involvement, and developing or validating life purpose. This requires that the relationship between advisor and advisee be: (1) ongoing and purposeful, (2) challenging for the student, but also supportive, (3) goal-oriented, and (4) intentional, as it maximizes the use of university resources (p. 119). Similarly, Tinto (2004) states that effective advising is an "essential" part of any retention program for these students (p. 8). He identifies the following elements of a successful program by providing students with: (1) clear guidelines, (2) support for academic and career decision-making, (3) knowledge on how to navigate postsecondary education, (4) empowering students to access support when needed, and (5) making sure the support program is connected to everyday student learning needs (p. 8).

Pritchard and Blouschild (1970) concentrated more on the psychological characteristics of underprepared students and identified the following traits for which advisors should be on guard: weak academic skills in one or more area; low academic self-concept; unrealistic graduate and career expectation; unfocused career objectives; extrinsic motivation; external locus of control; low self-efficacy; inadequate study skills for college success; belief that learning is memorization; and a history of passive learning. All of these characteristics provide examples of observable behaviors, emotions, or thinking that a student might manifest. As noted, advisors should be alert to these "triggers" when working with these students.

Examples of Triggers for Underprepared Students

1. Student has lower than institutional average for ACT or SAT scores.
2. Student has lower than institutional average for placement scores.
3. Student explains that it is difficult to study because of his off campus job which he needs to help pay for his college education.
4. Student declares a major that has the same core requirements as the student's area of academic unpreparedness.
5. Student is doing poorly in several or all courses after the first term.
6. Student transcripts show a pattern of poor grades in courses that share a common characteristic such as writing or a heavier reading load.
7. Student is doing poorly academically, admits she studies infrequently, but spends a great deal of time seeking out course professors to reconsider grades and permission to turn assignments in late.

8. Student expresses difficulty after first set of midterms, and from his record it appears he attended high school that has consistently low scores on statewide proficiency exams.

9. Student is a returning adult who expresses concern about pursuing a major that requires any amount of math or writing.

10. Student with high ACT scores and below average placement scores confesses concern about how to study.

Clearly, the role and responsibility of the advisor as defined by Kuhn, Gordon, and Webber (2006) for working with underprepared students is much more aligned with the Explanatory, Developmental, and Mentoring advising roles. The role and responsibility of the advisor is much more than helping underprepared students interpret their placement test scores and enrolling them in the proper remedial course or courses. Hardin (1998) offers a typology of students who need developmental education. Those students include the *poor chooser*—students who, through poor choices, are misprepared rather than underprepared; the *adult learner*—students who have been away from the academic setting for an extended period; the *ignored student*—students who had academic or physical problems never detected in high school; *students with limited English proficiency*—a student who acquired their high school education in a foreign country (and perhaps now should also include those students who enter college from households that do not speak English as their primary language); and the *disabled student*—a student who has a physical or learning disability.

There are two groups of students whom Hardin suggests might not belong in higher education: *the user*—students who lack academic goals and are using the higher education system for their own goals, and *extreme cases*—students with extreme emotional, academic, and psychological problems. Clearly, students in these last two groups should be referred to counseling.

The scope of the advisor's role is also reflected in the breadth of resources they need to access. Boylan (1995) stated, "In developmental education, remediation is only one of several possible options along a continuum of interventions ranging from occasional tutoring to brushing up on forgotten material to complete in-depth remedial courses" (p. 2). Resources in a developmental education program that would be helpful for advisors to draw upon include student support groups, frequent or required advising, mentoring programs, tutoring programs, supplemental instruction, effective assessments, and counseling. Courses that use collaborative teaching strategies, learning communities, and linked classes in which one class is developmental in nature, offer better support to these students' learning needs and styles (Tinto, 2004).

CONCLUSION

Advisors working with undecided, major-changing, and underprepared students during college face a variety of common and unique series of transitional issues.

Some of these transitions are not anticipated. In other cases some anticipated events do not occur. It is critical that advisors be perceptive in detecting these transitions and support students through challenging experiences.
Any individual student may share characteristics found in any one of these
populations. Kuhn, Gordon, and Webber's Continuum of Advisor-Counselor
Responsibilities offers a conceptual model for identifying the scope and types
of interventions. In the end, students in all three of these groups can succeed
in college, and it is in the interests of the students as well as the institution
and society that they do so. Good academic advising is often the critical component in helping achieve this important goal.

References

Alliance for Excellent Education. (2006). *Paying double: Inadequate high schools and
community college remediation.* Alliance for Excellent Education Web site. Retrieved
August 8, 2007, from http://www.all4ed.org/publications/remediation.pdf

Appel, V., Haak, R., & Witzke, D. (1970). Factors associated with indecision about collegiate major and career choice. *Proceedings, American Psychological Association, 5,*
667–668.

Baird, L. (1967). The undecided student—How different is he? *ACT Research Report,*
No. 2. Iowa City: American College Testing Program.

Beck, A. (1999). Advising undecided students: Lessons learned from chaos theory,
NACADA Journal, 19 (1), 45–49.

Berrios-Allison, A. C. (2005). Family influences on college students' occupational identity. *Journal of Career Assessment, 13* (2), 233–247.

Bertram, R. M. (1996). The irrational nature of choice: A new model for advising
undecided students? *NACADA Journal, 16* (2), 19–24.

Boylan, H. R. (1995). Making the case for developmental education. *Research in
Developmental Education, 12* (2), 1–4.

Brier, E. (1984). Bridging the academic preparation gap: A historical view. *Journal of
Developmental Education, 8* (1), 2–5.

Chronicle of Higher Education. (2007). Almanac issue 2006–08. *Chronicle of Higher
Education, 54* (1), 4, 16.

Cross, K. P. (1976). *Accent on learning.* San Francisco: Jossey-Bass.

El-Khawas, E. (2003). The many dimensions of student diversity. In S. R. Komives,
D. B. Woodard, Jr., & Associates (Eds.), *Student services: A handbook for the profession* (pp. 45–64). San Francisco: Jossey-Bass.

Ender, S. A., & Wilkie, C. J. (2000). Advising students with special needs. In
V. N. Gordon, W. R. Habley, et al. (Eds.), *Academic advising: A comprehensive
handbook.* San Francisco: Jossey-Bass.

Enright, G. (1994). College learning skills: Frontierland origins of the Learning
Assistance Center. In M. Maxwell (Ed.), *From access to success: A book of readings
on college developmental education and learning assistance programs* (pp. 1–20).
Clearwater, FL: H & H Publishing.

Foote, B. (1980). Determined- and undetermined-major students: How different are
they? *Journal of College Student Personnel, 21* (1), 29–34.

Fuqua, D. R., Seaworth, T. B., & Newman, J. L. (1987). The relationship of career indecision and anxiety: A multivariate examination. *Journal of Vocational Behavior, 30* (2), 175–186.

Gaffner, D. C., & Hazler, R. J. (2002). Factors related to indecisiveness and career indecision in undecided college students. *Journal of College Student Development, 43* (3), 317–326.

Gianakos, I., & Subich, L. M. (1986). The relationship of gender and sex-role orientation to vocational undecidedness. *Journal of Vocational Behavior, 29* (1), 42–50.

Goodstein L. (1965). Behavior theoretical views of counseling. In B. Steffre (Ed.), *Theories of counseling* (pp. 140–192). New York: McGraw-Hill.

Gordon, V. N. (1992). *Handbook of academic advising.* Westport, CT: Greenwood.

Gordon, V. N. (1998). Career decidedness types. *The Career Development Quarterly, 46* (4), 386–403.

Gordon, V. N. (2006). *Career advising: An academic advisor's guide.* San Francisco: Jossey-Bass.

Gordon, V. N. (2007). *The undecided college student: An academic and career advising challenge* (3rd ed.). Springfield, IL: Charles C Thomas.

Gordon, V. N., & Kline, D. (1989). Ego-identity statuses of undecided and decided students and their perceived advising needs. *NACADA Journal, 9* (1), 5–15.

Gordon, V. N., & Polson, C. (1985). Students needing academic alternative advising: A national survey. *NACADA Journal, 5* (2), 77–84.

Green, J., & Winters, M. (2006). *Leaving boys behind: Public high school graduation rates.* New York: Manhattan Institute.

Hagstrom, S. J., Skovholt, T. M., & Rivers, D. A. (1997). The advanced undecided college student: A qualitative study, *NACADA Journal, 17* (2), 23–30.

Hardin, C. J. (1998). Who belongs in college? In J. L. Higbee and P. L. Dwinell (Eds.), *Developmental education: Preparing successful college students* (pp. 15–24). Columbia: University of South Carolina, National Resource Center for the First-Year Experience and Students in Transition.

Harren, V. A., Kass, R. A., Tinley, H. E. A., & Moreland, J. R. (1978). Influence of sex role attitudes and cognitive styles on career decision-making. *Journal of Counseling Psychology, 25*(5), 390–398.

Heppner, M. J., & Hendricks, F. (1995). A process and study examining career indecision and indecisiveness. *Journal of Counseling and Development, 73* (4), 426–437.

High School Survey on Student Engagement [NCES]. (2005). *HSSSE 2005 overview* Indiana University, HSSSE Web site. Retrieved August 8, 2007, from http://ceep .indiana.edu/hssse/pdf/hssse_2005_report.pdf

Holland, J. L., & Holland, J. E. (1977). Vocational indecision: More evidence and speculation. *Journal of Counseling Psychology, 24,* 404–414.

Kimes, H. G., & Troth, W. A. (1974). Relationship of trait anxiety to career decisiveness. *Journal of Counseling Psychology, 21* (4), 277–280.

Kramer, G. L. (2000). *Advising students at different educational levels.* In V. N. Gordon, W. R. Habley, et al. (Eds.), *Academic advising: A comprehensive handbook.* San Francisco: Jossey-Bass.

Kramer, G. L., Higley, B. H., & Olsen, D. (1994). Changes in academic major among undergraduate students. *Colleges and University, 69,* 88–98.

Kuhn, T., Gordon, V. N., & Webber, J. (2006). The advising and counseling continuum: Triggers for referral. *NACADA Journal, 26* (1), 24–31.

Laanan, F. S. (2006, Summer). Editors note: Understanding students in transition: trends and issues. *New Directions for Student Services, 114*, 1–6.

Layton, C. A., & Lock, R. H. (2003) The impact of reasoning weakness on the ability of post secondary students with learning disabilities to select a college major. *NACADA Journal, 1 & 2*, 20–29.

Lewallen, W. C. (1993). The impact of being "undecided" on college-student persistence. *Journal of College Student Development, 34* (2), 103–112.

Lumina Foundation. (2007). Returning to learning: Adults success in college is key to America's future. New Agenda Series Web site. Retrieved August 8, 2007, from http://www.luminafoundation.org/publications/ReturntolearningApril2007.pdf

Luzzo, D., & Andrews, M. (1999). Effects of Strong Interest Inventory feedback on career decision-making self-efficacy and social cognitive career beliefs. *Journal of Career Assessment, 7* (1), 1–17.

Mau, W. (1995). Decision-making style as a predictor of career decision-making status and treatment gains. *Journal of Career Assessment, 13* (1), 89–99.

Maxwell, M. (1985). *Improving student learning skills.* San Francisco: Jossey-Bass.

McCalla-Wriggins, B. (2000). *Integrating academic advising and career life planning.* In V. N. Gordon, and W. R. Habley, et al., *Academic advising: A comprehensive handbook* (pp. 162–176). San Francisco: Jossey-Bass.

Newman J. L., Fuqua, D. R., & Minger, C. (1990). Further evidence for the use of career sub-types in defining career status. *Career Development Quarterly, 37* (2), 221–231.

Noel, L. (1985). Increasing student retention: New challenges and potential. In L. Noel, D. Levitz, et al., *Increasing student retention* (pp. 1–27). San Francisco: Jossey-Bass.

Orlofsky, J. L. (1978). Identity formation, achievement, and fear of success in college men and women. *Journal of Youth and Adolescence, 7* (1), 49–62.

Pearson, C., & Dellman-Jenkins, M. (1997). Parental influence on a student's selection of a college major. *College Student Journal, 37* (3), 301–313.

Pritchard, R. W., & Blouschild, B. (1970). *Why college students fail.* Mahwah, NJ: Funk & Wagnalls.

Rose, H. A., & Elton, C. F. (1971). Attrition and vocational undecided student. *Journal of Vocational Behavior, 1* (1), 99–103.

Salamone, P. R. (1982). Difficult cases in career counseling: II—The indecisive client. *Personnel and Guidance Journal, 60*, 496–499.

Savickas, M. L., & Jorgourna, D. (1991). The career decision scale as a type of indicator, *Journal of Counseling Psychology, 38* (1), 85–90.

Schein, H. K., & Laff, N. S., (1997). Working with undecided students: A hands-on strategy. *NACADA Journal, 17* (1), 42–48.

Schlossberg, N. K. (1989). *Overwhelmed: Coping with life's ups and downs.* Lanham, MD: Lexington Books.

Schlossberg, N. K., & Robinson, S. P. (1996). *Going to plan B: How you can cope, regroup, and start your life on a new path.* New York: Simon & Schuster.

Schlossberg, N. K., Waters, E. B., & Goodman, J. (1995). *Counseling adults in transition: Linking practice with theory* (2nd ed.). New York: Springer.

Serling, D. A., & Betz, N. E. (1990). Development and evaluation of a measure of fear of commitment. *Journal of Counseling Psychology, 37* (1), 91–97.

Srsis, C., & Walsh, W. B. (2001). Person-environment congruence and career self-efficacy. *Journal of Career Assessment, 9* (2), 203–213.

Steele, G. E. (1994). Major changers: A special type of undecided student. In V. N. Gordon (Ed.), *Issues in advising the undecided college student* (pp. 85–92). Columbia: University of South Carolina, National Resource Center for the First-Year Experience and Students in Transition.

Steele, G. E. (2003). A research-based approach to working with undecided students: A case study illustration. *NACADA Journal, 1 & 2,* 10–19.

Steele, G. E., & McDonald, M. L. (2000). Advising students in transition. In V. N. Gordon, W. R. Habley, et al. (Eds.), *Academic advising: A comprehensive handbook,* (pp. 144–161). San Francisco: Jossey-Bass.

Taylor, K. M., & Betz, N. E. (1983). Application of self-efficacy theory to the understanding and treatment of career indecision. *Journal of Vocational Behavior, 22* (1), 63–81.

Tinto, V. (2004). *Student retention and graduation.* Pell Institute Web site. Retrieved August 8, 2007, from http://www.pellinstitute.org/tinto/TintoOccasionalPaperRetention.pdf

Titley, R. M., & Titley, B. S. (1980). Initial choice of college major and attrition: The "decided" and "undecided" after 6 years. *Journal of College Student Personnel, 26,* 465–466.

Trabant, T. D. (2006). Advising syllabus 101. NACADA Clearinghouse of Academic Advising Resources Web site. Retrieved August 8, 2007, from http://www.nacada.ksu.edu/Clearinghouse/AdvisingIssues/syllabus101.htm

Van Matre, G., & Cooper, S. (1984). Concurrent evaluation of career indecision and indecisiveness. *Personnel and Guidance Journal, 62* (10), 627–639.

Wirt, J., Choy, S., Rooney, P., Provasnik, S., Sen, A., & Tobin, R. (2004). *The condition of education 2004* (NCES 2004–077). Washington, DC: Government Printing Office.

Zytowski, D. G. (1965). Avoidance behavior in vocational motivation. *Personnel and Guidance Journal, 43,* 746–750.

CHAPTER ELEVEN

Moving on from College

Jennifer Bloom

A s in the moving in and moving through stages, academic advisors are well positioned to guide students through the moving on stage. Chickering (1994) purports that academic advisors prepare students to "become effective agents for their own lifelong learning and personal development" (p. 50). Essentially, as advisors, our job during the moving on stage is to put ourselves out of business by teaching and preparing our students to "increase their capacity to take charge of their own existence" (Chickering, 1994, p. 50). In this chapter, we will be exploring a seven-step model for empowering students to proactively take control of the moving on phase, including specific ways that academic advisors can assist students as they depart from the institution.

Our job as academic advisors is to help students develop their uniqueness. As my colleague, John Wright, Sr., says, "Our job as leaders is to help people become better than what they think they can be" (personal communication, December 7, 2006). This is a tall order, and since this moving on phase means that we will not be as readily available to students once they leave campus, this transition means that we are also beginning to phase ourselves out of their lives.

POSTCOLLEGE OPTIONS

Each May and June at colleges and universities throughout the country, commencement speakers remind graduates that the ceremony marks not only the end of their undergraduate careers, but also the beginning of the next phase of their lives. Students' postgraduation plans vary, but typically involve pursuing full-time work, graduate or professional school, or volunteer and public service opportunities. These choices are not exclusive. For example, students will often pursue full-time work during the day and public service opportunities at night or on the weekends. As you have seen in the previous two chapters, academic advisors play a key role in preparing students throughout their college careers for future success in all of these arenas.

SEVEN-STEP SELF-AUTHORED MOVING ON MODEL

Baxter Magolda (2001) found that college students are heavily influenced by societal, parental, and peer pressures when making their initial career choices during college. This reliance on others to define themselves and their goals can be combated by promoting what Baxter Magolda calls "self-authorship" (p. 3). Baxter Magolda discusses how important it is for students to self-define who they are and where they are going. This emphasis on "the self as central to one's career choice" can also be emphasized by "giving students real responsibility in the counseling/advising relationship" (p. 311).

In order to accomplish this goal of self-sufficiency, I offer a Seven-Step Self-Authored Moving On Model that puts students in the driver's seat of their transition to their postcollegiate lives. This model is based heavily on John Kotter's (1999) work on how to successfully deal with change. The change model is pertinent because transitions are about change, and one of the biggest changes we undergo in life is the one from college to our first postcollegiate opportunity. In addition, the model relies heavily on the Appreciative Advising model (Bloom & Martin, 2002; Hutson, 2006) to help facilitate student progress through these changes. Appreciative Advising is the intentional collaborative practice of asking positive, open-ended questions that help students optimize their educational experiences and achieve their dreams, goals, and potentials. Based in part on the organizational development theory of Appreciative Inquiry (Cooperrider, et al., 2000), Appreciative Advising uses the four stages of Appreciative Inquiry—Discover, Dream, Design, and Deliver—to assist students with uncovering their strengths, dreaming about their future, designing a plan to make their dreams come true, and dealing with obstacles that they will inevitably encounter.

Step 1: Self-Assessment

Before students are able to convince employers or graduate or professional schools that they are ready to contribute to an organization's success, they must first know what makes them tick—their values, strengths, and skills. The Discover phase of Appreciative Advising is centered on helping students identify their passions and strengths.

Values. A values-based approach to a career is a powerful means of encouraging self-authorship and ensuring that students will make career choices that are in alignment with their most treasured values. Identifying and clarifying one's values is an invaluable exercise for college students to undertake.

Table 11.1. Values, Stories, and Questions Chart.

Values	Stories	Questions

Source: Adapted from Martin & Bloom (2003), pp. 5–6.

One exercise for doing so is to fill out the Values, Stories, and Questions (VSQ) Chart proposed by Martin and Bloom (2003). Advisors can assign students to fill out this chart and provide the following directions: In the Values column write the values that are most important to you—what are things without which your life would not be complete (e.g., independence, family, creativity, etc.). Once you have identified your values, in the Stories column jot down a story that demonstrates how you live out this value. In the Questions column, write at least two questions that you would ask a potential employer or school to ensure that they and the company or institution they represent have the same values as yours.

This chart will be invaluable to students throughout the job search process in that it will help them write a compelling cover letter, interview well, and negotiate an agreement.

Strengths. Marcus Buckingham (2006) quotes a Gallup Poll that asked Americans, "How many of you are able to play to your strengths at work a majority of the time?" Gallup data indicate that the answer is that less than two of ten people are able to use their strengths at work a majority of the time. Why is this important? Buckingham (2006) defines strengths as "what makes you feel strong" (disk 2). What do you look forward to doing? What makes you feel energized while you are doing it? What leaves you on a high after you are finished doing it? If everyone were able to use their strengths a majority of the time at work, then people would be happier, the workplace would be more productive, absenteeism would decrease, and job satisfaction would increase. Helping students become aware of what their strengths are is key. Buckingham's six-DVD series called *Trombone Player Wanted* is an entertaining way to help students identify their strengths.

Skills. Robert Quinn (2004) advocates that people write a description of when they are at their best. In order to do this effectively, he states that you cannot rely solely on yourself to identify your unique skills. Instead, he assigns his students to e-mail approximately fifteen people from all different facets of their lives (home, work, volunteering, friends, etc.) and ask them to help identify the student's unique skills. Once they receive the responses, Quinn directs his students to organize the responses into categories based on the themes that emerge. Finally, the students are instructed to write a one-page description that describes them when they are at their best.

Step 2: Develop a Vision

Terry O'Banion's (1994) seminal article about academic advising, which first appeared in the *Junior College Journal* in 1972, set forth the following key elements of academic advising:

1. Exploration of life goals
2. Exploration of vocational goals
3. Program choice
4. Course choice
5. Scheduling courses (p. 11)

The starting point involves exploring students' life and career goals instead of picking courses for the following semester without these important foundational pieces of information. The Dream phase of Appreciative Advising offers questions that advisors can use to accomplish this goal. Sample Dream phase questions from Habley & Bloom (2007) include:

- How is the world going to be a better place because of you?
- Twenty years from now, what does your ideal day look like?
- What are your top three life goals?
- What are your top three career goals?
- What are your top three goals for your undergraduate education?

Step 3: Design a Plan

In Appreciative Advising, the next phase is called the Design phase because this is the where the advisor partners with the student to devise a series of steps needed to accomplish the goals shared in Step 2. Advisors can help students by brainstorming with them about their options and referring them to appropriate resources on and off campus. These resources can include, but are not limited to, current students, alumni, faculty, campus administrative offices, community leaders, courses, and online resources.

As DeWitt Jones (1999), a photographer for *National Geographic*, points out in his video titled *Everyday Creativity*, "There is more than one right answer to a problem." He notes that anyone can come up with one right answer; the challenge is to not stop at the first right answer by continuing to brainstorm about other solution options. The importance of helping students identify multiple options is reiterated in the literature on academic hope (Snyder, Harris, Anderson, Holleran, Irving, Sigmon, et al., 1991; Snyder, Shorey, Cheavens, Pulvers, Adams, & Wiklund, 2002; Snyder, Feldman, Shorey, & Rand, 2002; Chang, 1998; Chemers, Hu, & Garcia, 2001). Academic hope is comprised of self-efficacy, the ability to set achievable goals, and the ability to devise multiple options for accomplishing goals. Therefore, explicitly emphasizing to students the importance of coming up with multiple ways to accomplish goals is key. Much time was spent in the two previous chapters discussing how to encourage students to take care of the wide variety of opportunities to grow and develop their skills, so just two important components will be briefly covered here: education and cocurricular activities.

Education. Throughout students' undergraduate careers, they should have been partnering with their academic advisors to strategically select courses that will be both personally and professionally beneficial. The students will need to do homework on their proposed line of work to uncover the educational credentials required to be hired to work in the field. Additional education may be necessary and that should be worked into the student's self-authored plan.

Cocurricular Activities. The National Survey of Student Engagement (NSSE) results (De Sousa, 2005) clearly indicate the positive relationship between student involvement in cocurricular learning opportunities and student academic success. For example, internship and practicum experiences are both powerful learning tools for students and excellent opportunities for them to get exposure to possible future employers. In addition, extracurricular activities such as volunteer duties, leadership positions in campus clubs and organizations, as well as participation in other events (intramural sports, church activities, etc.) are also important. It is often these extracurricular opportunities that help students gain insights into themselves and identify their passions. Future employers and graduate and professional schools often pay particular attention to the level and quality of student involvement outside the classroom as an indicator of the well-roundedness of the student.

Step 4: Creating a Personal Presidential Cabinet to Help Oversee the Process

Creating a "Personal Board of Directors" (Butler, 2006; Leider, 2000) is a concept that is more familiar to the business world than to academia. The main thrust of the idea is that just as organizations carefully select a diverse set of trusted people that have different strengths and perspectives to serve on the company's board of directors and guide the company, individuals should intentionally select people to sit on their own personal board of directors. However, the board of directors analogy is imperfect because the CEO reports to the board of directors and the board is responsible for making the decisions that the CEO must execute.

Shifting to a more self-authored analogy, I propose that advisors encourage students to form their own Personal Presidential Cabinet. This analogy is more appropriate because just as the president of the United States consults the presidential cabinet for advice on how to best proceed on a wide variety of issues, the student is the president of his or her own presidential cabinet and needs to seek advice from the trusted members of the Personal Presidential Cabinet. In cases of both the U.S. president and the student president, after obtaining advice from the cabinet, the president is the one who makes the final decision and is responsible for the outcomes.

This analogy helps students realize that there likely is not one superhero mentor out there who will have all the right answers for them. No one person is able to magically fulfill all the needs of his or her mentee. The Personal Presidential Cabinet allows students to fill the cabinet slots with trusted family, friends, university personnel, and others who will be available to consult when situations and problems arise.

Personal Presidential Cabinets are dynamic and ever-changing. The president can rotate people off the cabinet and bring on new people as warranted. The underlying power of this concept is that it reminds students that the decisions they ultimately make are their own. They can use their cabinet members to gather information and advice, but the final responsibility for all decisions made lies with the individual. This important aspect of the Personal Presidential Cabinet analogy is crucial to promoting self-authorship among students.

As academic advisors, our hope is that we can earn a place on our students' Personal Presidential Cabinet for at least the duration of their undergraduate careers and possibly beyond. Advisors need to always respect that the CEO of each student is not the advisor, but the student. Hanna Whitall Smith once said, "The true secret of giving advice is, after you have honestly given it, to be perfectly indifferent whether it is taken or not, and never persist in trying to set people right" (Booker, n.d.).

Below is a worksheet that can be given to students to fill out and then discuss with you.

Your Personal Presidential Cabinet

As the president and CEO of your life, you want to make the best decisions based on the very best information you can acquire. Just as the president of the United States has a cabinet to advise him or her on any subject relating to the cabinet member's expertise, you need to ensure that you surround yourself with people who are trustworthy and have expertise in a wide variety of areas. As president, you appoint cabinet members and you may dismiss individual cabinet members at any time.

Who is on YOUR cabinet? Who are your role models? Who do you trust for advice on a variety of different topics? The cabinet members serve as consultants and advisors, but you should take the best nuggets of information from each person and create the best solution for you. Always remember that there is more than one right answer. As the president, you make your own decisions because you are the one who has to live with the consequences of those decisions. Although there are nine slots in the chart below, you may have more or fewer cabinet members on your Personal Presidential Cabinet.

Step 5: Understand the Nature of Change and Transitions

Change is often difficult. Alan Deutschman (2005) wrote a fascinating article titled "Change or Die" that contained several examples of how patients who suffered heart attacks or had diabetes were unable to make changes to their eating and health habits even though they knew that not doing so would shorten their lifespan dramatically. Kotter (1999) notes that there are typically four reasons people are resistant to change: "a desire not to lose something

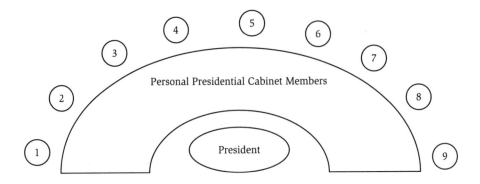

Figure 11.1

Table 11.2. Who Is on YOUR Personal Presidential Cabinet?

#	Cabinet Member's Name	I go to this person for advice on the following topics:
Example	Jane Smith	Career advice and ethical dilemmas
1		
2		
3		
4		
5		
6		
7		
8		
9		

of value, a misunderstanding of the change and its implications, a belief that the change does not make sense . . ., and a low tolerance for change" (p. 31). Advisors are ideally positioned to help students understand the complex nature of human reactions to change and transition. Armed with this knowledge, students can begin to understand why they may be procrastinating about implementing their postgraduation plans.

William Bridges (2003) differentiates between change and transition. He advocates that change is situational and that transition is psychological. Transitions are three-phase processes that "people go through as they internalize and come to terms with the details of the new situation that the change brings about" (p. 3). Bridges' transition model includes the following three stages: *Endings,* the *Neutral Zone,* and *New Beginning.* The Endings stage is often marked with feelings of disengagement, disidentification, disenchantment, and disillusionment (Tichy, 2002). Therefore, students are sometimes in denial that their undergraduate careers are coming to an end and thus avoid taking any steps toward preparing for life after graduation. One of the most powerful ways that advisors can create a sense of urgency is to teach students that the emotions that they feel are normal, yet simultaneously suggest "breakthrough strategies" to jump start them into the next stage. Tichy (2002) suggests the following breakthrough strategies to move out of the Endings phase—acknowledge your feelings about the ending, prepare for confusion, and seek stability and support to help you through the uncertainty. This is where the student's Personal Presidential Cabinet can be of assistance.

The Neutral Zone is a time when not much gets accomplished and people start to disconnect from the past and yet do not have a firm understanding of or connections to their postgraduation experience. People often feel confused and appear to alternate between being extremely happy and being deeply depressed. Tichy's breakthrough strategies for the Neutral Zone include taking time to reflect, symbolically moving from the old to the new, and using your support system. The last phase of Bridges' model is the New Beginning stage. This stage will be discussed in more detail in Step 7.

Step 6: Execute the Vision

In Step 2 the student created a vision, in Step 3 the student devised a plan to accomplish the vision, in Step 4 the student proactively put together a Personal Presidential Cabinet, and in Step 5 the student learned about the nature of change and some breakthrough strategies. In Step 6 the student needs to execute the plan. In Appreciative Advising, this is known as the Deliver phase. The advisor's job during this phase is to make sure that the student has developed concrete, incremental steps to accomplish the goals set forth by the student. Encouraging students to build momentum early by tackling the easiest goals first will help build the students' confidence and sense of efficacy. Remind students to celebrate the little victories along the way and not to wait to celebrate until they have been accepted into graduate school or secured a job.

Another important role that advisors can play during this step is to let students know up front that they will likely face unexpected problems and setbacks in the pursuit of their goals. DeWitt Jones (1999) encourages us to "turn problems into opportunities" and to proactively turn "win-lose" situations into "win-learn" opportunities. Helping students anticipate setbacks is crucial, as is letting students know that you care about them and want them to come see you when they run into these inevitable roadblocks.

Other substantive actions that advisors can take during this step include offering to write letters of recommendation, helping to edit students' cover letters and resumes, and possibly even conducting mock interviews. For the latter two items, it may be more appropriate to refer students to the Career Services Center on campus if the advisor does not have the expertise to assist with these activities.

Step 7: Successfully Transitioning into the New Opportunity

As students prepare to graduate and embark upon the next phase of their lives, the advisor's job is not over yet. Advisors should continue their teaching role by letting students know what to expect and providing them with breakthrough strategies. The last stage of Bridges' (2003) transition model is the

New Beginnings stage. In this stage, gaining confidence and self-confidence in the new role with an optimistic view of the future is key. This happens only after working through the Ending and Neutral Zone phases. Tichy (2002) notes that typical emotions during this phase include understanding, acceptance, hope, and fondness. Breakthrough strategies include taking bold new actions while also expecting some failures, as well as helping others who are having difficulty with the transition. The advisor can also encourage the student to form a Transition Team and a Transition Plan (Martin & Bloom, 2003). The Transition Team is composed of key people within the new work environment who are resources to help acclimate the graduate to the new environment as well as help the graduate avoid stepping on the culture by learning the company's unique cultural nuances. The Transition Plan will be developed in concert with the members of the Transition Team and will consist of goals and deadlines for meeting key constituents early and developing strategies for meeting performance expectations. Since the graduate will have already gone through this process with you earlier as they designed their collegiate plan, they can be reminded that they already enjoyed great past success with designing and following through on their self-authored plans.

CONCLUSION

Building on Baxter Magolda's research findings that students need to compose a self-authored career plan, this chapter has shared a model for giving students the tools to develop such a plan. In addition, specific mechanisms for advisors to partner with and support students through this process have been shared.

Vygotsky (1978), a nineteenth-century Russian philosopher, used a powerful analogy for parenting that he termed "scaffolding." In the advising context, *scaffolding* means that early in the relationship the advisor may need to be more hands on, double-checking that the student is heading in the right direction (Bloom, Cuevas, Hall, & Evans, 2007). However, as the advisor continues to teach the student about how to make good decisions and the advisee better understands the culture and system of higher education, the advisor carefully and strategically dismantles the scaffolding so that the advisee emerges as a graduate well positioned to make his or her own choices. Using the proposed seven-step plan will allow advisors to strategically take down the last pieces of scaffolding. The final product that emerges is a unique individual with a self-authored plan.

References

Baxter Magolda, M. B. (2001). *Making their own way: Narratives for transforming higher education to promote self-development.* Sterling, VA: Stylus.

Bloom, J. L., Cuevas, A. E. P., Hall, J. W., & Evans, C. V. (2007). Graduate students' perceptions of outstanding graduate advisor characteristics. *NACADA Journal, 27* (2), 28–35.

Bloom, J. L., & Martin, N. A. (2002, August 29). Incorporating appreciative inquiry into academic advising. *The Mentor, 4* (3). Retrieved September 9, 2007, from http://www.psu.edu/dus/mentor/020829jb.htm

Booker, P. (n.d.). Wisdom and practical philosophy. Retrieved September 10, 2007, from http://www.wisdom-and-philosophy.com/wisdom_quotes.htm

Bridges, W. (2003). *Managing transitions: Making the most of change* (2nd ed.). Cambridge, MA: De Capo.

Buckingham, M. (Director). (2006). *Trombone player wanted* [video]. Los Angeles: The Marcus Buckingham Company.

Butler, S. B. (2001). *Become the CEO of you, Inc: A pioneering executive shares her secrets for career success.* New Canaan, CT: Paribus.

Chang, E. C. (1998). Hope, problem-solving ability, and coping in a college student population: Some implications for theory and practice. *Journal of Clinical Psychology, 54* (7), 953–962.

Chemers, M. M., Hu, L.-T., & Garcia, B. F. (2001). Academic self-efficacy and first-year college student performance and adjustment. *Journal of Educational Psychology, 93* (1), 55–64.

Chickering, A. W. (1994, Fall). Empowering lifelong self-development. *NACADA Journal, 14* (2), 50–53.

Cooperrider, D. L., Sorenson, P. F., Whitney, D., & Yaeger, T. F. (Eds.). (2000). *Appreciative inquiry: Rethinking human organization toward a positive theory of change.* Champaign, IL: Stipes.

De Sousa, D. J. (2005). What advisors can do. National Survey of Student Engagement: Occasional Paper No. 11. Retrieved September 9, 2007, from http://nsse.iub.edu/institute/documents/briefs/DEEP%20Practice%20Brief%2011%20What%20Advisors%20Can%20Do.pdf

Deutschman, A. (2005, May). Change or die. *Fast Company, 94,* 53. Retrieved April 18, 2007, from http://www.fastcompany.com/magazine/94/open_change-or-die.html

Habley, W. R., & Bloom, J. L. (2007). Giving advice that makes a difference. In G. L. Kramer (Ed.), *Fostering student success in the campus community.* Bolton, MA: Anker.

Hutson, B. L. (2006). Monitoring for success: Implementing a proactive probation program for diverse, at-risk college students. Unpublished doctoral dissertation, University of North Carolina at Greensboro.

Jones, D. (Director). (1999). *Everyday creativity* [video]. Zepher Cove, NV: Dewitt Jones Productions.

Kotter, J. P. (1999). *John P. Kotter on what leaders really do.* Boston: Harvard Business Review.

Leider, R. (2000, February). Create a personal board of directors. *Fast Company.* Retrieved March 12, 2007, from http://www.fastcompany.com

Martin, N. A., & Bloom, J. L. (2003). *Career aspirations and expeditions: Advancing your career in higher education administration.* Champaign, IL: Stipes.

O'Banion, T. (1972). An academic advising model. *Junior College Journal, 42* (6), 62, 64, 66–69.

Quinn, R. E. (2004). *Building the bridge as you walk on it: A guide for leading change.* San Francisco: Jossey-Bass.

Snyder, C. R., Feldman, D. B., Shorey, H. S., & Rand, K. L. (2002, June). Hopeful choices: A school counselor's guide to hope theory. *Professional School Counseling, 5* (5), 298–307.

Snyder, C. R., Harris, C., Anderson, J. R., Holleran, S. A., Irving, L. M., Sigmon, S. T., et al. (1991). The will and the ways: Development and validation of an individual-differences measure of hope. *Journal of Personality and Social Psychology, 60* (4), 570–585.

Snyder, C. R., Shorey, H. S., Cheavens, J., Pulvers, K. M., Adams, V. H., & Wiklund. C. (2002). Hope and academic success in college. *Journal of Educational Psychology, 94* (4), 820–826.

Tichy, N. M. (2002). *The leadership engine: How winning companies build leaders at every level.* New York: Collins Business Essentials.

Vygotsky, L. S. (1978). *Mind in society: The development of higher psychological processes.* Cambridge, MA: Harvard University Press.

CHAPTER TWELVE

Students with Specific Advising Needs

Blane Harding

Over the past few decades, the make-up and diversity of students arriving on our campuses has changed drastically and requires new and innovative approaches to academic advising. All students, regardless of their preparedness and background, could be classified as special and deserve the very best our advising systems have to offer. However, there are several groups of students who present additional needs or who require advising services designed to address the specific characteristics that define them as special. These groups include high-ability students, student athletes, students with disabling conditions, first-generation students, adult learners, and lesbian, gay, bisexual, or transgender students (LGBT). Because of the wide range of characteristics and complexities of these groups, advisors must be trained and educated about these student populations and have the ability and sensitivity to build relationships with diverse student populations. This will allow us to empower students to take ownership of their education. The purpose of this chapter is to identify the specific needs of each group and to suggest approaches to maximize our advising techniques so these students' potential for success is enhanced.

Our responsibilities as advisors have become more problematic due to the fragmented nature of our college systems and structures. Each of these groups may have additional advisors (e.g., college athletes), advocacy offices (e.g., LGBT), campus-wide services, or special programs (e.g., honors programs, adult learning center) that require a coordination of efforts to best meet individual student needs. Advisors face the challenge of not only building personal relationships with this diverse group of students but also creating systems and structures that work together on behalf of student development and success.

Academic advisors play a critical role in implementing integrated collaborative approaches across campus. We must sustain partnerships over time based on institutional values and involve all stakeholders in defining the issues so that targeted advising approaches can be developed. It is necessary to facilitate cross-communication between offices and resources that may include advocacy offices, Trio Programs, athletic departments and their advisors, resources for disabled students, a central advising center, or resources that are unique to individual campuses. Advisors need to know the resources on their campus so that they can refer their advisees to these special programs and offices. Campus personnel must work together and complement each others' strengths.

It is impossible to place students into only one group, since one student might represent several types (e.g., first-generation athletes, GLBT high-ability students). This chapter will describe the general characteristics of each student population and their unique academic advising needs, and offer specific advising techniques to assist students in their academic careers. In addition, it will analyze the various campus systems and structures used by these student populations and suggest ways in which coalitions can be built to enhance our collective abilities to serve them.

The information presented in this chapter may seem not only complex but overwhelming at times. Advisors are asked to serve a very diverse population of students with special advising needs and master numerous approaches and strategies that may be specific to each group. Although it is important that advisors understand such issues as student identity theory, retention rates for each group, strengths and weaknesses, personal concerns, and the special needs of each group, the most important strategy is to treat the individual within the cultural context. Students cannot be treated simply as categories, statistics, or cultural entities. We don't need to know the statistics in relationship to LGBT students enrolling in college or their suicide rate, for example, in order to provide the best service to them. To treat students equally means to treat them individually. Three commonalities that exist when addressing advising approaches to these students are: (1) the need to establish coalitions and partnerships across campus, (2) our willingness to understand our own biases and level of cultural competency, and (3) our ability to build relationships with individual students.

COALITION-BUILDING

In order to maximize our effectiveness with students with special advising needs, it is necessary to first build coalitions and establish relationships with various campus resources. These students not only face unique challenges but fit into multiple populations that are serviced by a wide variety of campus offices and resources. It is necessary to use all available resources, and advisors can serve as "linking pins" between students and various departments and programs. Coalition-building requires a systematic process involving academic departments, faculty, and advising services in order to address the personal, career, and academic goals of these special students. Advisors must make a commitment to the whole student and recognize and appreciate the unique characteristics and individual differences of each student population. This should include a commitment to facilitating student development, success, and learning; providing quality services to meet individual student needs; and providing each student access and opportunity across our campuses. Effective coalitions and partnerships with other services must meet the following objectives:

- Mutually agreed-upon visions and goals
- Understanding and appreciation of one another's work
- Ongoing communication between various personnel
- The willingness and ability to learn from partners
- The creation and implementation of a shared inclusive decision-making process
- Respect, trust, and mutual understanding
- Sharing of resources
- Consistently advocating for one another
- A shared understanding of the general characteristics of students served

Coalition-building is an ongoing process that demands communication between partners on a regular basis. This provides a solid foundation and consistency over time that becomes embedded in our institutional structures and approaches as students with specific advising needs are served.

Cultural Competence

High-ability students, student athletes, students with disabling conditions, first-generation students, adult learners, and lesbian, gay, bisexual, or transgender students each have their own cultures and subcultures. It would be a monumental task for every advisor to know and understand the various cultures that are involved or overlap for each student. At times advisors may not even be aware of the various "hats" students wear, their situations, or the reasons they emphasize one subculture over another.

It is crucial for advisors and other campus staff to realize their own level of cultural competency in identifying and addressing the concerns and issues of their advisees. As academic advisors and individuals on the front line, we must be honest with ourselves and recognize where we are in terms of intercultural awareness. The following represents various levels of intercultural awareness:

- *Non-awareness* of difference refers to advisors who have no or limited experience with diversity. It is not that they do not recognize difference, but they place no value on it, and approach each student as an individual regardless of race, ethnicity, religion, class, sexual orientation, and so forth.
- *Awareness of difference* indicates that you not only recognize difference but realize that it actually holds some value to individuals and your

relationships with them. However, you may lack the training, expertise, and ability to apply the knowledge you have.

- *Acceptance/acknowledgement* of difference indicates that during this stage you have accepted that *different* does not mean deviant, and your responsibility as an advisor is to become more culturally competent.

- *Understanding cultural difference* indicates you have taken the necessary steps to increase your cultural knowledge through diversity training, workshops, discussions with others, and self-education to better understand and relate to the diverse students you serve.

- *Cultural adaptation* indicates that you now have the ability to apply what you have learned and can adapt your advising approach to the needs and communication styles of your diverse students.

- *Intercultural skillfulness* indicates you have expanded your comfort zone and have become a culturally competent advisor. You now have the tools, knowledge, and skills to relate to a wide range of students and feel comfortable in doing so. Although these skills have been gained, they need to be maintained. This is an ongoing process in which advisors continue to learn and expand our knowledge.

Once you have identified your level of awareness, you can begin to apply your knowledge to individual students. Cultural competency is as much internal as external, and by identifying your level of understanding you can begin to work on areas of weakness to better identify and relate to diverse students and their needs. Self-assessment of cultural competency can be problematic and requires an honest evaluation of where you fit on the levels outlined above.

The four components of culturally competent advisors are awareness, knowledge, skill, and respect. Advisors must have awareness of others and themselves as well as the ability to adjust to individual students. Advisors must have knowledge of difference, cultural competency, theories of integration, ethnic identity, and relationship-building. They must have the skills to adjust and apply what they have learned. Respect is extremely important, since without respect, awareness, knowledge, and skills become just tools and not an ideology that is internalized and applied. Honoring students' differences means treating them as subjects, not objects to which our training and theories are applied (Eagleton, 1998). Students' differences can be found not only in their level of assimilation or identification with their particular subcultures but also in their individual needs, desires, motivation, and goals. Once we have identified where we are in terms of our level of understanding, we can apply the various identity models developed for these populations (Walter & Smith, 1989; Cass, 1984). The next step is an ongoing process of establishing trusting relationships with students.

Relationship-Building

While all these students belong to identified groups that fall under the category of students with special advising needs, they are individuals first and foremost. Many may be lacking confidence or direction or be nervous and confused concerning their role on campus or in the advising process. They are placed in an environment that can be intimidating, and it is often difficult for them to ask for help. Regardless of how much time is provided for advising, gauging students' interest outside the classroom is important as well. Advisors can:

- Develop a series of questions that will allow relationship-building during the initial stages of your meeting.
- Inquire about the students' prior experience or activities they wish to pursue in college.
- Have a list of campus organizations to better direct the student to meaningful extracurricular activities.
- Introduce the student to programs and events that celebrate their interest in diversity or closely relate to their sense of identity.
- Inquire where the student went to high school to have a better understanding of the socialization and home environment.

Developing a series of questions will help advisors use the full range of campus resources (e.g., advocacy offices, disabled student services, honors programs) as they begin to develop relationships with students.

STUDENTS WITH SPECIAL NEEDS

Students with Disabilities

Students with disabilities may seem like the "invisible minority" on our campuses, and at times it is difficult for advisors to identify students in this population. Disabilities may include health-related issues, learning disabilities, partial sight or blindness, hearing impairment, physical impairments, or speech impairments. Section 504 of the Rehabilitation Act of 1973 and the Americans with Disabilities Act of 1990 were passed to establish legal requirements and eliminate architectural barriers so that this population of students could have equality of opportunity. These laws were also passed to address "issues of dignity, access and meaningful participation, dimensions of inclusive and supportive environments, institutional obligations for recruitment and admission, the value of and inclusion in out-of-class activities, strategies for career and academic advising, and the impact of financial resources on funding programs and services" (Belch, 2000, p. 1).

Due in part to this legislation and the focus on the needs of students with disabilities, the number of these students entering higher education between 1980 and 1998 tripled (Hehir, 1998). Although this student population is growing, a stigma remains, and individual students may choose not to identify their disability. According to a national survey of advisor's experiences, "approximately 91% of the survey respondents reported that students with invisible disabilities do not inform advisors of their particular disability until they are in significant academic trouble" (Preece, Roberts, Beecher, Rash, Shwalb, & Martinelli, 2007, p. 63). Advisors must encourage students to share their disability and the challenges they face in and out of the classroom. Advisors also should be aware of the various types of disabilities, the attitudes on their campuses toward disabilities, the resources available to students in this population, and barriers to their success. However, they "need not be trained as mental health therapists or as accessibility specialists" (Preece et al., 2007, p. 62).

According to Belch (2000, p. 2), "fair opportunity describes equality in which intentional intervention mediates the effects of discrimination, bias, or inequality." In order to mediate the effects of exclusion or inequality, advisors must understand and recognize the challenges faced by students with disabilities. These challenges include but are not limited to the following:

- Underrepresentation of the issues and concerns of students with disabilities
- Accommodations and faculty attitudes toward these students
- Career-planning opportunities
- Invisibility and equal participation on campus
- Quality-of-life issues
- Academic planning and course scheduling

To best meet each of these concerns, advisors need to establish partnerships with various offices (e.g., Office of Disability Services, Career Center) and recognize their own prejudices or levels of discomfort when working with this student population.

Advisors can help students with disabilities take command of their own education and become actively involved on campus. These students must develop a sense of identity and self-confidence and be willing to explore all the options campus life provides. This may include various student organizations, off-campus opportunities in the community, internships, student government, diversity programs, student ambassadors for the Admissions Office, and other activities that students without disabilities have the opportunity to experience. Once the barriers are removed, opportunities are offered, and accommodations are provided, these students can assume their rightful place at our colleges and universities and contribute as students and not as students with disabilities.

Adult Learners

The population of adult learners is also increasing, and according to the *Journal of Blacks in Higher Education* (2006, p. 59), 45 percent of black undergraduate students and 25 percent of whites are over the age of thirty. The terms *nontraditional* and *adult learners* have been used interchangeably, yet there are differences between these two groups. Nontraditional students possess at least one of the following characteristics: "they delay postsecondary enrollment one year or more after high school graduation, enroll part time, are employed full time, are financially independent of their parents, have dependents other than a spouse, are single parents, or do not have a high school diploma" (Compton, Cox, Laanan, 2006, p. 73). Adult learners have their own characteristics, goals, and motivations. Richardson and King (1998) state that, "given their diversity as a population, consideration of adult students and their needs should take into account a multiplicity of factors and not give credence to simplistic or reductionist notions" (p. 68).

According to Compton et al. (2006, p. 74), the following characteristics recognize adult learners as a distinct group:

- Adult learners are more likely to pursue a program leading to a vocational certificate or degree.
- Adult learners have focused goals for their education, typically to gain or enhance work skills.
- Adult learners consider themselves primarily workers and not students.
- Adult learners are more likely to be enrolled in distance education.
- Adult learners are more likely to speak a language other than English.
- Adult learners are more likely to leave postsecondary education without earning a degree.

Adult learners may have family- and work-related responsibilities that interfere with their academic goals and graduation requirements. The goal of academic advising is to help students remain in school, succeed academically, and eventually graduate. Adult learners "are more diverse than traditional students in their motivations, needs, expectations, and experiences with higher education" (Richardson & King, 1998, p. 66). According to Richardson and King, adult students are treated sometimes as if they lack the required skills to succeed in higher education. They suggest that "the idea that adult students are deficit in their study skills is meaningless because there is no one significant set of skills that constitutes effective studying in higher education"(p. 81).

Adult students face many challenges as they enter or reenter higher education. These challenges may include:

- Additional financial burden
- Lack of familiarity with campus resources
- Family obligations
- Time-management skills, or time constraints on graduation
- Lack of study skills
- Lack of confidence in academic abilities
- Lack of integration into the social life of the campus
- Lack of utilization of life experiences in and out of the classroom
- Lack of a support system between adult learners on campus
- Lack of class scheduling around their other responsibilities

The Council for Adult and Experiential Learning (2005) developed the following eight principles to guide the servicing of adult learners:

1. *Outreach.* The institution conducts its outreach to adult learners by overcoming barriers in time, place, and tradition in order to create life-long access to educational opportunities.

2. *Life and Career Planning.* The institution addresses adult learners' life and career goals before or at the onset of enrollment in order to assess and align its capacities to help learners reach their goals.

3. *Financing.* The institution promotes choice using an array of payment options for adult learners in order to expand equity and financial flexibility.

4. *Assessment of Learning Outcomes.* The institution defines and assesses the knowledge, skills, and competencies acquired by adult learners from the curriculum and from life and work experience in order to assign credit and confer degrees with rigor.

5. *Teaching-Learning Process.* The institution's faculty use multiple methods of instruction (including experiential and problem-based methods) for adult learners in order to connect curricular concepts to useful knowledge and skills.

6. *Student Support Systems.* The institution assists adult learners using comprehensive academic and student support systems in order to enhance students' capacities to become self-directed, lifelong learners.

7. *Technology.* The institution uses information technology to provide relevant and timely information and to enhance the learning experience.

8. *Strategic Partnerships.* The institution engages in strategic relationships, partnerships, and collaborations with employers and other organizations in order to develop and improve educational opportunities for adult learners.

In each of these categories, academic advisors can serve as "linking pins" between adult learners and the various campus offices and resources involved in this process, including Student Financial Services, academic departments and units, adult learning centers, advocacy offices, counseling centers, and career centers. Through campus-wide collaboration, adult learners will be able to use their skills, talents, and experiences. As Richardson and King (1998) point out, "they are capable of more effective and elaborative learning than younger students precisely because they are likely to be far more adept at examining and exploring their prior experience in order to make sense of new information and new situations"(p. 69).

Student Athletes

Student athletes often hold a unique position on campus because their participation in college athletics adds a complex layer to their college experiences and sense of belonging. They have adjustments similar to those of nonathletes in terms of intellectual growth, social activities, and commitment to their studies, yet they also have sports-related obligations in terms of practice, seeing trainers, travel, studying playbooks, and game days (Watt & Moore, 2001, p. 7). A typical advising site for student athletes looks much like this one at Colorado State University: http://www.casa.colostate.edu/advising/Faculty_Advising_Manual/Chapter2/student%20athletes.cfm.

When advising student athletes, keep in mind that they:

- Must be registered for a minimum of twelve credits at all times in order to practice and compete.
- Need to successfully complete twenty-four new credits toward their major per evaluation year—August to August. Eighteen of these twenty-four credits must be completed during the regular academic year (Fall or Spring semester), with six credits counting during the summer.
- Must complete at least six credits toward their major each semester.
- Must declare a major prior to the beginning of their fifth semester of full-time attendance.
- Must complete 40 percent of the course requirements in their specified degree program by the beginning of their third year, 60 percent by the beginning of their fourth, and 80 percent by the beginning of their fifth.
- Must remain in good academic standing according to the NCAA grade point average scale (must have a 1.8 cumulative grade point average [GPA]after two and three semesters, must have a 1.9 cumulative GPA after four and five semesters, and must have a 2.0 GPA all semesters thereafter). Individual institutions may require higher GPAs for eligibility.
- Have various time commitments with regard to class, homework, study hall, practice, competition, and travel.
- Must develop a long-range scheduling plan for subsequent semesters; this will allow scheduling of courses depending on sport season.
- Need assistance in identifying the qualities in the sport experience that will apply to their major and career choice.
- Need to discuss summer school courses prior to or during fall registration.

If the advising focus is simply to keep student athletes eligible to compete in intercollegiate sports, then it would be better to label them athlete students and not student athletes. Instead, the focus must be on guiding them based on their academic, personal, and career goals. This is especially true for students in revenue-producing sports. It is necessary to use advising strategies to help them remain academically eligible, but lifelong learning skills and the challenges they face as intercollegiate athletes must also be addressed. The challenges of student athletes include:

- Isolation from the nonstudent population outside the classroom.
- Inflexible and demanding schedules, especially during the season.
- A sense of inadequate preparation for college-level work, which leads to a lack of self-esteem outside sports activities.
- Stereotypes of athletes by campus personnel and other students.
- The possible conflict in the roles of student and athlete.

- Issues of time and energy devoted to the classroom and their sport.
- Lack of academic motivation.

Given the unique challenges faced by student athletes and the unlikelihood that these students will advance to professional sports, it is necessary for academic advisors to instill in them a sense of belonging and involvement. This will require an assessment of the athletes' motivation to succeed academically and the development of strategies to build academic skills and confidence. Working with their coaches or athletic counselors, advisors need to stress the role that academics play in their lives and beyond their playing career. Outside of their obligations to their individual sport and team, student athletes are no different than nonstudent athletes and require the utilization of all campus resources and the commitment and guidance of academic advising to be successful.

First-Generation Students

Like many students in this chapter, there is no single definition for first-generation students who remain invisible on our campuses unless they chose to identify themselves. The definitions of *first-generation* range from the first in their immediate family to attend college, to neither of the student's parents graduating from a four-year college, to the first in the family to pursue education beyond high school (Schauer, 2005). Regardless of the definition, first-generation students confront issues that are directly related to their socioeconomic status or inexperience with higher education. The following issues and concerns have been identified for many first-generation students. They:

- Are twice as likely to leave college before their second year.
- Typically enter college for the first time beyond their eighteenth birthday.
- Come from a lower-income family.
- Are married.
- Belong to an ethnic minority group.
- Attend college part-time.
- Tend to work full-time.
- Are more likely to enroll at two-year schools or community colleges.
- Are underprepared academically and have a feeling of low self-esteem.
- Have lower standardized test scores.
- May come from a home in which English is not the first language.
- Have insufficient parental or family support.

First-generation students are pioneers for their families and may enter college with mixed emotions. Some are role models for younger siblings or the next generation and may be leaving their family and community. These students may experience isolation and hesitancy once they arrive on campus and are uncertain of their fit or ability to succeed. Peters (2007) offers six practical suggestions that advisors can say or do to increase the success rate of first-generation students:

- *Develop positive friendships.* Students should be encouraged to seek others with similar goals who serve as a support system. This includes fellow students, faculty, staff, and professional organizations.

- *List important dates.* Time management is one of the keys to college success.

- *Develop a contact list.* First-generation students are often hesitant to seek help on campus. By developing a contact list of individuals from various departments, advisors can direct students to those who may have a more complete understanding of the needs of first-generation students.

- *Use technology to help students.* Use technology as an advising tool to stay in contact with advisees and to follow through on suggestions you have made.

- *Use all campus resources.* This includes national Trio programs, advocacy offices, writing centers, tutoring centers, and academic offices.

- *Help students persist.* Serve as an advocate for first-generation students, and assist them in maneuvering through the complexities of higher education.

In addition to the practical suggestions listed above, first-generation students need structure and guidelines in order to be successful. Hicks (2002) suggests implementing intensive counseling support groups; an intensive orientation program; involving parents in the process; offering a first-year experience course that introduces students to course expectations of faculty and the language of the university; organizing community-building activities such as first-year interest groups and living learning communities; and supplemental instruction. Academic advisors are critical in implementing these programs and in providing the support and guidance first-generation students may require throughout their academic careers. Coalition- and relationship-building serve as the keys for first-generation success.

High-Ability Students

On the surface it would seem that high-ability students are the least-demanding group to advise, are self-directed, and are far less "high maintenance" than students not classified as high ability. After all, these students enter colleges and universities with advanced academic skills, lofty career expectations, focus, dedication, and a drive to succeed. Gerrity, Lawrence, and Sedlacek (1993) reported that more high-ability student than non-high-ability students had college-educated parents, with 40 percent having graduate degrees. High-ability students are more likely to plan to attend graduate school than non-high-ability students. These young adults, however, enter our institutions with the same developmental needs as other students (Schwartz, 2006). Dougherty (2007) reports that high-ability students may lack good study skills, not have sound time-management practices, lack social maturity, possess unrealistic expectations for college, be experiencing immense pressures to succeed academically, and be experiencing burn-out. Dougherty (2007, p. 64) states that, "These students are often overlooked in the advising process because they typically excel in academics and appear to work in a self-reliant manner. Too often, educators mistakenly assume that high-achieving students do not require as much advising because they are autonomous, self-motivated, and know how to attain their goals." These students need developmental advising as much as other students to clarify their academic, personal, and career goals.

Digby (2007) provides guidelines for advising high-ability students:

- *Ease up on the reins.* Let students explore options and reach their own conclusions.

- *Encourage them to play.* Allow these students to expand their sense of personal choice and participate in activities not directly related to their career choice. This may include internships, study abroad, or major exploration courses outside their chosen field of study. Allow them the freedom to break beyond the structure and protection so many have experienced in high school.

- *Don't enter them into too many races.* Advisors should build personal relationships with these students and attempt to eliminate the tension that comes from being pushed toward too much competition.

- *Lead them to water but don't force them to drink it.* Serve as a guide, but allow students to make their own choices.

This approach allows high-achieving students to be more than their grade point average so they can truly experience all that a college education has to offer.

Although high-ability students may be the stars in the classroom, some may have difficulty establishing relationships with other students outside academics. High-achieving students also need the resources that the campus offers, such as specialized advising services (e.g., pre-med or pre-law), tutoring for some classes, the counseling center, or the career center. By relating to high-achieving students individually, academic advisors can determine which areas of developmental advising need the greatest focus.

Lesbian, Gay, Bisexual, and Transgender Students

Lesbian, gay, bisexual, and transgender (LGBT) students constitute students not only with special advising needs, but more importantly they are students who have struggled to find their place on campuses across the nation. Phrases such as "Safe Zones" and "LBGT Ally" indicate that it is not always a welcoming atmosphere for LGBT populations. The Federal government and thirty-five states do not include sexual orientation in their laws (National Gay and Lesbian Task Force, 2005). Students, such as Matthew Shepard, are targets of violence across the country. According to Moorhead (2005), "our profession has a central role to play in creating campus environments that can support the complexity of people's experiences." Academic advisors can assist in fostering a culture of equality for LGBT people by serving as allies and educating other faculty, staff, and students to dispel prejudice and discrimination.

Even more than other groups discussed in this chapter, it is necessary for academic advisors to establish partnerships with other offices to build credibility and a growing network of campus personnel that provide support and recognition for the increasing number of LGBT students. This is true not because this group merits or requires more than others, but rather because historically little has been done to serve their needs. More and more campuses are recognizing the needs of LGBT students, but others do not fund offices that provide needed services.

Academic advisors need to assist LGBT students in making sense of their lives on campus as they increasingly become an integral and crucial element of campus life in and out of the classroom. Most advisors have a general sense of the characteristics of student athletes, high-ability students, first-generation students, and students with disabilities. However, because LGBT students have been "silenced" for so long and often choose not to go public with their sexual orientation and identity, there is often a lack of understanding for this group.

Moorhead (2005) suggests the following advising strategies for LGBT students: Be aware of your language, and use appropriate labels and expressions; never assume heterosexuality, and use inclusive language and content; promote understanding by making an effort to learn about LGBT people, their issues, and concerns; ask questions, and rather than making incorrect assumptions, establish a relationship in which you are allowed to ask questions and make mistakes; instead of merely offering solutions, include students in the search for answers; facilitate and support students by empowering them to advocate for themselves, and be there to support their actions and decisions; be an advocate and ally for LGBT students throughout campus; treat students equally according to their own individual needs, desires, and objectives; and get involved on campus, since students always appreciate seeing faculty and staff at events, gatherings, and special graduations.

Brandy L. Smith (2006) suggests doing the following to increase our understanding of LGBT persons and the issues they face:

- Read affirming books that accurately portray LGBT people.

- Talk in a respectful way with people who are LGBT to learn about their experiences and struggles.

- Attend presentations that discuss LGBT persons' experiences or perspectives in an affirming way.

- Visit the Human Rights Campaign Web site at www.hrc.org.

- Connect with individuals who are LGBT to learn about them and how their sexual identities are integrated into their personalities rather than isolated from who they are.

Once our stereotypes and assumptions concerning this population have been challenged, meaningful relationships can be built with LGBT advisees as we assist them in reaching their academic, personal, and career goals. Like other students, LGBT students must be treated as individuals within their cultural context.

CONCLUSION

Students with disabilities, adult learners, student athletes, first-generation students, high-ability students, and LGBT students all have special advising needs. Although there are identity theories, case studies, statistical representations, retention rates, and other important information about each of these groups, knowing these will not necessarily make advisors more effective. The three most crucial areas to develop to become an effective advisor for all students, especially students with special needs, are coalition-building across campus, relationship-building with individual advisees, and cultural competence in terms of understanding our own intercultural awareness. The astounding and unique challenges these populations face, the multiple categories each group represents, and the extensive literature about each group can overwhelm even experienced advisors. First and foremost, advisors must understand that most students want to be treated as individuals and not as members of special groups with special needs. Advisors must always treat students as individuals within their cultural context and realize that they are the subject and not the object of advising. According to Boyer (1990), "a college or university is a just community, a place where the sacredness of each person is honored and where diversity is aggressively pursued."

References

Belch, H. A. (2000). Serving students with disabilities. *New Directions for Student Services, 91*.

Boyer, E. L. (1990). *Campus life: In search of community.* Princeton, NJ: Foundation for the Advancement of Teaching.

Cass, V. C. (1984). Homosexual identity formation: A theoretical model. *Journal of Sex Research, 20* (2), 143–167.

Compton, J. I., Cox, E., & Laanan, F. S. (2006). Adult learners in transition. *Understanding Students in Transition: Trends and Issues, 114*, 73–80.

Council for Adult and Experiential Learning. (2005). *Introduction to the adult learning focused institution initiative (ALFI).* Retrieved July 28, 2007, from http://www.cael.org/alfi.htm

Digby, J. (2007). Advising honors students. *Academic Advising Today, 30* (3). Retrieved July 7, 2007, from http://www.nacada.ksu.edu/AAT/NW30_3.htm

Dougherty, S. B. (2007). Academic advising for higher-achieving college students. *Higher Education in Review, 4*, 63–82.

Eagleton, T. (1998). Five types of identity and difference. In D. Bennett (Ed.), *Multicultural states: Rethinking difference and identity.* New York: Routledge.

Gerrity, D. A., Lawrence, J. F., & Sedlacek, W. E. (1993). Honors and nonhonors freshmen: Demographics, attitudes, interests, and behaviors. *NACADA Journal, 13* (1), 43–52.

Hehir, T. (1998). *High school "make or break" time for kids with disabilities.* Minneapolis: Parent Advocacy Coalition for Educational Rights.

Hicks, T. (2002). Advising the first-generation college student: Effective retention tools for colleges and universities. *The Mentor: An Academic Advising Journal.* Retrieved September 1, 2007, from www.psu.edu/dus/mentor

Moorhead, C. (2005). *Advising lesbian, gay, bisexual, and transgender students in higher education.* Retrieved August 12, 2007, from NACADA Clearinghouse of Academic Advising Resources. http://www.nacada.ksu.edu/Resources/index.htm

National Gay and Lesbian Task Force. (2005). *State nondiscrimination law in the U.S.* Retrieved August, 20 2007, from http://www.thetaskforce.org/downloads/nondiscriminationmap.pdf

Peters, L. (2007). Practical ways we can assist first generation students. *Academic Advising Today, 30* (3). Retrieved July 15, 2007, from http://www.nacada.ksu.edu/AAT/NW30_3.htm

Preece, J. E., Roberts, N. L., Beecher, M. E., Rash, P. D., Shwalb, D. A., & Martinelli, E. A. (2007). Academic advisors and students with disabilities: A national survey of advisor's experiences and needs. *NACADA Journal, 27* (1), 57–72.

Journal of Blacks in Higher Education. (2006). Racial differences in the age of under-graduate college students. *52,* 59.

Richardson, J. T. E., & King, E. (1998). Adult students in higher education: Burden or boon? *Journal of Higher Education, 69* (1), 65–88.

Schauer, I. (2005). Issues facing first generation college students. *Academic Advising Today, 28*(1). Retrieved August 6, 2007, from http://www.nacada.ksu.edu/AAT/NW28_1.htm

Schwartz, M. (2006). Preparing to advise high-achieving students. *Academic Advising Today, 29* (3). Retrieved August 1, 2007, from http://www.nacada.ksu.edu/AAT/NW29_3.htm

Smith, B. L. (2006). Gay, lesbian, bisexual, and transgender (GLBT) issues in advising situations. *Academic Advising Today, 29* (3). Retrieved August 3, 2007, from http://www. nacada.ksu.edu/AAT/NW29_3.htm

Walter, T. L., & Smith, D. E. P. (1989). *Student athletes.* In M. L. Upcraft & J. N. Gardner (Eds.), *The freshman year experience.* San Francisco: Jossey-Bass.

Watt, S. K., & Moore, J. L. (2001). Who are student athletes? *Student Services For Athletes. 93.*

CHAPTER THIRTEEN

Advising Students of Color and International Students

Evette Castillo Clark and Jane Kalionzes

Students from diverse backgrounds continue to experience unique challenges accessing and succeeding in higher education, despite their growing numbers in college enrollment and degree attainment. Chapter Twelve examined students with specific advising needs. This chapter discusses two more student populations that require special advisor attention. The academic, social, cultural, immigration, and transition challenges and concerns that both students of color and international students face warrant the attention of advisors committed to student success. Equally important to demonstrating an awareness of these issues and concerns is knowing how best to support these student populations without mega grouping (Anderson, 1995). *Mega grouping* is the tendency to homogenize the diverse characteristics within a group, such as language, class, generation, and academic achievement, to name a few. Advisors are at the forefront in helping students of color and international students understand the relationships and connections among the choices they make and the events they experience.

Students of color and international students on college campuses are two very distinct populations with varying needs, concerns, and backgrounds. This chapter will focus on the critical issues and advising perceptions of African American, Asian Pacific Islander American, Latino and Latina, Native American, multiracial and biracial, and international student communities in higher education. Although their challenges, experiences, and intercultural differences are recognized as unique, students of color and international students do share some cultural norms and racial experiences in higher education. The authors highlight both student groups and a full cultural contextual understanding of each in this chapter. Each is organized similarly to illustrate student status, cultural contexts, and advising perceptions, and ends with specific strategies and recommendations for advisors. Also included are distinguishable topics as they relate to the student of color and international student experience. It is important for advisors to use different approaches and demonstrate cultural awareness and competency to work successfully with these student populations.

ADVISING STUDENTS OF COLOR

Status of Students of Color in Higher Education

Throughout this chapter, the term *students of color* is used to identify students who are: members of racial or ethnic groups who have been historically underrepresented and underserved in America's educational system, and socially defined as minorities that are most likely to become targets of oppression, prejudice, stereotyping, and discrimination regardless of numerical status and distribution (Rendón, García, & Person, 2004). The terms *African American, Asian* and *Pacific Islander American, Latino* and *Latina, Native American,* and *Multiracial and Biracial* are specifically used to describe the various groups that comprise "students of color."

As demographics change and as demands for more of an ethnic and racially diverse society increases (Rendón & Hope, 1996), college student bodies will undoubtedly be more diverse, dynamic, and complex. Higher education professionals will need to be genuine and intentional about evaluating teachings, practices, service delivery, views, and approaches. According to Harvey-Smith (2005), in the past twenty years minorities have made significant progress in higher education, with larger proportions attending college. As the face of the American college-going population changes, however, students of color still trail behind their white counterparts in key areas such as high school achievement, college attendance, retention, and graduation. It is important to understand these trends because they inform the role of advisors in a learning-centered environment.

Participation

Table 13.1 shows that in fall 2005, Asian, Black, Latino and Latina, Native American, and white students were not equally distributed throughout the country's two- and four-year institutions. White, international, black, Asian, and Native American students show higher attendance rates at four-year institutions, while Latino and Latina attendance rates are higher at two-year institutions (52 percent) as compared with four-year institutions (48 percent). Black students on college campuses today comprise the largest population of students of color, with over two million students in both two- and four-year institutions. As indicated in Table 13.1, however, students of color in aggregate make up only a fraction of the entire undergraduate enrollment in the nation's college systems (participating in two- and four-year institutions) with only 13 percent for black students, 11 percent for Latino and Latina, 6 percent for Asians, and 1 percent for Native Americans.

Table 13.1. College Enrollment by Racial and Ethnic Groups, Fall 2005.

Race or Ethnic Group	Total Percent Undergraduate Enrollment (%)	Public/Private Four-Year (%)	Public/Private Two-Year (%)
Male undergraduates		63	37
Native American	1	54	46
Asian	6	62	38
Black	13	59	41
Latino and Latina	11	48	52
White	66	65	35
Nonresident alien	3	84	16

Source: *Chronicle of Higher Education* (Almanac, 2007–2008a).

Table 13.2. Degrees Conferred by Racial and Ethnic Group, 2004–2005.

	Total (%)	White (%)	Black (%)	Latino and Latina (%)	Asian (%)	Native American (%)	Nonresident Alien (%)
Associate degree	100	68.3	12.4	11.3	4.8	1.2	2.0
Bachelor's degree	100	72.9	9.5	7.0	6.8	0.72	3.2

Source: *Chronicle of Higher Education* (Almanac, 2007–2008b).

Degree Attainment

Associate and bachelor degrees conferred between 2004 and 2005 for white, black, Latino and Latina, Asian, Native American, and international students are shown in Table 13.2. Black students continue to be the largest population of students of color earning degrees at both two- and four-year institutions. White students continue to remain the majority in the attainment of both associate (68.3 percent) and bachelor (72.9 percent) degrees across the nation's campuses while Native Americans' associate (1.2 percent) and bachelor (0.72 percent) degree attainment is the lowest.

There is much attention given at the front end of recruiting students of color to college, which is to be applauded, but one cannot forget the emphasis needed for graduating them. Equally important to both access and graduation are the quality experiences and student learning that occurs during their college tenure. This is where the main responsibility and sphere of influence for advisors resides.

UNDERSTANDING CULTURAL CONTEXTS OF STUDENTS OF COLOR

The following offers specific background information and some recommendations for working with students of color. Additional recommendations are

provided that offer broad approaches to assist advisors as they work with specific student populations. Advisors will be more successful in their academic
advising work with students of color when they have a basic understanding
of each population as the demographics and concerns change, and when they
challenge their own stereotypes and biases.

African American Students

The focus on creating a strong and close community of African American
students, staff, and faculty is critical for the retention and success of African
American students. African Americans have historical links throughout the
world, representing many different countries. The ethnic realities of African
American students generally are grounded in African culture, with roots not
only in Africa, but also in the West Indies, the Caribbean, Canada, Central
and South America, and the United States (Lee, 2004; Rendón et al., 2004).

African American students who attend predominantly white institutions are
more likely to view the campus as alienating, hostile, unjust, and less supportive to their needs (Fleming, 1984; Schmader, Major, & Gramzow, 2002; White,
1998). African American students are fully aware of "race" and how it can
affect their academic success. Fries-Britt and Turner (2001) reveal that African
American students experience the stress of feeling intellectually inferior to
their white peers and may question their academic abilities. Compounding the
additional stress of facing racial stereotypes, their study indicated that African
American students undergo a "proving process" in order to validate their feelings of intellectual competence. If the classroom, work environments, and
other professional and academic settings are all examples of domains that
matter to African American students, then we as educators, must create positive learning climates that build confidence, self-esteem, and repair their "academic sense of self" (Fries-Britt & Turner, 2001, p. 426).

Much research about African American college students has been in the
areas of identity development as an aggregate group, comparing their experiences with other minority groups and issues they face on predominantly
white campuses. There is limited research on within-group differences among
African American students (White, 1998). This is an important factor because
it relates to how they view themselves in the context of others within their
community, their sense of belonging to the college community, and their overall persistence. White's groundbreaking study on how African American students perceive and interpret themselves and their community identity suggests
that: (a) African American identity is complex, ever-present, and situationally
determined; (b) African American students who have not been around their
peer group before college may have different social adjustment issues than
students from predominantly African American environments; and (c) African
American students have dual social relationships to the campus—their relationship to the campus as a "student" and their relationship to the campus as
"a black student" (pp. 95–96).

It is important also to examine and understand the increasing complexity
and development of an ethnic identity for second-generation black immigrants

because of the increase in nonwhite, voluntary immigrants to the United States since 1965 (Waters, 1994). Waters' study on second-generation West Indian and Haitian Americans in New York City revealed three types of identities evident among second-generation immigrants—"a black American identity, an ethnic or hyphenated national origin identity, and an immigrant identity" (p. 795). Waters' research found that first-generation black immigrants to the United States tended to distance themselves from American blacks; stress their national origins and ethnic identities as Jamaican, Haitian, or Trinidadian; and face overwhelming pressures in the United States to identify only as "blacks." Their children, however, who may lack their parents' distinctive accents, can choose to be more "invisible" as ethnics than their parents and will most often be seen by others as "American" rather than as black immigrants (p. 796). Second-generation black immigrant college students' experiences are complicated by American racism and its effects, and therefore must work to actively assert their identities. Second-generation black immigrants understand their racial and ethnic identities differently than those who identify as African American.

Malveaux (2005) writes that it is challenging to deal with issues of internal diversity in any community and to understand some of the tensions that may impede unity within communities. When educators on college campuses consider designing and implementing programs and services for African American and black immigrant students, they should be mindful of how they view themselves within their own cultural community and how it affects identity development and level of academic adjustment and success.

Asian and Pacific Islander American Students

Advisors are instrumental in addressing outcomes that relate to the integration of interpersonal and intrapersonal competence for Asian and Pacific Islander American students. The term *Asian* and *Pacific Islander American* applies to a highly diverse population encompassing Americans from East and South Asian backgrounds as well as the Pacific Islands. *Asian American* (or *Asian Pacific American* or *Asian Pacific Islander*) is now a term in common use in institutional data and throughout U.S. society (Hune, 2002). As a population that is rapidly growing and culturally diverse, many educators should be mindful of the various microcultures and complex issues faced within the Asian Pacific Islander American community. Asian Americans, however, share enough cultural similarities and common issues that they can be regarded as a unique student population (McEwen, Kodama, Alvarez, Lee, & Liang, 2002), but it is important to note the differences (e.g., income, ethnicity, culture, language proficiency, family size, and immigration patterns) that may shape their individual experiences.

Although Asian and Pacific Islander Americans are increasingly attending and graduating from higher education institutions (Suzuki, 2002), they are still invisible on U.S. campuses with respect to campus policies and programs (Hune, 2002). In fact, it would be far more accurate to measure progress of Asian and Pacific Islander Americans when international students from Asia are excluded from domestic statistics. It is also important to differentiate between the experiences of Asian Pacific Islander Americans that represent a racial minority group (e.g., Pacific Islanders, Lao, Hmong, and Cambodian) from the majority of Asian Pacific Islander Americans. Also, aggregate data may show that Asian and Pacific Islander American college students are "success stories" or "model minorities." This stereotype carries negative consequences for many students and is often challenged by Asian American researchers and educators (Suzuki, 2002). Academic success may be hard for first-year Asian Pacific Islander American students to achieve if they are under pressure to perform. Eventually, for some, the pressure becomes such a burden and a challenge that they drop out.

Asian Pacific Islander Americans see themselves as individuals, but also as an integral part of a family. Conflict may occur as these first-year students are highly focused on community and family, and college campuses focus on individuality and competition (Chew-Ogi & Ogi, 2002). Choosing a major, for many Asian and Pacific Islander college students, may be more of a family decision than an individual one (Castillo, 2002). Understanding this family interdependence and decision-making process (Kodama, McEwen, Liang, & Lee, 2002) may help advisors adjust their practice and pedagogy in helping students frame discussions and communications with their families. What needs to be emphasized for Asian Pacific Islander American students and their families, especially for new immigrants, is to help them understand the total college experience such as living on or off campus, balancing work with studying, engaging in conversations with professors, and exploring different major choices and career options. In addition to the college experience, students and families need to know about available academic resources such as tutoring, learning, and advising centers. Attention given to advisors' training and education on the diversity and complexity of the many microcultures within the Asian Pacific Islander community and their specific challenges is essential in valuing the responsibility to the students and institutions that advisors serve.

Latino and Latina Students

To create meaningful learning experiences and ensure academic success, critical attention needs to be focused on Latino and Latina students' college experiences. Like African Americans and Asian and Pacific Islander Americans, Latinos are not a homogeneous group. There are more than twenty Spanish- and Portuguese-speaking countries in the Western hemisphere and Latinos self-identity is based on their country of origin (Brown & Rivas, 1995). The terms *Latino* and *Latina* and *Hispanic* are often used interchangeably. The terms *Latino* and *Latina* are believed to be more inclusive and to encompass Latin American countries. The government adopted the term *Hispanic* in the seventies to keep population statistics and monitor compliance to Affirmative Action laws (Granado, 2007). Some believe the term to be given externally and not to be an expression that comes directly from the population itself. Generally, either term is acceptable and depends on how the individual prefers to be identified. It is also helpful to distinguish between those who identify themselves as multi-generational and those who are recent immigrants.

In terms of economic status, few Latino and Latina students come from families in which both parents attended college and graduate school. They are often first-generation college students. A large number come from working-class, low-income families, in which college attendance may not be encouraged or even introduced as an option. If they do attend college, many Latino and Latina students apply to nearby institutions to be closer to their families (Rendón, 1992). In addition, many Latinos and Latinas live in predominantly ethnic minority communities (Gonzalez, 2002; Rendón et al., 2004).

Like African American students, Latino and Latina students also interpret the campus culture of predominantly white students as alienating, unsupportive, isolating, and hostile. It is common for Latino and Latina students to feel "out of place" and "ignored" (Attinasi & Nora, 1996; Gonzalez, 2002; Hurtado & Carter, 1996).

Attinasi and Nora's (1996) study describes "getting ready" and "getting in" as important concepts to consider in understanding and addressing Latino and Latina student retention. The getting-ready concept includes college staff communicating with parents about college preparation and expectations of going to college, students witnessing or not witnessing family members attending college, conversations with high school teachers and counselors about college, and visiting college campuses. The getting-in concept (or cognitive mapping) are the postmatriculation experiences associated with how Latino and Latina students manage their new environment (Attinasi & Nora, 1996). The overall transition in the first year may include students' experiences such as: (a) learning how to manage resources (e.g., time and money), (b) maintaining family support, and (c) finding their "fit" in the college community. Further, Hurtado and Carter (1996) found that if Latino and Latina students made a smooth transition into college in the first year, they are less likely to perceive college as a hostile environment in the second year, which can result in an overall positive sense of belonging in the third year. For Latino and Latina students, validating their desire to succeed, encouraging an optimistic outlook (Hernandez, 2000), and recognizing their achievement at the onset of college is essential to their overall success and retention.

Native American Students

It is important for advisors to continually educate themselves about the culture and needs of Native American students, who differ from mainstream students. Native Americans, according to Russell (1997), include 557 federally recognized tribes in the United States, and 220 of them are in Alaska.

There is salient lack of research and information about Native American student participation, cultural preservation, and educational struggles and how they meet these challenges. What is known about Native American participation in higher education is that it has revolved around notions of assimilation. Dartmouth College, the College of William and Mary, and Princeton University were founded as institutions with distinctive mission statements clearly stating their role to educate Indian people and "civilize" them (DeJong, 1993; Tierney, 1993; Wright, 1988). Given the effects of colonialism, some Native Americans are economically deprived, often come to campus less academically prepared, and may live in rural areas where access to postsecondary institutions is difficult (Rendón et al., 2004; Tierney, 1993). It is critical to understand how Native American students' lives are affected by life on the reservations, their values of harmony with nature, and the degree to which community and tribal goals supersede individual goals.

Multiracial and Biracial Students

It is important to know and understand multiracial and biracial students from their point of reference—that is, how they view themselves and their experiences. Many multiracial students may come to know this view of themselves and perspective only when they encounter a new environment, such as coming to college. What is most important to consider is that there is no end point or final stage to their identity development as there is with other groups of students of color. Various models illustrate that students have their own way of coming to terms with their multiracial heritage.

Renn's (1998) multiracial identity model delineates five patterns describing how students group themselves in terms of their identity. This porous and fluid framework results from the influence of campus culture and peer-to-peer interactions in these students' making sense of their racial identity. One way that first-year students choose to identify themselves racially is to choose one racial category with which to affiliate. A second way involves students moving between their different heritage groups and choosing not to identify with one racial identity all the time. The third approach is identifying themselves as "multiracial" depending on the campus support (e.g., clubs and organizations for multiracial students, mentoring, courses, and ongoing programs or events that explore multiracial student identity and experiences). The fourth category includes students who avoid being labeled as belonging to any racial group. The fifth and final category involves students who use one or more of the first four options when different situations suggest different ways of affiliation.

Developing an advising community that is welcoming to multiracial and biracial students requires commitment and support to increase interracial contact and provide requisite resources to achieve multicultural competence (Pope, Ecklund, Miklitsch, & Suresh, 2004). An initial approach for advisors may be to first find out where students are in their racial identity formation and how they view themselves and the world around them.

ADVISORS' ROLE IN AFFIRMING DIVERSITY AND TRANSFORMING INSTITUTIONS

It is one thing to be aware of our diverse students and to know how to address their issues thoughtfully and appropriately. It is an even greater task to learn to genuinely *value* and *affirm* diversity in advising work and commit to transform institutions to better support students of color. Rendón, Lee, Clark, and Tobolowsky (2007) published a set of *old beliefs* and *new agreements* that would help shatter barriers for students of color and guide institutions to affirm diversity (pp. 3–4):

Old Belief: The agreement to resist engaging the topic of diversity.

New Agreement: **Diversity is an institutional value.**

Old Belief: The agreement that diversity can be affirmed simply by making small, marginal changes.

New Agreement: **Diversity involves making structural changes throughout the entire institution.**

Old Belief: The agreement to disconnect excellence from diversity.

New Agreement: **Diversity and excellence can and do coexist on college campuses.**

How advisors can demonstrate cultural awareness and begin to affirm diversity in their day-to-day work first requires a shattering of prevailing belief systems about diversity on campuses. To do this requires an unveiling of those powerful, shared belief systems that everyone agrees to follow and adhere to (most of the time unspoken) and critically look at those policies, practices, and systems that have created injustices and inequity. From this, the next step is to work collectively with both academic affairs and student affairs as partners to create new belief systems that serve to better affirm diversity and address the needs of our diverse student populations. Given that these new agreements were published only in 2007, specific best practices across the United States have yet to be aligned with them. It is evident, however, that universities' fluid strategic plans, revised mission statements, campus climate studies, growth in diverse curriculum and pedagogy, newly created statements on diversity, required department- and campus-wide diversity training, and the hiring of new administrative positions specific to diversity and equity show that a major shift and change from old beliefs to new agreements that affirm diversity is taking place.

SPECIFIC STRATEGIES AND RECOMMENDATIONS FOR ADVISORS

When advising students of color, it is important to note that there are no set guidelines, one-size-fits-all, or clear-cut strategies. Nor should advisors and other university faculty and staff view the experiences and characteristics of all students of color monolithically in order to support their learning. In the earlier sections of this chapter, some specific recommendations were offered as they relate to each student population. The following items for action offer broader philosophies for working with students of color but need to be addressed with those specific cultural contexts in mind. For example, mentorship is critical for the success of male students of color, but specifically for Latino students. Mentors are most helpful when provided before college and during the first year of college, since retention is a concern. The overarching goal in advising students of color is that the advising be contextual, ongoing, educational, and developmental for both advisor and advisee. Recommendations for advisor action are discussed below.

Advise the Whole Student

Academic advising is more than just course scheduling and helping students understand graduation requirements. At the onset, students of color enter college with a complex range of family, economic, educational, language, and identity characteristics and issues that warrant working with them holistically. It is our responsibility to learn about their cultural as well as individual backgrounds and help them develop the confidence and competence to navigate a campus that they initially may view as unsupportive.

Understand the Student's Family Background

Advisors should make a conscious effort to understand the family structure and background of the student of color. Families can transcend the traditional biological mother and father roles and may also extend to relatives who are primary in their households, such as older siblings, aunts, uncles, stepparents, grandparents, and foster parents. Understanding the educational backgrounds of family members may offer some context as well. For example, students of color who are first in their family to attend college may have a different experience from students of color for whom both parents have Master's degrees. We know that families play a large role for most students of color. Advisors' understanding about students' family background and who the student deems as family can help them engage the student in learning about the values of college life.

Mentorship

Students of color need a person who can help them when they have problems, offer advice, and provide support. Mentors and mentor programs can enhance minority student satisfaction about university life and their academic performance (McMillan & Reed, 1994; Ting, 2000). Advisors can show care and concern, personalize their interactions with students, and genuinely understand the whole student and their background.

Build Trust to Make Personal Meaning

Building trust with the student is extremely important. Advisors need to understand the students' background and aspirations as they help students examine their choices (individually and those that have been made with their families). Provide as much time needed to help students of color understand the process of going to college, being in a community of different learners, faculty expectations, and the requirements to graduate—both emotionally and academically. After trust and a good working advisor-advisee relationship is established, advisors can help students of color to make purposeful meaning of their experiences by discussing options, majors, various career pathways, and campus involvement opportunities. They can also help them make sense of their environment—how they fit and belong—and explore various ways to enhance students' dialogue with their families, professors, and peers.

Understand Identity Development

Tierney (1993) states that minority students need institutions that will create conditions in which students not only celebrate their cultural and personal histories, but also help them critically examine how their lives are molded and shaped by society's forces. It is important to understand the experiences of students of color through their cultural backgrounds, views, values, and identity development. Advisors play a key role in helping students through this process by educating themselves about the student populations and understanding the lenses through which students look at their experiences and make decisions about their surroundings and relationships. One way to further their understanding would be to informally assign advisors to culturally based clubs and organizations. Similar to some advising structures in which academic advisors are assigned liaison responsibilities with colleges or schools across campus, this connection to cultural clubs and organizations would serve as a strong link between students' understanding of their academic advising experience and their relationship with their advisor.

Develop Multicultural Competencies

Advisors need to possess the appropriate attitudes, knowledge, and skills to support a diversity of students. To develop these multicultural competencies, advisors must engage in purposeful and ongoing training and education. Communication styles, beliefs, values, worldviews, and perceptions about students of color are just some examples to be explored and embraced. It is also critical to continue to support Ethnic Studies courses, which help students of color learn about their history, culture, and identity. For continuous education and development, advisors may consider attending or auditing such Ethnic Studies courses.

Be in the Students' World

There are real advantages for advisors to meet with students on more informal levels outside their offices, since students will see their advisors as "real" people with whom they can connect. Advisors will witness firsthand and more personally the world in which their students live. These meetings can occur anywhere, including residence halls, campus events, workshops, classrooms, club meetings, and the local coffee shop. Residence halls that embrace community and cocurricular activities such as clubs and organizations in particular (Johnson, Alvarez, Longerbeam, Soldner, Inkelas, Leonard, & Rowan-Kenyon, 2007) have contributed to a greater sense of belonging for students of color.

ADVISING INTERNATIONAL STUDENTS

Status of International Students in Higher Education

The prospect of studying higher education at colleges and universities in the United States has appealed to students in other countries for decades. The numbers of international students studying in the United States increased each year from the early 1950s until 2002 (Koh Chin & Bhandari, 2006), with a sharp increase during the 1970s and 1980s (Gooding and Wood, 2006). The attacks of September 11, 2001, proved to be a turning point, as the numbers of international students slackened and then declined (Koh Chin & Bhandari, 2006). Reasons attributed to this include harsh changes in U.S. visa policies that led to difficulty in obtaining student visas, the perception that the United States was no longer a safe destination (Bain & Cummings, 2005), as well as the increasingly high cost of tuition at U.S. institutions (Dassin, 2004). In addition, competition is rising from countries such as Australia, the United Kingdom, and Canada, whose lower costs and less restrictive visa policies make them more attractive choices (Starobin, 2006).

Demographics

Data from 2005 and 2006 demonstrate a possible resurgence in the international student population. According to a Web article from the American Council on Education (ACE, 2006), Allan E. Goodman, President and CEO of the Institute of International Education (IIE), indicates an 8 percent increase in the number of new students entering the United States:

> America's colleges have begun to see positive results from their proactive efforts to recruit international students and make them feel welcome on campus. With several thousand campuses able to host international students (ten times as many as any of the other leading host countries), the U.S. has a huge untapped capacity to meet the growing worldwide demand for higher education. (ACE, 2006, p. 18)

Still the total number of international students in the United States in 2005 and 2006 totaled 564,766, with these students and their families contributing over $13 billion to the U.S. economy that same year (Koh Chin & Bhandari, 2006).

While the overall numbers of international students appear to be once more on the rise, the demographics of the populations of international students remain constant. Asia sent the most students in 2005 and 2006, with 58 percent of the total enrollment of international students. India led as the individual country sending the most students, followed by mainland China, Republic of Korea (South Korea), Japan, and Taiwan. The most popular fields of study continued to be Business and Management, Engineering, Physical and Life Sciences, and Social Sciences. Although Mathematics and Computer Sciences declined from previous years, it remained strong at fifth place. Students were more likely to study in one of four states, California, New York, Texas, and Massachusetts (Koh Chin & Bhandari, 2006).

Topical Issues

The post 9/11 decline in the overall numbers of international students poses short-term concerns about how to improve the visa process and restore faith in the safety of the United States.

Bain and Cummings (2005) maintain additional concerns that are more disconcerting: (1) how to retain the levels of international graduate research assistants on which the United States depends for academic cutting-edge research; and (2) as financial resources become scarce, institutions rely on recruiting international students who are paying full tuition increases to make up the difference. Bain and Cummings further note that the loss of the on-campus presence of international students will take away the broadened worldview that prepares U.S. students to live productively in a world that is increasing daily in globalization.

Campuses have responded to these concerns through increased recruiting efforts or overall changes in their recruiting strategies. International offices on campuses often take the lead in international student recruiting efforts and are charged with developing detailed recruiting plans (Darrup-Boychuck, 2007). International recruiting tours and recruitment fairs in different regions of the world have become accepted means for attracting new students. Tours and fairs are organized by for-profit companies or by the U.S. Department of State (2007) global network of advising centers supported through the Bureau of Educational and Cultural Affairs at the U.S. Department of State.

Understanding Cultural Contexts and Advising Perceptions of International Students

Advisors who have a basic understanding of culture, the stages of cultural adjustment, and differences in cultural assumptions will feel more comfortable and may be more successful in their advising sessions with international students. In his book on survival while living overseas, Kohls (1979) did not use the word *culture* to mean the arts, such as literature or opera. He used it to include everything that a particular individual "thinks, says, does and makes—customs, language, material artifacts and shared systems of attitudes and feelings" (p. 17). He gives examples: manners, beliefs, laws (written and unwritten), language, values, ideas and thought patterns, and concept of self.

International educators often use the metaphor of an iceberg, as used in the AFS Orientation Handbook (1984), when orienting their newly arrived students to the meaning of the nature of culture. Much like a real iceberg, with its true shape below the waterline, the true nature of culture is hidden from view. On the iceberg model the outward, easily observed aspects of culture such as dress, language, fine arts, literature, and drama are shown on the ice above the waterline. The aspects of culture primarily out of awareness are shown below the waterline and are termed "deep culture." Some examples of "deep culture" on Kohls' list include eye behavior, notions of modesty, patterns of superior-subordinate relations, conception of justice, patterns of group decision-making, attitudes toward the dependent, approaches to problem-solving, roles in relation to status by age, sex, class, occupation, social interaction rate, conversational patterns in various social contexts, and time.

Advisors who become aware of the deep culture of other cultures may relate them to everyday advising situations with international students. An example is differences in conversational patterns that stem from differences in thought patterns and result in different linguistic styles. In discussing intercultural communication, Bennett (1988) notes that North Americans prefer a linear style of conversation. They come to the point quickly and in a straightforward manner. He explains that people from some other cultures, such as Asia and Africa, have a circular style of conversation, with more background provided that allows listeners a chance to derive their own conclusions. Bennett goes on to say that students from a circular style may find linear speakers to be "cold and patronizing" for stating the obvious; while linear speakers find circular speakers to be "tedious" and wish they would get to the point. Students from Japan often continue the circular style long after becoming linguistically competent and adjusted to studying in the United States. They may continually ask questions seeking answers that advisors may feel have already been answered.

Other conversational differences include the length of time someone speaks. In Brazil, it is acceptable for a person to tell a long uninterrupted story. Latin Americans generally tell their entire story uninterrupted; the other person then gives their uninterrupted answer for the same amount of time or longer in contrast to the more back and forth approach used in the United States. Similar conversation patterns are common in African countries, where it is not unusual for speakers at a conference to lecture on for several hours.

Althen's (1994a) chapter, "Cultural Differences on Campus" discusses the misinterpretations that international students encounter with the phrases Americans use in expressing "No." As an example, a student may ask someone in the bursar's office for additional time to pay his tuition. The person replies "I wish I could help you, but we don't have a way to do that" or "I'm sorry, but our policies don't allow that." Although domestic students will realize that the answer is no and accept it, as Althen points out, other cultures may view these answers as the beginning of negotiations instead of the final word on the subject. They may begin to negotiate for an answer that is more satisfactory. Americans may think that they are being unreasonable or pushy when in fact they have just misinterpreted the cultural cues. Saying "no" directly can often save a lot of time and energy.

There may also be confusion on the semantics of how questions are worded and the appropriate response to the questions. English learners still unsure of their abilities will find it hard to respond to questions worded as a negative question such as "Haven't you told your professor that you don't understand his lectures?" Students will do better with more straightforward questions such as, "Did you go to your professor's office?" "Did you tell him you did not understand the lecture?"

Advisors may find that the largest group of international students from one country on a campus poses its own set of concerns. This dominant group may be less likely to fully assimilate into the new culture and may form its own microcosm of the home country. When these students are from a country with a strong pattern of group decision-making, they may turn to their fellow nationals for advice rather than seeking it from campus advisors. In the tradition of strong group behavior, they may send a representative to act as a spokesperson on their behalf. They may also feel peer pressure within the group to live and act only in the manner accepted at home.

While the iceberg model (AFS, 1984) mentions eye behavior, head behavior also deserves note and can easily be added to the model. Head nods are cultural and can be confusing to international students. Students may not readily understand that the American custom of shaking the head side to side means no, and up and down means yes. In responding to students' questions, advisors should respond with "yes," not just a nod of the head. Students from India often use a head movement referred to as the "head bob." They learn quickly that Americans do not understand this type of head behavior and usually stop using it shortly after arriving in the United States.

Cross-Cultural Adjustment

Newly arrived international students go through a period of cross-cultural adjustment that varies in length and intensity with each student. The model of the U-curve of adjustment (Lysgaard, 1955) is often used to explain the cultural adjustment process to new international students. Oberg (1960) revised the model and was the first to describe adjustment to a new culture as "culture shock." He assigned four stages to the model: Honeymoon, Crisis, Recovery, and Adjustment. Newly arrived students in the Honeymoon Stage resemble newly married couples enchanted with each other, but in this case it is the host country that is the focus. In the Crisis Stage, the students become acutely aware of the differences between home and the host culture and may respond with frustration and anger. Students begin to function without problems in the Recovery Stage. In the Adjustment Stage they function without problems, and begin to enjoy the new culture.

In their work on counseling student sojourners, Thomas and Harrell (1994) point out that the students are not always at the same level of adjustment in every part of their life. Students doing well academically may be in the "adjustment" stage in their academic life, but if lagging socially can be caught in the "crisis" stage of their personal and social life. They recommend that advisors use the U-curve as a starting point for discussion on cross-cultural adjustment. Thomas and Harrell note further that the stages are not static but are based on the student's past experience adapting to a new culture, their own personal adaptability level, and the types of experiences they encounter. They may experience none or all of the stages, may skip a stage, or may experience one or more of the stages repeatedly. The authors continue that any life event can change the student's stage of adjustment and the satisfaction they feel in the host culture.

Assumptions

All persons have implicit assumptions about how they approach their daily life based in part on their own personal "deep culture." Advisors bring these implicit assumptions to their jobs that unconsciously guide them in their daily advising practices. Advisors' assumptions often differ from those of their international students and can lead to confusion and misunderstanding during advising sessions.

Althen (1992; 1994b) discusses the different cultural assumptions American advisors bring to their work as well as the assumptions international students bring from abroad. In Althen's discussion of U.S.-based assumptions, he notes that U.S. advisors view their institution's rules and requirements to be legitimate and to generally be fair. He goes on to state that U.S. advisors assume that people working in campus offices are hired for their qualifications and promoted for their competence. They expect their students to be given reasonable treatment as long as "they (1) behave politely (by local standards) (2) follow standard procedures (which may involve filling out certain forms) and (3) tell the truth. (There is a truth)." Furthermore, clients "should speak for themselves, and not allow husbands, older siblings or friends to speak for them" (Althen, 1994a, p. 64). They expect students to accept their decisions since they are objective and follow the rules.

Althen notes that international students perceive campus staff to hold a lot of power and adds that they control many things students want—for example, letters for their home government, jobs on campus, and credit for courses taken at home. International students may assume males and older advisors have more power and ability to make decisions than female or younger counterparts. They may wish to speak only to the boss, who they may believe fits these qualifications. Althen (1992) comments that "facts and truths" may be relative, and that international students may seek the sympathy of staff members, who they believe should take time to talk with them. They think that what they ask for is important, and if an advisor will not give them the answer they are looking for, they will continue until they find someone who will.

In contrast to the U.S.-based assumptions are some of the assumptions that international students have because they have no experience with them in their home country. In some countries it is standard practice for the elder brother to speak on behalf of his younger siblings, or for the husband to do all the talking while the wife sits silently even though the discussion is about her admission to the institution. There may not be the same standard of truth, so they see no problem with offering another reason or answer if the first one does not produce the desired effects.

ADVISING PERCEPTIONS OF INTERNATIONAL STUDENTS IN TERMS OF THEIR IMMIGRATION STATUS

Many international students worry that they may inadvertently violate the terms of their F-1 or J-1 non-immigrant visa status while in the United States. The concern is so great that it may cause them to make seemingly irrational, unusual, inexplicable, or unreasonable requests. To maintain their status, students must enroll in a full-time course load each academic term. Advisors should be cognizant of the implications of an international student taking less than a full course load and how it could indeed lead to problems with their visa status. Should academic problems become a concern, advisors might recommend a reduction of course load to their students, which students may feel reluctant to do. Students faced with academic suspension will often express as much concern and even fear about losing their immigration status as about their academic failure. Their perception that one "mess-up" and they are deported from the United States may be exaggerated, but the reality is they must closely follow the regulations imposed on them through the Department of Homeland Security.

Because immigration regulations are complex and ever-changing, it is critical that advisors consult regularly with their institution's designated school officials (DSO) to ensure compliance with appropriate federal regulations. Developing and maintaining an open working relationship with the DSOs before a crisis event will aid in a stronger and better response to any severe problems that students may face.

STRATEGIES AND RECOMMENDATIONS FOR ADVISORS WORKING WITH INTERNATIONAL STUDENTS

Internationalizing the Campus

As discussed earlier in the chapter, many institutions are actively seeking ways to internationalize the campus and the curriculum. Advisors can use many strategies to become more aware of their campus' efforts:

- Learn what efforts toward internationalization are being made on your campus. Find out whether there are campus-wide initiatives that are currently being developed or implemented on the campus to further the internationalization of the campus. Learn how to become part of these efforts.

- Many institutions annually organize a series of internationally themed events during International Education Week, held the second week of November each year (International Education Week, 2007) as a part of their campus internationalization efforts. Advisors are encouraged to attend these events to increase their awareness of the steps toward internationalization being taken on their campus.

- Review and consider implementing activities listed in NAFSA's Intercultural Activity Toolkit (NAFSA, 2007), which is a collection of hands-on, group-oriented activities that can be used by international educators with the goal of internationalizing the campus.

- Join a campus professional organization or honor society that focuses on internationalization. Many campuses have a branch of the Phi Beta Delta international honor society, and will accept both faculty and staff as members. The society generally holds meetings and lectures on internationally related subjects given by faculty, staff, or visiting international faculty involved in international projects or exchange programs.

- Become knowledgeable about the curriculum changes and programs being developed to further the campus internationalization efforts. Steer students toward any of these new, often multidisciplinary, majors.

- Find ways to advocate for international students on campus. Look for ways to change policy or procedures that could improve student services for international students. A simple policy change demonstrates the institution's commitment to international students and their concerns.

Increasing Cross-Cultural Awareness and Cultural Sensitivity

- Participate in events organized through the international office or an international student club. International offices and clubs hold events throughout the year that showcase cultural artifacts, food, clothing, or dancing from their culture. International students are delighted when advisors take the time to attend these events.

- Show an interest in learning more about a student's country or culture. Ask international students questions about their country. Use a globe or map of the world as a way to begin a conversation. Even short discussions about a student's home country can demonstrate an advisor's interest in their culture and vastly improve the advising relationship.

- Hold a training program or workshop on advising international students for all advisors on campus. Invite the staff from the international office to be speakers or serve as resource persons. Plan to discuss cultural norms, cultural and academic adjustment issues, and specific strategies for improving advising sessions with international students. The staff from the international offices are often highly trained and experienced in these issues.

- Become a mentor to an international student or host an international student for a holiday or upon arrival to the institution.

- In many cities in the United States it is possible to expand knowledge of other cultures through festivals or holiday celebrations organized by local immigrant communities.

Specific to Small Institutions

Advisors at small institutions may not find the resources on their campuses to institute the recommendations listed here. Advisors at these schools will need to seek out and at times develop their own ways to become more skilled advisors to international students. Although campuses may be limiting, the wealth of information available on the Internet is limited only by the time and the willingness of advisors to sort through the information available. Review the Web sites of professional organizations such as NAFSA and NACADA, and those involved with international student advising such as the Association of International Educators for information on all aspects of international education. Many of these organizations offer information and advice, publications on areas of international education, as well as discussion groups and "Webinars" to further the knowledge of international education.

CONCLUSION

As advisors, it is important to use specific advising approaches and demonstrate cultural awareness and competency to work successfully with students of color and international student populations. Given that these student groups are dynamic, increasing, multifaceted, and complex, advisors' careful attention, understanding, open-mindedness, and willingness to be a learning colleague with students are requisite to having successful and meaningful advising relationships. It is a privilege and responsibility as educators in higher education to be sensitive to the role of culture and background that affect student academic achievement.

This chapter illustrated areas that concern marginalization, access, recruitment and retention, community and family obligations, moving from old beliefs about diversity to new agreements, assumptions, identity, cross-cultural adjustment, and barriers to academic achievement. These issues require advisors and campus leaders to reevaluate practices and programs with regard to students of color and international students and to intentionally transform higher education in the effort to create an enriched community of learners.

References

ACE: American Council on Education. (2006, November 13). Monday buzz: New report documents reversal in international student enrollment declines, continued growth in number of U.S. students studying abroad. Retrieved January 6, 2008, from http://www.acenet.edu/AM/Template.cfm?Section = News_Room&TEMPLATE = /CM/ContentDisplay.cfm&CONTENTID = 18903

AFS Orientation Handbook. (1984). *The iceberg conception of the nature of culture. Resource III–A, A Workshop on Cultural Differences*. New York: AFS Intercultural Programs.

Almanac. (2007–2008a). College enrollment by racial and ethnic group, selected years. *Chronicle of Higher Education*. Retrieved December 29, 2007, from http://chronicle.com/weekly/almanac/2007/nation/0102002.htm

Almanac. (2007–2008b). Degrees conferred by racial and ethnic group, 2004–5. *Chronicle of Higher Education*. Retrieved December 29, 2007, from http://chronicle.com/weekly/almanac/2007/nation/0102002.htm

Althen, G. (1992, February). The American educational administrator: Examining some assumptions. Presidential perspectives: the state of foreign student/scholar advising. *NAFSA Newsletter*. Retrieved September 9, 2007, from http://www.presidentialperspectives.info/assumptions.php

Althen, G. (1994a). Cultural differences on campus. In G. Althen (Ed.) *Learning across cultures* (pp. 57–71). Washington, DC: NAFSA: Association of International Educators.

Althen, G. (1994b). Recurring issues in intercultural communication. In G. Althen (Ed.) *Learning across cultures* (pp. 185–196). Washington, DC: NAFSA: Association of International Educators.

Anderson, J. A. (1995). Toward a framework for matching teaching and learning styles for diverse populations. In R. R. Sims & S. J. Sims (Eds.), *The importance of learning styles: Understanding the implications for learning, course design, and education.* Westport, CT: Greenwood Press.

Attinasi, L. C., & Nora, A. (1996). Diverse students and complex issues: A case for multiple methods in college student research. In C. Turner, N. Garcia, A. Nora, & L. Rendón (Eds.), *Racial and ethnic diversity in higher education* (ASHE Reader Series, pp. 545–554). Needham Heights, MA: Simon & Schuster.

Bain, O.& Cummings, W. K. (2005). International students gone? *International Educator, 14* (2), 19–26.

Bennett, M. J. (1988). Foundations of knowledge in international educational exchange: Intercultural communication. In J. M. Reid (Ed.), *Building the professional dimension of educational exchange.* Yarmouth, ME: Intercultural Press, pp. 121–135.

Brown, T., & Rivas, M. (1995). Pluralistic advising: Facilitating the development and achievement of first-year students of color. In M. L. Upcraft & G. L. Kramer (Eds.), *First-year academic advising: Patterns in the present, pathways to the future* (Monograph No. 18, pp. 121–137). Columbia: University of South Carolina, National Resource Center for The Freshman Year Experience & Students in Transition.

Castillo, E. J. (2002). Bridges over borders: Critical reflections of Filipino American college students on academic aspirations and resilience. Unpublished doctoral dissertation, University of San Francisco.

Chew-Ogi, C., & Ogi, Y. (2002). Epilogue. In M. K. McEwen, C. M. Kodama, A. N. Alvarez, S. Lee, & C. T. H. Liang (Eds.), Working with Asian American college students. *New Directions for Student Services*, 97, 91–96.

Darrup-Boychuck, C. (2007). Measuring return on investment in international student recruitment. *International Educator, 16* (3), 64–68.

Dassin, J. (2004). Promoting access and equity in international higher education. *International Educator, 13* (3), 3–5.

DeJong, D. H. (1993). *Promises of the past: A history of Indian education.* Golden, CO: North American Press.

Fleming, J. (1984). Summarizing the impacts of college on students. In *Blacks in college: A comparative study of students success in black and white institutions* (pp. 161–194). San Francisco: Jossey-Bass.

Fries-Britt, S. L., & Turner, B. (2001). Facing stereotypes: A case study of black students on a white campus. *Journal of College Student Development, 42* (5), 420–429.

Gonzalez, K. P. (2002). Campus culture and the experiences of Chicano students in a predominantly White university. *Urban Education, 37* (2), 193–218.

Gooding, M.& Wood, M (2006). *Finding your way: Navigational tools for international student and scholar advisers.* Washington, DC: NAFSA: Association of International Educators, 1–3, 95–98.

Granado, C. (2007). "Hispanic" vs. "Latino": A new poll finds that the term "Hispanic" is preferred. Retrieved December 29, 2007 from http://www.hispaniconline.com/hh/hisp_vs_lat.html

Harvey-Smith, A. B. (2005). *The seventh learning college principle: A framework for transformational change.* Washington, DC: National Association of Student Personnel Administrators.

Hernandez, J. C. (2000). Understanding the retention of Latino college students. *Journal of College Student Development, 41* (6), 575–588.

Hune, S. (2002). Demographics and diversity in Asian American college students. In M. K. McEwen, C. M. Kodama, A. N. Alvarez, S. Lee, & C. T. H. Liang (Eds.), Working with Asian American college students. *New Directions for Student Services, 97,* 11–20.

Hurtado, S., & Carter, D. F. (1996). Latino students' sense of belonging in the college community: Rethinking the concept of integration on campus. In F. K. Stage & G. L. Anaya (Ed.), *College students: The evolving nature of research* (ASHE Reader Series). Needham Heights, MA: Simon & Schuster.

International Education Week, U.S. Department of State, U.S. Department of Education. (2007). Retrieved September 8, 2007 from http://iew.state.gov

Johnson, D. R., Alvarez, P., Longerbeam, S., Soldner, M., Inkelas, K. K., Leonard, J. B., & Rowan-Kenyon, H. (2007). Examining sense of belonging among first-year undergraduates from different racial/ethnic groups. *Journal of College Student Development, 48* (5), 525–542.

Kodama, C. M., McEwen, M. K, Liang, C. T. H., & Lee, S. (2002). An Asian American perspective on psychosocial student development theory. In M. K. McEwen, C. M. Kodama, A. N. Alvarez, S. Lee & C. T. H. Liang (Eds.), Working with Asian American college students. (*New Directions for Student Services, 97,* 45–59).

Koh Chin, H. and Bhandari, R. (2006). *Open Doors 2006: Report on International Educational Exchange.* New York: Institute of International Education.

Kohls, L. R. (1979). *Survival kit for overseas living.* Chicago: Intercultural Press, pp. 17–21.

Lee, W. Y. (2004). Enhancing the first-year experience of African Americans. In L. I. Rendón, M. García, & D. Person (Eds.), *Transforming the first year of college for students of color.* (Monograph No. 38, pp. 93–107). Columbia, SC: University of South Carolina, National Resource Center for The First-Year Experience and Students in Transition.

Lysgaard, S. (1955). Adjustment in foreign society: Norwegian Fulbright grantees visiting the United States. *International Social Science Bulletin, 7,* 45–51.

Malveaux, J. (2005, November 3). Dimensions of diversity. *Diverse issues in Higher Education, 22* (19), 31.

McEwen, M. K., Kodama, C. M., Alvarez A. N., Lee, S., & Liang, C. T. H. (2002). Working with Asian American college students. *New Directions for Student Services, 97.*

McMillan, J. H., & Reed, D. F. (1994). At-risk students and resiliency: Factors contributing to academic success. *The Clearing House, 67* (3), 137–140.

NAFSA: Association of International Educators. (2007). Intercultural activity toolkit. Retrieved November 25, 2007, from http://www.nafsa.org/knowledge_community_ network.sec/international_student_3/campus_and_community/practice_resources_ 16/orientation/intercultural_activity_1

Oberg, K. (1960). Cultural shock: Adjustment to new cultural environments. *Practical Anthropology, 7,* 177–182.

Pope, R. L., Ecklund, T. R., Miklitsch, T. A., & Suresh, R. (2004). Transforming the first-year experience for multiracial/bicultural students. In L. I. Rendón, M. Garcia, &

D. Person (Eds.), *Transforming the first year of college for students of color*. (Monograph No. 38, pp. 161–174). Columbia: University of South Carolina, National Resource Center for The First-Year Experience and Students in Transition.

Rendón, L. I. (1992). From the barrio to the academy: Revelations of Mexican American "scholarship girl." In L. S. Zwerling & H. B. London (Eds.), First generation students: Confronting the cultural issues. New Directions for Community Colleges, *80*, 55–64.

Rendón, L. I., García, M., & Person, D. (Eds.). (2004). *Transforming the first year of college for students of color* (Monograph No. 38). Columbia: University of South Carolina National Resource Center for The First-Year Experience and Students in Transition.

Rendón, L. I., & Hope, R. O. (1996). *Educating a new majority: Transforming America's educational system for diversity*. San Francisco: Jossey-Bass.

Rendón, L. I., Lee, W. Y., Clark, E. C., & Tobolowsky, B. F. (2007). Shattering barriers: Affirming diversity in higher education. *Education Policy and Practice Perspectives, 3*.

Renn, K. A. (1998). Check all that apply: The experience of biracial and multiracial college students. Presented at the ASHE Annual Meeting, Miami, FL. (ERIC Document Reproduction Service No. ED 427 602.)

Russell, G. (1997). *American Indian facts of life: A profile of tribes and reservations*. Phoenix, AZ: Russell.

Schmader, T., Major B., & Gramzow, R. H. (2002, Spring). How African American college students protect their self-esteem. *Journal of Blacks in Higher Education, 35*, 116–119.

Starobin, S. S. (2006). International students in transition: Changes in access to U.S. higher education. *New Directions in Student Services, 114*, 63–71.

Suzuki, B. (2002). Revisiting the model minority stereotype: Implications for student affairs practice and higher education. In M. K. McEwen, C. M. Kodama, A. N. Alvarez, S. Lee, & C. T. H. Liang (Eds.), Working with Asian American college students. *New Directions for Student Services, 97*, 21–32.

Thomas, K., & Harrell, T. (1994). Counseling student sojourners: Revisiting the u-curve of adjustment. In G. Althen (Ed.), *Learning across cultures* (pp. 89–108). Washington, DC: NAFSA: Association of International Educators.

Tierney, W. G. (1993). The college experience of Native Americans: A critical analysis. In L. Weis & M. Fine (Eds.), *Beyond silenced voices*. Albany: State University of New York Press.

Ting, S. R. (2000). Predicting Asian Americans' academic performance in the first year of college: An approach combining SAT scores and noncognitive variables. *Journal of College Student Development, 41* (4), 442–449.

U.S. Department of State, the Bureau of Educational and Cultural Affairs (2007). Education USA, Your guide to higher education, Retrieved September 8, 2007, from http://educationusa.state.gov/fairs.htm

Waters, M. (1994). Ethnic and racial identities of second-generation black immigrants in New York City. *International Migration Review, 28* (4), 795–820.

White, L. S. (1998). "Am I Black enuf fo ya?" Black student diversity: Issues of identity and community. In K. Freeman (Ed.), *African American culture and heritage in higher education research and practice*. Westport, CT: Greenwood.

Wright, B. (1988). "For the children of the infidels?": American Indian education in the colonial colleges. *American Indian Culture and Research Journal, 12* (3), 1–14.

ORGANIZATION AND DELIVERY OF ADVISING SERVICES

Wesley R. Habley

Part Three lays the groundwork for the organization and delivery of advising services. In the pivotal Chapter Fourteen, Susan Campbell builds the case that the foundation of excellence in the delivery of academic advising relies on a carefully conceived and institutionally based mission statement. Campbell follows by describing the importance of goals and objectives derived from the institutional mission and sharing examples of these.

Excellence in advising requires that the mission is realized and the goals and objectives achieved through an appropriate, student-centered organization of services. In Chapter Fifteen Margaret King suggests that there are three basic constructs in the organization of services: centralized, decentralized, and shared. King presents and discusses seven organizational models, citing data on utilization and commenting on the particular strengths and possible concerns associated with each of the seven models. King builds a strong case for the implementation of the four shared models.

Chapters Sixteen through Nineteen provide insights into the various means by which advising services are delivered to students. Hemwall presents a strong argument for faculty advising in Chapter Sixteen. As both the most common and longest-standing means for delivering advising, Hemwall suggests that advising by faculty is a central component to the undergraduate experience. She suggests that a powerful strategy for approaching and engaging faculty more fully in the advising process is to focus on student learning.

Over the past five decades, the growth and increasing diversity of undergraduate enrollments as well as demanding and complex expectations of faculty members has led institutions to identify individuals who specialize in academic advising and also to rely on other members of the campus community to deliver advising. In Chapter Seventeen, Self discusses the following advisor types: professional advisors, counselors, peer advisors, graduate students, and support staff. Self shares advice on the utilization, the strengths of, and the concerns associated with each of these advisor types.

While Chapters Sixteen and Seventeen focus on the person-to-person delivery of advising services, Chapters Eighteen and Nineteen present delivery strategies that augment or supplement person-to-person advising. In Chapter Eighteen, Nancy King suggests that group approaches can be more than a relief strategy for overworked advisors. King shares a number of group advising strategies that are both viable and effective. In the final chapter of Part Three, Michael Leonard scans the horizon to share the technology available that can be used to both support and to deliver advising. Leonard provides a look into the future suggesting that the multiple technologies now available to advisors will converge and that the future of technology holds great promise for the future of advising delivery. But Leonard also sounds a word of warning, suggesting that advisors will need to adapt quickly to the new technologies or run the risk of becoming technologically obsolete.

CHAPTER FOURTEEN

Vision, Mission, Goals, and Program Objectives for Academic Advising Programs

Susan M. Campbell

Outstanding academic advising programs do not simply emerge. They are conceptually grounded—both theoretically and institutionally—and guided by statements of vision, mission, goals, and program objectives that codify the values, philosophy, approach, and central purposes of academic advising. These statements also provide both short- and long-term guidance for program initiatives, are central to the program planning process, and as such, must be dynamic, action-oriented statements. Taken together, the vision, mission, goals, and program objectives are an essential set of components for any academic advising program for they anchor the academic advising program, communicate the program's intentions to the institution, and provide the framework for the development of student learning and advising delivery outcomes that are at the heart of the advising program's assessment plan.

To set the stage for the consideration and design of statements of vision, mission, goals, and program objectives, it makes sense to first address the idiosyncratic nature of planning in higher education. This discussion facilitates an understanding of the importance of collaborative reflection and decision-making. From there, this chapter will elaborate on the importance of developing effective statements; highlight the relationship between the vision, mission, goals, and program objectives and the field of academic advising, one's institution, and among the statements themselves; provide guidance for the development of effective statements; and highlight some examples of statements for review and consideration.

SETTING THE STAGE: PLANNING IN HIGHER EDUCATION

In "The Emerging Third Stage in Higher Education Planning," George Keller (2007) widely considered the "founding father" of planning in higher education, addresses the complexity of planning in education. He confirms what is stressed here—that there is no "one way" to approach planning in higher education, for no two institutions are alike. He states that:

> it is abundantly clear that there can be no science of education planning. . . .
> Planning may have developed a few general principles, such as the need for an institution to pay attention both to its traditions and to the most consequential environmental factors pressing on it, or the necessity of knowing about competitors and competing distinctively among them. But to be successful, planning must also adapt to local, specific conditions and to the temper of the times. What this means . . . is that we must all be amateur anthropologists and historians of the present and the near-term future, as well as technicians of institutional change. (p. 61)

Rowley, Lujan, and Dolence (2001) agree and support Keller's conclusion that there is "no one model that can be applied like a cookie cutter" (p. xv). They go further by suggesting that conventional business models of planning—that is, mission-based and CEO-driven approaches—may not work effectively in colleges and universities. Rather than using a mission statement to drive planning efforts, these authors suggest the reverse, that a "statement of mission should be a derivative of planning rather than planning being a derivative of mission." They further stress that "a successful strategic planning process is marked by meaningful participation from across the campus" (p. xv).

Rowley et al. (2001) make two important and instructive points here. The first is that mission statements need to reflect an understanding of what Keller (2007) describes as the present and the near-term future. The second is that the process of planning and, hence, the development of effective vision, mission, goal, and program objective statements should be the result of dialogue among constituents. These essential components should derive from collaborative reflection, dialogue, and analysis, so that there is a collective commitment to them and they become part of the cultural fabric of the institution.

The vision, mission, goals, and program objectives serve a number of key purposes. The first is that they anchor the advising program, forming the foundation from which activities and initiatives are derived and guided. Without these foundational components, an unintended consequence is that the relationship between and among initiatives can be perceived by others as at best serendipitous and at worst of marginal importance or value. The vision, mission, goals, and program objectives therefore play important roles in communicating the purpose and intentions of the academic advising program to internal and external audiences—that is, the campus community and the community at large—and should be written with these audiences in mind. Further, as noted in planning, the vision, mission, goals, and program objectives frame action and guide the design of intentionally sequenced educational opportunities to support desired student learning and advising delivery outcomes. By identifying what is important with regard to student learning and advising delivery, the academic advising program is better able to develop strategies and actions, identify opportunities to learn, determine the qualitative and quantitative evidence that should be gathered to inform improvement and make decisions about vision, mission, goal, and objective achievement and effectiveness. Initiatives without the anchor of carefully crafted statements of vision, mission, goals, and program objectives are, as Drucker (1990, 2003) says specifically about mission statements, they are "nothing more than good intentions."

The Relational Nature of Vision, Mission, Goals, and Program Objectives

Statements of vision, mission, goals, and program outcomes for academic advising cannot stand in isolation. In this regard, to be effective they need to:

- be grounded in a philosophical and conceptual understanding of academic advising,
- be consistent with the vision and mission of the institution, and
- relate to each other from general to specific to guide action and assessment.

Relationship to the Field of Academic Advising. The vision, mission, goals, and program objectives must be grounded in relation to the field of academic advising. This relationship serves as the philosophical and conceptual basis upon which an institution frames its academic advising program. Three key documents from the National Academic Advising Association (NACADA) help to guide this philosophical and conceptual perspective, as described below.

NACADA Core Values (2007). Values are statements of belief regarding what is important and are used to guide and ensure the integrity of practice. For academic advising, the NACADA Core Values address the responsibility of advisors to:

- advisees,
- involve others, when appropriate, in the advising process,
- institutions,
- higher education,
- the broader educational community, and
- professional practice and personal development.

NACADA Concept of Academic Advising (2006). This statement provides the conceptual framework for the consideration of academic advising; it affirms a philosophical perspective that academic advising is a form of teaching and, as such, has a curriculum, pedagogy, and identified learning outcomes for students. The statement further explicates what each of these elements means with regard to academic advising. While confirming the contextual and individual nature of the design and delivery of academic advising, the NACADA Concept of

Academic Advising is clear about how academic advising is a holistic and developmental process that requires collaborative approaches to facilitate and support students as they enter and move through an institution toward achieving their educational, career, and life goals.

CAS Standards and Guidelines for Academic Advising (2007). The Council for the Advancement of Standards (CAS) has developed a set of guidelines for academic advising programs. These national standards serve as guides for institutions to audit their academic advising programs, help frame the development of programs, serve to align programs with national standards and also provide a way to demonstrate internal and external accountability and legitimacy. The CAS Standards and Guidelines for Academic Advising do not prescribe how advising is or ought to be organized. They do, however, identify critical areas for reflection, evaluation, and consideration. Beginning with *mission,* the CAS Standards offer guidance in thirteen areas and provide:

- clarity and context for the academic advising program goals,
- clarity regarding the role of the leader,
- clarity regarding the expectations of advisors, and
- a framework for the development of student learning outcomes.

The three documents discussed above are essential to consult and consider when developing statements of vision, mission, goals, and program objectives for an academic advising program. However, despite its importance, grounding an academic advising program's vision, mission, goals, and objectives is not enough. Additional considerations include the relationship to the institution's central purpose and mission and the interrelationship of the advising program's vision, mission, goals, and objectives.

Institutional Relationship. The vision, mission, goals, and program objectives of an academic advising program are inextricably intertwined with a college or university's central purpose and mission statement. This symbiotic relationship is an essential one, for without it the advising program stands on the periphery of the institution's core purpose and risks being marginalized. Figure 14.1 depicts, in elementary form, the relational nature of statements of vision, mission, goals, and program objectives. The figure illustrates the multidirectional ways in which each level influences and is influenced by the others. Each level needs to be integrated with the level above it, and all activities derive from and are informed by the institutional statement of mission, goals, and objectives. In situations when actions are "out of sync" with any of the levels, questions should be raised about the efficacy of the initiative and/or the efficacy of the statements of vision, mission, goals, and objectives for the advising program. Alignment among these is critical; alignment with the institutional mission is essential.

Interrelationship of Vision, Mission, Goals, and Objectives. Not only should the relationship among the vision, mission, goals, and objectives at various organizational levels be evident, the relationship between and among

Figure 14.1. Relationship between Institutional, School, College, and Division; and Program Missions.

the vision, mission, goals, and objectives themselves should be evident. Each of these components is interrelated, with each adding breadth or depth of meaning or both about the others. By design, these statements or components should: (1) be contextual; (2) be interrelated; (3) be in a deductive relationship and, in the inverse, an inductive one; and (4) be able to guide measurement at the level of strategy and action.

The contextual nature of statements of vision, mission, goals, and program objectives cannot be emphasized enough. Consistent with Keller (2007), Rowley et al. (2001), Drucker (1990, 2003), Habley (2005), and White (2000), there is no one statement of vision, mission, goals, and objectives that will apply to all academic advising programs. Institutional, environmental, and campus cultural differences make such a cookie-cutter approach impossible, impractical, and undesirable. In the end, it is from the conversation among key stakeholders that the most effective statements emerge.

These four key statements or components should be interrelated, mirroring, in a general way, the broader relationship among organizational levels. Figure 14.2, in a simplistic way, attempts to capture this relationship.

The triangle in Figure 14.2 also illustrates the deductive and inductive nature of mission, goals, and program objective statements. At the base of the triangle is the vision statement, which reflects the desired future for the program. Next is the mission statement, which is the general foundation from which more specific goals and program objectives are developed. Viewed inductively, Program Objectives are more specific than Program Goals, which are more specific than a Program's Mission Statement. The Vision Statement is a generalized view of a program's aspirations.

Finally, statements of vision, mission, goals, and program objectives should guide measurement at the level of strategy and action. In this regard, these components are not directly measurable; the strategies and actions that are put in place to achieve objectives and outcomes (student learning and advising delivery) are where actual measurement occurs. Measurement at the strategy and action level is used to gather evidence to support improvement and inform program objective, goal, and mission achievement.

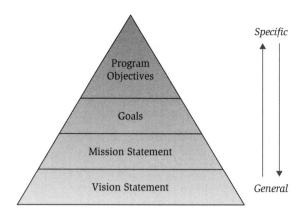

Figure 14.2. Relationship among Statements of Vision, Mission, Goals, and Program Objectives.

One final comment is in order here. It should be noted that, in reality, the relationship between and among statements of vision, mission, goals, and program objectives is much more complex than shown in the triangle in Figure 14.2. These components should be thought of as being nested within each other, rather than stacked on top of each other. This nesting captures the depth and breadth of the relationship.

DEFINING AND DESIGNING STATEMENTS OF VISION, MISSION, GOALS, AND PROGRAM OBJECTIVES

Discussions about statements of vision, mission, goals, and objectives always seem to spark heated debates about definition. Is "it" a mission statement or vision statement? Is "it" a goal or objective? What is the difference between a program objective and an outcome? Depending upon one's disciplinary perspective, the views may be different. The way to address this and to avoid what Heifetz and Linsky (2002) might consider a form of "work avoidance," in which participants divert the focus of the discussion from the important reflective work that needs to be done, is to identify the definitions that will be used in discussions. Developing a common language clarifies meaning and facilitates a richer, deeper discussion about what needs to be included in each of the components.

Starting with Vision

The prelude to a mission statement is a statement of vision. Essentially a vision is "a mental model of a desirable or idealistic future for an organization" (Nanus, 2003, p. 356). Vision statements are contextual. They result from reflection on the organization and its present and future. Visions are also inspirational—they reflect high ideals and generate enthusiasm and commitment to an organization's direction and purpose. Visions are also ambitious

Table 14.1. Vision Statements for Academic Advising.

Statement Definition	Example	Key Considerations
Vision statements reflect the aspirations of what academic advising can be on a campus. It represents a desired or ideal future.	The vision for academic advising is to develop a coordinated and responsive academic advising program that has regional and national recognition for excellence. *University of Southern Maine—College of Arts and Sciences*	Represents a desired future state Is inspirational Is ambitious yet realistic Generates enthusiasm Generates commitment to direction and purpose

and yet realistic in that they are shaped by information about the environment and reflect the distinctive character of the organization and what it is able to achieve. Vision statements may be realized or not, and they are subject to revision as conditions change (Nanus, 2003).

Translating this for academic advising, Table 14.1 provides both a working definition of vision as well as an example of a vision statement that has been shaped by an analysis of institutional considerations and goals and that challenges the academic advising program to a new standard of excellence.

Mission Statements

In contrast to vision statements, *mission statements* articulate purpose and direction. Value-laden, mission statements provide focus for action, provide guidance for the future, and inform immediate action. In many ways, a mission statement serves as the "roadmap" to one's vision, and while not presenting the portrait of a future in the same way as a vision, mission statements are, indeed, future-oriented.

Mission statements should be clear and concise. Drucker (1990, 2003) says they should "fit on a T-shirt" (p. 370). He also says they should inspire and be written in such as way that everyone can see how their actions contribute to the organization's purpose. While mission statements are designed to have some longevity, as actions are taken, initiatives completed, and goals achieved, they are (and should be) subject to revision. What should be kept? What has outlived its usefulness? In this way, the conciseness and simplicity of the mission statement remains intact.

According to Drucker (1990, 2003), mission statements need to reflect three things: opportunities, competence, and commitment. *Opportunities* represent needs that are to be addressed; *competence* relates to possessing the capacity and ability to make a difference; and *commitment* reflects the personal and collective belief in purpose. Table 14.2 translates this for academic advising.

The mission statement shown in Table 14.2 is concise, clear, repeatable, and identifies the purpose of the unit in assisting students in developing and

Table 14.2. Mission Statements for Academic Advising.

Statement Definition	Example	Key Considerations
Mission statements reflect the purpose of academic advising on the campus and serve as the roadmap to achieving the vision and affirming values.	The mission of University College is to assist new, transfer, and transitioning students, through academic advising, to develop and implement individual plans for achieving educational and life goals. *University of Utah*	Identifies purpose Is consistent with institutional mission Is long range Is clear and concise Is repeatable Is general in nature Is not measurable

implementing individual plans. It implies a particular understanding of academic advising that ought to be revealed in how the unit/program approaches its purpose. This example highlights some of the key considerations for mission development that have been outlined in the literature:

- *The mission statement should be broad and realistic.* As Habley (2005) says, the mission statement for academic advising is the umbrella for the delivery of services. As such, those in academic advising must be able to see how what they do "fits" and will support the purpose as reflected in the mission. While broad, the mission statement must also be realistic—that is, it must be achievable within the constraints of the resources available and consistent with the mission of the institution.

- *The mission statement must be short and concise.* The language used in the mission statement should be devoid of jargon and should be of sufficient length to be descriptive but *repeatable.*

- *The mission statement should be explicit and understandable.* As Drucker (1990, 2003) has so succinctly said, "(u)nless the mission is explicitly expressed, clearly understood, and supported by every member of the organization, the enterprise is at the mercy of events" (p. 371).

The question, then, is what strategies exist to help with designing an effective mission statement?

Approaches to the Design of Mission Statements

There is no one "best way" to begin to design a mission statement. The process, however, should be designed to encourage reflection on current practice as well as imagining a desired future. Keller (2007, p. 61) suggests thinking in both anthropological and historical terms; thinking about the cultural norms and institutional traditions as well as the "temper of the times." In translation, this requires careful reflection on what advising program, practices, and processes work or do not work, why those things work or have not worked, and the current contextual environment in which advising occurs. In this regard, a planning approach is most helpful when stakeholders are brought together to reflect on and brainstorm the current state of academic advising and to brainstorm and identify ideal concepts for academic advising at an institution. The challenge, of course, is to be creative and rational in this process; creative in the sense of not becoming trapped by traditions and rational by not posing ideas that are simply not feasible in the current organizational environment.

Strategy 1: Identify Key Stakeholders. Who needs to be at the table? Who should be involved in the discussions? Remember that this is not a solo activity or merely an administrative activity. Developing a mission statement from which goals, program objectives and learning outcomes can be derived is best done collaboratively and collectively to ensure commitment to, rather than merely compliance with, the mission.

Strategy 2: Brainstorm Current State of Academic Advising. The first task is to get a handle on perceptions of academic advising that currently exist. The process is a simple one. Record all the comments made by individuals in response to the question, "What terms, adjectives, concepts, metaphors, etc. could be used to describe academic advising at XYZ as it currently exists?" No discussion is had regarding any of the ideas presented, and stakeholders are encouraged to say what is on their minds, whether those are positive or negative comments. The recorder/facilitator may request clarification. All comments, whether duplicative or not, are recorded.

Strategy 3: Brainstorm and Identify the Ideal for Academic Advising. The second task shifts the discussion from the current state to the desired or "ideal" future for academic advising. Again, all comments are recorded to the simple question, "What would be ideal?"

Strategy 4: Synthesize the Ideal. Are there multiple concepts identified in the "Ideal" brainstorming materials? Can these be synthesized and more succinctly stated and still capture the intentions? To what extent are the values, principles, and concepts of the NACADA Core Values, the NACADA Concept of Academic Advising, and the CAS Standards for Academic Advising reflected in the ideal? How consistent with the mission and goals of the institution are the ideas being generated?

Strategy 5: Draft a Tentative Vision and Mission Statement. In terms of process, tentative vision and mission statements can be crafted at this point to guide the development of goals and program outcomes, or the group discussion can move to identification of desired outcomes for student learning before crafting them. Some may find that identifying desired outcomes for student learning add richness, depth, and focus to the tentative vision and mission statements as they are being developed.

A sample process that could be used to apply the strategies identified above in the development of a vision and mission statement is illustrated in the first five strategies depicted in Figure 14.3. Keep in mind that there is no "right" or "wrong" way to approach the development of these statements. In some situations, the vision might be clear from the beginning, in others reviewing the

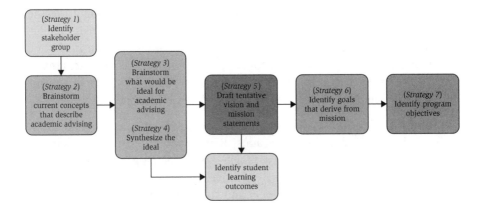

Figure 14.3. Sample Process Model for Developing a Mission, Goal, and Program Objective Statement.

current ideal concepts might lead to the development of a focused vision. The same holds true for mission statements (as well as goals and program objectives). The composition and "personality" of the stakeholder group will influence what approach is best to take. This suggests that the convener of the stakeholder group certainly needs to have an understanding of the nature of group process and be able to help the group navigate through the process to achieve the desired end result. This includes facilitating the group through the natural "bumps and hiccups" that all groups experience.

A substantial amount of time has been spent setting the context for developing statements of vision, mission, goals, and program objectives and specifically on developing mission statements. This is important work for, as has been suggested, the mission statement is the primary anchor for the academic advising program and serves as the vehicle through which one communicates to internal and external constituencies. Goals and program objectives add depth and meaning to the mission statement.

Goals and Program Objectives

Goals. Simply put, goal statements are expressions of the desired future state or "aims" of the organization or program. Goals are, by nature, both specific and long-range and are based on the mission statement. Table 14.3 offers an example of a set of goals.

These goals are broad and long-range. They support the concept of advising as teaching and indicate those general actions of importance to support the achievement of the mission. These goals represent the "aims" of the program and are derived from the mission. Finally, these goals are long-range.

When goals are met, the mission is achieved; students are engaged in learning, the advising program promotes students' success and fosters students' personal and intellectual growth.

Drucker (2003) indicates that goals need to be clearly defined, and it needs to be understood that from the goals, the strategies and actions and, in turn, a set of results should be able to be identified.

Table 14.3. Goal Statements for Academic Advising.

Statement Definition	Example	Key Considerations
Goal statements are long-range expressions of the desired future state of the organization or program. If met, they express what the organization would look like if the mission was achieved.	Engage students in learning Promote students' academic success Foster students' personal and intellectual growth	Represent the "aims" of the advising program Are long range Are clear Provide guidance for action Are not directly measurable Are general in nature, although more specific than the mission statement

Program Objectives. Finally, confusion often exists between what constitutes an objective versus what constitutes an outcome. Program objectives are more specific than goal statements but, like goal statements, are not directly measurable. Program objectives "identify content or learning parameters—what students should learn, understand, or appreciate as a result of their studies" (Maki, 2004, p. 61). Again, the language one uses is often dependent upon one's disciplinary perspective. However, in general, at the program objective level, the interest is in continuing to develop the overall portrait of the academic advising program to anchor it and to communicate the programmatic intentions to internal and external communities. Table 14.4 presents this definition of program objectives and offers an example for academic advising.

As noted previously, it is at the strategy and action level that measurement occurs. The strategies and actions are informed by the outcomes that have been developed for student learning and advising delivery. The program objective level provides an opportunity to illustrate this point. If one of the program objectives is to develop intentional partnerships in which students share responsibility for advising, what strategies and actions have been designed to facilitate achievement of this objective? How do these strategies and actions relate to the desired outcomes (student learning and advising delivery) for academic advising? What evidence (e.g., qualitative, quantitative, direct, indirect) is to be gathered to understand each strategy's and action's effectiveness in supporting the program objective? Actual measurement occurs at this more discrete, strategy and action level and is used to inform objective, goal, mission, and vision achievement.

Strategies for the Design of Goal and Program Objective Statements

Strategies 6 and 7 complete Figure 14.3 by addressing the key considerations in developing goal and program objectives for academic advising.

Strategy 6: Identify Goal Statements. Using the vision and mission statements as anchors, reflect on the following question, "Based on the mission statement (tentative or otherwise), what are the broad aims of the advising

Table 14.4. Program Objectives for Academic Advising.

Statement Definition	Example	Key Considerations
Program objectives articulate, in a general way, the expectations regarding how academic advising is delivered and what students are expected to demonstrate what they know and can do.	To develop intentional partnerships in which academic advisors are appropriately accessible and knowledgeable, in which academic advisors use their expertise to guide and facilitate student educational and life decision-making processes, and in which students share responsibility for advising. To offer a collective, collaborative process that makes use of appropriate university resources to support students' responsibility for their learning and success.	Specify the "intentions" of the academic advising program for student learning and advising delivery Reveal, in a general way, expectations for student learning. Inform and guide the development of student learning outcomes and advising delivery outcomes Are general in nature, although more specific than goals

program?" Using information from the CAS Standards for Academic Advising and the NACADA Concept of Advising statement is important here to ensure that goals are consistent with practice; using institutional information (e.g., vision, mission statements, etc.) is important to ensure consistency between the academic advising program and the institution.

Strategy 7: Identify Program Objective Statements. Program objective statements can be developed using an approach similar to that used for goals; however, the question is different and more specific—that is, "Based on the vision, mission and goals, what are the broad expectations regarding the delivery of academic advising and for student learning?" Framed another way, the question is, "What are the *intentions* of the academic advising program?"

CONCLUSION

Statements of vision, mission, goals, and program objectives represent the conceptual and philosophical foundations of any academic advising program. It is upon these critical statements that outcomes for student learning (i.e., what should students demonstrate they know, can do, and value as a result of participating the academic advising?) and the delivery of academic advising (i.e., how should academic advising be delivered?) are derived and on which specific strategies and actions (i.e., learning opportunities) are based. As the anchor, the vision, mission, goal, and program objective statements also serve as the primary basis upon which assessment plans are built. While assessment is addressed in another section of this volume, it is important to remember that these statements or components are at the center of the assessment cycle; they are used to guide the design of strategies and action and, in turn, the gathering of evidence to support improvement and change. Together, they indicate what an organization or program is about and wants to be, what it aims to achieve, and what specific intentions shape its aims.

References

CAS Standards and Guidelines for Academic Advising. (2007). Retrieved September 13, 2007, from http://www.nacada.ksu.edu/Clearinghouse/Research_Related/CASStandardsForAdvising.pdf

Drucker, P. F. (1990). *Managing the nonprofit organization: Principles and practices.* New York: HarperCollins.

Drucker, P. F. (2003). What is our mission? In *Business leadership: A Jossey-Bass reader.* San Francisco: Jossey-Bass.

Habley, W. R. (2005). *Developing a mission statement for the academic advising program.* Retrieved September 13, 2007, from http://www.nacada.ksu.edu/Clearinghouse/AdvisingIssues/Mission-Statements.htm

Heifetz, R. A., & Linsky, M. (2002). *Leadership on the line: Staying alive through the dangers of leading.* Boston: Harvard Business School Press.

Keller, G. (2007). The emerging third stage in higher education planning. *Planning for Higher Education, 35* (4), 60–64.

Maki, P. L. (2004). *Assessing for learning: Building a sustainable commitment across the institution.* Sterling, VA: Stylus.

National Academic Advising Association. (2006). *NACADA concept of academic advising.* Retrieved September 13, 2007, from http://www.nacada.ksu.edu/Clearinghouse/AdvisingIssues/Concept-Advising.htm

National Academic Advising Association. (2007). *NACADA core values for advising.* Retrieved September 13, 2007, from http://www.nacada.ksu.edu/Clearinghouse/AdvisingIssues/Core-Values.htm

Nanus, B. (2003). Where tomorrow begins: Finding the right vision. In J. M. Kouzes (Ed.), *Business leadership: A Jossey-Bass reader.* San Francisco: Jossey-Bass.

Rowley, D. J., Lujan, H. D., & Dolence, M. G. (2001). *Strategic change in colleges and universities.* San Francisco: Jossey-Bass.

White, E. R. (2000). Developing mission, goals, and objectives. In V. N. Gordon, & W. R. Habley (Eds.), *Academic advising: A comprehensive handbook.* San Francisco: Jossey-Bass.part Three

ORGANIZATION AND DELIVERY OF ADVISING SERVICES

CHAPTER FIFTEEN

Organization of Academic Advising Services

Margaret C. King

Effective academic advising programs identify what students should know and do as a result of academic advising and then implement the steps that will make those things happen. One of those steps is reviewing the organizational structure of advising. As the Council for the Advancement of Standards (CAS, 2006) indicates, advising programs must be structured purposefully and managed effectively; they must include development, evaluation, and recognition/reward; and the design of an advising program must be compatible with the institutional structure and its students needs. It is critical that the advising program have a mission statement that is consistent with the institutional program mission and have established outcomes and goals (see Chapter Fourteen: Vision, Mission, Goals, and Program Objectives for Academic Advising Programs).

There are a variety of trends affecting entire campus environments that are causing institutions to look more carefully at the services provided to help students become more engaged in their learning and to enhance student retention. Student demographics are changing. Students are more culturally and ethnically diverse, many have a disability, many come from homes characterized by physical violence and substance abuse, and more have low self-esteem, physical ailments, and psychological illnesses (Upcraft & Stephens, 2000). Many students come with high financial need, which causes them to work long hours, attend part-time, and borrow more money (Habley & Schuh, 2007). The National Center for Education Statistics suggests that as many as 75 percent of today's college students could be considered nontraditional, characteristics of which include "being over age 25, delaying enrollment, attending part-time, working full-time, being financially independent, having dependents, being a single parent, and lacking a high school diploma" (Habley & Schuh, 2007, p. 353). Increasing numbers of students require remediation in reading, writing, and math (Upcraft & Stephens, 2000).

Institutions are being held more accountable by their local, state, and federal officials in terms of graduation rates and time to completion. They are facing legal and financial issues. Technology is changing constantly, and there is an expectation that institutions will be on top of those changes and have state-of-the-art technology available to students, faculty, and staff. And curricula, especially at community colleges, are constantly changing to keep up with community needs. Advisors are expected to stay on top of these changes to help students achieve their goals.

FACTORS INFLUENCING THE ORGANIZATION OF ADVISING

A number of factors must be considered when reviewing how advising services are organized. The first is the institutional mission, which includes the control of the institution (public, private, proprietary), the level of educational offerings (associate, baccalaureate, graduate), the nature of the program offerings (liberal arts, professional, vocational), and the selectivity of the institution (open door vs. highly selective). The second factor is the student population. The more students are underprepared, undecided, diverse, first-generation, and commuter, the more important it is to have a highly organized system for advising. The role of faculty must be considered. What role should and will they play? (See Chapter Sixteen.) Here it is important to look at their interest in and willingness to serve as advisors. Programs and policies, such as the sequencing of courses, the complexity of degree requirements, the complexity of the general education requirements, and the degree to which an advisor must approve a variety of transactions must also be considered. As the complexity increases, the need for highly skilled advisors working in a well-defined advising organization increases.

Three additional factors must also be considered. The first is budget. Some organizational models and delivery systems are more expensive than others. For example, having academic advising as a requirement for full-time teaching faculty as part of their teaching load is less expensive than hiring full-time academic advisors. Using part-time peer or paraprofessional advisors is less expensive than using full-time advisors. If full-time advisors are the goal, are there resources to move in that direction? For further discussion of advisor types, see Chapters Sixteen and Seventeen. Facilities need to be factored in as well. If there is discussion about creating a new advising center, are there facilities to house the center or resources to build a new center? Organizational structure must also be considered. Who on the campus ultimately has responsibility for academic advising? If it is the Dean or Vice President of Academic Affairs, can the organizational structure include advising by staff in other divisions, and if so, how?

ORGANIZATIONAL MODELS OF ACADEMIC ADVISING

Much has been written about the seven organizational models of academic advising (Habley, 1983, 2004; Habley & McCauley, 1987), but a chapter on the organization of advising would be incomplete without a brief review of the models. Pardee (2000) classified the models as decentralized, centralized, and shared. In the decentralized models, advising services are provided by faculty and staff in their academic departments. While overall coordination may be centralized, advisors are accountable to their respective departments. In the centralized model, all advising takes place in an administrative unit such as an advising or counseling center with a director and staff generally housed in one location. In the shared models, advising services are shared between a central administrative unit and faculty or staff in academic departments. It should be noted that with the exception of the Faculty-Only model, the organizational models do not presume the use of a specific advisor type.

Decentralized Models

Of the two decentralized models, the Faculty-Only model (Figure 15.1) is the only one in which the model and the delivery system are one and the same. In this model, each student is assigned a faculty advisor. There may be a campus coordinator of advising, but advisors are accountable to their respective departments. Exploratory students are typically assigned to liberal arts or specially selected faculty. This model was being used by 25 percent of the institutions responding to American College Testing's (ACT's) Sixth National Survey of Academic Advising and is particularly strong in private two- and four-year institutions.

The Satellite model (Figure 15.2), sometimes referred to as the "multiversity model," finds advising offices maintained and controlled within academic subunits (schools, colleges). A satellite office specifically for exploratory students generally provides campus-wide coordination. Within this model, advising responsibilities may also shift from an advising office to specific faculty within the subunits. This model was found in 7 percent of the institutions surveyed by ACT and is more common in public universities. Strengths of this model include tying advising services to the individual school or college, which can help personalize the experience for the student. However, overall coordination may be an issue, as is the need to pay special attention to transitioning students who declare or change majors as well as to students with special needs.

Student   Faculty

Figure 15.1. Faculty-Only Model.
Source: Habley (1983).

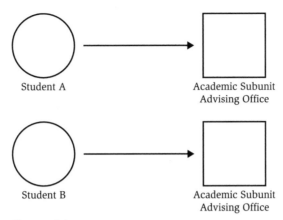

Figure 15.2. Satellite Model.

Source: Habley (1983).

Centralized Models

In the Self-Contained model Figure 15.3, all advising from orientation to departure takes place in a centralized unit such as an advising center or counseling center. The unit could be staffed with full- or part-time advisors, counselors, faculty, paraprofessionals, or peers, Sometimes called an administrator's delight, there is typically a dean or director who supervises all advising functions. This model was found in 14 percent of the institutions surveyed by ACT and is the second most popular model in community colleges. Strengths of this model include having trained advisors who have advising as a priority, being housed in a central location, having easy accessibility, and the ability to provide training, evaluation, and recognition and rewards more easily.

Shared Models

The first of the shared models is the Supplementary model Figure 15.4. In this model, faculty serve as advisors for all students, but there is also an office that assists faculty but has no original jurisdiction for approving academic transactions. Faculty assistance might include creation of an advising handbook, being an information clearinghouse, being a referral resource, providing training, and the like. In this model, the advising office is small, sometimes headed by part-time faculty or volunteer faculty with trained peer advisors. This model was found in 17 percent of the institutions surveyed by ACT and is the second most popular model in two- and four-year institutions. Strengths of this model include having an office to provide coordination. This model does require significant additional cost, and it is important that it have credibility with faculty.

The Split model Figure 15.5 divides the initial advising of students between an advising office and the academic subunits. The office advises specific groups of students, such as those who are exploratory or developmental. Once specific conditions are met—for example, choosing a major or completing developmental course work—students may be assigned to an academic subunit, where they could be advised by faculty, full-time advisors, paraprofessionals, or peers. In this model, a director or coordinator may have campus-wide

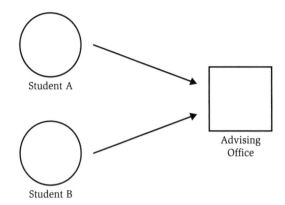

Figure 15.3. Self-Contained Model.

Source: Habley (1983).

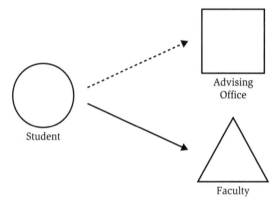

Figure 15.4. Supplementary Model.

Source: Habley (1983).

coordinating responsibilities and provide training, a handbook, etc. This model was found at 27 percent of the institutions surveyed by ACT and is the most popular model in public four-year institutions. Strengths of this model include having trained advisors with the skills to advise the higher-risk students. However, there is a need to have close coordination between the advising office and the academic units as well as the need to pay close attention to transitioning students from one advisor to another.

In the Dual model Figure 15.6, students have two advisors. Faculty advise regarding program and an advising office advises regarding general education requirements, registration procedures, academic policy, and the like. The advising office has overall coordinating responsibility and advises exploratory students. This model was found in 5 percent of the institutions surveyed by ACT. Advantages include having two delivery systems with the strengths of each. However, the responsibility of each advisor must be clearly articulated so students know who to see for what.

The last of the shared models is the Total Intake model Figure 15.7. In this model, all of the initial advising occurs through one office, which could be

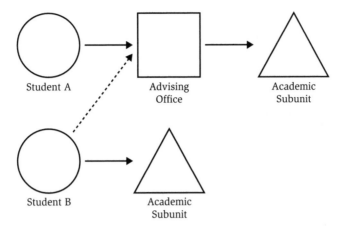

Figure 15.5. Split Model.

Source: Habley (1983).

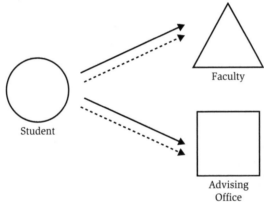

Figure 15.6. Dual Model.

Source: Habley (1983).

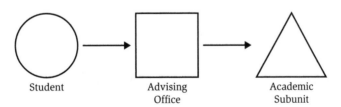

Figure 15.7. Total Intake Model.

Source: Habley (1983).

staffed by professional advisors, counselors, faculty, paraprofessionals, or peers. Students are assigned to faculty or academic subunits once specified conditions are met—for example, after their initial registration, after completion of the first semester, or after completion of 45 credits. The director of the office has campus-wide coordinating responsibility. The office may also have responsibility for the development and administration of curriculum and instruction and the development and enforcement of policies and procedures.

This model was found in 6 percent of the institutions surveyed by ACT. The key strength of this model is the ability to front load the system and to provide a strong start for students. Attention needs to be paid to transitioning the students from that initial contact to the assigned advisor.

TRENDS IN ORGANIZATIONAL MODELS

There have been a number of trends in the organizational models as documented by the Sixth National Survey on Academic Advising conducted by ACT (Habley, 2004). The use of the Faculty-Only model continues to decline, dropping from 33 percent in 1987 to 25 percent in 2003. The general trend toward shared responsibility for advising first noted in the 1998 ACT survey continues, but only partially. Use of the Dual, Total Intake, and Satellite models has increased slightly, but use of the Self-Contained model has increased as well (12 percent in 1998 to 14 percent in 2003) (Habley, 2004, p. 20). It should be noted, however, that the Self-Contained model can use a variety of delivery systems, so conceivably it could be viewed as a shared model. Given the complexity of academic advising, it is probably unrealistic to expect any one group of people to be able to know and do it all. It is also important that there be sufficient personnel available to address students' advising needs without unreasonable delay and to accomplish the mission and goals of the advising program. Sharing the advising responsibilities makes that much more feasible.

Other trends noted in the ACT Survey show that the dominant title for the person responsible for administration of the advising program is "Coordinator or Director of Advising." Use of this title has increased from 12 percent to 28 percent in two-year public colleges (Habley, 2004, p. 16). There has been an increase in those reporting to the Vice President or Dean of Academic Affairs or an Assistant or Associate Vice President or Dean (32 percent—39 percent), although in two-year public colleges 33 percent report through student affairs (Habley, 2004, p. 16). The Split model has been the most prominent organizational model across all campuses since the 1998 ACT survey.

KEY COMPONENTS OF EFFECTIVE ADVISING PROGRAMS

The Council for the Advancement of Standards (CAS) discusses the key components of effective advising programs. The first is coordination—someone must be in charge. Advising program leaders must be positioned and empowered within the administrative structure to accomplish the mission of the advising program. The academic advising program must have an articulated vision for advising, set goals and objectives, promote student learning and development, prescribe and practice ethical behavior, select and supervise staff, manage both the fiscal and human resources, and initiate collaborative interactions with other offices and individuals on campus. Effective advising is not a closed system and cannot be done in isolation.

Effective programs must have a strong advisor development component that focuses on informational, conceptual, and relational aspects. Advisor and advising program evaluation is also critical, as is advisor recognition and reward. Each of these topics is discussed more fully in Chapters Twenty through Twenty-Six.

Effective programs must have adequate funding to accomplish the mission and goals of the program and must demonstrate fiscal responsibility and cost-effectiveness consistent with institutional protocols. There must also be adequate facilities, technology, and equipment to support the mission and goals of the program. Advisors must have access to computing equipment, local networks, student data bases, and the Internet.

ADVISING AND OTHER CAMPUS SERVICES AND OFFICES

Academic advising is often referred to as the hub of the wheel with connections to all other campus offices and services. It cannot be successful without collaboration and cooperation among areas that deliver or support it. Academic advising is integral to the educational process, and depends upon close working relationships with other individuals, offices, and services. It is critical that the academic advising program establish, maintain, and promote effective relations with those offices and services. For example, advising needs to have close coordination with related processes such as admissions, orientation, placement testing, registration, and the like. It also needs to be coordinated with offices providing functional delivery of services such as career planning, learning assistance, supplemental instruction, first-year courses, and learning communities. And there needs to be close coordination with other units providing academic advising, including academic departments, schools, and colleges; disability services' honors programs; and developmental education.

One could list every office on campus and find some connection to academic advising. In the case of Institutional Research or Information Technology, staff in those offices help advisors do their job and help with assessment of advising. Faculty and staff in academic departments often advise students or serve as resources for full-time advisors needing in-depth information about programs or courses. In many cases, advisors and faculty and staff in other areas serve as resources for staff development for one another (e.g., providing training for working with disabled students or multicultural students or providing training for faculty in the relational components of advising). All serve as referral sources for students, whether it is an advisor referring a student for counseling support or a professor referring a student for more in-depth advising assistance.

Many institutions focusing on student success and student engagement stress the importance of redesigning and integrating student services as well as the importance of collaboration. Schuh (2003) notes that "students are served best when services, programs and learning opportunities are linked so that they can be accessed easily and build on one another, resulting in a robust learning environment for students" (p. 57). Recognizing that students often overlook opportunities for learning outside of class, Ardaiolo, Bender, and Roberts (2005) suggest that "students need to embrace the ethos that a college education is more than just attending classes, and institutional practices need to stimulate that understanding" (p. 91).

As institutions review the organization of advising services, it is important to look at the broader picture of an "interconnected, collaborative system of services that support student development and success" (Kramer, 2003, p. xi). Kramer (pp. xiv–xv) poses several questions institutions can consider as they look to improve their student services, all of which are applicable to academic advising:

1. How prepared are students for learning, and what academic support and services do they need?

2. How should students' readiness needs be addressed within the institutional environment?

3. At what point are students vulnerable to failure, and how should student academic services rally to support student development, growth, retention, and achievement?

4. What is meant by the student-centric view (vs. the department-centric view), and how can being student-centered lead to the creation of a seamless, integrated, horizontal, and collaborative student academic services environment?

5. How do we know that students are engaged in the learning process, are receiving the support they need, and are making progress?

6. What delivery model(s) work best for a given institution or mission? Where are the successful programs, and what critical success factors drive these best practices? What metrics do they use?

7. What is meant by managing and ensuring a collaborative student academic services enterprise?

8. Are standards for student services clearly defined? Who sets them, what should they be, and do they map to the campus culture?

9. How should existing and natural connections be managed among the various student academic services to ensure a maximally, personally, and coherently responsive system to address student needs, learning, and satisfaction?

10. What are the training issues involved in motivating and coordinating the work of service providers as they seek to deliver timely, comprehensive, and accurate academic services to students?

As mentioned earlier, academic advising is often described as the hub of the wheel, with connections to all other areas of the institution. As such, advising services are in a key position to take the lead in making sure that all services are interconnected and collaborative so that students are engaged in their learning and achieve their goals.

To be sure services are interconnected and collaborative, some institutions have created one-stop centers and portals, have created learning communities, and have focused on first-year success seminars and classes, all of which involve academic advising. Technology plays a key role. A study of six community colleges in Florida by the Community College Research Center (Jenkins, 2006) showed that the most effective institution in terms of practices that promoted student success not only increased its research but also created a "student success services program that uses the colleges' student information system to identify students who are struggling academically and then direct them to services that will help them stay in school" (p. 23). Technology is also a way to get information to students and serves as a valuable communication tool.

In focusing on the organization of advising services, it is important that institutions look at their student population and evaluate student needs and expectations. They should compare the match between existing services and student needs and develop concepts for what the new or altered advising services should look like. Then it would be important to look at facilities, staffing, and technology and at how advising services interconnect with other programs and services on campus. Collaboration is essential for student success, as is clear communication of who does what for which population and why. Successful advising programs can intentionally enhance a positive campus environment that will, in turn, impact student success.

References

Ardaiolo, F. P., Bender, B. E., & Roberts, G. (2005). Campus services: What do students expect? In T. E. Miller, B. E. Bender, J. H. Schuh, et al. (Eds.), *Promoting reasonable expectations: Aligning student and institutional views of the college experience* (pp. 84–101). San Francisco: Jossey-Bass.

Council for the Advancement of Standards in Higher Education. (2006). *CAS professional standards for higher education* (6th ed.). Washington, DC: Author.

Habley, W. R. (1983). Organizational structures for academic advising: Models and implications. *Journal of College Student Personnel, 24* (6), 535–540.

Habley, W. R. (Ed.). (2004). *The status of academic advising: Findings from the ACT Sixth National Survey.* (NACADA Monograph Series, no.10.) Manhattan, KS: National Academic Advising Association.

Habley, W. R., & McCauley, M. E. (1987). The relationship between institutional characteristics and the organization of advising services. *NACADA Journal, 7* (1), 27–39.

Habley, W. R., & Schuh, J. H. (2007). Intervening to retain students. In G. L. Kramer (Ed.), *Fostering student success in the campus community* (pp. 343–368). San Francisco: Jossey-Bass.

Jenkins, D. (2006). *What community college management practices are effective in promoting student success? A study of high-and low-impact institutions.* New York: Community College Research Center.

Kramer, G. L. (2003). Preface. In G. L. Kramer et al. (Eds.), *Student academic services: An integrated approach* (pp. xi–xxiii). San Francisco: Jossey-Bass.

Pardee, C. F. (2000). Organizational models for academic advising. In V. N. Gordon, W. R. Habley, et al., *Academic advising: A comprehensive handbook* (pp. 192–210). San Francisco: Jossey-Bass.

Schuh, J. H. (2003). The interrelationship of student academic services. In G. L. Kramer and Associates, *Student academic services.* San Francisco: Jossey-Bass.

CHAPTER SIXTEEN

Advising Delivery: Faculty Advising

Martha K. Hemwall

Throughout the history of higher education, faculty members have served in some advising or mentoring capacity. In the early years of our colleges and universities, faculty members seemed to fill a role somewhat like the beloved mentor, "Mr. Chips." Living near or on campus, faculty members were readily available to students, both formally and informally. Through numerous and long discussions with students, each teacher held the responsibility to provide "educational guidance, financial help, and health supervision" (Hardee, 1959, p. 3), and even to supervise living environments and worship habits (Frost, 2000).

Of course, this is no longer the case. This idealized role of the faculty-member-as-mentor eventually changed as universities grew larger and more complex. Faculty-student relationships became more formalized and systematic. By the middle of the twentieth century, class size had increased considerably, new media was changing teaching techniques, and an educator had become more of an "organization man" (Hardee, 1959, p. 3). Faculty members were expected to teach larger and more numerous types of classes, produce a substantial quantity of scholarly publications, and serve on a growing number of administrative committees. As their time became more formally structured, their relationships with students changed as well. It is in this changing context that the idea of formal faculty advising began to develop.

Faculty advising remains a central part of most of our institutions, and almost all faculty members are expected to advise as part of their faculty status (Habley, 2000, p. 39). Faculty advising varies widely, and can include both informal and formal contact with students at all stages of their education. Faculty advising also varies by the type of advising system—centralized, decentralized, or shared—in which they participate. (See Chapter Fifteen.) Nevertheless, faculty advising requires careful attention and support for at least two reasons. First, for more than twenty years, research has suggested how critical both informal and formal faculty contact is to student satisfaction, learning, and retention (Pascarella and Terenzini, 1991). Second, research has pointed to the importance of advising in students' lives, to learning, and to retention (Tinto, 1993). Richard Light (2001) concluded from his research that "good advising may be the most underestimated characteristic of a successful college experience" (p. 81). McGillin (2003) sums up the centrality of advising in a student's life:

> Academic advising is the single most important relationship offered to students by an institution of higher education. It is through this relationship that students will engage in a critical narrative process that will give shape and meaning to their curricular and life choices and through which they come to understand the interconnections of knowledge and the curricula. (p. 88)

Faculty members hold a basic and critical responsibility for the academic mission and the curriculum of the institution. Since they both determine and teach the curriculum, they remain central to how students come to understand connections between what they are learning and the overall purpose of their academic programs (McGillin, 2003). Even in institutions with advising responsibilities shared between faculty and professional advisors, the faculty are critical in helping craft a system that best supports the educational goals of the institution. An expectation that faculty should not remain responsible for academic advising by implication would distance them from this part of their central responsibility, potentially affecting not only the quality of the students' experience, but the integrity of the institution.

Given the importance of faculty to student learning, and the importance of advising to student learning, it seems reasonable to expect institutions to provide adequate support and guidance to faculty as they advise students. Such a conclusion might seem straightforward, but in reality, support and guidance for faculty advising is lacking on many campuses. This chapter will draw on current understandings of academic advising as learning-centered to suggest both small-scale and large-scale strategies for most effectively supporting faculty in their advising role. In doing so, the institution will benefit, faculty will come to better understand their role in helping students learn through advising, and students will benefit from the opportunity for increased learning and better understanding of their college experiences.

THREE STEPS TOWARD REALIZING THE POTENTIAL OF FACULTY ADVISING

Listening to faculty describe their academic advising responsibilities is telling. Despite differences in campuses, advising systems, and student populations, many responses are similar. Of course, positive stories about successful advising relationships are almost always described, but, at the same time, an underlying frustration is apparent through other commonly expressed themes: faculty don't get rewarded or recognized for advising students, faculty don't have time to do this task, and faculty can't really do advising because they aren't qualified. Such concerns are noted by others working with faculty. McGillin (2003), for example, points out that "the answer most frequently given is that faculty will seek out opportunities to advance as advisors if and when that activity is significantly recognized, evaluated and rewarded" (p. 88). The question when working with faculty, then, is not only how to inspire faculty but how to make academic advising an important and achievable task. Creating and maintaining an effective faculty advising system is not easy. It requires commitment on many levels—by the institution, by administrative staff, and by the faculty themselves. To achieve widespread commitment requires a comprehensive plan that addresses all levels of support; one includes at least three major steps: changing the concept and language of academic advising, supporting faculty advising through large-scale institutional strategies, and supporting faculty using small-scale daily strategies.

Step 1. Changing the Concept and Language of Academic Advising: Making the Link to Learning and Teaching

The first step is to change the framework used to talk about academic advising with faculty members by aligning it more closely with the institution's academic mission. Central to this effort is the current move away from a developmental model and developmental language, and toward a model for academic advising based on learning. This shift can be seen in recent publications (e.g., see Hemwall and Trachte, 2005; Lowenstein, 2005; Melander, 2005; Reynolds, 2004). This change is directly connected with changes in higher education. National conversations about higher education, for many reasons, have increasingly focused on student learning. The Wingspread Group on Higher Education (1993) concluded that learning needed to be the central focus of higher education, followed by other calls for postsecondary educators to adopt a learning paradigm. Barr and Tagg (1995) argued for a move from a focus on teaching to one on learning. National organizations such as the Association of American Colleges and Universities (AAC&U) and the American Council on Education (ACE), as well as the national accreditation associations, have increasingly focused on student learning, and learning outcomes, to discuss and evaluate the quality of our institutions.

Changing to a learning model is critical for faculty advising. The learning model puts academic advising back into a context that is both understandable and meaningful for faculty advisors. The previous approach, drawn from developmental and counseling models, marginalized faculty advisors in terms of both skills and interests. It is not surprising, then, that the literature reflects widespread skepticism about faculty as appropriate advisors (see, for example, King, 2000; Habley, 1995). These attitudes have been clearly communicated to faculty who, as a result, seem more than happy to relinquish responsibility for a task that seems so distant from their lives as scholars and teachers (see, for example, Paris and Ehlgren, 2006; Ender, 1994).

Shifting to a learning model of academic advising, however, allows academic advising to be discussed in a way that is consistent with the faculty members' other responsibilities. In viewing advising as a context for learning, the same questions can be asked that are asked by a faculty member when developing a course:

> Thinking about advising as student learning reorients the focus from the performance of the advisor, advising administrators and advising system, to the student. This rethinking leads one to ask both: "What should the student learn?" and "How might the learning take place?" In other words, the learning paradigm prompts consideration of the content of an advising curriculum and a more effective pedagogy for promoting student learning. (Hemwall & Trachte, 2003, p. 13)

The learning model not only affects the language used to talk about advising, but also can affect how advisors think about and do advising. The question of what the student should learn offers a provocative topic for conversations with faculty advisors. The academic goals of the institution should be readily identifiable from institutional documents such as mission statements and statements of purpose, and can be used to identify learning outcomes for advising students. An advising context offers the one formal place in the institution in which students formally pursue questions about their overall program and which allows them to take the time to think about interconnections among the things they are learning. The academic advisor becomes an important guide in this learning because "advising is the intersection of the teaching and learning experience" (Myers and Dyer, 2007, p. 284). As Marc Lowenstein argues, "an excellent advisor does the same thing for the student's entire curriculum that the excellent teacher does for one course" (2005, p. 69).

Clearly, the learning-centered model of academic advising is helpful, through both language and structure, in making academic advising a consistent part of the work of faculty members. This shift, then, is an important starting point in helping faculty find meaning in the advising task. Next, they likely will need guidance to understand the actual implications. Several articles might be useful reading for faculty advisors in thinking about advising, or as a focus for faculty discussion. Three examples are summarized here.

Hemwall and Trachte (2005), assuming a learning model, identify ten organizing principles for identifying an academic advising curriculum and developing advising pedagogies. Looking to mission statements and acknowledging the central importance of critical thinking, they argue, provide a useful core curriculum. The pedagogical principles focus on what should be understood about the nature of learning, what should be known about the student learners, and what practical approaches might be most effective in advising conversations.

Reynolds (2004), in a short but thoughtful article, draws on literature in education, and about the liberal arts, to argue for a learning-centered paradigm for academic advising. She describes how faculty can become involved in advising when it is seen as fostering learning. She argues that faculty should focus on the connections they help students make: connections with the institutional mission, connections with general education, connections with critical self-reflection and self-knowledge, and finally, connections with complexity. Embedded in her argument is how advising helps students develop critical-thinking skills, and thereby, understand the reasons for their academic work.

Lowenstein (2005) explicates the notion of academic advising as teaching within a learning-centered paradigm. He carefully examines various models for advising and then demonstrates how the notion of logic in the curriculum is critical to good advising. He argues that advisors are critical to the process of helping students make sense and meaning out of their academic experiences, concluding that, "the advisor is arguably the most important person in the student's educational world" (p. 69). He very effectively reframes the notion of academic advising for faculty.

In addition to articles such as these, faculty members should be introduced to the recent redefinition of the concept of academic advising, accepted by the National Academic Advising Association (NACADA). The Preamble begins, "Academic advising is integral to fulfilling the teaching and learning mission of higher education," and continues on to discuss the idea of an academic advising curriculum, an advising pedagogy, and student learning outcomes (NACADA, 2006).

Step 2. Changing the Support of Faculty Advisors: Large-Scale Strategies

The second step is to consider how faculty advising is supported by the wider institutional structures. Frequently, perhaps because they seem overwhelming and not easily achieved, large-scale strategies are not pursued. Habley and Morales (1998) reported that less than one-third of all campuses include advising in the evaluation of performance, or in a reward structure for faculty (Habley, 2000, p. 39).

While the hope is that small-scale strategies will make a difference, and add up to bigger change, change does not happen in a vacuum. To be effective, small changes must be guided by an overall vision. Alvin Toffler (personal communication, April 17, 2008) stated, "You've got to think about the big things while you are doing the small things, so that all the small things are going in the right direction." One of the big things guiding the strategies, of course, is the change to the learning model of academic advising addressed in the first step. The next step is to look at how the faculty advisor's work is reinforced, supported, and recognized by the institution. The case for institutional attention to faculty advising is more easily argued when academic advising is seen as part of the teaching responsibilities. The need to develop parallel structures for evaluating, recognizing, and rewarding academic advising is a logical outcome of this view of advising.

Attention to basic details of institutional structures can make a difference. This attention should begin with official recognition, on a number of structural levels, of the importance of academic advising. The following three suggestions go far to build advising into the institutional culture.

First, the central role of advising should be explicit from the beginning of discussions between potential faculty members and the institution. During interviews for positions, advising should be addressed as part of the larger teaching responsibilities. When negotiating contracts, advising should be made an explicit part of the discussion and appear in any official appointment letters. In *Academic Advising Today*, Thomas Edwards (2007) argues, "The hiring process reflects the values of our institution . . . if we value quality advising in the way we work, a simple first step is to practice it in the way we hire" (p. 1).

Second, the advising program should have a visible place in the university structure. First, as Hunter and White (2004) observe, "An advising program viewed as essential has an identifiable leader with authority over resources . . ." (p. 23). Next, this leader should be able to develop and direct resources toward an effective faculty advising program, by encouraging participation of faculty in overseeing advising through faculty advisory committees, newsletters, and other strategies (King, 2000; McGillin, 2003).

Finally, key leaders, such as the president, chancellor, provost, deans, and department chairs should officially acknowledge the integral part academic advising plays in the institution's mission, and discuss it in terms of a teaching responsibility. When advising workshops and training opportunities are available, they should encourage or expect faculty to attend and recognize those who do. This explicit recognition allows advising to become part of institutional culture, costs the institution no money, and offers significant potential benefits in terms of morale and attention to advising.

In addition to formally recognizing the role of academic advising, institutional strategies must include methods of rewarding effective advising. Habley, in a NACADA video discussion, reminds institutions that "what gets rewarded, gets done" (NACADA, 1999). Unfortunately, there has been a consistent decline since 1987 of all types of recognition and reward strategies (Kerr, 2000). Reinarz (2000) observes, "on many campuses, recognition of faculty for advising is sadly limited. This lack of recognition when coupled with competing demands for faculty time, can indeed lead some faculty to place less emphasis on advising" (p. 214).

This seems like a daunting situation. As previously discussed, academic advising requires acceptance as an integral part of the teaching responsibility of faculty (Creamer & Scott, 2000, p. 345). In addition, however, effective faculty advising systems must include a set of integrated, clear guidelines of advising responsibilities and tasks. These guidelines, in turn, should form the basis of systematic evaluation of both individual advisors and the advising system. Only after all this is developed can an appropriate, effective structure of recognition and rewards be created. Because all these levels—guidelines, evaluation, recognition, and rewards—are interconnected, the task appears overwhelming. The task can be deconstructed by considering its constituent parts.

Clear guidelines, consistent with the institutional mission, must be the first step. These guidelines, though perhaps drawn from and connected to the institutional mission and vision, need to be developed with input from faculty advisors. This is an opportunity to gather faculty opinion and perhaps use a faculty committee to suggest what might constitute advising responsibilities before any evaluation can be done (McGillin, 2003). Once the guidelines are developed and accepted, they must be clearly communicated in appropriate official documents such as letters of appointment, the faculty handbook, and in the annual report required of all teaching faculty. If faculty are required to advise, or at least expected to do some advising, common sense suggests that this responsibility would appear along with other duties in such communications. This costs the institution no money, and again, underscores the idea that advising is integral part of faculty members' responsibility. Below are several examples that illustrate how guidelines might be developed.

At Lawrence University, the president appointed a task force to examine the faculty advising system. Surveys and focus groups were conducted with faculty and students to review the philosophy of advising and to identify issues of concern and current strengths. Results were discussed at a faculty meeting. The final report was accepted by both the president and the faculty, leading to changes in several aspects of the advising system and providing better support for faculty advisors. Advising became part of faculty members' annual reports to the president and became the starting point for developing a system of evaluating advising. The statement of philosophy, the list of expectations of faculty advisors, and the summary of student perceptions of advising are printed in the advising handbook and discussed at the annual faculty advising meeting. (See Appendix A.) This approach led to faculty thinking more about advising, rather than viewing advising as a duty assigned by the administration.

The faculty of Fox Valley Technical College developed guidelines that include eleven elements. Each element provides the basis for regular advising discussions as well as for training modules (Schneider, 2002).

Western New Mexico State faculty developed explicit expectations about academic advising that are linked to faculty rank and shared widely over e-mail. These expectations are refined annually through regular faculty input (Vowell & Farren, 2004).

After the vision, official recognition, and clear guidelines are communicated, the campus is poised to begin evaluation; evaluation must be connected to rewards and individual recognition to achieve the institutional goal of encouraging effective advising. An institution must discuss with its faculty appropriate benefits for such duties. McGillin (2003) provides an excellent overview of evaluation and reward of faculty advising, and discusses how this information might be used on an individual campus; further information is available in Chapter Twenty-six of this book. She argues that the role of evaluation, and the ways in which good advising is recognized and rewarded, should vary both by campus, and also, by different faculty advisors.

Consideration in tenure, promotion, and merit evaluations is one critical strategy. This consideration is called by Kerr (2000), the "ultimate in extrinsic rewards" for faculty (p. 352). The idea of including advising in tenure and promotion decisions increases the need for a system for evaluation, with clear guidelines and articulated expectations. Once this system is in place, however, advising should become at least a small part of such evaluations of faculty. They already are juggling demands in classroom teaching, community service, and scholarship, and will not be able to take time to think about and be effective advisors without this consideration (NACADA, 1999; McGillin, 2003).

In addition, other large-scale rewards can be used by the institution: additional pay, release time, and reductions in the noninstructional load are just a few ways to add incentive on some campuses and in some advising systems (NACADA, 1999; Kerr, 2000; McGillin, 2003).

Step 3. Changing the Support of Faculty Advisors: Small-Scale Strategies

People who study change and leadership have long argued that leaders trying to introduce large-scale change should begin with making small changes that can affect institutional culture. Such changes in standard operating procedures eventually change perception and culture assuming, as Toffler (personal communication) cautioned, they are guided by a well-defined overall vision. When small changes are integrated with the overall goal or vision, they serve to symbolize and reinforce the overall change. This dynamic seems well supported by anthropological research, beginning in the mid-twentieth century (Barnett, 1953; Allison, 1971; Fernandez, 1972; Geertz, 1976). Efforts to create large-scale changes will be reinforced by attention to the small-scale details of the academic advising system.

Small-scale strategies rarely take much time or money but frequently reap significant benefits for the institution. It is surprising, then, that on most campuses routine recognition of academic advising is not pursued or included (Habley & Morales, 1998; Reinarz, 2000; Hunter & White, 2004). In part, the central importance of academic advising may not be well understood. When academic advising is focused on student learning and reframed to be consistent with teaching tasks, however, its importance is more apparent. If the first step in this process is successful, these smaller changes should be natural and logical outcomes. This approach points out the importance of developing small-scale strategies, such as the ones described below, that make sense and are meaningful to faculty members.

Provide Faculty with a Template for an Advising Syllabus. Just as faculty members develop a syllabus for a class, a syllabus can be developed for advising. This strategy actually reduces the time and stress placed on faculty advisors. The concept of an academic advising syllabus, and examples of advising syllabi from various types of institutions, can be found in the Clearinghouse on the NACADA Web site (see Appendix A). Finally, the advising syllabus is discussed in a NACADA Webinar, "Academic Advising Syllabus: Advising as Teaching in Action" (available on CD, see Appendix A). The advising syllabus should have two main parts: a statement of advising philosophy (definitions of advising, learning outcomes, role of advisor, list of advisee responsibilities) and practical information (contact information, resources, important dates in the academic year, when to seek advice, general recommendations). Many of the institutions cited in these sources provide a template for an advising syllabus for faculty advisors, an ideal small-scale strategy. In addition, to be useful, the syllabus has the practical benefits of easing workload and introducing the idea of advising as a teaching through a "standard operating procedure."

Develop Advising Forms for Students to Complete. Good advising forms encourage students to be thoughtful advisees and provide good information to advisors, which helps them get to know the student. The questions also provide a guide to the faculty advisor for advising meetings. Finally, the questions encourage both students and faculty to consider the institutional mission. Lawrence University, Colorado College, and a number of other colleges, ask new students to complete an advising information sheet before coming to campus, which asks them to discuss expectations, goals, concerns, and questions about beginning their college educations. Other colleges, such as Colorado College, Dartmouth College, Hope College, and Lawrence University, ask new students, midway through the first term of study, to complete a self-evaluation, which then is submitted to the faculty advisor during a required midterm advising session. The self-evaluation guides that discussion, a welcome benefit to many faculty advisors. Such forms can be put in the advising folder, whether paper or electronic, to be reviewed in the future (see Appendix A). Some campuses, such as Hope College and Dartmouth College, are using a similar reflective piece at different points during the first year and future years on campus to gain a longitudinal view, through advising, of student learning and change.

Redesign the Advising Handbook. Information given to faculty and students is an opportunity to communicate the learning-centered philosophy of advising that makes it a consistent part of teaching. The handbook can be structured around some of the advising curricular and pedagogical principles proposed by Hemwall and Trachte (2005) (see Appendix A) or around the connections described by Reynolds (2004) (see Appendix A). It also should include a description of potential learning outcomes and a template for an advising syllabus.

Provide Advisors with Timely and Accurate Information. This information provides the opportunity for training and development. Only about one-third of college and universities provide any type of training and development for academic advisors (Habley, 2000), and even fewer have these available for faculty advisors. Some have speculated that this lack of support for faculty is tied to the idea that faculty already are effective advisors, having learned through their own experiences (Selke & Wong, 1993). Other research suggests, however, that faculty desire better support and information in order to be more effective. Myers and Dyer (2007) argue that such opportunities increase faculty members' self-efficacy and, therefore, help them become more comfortable as advisors. A study at Winona State University (2007) found that faculty want more support, training, information, and resources to be better at advising. Such opportunities provide an ideal place to frame advising as learning-centered and to discuss the faculty advising guidelines. The guidelines could provide the basis for faculty brown bag discussion, forums, workshops, and other training and advising development opportunities (Myers & Dyer, 2007). Advising guidelines, for example, provide the basis of the topics covered in a series of two-hour advising training modules for faculty and staff advisors at Fox Valley Technical College. Other ideas and reflections on advisor training are available in the Clearinghouse on the NACADA Web site.

Create Contexts That Are Conducive to the Open and Informal Exchange of Ideas and Experiences about Academic Advising. In this spirit, food really must be included as an important small-scale strategy. If you feed them, they will come! Food is not infrequently mentioned in NACADA discussion and reports. In the NACADA video discussion, for example, Harry Cook states, "we found at SMSU that feeding faculty seems to get them there [to advising workshops]." Eric White agreed, and Nancy King suggested to others that "you feed participants well!" (NACADA, 1999). Other institutions report including food at most advising functions, including candy, refreshments at meetings, and more formal meals for special events.

Establish Advising Awards on Campus. Awards can be effective positive reinforcement. Awards need to be numerous or regular enough so that the hope of receiving one does not seem unrealistic, and they must be appropriate to specific campuses (McGillin, 2003). They can be based either on student feedback or institutional load or on a formal nomination process. The University of Alabama-Birmingham, for example, uses a nomination and reward process for several awards. This campus has an outstanding faculty advising award given each year in an Advising Awards Program sponsored by the Provost. This award, like those given for a new advisor and for a professional advisor, is selected by a panel of staff advisors, faculty, and administrators from a general resume related to advising and a letter of nomination from a colleague. The winner then is nominated by the university for the NACADA national award. The Provost's office, in addition, puts financial resources behind the award by paying for the winner to attend the NACADA conference (see Appendix A). This campus reports that this award has helped to stimulate more interest in advising among faculty, which, in the past had been limited. Many other campuses, particularly larger institutions, have instituted awards and are discussed further in Chapter Twenty-six.

Different strategies will be effective on different campuses and with different advisors. Whatever the appropriate approach in the structure of an advising system, few small-scale strategies require significant financial or time commitments. Many strategies, such as handbooks, printed materials, forms, and syllabi, in fact, save time for both the faculty advisor and the advising office. The ideal small-scale strategy reinforces the institutional understanding of academic advising and acknowledges the importance of advising. An added, and critical, benefit is that such strategies offer a regular opportunity to make advising a consistent and seamless part of faculty member's lives as teachers, and part of the institutional culture.

IMPLICATIONS

Faculty are central to successful achievement of the academic mission of our institutions, and in this role are important to the academic advising system. Whether in formal or informal advising, faculty's guidance of students in making meaning out of their experiences in higher education is critical to learning as set out in the institutional mission. As such, our institutions need to recognize, value, and support faculty advising. When faculty advising is incorporated as a central part of our campus, then we are well on our way to realizing faculty potential.

Faculty, of course, need to view advising as central to their roles as scholars and teachers. This requires reframing ways of thinking and talking about academic advising. Advising should be viewed as learning-centered and about student learning, as a task consistent with faculty responsibility to the institution. Many faculty members are already effective advisors, and this approach to advising gives them the language and framework to understand why and how they advise. If academic advising is understood as central to student learning, the work of both faculty and professional advisors becomes connected to the central academic mission of the institution (Hemwall & Trachte, 2005). Then the sharing of the same goal, creating a learner-centered environment through academic advising, may allow faculty and professional advisors on campuses to develop closer working relationships.

Academic advising may no longer seem almost impossible in this context, and with the strategies discussed in this chapter. By viewing advising as learning, responsibility is shifted to the advisees to prepare and think about what they can learn through advising. And, for the faculty advisor, academic advising contacts need not be overly time-consuming to be effective. It is the nature of the questions asked, not the length of the advising session, which will be most important to student learning.

The power of the faculty advisor in guiding student learning is enormous. A student in Richard Light's book, *Making the Most Out of College* (2001), described his first advising session as a freshman, which began with the faculty advisor asking "Why are you here?" The resulting discussion, and his thinking about that question of "why?" was influential. The student concluded that "there is no doubt at all that when I reflect on choices I made here, I can still hear his hard question from that first week, ringing in my ears"(pp. 88–89). Not insignificantly, Light found that successful students in colleges consistently mention the importance of faculty advising.

The research has shown that both academic advising and faculty are important to student learning. Our institutions will benefit from understanding the links between the two and creating a learner-centered context, which allows faculty to realize their potential as advisors.

Appendix 16. A: Web Resources

NACADA concept statement on academic advising:

http://www.nacada.ksu.edu/clearinghouse/Advisingissues/Concept-advising-introduction.htm

Academic advising handbooks based on the idea of advising as learning:

http://www.lawrence.edu/dept/student_acad (click on "Faculty Advising Handbook")

http://www.hope.edu/admin/registrar/Freshman/Connect_stu_2007.pdf

Examples of student self-evaluations:

http://www.lawrence.edu/dept/student_acad/forms.shtml

http://www.coloradocollege.edu/academics/FYE/pdfs/student_self_eval_prereq.pdf

http://discus.hope.edu/general/html/messages/156/2095.html?1141416951

Examples of advising syllabi:

http://www.nacada.ksu.edu/clearinghouse/Links/syllabi.htm

A discussion of advising syllabi:

http://www.nacada.ksu.edu/Webinars/AdvSyllabus.htm

Examples of advising awards system:

http://www.main.uab.edu

General Resources NACADA Clearinghouse:

http://nacada.ksu.edu/Resources/index.htm

Academic Advising Webinars:

http://www.nacada.ksu.edu/videos/index.htm

References

Allison, G. (1971). *Essence of decision*. Boston: Little, Brown.

Barnett, H. (1953). *Innovation: The basis of cultural change*. New York: McGraw-Hill.

Barr, R. B., & Tagg, J. (1995). From teaching to learning: A new paradigm for undergraduate education. *Change, 27* (6), 12–25.

Creamer, E. G., & Scott, D. W. (2000). Assessing individual advisor effectiveness. In V. Gordon, & W. Habley (Eds.), *Academic advising: A comprehensive handbook* (pp. 349–362). San Francisco: Jossey-Bass.

Edwards, T. S. (2007). Practice what we preach: Advising and the hiring process. *Academic Advising Today, 30* (1), 1–2.

Ender, S. C. (1994). Impediments to developmental advising. *NACADA Journal, 14* (2), 105–107.

Fernandez, J. (1965). Symbolic consensus in a Fang reformative cult. *American Anthropologist, 68*, 902–929.

Frost, S. H. (2000). Historical and philosophical foundations for academic advising. In V. Gordon, & W. Habley (Eds.), *Academic advising: A comprehensive handbook* (pp. 349–362). San Francisco: Jossey-Bass.

Geertz, C. (1959). Ritual and social change: A Javanese example. *American Anthropologist, 61*, 991–1012.

Habley, W. R. (1995). Faculty advising: Practice, performance, and promise. In G. L. Kramer (Ed.), *Reaffirming the role of faculty in academic advising*. (NACADA Monograph Series, no. 1.) Manhattan, KS: National Academic Advising Association.

Habley, W. R. (2000). Current practices in academic advising. In V. Gordon, & W. Habley (Eds.), *Academic advising: A comprehensive handbook* (pp. 349–362). San Francisco: Jossey-Bass.

Habley, W. R., & Morales, R. H. (1998). *Current practices in academic advising: Final report on ACT's fifth national survey of academic advising*. (NACADA Monograph Series, no. 6.) Manhattan, KS: National Academic Advising Association.

Hardee, M. D. (1959). *The faculty in college counseling*. New York: McGraw-Hill.

Hemwall M. K., & Trachte, K. C. (1999). Learning at the core: Toward a new understanding of academic advising. *NACADA Journal, 19* (1), 5–11.

Hemwall M. K., & Trachte, K. C. (2003). Academic advising and the learning paradigm. In M. K. Hemwall, & K. C. Trachte (Eds.), *Advising and learning: Academic advising from the perspective of small colleges and universities*. (NACADA Monograph Series, no. 8.) Manhattan, KS: National Academic Advising Association, pp. 13–19.

Hemwall M. K., & Trachte, K. C. (2005). Academic advising as learning: Ten organizing principles. *NACADA Journal, 25* (2), 74–83.

Hunter, M. S., & White E. R. (2004, March–April). Could fixing academic advising fix higher education? *About Campus*, pp. 20–25.

Kerr, T. (2000). Recognition and reward for excellence in advising. In V. Gordon, & W. Habley (Eds.), *Academic advising: A comprehensive handbook* (pp. 349–362). San Francisco: Jossey-Bass.

King, M. C. (2000). Designing effective training for academic advisors. In V. Gordon, & W. Habley (Eds.), *Academic advising: A comprehensive handbook* (pp. 349–362). San Francisco: Jossey-Bass.

Light, R. J. (2001). *Making the most of college: Students speak their minds*. Cambridge, MA: Harvard University Press.

Lowenstein, M. (1999). An alternative to the developmental theory of advising. *The Mentor. 1* (4). Retrieved March 25, 2008, from www.psu.edu/dus/mentor

Lowenstein, M. (2005). If advising is teaching, what do advisors teach? *NACADA Journal, 25* (2), 65–73.

McGillin, V. A. (2003). The role of evaluation and reward in faculty advising. In G. Kramer (Ed.), *Faculty advising examined: Enhancing the potential of college faculty as advisors* (pp. 88–124). Bolton, MA: Anker.

Melander, E. R. (2005). Advising as educating: A framework for organizing advising systems. *NACADA Journal*, (2), 84–91.

Myers, B. E., & Dyer, J. E. (2007). A comparison of the attitudes and perceptions of university faculty and administrators toward advising undergraduate and graduate students and student organizations. Retrieved March 25, 2008, from www.nacada.ksu.edu/clearinghouse/AdvisingIssues/faculty_adv.htm

NACADA. (1999). Frequently asked questions regarding faculty advising from: Academic advising: campus collaborations to foster retention, pp. 1–5. Retrieved September 10, 2007, from www.nacada.edu/clearinghouse/AdvisingIssues/faculty_adv.htm

NACADA. (2006). Concept of academic advising. Retrieved January 5, 2008, from http://nacada.ksu.edu/clearinghouse/AdvisingIssues/Concept-Advising.htm

Paris, D. C., & Elgren, T. E. (2006). Advising: Is less more? *Inside Higher Education.* Retrieved March 25, 2008, from http://insidehighered.com/views/2006/09/29/paris

Pascarella, E. T., & Terenzini, P. T. (1991). *How college affects students: Findings and insights from twenty years of research.* San Francisco: Jossey-Bass.

Reinarz, A. G. (2000). Delivering academic advising: Advisor types. In V. Gordon, & W. Habley (Eds.), *Academic advising: A comprehensive handbook* (pp. 349–362). San Francisco: Jossey-Bass.

Reynolds, M. (2004). Faculty advising in a learner-center environment: A small college perspective. *Academic Advising Today, 27* (2), 1–2.

Schneider, S. (2002). FVTC's faculty advising program in Appleton, WI. *Academic Advising Today, 25* (2), 5–6.

Selke, M. J., & Wong, T. D. (1993). The mentoring-empowered model: Professional role functions in graduate student advisement. *NACADA Journal, 13* (2), 21–26.

Tinto, V. (1993). *Leaving college: Rethinking the causes and cures of student attrition.* Chicago: University of Chicago Press.

Vowell, F., & Farren, P. J. (2003). Establishing clear expectations for advising, excerpt from expectations and training of faculty advisors. In Kramer, G. (Ed.), *Faculty advising examined: Enhancing the potential of college faculty as advisors.* Bolton, MA: Anker. Retrieved September 10, 2007, from www.nacada.ksu.edu/clearinghouse/AdvisingIssues/faculty_adv.htm

Wingspread Group on Higher Education. (1993). An American imperative: Higher expectations for higher education. Retrieved January 5, 2008, from http://www.johnsonfdn.org/American Imperative/index.htm

Winona State University. (2007). Creating the case for a new academic advising model at Winona State University: A review of the literature, pp. 1–34. Retrieved September 10, 2007, from www.winona.edu/21stcentury/innovation/documents/oertel%20report.doc

CHAPTER SEVENTEEN

Advising Delivery: Professional Advisors, Counselors, and Other Staff

Casey Self

Academic advising is a function performed by many individuals in various roles at institutions of higher education. Historically, faculty members have provided the primary function of assisting students with their academic success, and at times, personal success at college. While faculty members continue to play significant roles in academic advising, many colleges and universities have chosen to employ nonfaculty staff whose primary focus is the academic success of students. This chapter will identify many types of these staff members, and discuss the benefits and challenges that are associated with each.

A clarification may be in order to make distinctions between faculty academic advisors and other professional staff academic advisors. For the purposes of this chapter, *faculty advisors* are those individuals whose primary responsibility at the institution is to teach or conduct research. Providing academic advising to a caseload of students may be one of many additional responsibilities assigned to faculty members. Academic advising provided by faculty members may focus on the academic curriculum or career opportunities related to a specific major or area of study, along with time and attention to addressing student development and success issues. Faculty members also provide excellent mentoring roles within the specific academic disciplines. For a further discussion of faculty advisors, see Chapter Sixteen.

Professional staff academic advisors, on the other hand, are individuals who have been hired to focus primarily on academic advising activities that promote the academic success of students, with additional attention to general student development at the institution. While some teaching responsibilities may be included in a general job description, professional academic advising staff spend the majority of their time meeting with individuals and groups of students regarding academic curriculum requirements of one or many academic majors or areas of study and general academic and personal success strategies, and addressing overall developmental issues with students in their pursuit of a college education.

The most recent ACT Survey (Habley, 2004) information regarding academic advising models used by institutions of higher education indicates that the Faculty-Only model of advising (see Chapter Fifteen) is declining. The Split model—in which specific groups of students, such as exploratory/undeclared, underprepared, etc., are advised in an advising office, and all other students are assigned to academic units and/or faculty advisors—has become the most prominent organizational model across all campuses. Yet the most widely used model in two- and four-year private colleges is the Faculty-Only model (Habley, 2004). ACT Survey results also suggest that while 99 percent (80 percent in all departments and 19 percent in some departments) assign faculty advisors in a least some of their departments, there are also indications of a steady upward trend in the use of full- and part-time nonteaching advisors in at least some departments (Habley, 2004, p. 28). In addition, the ACT Survey indicates a steady increase in the use of professional staff advisors as primary and secondary providers in advising offices (pp. 64–65). It appears that while faculty are still major providers of academic advising, there are steady increases in the numbers of institutions who are using some capacity of professional staff academic advisors to serve their students.

As with other chapters in this section of the handbook, the institutional mission should guide decisions on the selection of an appropriate academic advising model as well as which individuals should deliver academic advising. With increasing attention to and the importance of institution graduation and retention rates, the role of academic advisors has never been more critical in assisting students in their academic success. In reality, institutions seeking to provide quality academic advising systems should consider deploying more than one type of advisor to meet the variety of student backgrounds and needs on campuses today. Each of the following segments will provide specific thoughts regarding nonfaculty advising roles intended to assist institutions that may be exploring the variety of academic advising service options for their specific campuses.

PROFESSIONAL ACADEMIC ADVISORS

The emergence of the professional staff academic advisor is perhaps indicative of recent National Academic Advising Association (NACADA) growth trends. NACADA data indicate that members identifying as academic advisors or academic counselors (professional advisors) increased from 2,236 in February 2001 to 5,207 in February 2007 (133 percent increase). In this same time period, 243 members identified as faculty advisors in 2001 and increased to 528 in 2007 (117 percent increase). In addition, 1,520 members identified as advising administrators in 2001, which increased to 2,312 in 2007 (52 percent increase) (NACADA, 2007). The tremendous growth in all general NACADA membership, now surpassing the 10,000 total membership mark, certainly indicates a significant increase in the number of individuals interested in academic advising issues and resources, many of whom indicate full-time academic advising status.

Professional academic advisors are generally employed to devote the majority of their workday to meeting directly with students to address academic curriculum requirements, college policies and procedures, and general student development and success issues. Professional advisors seek to teach their advisees the skills and knowledge that will ultimately result in the students' succeeding in their academic and personal goals.

The professional academic advisor may be a full-time or part-time employee, and may even be a seasonal employee, providing assistance during peak periods of the academic year. These advisors may be employed in a specific academic department serving as the sole staff person in a small department, or part of a team of professional and possibly faculty advisors who serve an entire department or college. Many professional academic advisors are part of centralized advising centers that serve a wide variety of specific populations of students. Among these are freshmen, exploratory students or those with undeclared majors, or students admitted to the institution who might have been identified for specific academic assistance programs. As with faculty advisors, professional staff advisors may be assigned a specific caseload of students or may be part of a team of advisors who are assigned a population of students. At many institutions, the professional academic advisor may be the initial contact for students who are seeking assistance in the process of exploring a major and a career.

Academic and professional requirements for the professional staff advisor vary across institutions. Academic advisors are also now able to enhance their academic background through specific academic programs focusing on the academic advising profession, such as the NACADA/Kansas State University Academic Advising Certificate and a Masters Degree in Academic Advising.

Strengths of Professional Academic Advisors

The presence of professional academic advisors on campuses has many benefits associated with promoting student academic and personal success. Unlike faculty advisors, whose primary focus is on teaching or research, professional academic advisors are able to spend the majority of their time and availability meeting with students or participating in advising-related activities. Advisors must balance the needs of their specific responsibilities, which may include some nonadvising activities. However, the primary focus is to be available to meet the needs of students. Likewise, professional advisors are able enhance their skills, knowledge, and experience through participating in campus, regional, and national and international professional development activities focused on academic advising. With the emergence of advising as a profession, NACADA is providing more resources and development experiences that enhance the professional advisor role.

Other benefits of professional academic advisors include their ability and willingness to obtain and share knowledge across multiple academic disciplines and knowledge of overall college and university policies and procedures. Professional advisors are able to keep up to date on skills and knowledge in using the most recent technologies that enhance the academic advising experience such as student information systems and degree audit programs. Professional advisors, with appropriate resources and training, deliver academic advising through one-on-one meetings, through group or workshop activities such as new student orientation, and through technology. In addition, professional academic advisors enhance their skills to include basic assistance in areas such as career exploration and development activities, transfer student articulation and policies and procedures, and general admission and recruitment responsibilities when their specific job function may require these needs. Faculty advisors are certainly capable of these types of advising activities and strategies but may find them a challenging because of their focus on the classroom or research.

Challenges of the Professional Academic Advisor

Although the professional academic advisor may become a primary resource for students and administrators in meeting the many advising related needs, there must be point at which professional advisors understand that they cannot be all things to all people. Professional advisors should use their referral skills in getting students to appropriate resources when the need is beyond the scope of the academic advising role or beyond the skills of the specific academic advisor. Some examples of this may be when a student requires the professional assistance of a licensed counselor or the expertise of a financial aid counselor.

Another challenge for professional academic advisors may be the lack of a career progression ladder at their institution. While many individuals choose to remain in academic advising roles through retirement, the need for advisors to progress into other roles and responsibilities is evident, yet lacking, on many campus. Perceptions of professional advisors' roles may also be an issue on campuses where faculty have historically delivered academic advising. It can be difficult to educate and explain to others who may not understand the general responsibilities and roles of professional academic advisors and the value and importance of their presence. It is often the case that when campus administration identifies issues and strategies that include increasing student contacts, the academic advisors are expected to take on these new efforts on top of what is already expected of them. Some institutions may also not have included advisors in policy decisions affecting them, which may affect the overall outcome of how professional advisors are able to perform their duties. This may be due to a general lack of understanding of how advisors spend their time and efforts with students. Finally, hiring individuals to perform academic advising duties in full-time positions requires a significant financial commitment from the institution. Nearly all campuses require professional advisors to have completed a bachelor's degree, and many require a master's degree, which results in the need to offer competitive salaries to obtain and retain advisors.

Effective Uses of Professional Advisors

Institutions wishing to provide a focus on specific student populations who may need routine, or perhaps even intrusive, continuous follow-up should consider professional staff academic advisors. This will allow the academic advisors to provide consistent, continuous support and follow-up regarding the academic curriculum and other developmental issues. Colleges and universities whose faculty are primarily focusing on research and teaching will also benefit from having professional advisors. Professional advisors are able to address the complex and more time-consuming issues that faculty may not be able to handle. In doing so, professional advisors enable faculty to spend more time in their roles as student mentors.

PROFESSIONAL COUNSELORS

The use of professional counselors in advising roles occurs in all institutional types, but is far more prominent in community college settings. The Self-contained advising model grew out of the guidance office concept common in public schools at the time when many community colleges were being created. That model provides that all advising take place in a centralized unit, typically an advising or counseling center, and advising often reports through the Dean or Vice President of Student Affairs (King, 2002). Professional counselors in these settings commonly wear multiple hats, which may include traditional academic advising duties along with typical professional counselor duties such as career counseling, addressing student crisis-related issues, and general mental health issues.

Strengths of Professional Counselors

Counselors have excellent skills and training through their educational and clinical background for offering a variety of services to students. The most applicable skill is their professional training and experience in working with students with a variety of questions, issues, and personal backgrounds. Counselors have the ability to meet students at their developmental level to assist with personal counseling, career counseling, and holistic developmental approaches, which go beyond the typical academic advising needs. And counselors at many institutions receive training to develop expertise on academic curriculum and programs, transfer articulation, and general campus referrals more common to the skills of professional academic advisors.

Students who visit advising and counseling centers may receive a variety of services, quite possibly from the same person. This allows students and their counselors to build an even stronger connection, permitting counselors to get to know their students and assist them with a wide variety of issues. Counselors are able to make general assessments of students, even if the reason for the appointment is to answer academic advising-related questions, and they end up assisting the students with other critical personal issues. Counselors are also accessible on a daily basis and can dedicate their schedules to addressing the different needs of students based on the institution academic calendar.

Challenges

Counselors typically have to balance students' needs for personal counseling with the need for academic advising and registration with limited time or access to the student. When a student has a personal crisis during a peak academic advising period, counselors may have to adjust their schedules to address the issues related to the academic calendar and the demands of specific students' needs. When an advising and counseling center is minimally staffed because of budget limitations, the stress of meeting the variety of student needs may increase as students' demands increase. As with professional advisors, educating the campus community regarding roles and responsibilities related to academic advising and personal counseling may be challenging. Counselors are typically individuals licensed by the state, many of whom have completed doctorate-level education. Providing a sufficient number of counselors to offer academic advising may prove a fiscal challenge to the institution.

Student perceptions of counseling as opposed to academic advising may also be a challenge. The stigma of "going to counseling" may be challenging enough for students to overcome, and when it occurs in a public center fulfilling academic advising and counseling needs, the anxiety of being seen by peers may create additional stress.

Effective Uses of Counselors

Counselors who provide academic advising as well as other general counseling-related services are beneficial in many campus settings. Community colleges, small campuses, and campuses with general advising centers may benefit from having the professional counselor's skills and experience to assist with addressing a variety of student needs. Advising offices that also address career counseling and career-exploration activities would also benefit from having trained counselors. Collaborations between academic advising units and counseling offices can be highly effective for coordinated events activities and making cross referrals for students. Having academic advising and counseling centers close to each other, if not sharing space, would also be beneficial. Administrators responsible for these units should take proactive measures to ensure that communication channels are in place between units.

GRADUATE STUDENT ADVISORS

Graduate student advisors are those seeking opportunities to help fund their education through assistantships, internships, or practicum experiences that enhance their educational experience and prepare them for careers. Departments and schools may choose to provide academic advising for undergraduate students by hiring graduate assistants to supplement faculty or professional advisors, or to be the sole advisors for the department.

Strengths

Using graduate student advisors offers departments an economical option since graduate students are not as expensive as full-time professional or faculty advisors, and the option to employ graduate students for shorter time periods (one or two semesters) may be more conducive to some departments' academic calendar needs. If the graduate student advisor has an undergraduate degree in a similar area of study or from the same institution as the advisee, the advisor is able to offer personal experience to undergraduates. Graduate students are usually more flexible in their availability to hold office hours, and may also possibly be available to offer more time during peak advising periods or summer orientation programs. If graduate advisors are being used to supplement professional or faculty advisors, the graduate advisors may deal with more routine advising tasks, allowing the professional and faculty advisors to spend their time on more critical and complex issues. The benefit of providing graduate students with practical experience and professional development is irreplaceable.

Challenges

Graduate students must make finishing their degree a priority; therefore, issues relating to availability and dependability may arise at certain times of the semester. Because graduate students spend only two or three years finishing their degrees, it is not realistic for them to establish long-term relationships with students or long-term commitments to the advising office and institution. And, because of the turnover, the selection process, training, and supervision of graduate students must be a priority for someone in a full-time professional or faculty position. The supervisor must be available continually to lead meetings, provide training, and initiate communication that ensures appropriate, accurate advising. For some graduate students, academic advising may not be viewed as professional or career possibility—only as a means for financing graduate school. Careful attention must be given to make sure individuals hired to fulfill graduate advisor roles demonstrate commitment to students and to providing sound academic advising. Institutions looking for academic advisors to establish consistent, ongoing, somewhat intrusive advising activities may also struggle with the use of graduate assistants because of their own personal time-commitment issues and availability for the long term. Graduate students are also less likely to establish a strong knowledge base of undergraduate student campus resources and other academic programs because of limited exposure to the campus over the course of one or two years.

Effective Uses of Graduate Assistants

Academic departments that desire to hire individuals who provide general assistance or basic advising functions throughout the academic year, during peak advising periods, or during key programmatic functions such as orientation programs should consider graduate student advisors. Academic programs with large graduate and undergraduate populations may benefit from using graduate student advisors. Master's and Ph.D. programs such as counseling, student personnel administration, and education should also promote the use of their students in academic advising roles through assistantships, internships, and practicum experiences. It seems there is an increasing number of students who are interested in pursuing academic advising as a career in the graduate and even undergraduate levels.

PEER UNDERGRADUATE ADVISORS

Using peer undergraduate students in various roles to support academic advising efforts is increasing according to ACT surveys (Habley, 2004, pp. 28–29). Peer undergraduate advising is one of the many types of paraprofessional positions for which students are selected and trained to offer services to their peers. Four common types of peer advising programs are friendly-contact programs, programs that pair peer advisors and faculty or professional staff advisors, peer advisors as paraprofessionals within a centralized advising center, and peer advisors as paraprofessionals within residence halls (Koring & Campbell, 2005). As colleges and universities explore creative options to assist students, using the knowledge, experience, and energy of undergraduate peers may be a legitimate answer.

Strengths of Peer Advisors

Most people trust others who have had experiences similar to their own, rather than words from those who cannot relate through current personal experiences. Peer advisors may be able to communicate more appropriately and effectively with students on some issues than individuals who finished college decades earlier. Students like interacting with other students, and if this interaction can work to benefit students by helping them to succeed academically, it should be considered. Peer advisors who receive training and supervision can compliment professional and faculty advising roles through a variety of strategies such as orientation assistants, registration assistants, and learning community leaders. Having peer advisors fulfill appropriate, time-consuming tasks allows professional staff to focus on more critical needs of individual students. Peer advisors may also fit better in units with tighter budgets that cannot afford additional professional advisors by helping with more general tasks and interactions, and possibly group settings. Creating peer advising programs also provides excellent opportunities for leadership and professional growth that prepare them to take on additional vital roles on our campuses and in society in general. Peer advisors may also assist advising programs in recognizing problems and challenge inadequacies in the advising system because they are more attuned to the effect that the advising program has on students (Habley, 1979).

Challenges

Although peer advising programs may offer a number of benefits, it is critical to consider the time and energy of the professional staff person(s) responsible for selecting, training, and supervising peers. It is not acceptable to initiate a peer advising program without identifying a professional staff or graduate student who will have the time and authority to administer the program effectively and hold the peer advisors accountable for fulfilling their roles. Peer advisors may be more experienced than the students they are assisting, but they are also still students who are learning and growing. Training on critical topics such as the Family Educational Rights and Privacy Act (FERPA), specific job responsibilities, and balancing peer advisor roles and school are crucial to an effective peer advising program. As with graduate students, peer advisors are not long-term employees; therefore, it will be a cyclical process with each new peer advisor. Continuity will continue to be a challenge, as it is with other student worker positions. It may also be the case that some students and parents will not be comfortable with or trusting of peer advisors; therefore, educating students and parents regarding the roles and responsibilities of peer advisors should occur prior to interactions.

Effective Uses of Peer Undergraduate Advisors

Many campuses have created strong, unique programs using peer advisors, which are highlighted in *Peer Advising: Intentional Connections to Support Student Learning* (Koring & Campbell, 2005).

ADVISING SUPPORT STAFF

This chapter would not be complete without addressing the significance of staff members who fulfill various roles of support staff in academic advising settings. Too many times, college and university administration, faculty, and staff underestimate these critical roles, especially when these individuals spend significant time in direct contact with students in person, on the phone, or through other mediums of communication. Examples of support staff that play a major role in the success of an academic advising program are:

Office managers: persons responsible for the overall daily operations of general advising centers or department or college offices. In addition to providing operational support for advisors and administrators, office managers should understand the significance of customer service functions critical to student satisfaction with the academic advising experience. Office managers need to be very knowledgeable regarding other resources on campus that fulfill key roles so students are able to get the specific assistance they need at the appropriate place.

Secretaries/receptionist: key players in making direct student contact in person or via the telephone. It is crucial that students have a positive encounter throughout the advising experience. Making appointments, receiving reminder phone calls, and receiving professional, friendly greetings when visiting the academic advising office are critical elements of the advising experience. Secretaries and receptionists may also fulfill triage roles in order to determine which students may need specific assistance at specific times or by specific advisors.

Clerical staff: individuals who play critical, behind-the-scenes roles such as basic clerical support to advising administrators and academic advisors, being specialists for providing critical data reports, and maintaining communication links to other key offices. Though many times these individuals may not be in the public eye, their roles are significant to the overall positive academic advising experience for students and parents.

Technical staff: specialists who support critical efforts in using technology in the academic advising environment. Technical support staff have become instrumental in the success of academic advising efforts in recent years, especially since our students expect a more technically oriented, online service as they now have in almost every other aspect of their lives.

Just as academic advisor professional development and training is critical to the success of academic advisors in their daily contact with students, so is the development and training of support staff. Many training topics will be similar to those of academic advisors, and some additional areas such as role clarification (academic advising vs. general assistance), FERPA, and customer-service-related skills should be included. For individuals on the front lines greeting students in person and through phone interactions, training to enhance communication and people skills should be provided. Support staff need to have an understanding of the goals and objectives for academic advising and should be able to articulate to students and parents what will be included in the academic advising experience. Inclusion of support staff in shadowing advising appointments, orientation programs, workshops, and other office-related services is one strategy to help them gain a good understanding of the overall advising process. In addition, team-development activities, retreats, and staff meetings should include critical support staff team members. Administrators and academic advisors should not underestimate the significance of how support staff team members contribute to the overall success of academic advising operations and processes. Students will remember their entire academic advising experience, which includes interactions with support staff.

ADVISING FUNCTIONS IN NONADVISING OFFICES

Colleges and universities employ many individuals in a variety of offices whose responsibilities may include directly assisting students in their general success at the institution. In most cases, academic units are charged with providing the advising functions related to curriculum. It is not uncommon, though, for other units across campus to include job functions related to supporting the academic success of students. These functions may, at times, resemble academic-advising-related efforts in addressing academic curriculum and developmental issues. It is imperative for any college or university employee who attempts to provide academic curriculum assistance for students to receive appropriate training and development. If the institution has an individual or office responsible for general oversight of academic advising, this individual or office should also facilitate discussions regarding role clarifications and training for individuals in nonacademic units providing "academic advising." Examples of offices that may have staff members performing some academic advising related services are:

Admissions office: Recruiters often engage in academic curriculum discussions with prospective students and parents. Recruiters targeting potential transfer students may be asked to address articulation and curriculum applicability questions from prospective students during the admissions process.

Course schedulers: People responsible for scheduling courses may participate in scheduling blocks of courses commonly known as Freshmen Interest Groups (FIGs). These individuals must have a basic understanding of curriculum and graduation requirements to appropriately schedule these clusters of courses. Ideally, course schedulers would work along side academic advisors in preparing these clusters of classes.

Disability resources: These staff members assists students with disabilities and provide assistance in meeting the students' specific needs related to their disabilities. On occasion, disability resource staff members may be assisting students with courseload or class placement issues. Collaboration with specific major and department academic advisors is critical to ensure that specific requirements are not overlooked.

Intercollegiate athletics: These offices may hire individuals to be academic coaches for college sports teams. These individuals often work in tandem with college advisors to make sure that student athletes are meeting eligibility requirements as well as graduation requirements.

Multicultural student centers: These often provide offices on campus whose charge is to specifically target underrepresented student populations for academic and social success. Staff in these roles may offer assistance to students with registration, course scheduling, and academic course load issues.

Honors program: Students participating in college honors programs may have requirements above and beyond the traditional academic curriculum. Honors program staff may be assisting students to identify classes that may meet both major and honors program requirements.

All college and university faculty and staff are committed to student success. Collaboration between and among various academic and student services units is critical to meet the ultimate goal of students' academic success and graduation. Academic advisors and advising administrators should work closely with their allies across campuses to facilitate dissemination of appropriate information regarding curriculum to promote these collaborations in support of student success.

CONCLUSION

Colleges and universities must consider the mission of their institution and their departments in determining an appropriate academic advising delivery. As faculty members are pressured to spend more time on teaching and research activities, colleges and universities are looking to others, such as professional advisors, counselors, and graduate and undergraduate students to fulfill academic advising functions. Regardless of who fulfills academic advising roles, institutions should ensure that these individuals receive the appropriate development and training to effectively benefit students they are advising. The National Association of Academic Advising (NACADA) provides a wealth of resources, publications, and professional development opportunities for all types of academic advisors and advising administrators.

References

Habley, W. R. (1979). The Advantages and disadvantages of using students as academic advisors. *NASPA Journal, 27* (2), 46–51.

Habley, W. R. (Ed.). (2004). *The status of academic advising: Finding from the ACT Sixth National Survey.* (NACADA Monograph Series, no. 10.) Manhattan, KS: National Academic Advising Association.

King, M. C. (2002). *Community college advising.* NACADA Clearinghouse of Academic Advising Resources Web site. Retrieved August 1, 2006, from http://www.nacada.ksu.edu/Clearinghouse/AdvisingIssues/comcollege.htm

Koring, H., & Campbell, S. (Eds). (2005). *Peer advising: Intentional connections to support student learning* (NACADA Monograph Series, no. 13). Manhattan, KS: National Academic Advising Association.

National Academic Advising Association. (2007). Membership data 2001—2007. Unpublished raw data.

CHAPTER EIGHTEEN

Advising Delivery: Group Strategies

Nancy S. King

Individual or one-on-one advising is still regarded by most as the preferred method of delivering academic advising. Increasingly, however, group advising is being considered to be a viable option. Indeed, there are situations in which advising a group can be extremely effective in enhancing and augmenting advising services. Certainly, advising groups should not replace one-on-one advising on a campus, but it is important to recognize that there are some compelling reasons to incorporate group advising into a comprehensive advising system. Indeed as advising is viewed more and more as a form of teaching, the group advising model should gain even wider acceptance. As Woolston and Ryan (2007) point out, group advising is more closely related to classroom teaching and less aligned with counseling than is one-on-one advising (p. 119). In fact, many faculty advisors may initially feel more at home in a group advising session because the format is familiar to them as classroom teachers. Faculty are extremely comfortable sharing information in a group and engaging in dialogue with students in a classroom setting. The group model works exceedingly well in giving information, but there are other advantages as well. For example, innovative group advising methods may offer retention value by connecting students with both their peers and an advisor. Regardless of whether advising is done individually or in a group, however, it is important to remember that many of the underlying principles of developmental advising theory still apply. Grites (1984) notes that a group advisor, like a classroom teacher, "facilitates discussion, suggests alternatives, and answers specific questions; this is developmental advising at its peak" (p. 221).

CHARACTERISTICS OF SUCCESSFUL GROUP ADVISORS

In both one-on-one advising and group advising, it is critical that the advisor view the process as student-centered. As Crookston (1972) points out, developmental advising "contributes to students' rational processes; environmental and interpersonal interactions; behavioral awareness; and problem-solving, decision-making and evaluation skills" (p. 16). The developmental model of including exploration of life goals and educational and career goals in addition to making referrals and giving accurate information is still relevant for group advising. The hallmarks of a successful advisor—knowledge, accessibility, and a caring attitude—are also characteristics of the successful group advisor. In fact, one might well make the case that these attributes are typical of outstanding classroom teachers as well. There are some additional characteristics that group advisors need that are common to the most effective classroom teachers. For example, the successful group advisor must demonstrate excellent presentation skills. In the same way that classroom teachers need an animated, engaging delivery style and the ability to solicit questions and comments from the students and keep the class on task, an advisor of a group likewise should exhibit these traits. In both group and one-on-one advising the advisor and the students have a shared responsibility in the advising process.

In his seminal article on advising, Crookston (1972) defines teaching as any experience that "contributes to individual growth and that can be evaluated. The student should not be a passive receptacle of knowledge, but should share responsibility for learning with the teacher" (p. 12). When group advising is done well, the advisor is indeed teaching. Classroom instructors increase their effectiveness as they master various teaching techniques and as their understanding of various learning styles and student-development theories increase. In much the same way, academic advisors are more effective in both individual and group advising when they expand their knowledge of advising techniques and developmental theories. For example, understanding Chickering's (1969) seven vectors of college students' developmental tasks allows advisors to see more clearly the direct connection between advising and three of these vectors (Gordon, 1988, p. 109):

- Developing competence, or increasing the intellectual, physical, and social skills that lead to the knowledge that one is capable of handling and mastering a range of tasks

- Developing autonomy, or confronting a series of issues leading ultimately to the recognition of one's independence

- Developing purpose, or assessing and clarifying interests, educational and career options, and lifestyle preferences and using these factors to set a coherent direction for life

An advisor who is knowledgeable about student-development theories can assist students in increasing their competence, autonomy, and purpose in advising groups that augment individual contact between advisors and students.

REASONS FOR USING GROUP ADVISING

There are many reasons why institutions may decide to include group advising as a part of their delivery system. Perhaps the most common reason is that there are situations in which individual advising is simply not a viable option. For example, when the number of students to be served far outweighs the number of available advisors, group advising becomes a workable alternative. Bentley-Gadow and Silverson (2005) describe the Sequential Advising Model in the College of Education at the University of Northern Iowa that was created as a cost-efficient, manageable delivery system that incorporates group advising. In this model, students participate in two phases of advising sessions. Phase I consists of two large group advising periods: New Major Orientation and a Pre-Registration meeting. Phase II sessions are conducted with small groups and involve Academic Planning Meetings. This two-phase approach to group advising has been used by the college to meet the advising needs of both first-year students and transfers.

Serving large numbers of students with a limited pool of advisors is but one of the challenges many campuses face in providing advising services. Some student populations have special time restraints, and group advising sessions can be a helpful solution. For example, nontraditional commuters who are balancing jobs and family responsibilities with school frequently cannot connect with their advisor at a mutually agreeable time. However, giving these students the option of a group session may assist both the student and the advisor in addressing the time pressures that are so prevalent among today's students and advisors.

Not only is group advising a valuable way to meet the challenges of numbers and time, but it can also be an extremely efficient and effective means of sharing important information. Rather than repeating the same information again and again in one-on-one settings—an exercise that may very well become tedious and time-consuming for the advisor—using groups can enable advisors to convey important information to several students at the same time, thus freeing them to spend one-on-one advising time addressing individual needs.

There are a number of topics that can be covered quite well in a group setting, such as a review of general education (both the purpose and requirements); instructions regarding the registration process, course selection, policies and procedures; offering general career-planning advice; and providing a framework for selection of a major. For example, many institutions offer a variety of group sessions in which students are given information about degree requirements, program of study options, and career opportunities for a particular major. By attending one of these "major sessions," students are in a better position to make informed choices about a program of study. Ideally, there would be representatives from the administration, faculty, and students in each of these majors available at these information sessions.

Perhaps the most compelling reason for using groups to advise relates to the establishment of peer groups. Unquestionably, peers exert a powerful influence on student success, especially in the critical first year. Peers play a vital role in how students view themselves and the connection they make with the institution. In addition, they influence students' attitudes toward academic goals and values. By creating advising groups, the advisor becomes, in Rice's (1989) view, "an agent for social change whose primary task is to engineer ways for students to interact with student peer groups and faculty" (p. 326). Commuter students, who typically find it more difficult than residential students to establish peer-group relationships, will especially benefit from an advising group.

It is not simply the opportunity to interact with peers that offers the most important advantage, however. Many students feel a sense of isolation on college campuses. Tinto (1993) cites isolation as one of the primary reasons for attrition. That is particularly true of certain groups, such as probationary or exploratory students. Having the opportunity to meet with other students like themselves who are facing many of the same challenges is extremely comforting to students who are feeling alone. In an article titled "What Can Academic Advisers Learn from Alcoholics Anonymous?" Allen (2002) explores what group advising has in common with AA. One of the dominant reasons for the success of AA is the fact that participants are meeting with others who share the same challenges and are able to give one another the support that they need. Light (2001) makes clear that students are less able to succeed if they are facing their academic and social challenges alone. Furthermore, groups that are made up of students with common interests can also be extremely effective because they offer an opportunity for students to establish relationships with their peers. Group advising with special populations, then, serves a dual purpose: it is a means of sharing information and a way of establishing relationships with peers, who share a common need or interest, as well as with an advisor-mentor. These connections directly impact student persistence and success.

It is also far easier for many students to discuss their questions in a group not only because they feel they are with others who understand their issues but also because it removes the intimidation factor that some may feel in an individual appointment with an advisor. In addition, students often get more from a group advising session as a result of hearing other students' questions or comments. Often a question or comment may be raised that has never occurred to many of the students in the group. Some are reluctant to raise a question in a group, and hearing it asked by a peer is reassuring. Woolston and Ryan (2007) observe that "for students hesitant to approach an advisor, group meetings offer both the power and safety of peers. . . .[They] hear peers ask questions or receive resolutions to their problems [and] realize that not only are they not alone in their concerns but that advisors are approachable and helpful" (p. 122). As a result, a student who participates in an advising group may feel more comfortable following up with a one-on-one meeting with the advisor.

FORMATS FOR DELIVERING GROUP ADVISING

Orientation Program

The methods of delivering group advising vary widely; many options already exist on most campuses or can be easily developed. For most students their first introduction to campus life comes during new student orientation. Since one-on-one advising may not be feasible for all orientation sessions, advising groups are often used. According to *ACT's Sixth National Survey of Academic Advising* (Habley, 2004, pp. 32–33), group advising during orientation or registration, although declining, continues to be a common delivery strategy. In the 1987 survey, this strategy was used in at least some of the departments on 93 percent of campuses. In 2003 that percentage declined to 79 percent overall (at two-year public colleges, 74 percent; two-year private, 90 percent; four-year public, 87 percent; and four-year private, 75 percent). These small group meetings during orientation can serve the purpose of informing students about the curriculum, assisting them in planning a first-semester schedule, and introducing the basics of the registration system. Peer advisors and orientation leaders make excellent facilitators to lead these group sessions. New students are likely to pay attention to a peer, especially if this person has received training as a group facilitator. Transfer students present some unique problems and can benefit from an orientation to the institution apart from the new first-time students. Many of the transfer students' questions can be answered in a group advising session prior to their meeting with an advisor to address their individual situations.

The First-Year Seminar and Group Advising

Another excellent venue for group advising is the first-year seminar course. The instructor for this class usually serves the dual role of teacher and mentor. Since a great deal of the course content is clearly related to advising goals, the first-year seminar instructor serves as an informal advisor. In some first-year seminar programs, the instructor is also formally assigned as the academic advisor for the group. Topics frequently covered in a first-year seminar include goal-setting; developing study skills and effective time-management skills; exploring individual interests and aptitudes and career options; introducing students to all of the resources of the institution; encouraging student involvement in out-of-class activities; examining the purpose of higher education; and encouraging student growth in all of the dimensions of wellness. Because many of these topics are definitely part of a developmental advising model, using the first-year seminar as a forum for advising is a logical and effective strategy. Certainly the class sessions can be supplemented by individual meetings with the instructor or advisor, but the classroom setting becomes a valuable avenue for group advising. In the process of group discussions about these advising issues, students not only gain information, but they also learn from one another. In sharing their questions and common experiences, a sense of group identity begins to develop that is important to the success of the class.

Advising and Learning Communities

In the past decade, a dramatic increase has occurred in the number of colleges and universities that are using learning communities as a vehicle to enhance students' academic success and social adjustment. According to the Learning Communities National Resource Center at Evergreen University (http://www.evergreen.edu/washcenter/lcfaq.htm#21) in Olympia, Washington, there are three common types of learning community structures: student cohorts/integrative seminar; linked courses/course clusters; and coordinated study. Regardless of the structure of the learning community, Laufgraben (2005) notes that "they strengthen and enrich students' connections to each other, their teachers, and the subject matter they are studying" (p. 371). Others (Tinto, Goodsell Love, & Russo, 1994) have pointed to the connection between learning communities and student persistence. One learning community model, a cohort in large courses or freshman interest groups (FIGs), has worked especially well at large universities according to Goodsell Love and Tinto (1995). The FIG at the University of Oregon, established in 1982 by the Office of Academic Advising and Student Services, is a prototype of a learning community. The FIG program at the University of Washington is another example of such a program (p. 84). Groups of about twenty students are enrolled during their first term in a cluster of three courses that are linked by a common theme. The FIG members also participate in meetings that are facilitated by a junior or senior peer advisor. One of the major advantages of learning communities and FIGs is the social interaction that they afford among peers both inside and outside the classroom. In the opinion of Goodsell Love and Tinto (1995), "of special importance at large institutions, learning communities allow students to aid each other with one of the key points of transition—learning their way around campus and meeting people" (p. 85).

As Bennett (1999) points out, academic advisors are uniquely qualified to be key players in the learning community. He identifies six functions in the design and implementation of learning communities that can benefit from the expertise and participation of advisors: making decisions about the structure of the learning community, especially as they relate to curricular concerns; assisting students with the selection of an appropriate learning community; selecting peer leaders; helping to administer the program; teaching a student success seminar as a component of the learning community; and helping to identify the support needs of both students and faculty in the community (p. 72). Because advisors are in an excellent position to assist students in making connections within the institution, their participation in the learning community can contribute to the success of the program.

Advisors do play a key role in many learning communities. At La Guardia Community College's New Student House (Schein, 1995, p. 87), three faculty members and one advisor teach a group of students who are divided into three course sections. The advisor meets with the group in a seminar format and the advisor and faculty members meet regularly to discuss student progress. The advising group is used to administer and interpret learning skills tests, to teach study skills techniques, and to advise for registration the following term. At Wofford College, Kuh, Kinzie, Schuh, and Whitt (2005) observe that "first-year students identify themselves by the LC [learning community] they are in as often as they claim affiliation with a Greek organization. And the identity sticks" (p.144). Clearly these groups have the potential for connecting students to the institution, faculty, advisors, and one another.

Advising in Residence Halls

Learning communities can be especially useful on commuter campuses as a way of helping students establish meaningful relationships with their peers. At residential institutions, however, the structure naturally exists for creating advising groups. According to Schein (1995), the residence hall environment offers a possible solution to "the problem of introducing the life-skills approach that developmental academic advising theory advocates. This setting has great potential for supporting interaction between students and advisors. Residence halls also facilitate group advising in an environment where peer-support is already built into the participants' social structure" (p. 120). In order for this approach to work, however, there must be intentionally designed advising interventions. Some institutions are locating advising offices within residence halls; others have schedules set up for advisors to meet with groups at specified times during the week or have "advisor-on-call" systems in place.

Senior Capstone Courses

Although advising groups like FIGs are especially helpful for first-year students making the critical transition into college, they are also useful for students in the last year of their college career. Senior capstone courses, for example, offer a similar opportunity to assist students with another important transition from college to the world of work. Once again, a senior capstone instructor, like the first-year seminar teacher, may serve not only as an instructor but also as an advisor-mentor. Students' sharing their concerns and excitement about their impending graduation creates a supportive environment for successfully navigating this transition. Bringing in alumni and individuals from various careers to serve in an advisory role for the group also assists in preparing students for moving into the next phase of their lives. In much the same way that juniors and seniors may serve as peer mentors in the first-year seminar, these alumni and individuals from various careers can help prepare seniors for their transition from the college into their careers.

GROUP ADVISING FOR SPECIAL POPULATIONS

Methods for delivering group advising include providing group experiences for specific populations of students who may have some special needs. For example, many institutions have successfully used regular group meetings to address the needs of students on probation. Such groups are frequently led by counselors, faculty, or full-time advisors. Group meetings with these students have several purposes. First the advisor-group leader helps students understand the common reasons that lead to students being placed on academic probation. The objective is to help students achieve some self-understanding and accept responsibility for their actions. However, the advisor should also assist the students with developing strategies that will enable them to succeed. Self-esteem issues are important in these groups because students who are in academic difficulty often feel down on themselves. Getting to know others in the group is beneficial because students realize that they are not alone; others are facing similar challenges. The interaction among the students in the group can be a vital contributor to building self-esteem and setting achievable goals as well as holding one another accountable for meeting their goals. These advantages of a probation group may outweigh any stigma that may be attached to a group composed of students in academic difficulty.

Another specific population that may well benefit from group advising is honors students. Although these are high-achieving students, they, too, profit from interaction with peers who are part of the honors program. Coming together to discuss coursework, to establish a sense of camaraderie, and to meet informally with a faculty member-advisor adds value to the in-class honors experience. These same advantages of group meetings also hold true for other specific populations. Students with disabilities, members of minority groups on campus, international students, and returning adults all can benefit from frequent group meetings not only as a means of information-sharing but for purposes of establishing relationships with peers as well.

Two other populations that lend themselves quite naturally to group advising are oversubscribed majors and undeclared or exploratory students. From a practical standpoint, group advising for oversubscribed majors helps to alleviate the logistical problem of providing services for large numbers of students. Using groups to provide information can supplement individual sessions at the same time that students are able to meet with fellow students who share their program of study.

Advising groups can also be established for students who have not decided upon a major. In addition to providing an opportunity for them to explore available options and receive assistance in the decision-making process, these groups provide a means to deliver noncognitive assessment focusing on interests, values, and motivation. The groups also reassure undecided and exploratory students that they are not alone in their confusion about a major and career direction. In addition, groups can be established for students who fail to be admitted to the major of their choice. Knowing that others also face making alternative plans can be reassuring to students who are denied admission to their first-choice major. The advisor can work with these students to help them explore viable options, gather relevant information, and make informed decisions about other possible majors. Having this help available may well prevent a student's leaving the institution in discouragement over not being admitted to a particular major.

A variation of group advising that works well, particularly with specific populations, is the chat room. Following a group meeting, participants may continue to interact electronically. These chat rooms offer students ongoing contact with other group members and the advisor. Students may provide reactions and insights to group discussions or pose questions or topics to discuss during the next meeting. These "virtual" groups are a way for students who are initially reticent about asking questions or offering their opinions in the group's meetings to become involved in the discussion. They also provide a way for students to post questions and replies as they occur to them. With a growing dependence on technology in advising, one can expect to see an increase in chat rooms that are in reality an extension of advising groups. In addition there is a growing use of listservs, e-newsletters, instant messaging, and other electronic methods among today's advisors. (See Chapter Nineteen for additional information on technology and advising.)

KEYS TO SUCCESSFUL GROUP ADVISING

In "A New Adviser's Journal" Patrick Lynch (2005) reveals that "he was a fan of group advising until I had to do it. Now I don't know how I feel about it" (p. 3). Two of the major problems he encountered were attendance and the attitudes of some of the students in the group. Clearly, not all students are ideally suited to the group setting because individuals respond to different teaching methods. With regard to the attendance issue, Woolston and Ryan (2007) suggest that there are only three means to ensure attendance: making the sessions mandatory by placing registration holds on students, refusing individual appointments until a student attends a group meeting, or convincing students that the group advising sessions are time well spent. There are also methods that can be used to make group advising more successful. Woolston and Ryan (2007, p. 120) offer a number of practical tips to making group advising effective that a group advisor would be wise to follow. The first step is appropriate planning. In much the same way that a classroom instructor needs to engage in planning for a class, the group advisor must also spend some time preparing for a group advising session. Some of the preparations an advisor needs to make include:

- Locating a space that is functional for group advising
- Informing students of the session using multiple means of communication, such as e-mails, student newspapers, and flyers strategically placed
- Preparing engaging materials and handouts that students can take with them to refer to later (e.g., worksheets, curriculum guides, lists of important dates and campus resources)
- Developing a clear agenda for the meeting. Consider these questions: What is the primary purpose of today's session? Is the material to be covered suited to the time allotted? Advisors should also anticipate questions that students might raise and make certain they are prepared to give correct answers.

Furthermore, the advisor needs to be aware of strategies for successful group facilitation. First, the introductions and icebreakers are critical to establishing a climate in which students feel comfortable. Winston, Boney, Miller, and Dagley (1988) caution that the icebreakers, which are designed to alleviate anxiety, are frequently misused. Their purpose is not solely entertainment value, but rather they should be directly related to the group's goals and they should promote a feeling of identity with the group (p. 132). Other keys to facilitating a successful advising group include learning the names of all the group members (name cards are helpful) and using them frequently, establishing a climate of trust and respect between the advisor and the students and among the group members, and not allowing one group member to dominate the questioning and discussion.

The advisor should also be aware of some of the same cautions that apply to one-on-one advising meetings. For example, one should begin the group by discussing the broader purposes of advising as a means of assisting students in establishing appropriate and meaningful educational plans. After helping students to understand and appreciate the value and goals of advising, the advisor may then move to more specific questions related to course scheduling or major requirements. Advisors should avoid supplying all the answers instead of encouraging students to think for themselves. Certainly advisors need to give guidance in the decision-making process, but their overarching goal is to assist students in making informed choices and taking responsibility for their decisions. A group in which the advisor lectures the students as opposed to interacting with them is clearly less effective than a situation in which the advisor acts in more of a coaching role. One of the characteristics that effective advisors share with successful coaches is the ability to motivate and encourage. College life, especially when combined with job and family responsibilities, can be stressful. A group advisor can be an excellent sounding board for students to help alleviate some of their stress and confusion.

Group advisors also need to be aware of the necessity of collaboration with other areas of the campus. It is equally important for both one-on-one and group advisors to be familiar with all of the resources of the institution and to make appropriate referrals when necessary. In order to refer students correctly, advisors must be knowledgeable about all available resources, but they should also be skilled at reading group members' needs. For example, if a student is having difficulty relating to other members of the group or seems particularly withdrawn, the advisor should meet with the student outside the group and perhaps make a referral to the counseling center.

At the conclusion of the group session, it is important for advisors to encourage students to follow up with the advisor. Many questions can be handled very effectively with e-mail or by phone, but there are also times when a student definitely needs to meet individually with the advisor following a group meeting. Citing the practice of AA members meeting in groups as well as with an individual sponsor, Allen (2002) draws the analogy of group advising experiences coupled with one-on-one meetings with an advisor as necessary. During the group sessions the advisor should always encourage students to meet individually to discuss questions or concerns that may not be appropriate for group discussion. In addition, it may be helpful to suggest some concrete strategies for following up, such as asking a student to come to the one-on-one session with questions or issues that need to be discussed with the advisor written out. It is also important to stress the fact that students need to do some preparation for the individual appointment as a way of underscoring advising as a shared responsibility between advisor and advisee. Since the group meetings often serve the purpose of breaking the ice, students may feel much more comfortable in a one-on-one session with the advisor than they might have felt without the group experience.

ASSESSMENT OF GROUP ADVISING

As is the case with all advising services, assessment is a necessary component of group advising. Certainly the group advisors should be consulted for their perception of the group's effectiveness and their role in the advising process. The coordinator or administrator in charge of the program should conduct both formative and summative evaluations. Formative evaluation is ongoing. Determining the group's effectiveness while it is still in existence allows for changes and midcourse corrections that will improve its value for participants. Information can be collected in an informal way through written or oral feedback from group members. In contrast, summative evaluation, which is generally more formal, occurs at the conclusion of the group's experience and focuses on the outcomes and final judgments about the efficacy of the group. Administrators may use the summative evaluation to make decisions about the group's effectiveness and to make decisions about continuing the program. Both formative and summative methods are important in evaluating the value of group advising.

In assessing the feasibility of group advising, one should consider the interests of three major campus constituencies—administrators, students, and faculty. Each has a vested interest in group advising services. From an administrative perspective, group advising helps to address the issue of limited resources and makes for an efficient delivery of advising services. In addition, advising groups are related to retention because they connect students to a peer group and a mentor. These connections are invaluable in establishing a student's sense of connection to the institution, a critical factor in retention.

Students who participate in group advising have the opportunity to interact with peers as well as with an advisor; and this interaction is one of the most important contributors to institutional fit (Bean, 1985). For students, the feeling of not being alone on the campus can be a powerful by-product of the group experience. In addition, participation in group advising may well reduce the intimidation that meeting individually with an advisor poses for some students.

The faculty—and the majority of advising is still delivered by faculty—can relate to the value of group advising with regard to time issues. Because of the multiple demands of teaching responsibilities, research, and other institutional commitments, many faculty view group advising as an efficient use of their time. It can certainly free an advisor from the boring monotony of repeating the same information multiple times, but there are other advantages as well. Ideally, faculty may be led to see the similarity between teaching in the classroom and in an advising group. The introduction of an advising syllabus can be extremely useful in developing this advising-as-teaching view. An advising syllabus, like a course syllabus, contains the purpose and goals of academic advising along with a schedule of activities and tasks that relate to advisement. An advising syllabus is useful in helping an advisor view academic advising in its totality with a clear purpose and goals as well as learning outcomes for students. For example, as a result of advising-as-teaching, what would an advisor want students to know, to be able to do, and to value?

CONCLUSION

Although it is true that the relationship between an advisor and advisee most commonly develops during an ongoing one-on-one advising process, there is a definite place for group advising in an institution's overall advising program. Erickson and Strommer (1991) argue that group advising "does not, as some fear, make advising impersonal, but rather supplements the one-to-one advising meeting with the strengths of a seminar, fostering connections among students sharing similar academic interests, prompting a deeper exploration of career and personal issues, and encouraging more probing questions of academic issues" (p. 191). Group advising is not the answer for all students' advising needs, but it definitely deserves a place in a comprehensive advising program because of the benefits it offers for both advisors and students. Clearly faculty may be more prone to see the similarities between advising and teaching when advising is delivered in a group setting. When it is done well and with the appropriate attention to preparation and techniques, group advising can indeed aid retention, address time and resource constraints, complement the individual advising meetings, and enhance students' overall advising experience.

References

Allen, C. M. (2002, September 23). What can academic advisors learn from Alcoholics Anonymous? *The Mentor.* Retrieved August 2007, from www.psu.edu/dus/mentor

Bean, J. P. (1985). Interaction effects based on class level in an explanatory model of college student dropout syndrome. *American Educational Research Journal, 22* (1), 35–64.

Bennett, J. W. (1999). Learning communities, academic advising, and other support programs. In J. Levine (Ed.), *Learning communities: New structures, new partnerships for learning.* (National Resource Center Monograph Series, no. 26.) Columbia: National Resource Center for the First-Year Experience and Students in Transition, University of South Carolina.

Bentley-Gadow, J. E., & Silverson, K. (2005). The sequential advising model for group advising: Modifying delivery venues for freshmen and transfer students. National Academic Advising Association Clearinghouse of Academic Advising Resources Web site. Retrieved August 2007 from http://www.nacada.ksu.edu/Clearinghouse/AdvisingIssues/Group.htm

Chickering, A. W. (1969). *Education and identity.* San Francisco: Jossey-Bass.

Crookston, B. B. (1972). A developmental view of academic advising and teaching. *Journal of College Student Personnel, 13*, 12–17.

Erickson, B. L., & Strommer, D. W. (1991). *Teaching college freshman.* San Francisco: Jossey-Bass.

Goodsell Love, A., & Tinto, V. (1995). Academic advising through learning communities: Bridging the academic-social divide. In M. L. Upcraft & G. L. Kramer (Eds.), *First-year academic advising: Patterns in the present, pathways to the future.* (NACADA Monograph Series, no. 3.) Manhattan, KS: National Academic Advising Association.

Gordon, V. N. (1988). Developmental advising. In W. R. Habley (Ed.), *The status and future of academic advising: Problems and promises.* Iowa City, IA: American College Testing Program.

Grites, T. J. (1984). Techniques and tools for improving advising. In R. B. Winston, Jr., T. K. Miller, S. C. Ender, & T. J. Grites (Eds.), *Developmental academic advising.* San Francisco: Jossey-Bass.

Habley, W. R. (Ed.). (2004). *The status of academic advising: Findings from the ACT Sixth National Survey.* (NACADA Monograph Series, no 10.) Manhattan, KS: National Academic Advising Association.

Kuh, G. D., Kinzie, J., Schuh, J. H., & Whitt, E. J. (2005). *Student success in college: Creating conditions that matter.* San Francisco: Jossey-Bass.

Laufgraben, J. L. (2005). Learning communities. In M. L. Updegraft, J. N. Gardner, & B. O. Barefoot (Eds.), *Challenging and supporting first-year students: A handbook for improving the first year of college.* San Francisco: Jossey-Bass.

Light, R. J. (2001). *Making the most of college: Students speak their minds.* Cambridge, MA: Harvard University Press.

Lynch, P. C. (2005, September 27). A new adviser's journal. *The Mentor.* Retrieved August 2007 from www.psu.edu/dus/mentor

Rice, R. L. (1989). *Commuter students.* In M. L. Upcraft & J. N. Gardner (Eds.), *The freshmen year experience: Helping students survive and succeed in college.* San Francisco: Jossey-Bass.

Schein, H. (1995). University residence halls in the academic advising process. In R. E. Glennen & F. N. Vowell (Eds.), *Academic advising as a comprehensive campus process.* (NACADA Monograph Series, no. 2.) Manhattan, KS: National Academic Advising Association.

Tinto, V. (1993). *Leaving college: Rethinking the causes and cures of student attrition* (2nd ed.). Chicago: University of Chicago Press.

Tinto, V., Goodsell Love, A., & Russo, P. (1994). *Building learning communities for new college students.* University Park, PA: The National Center on Postsecondary Teaching, Learning and Assessment.

Winston, R. B., Boney, W. C., Miller, T. K., & Dagley, J. C. (1988). *Promoting student development through intentionally structured groups.* San Francisco: Jossey-Bass.

Woolston, D., and Ryan, R. (2007). Group advising. In P. Folsom, & B. Chamberlain (Eds.), *The new advisor guidebook: Mastering the art of advising through the first year and beyond.* (NACADA Monograph Series, no. 16.) Manhattan, KS: National Academic Advising Association.

CHAPTER NINETEEN

Advising Delivery: Using Technology

Michael J. Leonard

Technology has had and will continue to have a profound effect on academic advising. In fact, there is probably nothing else that has had as significant an impact on advising in the past ten years as the introduction of new technologies.

Furthermore, nothing changes as rapidly as technology. The first edition of this book was published in 2000. Since then, the iPod was introduced in 2001, Facebook (a social networking site) in 2004, YouTube (a video-sharing Web site) in 2005, and the iPhone in 2007. Cell phones were not as common as they are today, and the use of instant messaging in advising was rare. Now all of these technologies are having, or will have, a significant impact on advising and other forms of teaching in higher education.

This chapter will: (1) provide an overview of technology in academic advising, (2) focus on the uses of technology that support advising systems, such as student information systems and degree audit programs, (3) deal with technologies that support the actual delivery of advising, including instant messaging and social networking, and (4) examine some future trends in the uses of technology in advising.

OVERVIEW OF TECHNOLOGY IN ADVISING: A DIFFERENT KIND OF DIGITAL DIVIDE

The term *digital divide* has been used to refer to the gap between those who have access to technology (especially computers and the Internet) and those who do not. This divide often falls along socioeconomic or racial lines. At least among today's college students, however, that divide seems to no longer exist, although there may be differences in the frequency with which various subgroups of college students use the technology to which they have access (Among Freshmen, a Growing Digital Divide, 2005).

A different kind of digital divide does seem to exist between *digital natives* (those who have grown up with technology) and *digital immigrants* (those who have come to technology later in their lives/careers) (Prensky, 2001a). In higher education today, the digital natives are primarily traditional-aged students, while academic advisors are primarily digital immigrants. Prensky (2001a) postulates that digital natives think and process information fundamentally differently from their predecessors. Prensky (2001b) goes even further by asserting that the brains of digital natives are physically different from the brains of digital immigrants. It is as if students and advisors were raised in different cultures and speak different languages. Certainly, it seems clear that their preferred learning styles are different.

As characterized by Lipschultz and Leonard (2007), digital natives "are accustomed to receiving information at high speeds, process information simultaneously and/or in parallel, tend to multi-task, prefer random (that is, non-linear) access to information, and crave frequent interactivity" (p. 73). On the other hand, digital immigrants "receive information slowly and carefully, process information step-by-step, like to work on one thing at a time, prefer linear access to information, and are accustomed to lectures" (p. 73). This may, in part, explain why some older advisors have difficulty accepting and adjusting to new technologies, while younger students see these technologies as simply an extension of the way they live.

In an MSNBC segment, Popkin (2007) quotes Andrew Davidson, an MTV vice president, as saying, "Young people don't see 'tech' as a separate entity—it's an organic part of their lives. Talking to (young people) about the role of technology in their lifestyle would be like talking to kids in the 1980s about the role the park swing or the telephone played in their social lives—it's invisible" (p. 4).

If digital natives (students) think differently and learn differently from digital immigrants (advisors), then advisors need to take these learning styles into consideration as they develop effective advising programs and decide on the best ways to reach (and teach) their advisees.

What is Technology Good for Anyway?

Luddites notwithstanding, technology itself is neither good nor bad—but the ways in which technology is used could be either appropriate or inappropriate. When is the use of technology in advising appropriate? When it enhances the advisor-advisee relationship, especially when it raises the discourse of advising to a level beyond information giving by expediting, simplifying, or increasing access to information. Eric White (2005), former president of NACADA, wrote, "We talk about the power of computers and how technology can free us. . . . What we must now do is take advantage of the freedom the technology provides and deliver on the promises that are inherent in sound academic advising" (p. 2).

Some advisors thrive on technology—they are comfortable with it, they like using it, and they find that it enhances their relationship with advisees. Other advisors abhor it. What, then, are advisors who are digital immigrants to do about their fear or dislike of using technology in their work? Perhaps the best answer comes from a respondent to the 2000 technology survey conducted by NACADA and its Technology in Advising Commission (Leonard, 2004): "I realize that [technology] is coming and will play an integral role in future advising. . . . I feel it is my obligation to my students and my profession to learn and try to use this technology to the best of my ability" (p. 31).

Leonard (1996), in a prognostic article addressing the (then) present and future of online advising applications, wrote:

> One of the goals of these computer-assisted advising modules is *to enhance the advisor-advisee relationship* by emphasizing the importance of advising in the educational process, by anticipating and managing some of the routine activities that now occur in traditional advising situations (for example, providing basic information and referrals), and better preparing the student for advisor contact and subsequently elevating the advising interview from a mundane to a more meaningful and substantial interaction. Computer-assisted advising provides distinct advantages over traditional advising including convenience (no need for an appointment or to wait until office hours), availability (24 hours a day), accessibility (from anywhere in the world), accuracy (instantaneous updates of system-wide information), anonymity (in cases where a student feels uncomfortable working with an advisor in a one-on-one relationship), consistency (policies and rules are interpreted in a uniform way to all students), and expert consensus (the collective opinions, knowledge, and experience of many advisors comprise the advice provided to the student). (p. 49)

USES OF TECHNOLOGY THAT SUPPORTS ADVISING SYSTEMS

Advising Web Sites

The technology that has likely made the biggest impact on academic advising in the past ten years is the World Wide Web. Now, most students and advisors can locate academic information by simply clicking on an institution's Web site. College catalogs, academic policies and rules, and advising handbooks, formerly available only in print, are now accessible from any PC via the Web.

Institutions, colleges, and advising centers should carefully consider what academic information their students need and should strive to make that information available to them in a format that is easy to access, navigate, and interpret. According to Steele and McDonald (2003), "It is critical that the advisor perspective is added to the campus discussion regarding the development, selection, and implementation of these services" (p. 1). Individual advisors may also want to consider developing their own Web pages as a way to connect online with their advisees.

For a list of award-winning academic advising Web sites, see the NACADA advising technology innovation award recipients at http://www.nacada.ksu .edu/Awards/EPub_Winners.htm.

Student Information Systems

A student information system (SIS) is typically a large-scale, institution-wide program that provides electronic access to student records (grade reports, transcripts, course schedules, advising notes) and processes (course registration, course drop and add, course late drop, withdrawal, declaration of major). Advisor-specific functions may include online advising rosters and access to advising notes and electronically scanned paper documents. Student-specific features may include financial aid summaries and tuition billing.

Many institutions use commercially available SISs, such as PeopleSoft or Banner, though some institutions have developed their own systems or have adapted commercial software for their own uses. The primary advantage of all of these systems, in addition to the access they provide to academic records, is that they are usually integrated. That is, they share a common institutional database of academic and student information, making data management easier for the institution.

Although selecting, installing, and learning to use a new SIS can be a trying experience, the initial problems and limitations are usually overcome with time, resulting in a more efficient way of accessing student records and processes.

DEGREE AUDIT PROGRAMS

According to McCauley (2000), a degree audit program "matches completed coursework with sets of degree-program requirements, tracking student academic progress from declaration of major to completion of a degree" (p. 240). The results of this matching (the audit) may be displayed on screen or produced in paper form. In addition to listing required courses, a degree audit may include other types of requirements (such as entrance-to-major, course grades, and grade-point average). Audits may use different codes, colors, or graphics to indicate which requirements have been completed or need to be completed.

Most audit programs will allow students to do "what if" audits to see how the courses they have completed (and, in some cases, are planning to take in an upcoming semester or term) will count in majors other than the ones in which they are enrolled. This is particularly helpful for students who are contemplating changing majors and for students who have not yet declared a major. Although degree audit programs provide consistent evaluations of progress toward graduation, they are generally flexible enough to allow for substitutions and exceptions to be entered into the system for specific students and situations.

Commercially available degree audit programs include Degree Audit and Review System (DARS), Degree Navigator, and Oracle/PeopleSoft. Some institutions have developed their own degree audit programs or have adapted commercial programs.

Degree audit programs have freed academic advisors from the drudgery of manually assessing a student's progress toward meeting graduation requirements. Audit programs give advisors the chance to use a student's progress as a springboard for more in-depth discussions rather than as the actual event and content of an advising session.

TRANSFER ARTICULATION SYSTEMS

Transfer articulation systems "are designed to reduce the time expended by transfer credit evaluators and to provide consistent and accurate course equivalency data for all students (regardless of the number of institutions attended)" (McCauley, 2000, p. 243). Some states have statewide articulation systems so that students can determine how courses taken at any college or university in the state will transfer to any other college or university in the state (ASSIST, n.d.). These intrastate articulation agreements are especially common between community colleges and four-year public institutions within the state (Virginia's Community Colleges, n.d.).

Once the course transfer articulation agreements are made among the participating institutions, the equivalencies can be published and made available to students and advisors. Preferably, the course equivalency information is made available via the Internet rather than in printed form, which can quickly become outdated.

CAREER GUIDANCE PROGRAMS

Academic advisors, career counselors, and students now have access to a wide variety of computer-based career exploration tools. Career guidance programs such as DISCOVER (www.act.org/discover) and SIGI PLUS (www.valparint.com/sigi.htm), and self-assessment instruments such as the Self-Directed Search, Myers-Briggs Type Indicator, and Strong Interest Inventories are now generally available online.

Career guidance programs may include one or more of the following components: self-assessments of a student's interests, abilities, and values; self-assessments of a student's personality type; matching a student's self-assessments to related majors and careers; general information about the world of work; databases of majors and occupations; and career decision-making strategies.

Students often have the misperception that career programs will tell them what they should do or what they should be, even though academic advisors and career counselors make it clear that this is not the purpose of these programs. Some students with uncrystallized interests may also be disappointed when the results of the surveys and inventories result in a flat profile, simply confirming that the student's interests are not particularly strong in any one area and, thus, cannot be matched to specific majors or careers.

WEBINARS

A Webinar is a Web-based seminar in which the attendees, who can be anywhere in the world, use a Web browser to hear and view a live presentation given by a presenter (or group of presenters), who can also be anywhere in the world. Also referred to as a Webcast or a Web conference, a Webinar typically includes audio and still pictures; it may also include live video or animations, although some participants may have difficulty viewing live video due to slow Internet connections. Webinars allow participants to communicate with the presenter either by typing their questions online or by speaking over telephone lines. A Webinar in which the communication is one-way only (that is, the presenter can "talk" to the participants, but the participants cannot respond to the presenter) is referred to as a Webcast.

Some Webinars are archived online so that they can be viewed again at any time, which is particularly helpful for those who cannot attend live presentations. Webinars can also be archived on CDs and DVDs, although interaction between the presenter and the viewer of any archived presentation is obviously not possible.

USES OF TECHNOLOGY THAT SUPPORT THE DELIVERY OF ADVISING

This section provides brief description of several types of technologies. Table 19.1 provides suggested advising applications for each technology as well as some pros, cons, and cautions related to their use in advising.

Instant Messaging

Instant messaging, usually abbreviated IM, is a way for two (or more) people to communicate "live" over the Internet. Much like e-mail, IM is primarily a text-based form of communication in which one person types a message on a PC and sends it to another person who is also online. That person will receive the message instantly and can respond to the sender, who then receives the reply instantly. Since the users do not have to continually check to see if there are any new messages (as they usually do with e-mail), the communication really can be instantaneous.

Social Networking Sites

Social networking sites, such as Facebook (www.facebook.com) and MySpace (www.myspace.com), are online communities of interlinked personal Web sites through which people can post photos, profile themselves (tell about their interests, religious and political affiliations, and so on), and "friend"

Table 19.1. Technologies, Advising Applications, and Pros, Cons, and Cautions.

Technology	Advising Applications	Pros, Cons, and Cautions
Instant Messaging	1. Communicating with assigned advisees at times when advisors do not have scheduled appointments 2. Answering students' questions through an on-duty, online advisor 3. Communicating with students who have speech impediments that make ordinary in-person communication difficult or stressful 4. Providing an icebreaker for shy or reticent students See: http://communication.utexas.edu/current/AcademicAdvising/ DEV75_007369.html for information about the use of IM in advising at the University of Texas.	1. Cannot identify someone through an IM name the way it is possible to associate an e-mail address with a specific person. 2. Both parties have to know the other's IM name. 3. Confidential issues should be avoided.
E-mail and Listservs	1. Reaching out to one, selected, or all advisees quickly, easily, and efficiently 2. Distributing academic information to groups of advisors quickly, easily, and efficiently	1. Students tend not to use e-mail and may miss important announcements. 2. E-mail is typically not archived online for later reference.
Social Networking Sites	Individual Profiles: 1. Meeting students where they are 2. Making advisors seem more approachable, providing a way to post not only tastes in music, books, and movies, but also advising philosophies, office hours, advising news, and so on	1. Privacy: this problem has been mitigated by giving members privacy controls, though some students still maintain open profiles for anyone to view. 2. Persona: Does the online profile truly represent who that student is?

3. Ethics: Should advisors check the profiles of their advisees? What are an advisor's obligations if he or she sees evidence of inappropriate behavior in a student's profile?

1. Uses a format that students will be familiar with through their courses.

3. Modeling appropriate online behaviors for students

Groups:

1. Creating professional discussion groups; Facebook already includes several NACADA groups

Course-Management Systems

1. Giving advisors the power to create a Web presence without knowing how to create or manage Web sites

2. Giving advisors a way to create groupings of advisees as a way of staying in touch, chatting online, and e-mailing

See: "Public Forums" on Providence College's ANGEL site at http://angel.providence.edu/frames.aspx

Advisor to Student:

Podcasts

The University of Washington (2007)—audio podcasts for students in which presenters address academic topics, including the use of the degree audit system, the advising relationship, and the value of podcasting for academic advising

Student to Student:

Penn State's Division of Undergraduate Studies (2007)—audio podcasts for prospective and current first-year students; topics include advice for high school seniors, exploring majors, and balancing academics with cocurricular activities

(Continued)

Table 19.1. *(Continued)*

Technology	Advising Applications	Pros, Cons, and Cautions
Cell Phones	1. Posting important academic information, much as college administrators have been experimenting with posting course syllabi, assignments, and deadlines (Fischman, 2007) 2. Providing interactive applications (course registration, making advising appointments, and so on) through Web sites designed specifically for cell phone access	1. Students will not experience the same type of interactions that on-campus orientation programs provide. 2. Institutions can save time and money.
Online Orientation	1. Orienting distance learners who are location-bound 2. Orienting future on-campus students, especially those for whom the cost of a trip to campus for one or more days in the summer would be a financial burden	
Blogs	1. Posting academic information on a regular, rolling basis 2. Posting agendas, meeting notes, works in progress, and outcomes for advising meetings 3. Engaging students in discussions of academic topics See: North Lake College's advising blog (http://blog.northlakecollege.edu/advising), University at Buffalo's pre-law blog (http://prelaw.buffalo.edu), and Thomas Nelson Community College's academic advising task force blog (http://www.tncc.edu/blogs/index.php?blog = 11)	
RSS Feeds	1. Providing up-to-the-minute updates on changes in university policies and procedures and other academic issues 2. Providing announcements about changes to advising Web sites 3. Providing updates about new episodes in a podcast; see University of Washington (2007) and Penn State (2007)	

(link to) other members of the site. These sites give almost anyone the ability to create a Web presence without knowing how to create or post Web pages. Individual members can usually control who can view their personal information and photos, while still making themselves known as a member of the network so others can find them on that network. These sites have become very popular with college-aged students as a way to stay connected with friends and classmates not only at their own schools but also at other institutions.

According to Crane (2007), "Today, over half (54%) of college students visit social networking sites every day. In fact, social networking sites are the preferred mode of communication among today's college students for staying in touch with friends (27%) and reconnecting with friends from the past (31%)" (p. 4).

E-Mail and Listservs

In a now-famous article appearing in the *Chronicle of Higher Education* ("E-Mail Is for Old People"), Carnevale (2006) wrote that traditional-age college students now see e-mail as an antiquated technology, and they prefer to use instant messaging and social networking sites as ways to contact their friends and others online. Institutions of higher education, on the other hand, see e-mail as an efficient way to send information to students quickly, easily, and inexpensively, often sending out thousands of e-mails each week. This is another example of the differences in expectations and modes of operation that exist between digital natives and digital immigrants.

Listservs, or lists of multiple e-mail addresses, are efficient ways to reach selected, and often large, numbers of people simultaneously. By sending one e-mail message to the "list," all e-mail addresses on the list will receive the same message. (Technically, LISTSERV is a licensed product of the L-Soft company, but the term *listserv* is often used generically to refer to e-mail lists or the software used to manage them.)

Listservs can be used as a one-way delivery medium (only managers of the listserv can send information to the list) or as an online discussion medium (anyone can send information to the list, which can be used to pose questions, receive answers, and discuss topics of interest).

Course-Management Systems

Course-management systems (CMSs; sometimes called learning-management systems), such as Blackboard/WebCT (www.blackboard.com) and ANGEL (www.angellearning.com), were designed to support the teaching functions of classroom instructors. Typically, CMSs allow instructors to post course materials online (syllabi, calendars, assignments), manage class rosters and grade books, establish teams of students within a class, chat with students outside of (or instead of) class meetings, and create online quizzes and tests, all without knowing how to create a Web site.

Although CMSs tend to be course-driven (that is, students are linked by virtue of their common enrollment in a course), they can also be used to create other groups of individuals who share a common interest or bond. Many of the same course functions (such as posting information, managing rosters, and creating quizzes) can be used in groups established by almost anyone (students, advisors, staff) who have access to the institution's CMS.

Podcasts

As commonly used, the term *podcast* refers to an audio or video file that can be played or downloaded from the Web. Technically speaking, however, a podcast is distinguished from other online audio and video files by being a *series* of audio and video files to which users can *subscribe*. Podcasts are also usually information-rich, while many other audio and video files tend to be oriented toward music or entertainment. Every time a new episode (file) in a podcast series is made available, the podcast subscriber is notified via the Internet of its availability. Depending on the software being used to manage one's podcast subscriptions (for example, iTunes or an RSS news reader), the subscriber can choose to automatically download each new episode as it is posted to the Internet or can decide whether to download each file manually after being notified of its availability. Podcast files can be listened to or viewed on the Web, downloaded to a PC for later listening or viewing, or downloaded to a portable audio or video player, such as an Apple iPod.

Cell Phones

According to a survey by Harris Interactive (Crane, 2007), "Cell phone ownership among college students continues to rise. Virtually all (93 percent) college students today own cell phones compared to less than seven in ten (69 percent) in 2002. And college students today use their cell phones for more than just talking. Eight in ten (81 percent) use their cell phone for something other than conversations. Nearly seven in ten (69 percent) college cell phone owners use text messaging capabilities on their cell phones" (p. 4). The percent of students who own cell phones is likely to be even higher on some campuses (Fischman, 2007).

But what can colleges and universities do, if anything, to harness the power of this ubiquitous communication device? According to Fischman, "Colleges are pressing ahead despite the bumps because they realize that cellphones are the best, and often the only, way to reach their students."

Online Advising Orientation

The traditional summer orientation for new students, which typically takes place on campus, can also take place at a distance. The winners of the 2007 NACADA Advising Technology Innovation Award (the University of Louisville and Metropolitan State University) have produced exceptional online academic orientations. Louisville's STOMP (Student Tutorial Online Module Program) includes an academic orientation video that uses a humorous talk-show format to provide information about topics such as the institution's course catalog, making an advising appointment, opportunities for learning outside the classroom, and more. One of the five sections of this video, a sketch based on a film noir plot, cleverly illustrates the advisor-advisee relationship. Other videos in the STOMP (http://www.s4.louisville.edu/stomp/index.html) series include general education, faculty-student interaction, and academic services.

Metropolitan State's online orientation (www.metrostate.edu/orientation/ portal) also uses video, but in this case the videos supplement text-based Web pages that include quizzes to test students' knowledge of the topics discussed. Modules in this orientation package include program planning, learning resources, success strategies, and registration. Each module features a video of a different presenter, who introduces that module's topics. The academic program-planning module, for example, includes information about degree components, exploring majors, choosing and declaring a major, and declaring a minor.

Blogs

The easiest way to conceptualize a blog (a contraction of *Web log*) is to think of it as an online diary or journal. Blogs tend to be text-based, but may include personal photos, videos, audio files, and graphics. The creative part of blogging is allowing readers to respond, online, to a person's (blogger's) writings. These responses then become part of the blog, as do responses to the responses. A blog can become a running dialogue between the blogger and his or her readers. There are now many Web sites (for example, Blogger: www.blogger.com; Blogware: home.blogware.com; and TypePad: www.typepad.com) that provide free or low-cost space and the tools needed for users to write their own blogs.

RSS News Feeds

An RSS (really simple syndication) news feed is an automatic announcement that there is something new on the Web that may be of interest to a news subscriber. For example, if someone were interested in keeping up with breaking news on the MSNBC Web site but did not want to keep checking the site every few minutes just to find out if there was something new there or not, he or she could subscribe to a news feed on the MSNBC Web site. Then MSNBC would automatically let that person know when breaking news had been added to the site.

To be able to subscribe to and read news feeds requires software known as an RSS news reader or news aggregator. Some news readers are stand-alone programs, while others are incorporated into Web browsers. Most readers allow a person to display news from multiple sources at once (for example, from MSNBC, the *New York Times,* ESPN, and the *Chronicle of Higher Education,* all of which offer their own RSS news feeds).

For more information, see "News feeds—what are they and how can I use them?" at http://www.ossite.org/collaborate/open_news/weblog.help/about-rss.

FUTURE TRENDS

One significant future trend of technology will be convergence—more and more services being integrated into smaller and smaller devices. This trend is already being seen in products like the iPhone, which integrates cellular phone service, Web browsing, audio and video file playing, digital photography, e-mail, text messaging, and more, all in one small, wireless, touch-screen device. Convergence will continue as more functions and new functions are integrated into a single device, or perhaps into a few different customizable devices. Improvements in hardware and software will make these devices ultraportable and less expensive, even with the convergence of additional functions.

In terms of software, one future trend may be three-dimensional virtual reality worlds, such as Second Life (secondlife.com). Some institutions have already begun developing their presence in such Internet worlds, and it seems likely that there is a place for academic advising and academic advisors in that world as well, if this technology succeeds.

On the institutional level, one future trend should be toward offering more academic advising functions via the Internet. For example, it is possible, using artificial intelligence, to develop interactive advising modules that simulate for students personalized discussions with advisors on specific topics (such as late dropping of a course, withdrawing from the institution, and choosing a major) (White and Leonard, 2003). While many institutions already offer online degree audits, transcripts, course registration, and grade-point-average calculators for students, not many have ventured into the realm of advising applications that use artificial intelligence. The reason is simple: it takes much longer to develop an expert-based, interactive advising module than it does to create, for example, a grade-point-average calculator.

For individual advisors, the future trend will be toward multiple channels of communication with advisees. It simply will no longer be acceptable or efficient to expect e-mail to be the only digital way that advisors routinely communicate with their advisees. It will be one way—but it will not be the only way.

At the student level, a future trend will be toward increasing expectations: students will expect the institution, including academic advisors, to use available technology to communicate with them, to provide advising programs, and to help them navigate the educational system. This is the world that eighteen-year-old students have grown up in. They know no other world. They live in the digital realm, and they expect others to do the same.

CONCLUSION

Although technology will continue to change (probably more quickly and in ways that most of us cannot imagine), the main message that readers should take away from this chapter is that many technologies can be appropriately adopted and adapted for academic advising purposes. If academic advisors want to reach their advisees, and their advisees are living in a digital world, then advisors need to become part of that world as well. Perhaps the best way to reach students in this world is not really in one way, but rather in multiple ways, through multiple methods to suit different learning styles, personalities, and opportunities for interaction. This could mean being present to students through not just e-mail but also instant messaging, social networking sites, course-management systems, personal Web sites, podcasts, cell phones, and other forms of communications technology that will be developed in the future. The more ways an advisor reaches out, the more likely it is that the advisor will reach more students. Not everyone—particularly a digital immigrant—is going to be comfortable with this approach. But as the profession of academic advising matures and its digital immigrants are replaced by digital natives, the use of technology in academic advising will not be a question of whether—it will be a question of how.

References

ASSIST. (n.d.). Welcome to ASSIST. Retrieved September 23, 2007, from http://www .assist.org/web-assist/welcome.html

Among freshmen, a growing digital divide. (2005, February 4). *The Chronicle of Higher Education*, p. A32.

Carnevale, D. (2006, October 6). E-mail is for old people. *The Chronicle of Higher Education.* Retrieved September 15, 2007, from http://chronicle.com/weekly/v53/ i07/07a02701.htm

Crane, L. (2007, April). On campus and beyond: College students today. *Trends and Tudes, 6* (6), 1–4. Retrieved September 15, 2007, from http://www.harrisinteractive .com/news/newsletters/k12news/HI_TrendsTudes_2007_v06_i06.pdf

Fischman, J. (2007, May 11). The campus in the palm of your hand. *The Chronicle of Higher Education.* Retrieved September 15, 2007, from http://chronicle.com/ weekly/v53/i36/36a04101.htm

Leonard, M. J. (1996). The next generation of computer-assisted advising and beyond. *NACADA Journal, 16* (1), 47–50.

Leonard, M. J. (2004). Results of a national survey on technology in academic advising. *NACADA Journal, 24* (1& 2), 24–33.

Lipschultz, W. P., & Leonard, M. J. (2007). *Using technology to enhance the advising experience.* In M. S. Hunter, B. McCalla-Wriggins, & E. R. White (Eds.), *Academic advising: New insights for teaching and learning in the first year.* (NACADA Monograph Series, no. 14.) Manhattan, KS: National Academic Advising Association, pp. 71–86.

McCauley, M. E. (2000). Technological resources that support advising. In V. N. Gordon, & W. R. Habley (Eds.), *Academic advising: A comprehensive handbook* (pp. 238–248). San Francisco: Jossey-Bass.

Penn State, Division of Undergraduate Studies. (2007, March 23). DUS podcasts. Retrieved December 30, 2007, from http://www.psu.edu/dus/podcasts

Popkin, H.A.S. (2007, July 26). How technology has ruined life for our kids. MSNBC. Retrieved September 23, 2007, from http://www.msnbc.msn.com/id/19983210

Prensky, M. (2001a, October). Digital natives, digital immigrants. *On the Horizon, 9* (5). Retrieved September 15, 2007, from http://www.marcprensky.com/writing/ Prensky%20-%20Digital%20Natives,%20Digital%20Immigrants%20-%20Part1.pdf

Prensky, M. (2001b, December). Digital natives, digital immigrants, part II: Do they really think differently? *On the Horizon, 9* (6). Retrieved September 15, 2007, from http://www.marcprensky.com/writing/Prensky%20-%20Digital%20Natives, %20Digital%20Immigrants%20-%20Part2.pdf

Steele, G., & McDonald, M. (2003). Designing a career and advising Web site. *NACADA Clearinghouse of Academic Advising Resources.* Retrieved September 23, 2007, from http://www.nacada.ksu.edu/Clearinghouse/AdvisingIssues/CareerWebSite/home.htm

University of Washington. (2007, April 24). *iHelp: The value of podcasting for academic advising.* Retrieved September 15, 2007, from http://depts.washington.edu/advpdcst/new/wordpress/?p = 13

Virginia's Community Colleges. (n.d.). *Guaranteed transfer.* Retrieved September 23, 2007, from http://www.vccs.edu/Students/Transfer/tabid/106/Default.aspx

White, E. R. (2005, February). Academic advising and technology: Some thoughts. *National Academic Advising Association Newsletter, 28* (1).

White, E. R., & Leonard, M. J. (2003). Faculty advising and technology. In G. L. Kramer (Ed.), *Faculty advising examined: Enhancing the potential of college faculty as advisors* (pp. 259–284). Bolton, MA: Anker.

PART FOUR

TRAINING, ASSESSMENT, RECOGNITION, AND REWARD

Wesley R. Habley

INTRODUCTION

As underscored by ACT's Six National Surveys of Academic Advising, the most critical elements of effectiveness are training of advisors, the assessment of the advising program and individual advisors, and recognition and rewards for those who deliver advising. Part Four focuses on these elements.

Chapters Twenty and Twenty-one cover the first critical elements of effective advising: training and development of advisors. In Chapter Twenty, Thomas Brown provides an overview of the critical components of effective advisor training. Brown asserts that effective training requires a balance and blend of content, participant factors, and techniques. His primary focus is on the three critical content areas: conceptual—the things advisors must understand; informational—the things advisors must know; and relational—the skills advisors must exhibit. In Chapter Twenty-one, Pat Folsom provides a compendium of the tools and resources that are available to guide trainers in the implementation of the conceptual, informational, and relational content areas. In addition, she provides a master plan that can be implemented either as a guide for the trainer of groups of advisors or as a self-guided training tool for individual advisors to use in a self-development approach.

Because advising is primarily a relationship, it follows that effective advising will not take place unless the advisor demonstrates the skills necessary to build and maintain a one-to-one relationship with students. In Chapter Twenty-two, Rusty Fox provides an overview of the essential elements of relationship-building. He stresses the importance of communication skills, particularly listening and paraphrasing, and closes the chapter with a review of the Five "Cs" of skilled advising.

Chapters Twenty-three to Twenty-five cover the second element of advising effectiveness: assessment. As higher education continues to focus on the assessment of learning outcomes, it is incumbent upon advising programs to document the contribution they make to student learning. Focusing on the CAS Standards for Academic Advising, John H. Schuh provides insight into the role academic advising plays in the achievement of student learning outcomes in Chapter Twenty-three. He describes the importance of advising in student learning, discusses the ways in which advising contributes to learning outcomes, and uses two scenarios to illustrate how advising contributes to student learning.

In Chapter Twenty-four, Joe Cuseo provides a template for the assessment of individual advisor performance. In that template, Cuseo provides a step-by-step strategy for the development, collection, analysis, and uses of assessment, making the case that student input into advisor importance can provide far more than information on student satisfaction. Cuseo rounds out advisor assessment by sharing insights on the use of qualitative methods, analysis of student behavior via institutional records, and advisor self-assessment.

In Chapter Twenty-five, Wendy Troxel suggests that the evaluation of the advising program must focus on three critical areas: Efficiency—the degree to which the advising program is productive in relationship to the resources it uses; Effectiveness—the degree to which program goals have been realized; and Impact—the degree to which changes have occurred. In addition, Troxel presents and discusses a five-stage planning model to guide practitioners in the implementation of program assessment.

In the final chapter, Chapter Twenty-six, Jayne Drake presents and discusses six principles of effective systems of recognition and reward. Drawn primarily from management literature, the six principles are: create a positive and natural reward experience; align rewards with program goals; extend people's line of sight; integrate rewards; reward individual ongoing value with base pay; and reward results with variable pay. Drake also includes discussion of the results of a survey on rewards valued by members of NACADA.

CHAPTER TWENTY

Critical Concepts in Advisor Training and Development

Thomas Brown

Academic advisors serve as lights in the labyrinth to students. Advisors—whether instructional faculty members, professional advisors, counselors, or paraprofessionals—help students make sense of the past as they plan their futures. No student service is mentioned more often in research on student persistence than academic advising (Hossler & Bean, 1990). For community college students, frequent interactions with faculty and advisors had a positive impact on preventing students from dropping out (Deil-Amen, 2005).

Effective academic advising requires preservice and in-service development programs that define roles and responsibilities, set expectations (i.e., institutional, program, and students), and provide opportunities for the development and enhancement of attitudes, skills, and behaviors essential to creating effective advisor-advisee relationships. Instructional and administrative faculty are expected to have relevant competencies before commencing their work with students; however, many key competencies are developed only after these educators arrive on campus (Brown & Ward, 2007). If colleges and universities are to expect competent academic advising, they must provide structured professional-development programs for all faculty and staff who advise students.

In a survey of advising needs, educators at 224 U.S. colleges and universities identified the following as the five advisor education topics of greatest concern: the relationship between advising and retention, going beyond class scheduling in advising, early identification of student needs, engaging faculty in advising, and enhancing communication and relational skills (Noel-Levitz, 2006a).

This chapter describes the elements that constitute comprehensive advisor development programs. In addition to outlining content and recommending strategies and techniques, it will also suggest some of what academic advisors might share with students to help them shape their perspectives, values, and attitudes toward learning and higher education. Students hear a great deal about what is necessary to get into college, and academic advisors assist their advisees to understand what they must do to successfully move through and move on from college.

This chapter considers how relational and informational issues must be on the agenda for advisor development programs; however, the primary emphasis is on the conceptual principles that are essential to preparing effective academic advisors. In Chapter Twenty-two, Rusty Fox provides a summary of relational skills that lead to the establishment of effective relationships with students. In Chapter Twenty-one, Pat Folsom provides a detailed overview of the informational tools and resources advisors need to do their work and discusses how these can be used to enhance advisor training.

THE STATUS OF ADVISOR DEVELOPMENT IN U.S. HIGHER EDUCATION

Since 1979, six ACT national surveys have reported on the status of academic advising on U.S. college and university campuses. In the second survey, Crockett & Levitz (1983) observed that training was a cornerstone of performance for every field or job. In the subsequent national surveys (Habley 1987, 1993, 2004; Habley & Morales, 1998), the lack of advisor training has been identified as one of the major weaknesses in academic advising programs.

Faculty continue to be the primary providers of academic advising to students. Nonetheless, Yolanda Moses (1994) observed that faculty, who have received little or no training, are often judged to be inadequate advisors. According to Habley (2004), less than one-third of campuses mandate faculty advisor training in all departments, and 35 percent of campuses neither mandate nor offer training. Two-year public colleges were most likely to require advisor training in all departments (42 percent), while only 16 percent of four-year public colleges had such requirements.

A study of nearly 2,000 mostly faculty advisors at two- and four-year institutions (Brown, 2007) found less than a third of respondents agreeing that they had adequate preparation and training before beginning to advise students. Many respondents said they learned by trial and error or gleaned what they could from colleagues—most of whom likely acquired their backgrounds the same way.

The absence of consistent and systematic training weakens the quality and effectiveness of academic advising. The lack of training also contributes to misperceptions about advising and serves to undermine the status of advising and advisors on many campuses, especially among instructional faculty. While advisor-development programs typically are scheduled for half a day or less at the beginning of the academic year (Habley, 2004), comprehensive advisor development should be an intentional, ongoing process that supports advisors in the acquisition of the perspectives and tools needed to expand their understanding, knowledge, and skills to enhance student learning, engagement, and success.

FACTORS IN PLANNING ADVISOR-DEVELOPMENT PROGRAMS

Advisor-training programs need to establish goals and outcomes that are SMART: Specific, Measurable, Achievable, Realistic, and Tangible (Brown, 1998; King, 2000). Examples of SMART outcomes for advisor development would include increasing advisor knowledge and satisfaction with advising, increasing the frequency and quality of advisor-advisee contacts, reducing advising-related errors that can increase time to program completion, or increasing referrals and use of resources and services that can enhance student success. Each of these goals is specific and realistic, is measurable, and could have a tangible impact on the effectiveness of advisor-advisee interactions.

Those responsible for advisor development activities need to consider:

- *Content*—what will be included on the agenda
- *Audience*—skill levels, experience, advisor type (faculty, professional, counselor, etc.)
- *Techniques and format*—what the most appropriate methods are to deliver programs so as to maximally engage participants

Whether advisors are instructional faculty members, counselors, or professional advisors, there are some common elements that should be incorporated into the content of training and development programs. These have been identified as conceptual, relational, and informational issues (Habley, 1986; King, 2000; Brown, 1998).

King (2000) observed that conceptual elements include what advisors need to understand about the students they serve, as well as about their work as advisors. Informational elements are specific details regarding institutional policies, procedures, and programs that advisors need to know in order to provide timely and accurate advice to students. Relational elements are the skills and attitudes advisors need to use to engage students in academic goal-setting, planning, and decision-making.

New advisors often are concerned that they lack the information necessary to advise their students. However, the quality of relationships advisors develop with students are often more important than the quantity of information they may, or may not, have. Informational issues are most frequently included in advisor-development programs (Habley, 2004); however, greater emphasis must be placed on conceptual and relational elements if advising is to be viewed and valued as more than a clerical activity directed at helping students to schedule classes.

All advisors should understand the critical role they play in supporting students to value education as more than preparation for a job, to help students distinguish between grades and learning, and to enable advisees to view education as a lifelong process, of which college is but one part.

CONCEPTUAL ISSUES IN ADVISOR DEVELOPMENT

Advisor-development programs should begin by defining (or redefining) academic advising and its relationship to an institution's mission and student learning. Gordon (1992) recommended that programs include historical and philosophical perspectives on academic advising, although she pointed out that these aspects of advising were rarely included. The facilitator should review the institution's mission statement for academic advising, or The Concept of Academic Advising, which can be found through the National Academic Advising Association (NACADA) Clearinghouse (www.nacada.ksu.edu).

As part of the process of defining advising more broadly, participants should be provided with a framework to guide their work with students. Terry O'Banion (1994) offered a hierarchy of advising that remains relevant because it describes academic planning and decision making as a process wherein the advisor and advisee move through five sequential steps:

1. Exploration of life goals, values, interests, aptitudes, and limitations
2. Exploration of vocational/career goals consistent with goals, values, etc.
3. Choice of program or major
4. Course selection
5. Scheduling classes

While a scheduling and registration approach to advising starts at the bottom of the hierarchy, O'Banion's model proposes a developmental learner-centered model of academic advising that begins by asking about goals, values, interests, etc.

A second conceptual outcome for advisor development is supporting participants in understanding and appreciating that academic advising is more than scheduling classes or tracking progress toward satisfaction of degree and program requirements. This can be done by considering some of the shared goals of teaching and advising, such as those set forth by Drew Appleby in Chapter Six.

Susan Frost (1991) suggested that academic advising is more meaningful when viewed as a teaching process rather than as a one-time event related to course scheduling. Vowell and Farren (2003) noted that for many instructional faculty, advising is regarded as a low status activity or an add-on to a faculty load already full of other obligations. Brown-Wheeler and Frost (2003) concluded that casting academic advising as an obligation rather than as a form of teaching might actually lead to the attitudes identified by Vowell and Farren. Similarly, counselors often resist serving as advisors because they do not see how "class scheduling" is the best use of the educational backgrounds and skills they have developed to support student development.

Development programs should encourage advisors to understand that part of their role is assisting students to understand what is required to be successful in college and helping them to identify skills and habits that produce higher levels of achievement. Advisors should be encouraged to recognize the need to support and challenge their advisees to understand the commitment, hard work, and resilience that are essential to success—in college and in life.

An overview of student-development theories should be included among the conceptual elements of an advisor-development program. The extent to which students are able to become fully engaged with the planning and decision-making at the core of advising can be adversely affected by where they are in their personal development.

Theories of development reviewed should include adults (Schlossberg, Lynch, & Chickering, 1989; Taylor, Marienau, & Fiddler, 2000); racial-identity development (Torres, Howard-Hamilton, & Cooper, 2003); gay- and lesbian-identity development (Cass, 1984); and women (Gilligan, 1982; Belenky, 1997). Overviews of relevant theories can be presented by academic advising staff, psychology or education faculty members, or others who can share this information in a jargon-free and accessible manner.

Sharing national and institutional research regarding the relationship between academic advising and student persistence can be a powerful motivator for academic advisors. Brown and Rivas (1994) concluded that faculty advisors are on the front lines of higher education in supporting increased achievement and success for multicultural students. In *What Works in Student Retention*, Habley and McClanahan (2004) highlight information on successful practices in college student retention based on ACT's national survey of more than 1,000 colleges. They found academic advising to be among the campus interventions that survey respondents believe have the greatest impact on student persistence across all institutional types.

Advisor-development programs should also clarify advisor and advisee responsibilities. Effective academic advising requires students to share the responsibility for academic planning, to find their own answers and use their advisors as a sounding board (Frost, 1991). Students expect their advisors to be available, knowledgeable, and to care personally about them. Professional-development programs must set forth student expectations and delineate the responsibilities of academic advisors and advisees.

Figure 20.1 offers a model of shared responsibility based on the work of Creamer (2000), Lynch (1989), Brown & Rivas (1994), and Brown (2006).

This model suggests that advising needs and responsibilities evolve as students move into (see Chapter Nine), move through (see Chapter Ten), and move on from (see Chapter Eleven) college (Lynch, 1989). Creamer (2000) observes that students initially need information and guidance, but as they adjust to college, their advising needs shift, and they seek feedback or consultation from advisors. Brown and Rivas (1994) suggested that advisors often need to take the lead and be more prescriptive and directive with first-generation, multicultural,

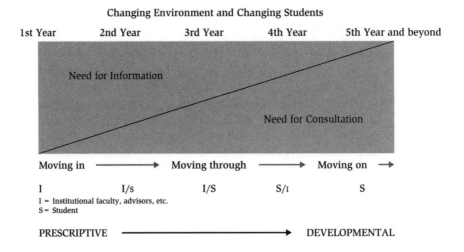

Figure 20.1. A Model of Shared Responsibility.

or other at-risk cohorts, especially at the outset of the advising relationship. Advisors must take the initiative to establish the advising relationship, with students sharing, then bearing the responsibility as they move through and move on (Brown, 2006). This model has been adapted for students in two-year community and technical colleges, with years one to five being modified to years one to three and beyond.

Effective academic advising should also ensure that students understand and are encouraged to use the full range of campus and community resources. Accordingly, advisor-development programs should support advisors in understanding referral resources and how to refer students to them. Faculty members often feel more comfortable and confident when they understand that a major part of their work is making effective referrals, rather than being personal and career counselors, for example.

Ongoing advisor-development programs should provide opportunities for in-depth interactions between advisors and support service providers, while shorter programs should allow advisors to hear briefly from staff in areas such as counseling, career services, academic support programs (e.g., tutoring, supplemental instruction, study skills), and offices serving specific populations (e.g., student athletes; multicultural, international, and lesbian, gay, bisexual, and transgender [LGBT] students; first-generation adults, and students with disabilities). Support service representatives should provide and discuss informational materials, synopses of services, and current and emerging issues. They should also suggest how advisors can refer students to campus and community resources.

Advisors play a key role in encouraging students to think beyond their majors or programs, and they should help students make meaning and see connections between curricular and cocurricular learning opportunities. Programs should encourage and empower advisors to help students develop fields of study (Schein, Laff, & Allen, 1987), rather than focusing narrowly on major requirements. This approach validates the worth of all coursework and integrates major courses, general education, elective, and cocurricular learning.

Effective academic advising is not only helping students to find the right answers, it must also challenge and support students to ask big enough questions. The question students seek to answer in advising is not, "What courses do I need to take?" Rather the question they should ask is, "How do I want to live my life, and what can I do in college to help me move toward that vision of my future?"

The focus on conceptual training topics has increased, but fewer than half of all advisor-development programs include these topics (Habley, 2004). A strong conceptual component is essential to effective advisor-development programs because it can reshape attitudes about academic advising and motivate faculty, counselors, and others to embrace advising as an essential part of higher education's mission, and an integral part of their personal and professional work to support student learning, engagement, and success.

RELATIONAL ISSUES IN ADVISOR DEVELOPMENT

The quality of academic advising is often determined by the quality of relationships that exist between students and their advisors. The skills that enable the establishment of effective relationships can be taught, developed, and enhanced.

In a continuing study of student priorities, Noel-Levitz (2006b) reported that after instructional effectiveness, academic advising is the next most important area of campus life for undergraduate students. Pascarelli and Terenzini (2005) refer to several studies that found that students' perceptions of faculty interest in them may be enough to promote increased persistence. Student experiences during recruitment often lead them to believe and expect that faculty, advisors, coaches, and other members of the campus community will be available to them and genuinely care about them once they enroll. When students leave college prior to completing their goals, it is often the gap between students' expectations and experiences that leads to dropping out.

Academic advisors must develop relationships with students that cause them to be more receptive to their advice, guidance, and referrals. In some of the earliest work in the field of social influence theory (Hovland, Janis, & Kelley, 1953), attractiveness, expertness, and trustworthiness emerged as three keys to influence. Each of these elements is at the heart of the work of academic advisors.

When students perceive that their advisors care about them (attractiveness), they respond and are more open to the advisor's advice (expertness). Students experience advisors as trustworthy when they perceive them to have students' interests at heart. Trustworthiness emerges when students feel confident that their advisors will be there for them when they fall short of goals, encounter disappointment, and need to develop strategies to overcome obstacles, or develop alternative plans.

Relational elements of advisor development should include effective one-to-one skills, including interviewing, rapport-building, making effective referrals, multicultural advising skills, and others that are discussed in Chapters Seven and Twenty-two. Advisor-development programs must provide specific guidance to enable advisors to engage students in meaningful discussions, rather than eliciting "yes" or "no" answers. Advisors should also be encouraged to consider how they communicate their caring (or lack thereof) for students by the extent to which they are prepared for advising sessions. Communication skills in advising are important, and none is more critical than effective listening. Advisors should be encouraged to recognize that good advising sometimes means sitting with students as they find the answers they need in the comforting silence of their advisor's office.

Perhaps the most important skills educators have are their life experiences and the ability to "tell stories" that can inform, inspire, and motivate students. Experienced educators know stories about students who have struggled and overcome obstacles; however, few stories are more compelling for students than our own appropriately self-disclosed times of struggle, failure, and doubt.

No issue in higher education has received more attention over the past quarter century than the issue of diversity and creating inclusive campus communities. Human beings often seek to economize on the energy required to make distinctions. Treating everyone the same may be equal treatment; however, it is not necessarily equitable treatment. Those who advise students should be expected to develop the skills and attitudes that will allow them to respond effectively to *all* students.

Effective professional development must support advisors in developing or enhancing their cultural competence so they can work effectively with multicultural students, international students, students with disabilities, LGBT students, first-generation students, older adults, and others who often find themselves at the margins of campus life. Chapters Twelve and Thirteen address many of the issues and skills advisors need to develop to work effectively with diverse populations.

INFORMATIONAL ISSUES IN ADVISOR DEVELOPMENT

An important part of academic advising is providing students with accurate and timely information about institutional and departmental programs, policies, and procedures. Nonetheless, making informational elements the central focus of advisor-development activities will only serve to reinforce the notion that advising is primarily a clerical activity related to providing information. The presentation of informational training topics has generally decreased, but informational topics continue to dominate (Habley, 2004).

In discussing informational issues, the focus should be on assisting advisors in becoming familiar with academic and cocurricular programs; institutional, departmental, and program policies, procedures, and requirements; referral strategies; student information sources; and support tools available to academic advisors. Programs should also communicate that it is important for advisors to support students in assuming the responsibility for knowing about policies, requirements, etc.

Advisors should be provided with an overview of key resources, including the campus catalogue and bulletin, degree audits, academic planning worksheets, class schedules, advising conference records, the Family Educational Rights and Privacy Act (FERPA), and campus advisor listservs. Advisor handbooks and Web sites that are concise and easy to navigate can also provide ongoing advisor development related to information issues. Again, a comprehensive consideration of information resources for advisor training is provided in Chapter Twenty-two. Advisors should be assisted in understanding how to use informational resources to support students to achieve their goals in a timely manner, with students coming to assume the responsibility for their own lifelong planning and decision-making.

DESIGNING PROGRAMS TO MEET ADVISOR NEEDS

Successful advisor-development programs integrate the content and format of professional development with the experience, skill level, and willingness of advisors to participate. Participation in advisor development might be an expectation for professional advisors, counselors, paraprofessionals, and peers. However, for instructional faculty, trainers must also be sensitive to the fact that faculty have significant demands on their time and that the effectiveness of academic advising is often not part of the faculty recognition and reward system (although it should be).

Rather than designing an advisor-development program based on external models, or even best practices, a good place to begin is to ask faculty and staff who currently advise students whether they had adequate preparation and training prior to beginning to advise. Needs assessments could list a number of conceptual, relational, and informational issues and ask advisors what they wish they had known before they began to advise students. Assessments might also identify students cohorts at risk for dropping out (e.g., first-generation students, undecided students, and student athletes) and ask faculty to identify those groups whose characteristics and needs they would like to know more about. Assessments enable program planners to develop an agenda appropriate to campus advising needs, and the feedback gleaned can be used to make the case for advisor development.

Table 20.1 presents two advisor development models that integrate advisor characteristics, content, and techniques for experienced and inexperienced advisors.

FORMATS FOR ADVISOR-DEVELOPMENT PROGRAMS

There are many approaches to advisor development, including group sessions, self-paced online programs, seminars, graduate programs, campus-based institutes, and Webinars. Habley (2004) reported that 52 percent of colleges and universities used individualized training based on advisors' needs, 35 percent provided a series of short workshops throughout the year, and 24 percent offered

Table 20.1.

Experienced Advisors	Inexperienced Advisors
Skill level: Moderate	Skill level: Low
Experience: High	Experience: Low
Willingness to participate: Moderate	Willingness to participate: High
Conceptual need: Moderate	Conceptual need: High
Informational needs: Low	Informational needs: High
Relational needs: Moderate	Relational needs: High
Program Techniques and Formats	
External presenters	Internal presenters
Readings/discussions	Reading/discussions
Panel presentations	Pre-test knowledge
Simulations/role plays	Brainstorming needs and issues
DVD/Video vignettes	DVD/Video vignettes
Group discussions	Group discussions
Case studies	Questions and answers

single workshops. Interestingly, the Advising Needs Survey (Noel-Levitz, 2006a) found that 84 percent of respondents expressed a preference for training provided in group settings, while only 8 percent and 5 percent respectively, indicated a preference for online programs or Webinars.

Formats for advisor-development programs that have been used successfully include panel discussions by experienced and new advisors, simulation exercises and role-plays, and brown bag lunches with group discussions based on readings or critical issues identified by academic advisors and students. An increasing number of campuses invite nationally recognized experts to address academic advising issues as part of campus colloquia or programs for faculty. Finally, the National Academic Advising Association (NACADA) offers regional and national conferences, institutes, DVDs, and other resources that provide opportunities for program enhancement, individual advisor development, and exposure to best practices in advisor training and development.

Increasingly, faculty advisor development is being included as part of the professional-development activities provided through campus-based teaching and learning centers. Rochester Institute of Technology, Tacoma Community College, Prairie View A&M University, North Shore Community College, and the University of Nevada, Reno, are among the campuses whose faculty development offices have focused on academic advising in recent years.

The University of Washington provides a comprehensive curriculum leading to certification for academic advisors that includes a series of readings, workshops, and colloquia. Similarly, the Office of Undergraduate Advising at Virginia Tech offers a regular series of workshops and programs for professional and faculty advisors throughout the academic year.

Whatever formats are used, it is important to share with the campus community how advisor development can increase the quality of academic advising, and support efforts to enhance student development, learning, and persistence.

IMPLEMENTING ADVISOR-DEVELOPMENT PROGRAMS

Developing and implementing effective advisor-development programs is a process that requires commitment, dedication, hard work, and resilience. Like most successful activities in a campus community, it is important to involve key stakeholders in the process of assessing needs, planning, implementation, and evaluation. Those responsible for planning should emphasize that the program is being developed as part of institution-wide efforts to enhance student achievement and success. Unless there is evidence to the contrary, the basis for offering programs should be to develop and enhance advisor knowledge, skills, and effectiveness, rather than communicating a negative assessment about the commitment or current work of advisors.

It would also be valuable to consider targeting initial advisor development programs for specific groups of academic advisors, such as first-year seminar instructors and advisors and faculty and staff advising specific populations (e.g., student athletes, international students, and underprepared students).

The following are some recommended steps in the process of program implementation.

1. Form a representative planning group that can identify important academic advising needs and issues and have the group appointed or commissioned within the existing governance structure to ensure its standing and credibility. Members of the planning group should include faculty and professional advisors, students, and representatives from offices with which advising is linked (e.g., admissions, counseling, career services, multicultural programs).

2. At the initial meeting, the advising administrator should share information about the status of academic advising—nationally and at her or his campus. She or he should also introduce the conceptual, informational, and relational elements of advisor development, to ensure a broader focus for program planning and implementation.

3. On campuses where the results of program assessment, advisor evaluation, or other advising use and satisfaction data are available, these can be examined to identify areas of effectiveness and topics for inclusion in advisor development. Once an agenda for the program has been developed, input from academic advisors should be encouraged.

4. Enlist the support of academic leadership, deans, department chairs, program heads, and others for the proposed professional-development program, perhaps with invitations to faculty and staff being issued by these individuals in conjunction with the academic advising administrator.

5. Publicize the program widely, stressing the benefits of participation; schedule the program to avoid conflicts, and offer multiple sessions; select an appealing location away from distractions with refreshments available throughout the program.

6. Acknowledge participant attendance to them, their colleagues, and their supervisors.

7. Assess and evaluate the program, and use the findings for continued development and improvement. In addition, if advisor development is a new or expanded endeavor on a campus, communicate this fact to participants and let them know that their feedback will be sought about what works and what needs to be added or improved.

Effective advisor development is very much connected to issues of advisor evaluation, recognition, and reward—the latter being the only areas that consistently receive lower ratings than advisor development and training on the national surveys of the effectiveness of advising programs (Habley, 2004). What an institution values is evident in its public proclamations, how resources are allocated, and what it recognizes and rewards through institutional systems such as rank and tenure, administrator evaluations, etc.

In many ways, advisor development is the foundation upon which evaluation, recognition, and reward are based. It is not equitable to hold people accountable when they have not received adequate training and preparation, and there can be no meaningful recognition and reward for academic advising without advisor evaluation.

Academic advising plays a powerful role in helping students to develop and achieve their personal, academic, and career goals. Effective advising and effective advisors emerge as the result of intentional planning and development. Therefore, all individuals engaged in academic advising should be expected to participate in preservice and in-service programs that set expectations and develop the attitudes, skills, and behaviors that produce the kinds of academic advising that students expect and need. Without such programs, competent and effective academic advising may not come to exist.

References

Belenky, M. E., Clinchy, B. M., Goldberger, N. R., & Tarule, J. M. (1986). *Women's ways of knowing: The development of self, voice, and mind.* New York: Basic Books.

Brown, T. E. (1998). Designing advisor training/development programs. In *NACADA/ACT Academic Advising Summer Institute Session Guide.* Manhattan, KS: National Academic Advising Association.

Brown, T. E. (2006). Designing and implementing effective advisor development programs. In *NACADA Academic Advising Summer Institute Session Guide.* Manhattan, KS: National Academic Advising Association.

Brown, T. E. (2007). Academic advising survey. Unpublished study. St. Helena CA: Thomas Brown Associates.

Brown, T. E., & Rivas, M. (1994). The prescriptive relationship in academic advising as an appropriate developmental intervention with multicultural populations. *NACADA Journal, 14* (2), 108–111.

Brown, T. E., & Ward, L. (2007). Preparing service providers to foster student success. In Kramer, G. L. (Ed.), *Fostering student success in the campus community*. San Francisco: Jossey-Bass.

Brown-Wheeler, K. E., & Frost, S. H. (2003). Evolution and examination: Philosophical and cultural foundations for faculty advising. In G. L. Kramer (Ed.). *Faculty advising examined: Enhancing the potential of college faculty as advisors*. Bolton, MA: Anker.

Cass, V. C. (1984). Homosexual identity formation: A theoretical model. *Journal of Homosexuality, 4,* 219–235.

Creamer, D. G. (2000). Use of theory in academic advising. In V. G. Gordon, W. R. Habley, & Associates, *Academic advising: A comprehensive handbook*. San Francisco: Jossey-Bass.

Crockett, D. S., & Levitz, R. S. (1983). *Final report on ACT's Second National survey of Academic Advising*. Iowa City: ACT Inc.

Deil-Amen, R. (2005, April). Do traditional models of college dropout apply to non-traditional students at non-traditional colleges? Presented at the annual meeting of the American Sociological Association, Philadelphia, PA.

Frost, S. H. (1991). *Academic advising for student success: A system of shared responsibility*. (ASHE-ERIC Higher Education Report no. 3.) Washington, DC: The George Washington University School of Education and Human Development.

Gilligan, C. (1982/1993). *In a different voice: Psychological theory and women's development*. Cambridge, MA: Harvard University Press.

Gordon, V. N. (1992). *Handbook of academic advising*. Westport, CT: Greenwood.

Habley, W. R. (1986). Designing advisor training programs. ACT National Conference Series unpublished participant notebook: *Academic advising as a critical element in student growth and development*. Iowa City: ACT, Inc.

Habley, W. R. (1987). *The status and future of academic advising*. Iowa City: ACT, Inc.

Habley, W. R. (1993). *Fulfilling the promise: Final report of ACT's Fourth National Survey of Academic Advising*. Iowa City: ACT, Inc.

Habley, W. R. (2004). *Current practices in academic advising: Final report of ACT's Sixth National Survey on Academic Advising*. (NACADA Monograph Series, no 10.) Manhattan, KS: National Academic Advising Association.

Habley, W. R., & McClanahan, R. (2004). *What works in student retention? All college survey*. Iowa City: American College Testing Program.

Habley, W. R., & Morales, R. (1998). *Current practices in academic advising: Final report of ACT's Fifth National Survey of Academic Advising*. (NACADA Monograph Series, no. 6.) Manhattan, KS: National Academic Advising Association.

Hossler, D., & Bean, J.P. (1990). *The strategic management of college enrollments*. San Francisco: Jossey-Bass.

Hovland, C. I., Janis, I. L., & Kelley, H. H. (1953). *Communications and persuasion: Psychological studies in opinion change*. New Haven, CT: Yale University.

King, M. C. (2000). *Designing effective training for academic advisors.* In V. G. Gordon, & W. R. Habley, & Associates, Academic advising: A comprehensive handbook. San Francisco: Jossey-Bass.

Lynch, A. Q. (1989). Moving in, moving through, moving on. In Schlossberg, N. K., Lynch, A. Q., & Chickering, A. W. (Eds.), *Improving higher education environments for adults.* San Francisco: Jossey-Bass.

Moses, Y. T. (1996). Quality, excellence, and diversity. *New Directions for Institutional Research, 81,* 9–20.

Noel-Levitz. (2006a). *2006 Advising needs report: Summary of findings from National Advising Needs Survey.* Retrieved February 1, 2008, from https://www.noellevitz.com

Noel-Levitz. (2006b). *2006 Student satisfaction inventory and priorities report.* Retrieved February 1, 2008, from https://www.noellevitz.com

O'Banion, T. (1994). An academic advising model. *NACADA Journal, 14* (2), 10–16.

Pascarelli, E. T., & Terenzini, P. T. (2005). *How college affects students: A third decade of research.* San Francisco: Jossey-Bass.

Schein, H. K., Laff, N. S., & Allen, D. R. (1987). *Giving advice to students: A road map for college professionals.* Alexandria, VA: American College Personnel Association.

Schlossberg, N. K., Lynch, A. Q., & Chickering, A. W. (1989). *Improving higher education environments for adults.* San Francisco: Jossey-Bass.

Taylor, K., Marienau, C., & Fiddler, M. (2000). *Developing adult learners: Strategies for teachers and trainers.* San Francisco: Jossey-Bass.

Torres, V., Howard-Hamilton, M. F., & Cooper D. L. (2003). *Identity development of diverse populations.* (ASHE-ERIC Higher Education Report, volume 29, no. 3.) San Francisco: Jossey-Bass.

Vowell, F., & Farren, P. J. (2003). Expectations and training of faculty advisors. In G. L. Kramer (Ed.), *Faculty advising examined: Enhancing the potential of college faculty as advisors.* Bolton, MA. Anker.Part FOUR

CHAPTER TWENTY-ONE

Tools and Resources for Advisors

Pat Folsom

hapter Twenty builds the case that advisors need to understand and ultimately master the conceptual, informational, and relational components
of advising regardless of the student populations they serve, their institutional settings, advising positions (faculty, nonfaculty, or peers), or advising
delivery system (face-to-face, group advising, or distance advising). This chapter focuses on the tools and resources to help them gain this mastery. Because
there is so much diversity in advising settings, positions, student populations,
and delivery systems, not all advisors will need the same topics delivered in
the same way, so tools and resources are defined broadly in this chapter and
include written and electronic formats as well as individuals, campus offices,
and professional organizations. In addition, because advisors gain excellence
over time, student by student, through an experiential synthesis of the conceptual, informational, and relational components of advising, much of their
development occurs after the initial training program. Advisors, therefore,
need tools and resources that support their continued development as well as
tools and resources for their initial training.

ADVISING TOOLBOXES: THE BASICS

There are three comprehensive resources that can be useful to faculty or nonfaculty advisors in any setting. These are described below.

- This *Handbook* and its predecessor (Gordon & Habley, 2000) are
  authoritative resources on virtually every aspect of academic advising,

including its history, advisor training and development, advising specific student populations, advisor types, and advising program models and assessment. The *Handbook* provides a conceptual, research, and theory-based approach from authors with years of experience in the field. This is a resource both new and experienced advisors can return to and learn from year after year.

- *The New Advisor Guidebook: Mastering the Art of Advising through the First Year and Beyond* (2007) is a National Academic Advising Association (NACADA) monograph that offers a practice-based approach to advisor training and development. It functions as a curriculum for advisors who are managing their development and serves as a resource for trainers to enrich their ongoing advisor development programs. The monograph includes a New Advisor Development Chart outlining long-term developmental goals as well as realistic expectations for the skills advisors can acquire during their first year of development. The chart can be used to train as well as to assess advisor development over time.

- The resources available through the National Academic Advising Association (NACADA) provide career-long developmental support and include numerous advising-focused publications such as *The NACADA Journal, Academic Advising Today,* and monographs as well as the NACADA Clearinghouse of Academic Advising Resources (n.d.). The Clearinghouse is a central location within the NACADA Web site for the collection, organization, and dissemination of information and resources to assist advisors. It features a searchable Web site that includes research and practice-based resources and examples of best practices for all aspects of advising. New advisors should be encouraged to explore its riches; experienced advisors should visit it frequently; and trainers should return to it routinely to identify materials for ongoing advisor-development programming.

NACADA commissions and interest groups offer the opportunity for advisors to network and ask questions of other advisors with similar advising interests or advising focus. One interest group specifically targets new advisors. NACADA national and regional conferences and institutes also offer networking opportunities as well as the opportunity to learn about best practices or the latest research on advising.

These comprehensive resources should be in the toolboxes of all trainers and advisors. Advisors new to the field who do not have access to formal training programs can use the *Handbook* to gain a conceptual understanding of the history, role, and practice of advising, and then use the *Guidebook* to map out a practice-based self-development plan and chart their growth. Subsequently they can search the Clearinghouse resources to deepen their knowledge base and address specific advising issues that arise. Given the tight timeline typical for getting new advisors prepared to work with students, trainers might want to begin with the more practice-based *Guidebook* followed by ongoing advisor-development programming that uses the *Handbook* to assist advisors in gaining a profession-wide perspective and Clearinghouse resources related to specific advising issues or student populations.

In addition to these comprehensive tools, there are more specifically targeted resources that can assist advisors in mastering the conceptual, informational, and relational components of academic advising.

CONCEPTUAL COMPONENT: THE BROAD PERSPECTIVE

Academic advisors enter their role from a multitude of backgrounds. Some advisors have backgrounds in traditional liberal arts (history, English, or biology); others have professional degrees in nursing or education; still others have degrees in counseling, student development, or higher education. While new advisors may remember their own advising experiences as students, or may have some notion of what constitutes academic advising, many would be surprised to find that there is a body of literature devoted to academic advising that includes conceptual content and standards. And few have a full understanding of their institution's expectations for advising with respect to student success and student retention. Yet, it is this conceptual component of advising that provides a framework for the work advisors do as well as the context within which advisors work.

Tools and resources for the conceptual component of advising help advisors answer the following questions about academic advising: What is academic advising? What do academic advisors do, and what are their responsibilities? Why is academic advising important?

Four documents endorsed by NACADA address these questions and support advising for all types of institutions and advising delivery systems. These documents, available for downloading through the NACADA Clearinghouse, should be part of every advisor's toolbox:

- NACADA's Core Values are delineated in *The Statement of Core Values of Academic Advising*. The core values provide a framework to guide professional practice and remind advisors of their responsibilities to students, colleagues, institutions, society, and themselves.

- NACADA *Concept of Academic Advising* affirms that academic advising is integral to fulfilling the teaching and learning mission of higher education and outlines three components of advising as teaching: curriculum, pedagogy, and student learning outcomes.

- The Council for the Advancement of Standards in Higher Education (CAS, 2006) *Standards and Guidelines for Academic Advising Programs* outlines the standards for academic advising programs, including mission, outcomes of student learning and development, advisor responsibilities, leadership, human resources, and financial resources. Advisors will find the sections on advisor expectations and student learning outcomes helpful in answering the questions posed above.

- The *NACADA Standards of Advising Distance Students* should be in the toolbox of advisors working in distance relationships with students.

Chapters in Part One of this *Handbook* define academic advising, address the theoretical underpinnings of advising, outline the role of advisors as teachers, and provide a historical context for the field. In addition to the Clearinghouse, other excellent resources that offer substantial conceptual information include:

- *Foundations of Academic Advising I: What is Academic Advising?* (NACADA, 2006). This CD provides an alternative training format to a text-only format. Each unit is about 10 minutes so can be tailored to short, workshop style training programs.

- *The Mentor: An Academic Advising Journal* (Center for Excellence in Academic Advising, n.d.) is a free, Web-based scholarly publication about academic advising in higher education. The publication's goal is to provide a mechanism for the rapid dissemination of new ideas about advising and for ongoing discourse about advising issues. This publication includes numerous articles on developmental advising, faculty advising, advising as a profession, and a series by Drew Appleby (2001) on "The Advising-Teaching Connection." Articles are short, thereby lending themselves easily to ongoing advisor-development workshops.

- *Advising: New Insights for Teaching and Learning in the First Year* (Hunter, McCalla-Wriggins, & White, 2007) is a monograph that explores advising as a rich form of one-on-one teaching for first-year students.

Whether advisors are self-managing their development or participating in formal training programs, they can use the resources listed above to develop a personal definition of academic advising or to create an advising syllabus to use with students. Advisors should receive and use these conceptual resources during training and should be encouraged to return to them frequently throughout their tenure as advisors. The definitions of advising and the syllabi they develop will most certainly change as they gain advising experience. These changes offer a tangible indication of their growth as advisors.

CONCEPTUAL COMPONENT: THE CAMPUS PERSPECTIVE

Tools and resources at the institutional and departmental or unit level should provide advisors with the answers to the following questions: How is academic advising defined at my institution? As an advisor, what is my role as an educator within the institution? What role does advising play at my institution?

Good resources to answer these questions include the institutional mission or strategic plan and the advisor's departmental or advising program mission and philosophy statements. The institutional mission can be found in both printed and electronic formats and usually are readily available on the institution's Web site. Thurmond (2006, p. 30) suggests that new advisors:

- Find the mission, philosophy, or strategic plan on the institution's Web site.

- Acquire an organizational chart on the central administration Web site.

- Review the general catalogue and admission materials (mission statements often are incorporated into admissions materials).

To find out where advising programs fit into the institutional mission and structure, Thurmond further suggests that advisors-in-training review the advising unit's mission statement. If there is no mission statement, advisors-in-training should talk with their advising supervisor to determine where the advising unit fits within the institution and the role of academic advising in achieving the institutional mission and goals.

Armed with this information as well as the broad conceptual background, advisors can begin to develop a personal philosophy of advising to guide them in their work with students. Nikki Dyer (2007, p. 30) provides a step-by-step account of how to develop a personal advising philosophy. Dyer's exercise and others like it familiarize advisors with their institution's mission, give them a positive picture of how their daily work helps students, and also supports the broader educational goals of the institution. Advisors should be encouraged to revisit and revise their personal philosophy and monitor how it changes as they gain experience. Patrick Lynch's account (2005) of his emerging understanding of advising during his first year as an advising professional offers a good model.

CONCEPTUAL COMPONENT: ADVISOR PERSPECTIVE

Advisors need a clear definition of their roles and responsibilities and their students' responsibilities. Developmental tools and resources should answer questions such as: What are my specific responsibilities to my students and to my department or advising unit? What are the expectations for advisors and for advising within my unit?

Written or electronic resources that address this question include faculty handbooks, advising-unit training manuals or handbooks, advisor job-description position notices, and advisor-evaluation materials. Evaluation standards should be given to all advisors so that they have a solid understanding of the skills and knowledge trainers and administrators are looking for as they assess advisor effectiveness. The pathway for reaching these standards should be clearly delineated in the initial training and through ongoing advisor development.

The "New Advisor Development Chart" is a tool that provides such a pathway. The chart addresses the core functions of advising by asking: What should advisors know and be able to do in their first year, in year two and beyond—regardless of their institutional setting or the type of student they advise? (Folsom, 2007a). It delineates long-term goals for each of the major components of advising—conceptual, informational, and relational—but also offers advisors explicit, realistic short-term goals for skill development within the first year. For example, the section of the chart shown in Table 21.1 outlines first-year expectations and long-term goals for making effective referrals.

The substantive difference in these expectations is experience. The New Advisor Development Chart can be molded or adapted to any advisor-development program. New advisors can use the chart to create an initial self-development plan, and trainers can use the chart to assist new advisors in

Table 21.1. Making Referrals: Expectations and Goals

Year One	Year Two and Beyond
Usually capable of matching students with appropriate resources	Demonstrate advanced referral skills
Able to provide students with standard information about referrals and resources (standard information is gained through printed resources and Web sites)	Integrate fully the detailed knowledge of resources and working knowledge of student to match specific student needs
Competent at seeking information and asking for help to ensure effective match of student and referral	Prepare a student for referral

Source: From the University of Iowa New Advisor Developement Chart. *The New Advisor Guidebook*

identifying areas for improvement. Like the philosophies of advising and advising syllabi developed by advisors, these plans will change as advisors begin to synthesize the conceptual, informational, and relational components in their work with students. Development in each component, however, does not necessarily move forward at an identical pace. The chart allows trainers or advisors themselves to work on individual components as they manage professional development.

TOOLS AND RESOURCES FOR TRAINING ON THE INFORMATIONAL COMPONENT

Academic advisors must be familiar with all aspects of their institution, even if they specialize in a particular major or type of student. Therefore it is understandable that preservice training programs have a heavy focus on the informational component of advising. In order to be credible, academic advisors must give students accurate, up-to-date information about majors; courses; departmental, collegiate, and institutional policies; and procedures, and institutional support services and resources. In addition, they must be knowledgeable about the students at their institution and the student populations they advise. Goodner (2007) recommends that tools and resources to help advisors gain both institutional knowledge and knowledge about the student populations they advise should assist new advisors in three critical ways: acquiring essential information, organizing information, and over time, expanding and deepening this knowledge base.

Acquiring and Solidifying Basic Institutional Information

Because advisors are frequently responsible for introducing students to and teaching them how to use institutional resources; they should learn from and be adept in using those resources. Such resources may include, but are not limited to general catalogs, course-enrollment tools, student policy, procedure, and codes of conduct handbooks, all of which may be in printed or electronic formats. Given the wealth of Web-based institutional information, it is also imperative for new advisors to know which of the informational resources is considered the official record for academic policies and requirements.

Checklists, if used as tools and not as the focus of advising sessions, help advisors master the complexity of the information they need to share with students. Checklists create a visual outline of a major, minor, or certificate program and can be used in tandem with standard institutional references. For example, an advisor may pull up major requirements from the online catalogue, then use the checklist to review the requirements the student has already completed. The repetition of this process, student by student, helps advisors solidify basic knowledge and ensures that they have covered all relevant points with the student. Many institutions have degree evaluations or electronic audits (see Chapter Nineteen) that serve the same purpose. Checklists should be visually clean and clear and contain all relevant information for the program (major, minor, certificate), including prerequisite courses and requisite grade points for selective programs. Other exercises that trainers can use to assist advisors in acquiring basic information are described below.

- *Campus maps.* Advisors must be able to locate the departments and campus offices. Trainers should ask advisors to describe how to get to the referral office from the advising session.

- *Campus resources scavenger hunts.* In this exercise, advisors match a list of student questions with the appropriate campus resources. Advisors subsequently visit these offices and collect sample handouts and materials. This exercise provides materials for advisors' own informational files and allows them to make more detailed referrals for students.

- *Virtual scavenger hunts.* Advisors complete a scavenger hunt by visiting the Web sites of offices to which students are commonly referred.

- *Referral handout that includes the offices to which new advisors are most likely to refer students.* The handout should include all contact information for each office as well as office hours. This is a tool that assists advisors in organizing information about campus and a tool to which advisors can return repeatedly to use in advising sessions and hand out to students.

Organizing Information

As Mark Goodner (2007) notes in his article on managing information, "Advisors cannot use information if they cannot find it, and until new advisors internalize information, the pace and quality of their advising depends on how quickly they can access information. The speed at which new information comes at advisors does not stop with training. Advisors need to develop a system to manage information during training so that they have a system in place as they begin to see students" (p. 53).

Advisors must create both electronic and paper filing systems and must organize their offices in ways that allow them to efficiently retrieve information when they are working with students. Trainers can use the training program topical organization as a template for information organization for new advisors. Advisors also can be encouraged to look at how other advisors organize their desks and files—whether paper or electronic. Trainers may also want to create a list of tips and strategies for organizing information. There is an ancillary benefit to developing good organizational systems. Goodner emphasizes that "Developing an organization scheme for information provides yet another way to internalize and learn the information: each time an advisor reads and files material he or she undergoes another informational review" (p. 55).

Deepening and Broadening the Institutional Knowledge Base

Advisors solidify their basic institutional knowledge through repetition of information in advising sessions, but advisors can use individual advising sessions to build on their knowledge as well. For example, reviewing students' course syllabi during an advising session is beneficial to both advisor and student. Advisors increase their knowledge about each course as they teach students how to read and use a syllabus. Through effective interviewing skills, advisors gain substantial information about courses, campus resources, and policies from a student perspective and frame questions that encourage students to talk about their experiences. Such questions signal that the advisor is interested in them. Advisors who work with exploratory students may want to meet with instructors to learn more about introductory courses in majors. And trainers should encourage advisors to keep an advising information log in which they write down information they have gleaned from students during advising sessions. Reviewing their advising information log weekly assists advisors in solidifying and deepening their knowledge base. Just as important, this tool offers them a tangible record of their developmental growth in advising knowledge.

Advisors, as teachers, are responsible for helping students bring meaning to their educational experience, yet advisors may struggle to use the specific information they have gained about academic programs to articulate the purpose and value of academic program requirements (including general education programs) to students. The American Association of Colleges and Universities has numerous publications focused on the meaning of a liberal education. *Why Do I Have to Take This Course? A Student Guide to Making Smart Educational Choices* (Shoenberg, 2005) provides excellent practical talking points for teaching students about knowledge and skills they gain through their collegiate academic experience.

Trainers also may want to return to tools used in the initial training but use them with a different developmental emphasis. Take, for example, the physical-resource scavenger hunt described earlier. Midway through a new advisor's first year, trainers could repeat the matching quiz with more nuanced questions. Goodner suggests possible components for the repeat scavenger hunt to a career center (2007, p. 55):

- Walk by the building to gain familiarity with recognizable features such as signs and entryways. Walk through the building and learn where the lobby is located, where students sign up for counseling appointments, and where the library is located in relation to the entry and to get a sense of the traffic flow and the feeling of the center.

- Think about the office from a student's perspective. What happens when students enter the center? What will the staff ask them or expect of them?

Goodner (p. 56) also suggests the following strategies for deepening knowledge about a career center:

- When calling or e-mailing the center to ask questions, try to develop a relationship with one or two specific staff members to serve as regular contacts for learning more about the center and to use as resources for students.

- Use these contacts to learn about the specific goals and tasks of career counselors and how their jobs differ from those of academic advisors.

All of this knowledge helps the advisor give students a much more detailed, first-person description for a referral that will make students feel more comfortable with and more likely to follow through on the referral.

Acquiring Basic Information about Students

New advisors need access to tools and resources that give them an understanding of the institution's student body, the specific subgroup of students with whom they work, and the specific students they advise. Susan Kolls (2007) notes that new advisors must seek to gain as much information about their students as they do about the policies and programs of their institution. The institution may provide the content for teaching students, but if advisors do not understand who they are teaching and how their students learn, it will be difficult for them to master the synthesis of advising skills that leads to excellence in advising. Kolls likens gaining advising knowledge about students to "looking into a box of a 1,000 piece puzzle," noting that new advisors who "systematically seek out available information on students" to put together the pieces will be able to work with students more effectively (p. 59).

As part of training, advisors should receive the student data essential for them to begin working directly with students. The tools used to deliver this data should answer the question "Who are the students at my institution?" Whether the information is provided through a handbook, profile, in print, or online, it should provide a comprehensive picture of the student body, including, but not limited to the following information:

- Average ACT/SAT, high school class rank, and high school grade point average

- Percent of students admitted who do not meet admission requirements

- Percent of students who enter with Advanced Placement, College Level Examination Program Test (CLEP) test scores, or college coursework completed while in high school.

- Percent of resident and nonresident students and geographical distribution of student body

- Demographic composition of the student body
- Ratio of commuters to residential students
- Percent of traditional-age as opposed to non-traditional-age students
- Assessments such as institutional placement exams, College Student Inventory (Noel-Levitz), ACT Student Profile

National and institutional student surveys are rich resources for learning about student levels of engagement, satisfaction, and college expectations. Some national surveys, such as the National Survey for Student Engagement (NSSE) and the Cooperative Institutional Research Program (CIRP) issue national reports and provide institutional reports for participating institutions.

Trainers should provide similar profiles for the specific subpopulation with whom their advisors work. Again, the tools can be advising handbooks, unit, departmental or collegiate student profiles, and student profiles extracted from external tools and resources such as the surveys and assessments listed above. Using these tools, advisors should be able to answer the question "How do the students I advise compare to those at the institution as a whole?"

Advisors typically have multiple tools and resources to learn more about the individual students they advise—even before they meet with the students. These tools include student information systems, degree evaluations, and grade reports (see Chapter Nineteen). Grade reports reveal information about the student's academic performance (e.g., whether the student has been on probation, dismissed, reinstated, or made the Dean's list), specific areas of academic strengths and weaknesses, and patterns that suggest that an advising intervention is needed (e.g., a substantial drop in grades). Student information systems typically provide advisors with testing and placement results, high school information, and enrollment histories that show patterns of major changes and changes of registration. And student files, whether in electronic or paper format, contain a wealth of information. The student's folder may include their admissions essay and advising session notes that reveal the reasons behind a change of major or a recent drop in grades.

Training should provide opportunities for new advisors to become adept at interpreting and using these tools. For example, trainers might ask new advisors to use the tools described above and write down what they discover from each tool or resource. Advisors then should be asked to create a student profile or narrative from what they have learned about the student.

Finally, advisors should develop a list of questions to ask the student in an advising session. If a new advisor is paired with an experienced advisor, they could both complete the exercise and compare results. Exercises like this allow advisors to see the limitations of using one source of information about students while simultaneously improving their ability to integrate information from several sources. Case studies present another excellent tool for learning to interpret and synthesize information from these tools and the data profiles described above and are addressed later in this chapter. Finally, the best resource for learning about each student is the student. Tools for developing the relational skills necessary to elicit critical information from students also are addressed later in this chapter.

DEEPENING ADVISING KNOWLEDGE ABOUT STUDENTS

Just as advising sessions present advisors with new and more complex informational challenges, they also present advisors with unanticipated and complex student situations. Advisors quickly discover that they need to gain a deeper knowledge of their students than the informational profiles, assessments, and surveys have afforded them. Many academic advisors, including faculty advisors, are hired because of their specific academic background and credentials as opposed to their understanding of student development, yet to advise and teach students effectively it is important for advisors to understand and to meet students where they are developmentally. Fortunately, there are excellent resources available. Part Two of this *Handbook* addresses student needs as they transition into, through, and out of the institution. *The New Advisor Guidebook* (Folsom, 2007b) includes articles and tips on learning about student development that are practice-oriented and that trainers or new advisors can digest relatively quickly. Kim Roufs (2007) offers a clear, succinct explanation of a number of student-development theories and walks through a case study to show how Chickering's (1969) Seven Vectors might play out in an advising session. Opatz and Prestwich (2007) discuss adapting to the stressed, tech-savvy, achieving, multitasking, protected, entitled, and diverse (or "stamped") generation, and Hurley (2007) offers tips for applying concepts of developmental advising in practice. Advisors can deepen their knowledge base about and stay current on the latest research on students, student development, and advising students through two scholarly, research-based journals: the *NACADA Journal* and the *Journal of College Student Development.* Trainers could assign an article on student development from the *Handbook,* the *New Advisor Guidebook,* or one of the journals, and then ask advisors to use the case study or advising notes that reflect specific student-development theories or the latest research on student behavior. This is an exercise that can be done individually or as a group activity and will help advisors learn to identify and respond to theory in action during advising sessions.

Excellent print resources are published by The National Resource Center for the First-Year Experience and Students in Transition and by NACADA and found in *The Journal of College Student Development.* In addition, NACADA produces a CD series that includes a program that focuses on student diversity, and a set of Webinars are available in CD version. These resources provide advisors with the opportunity to learn more about specific student populations such as underrepresented minorities; first-generation students; lesbian, gay, bisexual, and transgender (LGBT) students; commuters; honors students; students on probation; and students with disabilities. Finally, the "Advising Issues & Resources" page of the NACADA *Clearinghouse* includes links to resources on thirty different student populations. The links lead to Web sites, topical overviews, annotated bibliographies, and answers to frequently asked questions.

NACADA commissions, interest groups, and conferences afford advisors yet another resource for deepening their knowledge of students. NACADA commissions are charged with proposing and facilitating activities, networking, and providing resources to advance the professional development of members while focusing on the specific area of the commission. Interest groups are created to focus on specific issues or represent a particular interest of NACADA members. Many of the thirty-four commissions and interest groups are devoted to advising special student populations. And NACADA national and regional conferences include sessions on specific student populations. Advisors should consider joining a commission or interest group in order to network with advisors who serve or have an interest in similar groups of students. These resources are particularly important for advisors who do not have the support of a training program as well as those who are sole practitioners within their administrative or departmental unit.

Finally, advisors should recognize that one of the best resources for expanding their knowledge about students is through individual advising sessions. Student by student, advisors come to understand, learn to recognize, and to respond appropriately to the attitudes, behaviors, and cultural issues presented by an increasingly diverse student body. As a means to further understanding, advisors should keep an advising log for more systematic self-reflection on student interactions to facilitate growth in their knowledge about and understanding of students.

Tools and Resources to Build Relational Skills

Building a positive working relationship with students is a prerequisite for successful advising. If students do not trust or have confidence in their advisor, they will be neither candid about their personal goals and the factors that affect their academic performance nor accept their advisor as offering credible advice. Experience as an advisor does not, in and of itself, build strong relational skills. Advisors must intentionally develop them. Relational skills include active listening, interviewing or questioning techniques, body language, and cultural competency (see Chapter Twenty Two). Tools to assist advisors in developing and improving their relational skills should address the following questions: How can I establish rapport with my students? How can I achieve cultural competency in working with all of my students?

Learning about Relational Skills

The comprehensive resources—this *Handbook* (Chapter Twenty-two), the *New Advisor Guidebook,* and NACADA's *Clearinghouse* conferences and publications—offer advisors and trainers excellent resources for learning about the basic relational skills necessary for academic advising: active listening, the art of effective interviewing, the messages body language communicates to students, and gaining cultural competency.

The application of relational skills may vary somewhat according to the advising context, such as group or one-on-one advising. And, it may vary according to advising approaches: advising as teaching, strength-based advising, and appreciative advising. Resources that address the various approaches to advising include:

- *Strengths-Based Advising: Going Beyond Course Scheduling With Developmental Advising* (Schreiner, 2007), a Webinar CD that provides an introduction to the strengths-based approach; and

- The Noel Academy for Strength-Based Education and Leadership (Azuza Pacific University, n.d.), a Web site with many downloadable resources on the strengths-based approach in teaching and advising.
- "Incorporating Appreciative Inquiry into Academic Advising" (Bloom & Martin, 2002)
- The NACADA Concept of Advising
- "The Teaching-Advising Connection" (Appleby, 2001)
- Chapter Six of this *Handbook*
- *New Insights for Teaching and Learning in the First Year* referred to earlier in this chapter (Hunter et al., 2007)
- *Advising As Teaching* (King, 2006)
- *Academic Advising Syllabus: Advising as Teaching in Action* (Thurmond, 2006)

In order for advisors to build strong relational skills, though, they need to experience them and practice them as well as read about them. There are a number of experiential tools and resources that facilitate building relational skills that can be used during initial training as well as during ongoing advisor-development programs.

Building Relational Skills: Experiential Tools and Resources

Simulations, role-plays, and case studies are excellent experiential tools for training new advisors on relational skills through experiential learning. In simulations, trainers create or reenact an advising session. Subsequently, advisors-in-training discuss or parse the relational skills of the advisor in the simulation and suggest alternative modes of questioning, listening, or using body language. Role plays involve advising-session scenarios as well. However, the advisor-in-training usually plays the advisor role, responding in real time to the student, a role typically played by a trainer or experienced advisor. Case studies are similar to simulations, but they are written exercises. Advisors read the case study and then discuss the situation in terms of the positive or negative communication that occurred.

Each of these tools assist advisors in building relational skills in a safe situation among colleagues. All three tools are effective in ongoing advisor-development programming as well. Experienced advisors will pick up nuances of a simulation or case study that they missed during their initial training. When possible, it is helpful to have new advisors and experienced advisors participate in these activities together; new advisors will quickly pick up questioning techniques and learn about various advising approaches from experienced advisors.

Experienced advisors serve as excellent resources for building relational advising skills. If advising-session observations are not part of their training program, new advisors should ask to observe the advising sessions of experienced advisors. It is important for new advisors to see that good relational skills emanate from different styles and by using varying approaches—that one advisor's relational approach is very informal, while another's is more serious and earnest, but that both approaches can work with students. Observations also help new advisors pick up ideas for questions to ask and questioning techniques that they can put into their own toolbox. Advising-session observations help new advisors try out different advising approaches as they develop their own advising voice.

While trainers can build experiential learning exercises using institution-specific examples, there are excellent external resources as well.

- The NACADA *Faculty Advising Training Video* includes eight advising vignettes and *Academic Advising for Student Success and Retention,* (Noel-Levitz, 1997) includes four videos with everyday advising scenarios from which advisors can see relational skills in action and which can serve as springboards for discussion.

- Webinars offer a form of experiential learning as well because advisors hear the spoken tone as well as learn about relational technique. *Relating to Students Through Advising* (Grites, 2007), a Noel-Levitz Webinar, provides an overview of relational skills in advising sessions. The Webinar comes in two versions: one for four-year institutions and one for two-year institutions. And a NACADA Webinar, *Expanding Your Comfort Zone: Strategies for Developing and Demonstrating Cultural Competence in Academic Advising* (Harding, 2007), discusses relational skills for working across cultures.

- *The Mentor* also includes interactive materials for relational skills. Each issue includes the "Advising Forum," in which an advising issue, topic, or case study is posted for readers to respond to and discuss. The case studies or topics can be used in formal advisor development programming, but they also provide a means for advisors who are self managing their growth to make virtual connections to and learn from other advisors.

Finally, because relational skills are important in the workplace, trainers can look beyond advising-focused materials for resources. On-campus professional-development opportunities may offer programs that will assist advisors in developing strong relational skills. Workshops on dealing with difficult people or Safe Zone and diversity training sessions may not focus directly on the practice of academic advising, but the these programs target important communication skills that add new tools to advisors' relational toolboxes. External training materials on general communication skills such as those offered by HRDQ (n.d.) may be applied to academic advising as well. Seeking campus-wide or external resources is important for advisors who do not have advising colleagues or have access to an advisor training and development program.

TRAINING RESOURCES AND TOOLS FOR ADVISING SESSIONS

The advising session requires advisors to "put it all together," synthesizing the conceptual, informational, and relational components of academic advising. The NACADA *Clearinghouse* has some excellent resources on conducting an effective advising session as well as specific strategies for the various components of an advising session—preparation, welcome and building rapport, advising discussion, and conclusion plus advising notes. Woolston and Ryan (2007) offer a step-by-step walk through an advising session in the *New Advisor Guidebook,* and the *Handbook* has chapters on both one-on-one and group advising.

After new advisors understand the basic components that comprise an advising session, the experiential tools used to build relational skills can also be used to develop skills in conducting effective advising sessions, including simulations, role-playing case studies, advising-session observations, and the other printed and electronic resources outlined above. Finally, trainers should not overlook experienced advisors as an effective resource for new advisors, especially after new advisors begin to see students. Experienced advisors can serve as mentors or working partners, providing on-the-spot assistance for informational and relational questions as they arise for new advisors.

Technology in Advising Sessions

The extensive use of Web-based resources and student information systems presents implications for advising sessions and for the advising relationship. Advisors must be able to move easily among various systems, and students must be able to easily read and follow information that is on the computer screen. Simulations and role-plays should include training on and opportunities to practice how to effectively incorporate use of the computer into advising sessions and still maintain good relational skills (e.g., eye contact and attention to students' body language).

Advising-Session Notes

Advising-session notes create a history of advisors' interactions with students. Notes enable advisors to recall salient discussions, actions, and decisions from previous student sessions, and protect both students and advisors by providing documentation of important decisions, actions, and referrals. Instruction on the content and style of advising notes should be included in training programs. Trainers can draw on the materials from the Faculty/Advisor Resource Center at Missouri State University (n.d.), which provides guidelines as well as a list of do's and don'ts for writing advising notes. When possible, trainers should have new advisors observe the advising session of an experienced advisor. Following this session, new advisors create conference notes for the session and subsequently compare these notes with those of the experienced advisor. An alternative activity for advisors-in-training is to watch a video vignette or real-time simulation of an advising session, write advising notes, and compare their notes to the guidelines or review their notes with experienced colleagues or supervisors.

Charting Progress: Assessment of Advisor Training and Development

Assessment of advisor training and development programs should answer the following questions: Have advisors-in-training acquired and sufficiently mastered the conceptual, informational, and relational skills for beginning to work directly with students? Are advisors who have taken the training continuing to develop according to expectations? How effective was the delivery of the program, and how can delivery be improved? Answering the first two questions requires tools that chart advisor growth; answering the last questions involves tools for gathering feedback from both participants and trainers.

Tools for Assessing Advisor Growth

Teaching tools such as quizzes and a two-minute paper describing three things the advisor learned in the training session are effective for immediate feedback as to whether advisors are learning the requisite material. The experiential tools described earlier—case studies, simulations, and role-plays—provide trainers with feedback on how well advisors are synthesizing the conceptual, informational, and relational components of advising. Case studies can be simple—a step above a quiz—focusing on the right course placement for a student, or they can be quite complex, involving for example, course placement, regression and duplication, referrals, and ethical issues.

Advisors should have their conferences and advising notes reviewed annually. These reviews provide critical feedback for trainers, supervisors, and advisors on advisor growth and development. Trainers and supervisors need to provide clear written guidelines regarding expectations for the advising sessions and advising notes.

Throughout their careers, advisors need opportunities to reflect on and assess their growth. The "New Advisor Development Chart" (Folsom, 2007) is an example of a tool that that enables advisors to create a road map for their development. The chart also gives administrators, trainers, and advisors the means to assess advisor growth. A good exercise is to have an advisor, trainer, and supervisor each indicate where the advisor is on the growth chart, compare results, then map out a plan for growth. A clear sign that training and development programs are meeting their objectives is when advisors are meeting expectations for their growth and development.

Tools for Assessing Advisor Development Program Delivery

Advisors work in a constantly changing environment. Academic programs revise their requirements, a new generation of students brings a different perspective to college and new approaches to advising arise. Training programs, therefore, need to be evaluated annually to ensure that they are producing effective advisors. Feedback should be sought from the advisors who have participated in training as well as the trainers who have run the training programs. Trainers should seek regular written and oral feedback on training materials and activities. Feedback can be collected through surveys, focus groups or debriefing sessions, or two-minute papers. Feedback on training should be collected again from participating advisors at least six to twelve months after the training, when advisors can better assess how well various training activities prepared them.

CONCLUSION

There are rich resources available for advisor training and development, whether that development is through a formal program or is self-managed. The aim of this chapter has been to highlight a variety of resources, a variety of formats (print, video, online, CD, Webinar) and to offer ideas for how they might be used. Because advisors in the field—and their trainers—typically carve out developmental time from busy schedules, this chapter has targeted tools that are easily accessible, offer search functions, and are relatively short. Individual advisors who seek more comprehensive training should consider the certificate program through NACADA or the video training programs offered by NACADA or Noel-Levitz. All of these are suitable for faculty or nonfaculty advisors. The resources selected for this chapter also are applicable to all types of advisors and advising situations. For example, an article or case study from *The Mentor* can serve as development for an individual advisor who, after reading it, joins the online discussion; this same article or case study can serve as the focus of an advisor-development session within a professional advising center or as the focus of a cross-campus faculty advising workshop. Trainers and advisors should return to these resources regularly as they seek to grow as advisors and improve advising on their campuses.

References

Appleby, D. (2001). The teaching-advising connection: Main (overview and table of contents). *The Mentor: An Academic Advising Journal, 3* (1).

Azuza Pacific University. (n.d.). *Noel Academy for Strengths-Based Leadership and Education.* Retrieved March 29, 2008, from http://www.apu.edu/strengthsacademy/about

Bloom, J. L., & Martin, N. A. (2002, August 29). Incorporating appreciative inquiry into academic advising. *The Mentor: An Academic Advising Journal.* Retrieved March 28, 2008, from http://www.psu.edu/mentor

Center for Excellence in Academic Advising, Pennsylvania State University. (n.d.). *The Mentor: An Academic Advising Journal.* Retrieved March 29, 2008, from http://www.psu.edu/dus/mentor

Chickering, A. W. (1969). *Education and identity.* San Francisco: Jossey-Bass.

Council for the Advancement of Standards in Higher Education. (2006). Standards and guidelines for academic advising programs. Retrieved April 17, 2008, from http://www.nacada.ksu.edu/Clearinghouse/Research_Related/CASStandardsForAdvising.pdf

Dyer, N. A. (2007). Advisement philosophy. In Folsom, P. (Ed.), *The new advisor guidebook: Mastering the art of advising through the first year and beyond.* (NACADA Monograph Series, no. 16.) Manhattan, KS: National Academic Advising Association.

Folsom, P. (Ed.). (2007a). The new advisor guidebook. *Academic Advising Today, 30* (2), 12, 27.

Folsom, P. (Ed.). (2007b). *The new advisor guidebook: Mastering the art of advising through the first year and beyond.* (NACADA Monograph Series, no. 16.) Manhattan, KS: National Academic Advising Association.

Goodner, M. (2007). Institutional information. In Folsom, P. (Ed.), *The new advisor guidebook: Mastering the art of advising through the first year and beyond.* (NACADA Monograph Series, no. 16.) Manhattan, KS: National Academic Advising Association.

Gordon, V. N., & Habley, W. R. (Eds.). (2000). *Academic advising: A comprehensive handbook.* San Francisco: Jossey-Bass.

Grites, T. (2007). *Relating to students through advising* (version for four-year institutions). (Noel-Levitz Academic Advising Webinar Series.). Available from http://www.noellevitz.com.

HRDQ. (n.d.). Available from http://www.hrdq.com/topics/topiccommunication.htm

Hunter, M. S., McCalla-Wriggins, B., & White, E. (Eds.). (2007). *Academic advising: New insights for teaching and learning in the first year.* (Monograph no. 46.) Columbia: University of South Carolina, National Resource Center for The Freshman Year & Students in Transition.

Hurley, M. (2007). Advising in practice. In Folsom, P. (Ed.), *The new advisor guidebook: Mastering the art of advising through the first year and beyond.* (NACADA Monograph Series, no. 16.) Manhattan, KS: National Academic Advising Association.

King, N. (2006). *Advising as teaching.* (NACADA Webinar.) Available from NACADA at http://www.nacada.ksu.edu/Monographs/audiovisual.htm

Kolls, S. (2007). Informational component: Learning about advises putting together the puzzle. In Folsom, P. (Ed.), *The new advisor guidebook: Mastering the art of advising through the first year and beyond.* (NACADA Monograph Series, no. 16.) Manhattan, KS: National Academic Advising Association.

Lynch, P. C. (2005, November 22). A new adviser's journal. *The Mentor: An Academic Advising Journal.*

Missouri State University. (n.d.). *Advising notes guidelines.* Retrieved August 7, 2007, from http://www.missouristate.edu/advising/43164.htm

NACADA. (n.d.). *Clearinghouse of academic advising resources.* Retrieved March 29, 2008, from http://www.nacada.ksu.edu/Resources/index.htm

NACADA. (2006). *Foundations of academic advising I: What is academic advising?* Manhattan, KS: National Academic Advising Association.

Noel-Levitz. (1997). *Academic Advising for Student Success and Retention* (package of four videos and resource guide). Available from Noel-Levitz at https://www.noellevitz.com/Our + Services/Professional + Development/Academic + Advising

Opatz, L., & Prestwich, N. (2007). Adapting advising to today's stamped generation. In Folsom, P. (Ed.), *The new advisor guidebook: Mastering the art of advising through the first year and beyond.* (NACADA Monograph Series, no. 16.) Manhattan, KS: National Academic Advising Association.

Roufs, K. (2007). In theory, advising matters. In Folsom, P. (Ed.), *The new advisor guidebook: Mastering the art of advising through the first year and beyond.* (NACADA Monograph Series, no. 16.) Manhattan, KS: National Academic Advising Association.

Schreiner, L. (2007). *Strengths-based advising: Going beyond course scheduling with developmental advising.* (Academic Advising Webinar Series.) Available from http://www.noellevitz.com

Shoenberg, R. (2005). *Why do I have to take this course? A student guide to making smart educational choices.* Washington, DC: Association of American Colleges and Universities.

Thurmond, K. (2006). *Academic advising syllabus: Advising as teaching in action.* (NACADA Webinar Series.) Retrieved April 17, 2008, from http://www.nacada.ksu .edu/Webinars/onDisk.htm#02

Woolston, D., & Ryan, R. (2007). Group advising. In Folsom, P. (Ed.). *The new advisor guidebook: Mastering the art of academic advising through the first year & beyond.* (NACADA Monograph Series no. 16.) Manhattan, KS: National Academic Advising Association.

CHAPTER TWENTY-TWO

Delivering One-to-One Advising: Skills and Competencies

Rusty Fox

The joy of advising, the deeper sense of why many choose to advise is the human element; being witness to that sacred moment when a student, "really gets it," really risks, really faces something challenging, or really succeeds! Whether you are a faculty member, an administrator, or a full-time advisor, it is that unique, rare moment, shared personally, one-to-one, that brings academic advisors back day after day. It's also the core of what's best about holistic academic advising. The significance of academic advising is evident in various forms, formats, and styles. However, the crux of it, the heart of good academic advising must always include at least a component of advising that occurs one-on-one between a student and a caring, competent professional. This chapter, then, is an exploration of that significant component.

THE ADVISING RELATIONSHIP MATTERS

Academic advising is a recognized discipline requiring significant relationship-building skills. It is neither a registration nor a counseling function, though it works in close proximity with both functions. It is not a data-entry job or simply about scheduling classes, though those tasks are required components. Carol Ryan (1992) identified the parallels between academic advising and classroom teaching and how many professional skills each have in common. Others write extensively about the impact it has on retention. Academic Advisor is a professional position, regardless of title, requiring an awareness of basic student-development theory, communication techniques, and problem-solving skills. Beyond any personal value inherent in academic advising, research also shows that advising is likely one of the most significant factors in increasing student retention as well.

When considering the responses from *all* institution types in the 2004 ACT survey of *What Works in Student Retention?* (Habley & McClanahan, 2004), Academic Advising is listed in the top three categories of interventions responsible for "the greatest contribution to retention." The survey verifies that, "academic advising, including advising interventions with selected student populations, increased advising staff, integration of advising with first-year transition programs, academic advising centers, and centers that combine academic advising with career/life planning," were among the most important things *all* institutional types could focus on to impact retention of students.

In the early 1970s, working independently of each other, Drs. Terry O'Banion (1972) and Burns Crookston (1972) began exploring the concept of a more developmental approach to academic advising. What collectively came from their individual starts was a definition, a broader conceptualization, and eventually a movement that would enhance the role and the understanding of the role of academic advising at colleges and universities nationwide. While a focus on the content of each advising session was crucial, each understood the importance of the relationship between the student and the advisor. It was from this core shift in our thinking about academic advising that other related concepts began to develop.

INFORMATIONAL, CONCEPTUAL, AND RELATIONAL ROLES

One such concept became more clearly defined in the mid-1980s, when Dr. Wes Habley (1986) outlined a framework for three major components central to the quality academic advising experience. Habley defined those as Informational, Conceptual, and Relational, and explained how there were essential components of the advising session. (See also Chapters Twenty and Twenty-one.) This approach, which explained that building relationships one-on-one with a student might be significant, became further differentiated by considering information, previously the sole component, as only one of three interconnected parts. Conceptually, the advising session had to include the bigger picture, first for the student within the academic world and then the world of work, and secondly for the advisor, who benefited from seeing the student through student development and learning theories. Finally, this broader construct of advising included the definition of a third component, Relational, which emphasized how the presence of a interpersonal relationship between advisor and advisee impacted the student's understanding, his or her ability to assimilate information gained, and the learned skills of how to apply some of this new knowledge in the world outside of the advising session.

ADVISORS ALREADY KNOW WHAT TO DO

It could be argued that in many cases advisors already know what needs to be done. At least in part, there is an innate sense in advisors of just wanting to help students. There is a natural valuing of student learning and genuine pleasure when a student learns a new, practical skill.

However, if innate skill and current knowledge are tweaked just a bit, then mixed with theory about student's development and blended with new skills about building an environment where risk and learning are encouraged, this creates a strong basis for establishing a helpful advising environment. Reviewing what is already known, consider for a moment a few examples of comments or questions which could work to establish this foundation with advisees.

Take a Genuine Interest in Students

It could easily be argued that the most important characteristic to search for when hiring an academic advisor is their genuine desire to help students. If that is missing, sharing information, relaying concepts, or attempting to build a constructive relationship are not likely to occur. The concept of relationship-building and demonstrating care and concern is not new. Ender, Winston, and Miller (1982) were writing two decades ago that the best models for academic advising are grounded in the theory discussed here and have a foundation based on a caring relationship with the student. Among their seven conditions essential to advising, they assert that advising must, "concern itself with quality-of-life issues," and that it, "requires the establishment of a caring human relationship," and necessitates advisors being "models for students to emulate, specifically demonstrating behaviors that lead to self-responsibility and self-directedness" (p. 7). However, all this is not enough. While there does need to be a genuine desire to help, there also needs to be a clear understanding of what behaviors are helpful and how to recognize and foster them in students. There must also be professional level skills that promote growth. Specific tips for communicating interest and concern are: (1) set the welcoming tone of the session with the very first interaction in greeting the student, and (2) demonstrate a genuine smile, make eye contact, and approach the student as though you have been waiting to see him or her. Briefly ask how the student is, and actually wait for a response.

Focus on Student Needs

What are a human's basic needs? Food, shelter, clothing, and safety. Each of these is essential to survival. Basic needs must be considered before being able to address other needs—these core needs have to be in place. Likewise, it could be argued that there are psychological needs that are basic to our survival and health. Assessing and addressing issues of psychological need are the responsibility of a professional counselor; however, awareness is completely appropriate and in fact useful for a faculty or professional advisor. Perhaps issues such as belonging, mattering (Schlossberg, 1989), the need for involvement (Astin, 1985), and the need for inclusion are helpful in student advising. It is critical that people know their personal value, that there is a purpose to being here or that our existence is of value.

This is evident even in the most simple of childhood nursery rhymes, "little Jack Horner sat in the corner." All Jack wanted was to, "put in his thumb, pull out a plum," and say, "what a good boy am I." Jack wanted someone to notice him and what had been accomplished. There was a desire to be recognized for an action that had been taken and the positive result it produced. This is a rather basic need for all people. It is so basic that the importance of it is often forgotten. However, without fanfare, without high praise, with just simple recognition, when a small accomplishment or a small positive action of one of our advisees is recognized, the result is much the same. The student wants to be noticed for being a "plum of a guy." When the placement test is taken and the score places him into freshmen English, the power of simply saying, "Hey congrats on your score, that's sometimes an intimidating process," often is transformational. Besides building a relationship with him, it tends to cause him to trust the advisor more because someone picked up on something significant to him. Someone recognized in him something important. In essence, someone recognized that the student himself was important. It does not have to be monumental. It does not have to include search for deep meaning; simple recognition is a powerful way to build trust between an advisor and an advisee. Notice what the student brought to the session. Though it may seem simple, say, "You've brought your degree plan with you today." Or say, "You have a backpack full of books with you today, don't you?" Then note how the student responds. "You've mentioned a visit to the math lab. I think we talked about that a little last time as well?" Besides being validating to the student, it is a great way to begin a conversation while placing the focus on the student. Specific tips for attending to student needs are: (1) though the agenda is to create a degree plan, address an academic problem, or begin career exploration, first validate whatever issue the student starts the session with, even if only quickly; (2) give the student a chance to set the direction for the session; and (3) assist by restating what was brought as the primary issue. If rambling or off-track, it is perfectly fine to redirect with a statement such as, "Okay, now let's take at look at your plan for the fall. How can I help you get ready there?"

Involve Students in the Process of Academic Advising and Learning

When possible, give the student a chance to discover or uncover the direction or answer needed. Give choices or options wherever possible and even if small in scope. "You could take your history now or next semester. A lot of our students prefer to take 1301 in the fall, but what is your sense?" Try to frame a statement in the form of a question. Instead of saying, "What you want is a degree plan in Business." Instead, try saying, "It sounds as if a degree plan in Business might be exactly what you are looking for. What do you think?"

Guide Students through the Process, Rather Than Simply Directing

Interestingly, students will bring completed degree plans that are clearly understandable, and say, "I just wanted to go through my degree plan with you again." When this occurs, it is rarely about the degree plan. It is instead about confidence, or uncertainty about the next step. Telling them what to do, will only cause them to return for more direction at the next step. Instead, try to think in terms of process, and in terms of the larger picture. Even if there is little time, or the student is unable to grasp the larger picture, at least introduce it. Explain that today's work is step one of four, and that future meetings will consist of such and such. Help lay out a plan, even if only a step or two ahead.

COMMUNICATION BASICS

Advising as a Transaction

In the annals of speech communications theory there is a model referred to as the Transactional Model (Heath & Bryant, 2000). This model is useful in that it simplifies and explains the basics of communication, and how communication involves not only the sender and receiver of information, but also the encoding and decoding of the message. It includes the contexts in which the message is both sent and received, and the impact of interpretation by the received, as well as the influence of feedback on the sender. This model illustrates the impact of outside noise on communication. While noise can mean literal audible distractions, it also means unspoken thoughts, opinions, fears, and previous conversations—anything that is distracting to the sender or the receiver of information.

The way this model may be of use to academic advisors is as a reminder that the context is often forgotten or muddled in noise. The noise is what surrounds the communication, the impact of students trying to translate what the advisor is saying into words or awareness that the student already has in place. The noise many students experience is also the noise of fear. Not knowing what to expect, or making the assumption that everyone else is smarter. How many students think that everyone is capable of college except for them and that they only "lucked into" college? Still other noise can be the opinions of new boyfriends, the advice of old uncles, and the concerns of complex histories in which the student remembers failures and frustrations.

In addition to external noise, another factor impacting clear communication between advisor and advisee is interpretation. Sometimes this is literal, meaning that dialect, accent, or even language may impact the information shared. But the other impact of interpretation is how students attempt to understand what is being said in the context of their lives and their experiences. If certain words are unfamiliar or a concept foreign to them, students try to assimilate those words through their own experiences thus far. Students will try to make it fit within the world they already know. Therefore, the context surrounding the communication is significant. The noise that can interfere with a student receiving the advisor's message is powerful. The challenges of students' interpretations of the message through the limits of their current knowledge and experience are dramatic. As academic advisors, it is helpful to consider how the receiver might perceive the information and how the information fits within their current experience or level of knowledge about a college. This is done through genuine connection, active listening, involving the student in the direction of the session, and building a professional relationship between academic advisor and advisee.

Active Listening: The skills of active listening are deceptively complicated. Most of daily conversation consists of dialogue, not monologue. The moment someone begins to speak, the listener's brain begins searching for common material that fits with what the sender is discussing. The typical first response is not to note what has been said, but to immediately compare with current knowledge so the point can be shared in conversation. For example, a student may say, "Wow, my history teacher is tough." The other's brain starts searching at the speed of light, and finds history, history classes, difficult teachers, previous experiences with difficult teachers, specific stories of previous experiences with difficult history teachers, and then responds, "Yeah, last year I had Dr. Keller, and his class was killer!" What has occurred is not bad. In fact, in the context of daily conversation it is the more appropriate response. However, it is dialogue. It is focused on both parties, and its intent is to share a topic, rather than to fully communicate and address one person's specific topic.

In the context of an academic advising session, the goals are student-focused. The goal of the conversation is to learn as much as possible about the student's immediate need as quickly as possible in an effort to either explore, challenge, or address that need. If an advisor can become more active in listening, the dialogue can be shaped in the beginning to generate more productive information coming from the student. Active listening means the student presents information. As a way to verify understanding, the advisor gives the information back to the student, verifying the advisor's understanding. The student processes the response, and then gives the message back to the advisor again with clarification. It some respects, it parallels the Delphi Method of research, in which experts are asked their opinions, the research summarizes all the opinions and reports back to the experts (Franklin & Hart, 2007). The experts, in turn, share the information again, including what was accurate, but clarifying where information was missed or is wrong. Active listening is about getting to the truer message through focusing on the student, clarifying the questions, and validating the student's communication. It is a useful tool for academic advisors.

Attentive Listening: If the power of good attentive listening is ever questioned, all one has to do is to try it. Dedicating the focus solely on the other person, asking about his or her day and waiting for a response, restating key points of the conversation, and not interrupting with a personal story, will make the power of this technique quite evident. So much of daily conversation is dialogue. One person tells a story. Then, taking turns, the other person tells his or her story. For daily conversation this works, but in an advising situation there might be better approaches. If an advisor occasionally makes use of the skills of good attentive listening and reflection when working with a student, there will be transformation in the communication pattern, and likely in the level of work coming from the session. It is amazingly validating to have the focus solely on the student. Because it occurs so rarely in daily life, the impact is significant. This simple technique will expedite the advising session, will validate the role of the advisees in planning their academic careers, and will energize the advisor.

Listening for Patterns: Students often tell what is most important in circuitous ways. A long story may be told to one's faculty advisor about Great Aunt Kate to get around to the fact that her Botany course is closed. Sometimes a long story is a sign the student is having difficulty focusing on an issue. However, if the same story is told each time, it may be that the student is conveying a bit more meaning in the tale than the advisor recognizes. As academic advisors, attempting to analyze and interpret the meaning behind each conversation is not necessary and is not within the advisor skills set. There are hundreds of psychological theories that still argue over the root of meaning and which interpretation is most meaningful. Instead, the advisor should simply point out the pattern and seek guidance from the student on possible meanings. For example, if the student always grins when telling a certain tale, and it occurs the same way repeatedly, there may be more to the story than the story itself. It is likely significant to the building of that relationship if the academic advisor simply says, "The last three times you've talked about Chemistry you have almost grinned. Isn't that interesting?" Again, as in previous paragraphs, it signifies that the advisor has been listening, that core needs are recognized, and that the student matters. It also means that perhaps helpful information will be given back to them that can be apply to their interaction, and their journey through advising. This works because the student better hears the message, knows the advisor also hears it, and can begin to truly address core issues of planning for success in college. Another tool is the unfinished sentence technique. Start a sentence addressing a key issue, but then leave it for the student to finish. "Goodness, you are only five classes away from graduating! Man, I bet that's. . . ." Usually the student will complete the sentence with a true emotion or thought. If they are not able to, the advisor can prompt with a few words such as, "exciting, scary, thrilling, freaky?"

Paraphrasing: Often underestimated, one of the more complex and high-impact skills is assisting students with academic advising, which appears to be the most simple. The skill of paraphrasing what students are saying is surprisingly important. First, paraphrasing verifies that the advisor has correctly understood what the student has said. Secondly, paraphrasing assists the student by clearly reframing or presenting again what appears to be the issue at hand. While it seems rather simple, skillful paraphrasing involves quickly sorting through multiple issues and identifying the most important ones needing to be addressed in that particular advising session. When done correctly, paraphrasing redirects the content of the session toward the issues most vital to the student's success, while still involving the student in the choice of content for the advising session.

When attempting to paraphrase what the student presents, the advisor must first attempt to pull out two or three key issues that have been presented. At times, this may actually mean interrupting a student who has gone on for some time or has presented many issues at once. It is appropriate for an advisor to say, "Let me stop you for a moment. I want to be certain I understand. The main issues we want to address today are. . . ."

Likewise, paraphrasing allows the advisor to check his or her assumptions with the advisee. What may appear to be an obvious conclusion to the advisor may not be accurate at all for the advisee. An illustration of this would be a student who after five semesters decides to change her major and says, "Wow, I guess that's really a dramatic change isn't it?" If the advisor says something like, "I know you must be concerned about how many hours you may lose." By contrast, the advisee might say, "Gosh no. I am so pleased to finally have figured out the direction, it doesn't matter if it takes an extra year. It is so significant and new to finally feel I am on track with my degree plan." Instead, the advisor could choose to paraphrase slightly and seek clarification from the student. "Wow, you said that change of major seems rather dramatic. What about that change is the most intense for you?" In this case it would redirect what might have been fifteen minutes exploration of electives and how courses transfer, into fifteen minutes of discussing who to speak to in the new academic division major, and what the Career Center could offer in service learning or information about the career field.

THE FIVE C'S OF THE SKILLED ACADEMIC ADVISOR

Several key concepts have been discussed related to quality academic advising. The importance of being a facilitation expert and not relying on content expertise only has been explored. Basic student-development theory has been considered, and the use of involvement and mattering to assist students in skill building and personal development has been discussed. New advisor skills such as active listening, models of communication, and listening for patterns have also been reviewed. As each of these issues and skill sets is considered, perhaps the most concise way to clearly define tasks of academic advisors would be through the following five C's of a skilled academic advisor. The skills and competencies needed to establish a quality ongoing relationship with an advisee are:

1. Competence
2. Confidence-building
3. Cordial
4. Credible
5. Creative

First, the advisor must be competent. Knowledge of the academic discipline, the institutional policies, and the application of degree plans, course content, transferability, and degree planning are at the center of the informational component of advising, a foundational piece in the advising process. Secondly, an advisor must be a confidence-builder for students. Through effective questioning, skillful reflection, and modeling appropriate behaviors, the advisor should assist students in gaining both confidence and understanding of self within the academic environment. The ability to act cordially and with a modicum of kindness to students is a foundation on which trust and confidence begin to build. There is a statement, attributed to multiple sources, that applies here: People do not care how much you know until they know how much you care. A student knowing she is of value to someone significant at the institution, an issue communicated through a cordial and supportive style, is at the heart of her being involved, connected, willing to take risks, and ultimately being successful in college. An additional factor, credibility, is of equal if not greater importance. Academic advisors must continually work to be well informed, connected to key personnel on campus, and respected for their work as an advisor. Faculty advisors recognize that their role as advisors must parallel their academic role in credibility. When a student learns that his or her advisor is someone of skill and authority and is respected among peers, that student is more likely to ask the questions that need to be asked and to trust the answers given. And finally, an academic advisor of high caliber must be someone of great creativity. Finding ways to assist students in exploring issues previously not considered, to attempt actions that were previously too scary to attempt, and to link students to resources and personnel that are new and unknown, requires that advisors be clever, quick, creative, and always exploring new ways of assisting students.

An additional "C" might also be that the skilled advisor includes culture as an important consideration. Brown and Rivas (1992) assert that a developmental approach, which uses the power of the one-on-one relationship between advisor and student, is instrumental in working with students from minority cultures. Some students from minority cultures face unique problems when attending college because they often lack a family history in or specific understanding of the higher education environment. Valdez (1993) explains these students directly benefit from the type of orientation to the academic environment found in the one-on-one interaction with their advisor. Fewer students now follow the traditional path, or resemble the traditional student, of only a few decades ago. Many students are more dependent on financial assistance, work while attending school, transfer between institutions, take longer than the traditional four years to complete college, commute from home, or return to college later in life. So the definition of a traditional student is changing as well (McLaren, 2004).

Each student brings her own personal culture to the advising session as well; not just her ethnic background, her family values, and her people's mores, but also her personal history, individual beliefs, sexual orientation, religious affiliation, personal level of understanding, and the influence of her circle of friends. The competent, credible faculty advisor, the caring creative professional advisor, will incorporate what the student brings from her culture to the advising session. The advisor will make use of the history introduced, and will validate the family patterns and beliefs that may impact the student's academic experience.

Skills beyond Empathy and Compassion

With these values and desires in place, the building of a strong professional relationship with students, and maximizing the dynamic of the one-on-one advising relationship, can begin. Perhaps it is a lack of confidence on the part of the academic advisor that is the greatest challenge at this juncture. Good skills are essential to good advising. In fact, to be a skillful academic advisor, Dr. Charlie Nutt (2000) suggests that there are four key skill sets required. Specifically, an academic advisor must possess: (1) knowledge about the specifics of the academic programs and the curricular requirements of their particular institution; (2) knowledge about the institutional resources available to students; (3) facility with good communication skills of subtle nonverbal cues the student may be giving that could indicate that important information is not being disclosed; and (4) strong skills with open-ended questions that encourage freer communication with students and indicate a sense of interest on the part of the advisor.

Each of these skills is central to supporting students in their exploration of career and life planning, degree plan, course selection, and even scheduling classes. Empathy and compassion are helpful when used in concert with Nutt's four components. Empathy and compassion are also significant when addressing issues of diversity, difference, and individual personality factors and choices. As students learn more about themselves, and then try to match that awareness with what is being learned about the world around them, the academic advisor plays a key role in considering how a student fits in that diverse world, how the student would like to fit, and how each can make changes to adapt themselves or portions of that surrounding environment.

Role Change: Information Expert to Facilitation Expert

For many academic advisors, knowing the institution, the degree plans, the course content, the transfer guides, the key people, and even the details of entry-level cut scores by discipline is central to the sense of being a good advisor. This massive base of knowledge comes from years of experience and a sincere dedication to absorb important minute details. In truth, this content is vital to advising students in the exploration of degree plans, course selection, and even career fields. However, knowledge in this area alone is not enough. Advising is not just course selection and degree planning. Advising is not a data-entry or clerical job, though it often includes these skills. Advisors have to make information meaningful to students. Academic advisors teach students about how information is relative to the learning environment and then applicable to the world outside the institution (Gordon & Habley, 2000). In truth, through advances in technology, a lot of content is already accessible to students. Some students literally grow up at their computer, many coming with highly advanced technological skills and often teaching the advisor how to access some of the core advising content.

As many as nine components have been identified as necessary to build this relationship between advisor and advisee, "prepping, attending, bonding, disclosing, laughing, counseling, normalizing, coaching, and continuing" (Smith, 2005, p. 9). When incorporated, student responses indicate that a "personalized relationship does impact students in a positive manner" (p. 4).

> Academic advisors and other student affairs professionals need to connect with students on a personal level in order for [sic] optimal outcomes. Educational personnel who work with students need to realize the power contained in forming "personalized" relationships and strive to attain such to benefit their student clients. (p. 2)

So the expertise of today's academic advisor has to include facilitation of information and not just possession of it. This means a likely change of role from a repository of data to an agent of facilitation. One who takes the data and makes them interesting, useful, and personalized for the student is the key to meaningful academic advising. This often is a challenging transition for advisors, who were viewed as *the* repositories of information and facts. Change occurs here through new programs and incentives linked to the role of facilitation agent.

Diana Boyd McElroy (2005) notes that there is a "paradox" in working with at-risk college students. Students at risk are most in need of support but are most likely to feel disconnected from the college. When the student finds a connection and senses their importance to the institution, their cognitive and affective development is stimulated, and the student becomes more likely to develop support resources and increase their potential to succeed. This occurs through stronger involvement and reliance on other people and functions at the college. A skillful academic advisor recognizes that this need for mattering and involvement is at the core of their interaction with students.

Nancy Schlossberg (1989) writes on the theory of *Marginality or Mattering*. She explains that students, such as those new to college, may experience "uneasiness" as major life transitions are experienced. At these times of transition, success or failure is strongly influenced by a feeling of whether or not one belongs in the environment. Through attention, a sense of importance to others, a sense of being appreciated, and ego-extension, or a sense of identifying with others, students succeed in part because of a feeling of value to others and the institution. Likewise, Alexander Astin's (1985) theory of *Involvement* explains that a student succeeds when becoming a more active participant in the college environment. Issues such as mattering and involvement can be easily overlooked, or assumed to be addressed by someone else at the institution. In truth, however, a skillful academic advisor is the perfect professional to facilitate the assessment and subsequent planning for students related to both of these skills sets. As a facilitation expert, this means that the academic advisor asks students for input on what brings them to college. It means explaining choices available to students and involving them in their planning. Plug and play, the old information-based paradigm, even when it seems the obvious choice, must give way to a more developmental or teaching-based process of assess, understand, and apply.

ADVISING . . . OR IS IT?

This discipline is called academic advising. Advising conjures up a wise old sage, directing the youth on the way to go. It creates a picture of the expert lecturing to the novice. This term tends to direct our thinking and set up a scene in which the advisor has the content and the knowledge about the right way and the student has the responsibility of listening and learning the rules of how to succeed. Perhaps then, advising is a misnomer. While an advisor does direct a student toward certain degree plans and through the maze of institutional policies and procedures, more often the advisor is listening attentively for patterns, facilitating the student's self-awareness through reflection, and incorporating new information into the student's learning. Creating a student-led experience in which students are exposed to ideas, information, and skills and choose for themselves how to apply this information is unique to the academic advising session, and is an instrumental piece of preparing them for success in college.

The challenges to building a strong relationship between advisor and student often cause institutions to resort back to the old and convenient model of academic advising as providing information and scheduling only. Virginia Gordon (1994) writes about the reasons or excuses that prevent colleges from making full use of this more developmental format. She explains that,

> 1) advisors do not have the time to become involved in the type of advising that requires frequent contact with one student, 2) Advisors do not have the background or expertise to handle the type of personal relationship required, 3) Students perceive that advising involves only scheduling and registration, 4) Many administrators neither understand nor support developmental advising and do not make funds available, 5) and Advisors lack training to help them acquire developmental advising expertise. (p. 71)

In a survey of faculty completed by Fox Valley Technical College (Perry, 2001), an institution with an advising history that includes multiple national awards, the majority of faculty state that advising is "necessary and beneficial," and that "direct contact with students presented them with the opportunity to have a positive impact on the student's educational experience." Their faculty recognized the importance of the advising relationship and already sensed much of what they needed to do. However, they also pointed out the need for their instructional administrators to "recognize the importance of advising, and provide more time for advising" (p. 5). Knowing of these concerns, college and university administrators responsible for advising face the challenge of educating their colleagues and clearly communicating the worth of advising to their own campus communities. Tinto (n.d.) explains that, "students are more likely to persist and graduate in settings that provide academic, social and personal support." He goes on to say they are also more likely to succeed if institutions "involve them as valued members of the institution."

Framing, Guiding, . . . Advising

An academic advisor will adopt many roles over the course of a career. Seldom do advisors strictly advise in that directive, instructional, authoritative manner one might anticipate. Instead, the academic advisor serves as a tour guide, hand in hand with the student exploring the catalog, the schedule, the student handbook, the meaning of the placement-test scores, and the resources available on campus—usually, symbolically taking the student to where the student needs to be, but sometimes literally walking with the student to meet the coordinator of the math learning lab or to make an active referral to a career counselor. The academic advisor serves as a facilitator as well. As a facilitator, the advisor takes the information brought by the student, incorporates the content learned with the advisor, and combines both to create a plan of action. Reminding the student of the awareness found and the issues reviewed together, the advisor guides the student through the process and facilitates the process when it becomes challenging. The advisor at times will serve as an interpreter as well, being careful to explain what certain scores mean, why certain prerequisites are necessary, and how certain majors may fit best for a particular student. Advisors will interpret the process for students, explaining when anxieties are normal, and how to cope when professors' behaviors are disturbing. Then the advisor helps the student put a plan into action. Often acting as a coach, the advisor does not just help the student create a plan, but encourages the student to enact the plan. This is done with very specific goals and very specific steps required of the student to accomplish short-term goals. As the student is guided, facilitated, coached, and supported, the student learns to assess on his own, and question on her own, and to begin to integrate learning into a larger career and life plan for him or her.

The reality of life on many of our campuses is that there is never really enough time to do all that is wanted with a student or to participate in the full conversation desired. However, there is some time, and there are interventions that can be made. Be genuine. Demonstrate care. Communicate that advising is far more than scheduling classes. Listen attentively. Redirect through paraphrasing. Facilitate learning about the academic environment on the part of the student advisee instead of simple rote memorization of lists or course schedules. There are specific skills and techniques that can be learned and used that make a powerful difference for students. Commit to learning three this month, trying two next week, sharing one with a colleague over lunch. Excellent advisors are made when the most is made of that little time, one-on-one.

References

Astin, A. W. (1985). *Achieving educational excellence: A critical assessment of priorities and practice in higher education*. San Francisco: Jossey-Bass.

Brown, T., & Rivas, M. (1992). Multicultural populations for achievement and success. *New Directions for Community Colleges, 21* (2), 83–96.

Crookston, B. B. (1972). A developmental view of academic advising as teaching. *Journal of College Student Personnel, 13*, 12–17.

Ender, S. C., Winston, R. B., Jr., & Miller, T. K. (1982). Academic advising as student development. In Winston, R. B., Jr., Ender, S. C., & Miller, T. K. (Eds.), Developmental approaches to academic advising. *New Directions for Student Services, 17*, 5–18.

Franklin, K. K., & Hart, J. K. (2007). Idea generation and exploration: Benefits and limitations of the policy Delphi Research method. *Innovation in Higher Education, 31* (4), 237–246.

Gordon, V. N. (1994). Developmental advising: The elusive ideal. *NACADA Journal, 14* (2), 71–75.

Gordon, V. N., & Habley, W. R. (Eds.). (2000). *Academic advising: A comprehensive handbook*. San Francisco: Jossey-Bass.

Habley, W. R. (1986). Advisor training: Whatever happened to instructional design? ACT workshop presentation. Iowa City: ACT, Inc.

Habley, W. R., & McClanahan, R. (2004). *What works in student retention?* Iowa City: ACT, Inc.

Heath, R. L., & Bryant, J. (2000). *Human communication theory and research: Concepts, contexts, and challenges*. LEA's Communication Series. Mahwah, NJ: Lawrence Erlbaum.

McElroy, D. B. (2005). Impact of outside-the-classroom involvement on cognitive and affective development for community college students. (Doctoral dissertation, University of Oklahoma.)

McLaren, J. (2004). The changing face of undergraduate academic advising. *Guidance & Counseling, 19* (4), 173–175.

Nutt, C. L. (2000). One-to-one advising. In V. N. Gordon, W. R. Habley, & Associates (Eds.), *Academic advising: A comprehensive handbook*. San Francisco: Jossey- Bass.

O'Banion, T. (1972). An academic advising model. *Junior College Journal, 42*, 62–69.

Perry, J. C. (2001). *Faculty advising survey results, 1996 to 2001*. Appleton, WI: Fox Valley Technical College.

Ryan, C. C. (1992). Advising as teaching. *NACADA Journal, 12* (1), 4–8.

Schlossberg, N. K. (1989). Marginality and mattering: Key issues in building community. *New Directions for Student Services, 48*, 5–15.

Smith, M. R. (2005). Personalization in academic advising: A case study of component and structure. Online submission. (ERIC Clearinghouse, ED490396.)

Tinto, V. S. (n. d.). *Taking retention seriously*. Retrieved December 22, 2007, from http://soeweb.syr.edu/academics/grad/higher_education/Copy%20of%20Vtinto/Files/TakingRetentionSeriously.pdf

Valdez, J. R. (1993). Community college culture and its role in minority student academic achievement. *Community Education Journal, 20* (3), 21–23.

CHAPTER TWENTY-THREE

Assessing Student Learning

John H. Schuh

W hile assessing student learning is an important topic on the contemporary higher education scene (see, for example, U.S. Department of Education, 2006), the fact is that assessing student learning has been advocated for more than twenty years in the higher education literature. Assessing student learning has become a central aspect for delivering services to students and, indeed, is an expectation for virtually all dimensions of colleges and universities, including academic advising (Lynch, 2000; Creamer & Scott, 2000). This chapter will begin by providing a historical view of assessing student learning and then will identify potential student learning outcomes. It will provide two case examples of how quite different institutions might go about conceptualizing student learning, and it will conclude with quantitative and qualitative measures designed to assess student learning. The comprehensiveness of this chapter is limited by space. That many of the topics are treated in a cursory manner should not be interpreted to mean that they lack depth. Instead, the chapter's approach has been to touch on a number of topics and provide resource materials in the reference list that can be used by the reader to examine the topics in greater detail.

A BRIEF HISTORICAL FRAMEWORK

A brief look at assessing student learning can be framed by several significant documents that have been released in the past twenty years. This review begins with the work of the Study Group on the Conditions of Excellence in

American Higher Education (1984), which released the report *Involvement in Learning*. In this report, the authors identified assessment and feedback as conditions of excellence in higher education. The authors asserted, "The use of assessment information to redirect effort is an essential ingredient in effective learning and serves as a powerful lever for involvement" (p. 21). They also provided five recommendations for assessment and feedback. One of their recommendations has direct application to the work of academic advisors as institutional staff members who should be concerned with student learning. They observed, "In changing current systems of assessment, academic administrators and faculty should ensure that appropriate instruments and methods used are appropriate for (1) the knowledge, capacities and skills addressed and (2) the stated objectives of undergraduate education at their institutions" (p. 57).

Alexander Astin, a member of the study group, built on this report with his volume *Achieving Educational Excellence* (1985). In his view of talent development, he observed "Assessing its [the institution's] success in developing the talents of its students is a more difficult task, one that requires information on change or improvements in students' performance over time" (p. 61). He reported, "I believe that any good college or university assessment program must satisfy two fundamental criteria: it must be consistent with a clearly articulated philosophy of institutional mission and it should be consistent with *some* [italics in original] theory of pedagogy or learning" (p. 167).

Focusing mostly on student learning and development outside the classroom, Kuh, Schuh, Whitt, & Associates (1991) advocated using an "auditing" process in "assessing the quality of the out-of-class experience" of students (p. 264). Their work provided a systematic approach to determine the extent to which the out-of-class experiences and learning of undergraduates were compatible with the education purposes of the institution they attended. Their work was consistent with that of Astin in that each emphasized that learning needs to be consistent with institutional missions and that it could vary from college to college depending on the goals and purposes of the institution.

The American College Personnel Association (1996) released The Student Learning Imperative in a special issue of the *Journal of College Student Development*. This document extended the work of assessment in measuring student learning. The document recommended that "staff should participate in institution-wide efforts to assess student learning and personal development and periodically audit institutional environment to reinforce those factors that enhance, and eliminate those that inhibit, student involvement in educationally-purposeful activities" (p. 121). Immediately following the publication of this document, Alexander Astin (1996) provided an update of *Involvement in Learning*. He asserted that "Assessment is a potentially powerful tool for assisting us in building a more efficient and effective educational program" (p. 133).

The National Association of Student Personnel Administrators (NASPA) and the American College Personnel Association (ACPA) published "Learning Reconsidered" (2004), a document whose purpose was to re-examine some widely accepted ideas about conventional teaching and learning, and to question whether current organizational patterns in higher education support student learning and development in today's environment. The need to do so is clear: few of the social, economic, cultural, political, and pedagogical conditions and assumptions that framed the structures and methods of our modern universities remain unchanged. (p. 1)

In this document the authors asserted, "Assessment must be a way of life—part of the institutional culture" (p. 26). They also urged campuses to "focus primarily on *student learning* [italics in original] rather than on student satisfaction" (p. 27).

More recently, Project DEEP (Documenting Effective Educational Practices), a study of twenty institutions with higher-than-predicted graduation rates and scores on the National Survey of Student Engagement, found that assessment played a central role in the life of these institutions. The institutions were committed, according to the study (Kuh, Kinzie, Schuh, & Whitt, 2005), to continuous improvement. The authors concluded that "most DEEP schools systematically collect information about various aspects of student performance and use it to inform policy and decision making" (p. 156).

The conclusion of these reports is clear. Assessment has become an increasingly central element in higher education. These persuasive documents assert that practitioners delivering support services to students cannot afford to ignore, obfuscate, or refuse to be engaged in assessment activities. And so, the discussion moves to how assessment can be accomplished in ways that ultimately will contribute to measuring the value of various student experiences. The next section of this chapter will discuss outcomes that are related to student learning and can be facilitated by academic advisors.

IDENTIFYING LEARNING OUTCOMES

Student learning is a central focus of institutions of higher education, along with inquiry and public service. In the eyes of some (see, for example, Wingspread Group on Higher Education, 1993; U.S. Department of Education, 2006), student learning must be placed at the heart of the enterprise, with an increased emphasis on outcomes. Regardless of one's perspective on this issue, there is no question that many organizations, including accrediting bodies, have an interest in student learning and measuring the extent to which institutions actually measure what students learn (National Commission on Accountability in Higher Education, 2005; Higher Learning Commission, n.d.).

What colleges and universities expect students to learn will vary from institution to institution, influenced to a great extent by the institution's mission and philosophy. Kuh et al. (2005, p. 27) observed, "Institutional philosophies serve as a compass, keeping the institution on track as it makes decisions about resources, curriculum and educational opportunities." Consequently, a private institution with a strong religious foundation and purpose may very well approach the centrality of faith development as a learning outcome for its undergraduates in a different way than the approach taken by a state university, which, in fact, may not even identify faith development as a learning outcome for its students.

What is important, however, is that institutions behave in ways that are consistent with what they indicate is important; that is, their enacted behavior must be aligned with their espoused behavior. This consistency of behavior was identified by Kuh et al. (2005) in their study of twenty high-performing institutions, and the finding is instructive for institutions of higher education. Student success starts with consistency of message and behavior. In identifying appropriate learning outcomes, colleges and universities are advised to identify those that are consistent with their institutional mission and philosophy.

The current edition of the *CAS Professional Standards for Higher Education* (Dean, 2006) includes sixteen domains of student learning and development that potentially could be addressed by an advising program (pp. 29–30). The outcomes are new to the 2006 standards and were not included in the 1997 version (Miller, 1997), but many of them can be traced to various seminal documents in student affairs practice, including *The Student Personnel Point of View* (1949) and *A Perspective on Student Affairs* (1987). Whether or not all of these outcomes would be appropriate for all institutions of higher education is not entirely clear, but many would be appropriate at most institutions. For example, the "Student Learning and Development Outcome Domains for Academic Advising Programs" (Dean, 2006) does not include a specific learning outcome related to an appreciation and understanding of foreign cultures, an outcome that has particular importance at a number of institutions of higher education (see, for example, Macalester College, 2006). The list includes the following:

- Intellectual growth
- Personal and educational goals
- Enhanced self-esteem
- Realistic self-appraisal
- Clarified values
- Career choices
- Independence
- Effective communication
- Leadership development
- Healthy behavior
- Meaningful interpersonal relationships
- Collaboration
- Social responsibility
- Satisfying and productive lifestyles

- Appreciating diversity
- Spiritual awareness

Definitions for each of these learning outcomes can be found in Dean (2006).

OPERATIONALIZING STUDENT LEARNING

The potential learning outcomes identified above provide an extensive list for the college student experience. Academic advisors are wonderfully positioned to work with students in developing plans to achieve many of them. In fact, Kuh (1999, p. 84) concluded that students' discussing "academic program matters with advisers . . . has been linked to desired outcomes of college." Realistically, it may not be possible for students to work with their academic advisors to develop plans so that they will have experiences designed to accelerate their learning in all of the categories identified above, and it is obvious, I hope, that some student experiences will result in learning in more than one category. For example, students who assume a senior role in an organization may very well improve their leadership skills and their oral and written communications skills, and as a consequence may have enhanced self-esteem.

More likely, students and advisors can work together so that learning can be enhanced in some of the categories but probably not all. Such an approach suggests that students and their advisors work closely together along the following dimensions:

1. Conduct an analysis of the student's strengths and areas of potential development upon entry into the institution.

2. Develop a plan to enhance existing strengths and improve areas of agreed-upon improvement.

3. Have an understanding of the assets of the institution that are available to facilitate each student's plan.

4. Use formative measurement techniques to assess the extent to which students are successful in making progress toward their desired goals while the student is enrolled and then use summative approaches as the student is ready to graduate.

Consider the following examples.

A Student at a Baccalaureate College

Sean is entering Selective College (SC), a very selective, baccalaureate, residential college located in the East. Sean's plan is to complete a bachelor's degree and then go to graduate or professional school. Sean's goals are not refined beyond those stated above, and he believes that the next four years will be an excellent opportunity to explore various subjects, develop a variety of important skills, and in the student's words, "learn a lot about all kinds of things."

Sean and Jean Kelly, a member of the advising staff, meet during the orientation period for new students at SC. They have a lengthy discussion about Sean's plans for college and how SC can provide experiences that will help Sean achieve the tentative goals that he talked about in applying for admission to the college.

Sean has some interest in the study of foreign languages and cultures and may even want to study abroad for a semester. SC is particularly proud of the opportunities it makes available to students who wish to study abroad, and Jean indicates that in addition to study abroad programs, SC has a number of clubs available on campus for students who wish to get to know international students. In addition, Jean provides information to Sean about speakers from overseas who will be on campus during the academic year to discuss their countries. She also lets him know that over holidays, domestic students sometimes will host international students because the international students often are not able to go home because of the cost of travel.

Jean also suggested to Sean that he consider talking a course on non-U.S. cultures to help meet his distribution requirements and also to build on his four years of study of Spanish to help meet general education requirements. Sean agreed to enroll in both courses. Jean reminds Sean to keep up with regular journaling and to feel free to drop in any time to talk.

Mid-term Follow-up

About midway through the term Sean stops in to visit with Jean. Sean reports that college has been exciting, that classes are going well, and that joining the international club has been very interesting. Sean is meeting students from all over the world and has planned to invite one of them to join him at his family's home for fall break. Sean has not met the international speakers as often as he thought he would, but promises himself that he will do better as the terms winds on. Jean and Sean talk about the journaling process, and while Sean has not been quite as diligent as he would like to in developing an entry each day, the fact is that there is a great deal of content to talk about at the next regularly scheduled meeting, which will be in November. At that time Jean and Sean will work on preparing a schedule of class for the spring semester.

Commentary

The process in which Sean and Jean are participating is virtually ideal and perhaps not too realistic. Here, the advisor and the student have conducted a preliminary assessment of the student's goals for college, have developed a plan for how to achieve some of the student's goals (that are consistent with the college's goals for students), and have begun to develop a process to assess the extent to which these goals are achieved (the journaling activity). Just one goal is presented in the example to illustrate how this process might work and how the advisor could work with the student to develop a plan using the same process. This approach assumes a resource-rich environment, in which an advisor could provide a "high-touch" approach to planning. In a less robust resource environment, this could be done online, although that approach would presuppose that students would follow through and take the initiative to engage in the kind of planning that Sean did with Jean. Consider the alternative scenario for a student at a metropolitan university.

A Student at a Metropolitan University

Sam is a returning adult student at Metropolitan University (MU), a state-assisted comprehensive institution located in the largest city in the state. Of the undergraduates attending MU, more than half are over the age of twenty-five and, therefore, might be classified as nontraditional, although at MU they are in the majority. The balance of the undergraduates are of traditional age, but virtually all commute from home and many work twenty-five hours per week or more.

Sam has two children and works thirty hours per week. She started her college career more than ten years ago, but marriage and her family intervened and only recently has she decided to return to college to complete her bachelor's degree in political science. She already works for the city government but knows that her opportunities for advancement are limited without completing the degree, and deep in her heart she'd like to pursue an MPA in the future. She has fifty-five credits completed toward her degree, so she plans to complete the degree in three years by going to college year-round.

Sam has a meeting planned with her academic advisor Charlie Lansdowne in a week to plan her academic schedule and also to talk about how she can best use her time so as to learn the most from her experience, realizing that her time is really limited.

During the meeting Charlie and Sam get acquainted. Charlie has reviewed Sam's academic record from State U (SU) where she attended before marrying, and he is impressed with her record. She did well academically, and she also let Charlie know that she had been quite active in residence hall government, an activity that will not be part of her experience at MU.

MU, as a metropolitan institution, is committed to the city and its surrounding area. What that means is that the institution's mission makes it clear that it is preparing people to serve the city in a variety of ways, through the school districts, health-care facilities, business and industry, and local government. Leadership development is a high priority for the institution, and it has developed an undergraduate minor in leadership in addition to providing a wide array of experiences for students to be engaged in the community.

Charlie and Sam talk about various experiences that will help her achieve her goal of completing her bachelor's degree but also develop leadership skills that will position her well for a career in the administration of the city. Clearly, being involved in student government or campus organizations or clubs simply will not work for Sam, since she has significant work and family commitments in addition to her coursework. But, two aspects of her academic program lend themselves to leadership development that will result in completing credit hours plus gaining valuable experiences. One is for her to participate in a strand of three service-learning courses that are part of the political science curriculum. These are designed to help students engage in activities related to local government. In Sam's case, since she already works for the city, the experience will be arranged with the county government so that she can understand the intricacies of how that governmental unit works, and she can develop contacts with several departments there that are likely to serve her well in the future.

Charlie also suggests that Sam explore the possibility of taking the leadership minor. If Sam plans her curriculum carefully, she can squeeze the minor into her program, although she may need to take more courses in the summer than she had planned so that she can finish according to her schedule. Sam agrees to consider this opportunity, although work and family may make a heavy summer load difficult for her to manage.

The other experience that Sam and Charlie discuss has to do with her participating in a senior honors seminar. If she continues to do as well as she did at SU, Sam is an excellent candidate for this kind of experience. She would be required to prepare a senior honors paper, and present it at the annual spring conference, where students and faculty share their work with the political science department and the larger university.

Commentary

Sam's experiences will be quite different from Sean's. Her development will be focused almost exclusively on what can be arranged for credit, whereas Sean will be engaged in lots of not-for-credit out-of-class experiences throughout the course of his academic career. Sean has ample time and few commitments other than attending college, whereas Sam has a very tight schedule and other important elements in her life that she must address. Jean, Sean's advisor, proposed that he engage in journaling, develop a form of a learning portfolio, and take advantage of the rich opportunities available at SC. Sam similarly will have rich experiences, but they will be built around for-credit activities. A learning portfolio is less practical for her, but Charlie will encourage her to keep a record of her experiences, especially through the service learning courses since what she learns in those are likely to have direct application to her career, and perhaps she can develop a more focused version of a learning portfolio as time allows.

MEASURING LEARNING

In the two scenarios the academic advisors worked closely with students and suggested potential experiences that will help them achieve their goals for their college experience. Please note that the advisors were careful to suggest experiences that were consistent with the institution's values and consistent with what was realistic for the students' available time, ability, and effort. But, how can one determine whether the experiences produced the desired outcomes? Several approaches are available to the advisors and their institutions.

Quantitative Approaches

Quantitative approaches often are defined as the administration of questionnaires to students with the results being compared with a norm group. A variety of standardized instruments are available to measure student experiences. Among them are the National Survey of Student Engagement, the College Student Experiences Questionnaire, Your First College Year, the College Senior Survey, the College Outcomes Survey, and other standardized instruments. Sometimes institutions might want to develop their own instrument. An example of a template for an institution-specific instrument was developed by Aulepp and Delworth (1976) and has been used on several occasions (Schuh & Veltman, 1991). The standardized instruments often provide evaluators with the opportunity to include institution-specific questions that examine topics of particular interest to a given campus.

Linking the instrument to central elements of the educational philosophy and goals of the institution is essential in selecting a questionnaire or preparing one from scratch. For example, items such as "Developing leadership skills,"

"Becoming an effective team or group member," and "Dealing fairly with a wide range of people" (items on the College Outcomes Survey (http://www .act.org/ess/fouryear.html) explore learning outcomes that are central to an MU education. Sam is planning to use her education to position herself for increasingly responsible positions in the administration of her city, and for her career to progress she will have to develop skills accordingly. Hence, the use of the College Outcomes Survey would be quite appropriate in measuring progress for the learning outcomes that Sam and Charlie have identified for her. So, whether an advisor is working with Sean or Sam, choosing an instrument that is well crafted in terms of its psychometrics (validity and reliability) and that measures constructs of value to the institution and its students are central to the measurement process.

Quantitative approaches can be particularly useful in that they can be used to develop data sets that can be compared with national or regional norms. Students at SC, the institution where Sean was studying, can be compared with those at other, similar institutions along selected dimensions of importance on the College Outcomes Survey. In Sean's case, his score and that of SC students as a group on the item "Interacting with people from cultures other than my own" would be important, given SC's emphasis on internationalism and understanding cultures other than those of the United States. Other items are included in this questionnaire that also would be of great value for this institutional goal ("Becoming more willing to consider opposing points of view" and "Becoming a more effective member in a multicultural society").

Scores on standardized instruments should be reviewed along at least three dimensions. First, for an individual student, the growth demonstrated along certain points in time can be valuable. Suppose that Sean spends a semester studying overseas. Administering an instrument to him before and after the experience could result in useful information about the growth he has experienced. Changes in scores certainly could provide a basis for in-depth discussions with Jean about his experiences. Second, the scores of SC students in the aggregate can be studied. Do they exhibit growth over time? Are some experiences more potent than others? For example, do students who participate in study abroad report greater gains in understanding cultures different from their own? This information is very useful in learning about the potency of certain experiences and can help advisors who work with students who have specific goals for their experience at SC, as was demonstrated by Sean's interest in international experiences. Finally, the scores of SC students, in the aggregate, who have completed a standardized instrument can be compared with the scores of students from similar institutions. How do the scores compare? Are SC students on track with their peers, or do they differ? Clearly, one needs to be careful in comparisons across institutions (see Bender & Schuh, 2002), but these can be useful conversation starters for those evaluating programs.

But using standardized instruments is not the only approach one might take. Qualitative approaches are another option.

Qualitative Approaches

Qualitative approaches also might be used in measuring student learning. Typical qualitative approaches include observing student behavior, reviewing documents, and interviewing people, either individually or in groups.

Various elements of student life lend themselves very well to the use of qualitative methods. For example, exploring issues such as asking students to make meaning of participating in experiences such as serving as volunteers, reporting what they have learned from service learning projects, and assuming leadership positions lend themselves very nicely to focus group discussions. In some cases a student's experience might be unique, so an individual interview might make more sense than a focus group that often includes five to seven participants. An example of this kind of experience might be for a student to report what he learned from serving on the governing board of the college. Another could be for a student to describe what she learned from serving as the plenary speaker at a student event.

Sam is interested in using her educational experiences at MU to position herself well for her career. She is a transfer student at MU and has two to three years of study before she will complete her program. Her advisor, Charlie, wants to make sure that she has the richest experiences possible. To keep track of what she is learning, Charlie suggests that Sam keep a weekly journal of reflections. The focus of the journal, Charlie explains, should be on what Sam learned each week. She should address such questions as, What was surprising? As a consequence of the learning, what will she do? What did Sam learn from other students? Charlie indicates that no more than a page or two of reflections is necessary and assures her that for some weeks Sam may have a modest amount of information to report.

Electronic Portfolios

Sean might want to work with Jean in the development of an electronic portfolio. Jean can provide assistance to Sean in identifying learning outcomes that are central to his learning experience at SC. For example, Jean might provide Sean with a list of potential learning outcomes that might result from his study abroad. Sean could develop essays or reflection pieces that could speak to some, or perhaps all, of the learning outcomes and then could identify artifacts that would support his conclusions about his learning experiences. Some of the artifacts might be papers he writes for his classes, field notes that he takes from service learning projects, and photos from his work at in his study abroad experience. A sample of electronic portfolios can be found at http://www.celt.iastate.edu/lt/eportfolio.html. Sean is planning on attending graduate or professional school after he finishes his baccalaureate degree, and the portfolio can be very helpful in providing evidence of what he has learned while enrolled at SC beyond his formal academic transcript. Chen and Mazow (2002) indicate that portfolios can be quite useful in the advising process in "engaging students in formative assessment of self-reflection and development." Garis (2007, p. 4) adds, "The intent of such (electronic) portfolios is not to support concrete applications such as employment; rather, they are more commonly less structured in supporting user learning through reflection." By providing Sean with broad learning outcomes that are consistent with what SC has in mind for the student learning experience, Jean can provide a basic structure for Sean, but he can decide how to address the learning outcomes and the artifacts that he will include in the portfolio.

Sam also might prepare a learning portfolio. Her approach is likely to be quite different from Sean's because her experiences are so much more than focused his. Sam might decide that her portfolio will center on how she has enhanced her professional skills through her courses and other experiences while enrolled at MU with a special emphasis on how she has been preparing herself for increasingly complex leadership responsibilities in city government. In addition to her courses and other experiences she could include artifacts and short reflection papers that would identify how the things she learned from these various learning experiences have contributed to her growth and potential in the field of public administration. Two examples of these could be a PowerPoint presentation she has made to the city's planning and zoning commission and her notes from a seminar she attended for public administrators across the county. The resulting portfolio has the potential to be quite helpful as her career in city administration advances.

From an advisor's perspective, the use of learning portfolios can be a very handy tool in measuring student learning. In addition to standardized tests and focus groups, learning portfolios can provide rich evidence of student learning. The evidence, then, can be compared with the learning outcomes that the advisor and student identified as the student matriculated and through ongoing conferences that they have while the student is enrolled. Combined with quantitative and qualitative assessment techniques, learning portfolios can provide wonderful assessment data for academic advisors.

CONCLUSION

This chapter has provided background on the development of interest in student learning over the past several decades through an identification of documents. It has also identified student learning and development domains discussed in the CAS Standards (Dean, 2006) for academic advising programs, providing two case examples of how students and their advisors might identify learning outcomes for their college experience. The chapter concludes with a few ideas about how student learning might be measured. Clearly, academic advisors are well positioned to measure student learning outcomes as part of the advising process. As part of their commitment to students, they must use assessment tools to help students have the most robust collegiate experience possible. Anything less will shortchange their most important stakeholders, students themselves.

References

American College Personnel Association. (1996). The student learning imperative. Retrieved April 16, 2008, from http://www.acpa.nche.edu/sli/sli.htm

Astin, A. W. (1985). *Achieving educational excellence*. San Francisco: Jossey-Bass.

Astin, A. W. (1996). Involvement in learning revisited. *Journal of College Student Development, 37,* 123–132.

Aulepp, L., & Delworth, U. (1976). *Training manual for an ecosystem model*. Boulder, CO: WICHE.

Bender, B. E., & Schuh, J. H. (2002). Using benchmarking to inform practice in higher education. *New Directions for Higher Education, 118.*

Chen, H. L., & Mazow, C. (2002, October 28). Electronic learning portfolios and student affairs. *Net Results.* Retrieved August 29, 2007, from http://www.naspa.org/membership/mem/nr/article.cfm?id = 825

Creamer, E. G., & Scott, D. W. (2000). Assessing individual advisor effectiveness. In V. N. Gordon, & W. R. Habley (Eds.), *Academic advising: A comprehensive handbook* (pp. 339–348). San Francisco: Jossey-Bass.

Dean, L. A. (2006). (Ed.). *CAS professional standards for higher education* (6th ed.). Washington, DC: Council for the Advancement of Standards in Higher Education.

Garis, J. W. (2007). E-Portfolios: Concepts, designs, and integration within student affairs. *New Directions for Student Services, 119,* 3–16.

Higher Learning Commission. (n.d.). *Institutional accreditation: An overview.* Retrieved August 28, 2007, from http://www.ncahlc.org/index.php?option = com_content&task = view&id = 37&Itemid = 116

Kuh, G. D. (1999). Setting the bar high to promote student learning. In G. S. Blimling, E. J. Whitt, & Associates, *Good practice in student affairs* (pp. 67–89). San Francisco: Jossey-Bass.

Kuh, G. D., Kinzie, J., Schuh, J. H., & Whitt, E. J. (2005). *Student success in college.* San Francisco: Jossey-Bass.

Kuh, G. D., Schuh, J. H., Whitt, E. J., & Associates. (1991). *Involving colleges: Successful approaches to fostering student learning and development outside the classroom.* San Francisco: Jossey-Bass.

Lynch, M. L. (2000). Assessing the effectiveness of the advising program. In V. N. Gordon, & W. R. Habley (Eds.), *Academic advising: A comprehensive handbook* (pp. 324–338). San Francisco: Jossey-Bass.

Macalester College. (2007). *Global citizenship at Macalester College: A timeline.* Retrieved August 2, 2007, from http://www.macalester.edu/globalcitizenship/timeline.html

Miller, T. K. (1997). (Ed.). *The book of professional standards for higher education.* Washington, DC: Council for the Advancement of Standards in Higher Education.

National Association of Student Personnel Administrators. (1949). The student personnel point of view. Retrieved April 16, 2008, from http://www.naspa.org/pubs/Stud_Aff_1949.pdf

National Association of Student Personnel Administrators. (1987). A perspective on student affairs. Retrieved April 16, 2008, from http://www.naspa.org/pubs/Stud_Aff_1987.pdf

National Association of Student Personnel Administrators. (1989). *Points of view.* Washington, DC: Author.

The National Association of Student Personnel Administrators and The American College Personnel Association. (2004). *Learning reconsidered: A campus-wide focus on the student experience.* Retrieved July 31, 2007 from www.naspa.org/membership/leader_ex_pdf/lr_long.pdf

National Commission on Accountability in Higher Education. (2005). *Accountability for better results: A national imperative for higher education.* Denver: State Higher Education Executive Officers.

Schuh, J. H., & Veltman, G. C. (1991). Application of an ecosystem model to an office of handicapped services. *Journal of College Student Development, 32,* 236–240.

Study Group on the Conditions of Excellence in American Higher Education. (1984). *Involvement in learning: Realizing the potential of American higher education.* Washington, DC: National Institute of Education.

U.S. Department of Education. (2006). *A test of leadership: Charting the future of US higher education.* Washington, DC: Author.

Wingspread Group on Higher Education. (1993). *An American imperative: Higher expectations for higher education.* Racine, WI: Johnson Foundation.

Sources of Instruments

National Survey of Student Engagement http://nsse.iub.edu/html/survey_instruments_2007.cfm

College Student Experiences Questionnaire http://cseq.iub.edu/

Your First College Year http://www.gseis.ucla.edu/heri/yfcyoverview.php

College Senior Survey http://www.gseis.ucla.edu/heri/cssoverview.php

College Outcomes Survey http://www.act.org/ess/fouryear.html

CHAPTER TWENTY-FOUR

Assessing Advisor Effectiveness

Joe Cuseo

THE CASE FOR ATTENTION TO ASSESSMENT OF ACADEMIC ADVISEMENT

Assessing the effectiveness of academic advisors delivers a strong and explicit message to all members of the college community that advising is an important professional responsibility; conversely, failure to do so sends the tacit signal that academic advisement is not valued by the institution and that the work of academic advisors is not worthy of evaluation, improvement, and recognition. Disturbingly, the results from five national surveys of academic advising reveal that only 29 percent of postsecondary institutions evaluate advisor effectiveness (Habley & Morales, 1998). Upcraft, Srebnik, and Stevenson (1995) state categorically that "the most ignored aspect of academic advising in general, and first-year student academic advising in particular, is assessment" (p. 141).

The major objective of this chapter is to address this shortcoming by outlining the development of a comprehensive plan for assessing advisor effectiveness. The plan begins by briefly identifying the key components of an effective advisement program that must be in place for effective advisor assessment to take place; this is followed by a short discussion of the foundational principles of effective assessment. The chapter then turns to an examination of the key components of a comprehensive advisor-assessment plan that includes multiple assessment methods and informational sources, namely: (1) student evaluations, (2) preassessment and postassessment strategies, (3) qualitative assessment methods, (4) analysis of behavioral records, (5) advisor self-assessment, (6) peer assessment, and (7) assessment by the program director. The chapter concludes with a discussion of

369

strategies for "closing the loop" of assessment—that is, transforming the results of assessment into actual improvement of advisor performance.

Rather than *evaluation,* the term *assessment* will be used predominantly in this chapter because it connotes a process that is more collegial than judgmental, and because it more accurately conveys the message that the primary purpose of the process is to generate constructive and productive feedback that may be used to improve performance.

KEY INITIAL STEPS IN THE DEVELOPMENT OF AN EFFECTIVE ADVISOR ASSESSMENT PROGRAM

Advisor assessment is embedded within a larger system of effective program practices. For effective assessment of advisors to take place, other supporting components of an effective advising system need to be in place. These supportive components may be viewed as concurrent or corequisite steps that ensure that advisor assessment is taken seriously by the institution and that motivate advisors to use assessment results to improve their performance. These corequisite steps include: (a) clarifying the meaning and purpose of academic advising; (b) providing effective advisor orientation, training, and development; and (c) providing recognition and reward for effective advisor performance.

These key elements of an effective advisement program will not be discussed in this chapter because they are covered more extensively in other chapters of this handbook. Nonetheless, they should be considered and coordinated with the initial development and eventual implementation of an advisor assessment plan.

FOUNDATIONAL PRINCIPLES OF EFFECTIVE ASSESSMENT

If the defining characteristic of effective assessment was summarized in a single word, that word would be *multiplicity.* Effective assessment serves multiple purposes, measures multiple outcomes, draws from multiple data sources, and uses multiple methods of measurement.

An effective assessment program can serve two key evaluative purposes, which have been historically referred to as: (a) *summative* evaluation—assessment that "sums up" and *proves* performance impact or value, and (b) *formative* evaluation—assessment that "shapes up" and *improves* performance quality (Scriven, 1967). Arguably, the latter is the most important purpose of advisor assessment because its primary goal is to promote positive change in advisor performance, which, ultimately, improves the quality of advising received by students.

Assessment becomes more comprehensive and complete when it measures multiple outcomes, which may be summarized in the form of an "ABC" mnemonic: A = Affective outcomes (e.g., student perceptions of advisor effectiveness), B = Behavioral outcomes (e.g., student use of campus resources), and C = Cognitive outcomes (e.g., student self-knowledge and curricular knowledge).

Comprehensive assessment also draws from multiple sources that include students, self, peers, and the program director.

Lastly, effective assessment uses multiple methods of measurement, which include quantitative methods that generate numerical data (e.g., ratings) and qualitative methods that generate "human" data (e.g., spoken or written words). It is an assessment axiom that multiple measurement methods, sometimes defined as "triangulation" (Fetterman, 1991), yield more reliable and valid results than any single method or data source (Wergin, 1988).

STUDENT ASSESSMENT OF ACADEMIC ADVISORS

Student ratings represent the most widely used method of measuring college teaching effectiveness (Seldin, 1993), and they have been the most extensively researched strategy for assessing college instruction (Cashin, 1995). This substantial body of research on student evaluations of college teaching may be adapted to inform the practice of advisor assessment, particularly given that academic advising is increasingly being viewed as a form of teaching (Cuseo, 2004; Lowenstein, 2005; Melander, 2005).

If a student-rating survey or questionnaire is well constructed and properly administered, it can serve as an effective centerpiece for a comprehensive advising-assessment plan. Developing an effective instrument for student assessment of academic advisors includes making informed decisions about: (1) content, (2) form or structure, (3) administration, (4) analysis and summary, (5) reporting results, and (6) "closing the loop"—that is, using the results to improve academic advising. Strategies for effective decision-making with respect to each of these key features of a student assessment instrument will be discussed in the ensuing sections of this chapter.

Determining the Content of a Student Assessment of Advising

A student assessment instrument may be "home grown"—created internally at and by the institution, or it may be "store bought"—imported externally from an assessment service or evaluation center. Standardized instruments do come with the advantages of having already-established reliability and validity, plus the availability of norms that allow for cross-institutional comparisons. On the other hand, home-grown or locally developed instruments have the advantage of providing a more sensitive measure of campus-specific objectives, issues, and challenges. The following recommendations are intended for the development and implementation of home-grown instruments.

Items should reflect specific advisor characteristics and behaviors that the institution deems indicative of high-quality academic advising. The items comprising the instrument should reflect qualities that the institution wants its advisors to aspire to and attain. Thus, an effective student assessment instrument functions not only as a tool for assessing the current reality of advisor performance (what *is*), but also serves as a catalyst for stimulating optimal or ideal performance (what *should be*).

Items should be grounded in systematic research on advisor characteristics that are valued by students. Upcraft et al. (1995) argue that "The first component of a comprehensive academic advising assessment program is the assessment of first-year student advising needs. This type of assessment is important because inadequate academic advising is often a result of offering advising services which do not match student needs" (p. 142). Research repeatedly points to the conclusion that students value academic advisors who are: (1) available and accessible, (2) knowledgeable and helpful, (3) personable and approachable, and (4) counselors and mentors (Winston, Ender, & Miller, 1982; Winston, Miller, Ender, Grites, & Associates, 1984; Frost, 1991; Gordon, Habley, & Associates, 2000; Smith & Allen, 2006). Each one of these "core" characteristics may be used to create specific content items.

Include items that ask students to report their behavior. Astin (1991) suggests a dual-category taxonomy for classifying the types of data that may be collected in the assessment process: (a) psychological data reflecting students' internal states (e.g., perceptions and feelings), and (b) behavioral data reflecting students' actions or activities. Traditionally, student evaluations of instructors have focused almost exclusively on gathering psychological data (student perceptions or opinions). However, given that one of the major goals of academic advising is to promote positive change in student behavior, assessment items that generate data on the use of campus services, or frequency of student participation in cocurricular activities, should be included in the assessment instrument.

Include items designed to assess student learning outcomes that advisors are expected to promote. Student surveys or questionnaires are commonly labeled as measures of student "satisfaction," carrying the negative connotation that they function much like customer satisfaction surveys. Yet, well-constructed student assessments are much more than satisfaction surveys. Results can provide meaningful data on student learning outcomes that come from the internal perspective of students. For instance, items may be included on student perceptions of how effectively their advisor contributed to any of the following learning outcomes: (a) self-knowledge or knowledge of curricular requirements, (b) understanding or appreciation of general education, (c) ability to think critically about educational choices, and (d) integration of academic and career plans.

Although these learning outcomes are self-reported (subjectively experienced) rather than performance-based (objectively observed), the systematic collection of such data from a large and representative sample of students provides evidence of the achievement of identified learning outcomes. Under the call for accountability that demands results and objective documentation of learning outcomes, student evaluations should not be summarily dismissed as merely subjective measures of psychological or emotional satisfaction.

Include items that ask students to rate their effort and effectiveness as advisees. Including such items serves to raise students' consciousness that they have a shared responsibility in the advisement process and to assure advisors that their performance evaluations include the conscientiousness and commitment of their advisees. This should reduce the degree of threat or defensiveness experienced by advisors about being assessed that normally accompanies any type of personal performance evaluation.

Obtain preliminary feedback from students and advisors on the proposed assessment instrument. This could be accomplished by having a sample of students complete the instrument and offer suggestions about items that should be added, deleted, or modified. Student focus groups may also be formed to obtain feedback on the instrument's strengths and ways in which the instrument could be improved. Soliciting student feedback prior to full-scale implementation of the assessment instrument serves two valuable purposes: it helps identify student issues, needs, or priorities that the assessment instrument may have failed to address, and it demonstrates respect for student input. Similar approaches should be undertaken with advisors, thus increasing their understanding of the process and enhancing their perception of assessment as something being done with or for them, rather than *to* them.

Determining the Form or Structure of the Assessment Instrument

The reliability, validity, and utility of an assessment instrument depend on its structure (form) as well as its content. The following recommendations are offered as strategies for structuring or formatting an effective student assessment instrument.

Collect demographic information from students. It is not uncommon for subpopulations of students to vary significantly in terms of their experiences, perceptions, and levels of satisfaction with the same educational program or service (Schuh & Upcraft, 2001). Including a short section on the instrument for students to report their demographic characteristics will provide an opportunity for cross tabulation of results for different groups of students.

Use a rating scale that includes five or seven response options. A rating scale containing five or seven options is likely to result in mean differences for individual items that are large enough in absolute value to provide discriminating data. Research on student evaluations of course instructors indicates that a rating scale with fewer than five choices tends to reduce the instrument's ability to discriminate between satisfied and dissatisfied respondents, while a rating scale with more than seven choices does not add to the instrument's discriminability (Cashin, 1990).

Have students rate both the perceived importance of advisor characteristics and their satisfaction with those characteristics. In effect, this enables the instrument to cofunction as a student *satisfaction* questionnaire and a student *needs assessment* survey.

Gaps between importance and satisfaction represent key target areas for performance enhancement.

Solicit written comments for each item. Item-specific prompts such as "please explain your rating" increase the number of written comments student provide. Prompted written comments also tend to be more focused, specific, and useful when they are anchored to a particular advisor characteristic or behavior (Cuseo, 2001). Providing students with the opportunity to explain or expand allows them to justify their ratings and also provides meaningful insights into advisor performance and direction for self-improvement.

Include at least two global items on the instrument to assess summative (overall) advisor effectiveness. The following two statements illustrate global items that are useful for summative evaluation purposes:

1. I would rate the *overall effectiveness* of this advisor as: (poor |← →| excellent).

   Reason for this rating:

2. I would recommend this advisor to other students: (strongly agree |← →| strongly disagree).

   Reason for this rating:

Responses to such global items provide an effective summative tool of students' overall assessment of the advisor. Research on students' course evaluations has repeatedly shown that global ratings are more predictive of student learning than student ratings given to specific aspects or dimensions of instruction (Braskamp & Ory, 1994; Centra, 1993; Cohen, 1986).

Include an open-ended question asking for students' general comments about the advisor's relative strengths and suggestions for improvement. Open-ended questions that are not tied to any particular advisor characteristic allow students to freely respond to any aspect of the advising relationship they choose to address, thereby allowing them to set their own agenda. Open-ended questions may provide distinctive information about the advisor and the advising process that may remain undetected by items in the assessment.

Keep the instrument short. Include no more than twenty items or questions. There is likely to be an inverse relationship between the length of the instrument and the depth of students' responses to it. It is probably safe to say that the longer the instrument, the less time and effort students will to devote to supplying the type of detailed written comments that are most useful for performance improvement.

Administering the Student Assessment Instrument

The effectiveness of an assessment instrument depends not only on its content and form, but also on its process of administration. The following recommendations are offered for administering a student assessment instrument in a manner that will improve the reliability and validity of the results generated by it.

Standardize the instructions delivered to students before administering the assessment. Research on instructor evaluations indicates that the wording of instructions can affect students' responses (Pasen, Frey, Menges, & Rath, 1978). For instance, if the instructions suggest to students that the assessment results are to be used for decisions about the instructor's retention and promotion, more favorable or lenient ratings are obtained than when instructions suggest that the results will be used for the purpose of course or instructional improvement (Braskamp & Ory, 1994; Feldman, 1979).

Instructions delivered to students should stress the role of the assessment process and the importance of student input in assessing college programs. To increase students' motivation for completing the assessment instrument and to improve the validity of the results obtained, it is recommended that the following elements be included in the administration instructions.

- Inform students that the assessment is an opportunity to provide input that can improve the quality of future advising.
- Explain the purpose of the assessment (e.g., to help advisors improve the effectiveness of their advising and the quality of the advisement program).
- Remind students that they should respond to each item *independently.*
- Emphasize that specific written comments are particularly useful.
- Assure students that their evaluations will be read carefully and taken seriously.
- Inform students about what will be done with their evaluations after they have been submitted.
- Assure them that their responses and their written comments will remain anonymous.

Give careful attention to when and where advisor evaluations will be administered. An effective assessment program requires both a sizable and a representative sample of respondents. Some have suggested that there is no tried-and-true method for the collection of student assessments of advisors, and as a result the choice of when and where to administer advisor assessment is institution-specific. Among those that have proven workable are administration: (1) in classes that meet during popular time blocks; (2) during selected classes within given majors; (3) as a condition of registration; (4) during group advising sessions; (5) at the conclusion of an advising appointment; and (6) at critical transition points in a student's academic career (e.g., change of major, completion of the sophomore year, graduation, etc.).

Analyzing and Summarizing the Results

Advisors should receive assessment summaries that allow them to compare their own advising performance with the ratings of all advisors. By aggregating results across all advisors and calculating the mean rating for each item on the instrument, individual advisors gain access to a collective reference point that can help them interpret their individual results. Sharing overall results can validate advisor behavior or it can provide an opportunity for formative self-reflection.

Provide advisors with information on students' response variance. Means tell only part of the assessment story. Advisors can gain significant insights into their performance by examining the consistency of student ratings by reporting ranges, standard deviations, and percentages of students choosing each rating option.

Reporting the Results

If the results are to be used for summative evaluation, report and attend to the information generated by global assessment items. It is imperative not to rely solely on the average of the ratings across individual items to obtain an overall assessment of advisor performance. This procedure is not only inefficient, but it is also an ineffective index of students' bottom-line evaluation of an advisor's effectiveness.

Abrami (1989) argues that it makes "conceptual and empirical sense to make summative decisions about teaching using a unidimensional [global] rating" (p. 227). Similarly, global items may be used to make summative (overall) assessments of academic advisors.

Make intentional decisions about the time and place where formative results will be shared and discussed. When and where assessment results are shared can affect how advisors react and how responsive they are to exploring strategies for self-improvement. For example, formative assessment data shared in an informal venue can create an atmosphere in which participants may review data and discuss improvement strategies in a relaxed and reflective manner. If a high-level administrator is a visible participant in the meeting, a strong message is sent to the college community that advising is a high institutional priority.

Report data generated by the advisor evaluation instrument in aggregate. If the focus is on individual advisor evaluation, the likelihood of defensiveness increases and the ability to focus on performance enhancements is compromised. When reviewing the results with advisors, "we" messages tend to keep the focus on *us* (the total program or advising team), whereas "you" messages place the focus on *them* (the individual advisors). Focusing on *collective* rather than *individual* strengths and weaknesses serves to depersonalize the assessment process and can reduce the defensiveness that often accompanies performance evaluation.

PREASSESSMENT AND POSTASSESSMENT METHODS

To gain a longitudinal perspective on changes in students' attitudes, knowledge, or behavior that may have taken place as a result of their interactions with advisors, an assessment instrument should be administered before the advising process begins and readministered after students have had experiences with their advisors. This design allows for the creation of a baseline against which change may be measured. To increase the likelihood that pre-to-post changes can be attributed to students' experiences with advising and not merely to their personal maturation or college experience in general, students' pre-to-post responses could be compared with the responses of students who did not meet with their advisors.

A less labor-intensive strategy for obtaining data relating to student changes that may be associated with their advising experiences would be to include an item that asks students to describe (in writing or through a rating scale) the degree to which changes in their attitudes, learning, or approaches to the college experience resulted from interaction with their advisor.

QUALITATIVE ASSESSMENT METHODS

The validity and comprehensiveness of assessment is enhanced when it includes a balanced blend of both quantitative and qualitative methods. Although quantitative and qualitative methods emerge from contrasting philosophical traditions and rest on very different epistemological assumptions (Smith & Heshusius, 1986), the data generated by these two methods of inquiry provide complementary sources of evidence, with the limitations of one method being counterbalanced by the advantages of the other. On student evaluation forms, students' written comments (qualitative data) can be used to help interpret the numerical ratings (quantitative data), while the average rating scores can be used to counterbalance the tendency to generalize from an individual's written comments that may be particularly poignant and memorable, but not representative of students as a whole.

Analysis of Students' Written Comments

Historically, student surveys and questionnaires have not been classified as qualitative research because they generate quantitative data. However, written comments made by students on the survey instrument represent a potential source of qualitative data that can provide insightful, in-depth information on advisors' strengths and weaknesses. Although written comments are difficult to summarize and manipulate statistically, their content may still be classified systematically and analyzed to discern trends or recurrent themes.

Even the volume of written responses students made in response to different items on a rating survey can itself serve as a rough measure of the importance or intensity of student feelings about issues addressed by particular items. Respondents with strong opinions about certain behaviors will state them if adequate space is provided. Mullendore and Abraham (1992) recommend that those conducting the evaluation "(s)ummarize written comments in detail; consider indicating the number of times the same negative or positive comments were made" (pp. 39–40).

Another potential source of written comments for use in advisor assessment is the one-minute paper, written in response to a focused questions that students complete after a learning experience. Examples of questions for one-minute papers include: "What was the most useful piece of information or skill you acquired in today's session?" or "What questions remain unanswered or on your mind following today's session?" One-minute papers provide immediate feedback in the form of qualitative data on what students may have learned during a specific advising episode. Furthermore, one-minute papers encourage students to actively reflect on and find personal meaning in their advising experiences, which, in itself, will increase the likelihood that students will learn from these experiences.

Focus-Group Interviews

A focus group is a small group (six to twelve people) that meets with a trained moderator in a relaxed environment to discuss a selected topic or issue, with the goal of eliciting participants' perceptions, attitudes, and ideas (Bers, 1989). In contrast to surveys or questionnaires, which solicit individual students' numerical ratings and written comments, focus-group interviews solicit students' oral responses. Students' oral replies to "live" questions posed to them in person can sometimes generate different, more elaborate data than students' written responses to questions posed to them in print.

Focus-groups may be a stand-alone assessment method or they may be used in conjunction with surveys. In one approach, interviews may be conducted as a follow-up to student surveys to acquire qualitative data that may be used to help interpret the survey's quantitative results. Focus-group questions would be directed at students' interpretations or explanations of survey ratings. In another approach, focus groups are conducted first to collect student ideas and perceptions to develop specific items for the advisor-assessment survey. Such combined use of qualitative and quantitative methods again reinforces the notion that these are complementary rather than contradictory assessment methods.

Finally, a tacit advantage of conducting focus groups is that it serves to validate students by sending them the message that someone at the institution is genuinely interested in their views and feelings about the quality of academic advising they are receiving and how it may be improved.

ANALYSIS OF STUDENTS' BEHAVIORAL RECORDS

Behavioral records of student activities outside the classroom can provide direct data on the incidence and frequency of productive student behaviors that may be influenced by academic advisors. Listed below are examples of records that are potentially relevant to the assessment of advisor effectiveness and impact:

- frequency of contacts between students and their advisors
- frequency with which students are referred to particular advisors
- the incidence or frequency with which certain advisors' students are referred to and use campus support programs

- incidence and frequency with which students *change to* and *from* individual advisors
- course enrollment patterns (adds and drops, major changes, degree completion, time to degree) as an indicator of academic progress
- use of student services such as academic support through trace audit system using student identification cards
- participation in on-campus clubs, student organizations, campus activities, and college-sponsored community service through the use of the student development transcript
- follow-through on advisor referrals

Caution must be exercised, however, when using systemic behavioral indicators such as student retention and academic performance (GPA) in a summative assessment of academic advisors. While useful in a formative assessment, such generic outcomes are influenced by a variety of factors that fall outside the responsibilities of an advisor and are not a reflection of the quality of advice or advisor competence.

ADVISOR SELF-ASSESSMENT

By engaging in self-assessment, advisors can become actively involved in and gain personal ownership of the assessment process. Comprehensive advisor self-assessment can be demonstrated in the form of an advising portfolio, which may include any or all of the following materials: (1) personal statement of advising philosophy, (2) narrative summary of key advising practices or strategies, (3) advising syllabus, (4) advisor responses to evaluations received from students or administrators, (5) advising materials created for use by students or advisors, and (6) advising-related professional-development activities.

Advisor reflection on, and response to, evaluations is a particularly important component of a comprehensive advising portfolio. Advisors could devote a section of their portfolio to their interpretations of student or administrator evaluations, their thoughts about why they received high evaluations with respect to certain advising functions, and strategies for addressing or redressing areas in which they were evaluated least favorably. Advisors who are given the opportunity to respond to evaluations are likely to view performance evaluation less defensively. They know they will have the opportunity to defend themselves in the event they receive negative evaluations that are unfair or unwarranted.

Another vehicle for promoting meaningful self-assessment is to ask advisors to complete the same assessment instrument as their advisees, responding to it as they see themselves or as they think their advisees would respond. Consistencies and discrepancies that emerge between advisor self-assessments and their students' assessments can provide advisors with a powerful source of assessment data. For example, advisors' written reflections on the mismatches that emerged between their self-perceptions and their students' perceptions may stimulate self-awareness and self-improvement.

Peer Assessment

Research in the area of faculty development strongly supports the effectiveness of peer feedback and collegial dialogue for promoting instructional improvement (Eble & McKeachie, 1985). It is reasonable to expect that peer assessment and feedback would be equally effective for advisor improvement. Disappointingly, however, national survey research indicates that peer evaluation is the least frequently used method of advisor evaluation (Habley, 1988, 2004).

An advisor evaluation instrument that is designed primarily for student assessment of advisors may also be used to inform peer assessment. For instance, teams of advisors could agree to review each other's student evaluations for the mutually supportive purpose of improving their professional performance. Peer assessment may also be conducted in a confidential manner by having advisors receive the student evaluations of an anonymous colleague and provide that colleague with constructive feedback; at the same time, the advisor who provides feedback anonymously to a colleague also receives feedback anonymously from a colleague.

Peer assessment can be a particularly potent performance improvement tool because it generates feedback from colleagues, which is likely to be perceived as less threatening and more credible than feedback delivered from above (a superior) or below (a student). Peer assessment represents horizontal feedback received from someone at the same professional level, performing the same duties, facing the same challenges, and working under the same conditions and constraints as the person being assessed.

ASSESSMENT OF ACADEMIC ADVISORS BY THE PROGRAM DIRECTOR

In addition to student, peer, and self-assessment, the program director also has a role to play in the assessment process. Comprehensive evaluation of an advisement program should include feedback from student advisees, peer advisors, and advising administrators (Frost, 1991). Through the collective review of assessments received by all advisors, the program director is uniquely positioned to interpret data that informs program assessment. Emerging trends or recurrent themes become visible when student assessments are aggregated and viewed as a composite. Glennen and Vowell (1995) recommend that a college should "evaluate its program of advising in addition to evaluating individual advisors. Student evaluations are one source that can be used to do this. Taken together [student evaluations] give an overview of student opinion and of reaction to the advising they receive" (p. 73).

The program director is also well positioned to identify critical incidents that, when viewed collectively and cumulatively, provide qualitative data for detecting common sources or causes of student complaints and grievances or recurrent reasons given by students for seeking a change of advisors. Themes that emerge from documenting and organizing these incidents may provide diagnostic data that can be used to troubleshoot weaknesses or kinks in the advising system.

CLOSING THE LOOP: USING THE RESULTS TO IMPROVE ADVISING

Transforming assessment results into demonstrable performance improvement represents the key final step that closes the loop in the assessment process, bringing it full circle and back to its original purpose—to improve advising effectiveness. Unfortunately, this last step is the one that is most frequently overlooked and typically receives the least attention in the assessment process (Cohen, 1990). Commenting on assessment of teaching effectiveness, Stevens (1987) notes that "the instructor must learn how to design and implement alternative instructional procedures in response to feedback, which means that a coherent system of instructional resources must be easily available to the instructor. Without such a system, the instructor may be unable to gain the knowledge or support that is necessary to effect change" (p. 37).

The following strategies are recommended for equipping advisors with information they need to close the loop and use assessment data to effect change in the quality of the advising they deliver to students.

Use Assessment Results to Guide Professional Development of Advisors

One way this can be accomplished is by identifying the items on a student assessment instrument for which advisors, collectively, receive the lowest average ratings. These items could then be used to prioritize and energize discussion of performance improvement strategies at professional development workshops for academic advisors.

Provide Specific Performance Improvement Strategies

Advisors should not only receive a descriptive summary of their assessment results, but they should also receive a prescriptive summary of specific strategies or a compendium of best practices, which they can use to improve their performance with respect to each dimension of advising that was assessed. The importance of providing specific performance feedback is reinforced by research on instructor evaluations, which indicates that the more specific the feedback, the more effective it is for helping instructors understand their evaluation results and improve their instructional performance (Goldschmid, 1978; Brinko, 1993). Furthermore, instructors report that they prefer feedback that is specific and focused on concrete teaching behaviors (Brinko, 1993).

Exceptional Advisors Should be Asked to Share Practices with Other Advisors

Another way to equip advisors with specific strategies for improving the quality of advising is by showcasing the practices of advisors whose performance is exemplary. For example, a panel of outstanding advisors could share the specific advising strategies or practices that they think contribute to advisor effectiveness. In addition to supplying other advisors with specific performance improvement strategies, an advising panel may serve as a vehicle for publicly recognizing and personally validating outstanding advisors. In addition, such a strategy raises the collective consciousness of advisors that effective advising is multidimensional and modifiable, not a monolithic and immutable character trait.

Advisors Should Provide Input into Overall Program Effectiveness

Advisors should be given the opportunity to assess the advising program from their perspective and suggest resources that would better enable them to transform their assessment results into improved advising. For example, academic advisors could assess: (a) the quality of administrative support they receive for advising; (b) the effectiveness of advisor orientation, training, and development they have received; (c) the usefulness of support materials or technological tools provided for them; (d) the viability of their advisee-advisor ratio; and (e) the effectiveness of administrative policies and procedures. Wes Habley (1995) notes that the need to obtain advisor feedback about program administration is especially important for delivering effective advising to today's diverse student population:

> In many cases, advisors do not (are not encouraged to) share with decision-makers the information which would lead to program, personnel, or policy modifications. This is particularly important in the case of the increasing diversity of entering students, because academic advisors may be the first to recognize how this diversity may influence programs, personnel, and policies. (p. 12)

There are two key advantages associated with allowing advisors the opportunity to assess the quality of administrative support they receive to do their jobs effectively: (a) It provides feedback to the advising program director that may be used for program improvement, and (b) it actively involves advisors in the assessment process, sending them a clear message that their input is valued and that they are not being treated as passive pawns or disengaged objects of evaluation.

CONCLUSION

The first step toward development of an effective advisor assessment plan is to ensure its integration with other key components in an effective advisement program. For effective assessment of advisors to take place, it must connect with other important elements the advising system that should be in place, namely: (a) a clear and coherent mission statement for the advisement program; (b) effective advisor orientation, training, and development; and (c) appropriate recognition and reward for effective advising.

Once this integration of key program components is established, a comprehensive advisor assessment plan is ready to be built on and driven by foundational principles of effective assessment, which may be encapsulated in one term: *multiplicity.* A comprehensive assessment plan accomplishes multiple purposes (formative and summative), measures multiple outcomes (affective, behavioral, and cognitive), embraces multiple data sources (students, peers, administrators, and self), and uses multiple measurement methods (subjective and objective, psychological and behavioral, qualitative and quantitative).

The final, key step in a comprehensive and effectively executed assessment plan is to close the loop by converting the results of assessment into actual performance improvement. This completes the cycle of assessment, bringing it back full circle to fulfill its original purpose: improving the quality of advising delivered by advisors and experienced by students.

References

Abrami, P. C. (1989). How should we use student ratings to evaluate teaching? *Research in Higher Education, 30* (2), 221–227.

Astin, A. W. (1991). *Assessment for excellence: The philosophy and practice of assessment and evaluation in higher education.* New York: Macmillan.

Bers, T. H. (1989). The popularity and problems of focus-group research. *College & University, 64* (3), 260–268.

Braskamp, L. A., & Ory, J. C. (1994). *Assessing faculty work: Enhancing individual and institutional performance.* San Francisco: Jossey-Bass.

Brinko, K. T. (1993). The practice of giving feedback to improve teaching: What is effective? *Journal of Higher Education, 64* (5), 574–593.

Cashin, W. E. (1990). Students do rate different academic fields differently. *New Directions for Teaching and Learning, 43,* 113–121.

Cashin, W. E. (1995). *Student ratings of teaching: The research revisited.* (IDEA Paper no. 32.) Manhattan, KS: Kansas State University, Center for Faculty Evaluation and Development.

Centra, J. A. (1993). *Reflective faculty evaluation: Enhancing teaching and determining faculty effectiveness.* San Francisco: Jossey-Bass.

Cohen, P. A. (1986). *An updated and expanded meta-analysis of multisection student rating validity studies.* Presented at the annual meeting of the American Educational Research Association, San Francisco.

Cohen, P. A. (1990). Bringing research into practice. *New Directions for Teaching and Learning, 43,* 123–132.

Cuseo, J. (2001). Course-evaluation surveys and the first-year seminar: Recommendations for use. In R. L. Swing (Ed.), *Proving and improving: Strategies for assessing the first college year* (Monograph No. 33) (pp. 65–74). Columbia: University of South Carolina, National Resource Center for The First-Year Experience and Students in Transition.

Cuseo, J. (2004, April). *The power of advising: Implications for student retention, learning, and educational achievement.* Presented at the NACADA Western Regional Conference, Pasadena, CA.

Eble, K. E., & McKeachie, W. J. (1985). *Improving undergraduate education through faculty development: An analysis of effective programs and practices.* San Francisco: Jossey-Bass.

Feldman, K. A. (1979). The significance of circumstances for college students' ratings of their teachers and courses. *Research in Higher Education, 10* (2), 149–172.

Fetterman, D. M. (1991). Auditing as institutional research: A qualitative focus. *New Directions for Institutional Research, 72,* 23–34.

Frost, S. H. (1991). *Academic advising for student success: A system of shared responsibility.* (ASHE-ERIC Higher Education Report no. 3.) Washington, DC: George Washington School of Education and Human Development.

Glennen, R. E., & Vowell, F. N. (1995). Selecting, training, rewarding, and recognizing faculty advisors (pp. 69–74). In M. L. Upcraft, & G. L. Kramer (Eds.), *First-year academic advising: Patterns in the present, pathways to the future* (pp. 3–14). (Monograph No. 18.) Columbia: University of South Carolina, National Resource Center for The Freshman Year Experience & Students in Transition.

Goldschmid, M. L. (1978). The evaluation and improvement of teaching in higher education. *Higher Education, 7,* 221–245.

Gordon, V. N., Habley, W. R., & Associates. (2000). *Academic advising: A comprehensive handbook.* San Francisco: Jossey-Bass.

Habley, W. R. (1988). The third ACT national survey of academic advising. In W. R. Habley (Ed.), *The status and future of academic advising: Problems and promise.* Iowa City: ACT National Center for the Advancement of Educational Priorities.

Habley, W. R. (1995). First-year students: The Year 2000. In M. L. Upcraft, & G. L. Kramer (Eds.), *First-year academic advising: Patterns in the present, pathways to the future* (pp. 3–14). (Monograph No. 18). Columbia: University of South Carolina, National Resource Center for The Freshman Year Experience & Students in Transition.

Habley, W. R. (2004). *The status of academic advising: Findings from the ACT Sixth National Survey.* (NACADA Monograph Series, no. 10.) Manhattan, KS: National Academic Advising Association.

Habley, W. R., & Morales, R. H. (1998). *Current practices in academic advising: Final report on ACT's fifth national survey of academic advising.* (NACADA Monograph Series, no. 6.) Manhattan, KS: National Academic Advising Association.

Lowenstein, M. (2005). If advising is teaching, what do advisors teach? *NACADA Journal, 25* (2), 65–73.

Melander, E. R. (2005). Advising as educating: A framework for organizing advising systems. *NACADA Journal, 25* (2), 84–91.

Mullendore, R., & Abraham, J. (1992). *Orientation director's manual.* Statesboro, GA: National Orientation Director's Association.

Pasen, R. M., Frey, P. W., Menges, R. J., & Rath, G. (1978). Different administrative directions and student ratings of instruction: Cognitive vs. affective effects. *Research in Higher Education, 9* (2), 1–167.

Schuh, J. H., & Upcraft, M. L. (2001). *Assessment practice in student affairs.* San Francisco: Jossey-Bass.

Scriven, M. (1967). The methodology of evaluation. In *Perspectives of curriculum evaluation.* (AERA Monograph Series on Curriculum Evaluation, no. 1.) Chicago: Rand McNally.

Seldin, P. (1993). How colleges evaluate professors, 1983 vs.1993. *AAHE Bulletin, 46* (2), 6–8, 12.

Smith, C. L., & Allen, J. M. (2006). Essential functions of academic advising: What students want and get. *NACADA Journal, 26* (1), 56–66.

Smith, J. K., & Heshusius, L. (1986). Closing down the conversation: The end of the quantitative-qualitative debate among educational inquirers. *Educational Researcher, 15* (1), 4–12.

Stevens, J. J. (1987). Using student ratings to improve instruction. *New Directions for Teaching and Learning, 31,* 33–38.

Upcraft, M. L., Srebnik, D. S., & Stevenson, J. (1995). Assessment of academic advising. In M. L. Upcraft, & G. L. Kramer (Eds.), *First- year academic advising: Patterns in the present, pathways to the future* (pp. 141–145). (Monograph No. 18.) Columbia: University of South Carolina, National Resource Center for The Freshman Year Experience & Students in Transition.

Wergin, J. F. (1988). Basic issues and principles in classroom assessment. *New Directions for Teaching and Learning, 34,* 5–17.

Winston, R. B., Ender, S. C., & Miller, T. K. (Eds.). (1982). Developmental approaches to academic advising. *New Directions for Student Services, 17,* 55–66.

Winston, R. B., Miller, T. K., Ender, S. C., Grites, T. J., & Associates (1984). *Developmental academic advising.* San Francisco: Jossey-Bass.

CHAPTER TWENTY-FIVE

Assessing the Effectiveness of the Advising Program

Wendy G. Troxel

Program assessment is not optional. The fundamental question for any comprehensive educational endeavor is "did it work?" Educators have a professional, ethical obligation to determine, through the systematic gathering and analysis of evidence, whether pedagogical interventions improved student learning and development in the ways for which the program was intended. Academic advisors work daily to help students achieve their academic and personal goals. Does it matter what had an impact and what fell on deaf ears? If the answer is "yes," all types and levels of stakeholders will ask for proof; if it is "no," be prepared to surrender institutional resources and support. While such a response may seem drastic, it is clear that increased pressure to prove impact has heightened our awareness of the challenges of assessing advising's contribution to student learning and development, both for internal improvement purposes and external accountability mandates.

A comprehensive advising system is a complex and often messy business. Barbara Walvoord (personal communication, November 4, 2007) often reminds educators involved in assessment that "a classroom [or other educational environment] is a place where every possible variable is actively varying." Not only do students represent widely diverse levels of preparation and motivation, but often many intended outcome statements of advising initiatives are actually subsumed under another department's or unit's intended learning outcomes (such as the competencies gained in a major field of study).

The thoughtful, professional response, however, is not to bemoan the vastness of the task, but instead to appreciate the scope of influence while also narrowing the focus of systematic inquiry to include those things that matter most. Given the complexity of the efforts, it becomes necessary to coordinate the assessment of interventions and activities of the academic advising program in order to gather appropriate evidence of effectiveness.

Program evaluation has its roots in educational research (Wholey, Hatry & Newcomer, 2004; Banta et al., 2002). A rigorous assessment process includes most, if not all, of the components of a research design. There is a purpose, a grounding in theory and past research, questions to be answered, appropriate methods tied to relevant evidence, analysis of results, conclusions drawn, and most importantly, recommendations for future action and study. Boulmetis and Dutwin (2000) define evaluation as the "systematic process of collecting and analyzing evidence in order to determine whether and to what degree program objectives have been or are being achieved" as well as to provide appropriate evidence "in order to make a decision" (p. 4). Program assessment borrows process from social science research and further examines program and project objectives to determine whether they have been achieved, judges the worth of ongoing programs, decides upon the usefulness of new programs or projects, and so forth (Black & Kline, 2002). Both program assessment and social science research require data (evidence and information) to help answer questions. But the design and intent of program assessment most closely resembles action research through its attention to change and improvement (Johnson, 2008).

The greatest value of assessment is the symbiotic nature of knowledge and subsequent use; that is, understanding (knowing, not assuming) if the mission, goals, and objectives of the advising program are being fulfilled, and then actually using the results to improve the program (Peterson & Einarson, 2001). Valuable time, energy, and resources can be wasted without a clear articulation of the intentional components of the educational process, as well as a commitment to systematic gathering and reviewing of evidence. Breaking the assessment process into pieces makes the work manageable, but the identification of possible gaps in the evidence can be seen only through the lens of the bigger picture.

CRITICAL ELEMENTS OF AN ADVISING PROGRAM

Assessing outcomes at the program level requires a broad look at the multifaceted nature of the advising function. A good place to start is the Council for the Advancement of Standards (CAS, 2006) that were discussed in Chapter Fourteen. The standards define expectations unique to academic advising under the following thirteen areas:

1. Mission
2. Program
3. Leadership
4. Organization and Management
5. Human Resources
6. Financial Resources

7. Facilities, Technology, and Equipment

8. Legal Responsibilities

9. Equity and Access

10. Campus and External Relations

11. Diversity

12. Ethics

13. Assessment and Evaluation

Note that while there is a specific section for "assessment and evaluation" (as there is in most educational accountability documents), the only way the previous twelve areas can be examined for compliance is through a process of assessment. Unfortunately, most assessment initiatives falter under the weight of the task.

A separate, full review of the twelve components would require a significant commitment of resources (both human and fiscal), and should be undertaken on a periodic basis (i.e., CAS Self-Study). The on-going process of overseeing the most critical elements of an advising program is manageable under a systematic framework of gathering and reviewing evidence. It is also necessary to recognize the nature of the educational program delivery, both immediate and long-term. Attention to these areas is necessary to be able to focus the lens through which evidence is created, gathered, and examined.

Assessing Efficiency, Effectiveness, and Impact

Choice of evidence and use of results depend on the nature of the inquiry. Elements of program assessment must coincide with decisions for action for both process improvement (efficiency and effectiveness) and outcomes improvement (impact). Each is defined as a matter of degree, which forces the assessors to make meaning of the evidence.

Efficiency. Efficiency can be defined as "the degree to which a program or project has been productive in relationship to its resources" (Boulmetis & Dutwin, 2000, p. 3). This involves an analysis of the costs (dollars, people, time, facilities, materials, etc.) that are expended as part of a program in comparison to either their benefits or effectiveness. The CAS Standards for Advising (2006) provide some guidance for administrators to assign advisees (caseload), but the institution must make annual determinations of resource allocations for each advising unit or department. Efficiency measures are often used in assessment reports (number of contacts per semester per student, number of students seen per advisor, cost expended per student each year). Assessing efficiency takes into account the process of carrying out the program. The logistical nature of program delivery cannot be overlooked in an environment of scarce resources, but those pieces of data cannot be viewed in isolation.

So, two important questions to reflect on with regard to documenting efficiency might be: (1) How are the details of the program carried out? and (2) What are the pieces of evidence that make the most sense for the unit or department to determine efficiency?

Effectiveness. Effectiveness, then, relates to the goals of the program and the determination of the "degree to which [they] have been reached" (Boulmetis & Dutwin, 2000, p. 3). While it is optimal to plan a program with the desired end state in mind and only then deliver the curriculum (Huba & Freed, 2000), most programs are fully functioning at the time that program assessment planning takes place. Rare is the opportunity to plan for collection of assessment data prior to implementing the program, so it is necessary to consider the intent of the activities and interactions when attempting to determine their effectiveness. Articulating intended outcomes, even after strategies and interventions have been implemented, is one of the most important elements of program assessment (Angelo, 1999). Educators are most concerned with substantive changes in knowledge, attitudes, or skills on the part of the students (see Chapter Twenty-three).

Appropriate evidence should be considered to answer two questions related to effectiveness: (1) Did the students learn what they were supposed to learn (intellectual growth, ability to communicate effectively, etc.)? and (2) Did the students develop in the affective domain (motivation and focus on academic goals, etc.)?

A word of caution: measures of efficiency and measures of effectiveness are often viewed in isolation. That is, the extent to which results are examined requires a sense of context and an understanding of how the process of delivering the program (logistics) and intended outcomes (student success, for example) work together. Consider one of the most typical (not necessarily the best) effectiveness measure tools: satisfaction surveys. The survey results reveal that Advisor X is far and above the rest of the advisors in terms of student satisfaction. Her students love her and give her consistently high marks for her level of caring, helpfulness, and engagement. At the next staff meeting, the director compliments Advisor X in front of her peers, and suggests to the rest that they can all learn something from X and the way in which she interacts with her advisees. Advisor X's colleagues applaud politely and glance at each other. What they know that the director doesn't is that while Advisor X is spending 45 minutes with each student, the others are forced to move much too quickly through the 37 other students who are in the lobby waiting to be seen. Advisor X is effective, but not efficient. The rest of the staff is efficient, but not effective in the interventions necessary to promote a positive interaction between the student and the advisor. The relationship between the mechanisms of program delivery and the quality of the services often must be considered together.

Impact. Whether advisors' interventions with students occur during the students, first year at the institution or their last, the ultimate goal is that advising services had a positive effect on student success. To assess impact, then, the program must be examined for "the degree to which [it] resulted in changes" (Boulmetis & Dutwin, 2000, p. 3). Faculty and staff spend too little time on this aspect of program assessment. One reason is that change takes time, and data-gathering activities tend to stop too soon. There is a tendency to rationalize that there are too many variables at play and too many other parts of campus involved in the education of students to prove that the time spent with them made a difference, either good or bad.

The collaborative nature of the college experience is critical to the holistic approach to student learning and development (Bresciani, Zelna, & Anderson, 2004; Banta & Kuh, 1998). It also makes the assessment of long-term outcomes complex and challenging. Involving advisors in a thorough and reflective examination of the place of advising interventions in the work of the institution is important not only to the context of program assessment, but it may also promote a sense of professional belonging and connection. Three questions are suggested for reflection of impact: (1) What activities and services are specifically designed to have long-term impact on students (such as learning strategies for personal goal attainment) rather than to address immediate needs (such as clear a block on a class)? (2) Can these changes be accounted for, and is evidence needed to determine the impact of each program objective? and (3) Can changes be attributed to this program, or is collaboration required to integrate assessment activities with other programs on campus?

While many outcomes take time to be revealed, the evidence of potential impact may be seen at the time of intervention (Smith, Szelest, & Downey, 2004). For example, an often-used program objective is to create and promote lifelong learners. Technically, the final assessment activity for this goal must take place at the end of a long life, which is neither practical nor desirable for most individuals. But behaviors can be observed (and documented) that can give educators a glimpse into future actions by students. What is really meant by that objective is that students can be encouraged to develop strategies and dispositions to take responsibility for their own learning. Advisors know what that looks like: it is not only rewarding and important to see students become more motivated and willing to do things that promote success, such as articulate personal academic and developmental goals, seek out resources when they need help, and find ways to study more effectively. The extent to which long-term, sustained impact can be assessed in advisees starts with documentation of educationally purposeful behaviors.

CREATING (OR REFINING) AN ASSESSMENT PLAN AT THE PROGRAM LEVEL

The good news: if the advising program is up and running, then many of the necessary components, tools, and skills are already available to document and implement the assessment plan. The challenge is to bring colleagues together to find the pieces of the puzzle, define the edges, and put the picture together in a systematic process. Gaps in the picture will be revealed, of course, but the task is likely to be less daunting because the vision of the goal will be much clearer.

The Assessment Process

Although there are many visual depictions of the assessment process in the literature (for example, Maki, 2002; Black & Kline, 2002; Huba & Freed, 2000), most models capture the critical elements of assessment design, as well as the

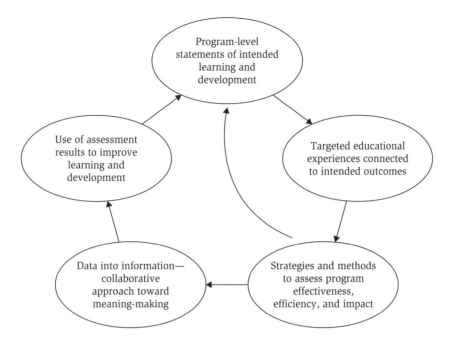

Figure 25.1. The Assessment Process Model.

points in the process for articulating and documenting learning and development. Terminology may be slightly different, but the concept of the circular nature of the process is typical (see Figure 25.1).

In addition, too much attention is often given to the tools and techniques for assessment without an examination of how the instruments best provide evidence for program improvement (Soundarajan, 2004). Assessing the full scope of a program is most effective when the process is viewed as an integrated curriculum, along with an understanding of the unique elements within the larger context. Administrators of academic advising programs should determine how best to involve staff in discovery and discourse throughout the process. Involvement of staff in the planning and development stage of an assessment plan leads to clearer definitions of terms to be used, collection of relevant evidence, and a stronger collaborative approach to using the data to make improvements. Each of the following critical elements has a literature base of its own, and it is intended to represent areas (and potential concerns) to be addressed when developing or revising a comprehensive assessment plan at the program level.

I. Intended Learning and Developmental Outcomes at the Program Level

A. Overview and description of individual intended outcomes as related to program goals, objectives, and intended outcomes.

1. Process for arriving at consensus—Use group decision-making techniques to articulate values, vision, goals, and intended outcomes.

2. Deal with bias—Have honest discussions with staff about the difference between assumptions based on intuition and systematic inquiry based on evidence.

3. Identify the connections—Often academic advising programs are connected to, or dependent on, intended outcomes of other departments or units (first-year students, major-declared and unde-clared or general students, upper-class students, major-based, etc.).

B. Initial decisions can now be made regarding appropriate methods, evidence, and criterion levels of performance of the articulated learning and developmental outcomes.

II. Instructional and Developmental Strategies

A. How is the program currently being delivered? Identify and document the intentional activities involving students.

B. Identify strategies for collecting this information from appropriate staff and faculty.

III. Strategies and Methods for Assessing Effectiveness, Efficiency, and Impact

A. Finalize the plan to gather data—Be intentional and realistic about strategies for collecting evidence for the different aspects of the program.

B. Strategies, questions, methods, and evidence—"How will you know it when you see it?" Consider the scope of data appropriate to academic advising outcomes (qualitative and quantitative types of evidence, direct and indirect measures).

1. Brainstorm how to get the data—What's already available? Who's already involved?

2. Generate data within the unit—Construct ways to aggregate data from the individual to the group level with a culture of intentionality designed to turn data into information; determine whether a sample of the population might be appropriate for a given topic.

3. Seek out and use institutional data—Enlist the assistance of insti-tutional research and assessment staff to help identify existing data relevant to program goals and outcomes.

IV. Processing the Results—Turning Data into Information

A. Determine who should be involved in the analysis of the evidence, and how often.

B. Document initial findings and emergent themes. What's the "story" to be told about the program overall?

C. Revisit criterion levels of performance—What's "acceptable" or "not acceptable" and why?

    D. What is known now that was only assumed before? What still needs more evidence? How should "surprising" results be handled?

    E. Document results and manage the data so it can be reviewed regularly.

V. Using the Results

    A. Who needs to have this information, for what purpose, and in what format?

    B. What's next? Document the process for planned changes and revisions to be made.

    C. Results can now be packaged for external accountability purposes as well. Determine additional venues for the results, such as brown-bag lunch sessions, institutional assessment workshops, and other public forums.

VI. Other Considerations for Program-Assessment Plans and Processes

    A. Find a way for the plan to become a dynamic, ongoing process as part of the academic advising unit.

    B. Promote and facilitate a "culture of curiosity" in the unit that leads to a "culture of evidence." What is discussed at staff meetings: program logistics or student outcomes? Are they proactive or reactive in nature?

    C. Determine the process for ongoing involvement. Who needs to be involved, how often (both formally and informally, both internal and external)?

    D. Schedule both special assessment activities (such as a CAS self-study) and regular program assessment processes. What needs to be monitored continually, and when should a more focused, deep approach be undertaken?

CONCLUSIONS

Assumptions are made about program effectiveness, efficiency, and impact, no matter what is currently known about the critical elements. An integrated, collaborative, intentional approach to unpacking program goals, intended outcomes, and results raises the level of understanding about the impact of academic advising strategies on student learning and development. This scaffolding effect, whereby a firmer knowledge base replaces previously held assumptions, results in a professional urgency that feeds the assessment process and brings meaning to the evidence.

Assessment plans and quality processes should be faculty and staff, program, and campus-driven (Huba & Freed, 2000). Pieces of the assessment puzzle are pulled together when intended, and actual outcomes are placed in context within the bigger picture of program goals and objectives that are articulated and valued by internal and external stakeholders. According to the CAS (2006) guidelines, the structure for program assessment should reveal:

1. Institutional culture that values involvement of all its members in decision-making—so program assessment requires involvement from all

2. Quality indicators that are determined by the institution—effective program assessment is an active, relevant process that makes a difference, so the evidence has to make sense for the faculty and staff within the program

3. Use of standards and guidelines in quality assurance—there are consistencies across academic-advising programs; good assessment practices lead to better accountability

4. Collection and analysis of data on institutional performance—multiple methods, types, and capture points provide evidence that allows advisers and administrators to know more and assume less about outcomes

5. Commitment to continuing improvement that presupposes freedom to explore and develop alternative directions for the future—closing the feedback loop, creating an assessment plan that provides a solid and consistent framework of intended outcomes, but also allows for innovation in "instructional" strategies to achieve higher levels of learning and development (CAS, 2006)

Properly administered program assessment offers faculty and staff the means to improve outcomes at all levels, provided they understand how to develop, refine, and use them. Data are turned into information with an implications approach to the goals and intended outcomes of the program. Distinctions can then be made between educationally based outcomes (student learning and development) and residual outcomes (retention and graduation rates) as indicators of student success.

In addition to providing a foundation for both process improvement and outcomes improvement, results can then be more easily compiled for accountability purposes, as well. A complete, relevant, and accessible repository of evidence is then available for multiple purposes and stakeholders. Further, finding ways to embed collection of evidence into the day-to-day operations of the department or unit provides advisers the opportunity to be more closely connected to the core values of the institution. As professionals, it is critical to know more and assume less about the effectiveness, efficiency, and impact of programs and services. And in this climate of diminishing resources, decisions to stay the course or revise strategies should be based on evidence rather than hunches, regardless of expertise and experience. Program-assessment processes should be transparent and all-revealing, involving advising administrators, advisors, and other staff, to promote a professional climate that moves the attitude from "it's not my job" to "it's everyone's job."

References

Angelo, T. (1999). Doing assessment as if learning matters most. *AAHE Bulletin, 51* (9), 3–6.

Banta, T. W., & Associates. (2002). *Building a scholarship of assessment.* San Francisco: Jossey-Bass.

Banta, T. W., & Kuh, G. D. (1998). A missing link in assessment: Collaboration between academic and student affairs professionals. *Change, 30,* 40–46.

Black, K. E., & Kline, K. A. (2002). Program review: A spectrum of perspectives and practices. In T. W. Banta (Ed.), *Building a scholarship of assessment* (pp. 223–239). San Francisco: Jossey-Bass.

Boulmetis, J., & Dutwin, P. (2000). *The ABCs of evaluation: Timeless techniques for program and project managers.* San Francisco: Jossey-Bass.

Bresciani, M. J., Zelna, C. L., & Anderson, J. A. (2004). *Assessing student learning and development: A handbook for practitioners.* Washington, DC: National Association of Student Personnel Administrators.

Council for the Advancement of Standards in Higher Education. (2006). *CAS professional standards for higher education* (6th ed.). Washington, DC: Author.

Huba, M. E., & Freed, J. E. (2000). *Learner-centered assessment on college campuses: Shifting the focus from teaching to learning.* Boston: Allyn & Bacon.

Johnson, A. (2008). *A short guide to action research* (3rd ed.). Boston: Allyn and Bacon.

Peterson, M., & Einarson, M. (2001). What are colleges doing about student assessment? *Journal of Higher Education, 72* (6), 629–639.

Smith, J. S., Szelest, B. P., & Downey, J. P. (2004). Implementing outcomes assessment in an academic affairs support unit. *Research in Higher Education, 45* (4), 405–427.

Soundarajan, N. (2004). Program assessment and program improvement: Closing the loop. *Assessment & Evaluation in Higher Education, 29* (5), 597–610.

Wholey, J. S., Hatry, H. P., & Newcomer, K. E. (Eds.). (2004). *Handbook of practical program evaluation.* San Francisco: Jossey-Bass.

CHAPTER TWENTY-SIX

Recognition and Reward for Academic Advising in Theory and in Practice

Jayne K. Drake

> *"The right results come from the*
> *right approach."*
> —*The Mental Game of Baseball*
> (Dorfman & Kuehl, 1989)

It seems simple enough. An advising center director, dean, provost, or president wishes to acknowledge the good work of professional and faculty advisors and so announces the creation of a tangible award for excellence in academic advising. It is a quick, easy, and powerful statement about the value the institution places on student success. It is an acknowledgment of the critically important work advisors assume in support of achieving the seamless navigation of students from freshman orientation through and beyond graduation. It signals the value an institution places on advising services, and it helps to improve overall delivery of such services by motivating advisors to reach a higher level of performance. An award, after all, reflects the continuing value that an institution places on advising and the contributions advisors make in support of student satisfaction and persistence. It seems simple enough.

Yet, establishing an advising award, while always laudable, does not automatically guarantee that it will achieve its intended purposes. A number of important elements factor into its development and implementation. Those who write about recognition and reward for outstanding performance tell us, for example, that an institution must be mindful to align its interest in rewarding performance to its own culture, mission, and values, and to ensure professional and faculty advisor buy-in or commitment by engaging them in the development, implementation, and ongoing assessment of the reward program. A reward strategy should be built within the larger context of a professional development and training program and a multistream assessment process for all advisors. Wes Habley (2007) underscores this important approach in "Putting Students First in the Campus Community: Pathway Five." "Without training there are no assurances that the appropriate tasks will be accomplished. Without evaluation, there are no assurances that the tasks are being done well, [and] without reward/recognition, there are no assurances that the tasks will continue to be done well" (p. 423). Building and supporting such a comprehensive approach provides a critical framework within which reward strategies can most productively and strategically be developed and sustained.

Particularly instructive and relevant to academic institutions or units interested in designing an awards program are the reward and recognition principles that characteristically operate in the corporate sector. These principles maintain that delivering quality services requires productive and engaged employees who have been provided the appropriate skill sets to meet the operational needs of the organization. They assert that a mix of both tangible and intangible rewards can legitimately be viewed as part of a coherent strategy within the mission of the organization, a strategy that acknowledges workforce similarities and differences, and one in which employees find value in the rewards and are active participants in determining the various reward benefits.

SIX REWARD PRINCIPLES

Reward theorists generally agree upon six principles that guide successful companies' business strategies. Organizational effectiveness, they suggest, relies on the human capital that people bring to the workplace—the skills and knowledge that help businesses improve their performance. What underpins these reward principles is a clear understanding of the needs of both the business and its employees, and from that understanding emerges shared values. Their applicability to the academy—and more particularly to academic advising settings—seems straightforward. Data from a recent survey of recognition and reward for advising, which appear later in this chapter, link these theoretical principles to actual current attitudes about and best practices in rewards for advising at institutions in the United States and Canada.

Reward Principle 1: Create a Positive and Natural Reward Experience

Leaders should take care to inform and educate employees about the reasons for and benefits of the reward plan, and engage them actively in its development, implementation, and ongoing assessment. Involving the people who potentially stand to gain from the reward ensures their understanding, acceptance, and commitment (Zingheim & Shuster, 2000, p. 6, among many others). An additional benefit from connecting stakeholders in this process is to provide a supportive culture that is in alignment with the company's overall strategic plan, mission, vision, and values. It is within this frame that the right design decisions can best be made (Lawler, 2000, p. 40).

Reward Principle 2: Align Rewards with Business Goals to Create a Win–Win Partnership

Both the management and employees need to gain something from the reward design. "To ensure a balanced win–win partnership, the company must provide clear direction, people must continue to add value, and the company must acknowledge their value with rewards" (Zingheim & Shuster, 2000, p. 7). Lawler (2000) also illustrates the importance of a win–win relationship in the context of what he describes as an Employability Contract:

If you:

- Develop the skills we need
- Apply them in ways that help the company succeed
- Behave consistently with our new values

We will provide:

- A challenging work environment
- Support your development [sic]
- Reward your contributions [sic]

And you'll be part of

- A high-performance organization (p. 62)

Through professional development, a supportive work environment, and a reward strategy that recognizes excellence, employees improve their skills and competencies, which, in turn, nurtures a culture of concern for personal growth and a workforce that is prepared and willing to meet the imperatives of the organization. In relating rewards to outstanding performance, companies cultivate the behaviors necessary to making the organization successful. Research study after research study concludes that pay, in particular, is a strong "source of motivation when it is tied to performance and seen as a form of recognition" (Lawler, 2000, p. 70).

Reward Principle 3: Extend People's "Line of Sight"

Reward theorists commonly use the expression "line of sight" to suggest that employees need to understand how what they do has an influence on other members of their organization. Zingheim and Shuster's (2000) advice is to move employees beyond a sometimes narrow view of their own work to see the larger influence they have on the organization and to "engage [them] in understanding how what they do affects the customer and how they can adapt to evolving customer needs" (p. 8). Motivation theorists also argue the critical importance of extending employees' line of sight as an important driver of behavior. This view leads to recognition that intrinsic rewards also serve a powerful function in building self-worth and personal satisfaction, and in improving performance. Especially when used in tandem with extrinsic rewards, intrinsic motivators are key elements in allowing an organization "to run the gauntlet of change, and come out stronger, more successful, and more competitive" (Flannery, Hofrichter, & Platten, 1996, p. 251).

Reward Principle 4: Integrate Rewards

It is important for organizations to determine—within the contexts of their missions, values, goals, and cultures—what sorts of rewards, both intrinsic and extrinsic, make sense for their workforces. Well-known management strategist W. Edwards Deming frequently made the point that all human beings inherently have intrinsic motivation, self-esteem, dignity, and eagerness to learn. However, he notes, "Our present system of management crushes that all out . . . by replacing it with extrinsic motivation, by constantly judging people" (1990, p. 39). While Deming was entirely correct in stressing that intrinsic motivators are strong elements in changing and supporting various behaviors, they are often, as Lawler and a number of other researchers point out, not sufficient to motivate all the behaviors needed in a successful organization, and "they fail to recognize that intrinsic rewards sometimes motivate the wrong behaviors" (p. 68).

Offering another layer of insight is expectancy theorist Victor Vroom (1964), who suggested that employee performance is predicated on personality, skills, knowledge, experience, and abilities. Vroom's point is that, even with differing sets of goals, employees can be motivated if they believe that:

- There is a positive correlation between effort and performance,
- Favorable performance will result in a desirable reward,
- The reward will satisfy an important need,
- The desire to satisfy the need is strong enough to make the effort worthwhile.

Reward Principle 5: Reward Individual Ongoing Value with Base Pay

This principle recommends using base pay as a reward strategy to emphasize the value an organization places on people performance—on the skills and competencies demonstrated by individuals to generate desired organizational outcomes, on employees' consistent performance over time, and on their value in the labor market. The key questions here are, of course, what constitutes an individual's value to the organization? And what are the appropriate pay thresholds for the top performers? It is a fact of life at many academic institutions across the country that professional advisors in particular often burn out all too quickly and leave because of weighty advising loads and the realization that there is little career advancement awaiting them. As a result, more and more institutional administrators are beginning to work with their Human Resources departments to create multilevel career advancement plans. In much the same way that faculty have a clear career ladder from Assistant, to Associate, and then to Full Professor, professional advisors can move through a level-based advising model in which they enter the college or university system in an entry-level position. With increasing experience and growing competencies, they move through higher levels to the position of Senior Advisor. The National Academic Advising Association's (NACADA's) Clearinghouse (n.d.) provides information on several institutions that use this classification construct, including Texas A&M, Iowa State University, University of California at Berkeley, and the University of Texas at San Antonio.

Reward Principle 6: Reward Results with Variable Pay

Advocates of merit-based pay argue that leaders can enhance the organization's success by developing pay systems that align employee's contributions to the organization's strategic goals. In short, merit pay rewards people for their performance. "Variable pay is best suited to reward results because it is agile, flexible, adaptable, responsive, and able to focus on key measures of success" (Zingheim & Shuster, 2000, p. 12). The effectiveness and impact of merit pay depends on having enough of it to differentiate among performance levels, as well as having an assessment model that adequately distinguishes the level and value of contributions to the organization's strategic goals. Lawler makes the point that even "small amounts of money can sometimes be important, particularly when the money is given in a way that involves recognition, goal achievement, and status" (p. 71).

Tangible Incentives and Intangible Recognition. The researchers who also focus on the value placed on tangible incentives and intangible recognition generally arrive at the conclusion that any such reward or recognition is made important by the way in which it is made public, whether it be by a news release, a reception, a formal dinner, or another gathering. Tangible or symbolic rewards especially are made more valuable by the frequency with which they are given. If awarded too frequently, they lose their value and status. If offered too infrequently, they appear to be unattainable and therefore have no significance as motivators or as emblems of achievement or excellence. The status that symbolic rewards carry is often marked by those who have received them in the past. The more respected and admired the recipients, the higher the value such rewards assume. For the reward to have its intended impact, it must also be meaningful in the culture. Selecting just the appropriate amount of money or the right plaque, trophy, or figurine can provide the intended high impact, high visibility, and high desirability. Finally, the process of selecting reward recipients must be credible and be conducted by respected members of the organization who have information on the performance and accomplishments of possible recipients (Lawler, 2000, p. 72).

Lawler points out that "the greatest amount of motivation is present when individuals are doing tasks that are intrinsically rewarding to them when they perform them well and that provide important financial and recognition rewards for performance . . . when individuals commit themselves to a goal, they become highly motivated to achieve it because their self-esteem and sense of self-worth get tied to accomplishing that goal" and "because a financial reward is tied to achieving it" (pp. 78–79).

From Theory to Practice. Habley (2007) makes the point that it is "incumbent upon institutional leaders to orchestrate a set of rewards, incentives, and recognitions, both tangible, and intangible, that encourage advisors to deliver quality advising" (p. 424). If institutional leaders hope to have their reward strategies motivate their advisors to meet certain goals and recognize them for achieving these goals, and if these leaders want to call attention to those who make a positive difference or celebrate the advisors' "value added" to the organization, they must determine what the advisors themselves value, take individual differences into account, and tailor a reward strategy accordingly. Sometimes people can be motivated by the opportunity to become the employee of the month, to get a letter of appreciation from their supervisor, or to receive a simple "thank you" (Lawler, 2000). There are many other "sources of fulfillment that contribute to employees' overall job satisfaction, such as learning, self-worth, pride, competence, and serving others" (Kouzes & Posner, 1995, p. 1). The point is that, to be a motivator, a reward or special recognition must be of particular desirability to the recipient.

Just how do these theoretical reward principles find practical application in advising settings?

How do institutions know which recognition and reward approaches will be most meaningful to their professional and faculty advisors? What precisely is the value advisors themselves place on various rewards, incentives, and recognitions?

SURVEY OF RECOGNITIONS AND REWARDS FOR ACADEMIC ADVISING

In June–July 2007, a survey was distributed to 8,769 NACADA members who were professional advisors, faculty advisors, or advising or university administrators, with a total of 1,969 respondents (22.5 percent of the total distribution list): 1,154 academic advisors, 99 faculty advisors, 344 advising administrators, 326 administrators with responsibilities over several areas, one of which is advising, 29 with institutional positions that support advising (registrars and admissions and financial aid counselors, for example), and 17 others affiliated with colleges or universities in positions other than those previously mentioned. The respondents represent 736 academic institutions across the United States and Canada (232 two-year, 235 four-year private, and 269 four-year public). The survey was designed to reflect the CAS Standards for Academic Advising (Council for the Advancement of Standards, 2005), which stresses the interrelatedness of the training, evaluation, and recognition and reward components in performance development. It moved from capturing basic demographic information on institutional types and sizes and on advisor types to a determination of current and best practices in the areas of professional development, evaluation, and recognition and reward strategies. And while the data presented here cannot be generalized to campuses nationally and are not, of course, representative of all advisors and advising administrators at all institutions, they do offer compelling snapshots of current advising issues, practices, and approaches. Posed as questions, the primary objectives were:

- What professional development, incentive, advisor evaluation, and recognition and reward options are currently used at institutions across the country?

- What is the level of importance and satisfaction with professional development, incentive, and recognition and rewards opportunities expressed by advisors?

Options Available to Professional Advisors for Training and Development

The first objective sought to determine what professional development and training options are currently available to professional and faculty advisors. The most frequently selected professional development opportunity for advisors was support for NACADA conference attendance, with 61 percent of respondents at two-year institutions, 57 percent of respondents at four-year private institutions, and 76 percent of respondents at four-year public institutions reporting this option. The second most frequently reported professional development opportunity open to advisors across all institutional types was regularly scheduled meetings on various advising issues, followed by a one-day, once-a-year advising workshop. Next, respondents at two-year public and private and four-year private institutions selected the advisor handbook as an important development and training tool.

When asked what professional development and training options not currently available would be most useful to them, professional and faculty advisors across all institutional types ranked as most important the tools they believe necessary in fulfilling their advising responsibilities: (1) an online advisor training manual, (2) an online advisor handbook, (3) an advisor handbook in hard copy, and (4) an advising newsletter. This information suggests that advisors want the training and other tools necessary to become better advisors and to ensure that they are guiding their students appropriately.

Importance of Incentives to Professional Advisors

Professional and faculty advisors were asked to select the incentives that encourage their participation in professional development opportunities. Advisors from all three types of institutions (two-year, four-year private, and four-year public) listed the same two responses as the most important incentives for encouraging professional development: 1) to assist students better, and 2) to cultivate their own professional and personal growth.

How do professional and faculty advisors rate their level of satisfaction with the incentives available to them? As might be predicted (and in direct correlation with the incentives available to them), advisors at all institutional types rated their highest levels of satisfaction with the incentives that are associated with "assisting students" and from those related to their "own professional and personal growth." Of least importance to advisors as an incentive to participate in professional development activities was any personal prestige or recognition that might accrue from their participation.

How Are Advisors Evaluated?

The majority of advisors are evaluated formally. Fifty-five percent of respondents at two-year colleges, 59 percent at four-year private, and 70 percent at four-year public institutions reported having some methods for evaluating individual advisor performance. The top methods in rank order are 1) Supervisor evaluation, 2) Continuing students' survey, 3) Individual student evaluation forms, and 4) Student exit survey at graduation. The least commonly employed options for evaluation advisor performance were alumni letters and other letters of support. The survey made no attempt to gather data on how frequently or consistently such methods were used as advisor evaluation tools.

Options Available to Professional Advisors for Recognition and Rewards

Professional advisors and administrators who oversee advising operations were then asked to indicate the recognition and reward options currently available to advisors.

As Table 26.1 indicates, the most frequently listed option available to professional advisors at all three institutional types was support for professional activities, such as NACADA membership or conference registration, with 34 percent of respondents at two-year institutions, 35 percent of respondents at four-year private institutions, and 44 percent of respondents at four-year public institutions indicating this option. Merit pay, an annual awards event, cash awards, and plaques or trophies trailed in distant second, third, fourth, and fifth positions. Twenty-nine percent of the 1,693 people who responded to this question reported that their institution offers no recognition or rewards to professional advisors. Broken down by institutional type, 43 percent of two-year, 38 percent of four-year private institutions, and 22 percent of the four-year public institutions have no recognition or reward strategies for their professional advisors. To state this information more positively—57 percent of two-year, 62 percent of four-year privates, and 78 percent of four-year public institutions do offer some form of recognition and reward for excellence in advising.

Importance of Rewards and Incentives to Professional Advisors

Professional advisors were then asked to rank how important the various recognition and reward options are to them. Their responses are unequivocal.

Table 26.2 clearly demonstrates that professional advisors most value support for professional activities such as NACADA membership and conference registration, with

Table 26.1. What strategies are currently employed in your unit/at your institution to recognize and reward PROFESSIONAL ADVISORS for academic advising? (Check ALL that apply.)

Professional advisors (n = 1,154), advising administrators (n = 297), or administrators with responsibilities over several areas (n = 242)

Rewards and Recognitions		Percentage of Responses		
	Total	Two-Year Public or Private College	Four-Year Private College or University	Four-Year Public College or University
Number responding	1693	301	330	1062
Professional support (e.g., NACADA)	40%	34%	35%	44%
None	29%	43%	38%	22%
Merit	24%	9%	22%	29%
An annual awards breakfast/lunch/ dinner/reception	24%	12%	14%	30%
Cash award	20%	4%	8%	28%
Plaque or trophy	19%	6%	7%	26%
Thank you letter	14%	13%	16%	14%
Certificate of appreciation	14%	11%	11%	16%
Other	11%	14%	14%	10%
News release	7%	4%	2%	10%
Secretarial support	7%	7%	7%	7%
Preferential parking	1%	0%	1%	1%

no significant differences among professional advisors' responses from two-year, four-year private, and four-year public institutions. Seventy-four percent of respondents consider support for professional development activities of most value to them; merit trailed a distant second at 56 percent, and one-time cash award at 45 percent. Interestingly, this information runs counter to prevailing notions that professional advisors' preferred rewards for excellence in advising are merit money and cash awards. Of little importance to professional advisors are certificates of appreciation, plaques, trophies, news releases, and preferential parking—the forms of recognition that carry no monetary value.

Options Available to Faculty Advisors for Recognition and Rewards

Faculty advisors and advising administrators were also asked to select the recognition and reward options currently available to faculty. The list of options

Table 26.2. As a PROFESSIONAL ADVISOR, how important are the following rewards and recognition to you?

Professional Advisors (n = 1,154)
Items ranked from high to low were
(4 = very important, 3 = moderately important, 2 = somewhat important, 1 = not important)

Rewards and Recognitions	Item Mean	Percentage of Responses			
		Very Important	Moderately Important	Somewhat Important	Not Important
Professional Support (e.g., NACADA)	3.63	74%	18%	5%	3%
Merit	3.37	56%	29%	11%	4%
Cash award	3.06	45%	27%	16%	12%
Secretarial support	2.71	30%	30%	21%	20%
Thank you letter	2.70	24%	35%	27%	13%
An annual awards breakfast/lunch/ dinner/reception	2.37	15%	31%	31%	23%
Certificate of appreciation	2.36	15%	30%	30%	25%
Plaque or trophy	2.12	12%	24%	28%	36%
News release	2.01	8%	23%	31%	38%
Preferential parking	1.89	12%	14%	23%	51%

remained the same as those for professional advisors, with one addition: consideration for promotion and tenure.

As Table 26.3 illustrates, at two-year institutions, the most frequently reported options are a thank you letter (20 percent), monetary support for professional-development activities (18 percent), certificate of appreciation (14 percent), an annual awards breakfast/lunch/dinner/reception (11 percent), and merit pay (11 percent), with certificates of appreciation, news releases, secretarial support, and preferential parking lagging farther behind.

At four-year private institutions, 34 percent offer consideration for promotion and tenure, 27 percent offer a thank you letter, an annual awards breakfast/lunch/dinner/reception comes in at 17 percent, and merit at 16 percent. Monetary support for professional-development activities came in at 12 percent. Faculty advisors at four-year private institutions reported little use of news releases (6 percent), plaques and trophies (12 percent), secretarial support (3 percent), and preferential parking (1 percent) but more frequent use of promotion and tenure considerations (34 percent).

Faculty advisors at four-year public institutions reported slightly higher uses of cash awards (29 percent), plaques or trophies (27 percent), and an

Table 26.3. What strategies are currently employed in your unit/at your institution to recognize and reward FACULTY ADVISORS for academic advising? (Check ALL that apply.)

Faculty advisors (n = 99), advising administrators (n = 331), or administrators with responsibilities over several areas (n = 249)

	Percentage of Responses			
Rewards and Recognitions	Total	Two-Year Public or Private College	Four-Year Private College or University	Four-Year Public College or University
Number responding	679	152	180	347
None	30%	40%	32%	24%
Considerations for promotion and tenure	24%	13%	34%	25%
Thank you letter	21%	20%	27%	18%
Cash award	20%	6%	14%	29%
An annual awards breakfast/ lunch/dinner/reception	19%	11%	17%	24%
Plaque or trophy	18%	8%	12%	27%
Professional support (e.g., NACADA)	17%	18%	12%	18%
Other	16%	16%	16%	16%
Merit	15%	11%	16%	17%
Certificate of appreciation	13%	14%	11%	14%
News release	7%	3%	6%	9%
Secretarial support	5%	5%	3%	6%
Preferential parking	1%	0%	1%	1%

annual awards breakfast/lunch/dinner/reception (24 percent)—monetary support for professional activities came in at a more distant 18 percent. Responses vary by institutional type: 40 percent of two-year institutions, 32 percent of four-year private institutions, and 24 percent of four-year public institutions offer no recognition or reward strategies for faculty advisors. To present this information in a more positive light—60 percent of two-year, 68 percent of four-year private, and 76 percent of four-year public institutions offer some means of recognizing and rewarding excellence in faculty advising.

Faculty advisors were also asked to rank the importance of the various rewards and recognition options available to them. Because those represented in Table 26.4 are faculty advisors who are members of NACADA, it would be natural to assume that they place a higher value on professional development opportunities. Interestingly, their responses are both resounding and

Table 26.4. As a FACULTY ADVISOR, how important are the following rewards and recognition to you?

Faculty Advisors (n = 99)
Items ranked from high to low were
(4 = very important, 3 = moderately important, 2 = somewhat important, 1 = not important)

Rewards and Recognitions		Percentage of Responses			
	Item Mean	Very Important	Moderately Important	Somewhat Important	Not Important
Professional support (e.g., NACADA)	3.47	63%	24%	9%	3%
Consideration for promotion and tenure	3.23	55%	24%	9%	12%
Merit	3.17	48%	33%	9%	10%
Cash award	2091	37%	31%	17%	15%
Secretarial support	2.71	28%	34%	19%	19%
Thank you letter	2.57	22%	31%	31%	17%
Certificate of appreciation	2.24	15%	22%	34%	28%
An annual awards breakfast/lunch/ dinner/reception	2.17	12%	27%	28%	34%
Plaque or trophy	2.00	8%	21%	32%	38%
News release	1.89	7%	20%	28%	45%
Preferential parking	1.87	10%	19%	19%	52%

unambiguous. More than cash awards, more than merit pay, and more than consideration for promotion and tenure, these faculty advisors most value support for professional activities.

Support for professional activities was selected as very important or moderately important by 87 percent of the respondents. Merit pay ranks in second place, with 81 percent of the faculty advisors considering it as very important or moderately important. The value that faculty advisors place on consideration for promotion and tenure ranks in a close third place, with 79 percent of respondents rating it as very important or moderately important. Of the monetary options available to faculty advisors, a cash award came in a more distant fourth place, with 68 percent of faculty rating it as very important or moderately important. Of least importance to faculty advisors (as well as to professional advisors) are the certificates of appreciation, an awards breakfast/lunch/dinner/reception, a plaque or trophy, news release, and preferential parking. Although faculty completing this survey are members of

NACADA, these respondents provide evidence of a shift from the attitudes faculty held about remunerative reward systems as recently as the 1990s:

> [The] decline in faculty acceptance of evaluation and reward systems became dramatic during the "assessment decade" 1990s when the preponderance of assessment efforts shifted from process (formative) to outcomes (summative). . . . This was also reflected in a shift in reward systems from those that promoted individual development and intrinsic motivation to teach and advise . . . to those that served as extrinsic rewards in a comparative competition (such as a decision on tenure, and winning or not winning an Outstanding Advisor Award). (McGillin, 2003, p. 96)

As reward and motivation theorists remind us, for any reward or recognition system to achieve its intended purpose, it must have value to the potential recipients. Clearly, what the faculty advisors who responded to this survey value most highly are the professional development opportunities that enable them to grow and develop as advisors in order to meet their students' advising needs more effectively.

The most compelling messages for institutional leaders to take away from the quantitative section of this survey are: (1) a vast majority of both professional and faculty advisors find a high level of personal satisfaction in assisting their students and becoming better at doing so; (2) they appreciate opportunities to cultivate their own professional and personal growth; (3) they particularly value support for professional-development activities (such as NACADA conference attendance)—this is money well spent; (4) of least importance to advisors—although still appreciated—are the nonmonetary forms of recognition such as news releases, plaques, certificates of appreciation, and awards receptions.

The survey also posed two open-ended questions, the first of which was: What one change would help your unit or your institution's recognition and reward of advising? A number of important themes emerged from the responses:

- Funding to support professional development activities:
  - Ability to offer monetary support and time off for professional development activities such as conference registration, etc. to advising conferences and Webinars.
  - Monetary and administrative support for attendance at, and participation in, outside advising networking and professional development meetings and events.
- Constructing a career ladder (or level-based salaries) for professional advisors:
  - A career ladder for professional full-time advisors. Promotion up the ladder would be dependent upon both merit (performance) and time in position. Similar to faculty-rank system.
  - Career pathway and compensation initiative for advisors for advancement; currently, the only way to significantly increase salary beyond

the pittance of 2.5percent annual wage increase is to "jump ship" and renegotiate in another unit.

- The need for administrators to understand and value advisors and advising:

  - Top administrators need to take a sincere interest in advising and attend a conference or at least a Webinar . . . to better understand our purpose and value (beyond "making students happy").

  - Recognition and acknowledgment of the importance of advisors and the advising process in the goals and mission of the university. This needs to come from the Provost and the College Dean level.

- The need for institutional respect of advisors:

  - Respect for advising as an integral part of the educational process could be demonstrated by acknowledging advisors as educators. . . . Over 89 percent of [our] advisors have a master's degree and many have their doctorates.

  - Just simply acknowledging the reality and value of our work with students, the challenges, listen to us, recognize our efforts, and thank us for our service above and beyond the call of duty.

Other refrains in response to this question included: (1) counting advising as part of teaching and acknowledging it as such in the merit, promotion, and tenure process; (2) offering variable rewards according to individual advisor's interests and needs; (3) developing a centrally administered university-wide evaluation instrument for all advisors, as well as student-satisfaction surveys; (4) constructing course release and overload pay programs for faculty advisors; (5) creating an advising mission statement as useful in giving advising the recognition it deserves; (6) making mandatory more on-campus professional development opportunities; and (7) asking administrators to acknowledge the importance of advising in a student's overall academic success by saying "thank you" with a simple handshake every once in a while.

The second open-ended question asked was: What one recognition and reward strategy not accounted for in this survey has worked well in your unit or at your institution? A number of respondents lamented that their institutions offer no recognition or rewards whatsoever. One institutional administrator's comments reflect those of several other respondents: "I do not believe in reward systems for doing what is expected as part of our job. Regular pay raises are expected for those who are performing well and meeting their goals." However, many hundreds more respondents reported strategies that often depend on little more than the good will and ingenuity of the giver and reflect the theorists' interests in designing a recognition structure appropriate to each situation:

- Vacation and work hour flexibility (flex time). One respondent said it best: "Giving free vacation days for recognition. People like money, but a day off is priceless!"

- Comp time for advisors who put in the extra hours during orientation and registration periods.

- Recognizing advisors during halftime at football and basketball games (this strategy is particularly appreciated at schools in which these sports, as one respondent put it, "reign supreme").

- Acknowledging advising award winners at graduation and convocation ceremonies.

- Establishing an "Advisors Wall of Fame" in a prominent location on campus—the student center, for example.

- Gift certificates donated by local restaurants and companies as thanks for a job well done.

- One advising administrator, whom we can all appreciate, wrote: "I take my own staff to lunch, send them for massages at 4 P.M. twice a year, we have team building every Friday afternoon during the summer, I respect, try to understand, and love them."

- Lots of positive verbal and written reinforcement from colleagues, administrators, and, most importantly, from students.

- Personal satisfaction and pride—those sometimes elusive intrinsic rewards—that come from the knowledge that advisors have had a positive effect on students' college experiences. This is the most valued of all rewards.

What conclusions can be drawn from both the reward and motivation theorists and the survey on academic advising? That for an advising reward or recognition to be effective, it must be relevant, affordable, and timely. It should represent the values, mission, and culture of the institution, involve employees in its development and implementation, be sincerely given, and serve as a motivator to others. It can be a handshake, a verbal or literal pat on the back, a public letter of appreciation, or some other form of celebratory acknowledgment. And what, more generally, might administrators do to cultivate a positive work environment and to show people just how much they count in the institution? They should take care to provide challenging and engaging work, opportunities to learn and advance, consistent, straightforward two-way communication, opportunities for employees to have some control over their work lives, make sure employees know that their work does make a difference, and offer rewards and recognition for outstanding performance.

The survey indicated that there is important work still to be done. While the percentage of institutions offering some sort of recognition or reward for academic advising is climbing quickly (with nearly 80 percent of respondents at four-year public institutions reporting some recognition or reward, for example), many advisors express concern at the lack of appreciation or attention from their institutional administrators. A substantial number of survey responses echo the sentiments expressed in the following comments:

"Academic advising is not really valued. The general impression here is that anyone can do this job." And, "We do not have any recognition and reward strategy set in place, so any improvement would be great."

This survey sounds some very positive notes about advisors and advising. Hundreds of colleges and universities recognize (or are coming to recognize), value, and acknowledge the important role advisors play in student success and persistence. Both professional and faculty advisors report that they want to do a better job of assisting students and are grateful for—more than a cash award or merit pay or a plaque or trophy or an awards luncheon—(1) support to participate in professional enrichment opportunities such as NACADA's annual or regional conferences, and (2) the tools—such as an advising handbook or an advising training manual—to perform their advising roles more effectively. Money allocated to such opportunities is a sound institutional investment because it ensures an engaged, educated, and motivated advising staff, who, all the while, strive to improve students' satisfaction with their college experience. Advisors also value and express a high level of satisfaction with the intrinsic rewards that come from seeing their advisees grow and flourish. It is an axiom among reward, motivation, and expectancy theorists that people, after all, work for more than money. Two survey respondents reflect this understanding well. "I feel I get the respect, recognition, and appreciation for this work, its importance and value for the institution and students." And "A simple 'thank you' and a smile or hug from my students is reward enough for me."

Note: Special acknowledgments to Dr. James Degnan, Director of Temple University's Research and Measurement Center, for his assistance in developing the Survey of Recognitions and Rewards for Academic Advising, in compiling and tabulating the data, and, along with Dr. Joseph Ducette, Temple Professor of Educational Psychology, in suggesting words.

References

Council for the Advancement of Standards (CAS). (2005). Academic advising: CAS standards and guidelines. Retrieved September 14, 2007, from http://www.nacada.ksu.edu/Clearinghouse/Research_Related/CASStandardsForAdvising.pdf

Deming, W. E. (1990, June 4). Deming's demons: The management guru thinks U.S. corporations are crushing their worker incentives. *Wall Street Journal,* p. 39.

Dorfman, H. A., & Kuehl, K. (1989). *The mental game of baseball: A guide to peak performance.* South Bend, IN: Diamond Communications.

Flannery, T. P., Hofrichter, D. A., & Platten, P. E. (1996). *People, performance, and pay: Dynamic compensation for changing organizations.* New York: The Free Press.

Habley, W. R. (2007). Putting students first in the campus community: Pathway five. In G. L. Kramer (Ed.), *Fostering student success in the campus community* (pp. 407–431). San Francisco: Jossey-Bass.

Kouzes, J. M., & Posner, B. N. (1995). *The leadership challenge: How to keep getting extraordinary things done in organizations.* San Francisco: Jossey-Bass.

Lawler, E. E., III. (2000). *Rewarding excellence: Pay strategies for the new economy*. San Francisco: Jossey-Bass.

McGillin, V. A. (2003). The role of evaluation and reward in faculty advising. In G. L. Kramer (Ed.), *Faculty advising examined*. Bolton, MA: Anker.

NACADA Clearinghouse. (n.d.). Advising issues and resources. Retrieved December 28, 2007, from http://www.nacada.ksu.edu/Clearinghouse/Links/Professional.htm#levels

Vroom, V. H. (1964). *Work and motivation*. New York: Wiley.

Zingheim, P. K., & Schuster, J. R. (2000). *Pay people right: Breakthrough strategies to create great companies*. San Francisco: Jossey-Bass.

PART FIVE

PERSPECTIVES ON ADVISING

Thomas J. Grites

INTRODUCTION

This section of the *Handbook* provides a variety of approaches and programs that facilitate good academic advising practices among public and private two-year and four-year institutions. One element for success that appears throughout these administrative perspectives is clearly that of campus collaboration. In addition, the editors have attempted to look beyond the horizon to forecast potential issues, concerns, and even remedies for what will shape the future of academic advising.

In Chapter Twenty-seven James Bultman describes the development of a successful faculty-based advising program at Hope College. The program emphasizes liberal arts values and skills, initially delivered through first-year seminars and culminating in senior seminars. Faye Vowell emphasizes the collaboration process among academic, student, and business affairs units of the four-year public institution to foster an overall learning environment. She extends the "advisor" role beyond academic matters to student clubs and organizations, career services, the registrar, and supervisors of student employees, all of which result in intentional learning interactions.

Jocelyn Harney reminds us of the mission and purpose of community colleges, especially as they serve a large diversity of students through open-door opportunities. She notes the special skills required of academic advisors in this environment, which is also under more scrutiny to demonstrate specific outcomes for local employers, for four-year institutions, and for local legislators. John Smarrelli and Susan Ames reinforce the collaborative efforts and adaptive (ameba-like) environment necessary in the small, private, liberal arts institution. They provide ten approaches to strengthen and integrate the process of academic advising on such campuses.

The authors in Chapter Twenty-eight provide the practical and operational aspects of managing advising programs that result in successful students and staff. Kathy Davis addresses a variety of campus-wide concerns likely to exist in public four-year institutions. She describes the critical elements in leading an effective advising office while also trying to maintain student contact, generate faculty support, and develop advising resources.

Dick Vallandingham reinforces the unique mission and wide diversity represented in two-year colleges. He addresses these characteristics through an analysis of the structure and delivery of academic advising services in this special environment. Philip Christman describes the multiple roles, and sometimes multiple reporting lines, that an academic advising administrator might face in a small private institution. He notes the knowledge base and "family" approach often required in such institutions. He also cautions all academic advisors about the potential for burning out when so many roles and responsibilities are undertaken.

Finally, in Chapter Twenty-nine the editors identify a number of challenges that higher education itself will face in the future. In addition, they note how the recent trends in the growing diversity of students and in their economic and educational planning practices will likely place new demands on academic advisors. They also identify potential ways to address the challenges at the macro (field of advising), the micro (institutional), and the individual advisor levels.

CHAPTER TWENTY-SEVEN

Campus Administrator Perspectives on Advising

PRESIDENT

James E. Bultman

Authors of other chapters have written about the theory and practice of academic advising. This perspective uses a case-study approach and examines academic advising in the specific context of Hope College, where an effective model of academic advising has been enthusiastically accepted.

Academic Advising at Hope College

Hope College in Holland, Michigan, is a distinguished four-year, liberal arts, undergraduate college chartered in 1866 and continuously affiliated with the Reformed Church in America. The curriculum offers a variety of courses in eighty-nine majors leading to a Bachelor of Arts, Bachelor of Music, Bachelor of Science, or Bachelor of Science in Nursing degree. During the 2007–2008 school year, Hope had 3,226 students from forty-five states and territories and thirty-one foreign countries.

History. Prior to 1977, all faculty were advisors for first- and second-year students, as well as for majors in their departments. Entering first-year students were assigned advisors based on the academic interest listed on their application. The number of advisees assigned to faculty could range from one to twenty. New students were registered for fall classes when they arrived on campus, with advisors providing guidance.

In 1977, a task force on academic advising created by the Academic Affairs Board recommended that thirty faculty members be selected each year by the registrar to serve as advisors to twenty new students each, that a core group of sixty faculty serve as advisors to new students, with new advisees assigned in alternate years, and that new students be registered by mail in the summer before their arrival. Each faculty advisor was given a budget of $200 to facilitate meeting their advisees informally over dinner, pizza, or coffee.

In 1987, the position of director of academic advising was created and filled by an adjunct faculty member who had served as an advisor and continued to teach. The director reports to the dean for academic services.

In 1998, as part of a revision of the general education curriculum, two-credit interdisciplinary seminars with an academic focus were required of first-year students in the fall semester. These are taught by faculty who also serve as advisors to the twenty seminar students. Declared majors have consistently been advised by faculty in their major departments and assigned by the department chair.

Until 1987, the registrar conducted advising workshops for faculty, typically before the start of the academic year. Since the appointment of the director of academic advising, the director has offered workshops and developed advising handbooks for faculty, for students, and for families of students. The director has attended department meetings to discuss advising issues and meets with new advisors. First-year seminar faculty members attend a summer workshop, part of which is devoted to advising issues. First-year faculty members do not serve as advisors, since teaching is their primary focus.

As is evident in this brief history, recognition of the importance of academic advising has grown at Hope. The college has moved from believing that all faculty should serve as advisors to new students to selecting faculty who are especially adept at connecting with students and working with them to enhance their skills. Hope College has also recognized that establishing relationships with advisees takes time: seeing students during orientation, meeting them for coffee or pizza at midterms, and being available for other meetings are not sufficient. Connecting academic advising with first-year seminars gives faculty and their students rich opportunities. Each comes to know the other well since seminars are limited to twenty students and meet for two fifty-minute classes throughout the semester. Further, the college has recognized the importance of academic advising and the time and effort needed to advise first-year students well by awarding four teaching credits to faculty who teach these two-credit seminars.

Purpose. Academic advising is an integral part of the mission of Hope College. A substantial number of credits (50 of the 126 required) are in general education core classes. Advisors are the embodiment of Hope's curriculum. "Perhaps the most urgent reform on most campuses in improving general education involves academic advising. To have programs and courses become coherent and significant to students requires adequate advising" (Task Group on General Education, 1988, p. 43). Academic advising at Hope College offers opportunities to embody the following liberal arts values.

Engaging actively. A strong liberal arts program demands engagement. Rather than simply memorizing or absorbing vast amounts of information, students are expected to develop skills of analysis, synthesis, interpretation, and integration. Through practice, they grow in their ability to communicate effectively in writing and speech. Academic advising lays the groundwork for the development of the above skill sets in students. Far from being nonvocational, such liberal arts skills are essential for the twenty-first century. When advisors listen to advisees' aspirations, ask them to set goals for the semester or year—which are not just goals for grades, but learning-oriented goals—and discuss their progress toward these goals, they encourage active and intentional involvement.

Reflecting critically. Through the liberal arts, as well as through academic advising, assumptions are scrutinized, discernment enhanced, and options considered. Students are expected to think. Certainly, advisors are expected to provide answers, but when they ask questions, advisors lay the groundwork for essential skills. "Graduating seniors report that certain kinds of advising, often described as asking unexpected questions, were critical for their success" (Light, 2001, p. 81). The art of asking the right questions also encourages students to think. Academic advising and the liberal arts foster habits of mind, which encourage lifelong learning and engagement with real-world questions. Through advising relationships, students can gain understanding and practice in "higher-order thinking skills that involve making decisions in situations of uncertainty and ambiguity" (Hemwall & Trachte, 2003, 15).

Forging connections. A hallmark of the liberal arts and of academic advising is connection. Students well-grounded in the liberal arts seek integration as well as application of what they are learning. Similarly, academic advising stresses making connections between and among classes and out-of-class experiences, among on-campus and off-campus resources, and between the students they are now and who they expect to become. Academic advisors ask thought-provoking questions, send their advisees to consult with others, and encourage advisees to look for connections between what they are learning and real-life issues. Also crucial to forging these campus connections is the prior ability of the advisor to establish a relationship—perhaps more appropriately, an investment—with each advisee.

Discerning vocation. Neither the liberal arts nor academic advising is an end in itself. Each beckons beyond itself and encourages consideration of important life questions, such as "Who am I? What are my convictions? What do I value? Where are my gifts? How do I live my vocation?" Academic advising encourages students to engage with these larger questions that they will have to ask and answer now and in the future as they make decisions.

In addition to providing the opportunity for students to embody the liberal arts values identified above, advising provides the opportunity to bring the mission statement from catalogue copy into the real world. Most students come to college because they want to earn a degree, which is a worthwhile goal. The mission statements of colleges, however, talk about very different goals for a liberal arts education, which we expect our advisees to understand. Yet, when asked, most students, even those at liberal arts colleges, were confused about what "liberal education" and "the liberal arts" involved (Humphreys & Davenport, 2005). Academic advisors can use the college mission statement to help students understand the purposes and values the college espouses. Can we expect that students will get the most from their education if we don't encourage them to consider the goals their college has set for their learning? Academic advising offers "perhaps the best opportunity for helping our students become more intentional about their own educations, as well as for helping them recognize the value of the liberal learning outcomes we seek to advance" (Laff, 2006, p. 36).

Advising also enables an explanation of "the logic of the curriculum" (Lowenstein, 2000). Faculty are in an ideal position to talk with students about the assumptions that support the curriculum and to explain not just the "what" but the "why" of the curriculum. Advising can be so much more than mere course selection; it is about making sense out of the curriculum—that is, to see its interconnections and the potential development of important skill sets that will serve students for an entire lifetime. This emphasis has had an unexpected but positive outcome: as more faculty teach and advise in the first-year seminar program and talk with students about the logic of the curriculum, they recognize the importance of emphasizing to students in the disciplinary courses they teach how their courses contribute to the liberal arts and how their disciplinary courses might connect with other courses required for general education. Making these connections more evident helps students and faculty see the coherence of the curriculum and helps requirements become more meaningful to students and less as obstacles to "get out of the way."

Invariably, students want to take courses that seem to have immediate applicability for their vocational or academic goals. Yet, student feedback affirms that explorations of academic material in areas that seem far removed from students' current goals or comfort levels often provide the best opportunities for stretching and challenging experiences that open new doors of interest and fulfillment. A teachable moment exists when advisors are able to encourage exploration and explain why the breadth of coursework in a liberal arts curriculum is enriching for future endeavors. On more than a few occasions, this interaction has provided the catalyst for students to abandon fields of expectation and pursue options that bring real fulfillment and enthusiastic contributions to society.

Challenges and Opportunities. When faculty view academic advising as a liberal arts skill, it is easier for them to understand its importance and to consider its relevance to their teaching and mentoring. Connecting advising for first-year students with their first-year seminars has enabled us to embed advising in an academic setting. Incoming students are asked during the summer to share what they plan to accomplish during their undergraduate education and to tell their advisor what skills they will work hardest to improve. This information provides a base for further discussion in advising interactions. A midsemester questionnaire encourages similar reflection.

During their first-year seminar, all students read Hope College's Philosophy of Education and write a three-page reflection exploring their personal goals, comparing their goals with the goals Hope College has set, or addressing the parts of this philosophy that are most important to them. The specific shape the essay takes is determined by the professor, but all essays are archived electronically; students will reread their first-year reflections during their required senior seminars and write a response. This assignment was piloted in five first-year seminars in 2005, and professors were delighted with students' responses; it became part of the first-year seminar curriculum in 2006. Beginning in 2010, during their senior seminar, seniors will reread the essays they wrote in their first-year seminar and reflect on their growth and development and anticipated deep understanding of the liberal arts. By embedding such activities in students' first semester on campus, we hope to make clear that advising is integral to an education at Hope College.

Academic advising cannot reach its potential if faculty advisors are expected to track degree progress. Hope has invested considerable resources in a degree-evaluation program to which students have access electronically. Advisors still must answer questions about requirements, of course, but no longer must they track degree progress or help students understand which classes meet requirements. Instead, they can talk about the philosophy behind the requirements and the connections among the courses. In addition, an advising handbook for students and another for faculty is updated annually.

Considering academic advising a liberal arts skill frees faculty from having to "know it all." Instead, faculty encourage their advisees to consult others, both on and off campus. At Hope, referrals might be to the CrossRoads Project, which is a center funded by the Lilly Endowment, Inc., that offers a series of opportunities for students to explore the interrelationships among faith, career, calling, and life; to the Center for Faithful Leadership; to Career Services; or to a host of other helpful centers.

Liberal arts skills are both practical and necessary for the twenty-first century, and few experiences support this notion more powerfully than internships. Slightly more than 50 percent of Hope students have at least one credit or noncredit internship before they graduate, in off-campus programs in Chicago, Philadelphia, New York, and Washington, DC, as well as in local placements. These internships help students make connections between classwork and the real world and enable them to identify skills they need to enhance, while providing opportunities to put to use the skills and habits of mind developed in their liberal arts education.

Conclusion

Every college president is interested in an effective advising system. It has major implications for student (and family) satisfaction, retention, and graduation. In an age of heightened expectations of the value received for the investment made, it is even more important that institutions deliver excellence in advising.

It is the right thing to do and it is time-intensive and, therefore, costly. Although most chief executive officers will not be intimately involved in the day-to-day advising system, it is crucial that they amplify its importance, support it with the necessary resources including time allowances, and recognize faculty and staff efforts through the college's reward system.

Advising is about coherence, that is, of making the parts whole. Ideally, we desire a synergistic relationship in which the whole is greater than the sum of the individual parts. When this exists we have achieved effective academic advising, which enhances retention, helps to ensure academic success, and overall makes a difference in students' lives. Students and parents expect and appreciate this; institutions should recognize and reward those who do it well.

CHIEF ACADEMIC OFFICER—FOUR-YEAR PUBLIC

Faye N. Vowell

In the June 2007 issue of *Academic Advising Today*, Patrick Terenzini discusses the need to think systemically about creating the best environment in which to enhance student learning. He specifically focuses on "the ability of the institutions and their faculty and staff members to look and think beyond the boundaries of their own units and activities and to understand the place and role of what they do in relation to the role and activities of others. The product is a coherent, integrated, intentional learning environment that serves the institution's students and its educational mission" (p. 20). This section will advance the idea that a focus on advising is one of the best ways for a chief academic officer (CAO) to initiate a coherent, integrated, intentional learning environment, which includes the active collaboration of academic, student, and business affairs.

Advising is a traditional activity for both student and academic affairs staff and faculty. It fosters a common good that faculty and staff agree is important. As the NACADA Concept on Academic Advising (National Academic Advising Association, 2006) asserts:

> Academic advising, based in the teaching and learning mission of higher education, is a series of intentional interactions with a curriculum, a pedagogy, and a set of student learning outcomes. Academic advising synthesizes and contextualizes students' educational experiences within the frameworks of their aspirations, abilities and lives to extend learning beyond campus boundaries and timeframes. (summary para.)

While faculty have traditionally thought of themselves as the prime deliverers of the teaching and learning mission of an institution, Kuh, Kinzie, Schuh, & Whitt (2005) and Pascarella and Terenzini (2005) have emphasized the importance of the teaching and learning experiences outside the class-room in the traditional student affairs areas and even beyond. All aspects of the student's experience contribute to or detract from the learning environment for each student.

Although higher education institutions face similar federal mandates and are impacted by the same popular culture, these institutions have different missions and histories and face different challenges in their state and local environments. The way each institution interprets its teaching and learning mission is influenced by its history and its state and local environment and will affect the kind of advising expected of its faculty and staff. A church-related school may envision its creation of a good learning environment for students very differently from a regional comprehensive school serving first-generation students from low socioeconomic backgrounds, and both may differ from the flagship research institution. While missions and advising delivery systems may be different, an integrated systems approach in which all aspects of the campus collaborate to create the desired student learning environment is crucial to success.

An example of this collaboration is when a faculty and staff team, cochaired by a faculty member and a staff member, draft the campus advising mission statement, the definition of advising, and the campus advising evaluation process. In many four-year institutions, departmental faculty provide advising for graduate students and upper-division majors, while advising for freshman and undeclared students is delivered through a "total intake" centralized advising model. The centralized advising center can model and enhance collaboration by welcoming both full-time staff and faculty advisors who may be given reassigned time to advise. Career counselors, international student advisors, and others can also be integrated into the advising center. All advisors should participate in training to enhance their knowledge and skill in working together. The CAO, along with the chief student affairs officer (CSAO) should support these efforts.

The advising center director could report to the CSAO or the CAO, but both must be equally knowledgeable and supportive of the activities. The director should evaluate the work of both the faculty and the staff advisors. The faculty member's evaluation should be included in annual evaluation, promotion, and tenure reviews. Both faculty and staff advisors should be encouraged to advise in summer orientation programs if they receive appropriate training. Both the academic and the student affairs offices should support the fiscal needs of the advising center, for example, the reassigned time for faculty and travel to regional and national advising conferences could be supported by the academic and the student affairs offices, respectively.

The CAO should be the leader in creating a system in which all stakeholders at the institution recognize the importance of their roles in advising students, all are trained, and all are welcome to participate in the shaping of the student learning environment. This approach fits the background and mission of many comprehensive universities, especially those that are primarily teaching institutions. Often these institutions serve many first-generation students, who did not prepare to go to college and, therefore, need a great deal of support to be successful. In times of declining student enrollment, student persistence and success is vital to all parts of an institution.

Ideally, the president and the vice presidents should all agree that advising is a form of teaching and that all parts of the institution have a role in encouraging and supporting student learning. This belief is supported by and can be operationalized using Terenzini's (2007) six findings about learning:

> learning: 1) requires an encounter with a challenge to the learner's current knowledge and belief structures; 2) requires active learner engagement with those challenges; 3) occurs best in a supportive environment that promotes reflection, consolidation, and internalization; 4) is relational and social, occurring best in the company of others and providing both enjoyable interaction and personal support; 5) is maximized in settings where both the learning activity and the learning outcome(s) have meaning for the learner; and 6) is neither time nor location bound. (p. 1)

Although the term *advisor* is most frequently associated with academic advisor, the advisor role is also shared by the faculty and staff who sponsor student organizations. This advising position can play a crucial role in fostering student learning outside the classroom by nurturing an "integrated, intentional learning environment." As students learn teamwork and practice their leadership skills in a student organization, they also learn and practice time management, goal-setting, and communication. Working with others to achieve a goal can challenge their current knowledge and belief structures and actively engage them. The faculty or staff advisor's role is to provide that supportive environment and give opportunities for reflection, consolidation, and internalization. The role of the institution is to foster that reflection about the importance of their role among both faculty and staff advisors and to encourage collaboration and sharing as they strive to become better advisors of student organizations—in other words, to create a systemic way of viewing their role.

Another example of an opportunity for an integrative, systems approach is in the collaboration of the delivery of career advising. Career advising is important to students at various times in their college experience. Working with first-year students to select or confirm the selection of a career, faculty advisors often must collaborate with career services staff to help their advisees learn more about their career options and how these fit into a choice of a major and ultimately in the selection of classes to take. Faculty advisors are crucial to the socialization of students into the discipline in which they choose to major and can provide students contacts in the field as they get closer to graduation. Career services is not only a place for students to go for help in scheduling interviews, writing resumes, and role-playing job interviews, but also is a place to help students achieve overall success.

Systematic collaboration among different parts of the institution is also important when attempting to build a user-friendly catalog or a current degree plan. The catalog and degree plan format frequently emanate from the registrar's office, while the content is often created by the faculty. The staff and faculty advisors have daily contact with students who are using the catalogue and degree plan; they often have the best grasp of the students' questions or problems when they use the catalogue or degree plan. They have the responsibility to create a system in which all parties collaborate in the sharing of information. Student input is also crucial to creating user-friendly documents.

Timeliness of the information contained in the catalogue and degree plans is also a consideration. All stakeholders must collaborate to provide the most current and accessible information.

One way to ensure this collaboration is for representatives from both the advising center and the registrar's office to attend the meetings of the faculty curriculum and instruction committee that makes the decisions about new courses, changes to course and degrees, as well as university policies. They can share their perspective of the impact of such decisions. Thus, all parts of the institution participate in the creation of new academic policies and understand the rationale behind them. For example, curriculum and instruction committee changes need to be communicated in time for summer orientation advising and can be broadcast via faculty and staff listservs. This systematic communication supports and fosters the sense that giving correct advising information is the role of the entire campus.

A final example of an opportunity for collaboration among all parts of campus can be seen in the role of student employees or work-study students. Work-study students are often awarded positions as a part of their financial aid. Students may work in a number of places from the business office, to the swimming pool, to a departmental office or lab, to the cafeteria or bookstore. In their jobs, students learn important life skills relating to customer service, cooperation, teamwork, timeliness, and responsibility. But rarely does an institution think of this work-study experience as part of the student learning environment. The work-study experience certainly could fulfill the requirements for student learning that Terenzini articulated. The responsibility of the CAO is to make those connections for all campus stakeholders and to create an integrated and systematic way of engaging the student, the employer, and the academic advisor in the reflection on student learning gained in the work-study experience. At one comprehensive university, an action committee composed of faculty, staff, and students collaborated to survey all campus employers and work-study students about the learning outcomes for these students and their learning environment and are working on a manual for both employers and students.

The communication necessary to support collaborative, integrated campuswide systems would be much harder without the use of technology such as a student information system, a campus portal, document imaging, and a degree audit.

Collaboration and communication in using this technology and understanding how its use can benefit students is an important aspect of supporting student learning. For example, information technology (IT) staff could create a software program to access all the information an advisor needs to help a student. It should be created with active input and collaboration from staff and faculty advisors. All new faculty members should be trained in its use, and continuing faculty and staff advisors should be offered refresher training each year. The role of the CAO is to ensure that users understand how using the technology enhances the student learning experience and that it is not just an end in itself.

A focus on processes, continuous quality improvement, and assessment is a way to achieve an integrated learning environment. Every CAO needs to consider the advising-related processes that cut across all parts of the institution. The process of getting a student enrolled involves admissions, advising, the registrar, financial aid, the foundation (scholarships), the business office (payment), and the IT organization. The early-warning process involves students, faculty, advisors, as well as various support and referral services (tutoring, counseling, special needs, athletics, etc.). Creating a safe environment for the discussion of such campus processes and how their efficient operation can better support the student is the role of the CAO. All stakeholders need to understand that the emphasis is on making the process better for the student and not in finding fault with a person or an office. Leadership from the top and collaboration among the president and the vice presidents is necessary to create this kind of safe environment.

Setting goals and assessing the progress of improvement is important to the health of the institution and to its continued improvement. Regional accrediting agencies have become aware of the importance of implementing quality-improvement processes and are providing opportunities to link accreditation to this kind of quality improvement. The U.S. Department of Education and many state legislatures are taking a more aggressive stance in regard to accountability.

CAOs are positioned squarely between the campus and the external bodies demanding accountability. All of the stakeholders, including students, parents, families, faculty, staff and administrators, legislators, and accrediting bodies have the same overarching objective: to ensure that students get a good education. The CAO's role is to provide leadership in collaboration with the CSAO, the faculty, staff, and students as they create the "coherent, integrated, intentional learning environment that serves the institution's students and its educational mission" Terenzini (2007) described, while ensuring outcomes that will satisfy external constituencies. Advising plays a crucial role in creating that learning environment.

CHIEF STUDENT AFFAIRS OFFICER—TWO-YEAR PUBLIC

Jocelyn Y. Harney

Academic advising holds great importance on community college campuses as an integrative process because of the unique mission of these institutions. Community colleges provide open access to students who might not otherwise have an opportunity to pursue higher education, and they provide an opportunity for education and training leading to preparation for baccalaureate education, preparation for the workforce, basic academic skills, English-language skills, or knowledge in an area for personal growth and development. The chief student affairs officer (CSAO) must remain aware of the mission of community colleges to ensure that meaningful advising services are made available to students who are diverse in a number of ways. In many community colleges, the positions of CSAO and CAO are held by a single individual.

CSAOs must also continue to reflect on the benefits of community colleges by remaining cognizant of the history of these institutions, which emerged during the twentieth century to provide increased numbers of high school graduates the opportunity for higher education. In 1996, more than 5.5 million of the nation's higher education students attended community colleges (Nettles & Millett, 2000). Chief administrators understand that affordability, adaptability, flexibility, and diversity are key features that contribute to students' access to community colleges (Alfred & Carter, 2000). Community colleges are predicted to experience an increase in student enrollment, an increased diversity of students, and to be of greater importance to nontraditional students in the twenty-first century (Nora, 2000). Community colleges must also remain learning-centered, as well as community-focused, including partnerships for workforce and economic development (Alfred & Carter, 2000).

Based upon the open access of community colleges, student populations remain extremely diverse in a number of ways. The stakeholders of community colleges demand that the CSAO be prepared to address the various presenting issues of the diverse student body. Giegerich (2006) described this diversity as follows: 32 percent of community college students are 30 years or older, with an average age of 29 years; 58 percent of community college students are female; 29 percent of community college students have an annual household income of less than $20,000; 85 percent of community college students are employed; and 30 percent of community college students are minorities. Further, many students enrolled are first-generation, and 61 percent of community college students attend part-time (Community College Survey of Student Engagement, 2006). Community colleges also include students with disabilities, as well as international, racial, and ethnic diversities.

The diverse ethnic populations are defined by national guidelines as African American, Hispanic, Asian American, and Native American (Harvey, 2001). According to national higher education enrollment trends, a greater number of minorities are enrolling in community colleges because of affordability and proximity to family and work, given that many students are of nontraditional age and have their own families. More than 60 percent of minorities enrolled in higher education are enrolled in community colleges (Nora, 2000). Specifically, more than half of Hispanic and African American students enter community colleges upon leaving high school.

For the CSAO, having competent advising staff capable of working effectively with diverse populations is imperative. Advising staff must be prepared to understand the cultural issues that are relevant and central to each student's identity and perceptions of their fit in the institution. Advisors must be able to help students set priorities and manage time, as well as offer strategies to address other barriers to academic success. The CSAO is responsible for ensuring the hiring and development of trained and competent advisors who can work effectively with diverse populations. In addition, the CSAO may need to consider specialized advising services to address relevant issues by working closely with students and their families through new student orientation, outreach programs, or bridge program efforts.

With this expected continual enrollment growth and a more diverse student body, community colleges will be repeatedly challenged to provide adequate and appropriate student services, especially in academic advising. Depending upon the level of academic preparation and college readiness of community college students, advising services may need to be extensive. Therefore, CSAOs will be challenged to ensure that staffing levels are adequate to provide the necessary advising services, and that advisors are appropriately skilled to address the issues of this ever-changing and growing population. This continual growth will require long-range planning by the CSAO to address the challenges of existing staffing and financial and facility resource constraints.

Along with these constraints, community colleges will also experience greater accountability for successful student outcomes. At times, some community colleges will continue to be challenged to do more and more with less and less. As community college enrollment numbers continue to increase and student populations become more complex in needs and diversity, CSAOs must ask the question, "What advising services are critical to student success?" It is nice to have advising specializations and services that often contribute to student retention and persistence, but they are frequently sacrificed or eliminated during times of fiscal constraints.

The community college stakeholders demand the accountability of successful student outcomes, while the CSAO must provide the necessary resources to facilitate expert and effective advising. These stakeholders include both internal and external entities. The internal community includes students, faculty, administrators, and boards of trustees. The external community may include local and state taxpayers, elementary and high schools, baccalaureate institutions, and finally, employers. All the stakeholders have an expectation that community colleges will educate students in preparation for transfer to baccalaureate institutions, for career employment, or for personal development. Whatever the intended destination or outcome, advising becomes crucial to assisting students in the identification of a plan to complete their identified goal and to identify assistance with services that aid in the completion of that goal.

Many community colleges are also under ever-increasing scrutiny by politicians, legislators, and the community to become more accountable in achieving successful outcomes, which requires students to receive accurate and appropriate advising. Expert and effective advising will lead to students identifying appropriate educational planning and to completion of their identified goals. Given rising tuition costs, the student's completion of educational and program goals becomes more important to ensure that needless courses are not attempted, especially since this may result in unnecessarily reducing the student's available financial aid or jeopardizing future eligibility. In addition, today's employers are seeking more accountability by demanding well-trained and competent workers from community colleges to help meet the community's economic workforce conditions within that same community.

The CSAO must provide the leadership to plan strategically for these eventual outcomes that also fulfill the accountability expectation of all stakeholders.

The CSAO must be concerned with extending resources to provide advising services to students who may or may not be pursuing academic coursework. The broad array of community college programming may include youth education programs, high school dual-enrollment programs, older adult programs, continuing education programs, and employer training programs. Non-degree-seeking students may also include those in need of improving basic academic skills with developmental education, adult basic education, English as a second language, and general education. Advising must also be able to address the wide array of programming needs that occur from pursuits of academic degrees and certificates to career and technical education programs.

Although the number of students entering community colleges with the intent to transfer to baccalaureate institutions has declined over the past twenty-five years, the number of associate degrees awarded in occupational and career technical education program areas has increased (Nora, 2000). The lower matriculation rate of community college students to baccalaureate institutions occurs for a number of reasons, including student characteristics, student socioeconomic status, retention, and articulation issues. It is because of these low transfer rates of community college students to baccalaureate institutions that transfer has become a focus for many state governments and federal policy-makers (Dougherty & Hong, 2005). The increased scrutiny of transfer rates by state governments and federal policy-makers demand that the CSAO work to ensure that students secure appropriate advisement assistance to facilitate matriculation to four-year institutions. This may require direct collaboration and partnering with other colleges and universities to facilitate articulation and transfer agreements by the CSAO, along with appropriate advising information to guide transfer preparation. In addition, advising services from or on behalf of the colleges and universities may need to be supported by the CSAO for delivery on the community college campus.

Community college students are typically first-generation, lower-income, female, from underrepresented backgrounds, are non-native-English-speakers and have children, are married or single parents, and are of non-traditional age. Many community college students are ethnic minorities who may see community college as their only opportunity to realize their hopes and dreams (Rendón, 2000). Students with disabilities are also seen as an underrepresented population. At one point 71 percent of students with disabilities in public institutions of higher education were enrolled in community colleges, with learning disabilities accounting for the largest category, followed by those with orthopedic and mobility disabilities, all requesting special accommodations (Barnett & Li, 1997).

Given these student characteristics, it is reasonable to expect that a student's advising needs may begin at their first contact with the institution, starting with assistance in the admission process, followed by the application process for financial aid, placement assessments, understanding the relevancy of placement assessments and the results, identification of specific coursework to meet identified goals, navigation of the intricacies of the college campus, transfer information, and finally, assistance with transition to a career. To address these needs, specific programming may be developed, such as recruitment activities, new student services, remediation services, transfer preparation, and career development. It is these types of services and activities that begin and continue the linkage of students with academic advising.

It is critical that CSAOs ensure that advisors' skills and knowledge are commensurate with the issues they will confront when assisting students, as well as the ability to collaborate with other student services and academic and program areas. In lieu of counseling services, many community colleges look to advisors to understand and address the complex issues students are facing while simultaneously pursuing their educational goals. Advisors are required to recognize serious issues presented by students and understand what issues are within their domain of expertise to address and recognize when it is appropriate to make referrals to other student service professionals or professionals in the community. Working collaboratively with other student-service professionals, advisors have the opportunity to become familiar with what assistance students can secure, from whom that assistance can be secured, as well as what indicators should signal that it is time to refer students to other professionals. In addition, the CSAO must be prepared to facilitate these internal and external linkages and integration of advising services. Specifically, linkages must be made with academic and program area faculty to access curriculum that extend to and facilitate the development of the whole student, such as civic responsibility, career information, internship, service learning, and cooperative education. And, if faculty share responsibility for advising, as is the case on many campuses, it is imperative that these linkages occur regularly to ensure students' access to accurate and relevant advisement, along with collaborating to provide the most effective and complete advising possible.

By helping advisors connect with other areas of the institution through professional development, partnership, and collaboration, CSAOs ensure the ability of advisors to connect students to the institution, which results in improved persistence of community college students. Although both new and continuing students need to feel a connection with the institution, it is extremely difficult to achieve when the institution has primarily a commuter population. One strategy to improve persistence is to encourage student engagement through advising, which establishes the connection with the institution when the student develops a meaningful relationship with a caring individual. The importance of this connection and the important role of advisors in facilitating this connection can be seen in a national survey of student engagement. According to the Community College Survey of Student Engagement (2006), students value advising from faculty (43 percent), followed by their friends, family, or other students (26 percent), nonfaculty advisors (10 percent), and online services (7 percent), and 13 percent of students indicate that they do not use advising services.

An integrative advising process contributes to appropriate student outcomes that include correct course selection, timely completion of programs and goals, persistence, retention, and successful performance. Advising services are frequently expected to ameliorate the barriers to success, persistence, retention, and outcomes through special design, delivery approach, and focus to target specific populations. Various issues unique to underrepresented, underprepared, nontraditional, and first-generation populations place students at risk for success, persistence, retention, and achievement. For the student intent upon transfer to a baccalaureate institution, this may mean failure to transfer, and for the career and technical education student this means not completing an identified program goal.

The intent of student affairs is, in part, to support the learning mission of the institution through direct support of each student, helping each student to develop fully for success in and out of the classroom. This student development may include areas such as intellectual, emotional, social, physical, academic, and vocational goals, needs, and interests. For advising to be effective in assisting the student to develop as a whole person, services must be effective and relevant to the issues students present. Services can be effective and relevant only if the institution's advisors maintain currency in their knowledge and skills. This can be achieved if environmental scans of the knowledge and skills of other student affairs staff, both within the institution and externally, are regularly performed with the direction and encouragement of the CSAO.

Continual environmental scans by the CSAO contribute to the supporting, encouraging, and championing of currency in the knowledge and skill of advisors by understanding the broader national, regional, and local economic labor market and economic workforce trends, along with the resultant employer needs of the institution's community. In addition, this environmental scan effort facilitates the ease with which students transfer to community colleges from high schools and from community colleges to baccalaureate institutions. The CSAO must be willing to participate actively in the development of partnerships with high schools and four-year schools—and for some, elementary schools—to create appropriate and relevant advising of community college students.

The CSAO's role is to ensure that advisement is accessible, accurate, and effective for the various populations of students pursuing myriad possible goals. Depending upon the institution, different advising models may be used—for example, faculty advisors, staff advisors, or a combination of both. No matter which advising model is used, the expectation is that the CSAO will ensure that appropriate advising services are available to each student. Since all stakeholders expect effective student learning outcomes from advising, accountability for achieving student outcomes will probably fall to the CSAO. Therefore, the CSAO's effort to integrate advising throughout the whole institution benefits the student and the institution and leverages existing fiscal and human resources to accomplish the necessary successful student outcomes.

Upon addressing the challenges of providing an integrative advising process, the CSAO's role and responsibilities in the community college setting may be described as charting the strategic direction of student affairs to align the division with the institutional priorities for advising; identifying issues confronting students that will be addressed by advising; providing leadership and facilitation of advisor competence for responsiveness and effectiveness; building strong partnerships with the internal and external college community; and remaining prepared and accountable for measuring and reporting the outcomes of the impact of academic advising.

CHIEF ACADEMIC OFFICER—FOUR-YEAR PRIVATE

John Smarrelli with Susan Ames

Today's student arrives on campus with hopes, expectations, and fears about the college experience, including the rigor of classes, relationships with roommates and professors, brand new coursework, and a 24/7 life rhythm. This student also arrives with a greater complexity of life experiences than previous generations, most of which will greatly influence academic success. These complexities range from the developmental, generational, and social, such as being highly advanced in technological communication yet uninitiated in how to interact with a roommate, having never before shared a bedroom, to academic, with a broader spectrum of profiles based on increasingly varied socioeconomic backgrounds.

Moreover, especially at the small private institution, traditional-age students are arriving with their parents as "coadvisors." Unlike any generation in recent memory, students and parents are a team, highly sensitized to the cost of college and its perceived effectiveness. They are assertive in their demands. "Be there for me and all of my needs," they say, "and make my education relevant to the world." Increasingly then, today's college students expect to be understood as unique whole individuals.

While education of the whole person is a common goal, old habits die hard, and students are often unwittingly segmented by previous frames of reference. The first inclination is to ask: What is your major? Where do you live? Are you an evening or a day student? Are you an athlete?

There is the tendency, particularly at the private liberal arts institution, to assume that a decentralized approach to advising is always preferable. The line of thinking is that such institutions are small enough to offer faculty accessibility, but with limited finances. Therefore, let the faculty, who hold knowledge of their disciplines, handle the bulk of the student advisee load. Granted, there is no replacement for the depth of knowledge imparted to the student from a veteran scholar within an academic field. However, the diversity of today's college population, the complexity of our students' academic and socioeconomic backgrounds, and perhaps most important, the hidden cost of attrition, should stimulate a much deeper reflection on what the student envisions and expects as "advising."

How can the expertise of all the campus resources be best used with regard to advising, from our faculty and all others who orient, develop, engage, and retain the students? Habley (1994) noted: "Academic advising is the only structured activity on the campus in which all students have the opportunity for ongoing, one-to-one interaction with a concerned representative of the institution" (p. 10). Advising, then, is the one constant that all students experience—whether the students are commuter or residential, traditional or nontraditional, or privileged or underprepared—from their arrival through their senior year.

Faced with a new breed of students who bring to campus such complex needs well beyond the departmental, academic advising can play a transformative role in students' lives, as academic advising's very definition relates to institutional missions. Together, those both in academic affairs and in student affairs should consider the importance of the shared development of students through an integrative approach to advising. These are holistic beings, and our advising efforts should also be holistic.

In their criticism of the teaching paradigm, Barr and Tagg (1995) used the metaphor that traditional pedagogy is "atomistic, the "atom" being the fifty-minute lecture, and the "molecule" being the one-teacher, one-classroom course" (p. 12). They further state that under the traditional model of teaching, "the college . . . exists to provide or deliver instruction . . . through . . . the fairly passive lecture-discussion format, where faculty talk and students listen" (p. 12) creating a rigid structure in which change is difficult and innovation is nearly impossible.

One could easily apply this metaphor to traditional ways of thinking about advising, with the advisor meting out "advice" and the student "receiving" it. To continue the scientific imagery, consider instead an approach to advising that is more akin to the ameba (from the Greek *amoibe,* meaning "to change"). Surrounded by its flexible outer membrane, the ameba moves as a whole without fragmentation and without rigidity, constantly changing in relation to its environment. In short, the ameba adapts. In recasting the role of advising at an institution, the chief academic officer (CAO), like a good scientist, may do best to observe the external environment, research the organizational system, and create a structure to respond to the environment (paraphrased from Kezar, 2001, p. 31). In doing so, the CAO will see that there are myriad resources that can be called upon to be part of a unique, integrated system to meet the students' needs.

Higher education institutions include great intellects, vast specialties, and creativity in all corners of campus. These attributes inevitably cross functional boundaries and, when taken together, are immensely powerful. They should be fully analyzed as to how they can all contribute by moving together as one toward crafting comprehensive advising programs. Therefore, an integrative approach to advising should involve faculty, student development and residence life specialists, academic affairs administrators, counseling staff, career and alumni services, and academic support staff, among others.

Perhaps most important, an integrative approach should also take into account unique institutional missions. Yet, why is there so much similarity in advising models despite the vast differences among our institutions? Kramer and

Spencer (1989) note that on many campuses, advising remains "unchanged" and "generally unsatisfactory" and, further, "Many institutions have no comprehensive statement about academic advising" (p. 103).

The essential job of the chief academic officer, then, is to identify and harness this intellect, these specialties, and this creativity among all units within the institution, based on its mission, and to provide an environment for integration to flourish. Otherwise, as Barr and Tagg (1995) suggest, "the college interacts with students only in discrete, isolated environments, cut off from one another. We must talk about changing the structure of advising, not just adjust its parts" (p. 18).

How can a CAO provide the vision for such change and encourage a culture of collaboration, especially at the small private institution, when it is only natural to hold fast to one's functional discipline? Senge, Roberts, Ross, Smith, and Kleiner (1994) wrote: "Changing the way we interact means redesigning . . . the hard-to-see patterns of interaction between people and processes. The disciplines of shared vision and systems thinking . . . are specifically aimed at changing interactions" (p. 48).

Consider the following ten approaches that a CAO might consider to strengthen the whole and integrate the advising process to benefit students, particularly at the smaller institution.

1. Define the role of advising, and connect it to the institution's mission. Current president of the American Association of Universities, former chancellor of Berkeley, and president of The University of Texas at Austin Robert Berdahl (1995) said: "Advising should be at the core of the institution's educational mission rather than layered on as a service." While good and dedicated advising may be happening on a campus, without a clear mission and a defined role, it will occur largely because of individual efforts by a small corps of champions. If it is not connected to the college's overall mission, advising will not be a part of the institution's culture. It is, at best, a service that can easily be fragmented and weakened depending on who is in charge. Bottom line: it will not have the financial and political resources to remain effective.

2. Develop clear language for a comprehensive and developmentally grounded advising program within the institution's strategic plan. Make goals and objectives for advising intentional. When written into a specific plan, these goals and objectives will necessarily identify those campus constituents who must be involved. Within five- and ten-year strategies, create specific benchmarks for advising to monitor success.

3. Institutionalize the advising role on campus. Create a position of authority, a highly visible directorship or deanship, for undergraduate advising. Ideally, choose a talented individual who understands the unique skills of both academic and student affairs staff, the faculty pressures and staff constraints. Find a savvy leader who can easily glide between both worlds and who can spot the political obstacles to collaboration. Having an individual who is well respected by both faculty and student affairs personnel will greatly elevate the importance of the position and, thus, create credibility for the function of advising campus-wide. With this highly visible person as the liaison, the small liberal arts institution, in particular, could easily marshal all resources in one room to monitor the continuing influence of academic advising in the students' development through a comprehensive academic advising committee structure. Conceivably, career services, registrar, faculty, advising, counseling, information systems, and academic support could meet regularly to discuss initiatives such as how to support and reward faculty who advise, how to mentor new advisors, and how to improve training for first-year advisors, based on their observations from the students they serve in their various capacities. Regular interaction among this core group, recognizing the value of all stakeholders equally, is key.

4. View advising as a living program, and encourage others to do so. Show by example that it is acceptable, in fact, desirable, for the advising program to evolve. Find out what is working, and humbly admit when something is not. In doing so, remember to make students an integral part of the conversation both up front and in program assessment. If small institutions have first-year seminars, for example, have students formally evaluate their courses and instructors, and create a protocol for evaluating advisors. In the assessments, try to involve all demographic representations on campus, such as international and domestic students, commuters and residential students, high achievers and probationary students, and first-year and transfer students.

5. Do not underestimate the power of faculty to shape and participate in the changes that will occur in advising as the student population continues to change. Mature faculty members possess a vast institutional memory regarding people and processes. Ask them: What was tried before that did not work? Was the idea attempted but not successful because of the plan, the process, or the person leading the charge? New faculty should be brought into the discussion as well. Demographically, they will be closer in age to the students. As such, they may have a very different view of the contribution of advising to student success. Encourage interested faculty to take on roles far different from their roles in the classroom. Have them assist with assessment, with advisor cultivation and training, and with being a part of student and parent orientation rituals related to academic issues. By calling attention to these broader faculty roles, an institution sends the message that advising is also a part of teaching and scholarship. Because of their size and accessibility, small institutions, in particular, can develop protocols that include advising as part of faculty training and development. Terenzini and Pascarella (1994) noted: "If undergraduate education is to be enhanced, faculty members, joined by academic and student affairs administrators, must devise ways to deliver undergraduate education that is as comprehensive and integrated as the ways that students actually learn. A whole new mind set is needed to capitalize on the interrelatedness of the in- and out-of-class influences on student learning and the functional interconnectedness of academic and student affairs divisions" (p. 32). Student success is everyone's job.

6. Create a structure for an advising clearinghouse on campus that can bring together in a single unit a broad range of services to support the work of both faculty advisors and student affairs administrators. Regardless of the campus advising model chosen, but based on an institution's mission, size, and culture, create an entity on campus that can be easily accessible to address problematic questions of requirements, training, faculty resources, registration, and the special needs of students. Such a clearinghouse, even if recognized informally, gives both students and faculty a place to vent and to acknowledge that there will be gray areas and that at times all the needed information may not be found within one source. Sometimes additional support is needed to resolve an issue.

7. Seek out small examples of the willingness to collaborate and publicly elevate the importance of these efforts. Often the traditional means of rewarding faculty include providing stipends and reduced courseloads to accommodate advising responsibilities. While these are extremely important and need to be championed aggressively, recognition should also occur when, for example, the information technology department streamlines a registration process, when a faculty member helps train first-year advisors, or when student life and academic affairs staff copresent at orientation. On one campus, first-year advisors are recognized for their special efforts at an annual luncheon at which their innovative advising ideas are exchanged among faculty.

8. Foster integration of the work of both academic affairs and student affairs from the time a student submits an admission deposit. Again, intentionality is the key. Ideally, there should be formal liaison established between academic and student affairs personnel so that both are working together to meet goals and deadlines at strategic points of student contact across the continuum, including preorientation, orientation, the first-year experience, major declaration, and the transitions to sophomore, junior, and graduate years. Do not look at these phases of the college experience as separate action points, but identify them as integral parts of a ladder-building process for each student. Small institutions can easily form strong alliances among advising, career services, and alumni programs, for example, because they can maintain close tabs on loyal alumni who often become career mentors. In turn, career mentors can work closely with academic advisors to help new students in their decisions regarding majors. To the student, college is a fluid, seamless experience, and our professional relationships with each other should reflect the student's meaning of this experience. How many times do students say that this is the third or fourth campus office they contacted for an answer? Better integration will alleviate the problem of having so many contacts.

9. Be aware of the surroundings and understand that creativity can come from anywhere. Be willing to accept input and even misinformation from disgruntled students and faculty and an increasingly vocal population of parents. Though the packaging of their comments may be less than desirable, they can offer valuable advice about what happened (or did not happen) to them, thus altering the institution's strategies from their unique lens. Pay particular attention to the needs and comments of transfer students, who often compare their former institution with yours. In those comparisons will be wisdom.

10. Finally, use disciplinary expertise. CAOs who are scientists, philosophers, psychologists, and management experts should not abandon their disciplines to become an institution's primary academic administrator. Use these strengths, and recognize the strengths in others that can be used across the institution.

With few levels of authority, the small private institution has the advantage of being able to talk across the aisle easily and whenever necessary and, thus, has great potential to be innovative on behalf of the student. The key is to view the institution as one comprehensive, ever-changing unit, moving together, and to establish strong lines of collaboration despite functional boundaries and limited human and fiscal resources.

References

James E. Bultman

Hemwall, M. K., & Trachte, K. C. (2003). Academic advising and the learning paradigm. In M. K. Hemwall, & K. C. Trachte (Eds.), *Advising and learning: Academic advising from the perspective of small colleges and universities.* (NACADA Monograph Series, no. 8, pp. 13–19.) Manhattan, KS: National Academic Advising Association.

Humphreys, D., & Davenport, A. (2005). What really matters in college: How students view and value liberal education. *Liberal Education, 91* (3), 36–43.

Laff, N. S. (2006). Teachable moments: Advising as liberal learning. *Liberal Education 92* (2): 36–41.

Light, R. J. (2001). *Making the most of college: Students speak their minds.* Cambridge, MA: Harvard University Press.

Lowenstein, M. (2000). Academic advising and the "logic" of the curriculum. *The Mentor, 2* (2). Retrieved September 13, 2007, from http://www.psu.edu/dus/mentor/000414ml.htm

Task Group on General Education. (1988). *A new vitality in general education: Planning, teaching, and supporting effective liberal learning.* Washington, DC: Association of American Colleges.

Faye N. Vowell

Kuh, G., Kinzie, J., Schuh, J., Whitt, E., & Associates. (2005). *Student success in college: Creating conditions that matter.* San Francisco: Jossey-Bass.

National Academic Advising Association. (2006). NACADA concept of academic advising. Retrieved January 6, 2008, from http://www.nacada.ksu.edu/ Clearinghouse/AdvisingIssues/Concept-Advising.htm

Pascarella, E., & Terenzini, P. (2005). *How college affects students: Vol. 2. A third decade of research.* San Francisco: Jossey-Bass.

Terenzini, P. (2007) From myopia to systemic thinking. *Academic Advising Today, 30,* (2). Retrieved May 25, 2007, from http://www.nacada.ksu.edu/AAT/NW30_2 .htm

Jocelyn Y. Harney

Alfred, R., & Carter, P. (2000). Contradictory colleges: Thriving in an era of continuous change. *American Association of Community Colleges, 6,* 1-15.

Barnett, L., & Li, Y. (1997). Disability support services in community colleges. *American Association of Community Colleges* (AACC research brief, no. 97-1).

Community College Survey of Student Engagement, Community College Leadership Program (2006). *Act on fact: Using data to improve student success.* Austin, TX: Author.

Dougherty, K. J., & Hong, E. (2005). *State systems of performance accountability for community colleges: Impacts and lessons for policymakers* (An Achieving the Dream Policy Brief). Boston: Jobs for the Future.

Giegerich, S. (2006, Winter). Barrier busters: Two-year institutions help students achieve their dreams. *Lumina Foundation Focus,* 4-25.

Harvey, W. B. (2001). Minorities in higher education 2000-2001: Eighteenth annual status report. (Report no. 309182.) Washington, DC: American Council on Education.

Nettles, M. T., & Millett, C. M. (2000). Student access in community colleges. *American Association of Community Colleges, 1,* 1-11.

Nora, A. (2000). Reexamining the community college mission. *American Association of Community Colleges, 2,* 1-7.

Rendón, L. (2000). Fulfilling the promise of access and opportunity: Collaborative community colleges for the 21st century. *American Association of Community Colleges, 3,* 1-15.

John Smarrelli with Susan Ames

Barr, R., & Tagg, J. (1995). From teaching to learning: A new paradigm for undergraduate education. *Change, 27* (6), pp. 12-25.

Berdahl, R. M. (1995). Educating the whole person. In A.G. Reinarz, & E. R. White (Eds.), Teaching through academic advising: A faculty perspective. *New directions for teaching and learning.* Report No.62. San Francisco: Jossey-Bass, 5-11.

Habley, W. R. (1994). Key concepts in academic advising. In *Summer institute on academic advising session guide.* Manhattan, KS: National Academic Advising Association.

Kezar, A. (2001, Winter). Organizational models and facilitators of change: Providing a framework for student and academic affairs collaboration. *New Directions for Higher Education, 116,* 63-74. Retrieved January 29, 2007, from the Academic

Search Elite database http://web.ebscohost.com/ehost/pdf?vid = 21&hid = 120&sid = 81953bc8-aa4a-4168-8ee9-fba350f86e7b%40sessionmgr107

Kramer, G. L., & Spencer, R. W. (1989). Academic advising. In M. L. Upcraft, J. N. Gardner, & Associates (Eds.), *The freshman year experience: Helping students survive and succeed in college,* pp. 95–107. San Francisco: Jossey-Bass.

Senge, P., Roberts, C., Ross, R., Smith, B., & Kleiner, A. (1994). *The fifth discipline fieldbook: Strategies and tools for building a learning organization.* New York: Doubleday.

Terenzini, P. T., & Pascarella, E. T. (1994). Living with myths: Undergraduate education in America. *Change, 26* (1), 28–32.

CHAPTER TWENTY-EIGHT

Advising Administrator Perspectives on Advising

FOUR-YEAR PUBLIC

Kathy J. Davis

An advising administrator at a public university must balance responsibilities as the supervisor of an advising staff while serving as an advocate for student advising concerns across campus. Providing leadership on both smaller and larger scales and attending to the mission of academic advising campuswide while focusing on details to make an office work productively can be challenging. This chapter will explore strategies for leading an effective advising office and for influencing the campus culture for student-oriented academic advising.

Campus-Wide Concerns

Academic advising administrators at public colleges and universities must be engaged with the advising process across the campus and be able to address concerns and develop programs that affect a variety of constituents.

Creating a Mission Statement. An advising administrator who is concerned about creating a positive campus climate for advising at a four-year public university may begin by developing an advising mission statement, if one does not already exist. A mission statement can provide direction, but it will be effective only if it is known and embraced by those who provide advising services. In the absence of a clear mission, advising practices are determined by tradition or circumstance (Abelman & Molina, 2006). Aspects of the institutional mission statement should be incorporated, and suggestions from the various providers of advising services should be requested. Stakeholders such as the advising council, faculty senate, and staff senate or administrative council may be involved. The new mission statement should be prominently displayed on advising documents and Web sites and included in the catalogue and other important university documents.

Assessing the Current Views of Advising across Campus. Another step in creating a positive campus climate for student-centered academic advising is to assess current beliefs and attitudes. That assessment can be done by faculty or staff, by supervised graduate students, or by a consultant, if funds are available. The advising administrator should ensure that the opinions of stakeholders such as faculty, students, staff advisors, and administrators are considered. Issues to assess are how advising is viewed (as schedule-building and clerical or as educationally oriented); how the quality of advising is perceived (the knowledge, assistance, and accessibility of advisors); and the effectiveness of the organizational scheme of advising (optional or required for all students or specific groups, and the overall functioning of the program).

This information will assist the administrator in understanding the current views of advising and in developing strategies for enhancing the campus culture. The administrator should avoid being defensive about the results and use any perceived weaknesses as opportunities for improvement. Simply conducting the assessment and sharing the results openly may bring attention and respect and could result in proposed changes in structure or staffing. Effective assessment may result in changed advising policies (Light, 2004).

Building Credibility for the Advising Program. One way to enhance the campus culture of advising is to build credibility of the program and the administrator. For decentralized advising programs, a well-respected administrator may serve as a resource person for advisors in other areas. As advisors review advising issues, personal relationships are built and the advisors are likely to develop an appreciation for the skills of the administrator. The administrator may develop presentations on advising skills or information and volunteer to visit departmental faculty meetings. Quality presentations will benefit the advising program and enable the administrator to be visible on campus. Serving on important campus committees, such as academic program review groups, also builds credibility. This service takes a significant amount of time and energy but often results in respect and good "word of mouth."

Balancing the Internal Role as Leader and the External Role as Advocate. An effective leader within an advising unit requires time in the office to attend to the professional development of each staff member, plan useful staff meetings, develop appropriate policies, manage a budget, and develop a productive environment, all while being available to the staff. However, to be an effective representative for advising across campus requires being away from the office to attend meetings, develop relationships with other constituents, and find ways to champion the importance of advising. Finding a balance among these important roles is critical to success as an advising administrator.

Developing Cooperative Efforts between Academic and Student Affairs. Many advising offices are housed under academic affairs, while others are part of student affairs. Because advising includes both academic decision-making and personal development, it has natural ties to both parts of the university. Advising administrators are in an excellent position to facilitate cooperative efforts. For example, the advising office that serves exploratory students may be in academic affairs while the career counseling office may be in student affairs. For students' best interests to be served, those two offices should be closely affiliated, regardless of the organizational structure.

Developing Influence. In centralized advising programs, the advising administrator usually has direct authority over advising policies and staff. In decentralized advising programs, the advising administrator may have only indirect or no official authority over advising policies and staff. In the latter case, the administrator must develop influence with those who do have such authority. Developing influence requires building solid relationships, communicating well, and developing camaraderie and common purpose.

Leading an Effective Advising Office

The administrator of an advising unit has primary responsibility for the operations and effectiveness of the unit. Many aspects contribute to its success.

Hiring Talented and Committed Staff. One key to leading an effective advising unit is hiring and nurturing a talented staff. When openings occur, qualified candidates should be recruited by targeted advertising, which can be done at low or no cost, through advising listservs and professional association Web sites. A diverse pool of qualified applicants must be sought.

Selection of search or screening committee members provides opportunities for current staff members to have a say in the selection of their future colleagues and allows interested colleagues from outside the advising center to learn more about advising. The administrator should make sure the committee fully understands its role in the decision-making process.

Once candidates are identified for interviews, the administrator should ensure that the applicants receive appropriate information to prepare for the interview. An interview process should be created to reflect the work environment. The interview schedule could include a writing sample, a presentation, or a role-play, because standard questions do not always discern the skills that are necessary for an excellent advisor in the specific unit. Appropriate constituencies should be included in the interview process. A panel of students can provide a valuable perspective on the candidates.

Building the Advising Office Team. Cohesive, effective advising teams do not occur by chance; they must be cultivated. An effective administrator can create conditions under which a strong team is likely to develop. Getting to know each staff member's strengths is a good place to begin. Advisors, administrative assistants, and student workers give their best work efforts if they believe they are valued and that their contributions shape the overall success of the operation. Effective administrators know how to delegate projects and then freely share credit for success.

Planning useful and informative staff meetings is an important responsibility. Staff meetings might include inviting department heads to speak on a rotating basis, having presentations on topics of interest by each staff member, and asking the staff to read and discuss a book related to student development.

Developing a fair balance of work among advising office staff members is an important challenge, especially to ensure that talented staff members do not become overworked. Staff members with excellent reputations across campus are often asked to serve on committees for other offices. Having advising representatives on campus committees can be valuable but must be monitored by the administrator. The advising administrator should review the advisor:advisee ratio, which is a key sign of quality in an advising program (Yudof, 2003).

The administrator should encourage advisors to participate in professional development activities. Attending and presenting at advising conferences and serving in professional associations assists staff members to build confidence, to gain a perspective on advising issues beyond their own campus, and to renew enthusiasm for their work. Low-cost alternatives include campus and local training programs.

When working on the team atmosphere of the advising office, the administrator must not neglect the development of administrative assistants and student workers. The reputation of the advising office will be influenced by the knowledge and attitudes of those who answer phones, handle certain problems, and make appointments.

Effective administrators take time to enjoy and celebrate the accomplishments of the office. Enhanced job satisfaction comes from sharing traditions and being recognized for achievements, which can result in better long-term productivity.

Training Advisors Campus-wide. The advising administrator, especially in a centralized model, is likely to be charged with responsibility for advisor training programs for all advisors on campus. Advisor training is an essential function that is often neglected. Effective advisor training programs may include annual workshops, ongoing advisor meetings or brown-bag lunch meetings, and Web-based information modules. Giving staff members appropriate opportunities to plan and present within the training program will contribute to their professional development while balancing the workload for the administrator.

Supervising and Evaluating Staff Members. One of the most rewarding aspects of administration is encouraging the professional development of staff members and helping them prepare for the next steps in their careers. Meaningful supervision requires regular individual contact with each staff member as well as group staff meetings to discuss the concerns and needs of the group. The administrator should foster an environment in which staff members feel comfortable approaching the supervisor with issues.

Advisors are interested in knowing how students perceive their work. The administrator should work with the staff to develop a system in which advisees can give periodic evaluations of their advising experience. The advisors should participate in developing or choosing the evaluation instrument and the method of distribution so that they will be more likely to accept the results. The supervisor must be aware that student satisfaction surveys are only one indicator of the quality of the individual advisor's work.

An important aspect of supervision is assisting each staff member in writing an effective annual appraisal and development plan. The plan must be both realistic and ambitious, and should reflect the priorities of the staff member and the supervisor. All staff members should be given significant responsibilities, reflecting their individual abilities, which will foster personal development and pride in their work. A formal annual evaluation conference gives the staff member and supervisor an opportunity to assess the success of the plan and make adjustments for the next year. The administrator should not wait for the annual evaluation conference to provide feedback; sufficient regular feedback should be built into the regular evaluation process so that any negative evaluation item will not come as a surprise.

Regardless of the quality of supervision, some staff turnover is inevitable and can be healthy. A skillful administrator will expect staff departures and may well support staff members who leave to pursue higher positions or advanced degrees. Advising administrators may advocate for appropriate career ladders for advisors. Advisors who are excellent at providing direct student service are often required to become administrators in order to advance. Different skills are necessary for success in administration, so that may not always be the best choice for a talented advisor. Administrators may find ways to use those experienced advisors and provide them with professional growth opportunities in positions such as advising trainer, senior academic advisor, or assistant director.

Budgeting Considerations. Many beginning advising administrators have considerable skills in student service and programming but may not enjoy or feel prepared for their budgetary responsibilities. The administrator should be proactive and learn as much about budgeting as possible. The administrator should make sure that the priorities of the advising office are reflected in how the money is spent. Sharing budget issues with staff and consulting with them about how resources will be used may minimize dissatisfaction about the resources available for individual priorities such as professional travel or new office computers.

Using Technology to Enhance Advising Operations. As with budgetary skills, the advising administrator may or may not have a particular interest or strength in technological issues. In either case, it is important to forge a strong relationship with the computer services personnel so that they understand advising goals and needs. The administrator should advocate for effective technological tools for advisors and should request that an advisor serve on the committee that makes decisions about the computer support on campus.

Although technological advances can enhance the delivery of advising services, the administrator should always work to ensure that individual contact between advisors and students is preserved. Timely e-mail messages, informative Web pages, and students' ability to view their own information can help students be well-informed self-advocates. Emerging technologies may change the way advisors interact with students (Steele, 2006). For making genuine, meaningful connections with students, though, many advisors will continue to prefer face-to-face advising sessions.

Challenges for Advising Administrators

Advising administrators are busy people. To maintain their effectiveness in providing students with quality advising, it is important to preserve some of the basic elements that characterize such quality.

Maintaining Student Contacts. Advising administrators are most effective and respected if they continue to have significant contact with students and if they are knowledgeable about current student characteristics. Although challenging, keeping an advising load helps administrators understand the concerns of both students and full-time advisors. Administrators may also benefit from teaching a course or serving as a sponsor for a student group.

Attending to Personal Professional Development. The advising administrator at a four-year public university plays multiple roles on campus. With the difficulty of attending to all the important duties, both within and outside the advising unit, it is easy for advising administrators to neglect their own professional growth. Advising administrators need to provide themselves time for professional pursuits, such as research and writing, leadership within a professional association, or pursuing an advanced degree.

Advocating for Excellent Faculty Advisors. Most advising administrators at public universities work in a system that includes faculty advisors. Those advisors are often poorly prepared for their advising role and may be resistant to the time demands of advising because of the pressures of teaching, research, and service. Increased workloads combined with other issues may create a system of institutional disincentives that prevents full participation by faculty members in academic advising when it may not be a significant factor in salary, tenure, and promotion standards (Swanson, 2006). Those advisors who are intrinsically motivated and are excellent advisors may be "rewarded" with heavier advising loads without receiving any institutional recognition.

Dillon and Fisher (2000) found that the majority of faculty surveyed believed that advising should be considered in promotion and tenure and that good advising should be rewarded. Administrators must recognize these concerns and advocate, whenever possible, for the recognition and support of faculty advisors.

Making the Case for a Fair Share of Resources. Scarcity of financial resources seems to be universal in higher education. Many of the administrator's initiatives may meet resistance because implementation would cost money. In the current climate, the administrator must be prepared to deal with accountability issues and to demonstrate the effectiveness of advising services. Connecting advising improvements to retention data is a practical way to make a case for resources. Advising administrators may want to partner with faculty members to conduct research, gather appropriate data regarding advising and student success, and share that information with decision-makers.

Representing the Interests of Advising in the "Big Picture." Finally, an overall challenge for the advising administrator at a public university is to represent the interests of advising without becoming single-minded. An advising administrator is, first and foremost, an educator and will support all educationally sound efforts on campus. Many advising administrators also have experience in and appreciation for classroom teaching, residence life, career counseling, student activities, adult student services, first-year programs, and others. The administrator should advocate for advising while maintaining perspective and appreciation for other important issues and priorities on campus.

An advising administrator who keeps a clear perspective as an educator and maintains an interest in campus-wide priorities will likely be successful both in leading an advising unit and in influencing the campus culture for student-centered academic advising.

TWO YEAR COLLEGES

Dick Vallandingham

The supervision and delivery of academic advising in the two-year college is impacted by the distinct mission of the institution, by the challenges presented by the diverse nature of the two-year college student population, and by the varied approaches by which advising is integrated into the institution's culture. Academic advisors within two-year colleges must be able to deal with students in specific technical and transfer programs as well as students undecided about their career paths. This portion of the chapter will focus on the challenges facing administrators working within the two-year college environment: to align the work of advisors with the mission of the college; to attract, train, and retain quality advisors who are able to deal effectively with the diversity of student needs; and to establish an integrative approach within the learning environment.

Defining the Two-Year College

Nearly half of all undergraduates in American higher education are enrolled at two-year institutions (Horn & Nevill, 2006). The term *two-year college* refers to all institutions at which the highest degree awarded is a two-year degree (e.g., associate of arts, associate of science, or associate of applied science). Within the realm of two-year colleges are junior colleges, technical colleges, and community colleges. Because the mission of two-year colleges varies among these sectors, a major challenge for administrators is to ensure that the advising mission aligns with the college mission and that the mission and function of advising integrates into the learning community of the institution.

Two-year colleges began around turn of the century as a result of changing educational needs related to urbanization, industrialization, and economic development. Until the 1970s, many of these institutions were called "junior colleges." Today, *junior college* has come to refer to an institution whose primary mission is to provide a general and liberal education leading to transfer and completion of the baccalaureate degree, although some junior colleges may also provide applied science and adult and continuing education programs.

Technical college refers to those institutions awarding no higher than a two-year degree or diploma in a vocational, technical, or career field. Technical colleges often offer degrees in applied sciences and in adult and continuing education. In addition, shorter-term certificate programs are typically available through the technical college in specific training areas. The mission of the technical college is related to teaching practical skills and applied sciences that are necessary to industry and business.

Generally, the term *community college* refers to a publicly funded institution offering general and liberal education, career and vocational education, and adult and continuing education. Most community colleges have open-door admission policies and provide credential training ranging from certificates to associate degrees. The mission of the community college is often stated in terms of meeting the ongoing educational, workforce development, and lifelong learning needs of the community. This mission reflects the need to react to the specific needs of the communities served. Thus, the mission may involve preparing students to enter or reenter the workforce, providing language and citizenship courses, and educating low-income and first-generation students along with the "traditional" roles of preparing transfer students for enrollment in four-year institutions and preparing students for the workforce.

A growing number of two-year institutions also offer opportunities for students to complete baccalaureate degrees at these two-year institutions through cooperative agreements with four-year institutions or through special approval from governing agencies.

Aligning Advising with College Mission. While these different types of two-year institutions share a goal to provide appropriate learning experiences for their students, the scope of these experiences is impacted by the specific mission. Understanding the mission of the college helps the advising administrator establish the focus of the advising process for the institution. For two-year colleges functioning as junior colleges, for example, advising in the context of the liberal arts general education core curriculum may become the emphasis. The advising administrator must ensure that strong communication connections with four-year institutions are established and maintained. In the case of the technical two-year college, the important connections are going to be with business and industry representatives. For the community college, both of these directions remain important, but an additional social and cultural niche may need to be included.

One tool that can be very helpful for the advising administrator when aligning the advising process with the college mission is an advisory board for advising that includes representatives from the various constituents impacted by the college mission. Such an advisory group might include students, teaching faculty, high school counselors, transfer institutions, area employers, and community groups, and could help define the goals and objectives of the advising process.

A second, equally important, tool for the advising administrator is utilization of the college's internal committee system. The advising administrator often becomes the advocate of advising as an integral component of the college experience for students within the academic and procedural decision-making structure of the college. By ensuring that advising, especially the developmental components of advising, is part of the discussion related to student learning, retention, and success, the effectiveness of advising, along with the inclusion of advising concepts in the curriculum, is increased.

Challenges

The various types of two-year colleges create a series of challenges when attempting to establish an effective academic advising program.

Student Characteristics. Two-year colleges that are designed to be open-door institutions enroll a much wider variety of students than four-year colleges and universities (Spellman, 2007). The range of students served includes those who are most likely to have academic, financial, and personal challenges, those who have dramatically varying goals, and those who have significant time commitments in addition to their studies (Kossoff, 2005). In addition, two-year colleges are major resources for students who are typically underserved in higher education, including first-generation students and students of color. For example, community colleges serve 47 percent of the nation's black undergraduates, 56 percent of the Latinos, and 57 percent of the Native Americans (Geigerich, 2006). Such diversity in the student population becomes a challenge for the advising administrator in terms of appropriate staffing, scheduling, and resource allocation.

Many two-year college students are considered to be nontraditional, or adult, students. In fact, people in their thirties or older account for almost half of the students enrolled in associate degree programs and are the majority of those in certificate programs (Spellman, 2007). One-third of adult students are married with children and one-fourth are single parents. Fifty-seven percent of students work more than twenty hours per week (Community College Survey of Student Engagement, 2005). For the advising administrator, these figures translate into the need for extended hours for advising and flexible scheduling for advisors.

Delivery Models. Models for delivering advising services may be categorized as centralized, decentralized, or shared. The majority of public two-year colleges use either a centralized self-contained model or a shared model (Pardee, 2004). Both models present challenges for the advising administrator to ensure that issues related to information-sharing are addressed.

A centralized model of advising in the two-year colleges allows for the creation of a "front door" for the college for new students with advisors involved in the initial contact on campus. The challenge for the advising administrator is to communicate to the institution the importance of academic advising as the foundational component of student involvement and engagement through the educational planning process and to ensure the integration of advising in the preadmission and orientation processes. When advisors are able to assist students in identifying educational and career goals, enrollment in classes becomes an end product of the planning process. Establishment of advising relationships that continue through the students' educational involvement with the college fosters student retention and success.

Another challenge for the advising administrator in a centralized delivery model is to ensure that communication channels between advising and academic areas are active. Centralized models of delivery require advisors to be knowledgeable about the entire range of options within the college. The advising administrator must ensure that collaborative connections are in place with academic areas and other student services areas to serve as information conduits to the advisor and from advising to other areas regarding program expectations and requirements, student learning opportunities, and college policies.

The shared model of delivery presents a very similar need for active communication channels. In addition, areas of expertise and responsibility must be identified and communicated. Often in the shared model, advising for specific program areas is assigned to faculty within that area while general studies or exploratory students are assigned to an advising center. The advising administrator is challenged to ensure that there is consistency across the campus in terms of college policy information, program expectations, and student resources. The administrator is also often challenged to ensure that all advisors have access to the professional development and support needed, that all advisors have a clear understanding of the advising philosophy of the institution, and that the efforts of all advisors are recognized and rewarded.

Staffing. The strength of academic advising in the two-year college is directly dependent upon the ability of the advising administrator to build a strong team of academic advisors. Regardless of whether the college mission relates to transfer to a four-year institution, technical training, or both, the academic advisor in the two-year environment must be able to address extremely diverse student needs and expectations.

Many students come to a two-year college without clear career goals. To assist these students, advisors are called upon to integrate career exploration and decision-making strategies into the academic advising process. The advising administrator must either hire advisors versed in these areas or provide professional-development opportunities that allow for skill development.

As noted previously, the two-year institution tends to attract a different student demographic than the four-year institution. Advisors in the two-year college, especially the community college, must be flexible enough to work effectively with students from different ethnic and social backgrounds, with different learning and communication styles, at various developmental levels both educationally and socially, and with educational and career goals from extremely focused to completely undecided. Such advisors need to be well versed in developmental theory and practice, educational and career decision-making and planning, personal growth and development mentoring, and teaching and learning approaches. Add the growing need for bilingual advisors, and the task of recruiting, training, and retaining academic advisors becomes a major challenge for administrators. These factors mean that the advising administrator must not only seek advisors through the usual channels of newspaper ads and professional publications, but also must often recruit through regional businesses and educational facilities. Some schools have found success using high school counselors as part-time or summer advisors, while others have approached area businesses for assistance.

Administrative Role. While the role of the advising administrator is in academic advising, it is not uncommon for the advising function in two-year colleges to report through the student affairs area (King, 2002). This emphasizes the role of the administrator in building bridges between advising and the academic areas of the college. The administrator may become the leader for the college in establishing information resources for both advisors and students, ensuring that these resources are readily accessible in a variety of formats, including online. In addition, the administrator may well serve as the major advocate for the importance of advising as part of the learning community within the two-year college structure.

If advising is delivered in a shared-model format, the administrator is also often challenged to build connections in evaluation measures for advising that connect with both staff and faculty advisors. In some public institutions, this process is made more cumbersome when the advisors are represented by different unions. The advising administrator must become familiar with the union negotiation process and include an advising rationale that is related to teaching objectives.

The advising administrator must develop the validity of advising within the learning community. One important reason for the use of assessment measures in advising is to demonstrate the effectiveness of advising in order to support advising services in the college budget process. The advising administrator is often called upon to justify the expenditures for advising in terms of student outcomes. Advising must compete for college resources for staffing, training, and technology and must connect budget needs with student success measures.

The advising administrator is often also asked to be a part of a larger team within the college that focuses on the delivery of student services. Working with other areas, including academic affairs, recruitment and enrollment services, financial aid, and student activities, is an important part of the administrator's job in order to create an effective college team for student success. This also encourages the inclusion of academic advising as a developmental learning experience for students within the college learning environment. The effectiveness of the advising administrator in establishing advising as an integral part of the learning environment will have direct rewards in terms of student engagement and student success in the two-year college environment.

Four-Year Private Institutions
Philip D. Christman

An advising administrator's job within a small college or university setting is often a solo operation involving multiple responsibilities. Since most small colleges use faculty in advising, the degree of involvement of the advising professional varies both within the institution and within various academic departments. This section examines how the advising administrator uses the institutional mission statement, faculty, and campus resources to serve as a student advocate in the small-college environment.

When working in the small-college environment one word comes to mind: family. Small colleges are very similar to a family model, embracing many of the traits of systems theory, in which the whole is different from the sum of its parts (Fenell & Weinhold, 2002). One cannot look at just one part of a small institution to understand it. Like a family, one must look at the entire college context to appreciate its dynamic. What are some of the important members of the small-college environment?

Common Institutional Components

Small private institutions share a number of characteristics that pertain to the academic advising aspect of student success. Some of these are described here.

Institutional Mission Statement. At the heart of advising in the small-college or university setting is its purpose, as expressed in the mission statement. In this environment the pragmatic can often conflict with utopia, with the academic advisor serving as a reference point to vivify student interests in a particular course, knowing that to do so might impact a student's life direction.

Small colleges and universities attempt to provide a more personal environment across disciplines that are often clearly delineated in the mission statement. "At the heart of Swarthmore's academic experience is the special relationship that exists between students . . . and the faculty with whom they work in and out of the classroom" (Swarthmore College, 2007). At St. Mary's College in California a core objective is "To create a student-centered educational community whose members support one another with mutual understanding and respect" (St. Mary's College, 2007). Collegial dialogue is welcomed outside the classroom experience, and it is not uncommon for this to be interdisciplinary. A student majoring in modern languages might enjoy a close relationship with a professor in the cognitive sciences.

While the goal of faculty, administration, and support staff is to embrace the core objectives of the institution, students may not be as cognizant of the value in embracing them, and it is the advising administrator who assists students in fostering a deeper understanding of the mission statement. This objective might also include a discussion of the relevancy of the core or general education requirements, for which courses are typically more specific within the small-college setting.

The mission statement might allow diversity in the required general education courses within certain disciplines. The articulation of such distinctions often becomes the responsibility of the advising administrator. Regular meetings with department chairs and faculty helps the administrator convey accurate information to students. The advising center often becomes the conduit through which requirements are shared with other student support offices, such as the registrar, career development, and student services.

Reporting Lines. Reporting lines in the small-college environment differ depending on the institution's philosophy regarding advising. Institutions whose focus is mainly on student retention might have advising report through an enrollment manager. If the institutional model slants toward student development, advising might fall under student services. For institutions that see advising as predominantly academic, the advising administrator might report to the chief academic officer. If advising is mainly considered a registration process, the office might report through the registrar.

The advising administrator needs to respond accordingly both in establishing an advising philosophy and in assessing student outcomes. Regardless of reporting lines, communication with department chairs and student support offices is paramount in order to disseminate accurate information to students. Doing so also gains access to any philosophical changes within departments that might eventually lead to curricular changes, allowing an advisor to be more proactive in advising students.

Advising Models. The models for delivery of academic advising used in small private colleges are varied and are likely to reflect the variability in reporting lines.

Faculty-Only Advising Model. In this model, advising is provided only by full-time faculty. Administrative responsibility typically rests with the academic dean or a designate, or possibly with a faculty member who is given release time. While most college catalogues have a statement such as, "Students bear the ultimate responsibility for decisions and actions that determine their success," under this model the fulfillment of the degree requirements rests within each department and is enforced by the registrar.

In order to best disseminate degree changes within a particular major or changes in advising policy to the rest of the small-college community, it is critical that the proper curricular procedure is maintained and that these changes are eventually reported to the full faculty. While some changes may be simply informational, recording them in this manner improves faculty awareness in other disciplines and helps avoid student confusion.

Faculty Advising Model with Professional Advising Support. This model includes any external person(s) or office in which nonfaculty or faculty have full-time advising responsibilities. As costs increased to recruit students, colleges became more concerned with student retention (Gardner, 2001). Across most institutions, advising has been invaluable in increasing persistence (Light, 2001), and this is particularly important with the less selective smaller colleges. Since small colleges look to students as "family," it was natural to examine how advising might decrease attrition. Consequently, this blended model of advising gained in popularity among smaller institutions (Habley, 2004).

If the advising administrator does not hold faculty rank, it is crucial that advisor training be channeled through the appropriate committee on faculty development.

Small colleges with a separate advising unit often include other institutional responsibilities with advising—for example, working with specific student populations such as undecided students, at-risk students, or students with special needs, and with career services, testing, and other support offices on campus.

In summary, the positive aspects of this model are to provide for centralized advising services, to provide a place where undecided students can explore majors, to reduce the routine aspects of advising for faculty, and to provide more consistent service to students and college personnel regarding advising questions.

The negative aspects of this model are additional costs, another level in the advising process, and potential misinformation if departments do not adequately communicate with the advising office.

Specific Institutional Components

Though some generalizations can be made about the nature of academic advising in small private institutions, each one must still must address its unique characteristics.

Accurate Faculty Representation. Small-college advising administrators "know" faculty through myriad contacts with students. Such knowledge is sometimes laced with sophomoric student comments; other times it carries high accolades. Recognizing individual strengths and weaknesses, the advising administrator uses this knowledge to represent faculty positively while maintaining healthy communication between students and various majors.

For example, if students widely communicate that others should avoid a particular professor "at all costs," the advising administrator must take steps to alleviate such ill will within the "family" of the small-college environment. Such action points to the necessity of an additional step in the advising process: dialogue. It is beneficial for the small-college advisor to create informal interactions with faculty, particularly those who teach first-year courses, in order to better connect student and faculty strengths and minimize discontent.

Knowledge across All Majors. Small-college advisors often work closely with undecided students and must be prepared to represent all majors to students. Students at smaller universities are typically allowed to explore all majors for which prerequisites have been met. It is not uncommon for some courses to be offered only once every two years. Small-college advisors need to pay particular attention to share with exploratory students how upper-level course prerequisites need to be considered early so as to not increase the risk of having to attend college longer than four years. It is not uncommon for undeclared students to default to taking only required general education courses. However, doing so can increase the risk of extending college beyond four years within some small colleges. The above examples highlight the importance of keeping objective, concise notes on advisees, to which later reference might chronicle the evolutionary process of student success.

Advisor-Student Relationships. Small colleges tend to refer to themselves has having a strong faculty-student relationship. Consequently, the majority have an organizational model centered on faculty advising (Habley, 2004). Faculty members are encouraged to meet with their advisees, whom they often also have in a class. Light (2001) points out the importance of this interaction in college achievement, and the small-college environment endeavors to foster this personal interaction, leading to faculty and student collaboration in the attainment of educational goals.

In representing the student (and often his or her family), it is important to listen, establish rapport, and learn what students want. Sharing stories can be an invaluable resource in better understanding students' backgrounds and long-range goals (Hagen, 2007). The pressure on the advisor for meaningful conversation in a short period of time, usually around registration, can be immense. Since individual personalization is foundational to the small-college environment, a few practical suggestions may be worthwhile: (1) define the time boundaries at both ends, that is, both current limits and future expectations; (2) value each student appointment, perhaps by reinforcing the student's importance in the process; (3) do not compromise by acquiescing to student wishes that may be inappropriate for their success; and (4) adhere to office hours to demonstrate availability and concern for students' welfare.

Self-Care: Avoid Burnout

In both advising models the increased time demands place a higher relevance on self-care. A common statement heard within the small-college environment is, "There is always something to do, whether writing a student reference for law school, talking with a concerned parent, scheduling a student, or working with an at-risk student; it is busy throughout the entire academic year." Often exasperated by a solo-office operation, small-college advisors wear many hats, have limited down time, and are subsequently at greater risk for burnout. Academic advisors in all institutional settings would likely benefit from the following discussion.

What are some telltale signs of burnout? According to Maslach (1993), who examined burnout in professional counselors, individuals who experience burnout will see signs of decreased energy, higher irritability with situations that typically do not produce stress, and feelings of exhaustion; they become emotionally tired and less productive or competent. Burnout is typically evident across multiple domains: cognitive, physical, emotional, relational, and mental (Much, Swanson, & Jazazewski, 2005).

Cognitive symptoms might include a negative attitude toward students, the inability to concentrate, forgetting appointments, self-doubt, or not looking forward to going to work. Physically, burnout can lead to heightened fatigue, insomnia, tenseness, or contracting any of myriad routine illnesses. Emotionally, symptoms include various psychological feelings, such as resentment, depression, anger, guilt, frustration, feeling overwhelmed, low self-esteem, or sobbing. One's relationships might become more and more distant from colleagues or disengaged from family and friends. Symptoms of mental burnout may include finding it more difficult to concentrate, daydreaming, forgetting appointments, overfocusing, and the like.

Recognizing the above symptoms is an important first step to avoiding burnout. Next is knowing certain prevention strategies, which fall into two categories: system-centered and person-centered (Much et al., 2005).

Within the advising workplace, system-centered strategies focus on improving the job-related factors mentioned above. Improvements might be additional financial resources, support personnel during peak advising times, or higher compensation. Person-centered strategies are subdivided into internal and external approaches. Internal approaches include restructuring daily peak efficiency times, completing more demanding assignments during high-energy times, and moving lower-energy assignments to less creative moments. Self-care is another internal, person-centered strategy, which involves proper eating, consistent exercise, getting adequate rest, and getting appropriate medical care. A final internal, person-centered strategy might involve spiritual or religious resources, which are available on most campuses.

External, person-centered strategies involve resources outside an individual and include involvement in a professional association, the reestablishment of boundaries around breaks or lunch, and support of peers (Lawson & Venart, 2005).

A final strategy not to be undervalued is the importance of play (Much et al., 2005). This might include developing a hobby, playing on a local sports team, playing an instrument in a local symphony, or any task that helps balance the pressure of the work environment with pleasure.

Final "Family" Comment. There is one more important note. While smaller institutions often use words synonymous with the family unit, it is critical to remember that it is not a family in the truest sense of the word and that a level of professional communication, integrity, and boundaries must be maintained and respected. While one may think of a student as a son or daughter, it is both healthy and important for the academic advisor (whether faculty or professional) to remember that, in reality, this is not the case. Professional roles and distances must always be maintained. It takes only one student misunderstanding to call into question years of successful advising or teaching.

CONCLUSION

This section has examined how a personalized approach to advising, present within the small-college or university environment, is integrated within common and specific institutional components. Since advising in this environment is often a solo operation, recognizing burnout and the importance of self-care were also discussed.

References

Kathy J. Davis

Abelman, R., & Molina, A. D. (2006). Institutional vision and academic advising. *NACADA Journal, 26* (2), 5–12.

Dillon, R. K., & Fisher, B. J. (2000). Faculty as part of the advising equation: An inquiry into faculty viewpoints on advising. *NACADA Journal, 20* (1), 16–23.

Light, R. J. (2004). Changing advising through assessment. *NACADA Journal, 24,* (1& 2), 7–16.

Steele, G. E. (2006). Five possible future work profiles for full-time academic advisors. *NACADA Journal, 26* (2), 48–64.

Swanson, D. J. (2006, April). Creating a culture of "engagement" with academic advising: Challenges and opportunities for today's higher education institutions. Presented at the Western Social Science Association Convention, Phoenix, Arizona.

Yudof, M. G. (2003). The changing scene of academic advising. *NACADA Journal, 23,* (1& 2), 7–9.

Dick Vallandingham

Community College Survey of Student Engagement (2005). Results portraying community college students. Retrieved August 8, 2007, from http://www.ccsse.org

Geigerich, S. (2006, Winter). Barrier buster: Community colleges and their students embrace challenges. *Lumina Foundation Focus,* 4–25.

Horn, L., & Nevill, S. (2006). Profile of undergraduates in U.S. postsecondary education institutions: 2003–04: With a special analysis of community college students. Washington, DC: U. S. Department of Education, National Center for Education Statistics.

King, M. C. (2002). Community college advising. *NACADA Clearinghouse of Academic Advising Resources.* Retrieved July 25, 2007, from http://www.nacada.ksu.edu/ Clearinghouse/AdvisingIssues/comcollege.htm

Kossoff, M. (2005, July). Fact sheet: Characteristics and challenges of community colleges. *Achieving the Dream: Community Colleges Count.*

Pardee, C. F. (2004). Organizational structures for advising. *NACADA Clearinghouse of Academic Advising Resources.* Retrieved September 4, 2007, from http:// www.nacada.ksu.edu/Clearinghouse/AdvisingIssues/org_models.htm

Spellman, N. (2007). Enrollment and retention barriers adult students encounter. *The Community College Enterprise* Web site. Retrieved September 4, 2007, from http://findarticles.com/p/articles/mi_qa4057/is_200704/ai_n19431963

Philip D. Christman

Fenell, D. L., & Weinhold, B. K. (2002). *Counseling families: An introduction to marriage and family therapy.* Denver: Love.

Gardner, J. N. (2001) Focusing on the first-year student. *Priorities, 17,* 1–18.

Habley, W. (Ed.). (2004), *Current practices in academic advising: ACT's sixth national survey of academic advising.* (NACADA Monograph Series, no. 10.) Manhattan, KS: National Academic Advising Association.

Hagen, P. (2007, September). Narrative theory and academic advising. *Academic Advising Today, 30* (3). Retrieved September 17, 2007, from http://www.nacada .ksu.edu/AAT/NW30_3.htm

Lawson, G., & Venart, B. (2005). Preventing counselor impairment: Vulnerability wellness, and resilience. *VISTAS Online 53,* 243–246. Retrieved September 7, 2007, from http://counselingoutfitters.com/vistas/vistas05/Vistas05.art53.pdf

Light, R. J. (2001). *Making the most of college:. Students speak their minds.* Cambridge, MA: Harvard University Press.

Maslach, C. (1993). Burnout: A multidimensional perspective. In W. B. Schaufeli, C. Maslach, & T. Marek (Eds.), *Professional burnout: Recent developments in theory and research.* Washington, DC: Taylor & Francis.

Much, K., Swanson, A., & Jazazewski, R. (2005). Burnout prevention for professionals in psychology. *VISTAS Online 46,* 215–217. Retrieved September 17, 2007 from http://counselingoutfitters.com/vistas/vistas05/Vistas05.art46.pdf

St. Mary's College. (2007). *Mission statement.* Retrieved September 7, 2007, from http://www.stmarys-ca.edu/lasallian-approach/mission-statement.html

Swarthmore College. (2007). *Teaching and learning in a community of scholars.* Retrieved September 7, 2007, from http://www.swarthmore.edu/x508.xml

CHAPTER TWENTY-NINE

Perspectives on the Future of Academic Advising

Thomas J. Grites, Virginia N. Gordon, and Wesley R. Habley

The preceding chapters in this book describe in detail the current concepts and practices of academic advising on American college campuses. Advisors should take pride in their past and current accomplishments, but it is also critical to look to the future and prepare for the challenges that academic advising will face in the next decade. How will changes in higher education impact the philosophy and delivery of advising? What factors will influence how advising will change? Who will be our advisors? How will technology affect future advising practices? How will the increasing diversity of college students influence our advising approaches?

Many authors have discussed the challenges that higher education is facing today and will face in the future (Avila & Leger, 2005; Bok, 2004; Hersh, Merrow, & Wolfe, 2005; Newman, Courturier, & Scurry, 2004). These issues are concerned with how postsecondary institutions will adapt to a world altered by changing demographics, globalization, and technology. Academic advising has become an integral part of higher education. The future agenda for academic advising will continue to be linked to the continuing and rapid change that characterizes the state of higher education.

The U.S. Department of Education Commission's report on the state of higher education (2006) indicated that the nation has become complacent in its satisfaction with our system of higher education and that many take our global postsecondary superiority for granted. While the Commission found much to applaud in the current system, it also warned that urgent reform is needed. It is imperative that advisors consider how the issues and trends cited in this and other reports will affect their relationships with students, coworkers, and institutional systems. This chapter will address not only the challenges that higher education is facing today but also the possible impact on the philosophy and delivery of academic advising and how informed planning can influence its future quality, content, and delivery.

CHALLENGES TO HIGHER EDUCATION

The great value of a postsecondary education for both individuals and society is well established. The individual with a bachelor's degree, for example, earns more than 75 percent more than a high school graduate. These additional earnings sum to over $1 million over a lifetime (Hill, Hoffman, & Rex, 2005). The advantages of a college degree go beyond increased income, however. College graduates enjoy higher levels of savings, increased personal and professional mobility, improved quality of life for their offspring, better consumer decision-making, and more hobbies and leisure activities (Institute for Higher Education Policy, 1998). The Carnegie Foundation reported that postsecondary students become more open-minded, more cultured, more rational, more consistent, and less authoritarian (Rowley and Hurtado, 2002).

Higher education also produces many societal benefits. Enhanced worker productivity can be traced to workers with greater educational attainment and skills. These productivity gains translate into higher output and incomes for the economy. Intergenerational social benefits may increase as degree attainment today translates into higher probabilities of degree attainment in future generations (Hill et al., 2005). If higher education is to meet the needs of the individual and society, the issues of access, affordability, accountability, financial aid, and quality of learning need to be addressed. Although these issues may not have a direct impact on academic advising, they do affect the environment in which advisors work and the students they serve.

Current Issues in Postsecondary Education

The most important issues facing higher education were identified and recommendations for change and improvements were reported in the U.S. Secretary of Education Commission's (2006) report on the future of higher education. The report identified the conditions discussed below as currently affecting higher education most significantly.

Access. The Commission found that access to higher education is severely limited by many factors. Substandard high school preparation was noted as a barrier to college entrance and success. Lack of information about college opportunities as well as persistent financial barriers were also cited. The nation's growing population of racial and ethnic minorities represent populations that have been less likely both to attend and to complete college than white students.

Affordability. Many students are dissuaded from attending college because of the rising costs. Still others are unwilling to incur what they believe will become an insurmountable debt. Although state subsidies have decreased on a per capita basis, the Commission believes that affordability is directly affected by a financing system that offers little incentive for colleges and universities to improve institutional efficiency in an aggressive manner. Many advisors have witnessed this financial burden on students, not only as it affects access and retention, but also how financial concerns can detract from academic involvement and concentration.

Financial Aid. The Commission found the current financial aid system to be confusing, inefficient, complex, and often not generally available to students who need it most. Although there are at least twenty separate federal programs providing financial aid or tax benefits to students, low-income families, especially, still have problems accessing financial assistance.

Learning. The quality of student learning at U.S. colleges and universities is inadequate, according to the Commission. "According to the most recent National Assessment of Adult Literacy, for instance, the percentage of college graduates deemed proficient in prose literacy has declined from 40 to 31 percent in the past decade" (U.S. Department of Education, 2006, p. 3). Employers often voice concern that many new graduates they hire are not prepared to work and are lacking the critical thinking, writing, and problem-solving skills needed in today's workplace. The Commission urges postsecondary institutions to make a commitment to develop new pedagogies, curricula, and technologies to improve student learning. Advisors can emphasize the importance of identifying and learning these basic, marketable skills as they help students select the academic programs and courses that might help them acquire and practice those skills.

Innovation. Numerous barriers to investment in innovation make it difficult for postsecondary institutions to address national workforce needs and compete in the global marketplace. The Commission recommends that colleges and universities embrace opportunities to be entrepreneurial, from testing new methods of teaching and content delivery to meeting the increased demand for lifelong learning. For-profit institutions have attempted to take the lead in the entrepreneurial effort, as evidenced by their overall average increase of 57 percent in stock prices in 2007, and more growth is predicted for the future (Inside Higher Ed, 2007). In addition to being advocates for innovative, new methods in teaching and in other institutional areas, advisors should embrace innovation in their own advising practices as well.

Accreditation. Another issue that has recently gained considerable attention is that of accreditation. Our nongovernmental accreditation system was designed as a self-regulatory mechanism relying on peer evaluation to ensure basic levels of quality in higher education programs. Schray (2006) noted three areas of concern associated with accreditation: (1) ensuring that performance consists of "a broad range of performance indicators, including access, productivity and efficiency, student learning, degree completion, and economic returns from postsecondary education" (p. 6); (2) open standards and processes issues involve "how accreditation standards and processes can be changed to be more open to and supportive of innovation and diversity in higher education including new types of educational institutions and new approaches for providing educational services such as distance learning" (p. 7); and (3) consistency and transparency issues "address how accreditation standards and processes can be made more consistent to support greater transparency and greater opportunities for credit transfer between accredited institutions" (p. 8). Advisors should be familiar with these and other accreditation issues and prepare to address them through short-term and strategic planning.

Higher Education Trends

In a report by the Society for College and University Planning (SCUP, 2007), many trends are cited that affect integrated planning in higher education institutions. Incoming students are making decisions about college attendance differently than their parents did. "Strength in intended major" and "financial aid availability" were viewed by students as most important when selecting a college (p. 2). Economically, students' and parents' concerns about loan debt affect whether or where students go to college. Part-time students, who are often older and have additional family and employment obligations, have minimal access to financial aid. Another trend noted in the report is that the current wave of millennial students value personal attention and the ability to customize their majors. Advisors are central to delivering this personal touch that today's students of all ages demand.

Online learning is now viewed as a growing learning trend and one of the few relatively unrestricted avenues for innovation in teaching and learning. The report cites blended learning, including gaming, virtual reality, text messaging, and social networking sites as new learning venues. Integrated planning will become even more important as campuses realize that learning occurs 24/7 and not just face-to-face (p. 11).

The authors of the SCUP (2007) report express concern about the trend of the increasing use of contingent faculty in all types of institutions. While graduation rates may be used as an accountability benchmark, they do not acknowledge the value of full-time tenured faculty in producing the results higher education needs.

Rhodes (2001) views the American university as an irreplaceable resource whose value must be preserved through renewal and reform. Rhodes states that the greatest catastrophe facing the university today is loss of community. Learning in community "will be expansive and informed, contested by opposing interpretations, leavened by differing experience, and refined by alternative viewpoints" (p. 45). Academic advisors are an integral part of this learning community and as such need to make sure the advising system on their campus is in tune with the paradigm shift that Rhodes describes.

Student Diversity

The issues and trends cited previously in this chapter suggest that higher education is facing formidable challenges. And, as critical as these challenges are, they are confounded and compounded by the ramifications of student diversity. It has only been during the final decades of the twentieth century that student diversity has assumed a new and expansive meaning. To explore these changes and their implications for academic advising requires a look to past interpretations of student diversity. To Havighurst (1954), *student diversity* referred to only two areas: academic aptitude and socioeconomic class. He reported that in 1940, 80 percent of upper- and upper-middle-class students, 20 percent of lower-middle-class students, and only 5 percent of working-class students entered college. He predicted that in the best-case future scenario, 50 percent and 40 percent of lower-middle-class and working-class students, respectively, would enroll in college. By 1962, McConnell and Heist identified several additional characteristics of a diverse student body: vocational interests, attitudes, and personality characteristics. It is clear from these mid-twentieth century examples that diversity was little more than a minor variation on homogeneity.

As we approached the end of the twentieth century, student diversity was already beginning to have an impact. Morrison, Ericson, and Kohler (1998) listed the important trends affecting higher education at that time. It is interesting to note that many of those trends are still evident, such as increased numbers of nontraditional and minority populations, increased community college enrollments, tuition increasing faster than household incomes, increased pressure for higher education to control costs, increased awareness of fitness and health, increased awareness of need for computer systems and information integrity, and increased demands for accountability.

In Chapter Eight, Kennedy and Ishler provide a current and comprehensive view of student diversity in the twenty-first century that provides a stark contrast to the homogeneous definitions of diversity offered by Havighurst and by McConnell and Heist. Simply stated, there is no longer (if there ever was) a definition of a typical student. Figure 29.1 captures that reality and demonstrates that assertion. It answers the question: "Out of every 100 undergraduate students, how many exhibit a specific characteristic or experience a particular outcome?" The forty-six data elements included in the figure provide a clear illustration of the complexities of student diversity. The figure is divided into three sections: Demographics, Pathways to College, and Experiences with College. Each characteristic is based on fact, on the combination of two or more facts, or on the best estimates available. The major sources of the elements cited in the chart include the *Chronicle of Higher Education Almanac* (2007) and multiple and the most recent reports from the National Center for Educational Statistics (NCES), the U.S. Census, the National Survey of Student Engagement (NSSE), the Cooperative Institutional Research Program (CIRP), and ACT data files. Virtually all of these data sources are cited and referenced elsewhere in this handbook. Due to the number and the complexity of possible citations (and accompanying references) formal documentation of each characteristic is not included here.

Demographics

• 1 is American Indian	• 34 delayed enrollment for more than one year after high school
• 7 are Asian	• 50 are financially independent
• 13 are Black, non-Hispanic	• 20 are financially independent students who report annual income of less than $20,000
• 10 are Hispanic	
• 65 are white	• 21 are married
• 4 are multicultural	• 16 are married with dependents
• 35 are first-generation	• 57 are women
• 30 come from single-parent families	• 11 will have a documented disability
• 25 come from blended families	• 10 are gay, lesbian, bisexual, or transgendered
• 30 will have moved within the previous five years	• 5 are international students
• 37 are over the age of 25	• 9 have high ability

Pathways to College

• 6 may have earned a general equivalency diploma (GED)	• 41 have enrolled in at least one advanced-placement course in high school
• 1 earned an international baccalaureate diploma	• 50 report an A-average in high school
• 6 were home-schooled in grades 9–12	• 26 have met ACT's College Readiness Standards in English, Mathematics, Science, and Social Sciences
• 40 have dual-enrolled in a college-level course while in high school	
	• 20 have spent less than one hour per week on high school homework

Experiences with College

• 63 will receive financial aid	• 10 work full-time
• 34 will attend one or more other colleges during their academic career	• 16 will fail at least one course during their first year
• 11 will simultaneously enroll at another college	• 85 will live off campus
• 20 will enroll in an online course	• 27 will seek personal counseling
• 28 will be required to take remedial education (range: 12 percent in four-year private colleges to 42 percent in two-year colleges)	• 25 will seek career guidance
	• 33 will not return to the same college for a second year
• 20 are undecided about a program of study	• 15 will not be enrolled in any college after three years
• 65 (or more) will change their mind about their program of study	• 35 will neither complete any degree nor be enrolled at any college six years after they first enroll
• 39 attend part-time	• 40 will not complete a degree at any college during their lifetime

Figure 29.1. How many of every 100 undergraduate students experience a specific characteristic?

As an advisor comes to know more about a student, an individualized and complex mosaic evolves—a mosaic that may result in overlap, confusion, or even conflict among multiple theoretical perspectives. It is one thing to advise an adult student, but as additional factors are introduced into the advising relationship, complexity increases and certainty decreases. For example, in addition to being an adult, the student may be a minority male, single parent who is undecided about a program of study, and whose entry credential is a GED earned more than a decade earlier. These multiple characteristics lead to complex variations and numerous permutations. Advising such a student presents a conundrum—a problem to which only a conjectural and contextual solution is possible.

Furthermore, if theory serves as a guide to practice, then advising practice is surely well served or, perhaps, advising practice might even be too well served. In the first edition of this *Handbook*, Creamer (2000, p. 28) identified more than twenty-five student-development and career-development theories that have applicability to academic advising. And, in Chapter Two of this *Handbook*, Hagen and Jordan provide us with fifty-one resources that support the theoretical foundations of academic advising. Theories have multiplied and diversified to the extent that a theoretical conundrum faces advisors. Each theoretical perspective, in its own right, seems plausible and useful, and many are supported by a significant body of research. The problem is that the diversity of student backgrounds, characteristics, and experiences defies the application of a single theory, as Hagen and Jordan argue in Chapter Two.

ADDRESSING THE CHALLENGES

Facing the issues and trends described above, the process of academic advising in higher education must continue to play a key role in responding and meeting these conditions. Every opportunity for this process to demonstrate its capacity for ensuring the success of students, institutions, and indeed higher education itself must be acknowledged and used.

The Field of Academic Advising

In the past thirty years, academic advising has become recognized as a viable and necessary component of higher education that results in the success of college students. The opportunity now exists for this component to stretch beyond its well-established foundation and assert its potential in multiple aspects of the higher education landscape.

Global Impact. Academic advising is not restricted to the local campus and advising office. Technology has enabled high-quality academic advising to reach a global audience. International conferences that focus on college students now occur more frequently, and the importance of academic advising must be shared with the higher education global community. The National Academic Advising Association (NACADA) has welcomed and fostered the advising community in

Canada for many years and more recently has engaged the same community from Great Britain. With increases both in international students studying in the United States and in study tours and international study programs for U.S. students, as well as global economies that require individual and family relocations to all parts of the world, effective links between college students who move or travel will be required.

Supporting Advisors. Another challenge could actually arise from the very success the field of academic advising has itself achieved. Increased recognition for faculty who advise well has been realized on a number of campuses. In some cases, an introduction to the expectation of the importance of this role has become part of graduate programs that prepare future faculty members. Concurrently, graduate programs in higher education have developed courses, tracks, and even complete degree programs that focus on academic advising. The challenge to the field will be to prepare, foster, and maintain the proper balance between faculty and nonfaculty academic advisors in order to provide the respective expertise of both that results in optimal student success.

Resources. Finally, the challenge of adequate fiscal resources for higher education will always exist, and the field of academic advising will likely remain a target for reductions when resources are dangerously scarce. As long as retention and graduation rates remain primary measures of institutional success and often the resultant funding, primarily in state institutions, academic advising will need to demonstrate its direct effect on these measures. Legislators and policy-makers need to know that good academic advising results in increased retention and graduation rates. Alternative measures of these concepts that have been discussed, proposed, and even implemented in some cases, and that may hold promise for academic advising, include increases in student performance and engagement, rather than simple retention rates—a value-added approach; and funding formulas based on numbers of graduates, rather than simple graduation rates—an approach that accounts for the degrees earned by transfer students. The latter concept has been recognized by the National Collegiate Athletic Association (NCAA) in calculating its graduation rates in two ways.

Research. In the summary and conclusions of the report on ACT's Sixth National Survey on Academic Advising, Habley (2004) suggested that, although advising is far more visible on the higher education scene than ever before, it remains in danger of not being able to claim a place at the core of the institutional mission. A primary cause for this dilemma is that although advising asserts that it makes a significant contribution to student success and institutional effectiveness, only a limited body of quality research substantiates that claim. If advising is to claim what many believe to be its rightful centrality in the institution, it is imperative that the field of academic advising undertake an aggressive research agenda. Such an agenda, led by NACADA, should include the following components.

Organize and fund an invitational research summit. The advising research summit should include some of the best research minds in higher education as well as NACADA members with a reputation in research.

Establish an ambitious five-year research agenda. Summit participants would be charged to develop a plan for a five-year research agenda for NACADA that identifies the topics to be studied, the scope of the studies, the preferred methods, and the direct and indirect costs.

Fund the five-year research agenda. NACADA currently supports advising research through its annual awards program. Although the research produced through grants and scholarships informs the field of advising, the topics are not those directed by NACADA. Rather, they are selected from those submitted. Funds for the current program should either be redirected to NACADA's research agenda or additional funds should be allocated to support the five-year agenda.

Seek matching grant support through foundations and other funding sources. The global economy and American competitiveness have contributed to significant public and foundation interest in improving postsecondary institutional effectiveness and college completion rates. NACADA should seek public- and private-sector collaborators who can augment the resources necessary to fulfill the research agenda.

Develop a request for proposals (RFP) to conduct the national studies. With the agenda established and funding in place, a detailed two-stage (preliminary and final) RFP process should be circulated to major research organizations, institutions with related graduate programs, and centers for the study of higher education.

Secure representative institutions to participate in the studies. Because national studies require broad-based and representative institutional participation, NACADA should work with member institutions to serve as research sites, provide data on students, and provide information on college practices.

Publish and disseminate research findings. NACADA should commit to publish research through its professional journal, along with its monograph series and other special publications. Most importantly, NACADA should devise strategies to share the research with individuals who make decisions on the allocation of resources.

Reaching All Stakeholders

Perhaps the three challenges to higher education to which academic advising can most effectively demonstrate its impact are learning, accreditation, and student diversity. Academic advising must result in improved student *learning* outcomes that enhance the institutional performance indicators that are reviewed for *accreditation* purposes and that are demonstrated across whatever *student diversity* mix exists on the campus. This will not be an easy task, however. Consider the challenge of demonstrating student learning outcomes that will be reviewed by almost every national or regional accrediting body.

The Commission Report (U.S. Department of Education, 2006) suggests the National Survey of Student Engagement (NSSE) and the Collegiate Learning Assessment (CLA) as viable potential instruments for all types of institutions to measure and demonstrate their learning outcomes for all types of students. Some critics have likened this suggestion to the No Child Left Behind Act that now drives elementary and secondary education. So, how does this affect academic advising?

Academic advisors have the most frequent opportunities to suggest and advocate for the most productive courses of study that will result in enhanced student engagement and performance. Advisors can encourage students to select options that provide learning experiences that engage them in higher-order thinking, problem-solving, writing, technology, and quantitative reasoning skills. Advisors can encourage and support student participation and involvement in a wide variety of campus and community events, which provide opportunities for civic and political engagement. To perform these tasks effectively, advisors will likely learn to play all the roles described later. Whether students accept and pursue the options proposed is another issue.

At the same time, however, other factors sometimes seem to militate against these opportunities. For example, the increase in baccalaureate completion programs at local community colleges further challenges academic advisors at both types of institutions to develop a coherent academic program that fosters optimal student learning outcomes when the array of degree programs, courses, and regular full-time faculty may be significantly diminished. Not every four-year degree option and not every course option to fulfill a degree requirement can be made available, and certainly not every instructor will be a full-time faculty member at these sites. These increased and often necessary conditions of convenience for many students simultaneously decrease the potential for their maximum learning and engagement. Advisors will face a greater challenge to assist their students in meeting these expectations of higher education.

The very nature of for-profit institutions may be a significant factor in realizing these opportunities. Abelman, Dalessandro, Janstova, and Snyder-Suhy (2007) found that the institutional mission and vision statements of the most rapidly growing institutions in the country tend to ignore efforts that encourage students to engage themselves beyond their specific course requirements. Consequently, academic advising is much more focused on specific career development than on student development. Academic advisors in these types of institutions will assume much different roles in trying to meet the challenges described above.

The impact of rapidly emerging technologies will continually affect all aspects of higher education, including academic advising. Steele (2006) presented an excellent description of the potential adaptations of these new technologies and potential resulting advisor roles across five advisor work profiles. He also acknowledged the likely interrelationship of these roles in the assessment of academic advising and in the training of academic advisors.

The phenomenon of the characteristic millennial student, who is extraordinarily reliant on parental support and the most recent technological advances, presents new challenges to the advisor who advocates for student responsibility and decision-making and the expectation of a more personalized relationship. Some institutions have further exacerbated this phenomenon by building residence halls with only single rooms, complete with every electronic device and convenience available at home, and even online take-out orders from dining halls.

Student diversity of another type, which is growing significantly, is the "swirling" transfer student who may have accumulated a substantial amount of student loan debt and is facing a job market that may not enable that debt and other life expenses to be met adequately, at least for more years than were anticipated when the loans were acquired. Perhaps the very nature of this student attendance pattern is a reflection of the affordability and financial aid challenges set out in the Commission Report (U.S. Department of Education, 2006). More students begin at one institution, transfer to another, and transfer again. The term *swirling* has been attributed primarily to those who transfer in and out of community colleges, but patterns of transfer in general are becoming more and more unpredictable, irregular—diverse—than what higher education has experienced in the past.

Where academic advising administrators and academic advisors can likely provide their most significant response to nearly all of the challenges is in reaching decision-makers, particularly on their own campuses. The following strategies would facilitate such a response:

1. Adopt the NACADA Concept of Academic Advising (National Academic Advising Association, 2006) as a standard for the campus. This document is accepted and recognized by the national professional association that represents the field of academic advising. The Concept establishes the link to the teaching-learning mission of every institution, demonstrates the integration of all campus constituencies, and articulates what students will know, value, and be able to do as a result of the academic advising experience at an institution. The Concept provides the framework under which every institution can develop its own individualized concept, definition, operational mechanisms, student learning outcomes, and assessment strategies that work best to achieve the institutional goals and objectives it has set for itself.

2. Remain cognizant of, and in fact even become involved in, the legislative and policy efforts that affect the advising process on the campus. As federal, state, accreditation, licensure, and other policies that affect student growth and learning are being developed, academic advisors need to apprise their own campus decision-makers of the potential impact of such action. Too often such actions are deemed necessary and ultimately enacted due to a single complaint or occurrence. Clearly, the response to such a limited event cannot be based on a single case, so advising programs need to maintain good information

about their students, their characteristics, and their behaviors. Simple cases and emotional responses to pending legislative action will not likely be adequate to support what would work best on a campus, or at least what would result in the least harm. The academic advising program needs to build and maintain its case for appropriate actions that might be imposed upon them.

3. Be able to demonstrate the cost benefit of a good advising program, whether that be in retention figures, student learning outcomes achieved, graduation rates, or funds acquired or saved. Often the legislative or policy actions result in additional resource needs or real-locations. The value of academic advising must be shown in multiple terms so that all stakeholders understand its significance.

Meeting the challenges of higher education through the strategic integration of campus human and fiscal resources is a "no-brainer." Using the campus academic advising program to facilitate, augment, and ultimately achieve meeting these challenges is a strategy that cannot be denied. The future of academic advising, perhaps of the success of our institutions in general, is in the hands of all those who have responsibilities for successful academic advising on each and every campus.

Academic Advisors

For academic advising to be successful at the local level, those responsible for advising programs, indeed individual academic advisors themselves, will be charged to meet the challenges described above as they affect their own advising units and individual students. Obviously, some challenges will have more direct effects than others, and some will not have an immediate or direct impact, but those responsible for academic advising must still be prepared to demonstrate how the academic advising process meets these challenges.

Armed with factual information and undergirded by theory, one might be tempted to think that advising is far more science than it is art. In many respects, institutions that view advising as a necessary but perfunctory process for ensuring that students efficiently process through a predetermined set of requirements in a linear and timely path to degree completion are institutions that do not understand the complexities and the nuances created by student diversity. Habley & Bloom (2007) suggest that there is little science to advising. It is not simply a "one size fits all" activity in which students are neatly compartmentalized and processed, but rather it is a teaching and learning function built on a quality relationship. They state that to develop a quality relationship, advisors must play several roles:

consumer advocate: assists the student to make wise choices

intervener: provides timely and assertive intervention

orchestrator: blends student characteristics and needs with institutional resources *dissonance mediator:* closes the gap between student expectations and realities

dissonance creator: challenges students to leave their comfort zones

boundary spanner: connects students to all pertinent institutional experiences

bellwether: anticipates possible roadblocks and pitfalls

cultural guide: assists in the navigation of institutional norms, policies, procedures, and the like

To fulfill these roles requires advisors who view advising not as a science, but rather as an art. Advice for individuals who want to practice the art of advising with an increasingly diversified student body includes the following:

1. Advisors have a primary responsibility to the individuals they advise. Academic advisors work to strengthen the importance, dignity, potential, and unique nature of each individual within the academic setting. Advisors' work is guided by their beliefs that students: (a) have diverse backgrounds that can include different ethnic, racial, domestic, and international communities; sexual orientations; ages; gender and gender identities; physical, emotional, and psychological abilities; and political, religious, and educational beliefs; (b) hold their own beliefs and opinions; (c) are responsible for their own behaviors and the outcomes of those behaviors; (d) can be successful based upon their individual goals and efforts; (e) have a desire to learn; (f) have learning needs that vary based upon individual skills, goals, responsibilities, and experiences; and (g) use a variety of techniques and technologies to navigate their world (NACADA, 2004).

2. Advisors should be grounded in theory, but not reliant upon a single theoretical perspective. It is critical for advisors to understand theory, the multiple theoretical perspectives that pertain to academic advising, and their potential applications to the advising process. Yet, it is equally critical that advisors not rely on a single theory or perspective as the only basis for achieving success with their students.

3. Advisors must not rely on generalizations. Two things are true about generalizations: (1) no generalization applies to all students; and (2) all students' needs are derived from the interplay among generalizations that are appropriate and generalizations that are inappropriate. Therefore, advisors must seek to learn each student's unique characteristics and qualities and respond accordingly, if not uniquely.

4. Advisors must take time to understand the presenting concerns. Borrowed from a medical term (the presenting symptoms), these are the concerns or group of concerns about which students worry or from which relief is sought. Because advisors are often pressed for time, it is relatively easy to take a shortcut to the solution without taking the time to listen to all of the circumstances and conditions affecting the concern.

5. Advisors should listen with the third ear. Virtually all conversations include a subtext. This subtext includes the student's overall body language, posture, demeanor, and pattern of speech. The subtext always provides clues to problem resolution, and in many cases, conveys stronger messages than the spoken word.

6. Advisors must check their value judgments at the door. Values are subject to individual interpretation and preference. The role of an advisor is not to impose a set of values, but rather to help students understand their values and apply those values to the issues to be resolved or the problems to be solved.

7. Advisors must consider the context before addressing the problem. Advisors need to be sure they understand both the facts and the motivations of the student in order to preserve the overall academic advising mission and reputation on the campus.

8. Advisors must not engage in overanalysis. While assuming a holistic approach to advising, advisors need to avoid the risk of appearing to be therapists, which could result in overdependency in their advisees.

Finally, how do academic advisors help meet these challenges as part of their commitment to the field of advising? As for the research agenda, advisors must advance this in two ways. First, they must remain informed of the research that affects their role and advance the results to those who need to know and can use them—the decision-makers. Informing others of findings that demonstrate the effectiveness of new or different programs and strategies that might be adopted on their own campus must occur.

Second, advisors should determine and communicate their own findings within their advising unit, within their own institution, and to the field at large. The demand for accountability provides both a challenge and an opportunity to document and verify that the work of academic advisors—and thus academic advising as an entity and process in itself—is a significant factor in student growth, learning, and success.

These are some of the challenges that potentially face the field of academic advising. Recognizing and preparing to meet these challenges rests with all who have a stake in the field. No one committed to the field of academic advising can afford to be apathetic. Active participation has been a trademark of the field, which has reaped significant benefits over the past several decades, and it needs to be advocated even more so in the future.

Thelin (2004) states that the challenge of higher education in the United States during the twenty-first century is to rediscover "its essential principles and values that have perhaps been obscured in the recent blurring of educational activities and commercial ventures" (p. 362). He suggests that by going back to its fundamental purpose, American higher education can connect its past and present so that an appropriate future can be created. The challenge to the field of academic advising is to remain true to the principles and values that have been at its core since its earliest days. That is, in spite of economic, social, and technological changes, the welfare and growth of students must always remain central to its mission.

References

Abelman, R., Dalessandro, A., Janstova, P., & Snyder-Suhy, S. (2007). Institutional vision at proprietary schools: Advising for profit. *NACADA Journal, 27* (2), 9–27.

Avila, R., & Leger, N. (2005). *The future of higher education—A scenario evaluation of its prospects and challenges.* Lincoln, NE: iUniverse.

Bok, D. (2004). *Universities in the marketplace: The commercialization of higher education.* Princeton, NJ: Princeton University Press.

Chronicle of Higher Education Almanac. (2007). Washington, DC: Chronicle of Higher Education.

Creamer, D. G. (2000). Use of theory in academic advising. In V. N. Gordon, & W. R. Habley (Eds.), *Academic advising: A comprehensive handbook* (pp. 18–34). San Francisco: Jossey-Bass.

Habley, W. R. (2004). *The status of academic advising: Final report of ACT's Sixth National Survey on Academic Advising.* (NACADA Monograph Series, no. 10.) Manhattan, KS: National Academic Advising Association.

Habley, W. R., & Bloom, J. L. (2007). Giving advice that makes a difference. In G. L. Kramer, & Associates, *Fostering success in the campus community* (pp. 171–92). San Francisco: Jossey-Bass.

Havighurst, R. J. (1954). Who should go to college and where? In E. Lloyd-Jones, & M. R. Smith (Eds.), *Student personnel work as deeper teaching* (pp. 15–31). New York: Harper.

Hersh, R. H., Merrow, J., & Wolfe, T. (2005). *Declining by degrees: Higher education at risk.* New York: Palgrave Macmillan.

Hill, K., Hoffman, D., & Rex, T. R. (2005). *The value of higher education: Individual and societal benefits.* Tempe, AZ: W.P. Carey School of Business, Arizona State University.

Inside Higher Ed. (2007). *Upbeat assessment of career college market.* Retrieved December 7, 2007, from http://www.insidehighered.com/news/2007/12/07/career

Institute for Higher Education Policy. (1998). *Reaping the benefits: Defining the public and private value of going to college.* The New Millennium Project on Higher Education Costs, Pricing and Productivity. Washington, D.C.: Institute for Higher Education Policy.

McConnell, T. R., & Heist, P. (1962). The diverse college student population. In N. Sanford (Ed.), *The American college: A psychological and social interpretation of the higher learning* (pp. 223–52). New York: Wiley.

Morrison, J., Ericson, J., & Kohler, L. (1998). *Critical trends affecting the future of higher education.* Retrieved March 15, 2005, from http://horizon.unc.edu/project/seminar/SCUP.asp

NACADA. (2004). NACADA statement of core values of academic advising. *NACADA Clearinghouse of Academic Advising Resources.* Retrieved November 30, 2007, from http://www.nacada.ksu.edu/Clearinghouse/AdvisingIssues/Core-Values.htm

National Academic Advising Association. (2006). NACADA concept of academic advising. Retrieved November 30, 2007, from http://www.nacada.ksu.edu/Clearinghouse/AdvisingIssues/Concept-Advising.htm

Newman, F., Courturier, L., & Scurry, J. (2004). *The future of higher education: Rhetoric, reality, and the risks of the market.* San Francisco: Jossey-Bass.

Rhodes, F. H. T. (2001). *The role of the American University—The creation of the future*. Ithaca, NY: Cornell University Press.

Rowley, L. L., & Hurtado, S. (2002). *The non-monetary benefits of an undergraduate education*. Ann Arbor: University of Michigan Center for the Study of Higher and Postsecondary Education.

Schray, V. (2006). Assuring quality in higher education—Key issues and questions for changing accreditation in the United States. An issue paper for the Secretary of Education's Commission's report, *A Test of Leadership: Charting the Future of Higher Education*. Retrieved August 12, 2007, from http://www.ed.gov/about/bdscomm/list/hiedfuture/reports/final-report.pdf

Society for College and University Planning (SCUP). (2007). *Trends in higher education*. Retrieved August 13, 2007, from http://www.scup.org

Steele, G. (2006). Five possible future work profiles for full-time academic advisors. *NACADA Journal, 26* (2), 48–64.

Thelin, J. R. (2004). *A history of American higher education*. Baltimore: Johns Hopkins University Press.

U.S. Department of Education. (2006). *A test of leadership: Charting the future of higher education*. A report of the Commission appointed by Secretary of Education Margaret Spellings. Retrieved August 12, 2007, from www.ed.gov/about/bdscomm/list/hiedfuture/reorts/final-report.pdf

PART SIX

EXEMPLARY PRACTICES IN ACADEMIC ADVISING

Virginia N. Gordon

This section offers descriptions of advising programs that illustrate practical applications of some of the topics covered in Parts One to Four of this book. The programs chosen to represent the topics in this Section (with one exception) are NACADA award-winning programs (http://www.nacada .ksu.edu/Awards/OP_Recipients.htm). Although not all of the book's chapters are represented, the following examples demonstrate how some institutions have put into effective practice many of the tenets and ideas presented by some of the chapter authors.

Part One—Foundations of Academic Advising. The advising practices described in this part illustrate how a theoretical framework (Appreciative Inquiry) can be applied to advising for remedial students (University of North Carolina, Greensboro); how one university addressed the retention problems of first-year students (North Carolina State); and how one program created an advising program to offer students more comprehensive career and life planning (Indiana University Purdue University at Indianapolis [IUPUI]).

Part Two—Student Diversity and Needs. To illustrate some of the topics in Part Two, the following descriptions deal with three special student groups: a unique help center for students who are confronted by their dual role of student and parent (University of Minnesota); a special program for first-generation students (University of Kentucky); and a special advising program to assist high-ability students in their pursuit of scholarships and fellowships (University of South Carolina).

Part Three—Organization and Delivery of Advising Services. Topics used to illustrate best practices in this section include how one advising center changed its organization over time to implement its student-centered goals and objectives (University of Minnesota, Duluth); how one program confronted the complexities and challenges of change in its organizational advising structure (Emmanuel College); and how one college successfully merged its academic and career advising services (Principia College).

Part Four—Training, Assessment, Recognition, and Reward. This part's best practices include an ongoing, comprehensive training program for professional and faculty advisors (University of Central Florida); an outstanding all-campus assessment program (Oregon State); and two examples of recognition and reward practices: a unique program that recognizes outstanding advising practices by rewarding academic departments (Shippensburg University) and a comprehensive advisor reward system (Howard Community College).

These award-winning advising programs are described in more detail below. For more information, please refer to the Web site when provided or e-mail the contact person listed at the end of each description.

EXEMPLARY PROGRAMS

Part One: Foundations of Academic Advising

Program Name: Strategies for Student Academic Success (SAS 100) http://web.uncg.edu/adv/sas100

Institution: University of North Carolina at Greensboro (UNCG)

Topic Connection: Chapter Two—Theoretical Foundations of Academic Advising

Program History. The SAS 100 program was introduced in the 1999–2000 academic year by UNC Greensboro's Student Academic Services office with a remedial study skills curriculum. Since then, several modifications have been made to meet the needs of students and the university based on program evaluation results. To better accommodate student needs at UNCG, the full-semester course was revised to an eight-week curriculum so that the course content is delivered before the midpoint of the semester. Mandatory individual student conferences are required to ensure communication between the instructor and the student. The Appreciative Advising approach was introduced in the curriculum in 2004 to guide the student conference and facilitate the instructor in emphasizing students' exploration of their personal and academic strengths in order to devise a plan for academic recovery.

Program Objective. The purposes of the program are: (1) to facilitate the development of student academic strategies; (2) to encourage students' self-reflections of their academic strengths and weaknesses; and (3) to provide support for students to achieve academic recovery.

Program Description. SAS 100 is required for all students who are on academic probation at the end of their first-degree-seeking semester at UNCG. It is an eight-week, pass/fail, noncredit course that combines mandatory classroom attendance with regular face-to-face meetings with the instructor.

The SAS 100 program assists students on academic probation in acting interdependently and gaining personal insight by taking responsibility, managing their behaviors, believing in themselves by actively reflecting on past successes, and setting goals accordingly. In addition, the program aims for students on academic probation to meet the academic good-standing policy for the institution.

The course starts at the beginning of the second week of classes so that all students have an opportunity to enroll in it. For students who need to take SAS 100, failing to register for the class or missing one class period will result in suspension. This extreme consequence forces students to take the course seriously, which is essential for the course to be effective (Kamphoff, Hutson, Amundsen, & Atwood, 2007).

The SAS 100 program emphasizes the use of Appreciative Advising, an advising approach highly influenced by Appreciative Inquiry, an organizational development model for engaging people across a system in renewal, change, and focused performance. The premise is to build organizations around what works, rather than trying to fix what does not. Appreciative Inquiry creates meaning by soliciting narratives of concrete successes from individuals, using these narratives to identify and understand an organization's strengths, and using these strengths to create an image of the organization's future (Cooperrider, 1990).

Bloom, Amundsen, and Hutson (2006) define Appreciative Advising as the "intentional collaborative practice of asking positive, probing questions that help identify and strengthen a student's ability to optimize academic performance." It mobilizes inquiry through constructing "unconditional positive questions" that focus on what works as it influences students' self-perception. In Appreciative Advising, the advisor solicits a narrative from students in which they describe a time when they were performing at their best. As students tell their story, the advisor listens for areas in which the students reveal strengths and passions, asking questions that lead students to describe them in detail. Subsequently, the advisor and student work together to align the student's strengths and passions with a course of study and a career path.

The intervention emphasizes the Appreciative theoretical framework for several reasons. Selective institutions such as UNCG have identified enrolled students as being capable of success and completing their degree, and under this assumption have invested resources in these students' efforts. This suggests that starting from a deficit-based paradigm (i.e., looking for areas of academic weakness or poor time management) may not be an adequate starting point since students should already have adequate preparation in these areas prior to matriculating. In addition, students in academic trouble typically have a very limited time in which to correct their status. Practically, it is quicker to correct this status by building on strengths and maintaining a courseload and engaging in academic and social behaviors that reflect these strengths, than it is to attempt to correct long-standing deficits (Hutson, Amundsen, & He, 2005).

In addition to the emphasis on Appreciative Advising, the SAS 100 program emphasizes group interaction among students. The students interact in a small-group setting in which reflection and self-disclosure occur regularly. Students are encouraged and guided to share their experiences with each other while other students provide support and guidance. A supportive environment is created for students to relate to other students in a similar academic situation (Kamphoff et al., 2007). Further, each student is required to meet with his or her SAS 100 instructor twice during the eight weeks of the course. In these meetings the student is asked intentionally positive questions that require them to tell narrative stories of past academic successes—for example, "Tell me about a time when you felt most alive in the classroom." This type of discussion reinforces past successes and allows the student to relive these positive experiences (Hutson et al., 2005).

Ongoing evaluation of the program not only facilitated the improvement of the program, but also illustrated the effectiveness of the SAS 100 program. After the implementation of the SAS 100 courses, the retention rate of academic probation students improved 18 percent. Additionally, when control and treatment groups were compared, the treatment group achieved a statistically significant GPA gain of .73 ($p = .03$) compared to the control group at .42 (Kamphoff et al., 2007).

Beginning in spring 2002 through spring 2005, SAS 100 students were surveyed before and after the course with the *Student Strategies for Success Survey* (Hutson, 2003) in order to measure changes in academic self-efficacy. The instrument has ten subscales: Social Behavior, Academic Preparedness, Time Management, Study Skills, Goal Setting, Connectedness to Campus, Interdependence, Dedication, Self-knowledge, and Confidence. There were statistically significant positive changes in nine of the ten subscales, indicating that the students had adopted behaviors that were more positive and were enjoying more success in their academic and personal lives. This information was cross-validated through face-to-face interviews before and after the course, and a high level of congruence was identified between students' survey and interview results (Hutson et al., 2005). Similarly, when longitudinal data from several semesters were examined, a trend toward overall effectiveness in the program was observed (Kamphoff et al., 2007).

Adaptability to Other Institutional Settings. The key to the success of this program is its responsiveness to student needs. This is achieved through assessing student requirements, beliefs, and perceptions at intervals throughout the course. As these data are analyzed, course facilitators adapt the curriculum to reflect the needs of their students. The SAS 100 program components were initially identified and have been modified annually because of information gathered through interviewing and surveying students and instructors about their experiences and their current needs. This data-driven approach has allowed the program developers to provide support that is targeted to the specific needs of this population. While the SAS 100 program itself is replicable at other institutions, it is suggested that institutions use the data-gathering approach illustrated by UNC Greensboro's Student Academic Services office to ensure that the program is responsive to student needs.

Bryant Hutson, blhutson@uncg.edu

Scott Amundsen, amundsens@uncw.edu

Program Name: The First Year College

Institution: North Carolina State University

Topic Connection: Chapter Five—Advising for Student Success

Program History. The First Year College (FYC) was created in 1994–1995 as a result of a requirement by university administrators to provide a more comprehensive experience for first-year undecided students. A task force was charged with improving retention and graduation rates and with reducing the number of students who switch majors. The task force recommended that the program design be supported by best practices exemplified in research on first-year students. The First Year College was created by combining two existing programs (the University Undesignated Program and the First Year Experience). The program design was enhanced and tailored to student needs by adding new support services.

Administratively, FYC is located in the Division of Undergraduate Academic Programs that reports, as an academic entity, to the Provost's Office. Initially, the program was looked upon competitively by some of the other college administrators and faculty. However, with intentional education, a concerted assessment process, and continuous communication of program outcomes, the FYC has grown to be more appreciated for the service that it provides to the other colleges and to the university.

Program Objective. The First Year College's mission is to "guide students through a structured process for transition to the University and selection of a major." The program is specifically designed for students who choose a year of study, major exploration, and guidance prior to selecting an academic major and for students who desire a first-year college experience that intentionally immerses them into the academic, social, and cultural university community.

Program Description. The FYC is one of nine academic colleges at NC State University, and was created to serve incoming freshmen who are undecided about an academic major. The FYC enrolls 15 to 20 percent of entering students who meet highly selective admissions criteria and identify themselves as "undecided" or "deciding." The hallmark of the program is cross-curricular advising, inquiry-guided teaching and learning, and a developmental approach that balances challenge and support for students. The program design is based on findings from many years of research about first-year students.

The assessment model is designed to refresh the program by aligning program goals and objectives with current research trends. The FYC has been recognized by the National Academic Advising Association, the Templeton Foundation, and the Boyer Institute for innovative and exemplary practices in academic advising and student service. The program has also been recognized locally for the graduation rates, academic success, and level of engagement and involvement of students who matriculate through the program.

The primary goals of the FYC are as follows:

- To encourage all First Year College students to collaborate with the entire NC State University community in order to enhance their own University experience;

- To encourage students to make an informed and timely decision regarding an academic major, and to explore related careers;

- To help First Year College students learn to apply higher-level thinking skills to academic and career decision-making;

- To help students become engaged members of the campus community through awareness of their own cultural values as they relate to others, and by helping students determine their strengths and weaknesses in valuing diversity;

- To positively impact academic success, self-reliance, first-year retention, and progress toward a degree through one-on-one advising and structured experiential teaching and learning; and

- To practice the use of sound advising strategies in First Year College programs and courses, as exemplified in the National Academic Advising Association's Core Values.

Components of First Year College
Intensive Advising Model:

- Developmental advising
- Personal relationship between advisor and student
- Cross-curricular advising
- Professional advisers
- Advising as teaching philosophy

Components:

1. Orientation courses taught by student's advisor
2. One-hour, two-semester, required, letter-graded course that includes units on

   Transition (issues)
   Academic Success
   Self-Exploration

Major and Career Exploration

Decision-Making

3. The Forum Series (extracurricular events that students must attend to expose them to new and different people, places, things, and thoughts)

4. FYC Student Council

5. FYC Web site

6. Linked First Year Inquiry (first year seminar course)

7. FYC Village Residential Community

8. Pack-Study (on-site study hall with walk-in tutors)

9. Cocurricular Programming (held in FYC Village to support curriculum)

10. Leadership Development and Service Events

11. Resident Mentors

12. Faculty Fellows

Results from the 10-Year (1994–1995 to 2004–2005) Assessment Report indicates that students who enter the university through FYC:

- Were retained at rates similar to the university cohorts and similar to or higher than the comparison group cohorts across most of the ten years. While the first-year retention rate is similar to the university comparison cohort, data for retention to the third and fourth years showed that significantly more FYC than the comparison group of students were retained. The lower first-year retention rate can be attributed to the fact that some students transfer to other institutions seeking majors that are not available at NC State once they become decided.

- Graduate as fast as, and several years faster than, the matched cohort of other university students, despite the fact that they take a year to explore majors. The percentage of FYC students graduating within four years has increased substantially.

- Have equal or better academic results on most measures compared to the matched university comparison cohort.

- Show an increased percentage transferring to a major their second year over the three most recent years (despite increasing intracampus transfer criteria).

- Are less likely to change majors than the university comparison cohort. (The percentage of comparison students with at least one major change was more than twice than, and in some cases more than three times, the percentage of FYC students with at least one major change. In most cases, the major change for an FYC student was within the same college.)

- Are more positive about their advising experience. (More than 75 percent of FYC students indicated that the advising system meets their needs more than adequately or exceptionally well, compared with 42 percent of students nationally.)

Adaptability to Other Institutional Settings. The FYC program model continues to be grounded by current research findings on first-year students and is supported by an extensive assessment plan. This assessment plan is the means by which other institutions, with similar student goals and objectives, can easily adapt the model for their own use. Interested institutions can review the FYC assessment plan, identify relevant learning outcomes, and use the parts of the model (and corresponding assessment plan) that suit their institutional needs to build their retention programs. The First Year College is a comprehensive program with several different components. Each program component has been developed with a corresponding assessment plan. This allows institutions to choose, by program component, the outcomes that best meet their institutional needs to build their own unique programs.

The key considerations for institutions desiring to develop similar programs should be given to the following factors.

- Commitment to the developmental approach to advising
- Commitment to extensive cross-curricular adviser training time and cost
- Early and broad-based communication with university constituents (faculty and administrators)
- Space conducive to student-adviser interactions
- Identifying appropriate students
- Commitment to strategic planning and assessment
- University commitment to enhancing undergraduate education

Carrie McLean, carrie_mclean@ncsu.edu

Program Name: Working Together for Student Success: Integrating Academic and Career Planning (http://uc.iupui.edu/students/academics/mccs.asp)

Institution: Indiana University Purdue University at Indianapolis (IUPUI)

Topic Connection: Chapter Seven—Advising for Career and Life Planning

Program History. As part of its mission to promote student success, retention and graduation, University College has always acknowledged and addressed the holistic nature of the student experience. Students' out-of-class experiences impact their in-class experiences, personal challenges affect educational achievement, and vocational goals impact academic choices. This program addresses the symbiotic relationship between academic and career planning.

The development of this program has occurred in stages. While working consciously toward the goal of integrating academic and career planning, we have also taken advantage of opportunities for organizational change and reallocation of resources. These opportunities include hiring a faculty member with a doctorate in career development as the Career Development Specialist for the Advising Center in 2000 and the organizational transition of the IUPUI Career Center from the student affairs division to University College in 2001. At this time, three positions were created in which the staff member works 50 percent as a career counselor and 50 percent as an academic advisor; this ensured that both the Advising Center and the Career Center had staff members who could help students along the continuum of academic and career planning without having to be referred to another office.

In 2003, a campus-wide task force on integrating academic and career planning was convened. The purpose of the task force was to create a context in which entering students make wise educational and career decisions, choose educational tracks that complement those decisions, and make connections with the faculty, staff, and programs that can support these decisions. In fall 2004, a working group of staff from the Career Center and Advising Center were charged with implementing the recommendations of the task force in collaboration with other campus faculty, staff, and students. In addition, in November 2004 the Advising Center and Career Center reported to the same administrator to formally align the units; in 2007 the two merged to become the Center for Academic and Career Planning.

Program Objectives. The overall goal of the program is to enhance student persistence and graduation by providing more thorough, integrated, and ongoing support for students' career and academic planning. Within this goal, the program strives to:

1. Add meaning and purpose to a student's collegiate experience by framing the academic experience within a student's life and career goals;

2. Expand the institutional definition and mission of advising to include career development issues;

3. Offer career and academic planning programs that serve students at different levels of readiness and at different points in the collegiate experience;

4. Provide ongoing training and support for academic advisors and career counselors to assist students in both academic and career planning; and

5. Make career development a significant part of the campus culture.

Program Description. Efforts to integrate academic and career planning include a variety of programs and services that meet the needs of individual students at their point of readiness while collectively seeking to change the culture of the campus so that a holistic approach to educational planning is reinforced throughout the student's experience. Program components are described below and are divided into two categories: (1) direct programs and services for students, and (2) training and support for staff. All programs and services are built on the IUPUI model of career decision-making, *STEP Ahead:*

S = Self-Awareness

T = Target

E = Explore

P = Plan

Direct Programs and Services for Students

Major/Career Connection Sheets. Six Major/Career Connections (MCC) sheets were developed—one for each of the Holland codes (RAISEC). Each MCC sheet includes a quick assessment for students to determine their fit with that code, a list of majors within that code, and sample careers. Additional information on choosing a major/career and campus resources are listed. Related Major Profiles have been developed for all IUPUI degree programs. The Major Profiles include a short assessment to determine fit with the career, a description of the career, a listing of sample courses and related majors, as well as employment outlook and salary projections.

First-Year Seminar Course. All beginning IUPUI students are required to enroll in a first-year seminar course. Several sections of the course for exploratory students are offered, and the content includes college success and career decision-making strategies. Sections are taught by an instructional team that includes a staff member from the Career Center and an academic advisor.

Themed Learning Community. Based on the theme "Career Perspectives: For Love AND Money," this block of four linked courses helps students gain perspective on their future by exploring majors and careers that would enable them to follow their heart and make a living. Through reading and writing assignments in a freshman English course, students examine and analyze the psychological and cultural influences that form their images of career and financial success. Using assessment instruments, writing, and research in their First Year Seminar class, students learn more about who they are and what majors and careers would help them reach meaningful life goals and pursue their passions. In the Introduction to Psychology as a Social Science course, they study theory and research that impact career development in areas of personality, motivation, learning, decision-making, life-span development, and job satisfaction. A math course builds logic, critical thinking, and problem-solving skills. Finally, going outside the classroom, students learn and practice networking, one of the most effective tools for major/career exploration and job searching.

Sophomore Career Course. This course is designed to assist sophomores who want or need to declare or change their major. In the course, students develop and execute an individualized plan of major and career exploration. The first eight weeks of the class are devoted to exposing students to the STEP model and developing their individualized plan; in the second eight weeks, students work independently to execute their plan. Students are required to attend individual meetings with the instructor and academic advisor. Experiential learning connects students with the people, activities, and resources that facilitate a realistic approach to major and career decision-making.

STEP Ahead to Your Future: A Guide to Choosing Majors and Careers. This workbook was developed by staff in the Advising Center and Career Center for use as a textbook with students enrolled in the learning community for exploratory students as well as a guide for advisors and career counselors when working individually with students.

STEP Ahead Workshops. Career counselors have developed workshops for each component of the STEP model. The Career Center offers these workshops on a regular basis. A brochure outlining the workshops is sent to all faculty members to encourage them to invite the Career Center to appropriate classes.

Career Exploration Day. Students have the opportunity to ask questions and gather information about programs and professions from IUPUI degree school advisors or career staff at an informal midday "majors fair."

Training and Support for Staff
Advisor Binder. Each advisor is provided with a binder of career information that includes: a list of all IUPUI majors; a listing of exploratory courses in each major (http://uc.iupui.edu/students/academics/ontrack_courses.asp.); a summary and comparison of IUPUI majors in health fields, computer-related fields and communication; information on the STEP Ahead model; information, tips and techniques for working with students who are exploring and evaluating major and career alternatives; and each Major Career Connection sheet and all Major Profiles. The binders are presented at a training session for advisors in which they learn about career decision-making and the role of the advisor in the career-exploration process.

Cross-Training for Career Counselors and Advisors. Staffs in the University College Advising Center and IUPUI Career Center meet monthly for cross-training and team-building. Meetings focus on identifying common areas of service as well as on in what services and knowledge advisors and career counselors specialize. Cross-training meetings address topics including the purpose and goals of integrating academic and career planning; the STEP Ahead model of career decision-making; career assessment tools, including a free online program advisors can easily use with students; academic policies and procedures that may impact major and career options for students; and "Plan B" advising and using strengths or asset-based approaches to academic advising and career counseling.

Campus-wide Conference and Workshops on Career Development. In 2005, a campus-wide conference on career development was held. Faculty and staff from around the campus gathered to learn about the significance of integrating academic and career development in relation to student persistence and to develop skills they could use in their own interactions with students. This work has continued with campus workshops on the same topic.

Adaptability to Other Institutional Settings. Because this program has many components, it is easily adaptable to other institutional settings. Colleges and universities can choose the components that best meet the needs of their students and fit within the institutional resources available. As was done at IUPUI, a comprehensive program to implement academic and career planning can be built over time.

Cathy Buyarski, cbuyarsk@iupui.edu

Part Two: Student Diversity and Needs

Program Name: Student Parent HELP Center (SPHC) (http://www.osa.umn .edu/help_center)

Institution: University of Minnesota, Twin Cities (U of M-TC)

Topic Connection: Chapter Nine—Moving into College (HELP for Low-Income Students Who Are Parents)

Program History. The Student Parent HELP (Higher Education for Low Income People) Center (SPHC) was founded in 1967 by the U of M-TC, General College, to meet the needs of all underrepresented, low-income students. Eventually, as other support programs evolved during the decade of the 1970s (TRIO and other similar programs), the one population left without support specific to their needs was the student-parent population. In 1983 the SPHC began exclusively serving low-income, student parents registered in any college of the U of M-TC. With the beginning of a new, five year, campus-wide strategic planning initiative, the host college was closed in 2006 and the SPHC was relocated administratively under the Office for Student Affairs.

Program Objective. The objective of this program is to assist low-income, undergraduate, U of M-TC students with children to meet and overcome specific challenges this group of highly motivated students typically face as they attempt to enter their first degree program. A secondary mission is to encourage participation in higher education among teen parents in the greater twin cities.

Program Description. The SPHC has a student- and family-friendly center located on the U of M-TC campus and offers a wide variety of services and programming, all designed to encourage both academic and family success. Facilities include a play area for children, kitchenette, computer center, resource and referral area, and lounge. The SPHC is staffed by master's level social workers and graduate social work interns. All SPHC staff members are familiar with a wide range of both campus- and community-based services.

The SPHC strives to provide a model, "one-stop shopping" service delivery and referral program to address the family and academic needs of our students. Some services include: academic advising, financial aid counseling and referral, crisis counseling and referral, child care, and emergency assistance grants. The SPHC sponsors various programs throughout the year that increase the visibility of student parents on campus, recognize the achievements of these students, and provide family-friendly alternatives for students. These include the Annual Student Parent Visibility Day, which features the hosting of over 100 teen parents from various community-based programs, an End of the Year Celebration and Graduation Party, participation in Tix for Tots events, and a weekly, staff-facilitated parent group that meets each week during regular terms. Currently the SPHC serves approximately 400 students, of which the majority are female, single, and between the ages of eighteen and twenty-four. Although the majority of students registered with the SPHC are single mothers, the program is open to all low-income, financial-aid-eligible, undergraduate parents, regardless of age, gender, or marital status. Participation with the SPHC is voluntary, and students either self-refer or are referred by other U of M-TC programs, staff, and faculty. Recruitment is conducted through our Web site, presentations, and mailings to a wide range of campus programs, word of mouth, and direct e-mail contact to students identified as having both dependents and economic need.

The SPHC is directly responsible for disbursing over $300,000 a year in child care assistance grants to U of M-TC student parents through the state sponsored Minnesota Higher Education Services Office (MNHESO), Post Secondary Child Care Grant (PSCCG), and the U.S. Department of Education, Child Care Access Means Parents In School (CCAMPIS) Grant.

An additional goal of the SPHC program is to encourage teen parent participation in higher education within the greater Twin Cities community. To meet this goal the SPHC provides off-site, college prep information presentations to teen parent programs in the metro area. In addition to providing basic college prep and child-care resources, referral, and assistance information, we also include our own SPHC students who were former teen parents themselves in these contacts. This interface between the teen parents and our own successful student parents provides significant encouragement and motivation for the next generation of potentially college-bound teen parents. Bringing these same teens to campus once a year for the annual Student Parent Visibility Day further enhances the access and exposure these young parents have to campus life. This event goes beyond recruitment to our university, but rather encourages participation in higher education at any level, as well as instilling a belief in these students about their ability to succeed academically. As most of the teen parents we work with are attending alternative programs outside of their home high schools, the SPHC is providing a service that many of these programs do not have the resources to provide themselves.

Adaptability to Other Institutional Settings. The SPHC could be adapted to any higher education institution serving students with children. In fact, the

SPHC model is ideal and can be replicated for any underserved or underrepresented student population. The key component, and for most institutions, the most difficult to find, is space. Having a designated, student- and family-friendly space is critical to making this typically "invisible" population of students feel they belong on campus. As SPHC director, and as a social worker who has served numerous under-represented populations, I believe this is the first step toward effectively serving any student group. All students (and people in general, one could argue) need a sense of community and belonging if they are to truly succeed in a new environment, especially one as daunting as a large Big Ten campus like ours. Having a place where students can both hang out together and receive the needed information, services, and tools required to succeed academically is important for any student population. The one-room center itself encourages the formation of a cohesive community of students with children that they might not find anywhere else in their four years at the university. The chances a student would ever sit next to another pregnant or parenting student in one of their classes, even on a smaller campus, would be very slim. By becoming involved with our center, studying in the SPHC computer lab, stopping in to eat lunch, or merely putting their feet up on the couch when they are pregnant, SPHC students are exposed to an entire community of learners who share similar challenges, successes, and concerns.

In addition to space, the training of staff is critical. When working with students who already have their own families, staff must be well versed in resources and opportunities on campus and in the greater community. Staff should be trained in regard to housing, child-care resources and referral, county welfare assistance programming (especially in regard to training and education benefits), parenting and child-rearing practices, basic screening for depression and other mental health issues, and group-facilitation skills.

The weekly parent group is consistently one of the most highly rated programs on student satisfaction surveys conducted by the SPHC. Allowing a consistent forum for students to build community, share what they have learned as both parents and as students, mentor each other, and receive needed academic and parenting information from trained staff is critical for students with children, especially those who are new to both parenting and collegiate life. The SPHC has been able to garner administrative support that allows us to provide a free, nutritional, hot lunch at these meetings, which goes a long way toward the initial recruitment of students for our group. Staff members do the grocery shopping and cook the meals in a crock pot each week, in order to keep costs for this part of our programming to a minimum. During lean budgetary years we have also been able to garner donations from local restaurants.

Child-care assistance grants are the final needed element for providing effective support for student parents in higher education. The ability to afford quality child care is "the make or break" factor for most student parents attempting to enter and remain in college. Finding resources that allow a program to provide ongoing child-care assistance funding to student parents is a very important, and perhaps the most daunting component when developing support programs for student parents in higher education. However, interested staff should not be intimidated by this task. The community-building aspects of the other components listed above will be enough to draw students. Child-care assistance tends to be "the icing on the cake" when, and if, programs can find it. The SPHC staff has improved their grant-writing and fund-solicitation practices over the course of four decades. There is time to go after the funding once you have the students. It never ceases to amaze me, as director, how often our physical space, family activities, and parent group are rated by students as high as or higher than our assistance grants. It is far more important to build the community of students and serve them well and then find the funding than to go after money without first having the student-service data. When programs provide needed services to enough students, the money follows.

Susan Warfield, warfi002@umn.edu

Program Name: Robinson Scholars Program (www.uky.edu/robinsonscholars)

Institution: University of Kentucky

Topic Connection: Chapter Twelve—Students with Specific Advising Needs (First-Generation Students); and Chapter Nine—Moving into College

Program History. In 1991, the University of Kentucky Board of Trustees approved a plan that set aside coal and timber royalties from a 5,000-acre section of the Robinson Forest to support economic and community development efforts in Appalachian Kentucky. The Board allocated a significant portion of those funds to provide scholarships to students in twenty-nine eastern Kentucky counties with historically low rates of college attendance. In 1996, the university approved a working plan for the Robinson Scholars Program (RSP), and the first class of Scholars was selected in the spring of 1997. Since then, the program has named 568 students as Robinson Scholars.

Program Objective. The RSP serves first-generation college-bound and college-enrolled students who have demonstrated the potential to succeed but who might encounter economic, cultural, or institutional impediments to their completion of four-year college degrees. The program's mission is to provide these students with support services and scholarship resources that empower them to complete a baccalaureate degree at the University of Kentucky and thereby increase the educational capital of their communities.

Program Description. In recognition of the potential obstacles facing these students, the program identifies Scholars in the eighth grade. This approach recognizes the importance of academic support, social mentoring, and college preparation throughout high school. Early intervention is a key to success for students from at-risk and traditionally underrepresented groups. Students submit application packets for the RSP as eighth-graders. Selection committees evaluate Robinson Scholars applicants on three criteria: first-generation status, demonstrated potential to succeed, and potential impediments to the completion of a four-year college degree. A certain number of students (typically four per county) participate in an interview process. Selected in the spring of 1997, the first class of Scholars consists of 162 students. The second class includes 116 students, the third class has 57 students, and all subsequent classes will have 29 students, one from each county in the service area. With a decrease in the number of Scholars and an increase in community awareness, the selection process has grown very competitive. In 2007, nearly 700 students vied for the 29 spots in the program.

High School Component. The Robinson Scholars Program seeks to provide support and enrichment opportunities to Scholars throughout their high school careers. Program officials continually assess students' academic and social needs and develop programs tailored to address those needs. The ultimate goal of the high school component is to prepare students for successful high school-to-college transitions. Program staff members understand that this requires a holistic approach and involves interactions with students, their families, their schools, and their communities. Below is a list of some of the programs and support services that the program administers at the high school level.

High School Visits. Staff members conduct high school visits at least once each semester. They meet with the students in group and individual settings as well as talk with guidance counselors and teachers. They discuss the students' overall high school experience, they engage in academic and personal planning, and they address any questions or concerns.

Weekend Programs. Each class of Scholars participates in at least one weekend program each semester. Freshmen and sophomore Scholars focus on study skills and academic assessment, and junior Scholars work on test-preparation skills and leadership development. Senior Scholars concentrate on college-transition issues and make two campus visits during which they have the opportunity to interact with current college Scholars, attend campus events, and sit in on actual college courses with their Scholar hosts.

Summer Programs. Each class of high school Scholars participates in a week-long summer enrichment program. Freshmen explore their Appalachian culture and consider the opportunities and challenges of their home communities. Sophomores study water-quality issues and then go back to their communities to implement community service projects of their own design related to water-quality concerns. Junior and senior Scholars participate in a Writers' Workshop on the campus of the University of Kentucky, where they work with college faculty and guest authors to produce both an argumentative essay like those required in freshmen composition courses and a creative piece. The workshop's location also exposes students to the university's campus and provides staff with the opportunity to address college-transition issues in both formal and informal settings.

College-Application Assistance. The program provides every senior with the Senior Year Checklist at the Writers' Workshop prior to the senior year. The Senior Year Checklist walks the students and their families through the paperwork involved in the high school-to-college transition. The program uses the Checklist, or "green sheet" as it is affectionately called, to guide students through the admissions, financial aid, and housing-application processes. Every time staff members and students come together during the senior year, they review the "green sheet."

Individual Services. RSP staff members are available anytime to Scholars and their families to address questions or concerns. The program serves as a conduit to school and community resources and when no resources exist, the program seeks to provide them. Individualized services have included tutoring, counseling referrals, testing referrals, social services referrals, and assistance to parents seeking to further their education.

College Component. Robinson Scholars who enroll at the University of Kentucky or any Kentucky Community and Technical College System (KCTCS) community college receive full scholarships (tuition and fees, room and board, and a book allowance) and a range of support services. The program seeks to connect students to the larger institution, to its people, to its services, and to its culture. It holds its Scholars to a high standard and expects them to perform well in the classroom, be involved in the campus community, and be committed to volunteer service. It equips students to perform at their highest levels, both as college students and in their lives beyond our institution, and it encourages students that they can and will succeed. With these goals in mind and with consideration for the challenges Scholars face, the program provides the following support and programming at the college level.

Transition Workshops. Beginning with a workshop at the close of their summer advising conference in June, incoming Scholars attend six transition workshops before the first day of class; parents participate in three of these workshops. During the workshops, RSP staff discuss a variety of topics including: important keys to college success; the family's role in a successful transition; practical information about the start of the term; the program's expectations for Scholars and the Scholars' expectations of the program; campus and community involvement; book buying; the city of Lexington; and student computer accounts.

Scholar Dinners. These dinners, held the evening before classes begin in the fall and spring semesters, bring all the college Scholars together and help to kick off the new term with food, fellowship, and entertainment. The dinners also provide RSP staff with an opportunity to share some last-minute details regarding the beginning of another semester.

One-on-One Meetings, Probation Meetings, and Consultations. Program staff members meet individually with every student during the course of each semester. First-year students meet monthly, graduating seniors meet three times a semester, students on scholarship probation meet every other week, and all other students meet twice per term. At these meetings, staff members discuss the student's overall university experience and his or her academic progress and campus involvement, they engage in academic and personal planning, and they address any questions or concerns. Staff members are also available for impromptu meetings or inquiries.

Monthly Small-Group Meetings. Each month, Robinson Scholars choose one of several small-group meetings to attend. The meetings provide the students with an opportunity to share ideas, questions, and concerns. The meetings also provide the RSP staff with a touch point to the students and with an opportunity to discuss pertinent and timely issues (exams, on-campus events, special opportunities, points of general concern, spring break cautions, etc.).

Student Mentoring Program. The program assigns each incoming Robinson Scholar a "veteran" Scholar, who serves as a mentor. The mentors touch base with their Scholars at least once a week, either by phone, by e-mail, or in person. The Scholars have the opportunity to meet their mentors for lunch or dinner at least once a month, and the mentors make themselves available for student questions or concerns. Students in the mentoring program also have the opportunity to participate in special social and cultural activities throughout the year.

Community Service Activities. Robinson Scholars participate in a number of individual and group service activities during the academic year. The program expects students to engage in at least five hours of community service each semester, but in the 2004–2005 academic year Robinson Scholars participated in over 2,500 hours of community service, far exceeding their goal.

Summer Opportunity Grants. The program awards a limited number of Summer Opportunity Grants (SOGs) each year. The SOGs are designed to encourage Scholars to pursue summer academic, career-development, and/or community service opportunities. The program recognizes that many Scholars may not be able to pursue these opportunities because many are unpaid experiences. A SOG may allow Scholars to participate in these opportunities despite their lack of compensation. In the past, RSP has awarded SOGs for a judicial internship, a television production internship, and funding for a literary magazine, among other experiences.

Rural Health Internship. The program has partnered with the Center for Rural Health in Hazard, Kentucky, to provide two summer internships for junior or senior Scholars interested in rural health issues. The interns spend eight weeks in residence at the Center, where they engage in rotations among the Center's agencies and conduct a research project.

Monday Morning E-Mails. Every Monday morning, the program sends an e-mail to the Scholars. These e-mails, which attempt to be fun, refreshing, and maybe a little corny, highlight on-campus events, special opportunities, upcoming deadlines, etc.

Robinson Scholars Program Office. The RSP Office provides a small, yet comfortable place for Scholars to relax, recharge, study, print a paper, gather with each other, or chat with staff.

Adaptability to Other Institutional Settings. Although the RSP is unique in the fact that it establishes an eight-year relationship with students and their families, many components of the program could be adapted to fit other institutional settings. While many institutions of higher education do not deal with high school populations, the college piece of the program could be adjusted to fit multiple groups of students and parents, whether in its entirety or by the individual program offerings.

Elizabeth Bryant, eabrya@email.uky.edu

Program Name: Office of Fellowships and Scholar Programs (www.sc.edu/ofsp)

Institution: University of South Carolina (USC)—Columbia

Topic Connection: Chapter Twelve—Students with Specific Advising Needs (High-Ability Students)

Program History. Prior to 1994, several University of South Carolina faculty members were scattered across campus serving as campus advisors for the Fulbright, Rhodes, and Truman Scholars programs. Even the most diligent students had difficulty ascertaining where to begin an application process for national fellowship competitions such as these. Both faculty and students wanted to engage in the dozens of national fellowship competitions available, but the university lacked a coordinated effort to identify and prepare candidates.

The Office of Fellowships and Scholar Programs was established in 1994 in order to provide a centralized national fellowship advisement process on campus. Organizationally, the office was placed under the supervision of the Vice Provost for Undergraduate Affairs illustrating the support by the central administration and providing clout in recruiting faculty to participate. Recognizing that the majority of students qualified to seek advisement for these awards were likely to be in the thousand-member Honors College, the new office was assigned physical space in the same building. Both decisions have proved critical to the success of the office.

Initially, the office staff consisted of a director and administrative assistant. A university advisory committee was established, composed of academic and administrative representatives throughout campus, as well as chairs of the newly established scholarship committees. The scholarship committees were designed to be the heart of the advisement and mentoring processes for awards requiring university nomination and provided individualized mentoring to students by faculty experts across the disciplines.

Shortly after establishing the office, the university president suggested that the unit assume responsibility for providing the top undergraduate scholarship recipients with an enhanced university experience. Thus, the Office of Fellowships and Scholar Programs was established. As the institution's finest scholarship students, Carolina Scholars were prime candidates for national fellowship competitions. In 1998 the national McNair Scholarship was established and an additional professional staff member was hired to direct Scholar Programs.

Program Objective. Our goal is to provide a central location for information and assistance in applying for national fellowships, to identify and support university students applying for national fellowships, and to serve as a university home for Carolina and McNair Scholars.

Three objectives shape our daily work.

- To advise and mentor students in the merits and requirements of various competitions and to facilitate the personal growth and development of candidates through the application and interview processes

- To facilitate faculty involvement with students outside the classroom through the nomination and preparation of students for national competitions and to facilitate the recognition and reward of their involvement

- To nurture the development of a community among Carolina and McNair Scholars and advise them of the various national competitions

Program Description. Our program is a developmental process from which students can learn and benefit in substantial ways. The program has three main components: awareness, advising, and mentoring.

Awareness. Our first goal is to raise the awareness of qualified university students regarding national fellowships and the support services available to them. This awareness is cultivated in a number of ways. Faculty and staff are encouraged to refer their best students to the office. Once referred, these students are personally contacted and invited to be advised about the opportunities. Public relations and marketing tools are used to extend the invitation for any academically talented undergraduate student to use the office services. These include *The Candidate* (our office newsletter); our Web site (www.sc.edu/ofsp); paid advertisements in the student newspaper; workshop flyers; and press releases to student media. Fellowships Night is an annual recruiting event, a dinner during which a former USC national scholarship winner speaks.

Advising. Individual and small-group meetings with students are offered to help them determine which competitions best fit their academic and career goals. At this time they complete a Candidate Card, providing general information for our database of more than 600 interested students. The database is our core directory of student profiles (major, GPA, fellowship interest) and communication system (mail and e-mail) with potential candidates. Because competition is keen, students must be carefully advised of fellowships for which they would be strong candidates. Ideally, this process begins as early as the freshman year. Students are encouraged to think broadly as they consider awards that best support their proposed academic and career goals.

Most advisement transpires in one of three ways: through one-on-one meetings with the director and assistant director, through programs, and through one-on-one advising sessions with individual faculty members. Drop-in hours are offered four days a week to meet with an advisor, and individual appointments may be made at any time, giving students ample opportunity to receive personal and focused attention.

Scholarship Workshops are offered each fall and spring for the fellowships that require campus nomination and the most-sought-after awards. The workshops are led by the faculty advisor for the Office of Fellowships and Scholar Programs staff. Details on a particular award are presented—everything from the qualifications to the actual application timeline are covered. Individualized follow-up with students is a priority.

Mentoring. The heart of our work is the philosophy that the consideration, application, and interview process for a national award be meaningful in and of itself. Although our ultimate goal is to see our students win prestigious scholarships and fellowships, we remain steadfast in the belief that the preparation process enhances academic and personal skills. This level of advising typically occurs at the mentoring stage of our program. Specific benefits include the students' obtaining: a better sense of professional interests, strengths, talents, career goals, and graduate school options; stronger interpersonal skills and interview techniques; experience and maturity in presenting and defending ideas in writing and before panels of faculty critics; improved ability in preparing applications for competitive positions; individual guidance from faculty; and recognition for outstanding efforts and accomplishments.

Once a student engages in a competition, a more personal mentoring process begins. For example, students nominated for a Goldwater Scholarship are paired with faculty members on the USC Goldwater Committee to advise them in fine-tuning and polishing their final application. The faculty member provides meaningful, personalized advice on the application and how that relates to a student's future academic and career plans. If a competition requires a selection interview, rigorous practice interviews are arranged for the candidates. Faculty experts from the candidates' discipline are invited to serve on the committees.

Mentoring continues after the posting of the competition winners. We celebrate the achievement of all applicants' personal best, whether or not they receive the scholarship. A celebration of all national fellowship applicants and the faculty and staff that supported them is held at our Year-End Reception, traditionally attended by the president and provost. All national fellowship recipients are recognized at University Awards Day and recorded on permanent plaques displayed in our building.

Our goal of providing a developmental experience for students engaging in the comprehensive process of a competition is realized again and again. The program has directly enhanced academic faculty and student involvement outside the classroom in a number of ways. Each year, an average of sixty faculty members serve on scholarship committees and practice interview teams, providing individual advising and support to national scholarship applicants. Dozens of additional faculty members support the process by nominating students to use the office or by writing letters of recommendation.

The placement of Scholar Programs in this unit has been a perfect blending of missions and also underscores the goal of increased faculty-student interaction. The First-Year Scholars Mentoring Program provides the framework for fifty students annually to become acquainted with a well-respected faculty member. These Carolina and McNair Scholars now represent about 27 percent of the students applying for national fellowships. Winners have included Goldwater, Fulbright, Udall, Rotary, Marshall, and Truman Scholars, among others.

The investment in the Office of Fellowships and Scholar Programs has resulted in substantial dividends for USC students, faculty, and staff. An average of 140 applications have been submitted annually, and not only have these applicants benefited from the rigorous preparation and introspection that are central components of the competitions, but also the institutional culture as a whole has been strengthened. By providing this support to our highest-ability students, academic rigor and discourse across the institution have been heightened. Since the office was established in 1994, more than 350 national fellowships have been won by university students and more than $10 million has been awarded for advanced academic study.

Adaptability to Other Institutions. The potential for transferability of this program to other institutions is excellent. The USC model for providing advisement and mentoring to students considering and applying for national fellowships and scholarships could be adapted at both large and small institutions. Although we believe strongly that program placement to clearly confirm central administration support is critical to securing faculty participation, this advisement service could be located in a career center, honors college, or a large college. Even the appointment of a half-time director could facilitate select services. The establishment of the National Association of Fellowship Advisors (NAFA) in 2001 illustrates the growth of this advisement area in higher education. This model could aid other institutions as more and more high-achieving students come to expect advisement for national fellowship competitions.

Novella F. Beskid, Director, novella@gwm.sc.edu

Part Three: Organization and Delivery of Advising Services

Program Name: Student Affairs and Advising Center

Institution: University of Minnesota Duluth (UMD) (http://www.d.umn .edu/~ clasa/main/index.php)

Topic Connection: Chapter Fourteen—Mission, Goals, and Program Objectives for Academic Advising Programs

Program History: The College of Liberal Arts' (CLA) Student Affairs and Advising Center (SAAC) was originally the "CLA Student Affairs Office," composed of one half-time student support staff and two student employees. This half-time staff position became full-time in 1995. In 1996, a full-time front-desk receptionist was hired, followed by the hiring of two additional professional positions in 1999 and 2004 dedicated to student support and the development of new initiatives. In 2003, the name of the office was changed from CLA Student Affairs to CLA Student Affairs and Advising Center to better reflect the mission of the office and communicate more effectively to students the services provided. The location of the office was also changed, giving us additional space and resources.

Program Objective: The Student Affairs and Advising Center's mission is to enhance the student experience by supplying the guidance, information, and education necessary to help students participate in CLA and UMD as confident, independent learners.

Values

- Student success is a comprehensive, transformative process that integrates academic learning and student development.
- Timely, accurate information regarding university policies and procedures is every student's right. Accessing this information is every student's responsibility.
- Positive student-faculty and student-staff interactions are essential to learning, growth, and satisfaction.
- Students are responsible for making independent and informed decisions regarding their academic careers.
- Parents and family members and the university are partners in student development.
- Technology-based advising resources are an essential cornerstone in a comprehensive, college-wide advising program.

Goals. The Student Affairs and Advising Center contributes to student success primarily by:

- Assisting students pursuing majors and minors within the College of Liberal Arts
- Collaborating with and aiding faculty academic advisors
- Supporting undecided students in their transition to college and the academic major exploration process

We are student-focused, within a context that recognizes and appreciates the contributions and needs of faculty, parents, and the university. Our focus allows us to make decisions that are in students' best interests, even if those decisions are not always seen by faculty and administration as in their best interests. We consider ourselves to be resources, while at the same time we regard the students ultimately to be responsible for their own success. Good advising is not intended to solve every student problem; it is intended to facilitate successful, independent learning.

Program Description. We take a comprehensive approach to advising that includes the following: walk-in advising sessions, Learning Community Program for approximately 320 new freshmen (about half of our freshman class each year), group and one-on-one faculty advisor training as well as departmental visits from SAAC staff to address broad advising concerns, a monthly newsletter sent to all faculty and staff that addresses components of the advisor-advisee relationship, a CLA transfer specialist who also administers an online transfer student orientation program (as with our Learning Community Program, this is unique to CLA), training for new faculty advisors, a shadowing process whereby new faculty assist experienced faculty at new student orientation, and individual advising for all returning students and students who have been academically dismissed but are working their way back into good academic standing.

We also make extensive use of technology-based advising tools. Examples include: (1) All transfer students have the option of attending UMD orientation or completing their orientation online. The online process incorporates self-taught materials with individual advising contact, facilitated by our CLA transfer specialist. In 2007 (the first time we made the system available), sixty-eight transfer students completed online orientation. (2) Each year CLA makes CD-ROM copies of our New Student Guide, which are distributed to all new students as well as mailed to their parents. (3) A new podcasting program for disseminating information to students is being piloted. Material from our CLA SAAC Web page is available for either downloading or for direct listening via the student's computer. Content includes advice from current CLA students about what they wish they had known coming into college, study strategies, upcoming deadlines, etc. (4) The SAAC Web site houses numerous online resources for students, including timely reminders of academic deadlines, current issues and processes, and links to degree resources, online forms, major exploration resources, and faculty advising resources.

Finally, we continually assess, adapt, and innovate. We try to approach ideas as though they were possible, rather than from the assumption that change is uncomfortable. Examples include: (1) SAAC is the only academic unit that requires its dismissed students who want to continue at UMD via Continuing Education to receive academic advising. This dramatically increases the advising workload of one SAAC advisor, but ongoing feedback from dismissed students showed us the importance of this requirement if we were serious about helping our dismissed students get off probation and back into good academic standing. (2) As a result of negative feedback from both students and faculty, SAAC improved the transfer-credit evaluation process by redesigning the form CLA department heads use to evaluate transfer credits, leading to better consistency, etc. (3) SAAC has made midstream changes to the CLA Online Orientation system in response to student feedback, including changing the password-reset process and revising text in the tutorial for improved clarity. And this year we are tracking incorrect answers on the online orientation worksheet and hope to identify any weak spots in the online orientation tutorial and make changes to improve the students' comprehension and information retention. (4) SAAC is currently undergoing a comprehensive critique of its at-risk student populations in an effort to better recognize these groups of students and design initiatives to help them succeed. (5) At about the fourteenth week of each fall semester, we conduct an online survey of freshmen in the Learning Community Program, aimed at determining the program's strengths and weaknesses. Those results are fed back into the program the following fall. One significant change that occurred during the fall 2006 program, for example, was the addition of more information on career-development options for CLA majors, as well as more discussion of how to choose majors and minors. All of the above are changes predicated specifically on student feedback.

Adaptability to Other Institutional Settings. CLA SAAC (3.5 full-time equivalent [FTE] Professional Advisors, one Executive Administrative Assistant, and the Associate Dean of CLA) oversees the advising needs of about 2,200 CLA students and 150 CLA faculty and staff, plus campus administrators, other advising offices, other campus functions, students' parents, and many students not in CLA but affected by CLA policies. Though we may be stretched to the limit of our resources, we are not stretched to the limit of our resourcefulness. Like many student-affairs functions across universities, we have developed policies and practices that may have been unique for a moment, but are certainly transferable to other units. For example: (1) This past fall another collegiate unit implemented CLA's policy on academic dismissals of first-year freshmen and is also using our New Student Guide to develop their own. (2) UMD's Advising Coordination Center plans to implement our 2002 faculty advisor survey campus-wide in 2008. (3) At least one other program at UMD (the online psychology major) is considering adapting CLA's online orientation program for use by their new transfer students. (4) Another college at UMD has created a faculty advising newsletter based on CLA's model. (5) CLA's student record exceptions form has been adopted across campus.

It is also likely that some of the initiatives that grow out of our current examination of CLA Students of Color and CLA at-risk student populations will catch the interest of other units. Clearly, a great deal of what we do is transferable; certainly some of what we do we "borrowed" from elsewhere. The only thing that stands in the way of advisement program innovation is the willingness of the staff to embrace change, not for the sake of change alone, but because needs exist that necessitate attention. In such cases, the first course of action should be to look around at what colleagues are doing both within and outside of our institutions and to identify practices that are consistent with our unique missions, practices, and cultures. There is seldom a clear need to reinvent the wheel when it comes to advising practices. Advising problems tend to be common across locations, and advising professionals tend to welcome the opportunity to share ideas and learn from one another. When you think about it, this sounds a lot like what a successful advising relationship is all about.

Jerry Pepper, gpepper@d.umn.edu

Program Name: Confronting the Complexities and Challenges of Change

Institution: Emmanuel College

Topic Connection: Chapter Fifteen—Organization of Academic Advising Services

Emmanuel College, founded by the Sisters of Notre Dame de Namur in 1919, is a coed, residential, Catholic liberal arts and sciences college located in the heart of Boston. Its beautiful seventeen-acre campus is neighbored by a world-class medical center, two major art museums, and Fenway Park. Its unique location allows students and faculty opportunities to explore real-world experiences through internships, research, and strategic partnerships within the Longwood Medical area and the city of Boston. Emmanuel is a community with a lifelong passion for teaching and learning rooted in the commitment to rigorous intellectual inquiry and the pursuit of social justice. Today, Emmanuel College continues to embrace its founding mission to transform lives and make a better world.

Program History. In 2001, Emmanuel's Academic Advising Program (AAP) faced an unusual challenge: a predicted 18.1 percent growth; a coeducational student body anticipated to reflect the unique descriptors of the millennials; and limited financial resources. Emmanuel's traditional student enrollment in 2001 was 694, and it has steadily increased each year, resulting in 1,741 in 2007. The AAP, which functions as an integral part of the academic affairs division of the college and has established strong links with offices throughout the institution, responded to this extraordinary growth in a manner that was pedagogically sound, fiscally responsible, and congruent with the appropriate delivery of services to students. The National Academic Advising Association's (NACADA) Core Values provided the framework, and the results flowed from the confluence of five factors: strong leadership, a sound organizational structure with theoretical underpinnings, clear goals and objectives, consistent professional development, and ongoing evaluation. A fourth academic advisor was hired in 2001 and a fifth in 2004. In 2007, academic advisors delivered services to approximately 1,100 first-year, transfer, and undeclared sophomore students.

Incoming students are randomly assigned and connect with a member of the Academic Advising Team during several of Emmanuel's two-day orientations in June. During the three to four semesters that follow, advisees meet regularly with their academic advisor in groups and individually.

Program Objective. The program's mission is "To challenge, support, and guide students as they become active participants in their own learning, and explore options, and make choices within the liberal arts and sciences curriculum." As a result, by the end of the first year, students should have:

- Established an effective working relationship with their academic advisor
- An understanding of Emmanuel College's academic policies and procedures as referenced in the Academic Catalog
- A clear understanding of the foundation skills and general and major requirements
- Learned how to read their Academic Evaluation Report and become familiar in the use of Online Academic Resources
- Created a working draft of a four-year academic plan
- Developed long-term educational plans
- Used the full range of campus resources

Program Description. The AAP reflects the blending of developmental, prescriptive and teaching components. Academic advisors are expected to be accessible, knowledgeable, and approachable. Factors that influenced programmatic success include a steady growth in the use of technology, the introduction of group meetings, and the development, implementation, and evaluation of a syllabus.

Steady Growth in the Use of Technology through:

- online placement testing and assessment of foundation skills during orientation
- partnerships with appropriate offices to provide academic resources in a consistent and timely manner for students and academic advisors
- ongoing electronic communication with students via First Class Communication Systems and intranet conferences during the summer and academic year
- online program assessment
- setting clear guidelines for students at the implementation of Web registration

Introduction of group meetings. These are meant not as a replacement for, but in addition to individual meetings in which general information is disseminated to students in a formal class structure, freeing academic advisors to spend time with individual students in more substantive ways.

Development, Implementation, and Evaluation of a Syllabus. The Academic Advising Team meets every three weeks for two hours, and individuals have weekly conversations with the administrator. This format builds collaboration

Academic Advising (AA 0101)

Abbreviated Syllabus

Semester One—Transition and Exploration	Semester Two—Exploration and Integration
Meeting 1—Group	Meeting 5—Group
Distribute catalogue, syllabus, and bookmarks; explain college and AAP missions; discuss advisee-academic advisors' responsibilities; reference technology links, Academic Evaluation Report, and SAS	Revisit advisee-academic advisors' responsibilities and technology links; introduce the Four-Year Plan and checklist; reference Visiting Classes Policy
Meeting 2—Individual	Meeting 6—Individual
Begin to build working relationship; Assignment 1, First Semester Thoughts, provides context for discussion	Discuss draft of Four-Year Plan (Assignment 4); make appropriate referrals to faculty and Career Services
Meeting 3—Group:	Meeting 7—Individual
Address catalogue questions from Assignment 2; discuss midsemester grades, implications of GPA, and pros and cons of withdrawing from a course; suggest strategies for academic success, including referrals; provide overview of Web registration; facilitate in-class Catalogue hunt activity; distribute Assignment 3	Address catalogue questions from Assignment 5; review midsemester grades; explain COF registration; anticipate summer study; and review Academic Evaluation Report
Meeting 4—Individual	Scripts are developed for each of these meetings and this ensures accurate dissemination of information.
Review Assignment 3, draft of spring schedule, and related questions regarding Web registration	These meetings do not preclude additional advisee-academic advisor contact at other times.

within the group and addresses the development of individual members. Team meetings begin with a discussion of a pertinent journal article or book chapter. Publications from NACADA, including its journals, monographs, and handbook, and other resources related to higher education, inform this segment of professional development. Four planning days punctuate the academic year—one at the close of fall semester and the remaining three in May.

Adaptability to Other Institutions:

- Provide workshops during orientation so that students will learn and use the various components of the institution's communication system.
- Establish an online academic advising system which includes FAQs, program syllabus, forms, etc.

- Monitor student progress through the use of Excel for data collection and analysis.
- Design, implement, and evaluate an academic advising syllabus.
- Schedule group and individual meetings.
- Provide opportunities for discussions and professional development for consistency in the delivery of services.

This program has had a profound impact on the students and faculty at Emmanuel College. It serves as an institutional model and an inspiration for faculty. Several departments have adopted it, and accolades from faculty continue to be forthcoming. In addition, two of our neighboring institutions have replicated aspects of this model to improve their academic advising programs.

Carolyn Caveny, caveny@emmanuel.edu

Program Name: Successful Merging of Academic and Career Advising

Institution: Principia College

Topic Connection: Chapter Fifteen—Organization of Academic Advising Services

Why merge academic and career advising? According to the National Leadership Council for Liberal Education and America's Promise in their booklet *College Learning for the New Global Century* (2007), higher education is going to have to think differently about its mission and learning outcomes for students in the twenty-first century (pp. 1–2). This report cites the Bureau of Labor Statistics, stating that "Americans change jobs ten times in the two decades following college." It urges institutions to offer students a liberal education that prepares them for the ever-changing global world by linking majors, general education, and skills needed for future careers (p. 16). Virginia Gordon states in her book *Career Advising* (2007), "The necessity for integrating academic and career advising is apparent in today's colleges because of the overwhelming number and scope of academic and career choices that students confront and the complexity of the changing work world they are preparing to enter" (p. viii).

Program History. In the fall of 2003, as director of the Academic Advising Center, I invited our college's Career Development Center director to attend the NACADA conference in Dallas, Texas, with the idea that we might explore ways to partner in our work with students. Conversations over the next couple of days and nights began to uncover a surprising number of links between the two departments. Among the key questions that arose were:

- How do students obtain information about exploring different majors?
- How do students link majors to possible careers?
- How do academic advisors support students with academic *and* career planning?

- What services can our centers provide to partner more effectively with faculty in educating students about connections between majors and careers?

- What can we do to educate students about the need to make those connections and prepare students with the knowledge and skills needed for the global world beyond college?

- How can students engage in preparation for their careers or graduate school in their freshmen or sophomore year, instead of waiting until the last half of their senior year?

By the time we returned to campus, we were both struck with the abundance of commonalities in our work with students and faculty. That enthusiasm was seen by others at the college, and in March 2004 the administration decided that the Academic Advising and Career Development Centers (CDC) would merge. The CDC director took another position at the institution.

Leading the merger as the new director, I was confronted with challenges immediately. How do we, as a four-year liberal arts college, avoid presenting ourselves as "vocational"? How will faculty advisors view the new department? What foundations do we want to lay for the new department? In consultation with our assessment office, we worked with the chapter, "Building the Vision" from the book *Built to Last* by James Collins and Jerry Porras (2004). To help bring the two office staffs together, this article provided the basis for our first joint office retreat, and it became the foundation of our core purpose and standards.

Program Objective. An article by Arthur Chickering (1994) ("Empowering Lifelong Self-Development") helped us see clearly that our new department's purpose was to help students into, through, and beyond college. Chickering discusses the importance of these three transitions and the need to provide adequate support as students move through their college experience. Several more retreats brought our team to conclude that it would promote and develop self-discovery, professionalism, and lifelong learning into, through, and beyond college.

Program Description. In the months following the creation of the new department, we found a new location and researched and polled students, faculty, and staff about a new name, which then became Academic and Career Advising (ACA). Our new department then reworked and combined our Web sites around Chickering's concepts. It also became clear to the entire staff that much of the work of the new department was to train academic advisors to help students with these three major transitions. An article that gave faculty new ways to think about this innovative approach to student advising was "Rethinking Liberal Arts Skills in the New Economy" by J. Bibbs Knotts (2002).

Over the next two years, we continued to work on becoming *one* department. It stretched us all mentally to think differently about the various areas we covered. Each time any of us was tempted to return to old, separate ways, we came back to the questions: What do we want students to gain from our services as they progress into, through, and beyond college? How do the various functions we provide overlap, and how can they be integrated? How can we help students (and advisors) understand the relationship of academic work to their preparation for a career "beyond" college?

The new department trains advisors to work with first-year students in a comprehensive advising program that includes academic planning, course selection, major exploration, and career planning. ACA also encourages new students to start thinking early about the link between their academic work and developing career-related skills. We have partnered with the college's student employment office by presenting resume workshops that encourage students to think about the skills and experiences they want to offer future employers. Students can then present their resumes when applying for jobs on campus, internships and externships, and during summer or other interim breaks.

The department researched and put together a newly integrated developmental self-discovery and self-assessment program, including several online tools. We were not surprised as students found it very natural that, as they were exploring majors, they would also want to explore possible careers. Academic advisors found that they had more information regarding major exploration, externships and internships, and career connections through ACA's presentations given at the mandatory Advisor Briefing meetings held before registration. These heightened advisor awareness of the importance of students becoming involved in work and other experiences during their undergraduate years. In working with faculty academic advisors within the majors, we quickly developed a cooperative partnership that helped students with specific details in self-discovery.

The ACA office has had more efficient staffing and resources, more consistent work flow, more visibility, and more contact with students and faculty since the merger. Although none of the student services the ACA office provides are mandatory, the merger of the two offices has been overwhelmingly successful.

In May 2007, a senior survey showed that (79 percent of seniors responded):

- 70 percent were first aware of ACA and its services during their freshman or sophomore year
- 93 percent stated advisors encouraged them to assume an active role in planning their academic program
- 83 percent of advisors gave accurate information or referred to other sources when needed
- 65 percent of advisors helped connect educational goals with career and/or graduate school goals

Also in May 2007, a review of ACA records regarding graduating seniors showed that:

- 73 percent had contact with ACA services (one-on-one appointments, conferences and seminars, etc.)
- 24 percent attended ACA's three-day Career Conference.

In fall 2007, results from the new student orientation survey indicated that (84 percent of students responded):

- 85 percent say they have a clear overview of Principia's academic program and degree requirements
- 90 percent stated their academic interests have been taken sufficiently into account

Adaptability to Other Institutional Settings. Several parts of our merged academic and career advising program can be adapted to other institutions. An important part of our program is training our advisors to be competent in discussing career connections with first-year students by linking academic work and the acquisition of career skills. Our mandatory Advisor Briefing meetings held before registration have heightened advisor awareness and provided information and techniques for discussing academic and career connections. Our integrated developmental self-discovery program includes several online tools. Our search of the Internet provided valuable information about how other institutions have integrated advising and career services. Like our program, these include self-exploration, academic planning, study-skill support, experiential learning opportunities, student employment, and career and graduate school services. In addition to our program, a few examples of merged offices include the University of Toronto, La Rouche College, and Keene State College.

Midge Browning, midge.browning@principia.edu

Part Four: Training, Assessment, Recognition, and Reward

Program Name: Academic Enhancement Program (AEP)

Institution: University of Central Florida

Topic Connection: Chapter Twenty—Critical Concepts in Advisor Training and Development

Program History. Created in the summer of 2001, the University of Central Florida's (UCF) Academic Advising Enhancement Program (AEP) was designed to provide direction and leadership for a continual program of academic advisor enhancement. UCF, the nation's sixth largest institution, is a public, multicampus, metropolitan research university currently serving over 48,000 students. Advisors must consistently remain current with the large volume of students and changing policies and advising practices that develop in response to growth and state-mandated requirements. The AEP was implemented to aid advisors in this process, allowing them to unite to discuss current issues, network, share best practices, and participate in professional development, all of which enhance UCF's advising services. Collaboration between the Division of Academic Affairs and Student Development and Enrollment Services, the AEP has provided services to over five hundred faculty and staff who have directly contributed to student progression, persistence, and success.

Program Objective. The purpose of the AEP is to provide a professional-development program for faculty and professional advisors. Program objectives are achieved through the following:

1. The AEP offers UCF professional advisors and faculty members a unique connection to university resources and learning opportunities. Monthly professional-development programs for advisors, training at new faculty orientations, and various workshops are offered as part of the program. Other resources created through the initiative include an academic advising handbook, online training sessions, and a Web site offering advising information. There is also the opportunity for continuous networking, communication, and collaboration among faculty and professional advisors.

2. The AEP allows UCF to more accurately assess the needs of the advising community. Following attendance at various AEPs, advisors are surveyed to determine whether the information imparted at the presentations was helpful to them in their positions. The programs are thus evaluated and adjusted accordingly.

3. Through professional-development training sessions, UCF's professional advisors and faculty receive up-to-date, accurate information regarding policies and procedures concerning the university. This is especially crucial in a university as large as UCF, where populations and policies change often and additional staff members are routinely hired.

4. Professional advisors and faculty obtain assistance with training on new technologies, due to the university's size and subsequent need for updated databases and online resources.

Program Description. Academic advising is an integral component of the educational process and is supported at all levels of the university. It is a developmental process that assists students in the clarification of life goals, and provides them with the opportunity to synthesize their goals and program choices into educational plans through which they can realize their maximum educational potential. Academic advising is an ongoing process of communication and information exchanges between advisor and student, a process whose power and impact cannot be underestimated. Thus, the AEP exists to ensure that this relationship between advisor and student thrives and achieves its ultimate potential. For this success to happen, the advisors must continuously receive professional-development training and professional support.

The AEP provides services and resources targeted to assist academic advisors in their quest to continually improve their knowledge and performance. Through discussions, networking opportunities, conferences, and other professional-development offerings, advisors receive the most accurate, current information and strategies in advising. Advisors attend workshops, go to monthly training programs, and gain a sense of community, leading to improved morale and greater communication and networking opportunities.

Colleges within the university rotate on a bimonthly basis to host the AEP. The Academic Advising Council, comprised of directors of advising units within UCF colleges and Student Development and Enrollment Services, invites guest speakers from within the university community to provide information and updates to the academic advisors. In addition, academic advisors are given the opportunity to recommend presenters or topics of discussion for future AEPs. Advising leadership in the colleges or university divisions encourage and support professional development of academic advising through participation in regional and academic advising conferences. They also encourage their advising staff to submit proposals for professional presentations at national and regional conferences.

As current faculty and advisors attend monthly training sessions and are afforded myriad networking opportunities, new faculty also benefit from the professional development offered with AEP. In collaboration with UCF's Faculty Center for Teaching and Learning, new faculty advisors attend hands-on workshops at the university's new-faculty orientation. These workshops provide instruction for new faculty advisors on university advising policies and the use of existing advising tools and related technology. In this collaborative effort led by professional advisors and Student Development and Enrollment Services, both new and existing faculty advisors are united in their professional development efforts and are supplied with the necessary information and tools for maximum advising efforts.

Program leaders conduct annual surveys to evaluate the success of the monthly training sessions and overall advising progress. Advising directors communicate with their staff to determine what needs could be enhanced through participation in the program. Through both the surveys and open discussions, advisors are able to provide input into the future topics and structure of the program.

Feedback from UCF advisors has indicated that the AEP has greatly facilitated professional advisors' ability to serve students. The program has increased their knowledge of campus advising policies, with over 95 percent reporting that the monthly programs benefited their performance. UCF students have indicated a decrease in erroneous information given in advising. Posttraining evaluation surveys have identified needs for future advisor professional-development training, thereby ensuring the continued success of the program and, ultimately, the greater success of UCF's advising efforts.

Adaptability to Other Institutions. Because the program uses existing resources and requires minimal funding, it can provide a low-cost professional-development opportunity for professional and faculty academic advisors at public and private colleges of varying sizes. The program can provide faculty and advisors with consistent, clear, and accurate advising information, in addition to offering an opportunity to explore the use of technology to implement and distribute advising resources. Finally, the program can create an avenue for involvement, recognition, and support from university-level administrators.

DeLaine Priest, dpriest@mail.ucf.edu
Judith Sindlinger
Mark Allen Poisel
Tina Smilie

Program Name: University-wide Academic Advising Assessment

Institution: Oregon State University

Topic Connection: Chapter Twenty-Five—Assessing the Effectiveness of the Advising Program

Program History. Oregon State University (OSU) is a research-intensive, land-grant institution with approximately 19,000 undergraduate and graduate students. Ten strong, independent colleges and the University Exploratory Studies Program provide academic advising to undergraduate students. Each college has a unique advising structure, and although each has a head advisor, their duties vary dramatically from hands-on advising to coordinating student services for their college. Some colleges have a centralized advising office staffed by professional advisors who work with all of the various majors in a respective college, while others have decentralized models in which the departments use faculty or professional advisors to address advising needs.

Program Objective. OSU academic advising reflects the institutional goal of excellence in teaching and learning and is focused on student success. We recognize that quality academic advising is integral to the academic development and well-being of students, and includes both the prescriptive elements and developmental aspects of advising.

In 2001, a visit by the Northwest Commission on Colleges and Universities (NWCCU), OSU's accrediting body, found advising of students to be less than ideal, noting inconsistencies and student confusion. They made a formal recommendation to rectify the situation. In April 2006, the NWCCU returned to Oregon State for an interim visit. The stern recommendation had been addressed fully and their outgoing comments to the president and provost were positive. The real acclaim came in their formal report which ended with a commendation for academic advising.

> Oregon State University has made dramatic progress in creating a culture where advising is valued and regarded as central to student success. The energy, enthusiasm, and commitment of those members of the OSU community engaged in advising are admirable. OSU is commended for the steps it has taken since the 2001 report to improve and promote advising, and for its success in creating a new university culture where excellence in advising is considered essential to student success. *The assessment plan for advising is the best we have observed for any university. [Italics in original.]*

Program Description. The approach to academic assessment at Oregon State University is elegant in its simplicity. It has three main steps: each unit

- articulates desired outcomes,
- gathers information about how well the outcomes are being met, and
- uses that information for program improvement.

We focus on the process versus the plan and recognize that full-cycle assessment is a valuable tool for reflection and decision-making. The following is a description of what those steps look like for university-wide academic advising.

First Critical Step: Articulate Desired Outcomes. In 2005, ten head advisors and two administrators attended the NACADA Academic Advising Summer Institute to determine best principles for advising at OSU. To shape this work, the team relied heavily on a few guiding documents, including the university's Strategic Plan and the national norms and standards outlined by NACADA and the Council for Advancement of Standards in Higher Education (CAS).

Best advising principles were made manifest, first with a vision and mission, then values closely aligning those of the institution, and finally with goals and learning outcomes for both advisors and students and a plan for measuring the outcomes. Intentionally built into this structure is the flexibility for departments and colleges to address expected outcomes for students, advisors, and delivery systems in ways most appropriate to the culture of each area.

This work was shared across campus in colleges and departments at brown bags, to various committees, and with the president and provost and their councils. The vision, mission, value, and goal statements were unanimously adopted by the Academic Advising Council, a committee of the Faculty Senate, followed by approval by the Executive Committee of the Faculty Senate.

Implementation strategies for the new principles have been framed by a few core concepts, as described below.

Institutionalizing Change. In order to realize improved advising and student success, OSU is investing in the following key areas: (1) reconceptualizing advisor time; (2) technology; (3) assessment; and (4) advisor development, training, and recognition.

- The group is negotiating the development of an expandable, comprehensive advising system prototype that will be funded by the provost and will serve the entire university.
- To jump start assessment efforts, three members attended the NACADA Assessment Institute.
- Funding has been secured and guidelines written for a Professional Advising Award (a Faculty Advising Award is already in place) to be given annually at University Day.

- Commitments have been made to offer local professional-development opportunities to faculty and professional advisors each year.

Implementation Principles

- Unified—supported by the university
- Consistent—used by all colleges
- Adaptable—to individual college needs
- Extendable—to community college students

College Investment for University Excellence in Academic Advising

- Adopt and promote these advising principles.
- Participate in developing an OSU strategy for advising technology.
- Encourage and support advisor development and training.
- Support assessment of advising learning outcomes.
- Recognize and reward excellent advising in your college.

Next Step: Develop Methods/Measurements and Gather Information. Assessment instruments were designed to monitor and direct program improvement. The goals and outcomes for academic advising were mapped to various advising activities as well as to a student's four-year college experience. The map provided a concrete visual of the complexity of a university-wide model for academic advising.

Once the essential learning outcomes for first-year students were identified, the team partnered with other campus units to develop several documents that put theory into practice. These are tangible products useful to both students and advisors.

- *Zero to Success in 77 Days* is a week by week list of things students need to stay on top of to enhance their chances of success.
- *Advisor-Advisee Responsibilities* shapes the role of each and acknowledges the partnership necessary for successful guidance.
- The *START Checklist* covers required and recommended tasks to be completed during START summer orientation as well as key information new students need to know.
- A *Vision, Mission, Values Poster* now hangs, matted and framed, in every advising office on campus, including athletics, international programs, equal opportunities, etc. It serves as a visible reminder of our commitment to excellence in advising.

These documents offer students a unified, campus-wide message—each document is used in every START session by every college and department. This work clarifies the expectations of advisors and advisees and identifies sites for assessment to ensure that intended outcomes are being met regardless of the discipline. The foundation of the design is the progressional shift of responsibility from the university to the student over the course of the student's college career, and from predominantly prescriptive advising to more developmental advising.

Data have been collected from the START Checklist and the START student evaluation, and First Year Student focus groups are conducted in the spring. An Academic Advisor Self-Assessment is given to advisors to gauge advisor perceptions about their own practice and the support provided to them by the university.

Last Step: Close the Loop by Reflecting on Data and Making Decisions. Each year the team has a summer retreat and a winter work session, both with dedicated time for reflection. This is essential to maintain focus, nurture creativity and collaboration, and commit to change. What do the data demonstrate? Where can energy be directed for greatest improvement? Is every college working toward achieving the goals and outcomes?

One result from this reflective time was the realization that head advisors have little control over many areas in which the outcomes are addressed. Learning takes place in areas not directly associated with academic advising. While not accountable for the work of others, the interdependence is clear, and partnering is necessary to reach our goals. Pairs of head advisors met with various units on campus to share the learning outcomes for advising and illustrate the role each unit plays in the successful achievement of each outcome. This action intensified the focus. Awareness alone promises some improvement, and often this outreach led to shifts in work and attitude of other units. Another result was the opportunity to share innovations at the college level—a new program for students on warning, an advising syllabus, a student survey, an "open house" degree fair, a forum for curricular change, and many others. The common feature of all the new practices is their grounding in the stated outcomes for academic advising at OSU. Assessment has come full circle.

Adaptability to Other Institutions. The approach we take at Oregon State could be easily adapted; it is not necessary to reinvent the wheel. It is rare that what works in one college or institution will be a perfect fit for another, but the basic format can serve as a template, spark interest, and save time and energy. This work is doable. Keep it simple, centered on students, geared toward continuous improvement, and most important, sustainable. Break it down into manageable pieces. Start small and do full-cycle assessment—every time!

Susie Leslie, Director of Academic Programs and Academic Assessment, susie.leslie@oregonstate.edu

Program Name: Advising Development and Resource Team: Advising Excellence Award (http://webspace.ship.edu/advising)

Institution: Shippensburg University

Topic Connection: Chapter Twenty-Six—Recognition and Reward for Academic Advising in Theory and Practice

Program History. Shippensburg University is one of fourteen institutions that make up the State System of Higher Education of Pennsylvania. A key characteristic that guides campus-wide advising practice is that the university is a collective bargaining institution. According to the terms of the bargaining agreement, academic advising is a faculty responsibility. Therefore, the framework for delivering advising services to students is a faculty-only, decentralized model. Students with a declared major are advised by a faculty member within their academic department, and undeclared students are advised through the Office of Undeclared Students.

It is the philosophy of Shippensburg University that good academic advising not only enhances the retention and satisfaction of students, it also enriches the professional experiences of advisors. The goal for the advising development program is continuous quality improvement. In spring 2000, the university's president charged the dean of the School of Academic Programs and Services with the task of improving advisement campus-wide. This commitment led to the formation of the Advisor Development and Resource Team (ADRT) to serve as a coordinating body to promote quality advising campus-wide and to create programs and services that assist faculty in their advising role. All academic departments are encouraged to designate a representative to serve on the team.

One of the significant initiatives to improve advisement campus-wide was the establishment of the Advising Excellence Award. In 2002, the provost announced the first competition. Her instruction was that a cash award be presented to the academic department that best demonstrates excellence and promotes best practices in academic advising. This remains the focus of the annual award. Since its inception, five different academic departments have earned the award.

Program Objectives. The Advising Excellence Award has two primary objectives: (1) to elevate the quality of academic advising campus-wide; and (2) to cultivate a campus culture that values advising as an integral component of the teaching and learning process. To achieve these objectives, the award process encourages academic departments to identify and share best practices that can be adapted by departments across campus. A copy of each year's winning application is placed in the university's library, and the winning department presents a campus-wide advising workshop. Other departments are encouraged to borrow ideas and adapt practices that are appropriate for their student's needs. In addition, faculty advisors from departments that have won the award serve as mentors to advisors across campus.

Program Description. The Advising Excellence Award is presented annually to the academic department that best demonstrates advising excellence as documented in supporting materials. The award is given to a department rather than to an individual advisor because of the belief that advising is programmatic and not a singular event and that effective advising is a collective effort. The ADRT develops the eligibility requirements, coordinates the application and selection processes, and recommends the recipient to the provost, who announces the award winner. A description of the program components follows.

Award. The $5,000 award is supported by the university president and provost and consists of $2,500 in funding from Academic Affairs and $2,500 from the President's Office. The only stipulation on the use of the award is that the funds are designated for the advancement of undergraduate teaching and learning. Any unspent foundation funds can be carried forward from one year to the next. Recipients of the award have used the funds for activities such as:

- student travel to regional conferences
- the purchase of educational materials
- a student field trip to the Dali Exhibit and the Philadelphia Museum of Art
- to purchase books for a reading circle
- to sponsor a student research competition
- an honors' reception

In addition to the cash award, the winning department receives campuswide recognition at the fall faculty convocation, is featured in an issue of the campus publication for faculty and staff and in the faculty advising newsletter, receives a plaque to display in their department, and is honored by a plaque displayed in the university's library.

Eligibility. The award is limited to academic departments. Previous winners are eligible to reapply only if two years have elapsed since their selection and their departmental advising program has been significantly modified or altered.

Criteria. Proposals are evaluated on the extent to which they provide evidence of each of the following criteria. In addition, a program description, a willingness to share best practices with the campus community, and an adherence to NACADA core values are key factors in the selection.

Innovative Quality—To what extent does the advising program represent unique approaches to best practices in effective academic advising?

Creativity—To what extent does the advising program demonstrate the creative use of resources (human, fiscal, and physical) in the delivery of academic advising services?

Currency—To what extent does the advising program address current departmental problems and issues in academic advising?

Institutional Commitment—To what extent does the advising program demonstrate commitment to advising throughout the department?

Impact—To what extent does the advising program provide definitive, qualitative, and quantitative assessment of positive student and departmental outcomes?

Professional Development—To what extent does the advising program address how faculty members prepare for their advising responsibilities?

Transferability—To what extent does the advising program display strategies applicable and adaptable to other academic departments?

Application Procedures. The call for applications is issued during the fall semester, usually in mid-October. The deadline for submissions to the chair of the ADRT is the end of February. Application materials and guidelines are distributed to each college dean and academic department chair. The coordinator of advising development and previous recipients of the award are available to assist departments in the application process. The application packet includes:

1. Five copies of the completed application with supporting materials;
2. A description of the department's understanding of the role and value of advising, practices used to achieve excellence in advising, and methods used to assess the effectiveness of the advising program;
3. A program narrative, no more than five pages in length that addresses the following:
   - the award criteria
   - how the program was developed (problems encountered, organizational concerns, budget and other practical considerations)
   - the goals and objectives of the departmental advising program
   - a program description with specifics on advisor/advisee ratio and how undeclared, minors, and transfer students are advised
   - procedures for program assessment, including quantitative and qualitative measures
   - results and outcomes that describe the impact on students and the institution
   - potential adaptations to other departments;
4. A completed application form with the appropriate signatures;
5. A letter from the department chair that outlines the mission, goals, and teaching philosophy of the department and explains how the advising activities support the department's philosophy;
6. Other supporting materials, such as student and alumni letters of support.

Selection Process. A subcommittee of the ADRT reviews and rates the applications. To avoid potential conflicts of interest, the readers are faculty advisors from academic departments not submitting a proposal. At least one of the readers is from a department that was a past recipient of the award. The chair of the subcommittee is a faculty member from a nonteaching department. The subcommittee ranks the applications using a standardized scoring rubric and reports the results of their work to the entire ADRT. A recommendation is forwarded to the provost, who announces the recipient in April and presents the award at the fall faculty convocation.

Adaptability to Other Institutional Settings: Transferability is a quality of excellent advising programs. One of the key features of this advisor recognition program is that it serves as a model that can be adapted to any institution. The implementation of the program does not require unusual resources of money or time. However, it should be noted that the Advising Excellence Award is an effective incentive to promote excellence in advising at Shippensburg University because of several factors.

1. It is a campus-wide initiative supported by the top administration—president, provost, and college deans—and not viewed as simply belonging to the advising program.
2. It is embraced by faculty advisors who are committed to excellence in advising.
3. It is administered through a coordinating campus-wide body (the ADRT) and not the responsibility of a single individual or advising center.

Stephen O. Wallace
David Henriques, dihenr@ship.edu

Program Name: Motivating and Rewarding Advising Staff: A Practical Approach

Institution: Howard Community College (HCC)

Topic Connection: Chapter Twenty-Six—Recognition and Reward for Academic Advising in Theory and in Practice

Program History. Howard Community College (HCC) reorganized its advising services in 1996. Until then advising was primarily provided by career and personal counselors with faculty rank who also taught various Human Development and Psychology classes. While counseling services received excellent ratings on yearly faculty and staff and student surveys, advising services were not as well regarded, and morale among counselor-advisors was poor and an increasing concern.

The new organizational structure created the Office of Admissions and Advising, uniting academic and transfer advising and admissions services. This unit includes outreach and recruitment; general, selective, and competitive admissions programs; international credit admissions; academic and transfer advising (including a new Transfer Center); transcript evaluation and degree audit; and the initial graduate petition process. This organizational structure enables students to be associated with one unit from the time interest is initially generated in the college to the point of graduation. Students, of course, can enter at any point in between. Since its inception, satisfaction with admissions and advising services has steadily risen, and the unit has continuously been among the top-rated campus services on both annual student and faculty and staff satisfaction surveys.

In the spring of 2006, along with all Maryland community colleges, HCC administered the Community College Survey of Student Engagement (CCESE) to its students. On this measure, advising was the top-rated service. In addition, minimal reports of errors or complaints are received through the multiple methods available to the college community for expressing concerns. Satisfaction has remained consistently high despite an overall enrollment growth of over 40 percent in the past five years and growth in advising contacts of 28 percent over the same period.

The bureaucratic structure is a seamless one that students regard highly. However, unit administrators believe through objective and anecdotal evidence that the significant improvement in and maintenance of staff morale has been at the heart of this unit's success and a significant factor in enrollment growth. Advising staff satisfaction has been achieved through the commitment of both the college and the unit to rewarding staff year-round in large and small ways. The decision to grow to meet the community's needs has been one of HCC's strategic objectives. Registration is basically ongoing year-round, including four summer terms. Realistically, this has led to an enrollment and programmatic growth rate that has outpaced, and continues to outpace, the addition of staff. Relying primarily upon the addition of staff as a basis for enhancing student satisfaction and employee morale would not be realistic, especially in light of the urgent need to hire more full-time faculty. Confident that the new organizational structure was one that would enhance student satisfaction, unit administrators turned their attention to staff morale and identified the following objectives:

1. Build upon the college's history as an excellent faculty- and staff-centered employer, which uses a merit-based compensation system and other institutional recognitions and awards.

2. Develop and deliver a robust staff-development program designed to increase advisors' knowledge base, enhance self-confidence, and increase student satisfaction and positive feedback.

3. Focus on hiring, team-building, individual interests and expertise, "ownership," staff participation in decision-making, and staff retention.

4. Provide career-advancement opportunities within the unit.

5. Provide time for team-building, meetings, administrative and follow-up work, individual appointments, creativity, and special projects.

6. Focus on wellness and stress reduction.

7. Educate students, faculty, and staff about the advising process.

8. Regularly assess staff and student satisfaction through formal and informal methods.

9. Minimize distinctions between budgeted and nonbudgeted staff, and full-time and part-time staff.

Program Description. Rewarding advising staff is not an isolated end goal, though it is certainly important. Instead, the focus is on creating a culture of recognition and reward that acknowledges expertise, work ethic, job-related stress, and staff feedback to achieve institutional objectives. Pragmatism is at the heart of the rewards and recognition provided. The methods used depend less on innovation than on consistency and "counterintuition." For example, while an obvious strategy for managing growth might be to expand the walk-in advising schedule, the urge to do so has been resisted in favor of getting more out of the hours the unit is open for walk-in advising.

Each of the following strategies fulfills one or more of the unit's objectives.

Access to Technology and Other Resources—The highest priority is placed on providing advisors with the latest in technology and other resources. Whether full- or part-time, all staff have access to the technology, space, supplies, and other tools they require.

Travel Opportunities—One of the first budget items cut by institutions when funds are tight is travel. Instead, the Office of Admissions and Advising views appropriate local, regional, national, and even international travel as essential to rewarding and renewing staff, encouraging new ideas, and networking with colleagues near and far. HCC's vice president of Academic Affairs has partnered with the unit to enable advisors to experience HCC's study-abroad opportunities firsthand. Advisors have a wonderful and energizing opportunity to travel and are far better positioned to inform and encourage students about study-abroad programs. All staff interested in travel know that they will eventually have this opportunity, including support staff. Local and regional travel to conferences and other institutions is also encouraged. Traveling builds camaraderie, infuses new information and ideas into the office, and often affirms what is already being done within the unit.

Membership in Professional Organizations—This may seem obvious, but many institutions or institutional units limit membership to administrators or full-time staff. HCC's Office of Admissions and Advising covers fees for all staff interested in membership in organizations such as NACADA. In addition to enhancing staff development, organizational memberships also reinforce professional identify and recognition.

Compensation Time—At HCC, advisors are professional staff and are not eligible for overtime compensation. Instead, immediately following peak periods an "enforced" rest period is granted. This must be taken within a four-week period and is not charged against leave. Part-time staff are generally granted a day while full-time staff are granted two days.

Office Schedule—Many advising units are open for walk-in advising or appointments around the clock. Finding time to work on special projects, conduct follow-up work, participate in various institutional activities, meet, or conduct staff-development activities is challenging at best. Based on this, HCC advising administrators decided to limit counter service-only one day per month, except in January and August. The office closes for advising between 3 and 5 P.M. each day before opening again in the evening allowing employees to catch up with paperwork, meet informally with coworkers, work on projects, or set up appointments with students, faculty, or other staff. Counter service-only is provided on Thursday evenings, which is set aside for special programs, information sessions, and other special events. Flexible scheduling is used to provide coverage as needed during peak periods.

Expertise and Ownership—Each advisor is assigned an area of expertise, generally based upon interest and specific abilities. While all advisors are required to have a general knowledge base, each becomes a specialist, liaison, problem-solver, and trainer in a particular area.

Hiring and Promoting—Hiring focuses holistically on how applicants will complement a team within the office and the unit as a whole. Entry-level positions are given increasing responsibility, and promotion occurs from within whenever possible. Supervisors are closely attuned to staff responsibilities and development and request reclassifications and top merit levels whenever warranted.

Institutional Recognition—Advisors are regularly nominated for institutional awards and other forms of recognition. This takes time and effort, but is crucial, whether or not the award or recognition is ultimately received.

Staff Development—Advisors and support staff are provided opportunities to enhance their resumes. Pursuing advanced degrees is strongly encouraged, and work-schedule adjustments are regularly made to accommodate this. Advisors are encouraged to participate in programs outside the unit and serve on committees whether directly related to the unit's core work or not. Feedback is provided through institutional student and faculty and staff surveys, comment cards, and student feedback cards returned to advisors and through other means. This provides continuous opportunities to adjust, improve, and reinforce.

Eat, Drink and Be Merry—Food and refreshments are a regular part of the office culture and integral to our peak-period planning, staff meetings, and staff development. Vouchers are provided for the college's coffee bar throughout the year to encourage staff to leave the office for a brief break with a colleague. Faculty and other units are included in our plans enabling all to "break bread" together.

Team Spirit and Collegiality—Above all, many efforts are made to foster collegiality. The unit has a large staff organized into "subunits" (i.e., allied health, transfer, international, etc.). Special focus is placed on ensuring that staff offices are not clustered according to area of emphasis. Members of each subunit are located throughout the office, enhancing team spirit, and all have access to various types of information. All staff meetings are scheduled monthly and are planned by staff randomly selected by a drawing at the beginning of each year. Providing staff a voice regarding working conditions in a broad range of areas helps to maintain a high level of satisfaction.

Adaptability to Other Institutional Settings. The Office of Admissions and Advising has been fortunate to have strong campus-wide support, including resources. This is a circular situation—the unit receives support because it has successfully contributed to the college's goals, and it has successfully contributed to the college's goals because it has received support. Distant travel may be an area that another institution's budget cannot support, but many of the "rewards" mentioned above are simple, easily enacted, and cost-effective—for instance, flexible scheduling, staff development, and time to develop projects. Ensuring that advisors understand that their expertise and job performance are valued is a key element of the institution's success. At Howard Community College, this understanding translates into the achievement of strategic goals and satisfaction with advising services for all sectors of the college community.

Barbara Greenfeld, bgreenfeld@howardcc.edu

PART SIX SUMMARY

Part Six has provided examples of award-winning advising programs that demonstrate how the ideas presented by some of the authors in this book can be practically applied. Basing advising on a theoretical framework such as "Appreciative Inquiry" can add structure and meaning to not only one-on-one contact with students, but may guide programming philosophy as well. The three program descriptions for advising special populations demonstrate how approaches can be designed to meet the very specific needs of these student groups.

Organizational designs must reflect the uniqueness of a campus size and culture. The programs described for Part Three of this book, however, offer practices that can be applied to any institution interested in improving the way it organizes and administers different aspects of its advising program. One of the most important components of any advising program is the type of advisor-development program it offers, the way it evaluates its mission and services, and how it recognizes the outstanding service that many advisors unselfishly provide. Many aspects of the two unique approaches to recognizing and rewarding outstanding advising practices offered as examples for Part Four of this book are adaptable to any institution interested in improving this important but often neglected area of its advising program.

The program descriptions given in Part Six are just samples of the many outstanding advising approaches created by institutions across the country.

Hopefully, the descriptions offered here will serve as an impetus to generate innovative program ideas and motivate administrators and advisors to adapt these practices that have been so successful for other advising programs.

References

Bloom, J. L., Amundsen, S. A., & Hutson, B. L. (2006, October). *Appreciative advising potential interest group.* Interest group session conducted at the Annual Conference of the National Academic Advising Association, Indianapolis, IN.

Chickering, A. (1994). Empowering lifelong self-development. *NACADA Journal, 14* (2), 50–53.

Collins, J. C., & Porras, J. I. (2004). *Built to last: Successful habits of visionary companies.* New York: Harper Collins.

Cooperrider, D. L. (1990). Positive image, positive action: The affirmative basis of organizing. In S. Srivastva, & D. L. Cooperrider (Eds.), *Appreciative management and leadership: The power of positive thought and action in organizations* (pp. 91–125). San Francisco: Jossey-Bass.

Gordon, V. N. (2007). *Career advising.* San Francisco: Jossey-Bass.

Hutson, B. L. (2003). *Student strategies for success survey.* Greensboro: University of North Carolina-Greensboro.

Hutson, B. L., Amundsen, S. A., & He, Y. (2005, April). *Monitoring for success: Implementing a proactive probation program for diverse, at-risk college students.* Presented at annual meeting of the American Educational Research Association, Montreal, QC.

Kamphoff, C. S., Hutson, B. L., Amundsen, S. A., & Atwood, J. A. (2007). A motivational/empowerment model applied to students on academic probation. *Journal of College Student Retention: Research, Theory, and Practice, 8* (4), 397–412.

Knotts, H. G. (2002). Rethinking liberal arts skills in the new economy. *NACADA Journal, 22* (1), 26–30.

National Leadership Council for Liberal Education and America's Promise. (2007). *College learning for the new global century.* Washington, DC: Association of American Colleges and Universities, 16.

APPENDIX A

NATIONAL ACADEMIC ADVISING ASSOCIATION

The National Academic Advising Association Board of Directors endorses three documents that champion the educational role of academic advising in a diverse world.

The three documents are:

- Concept of Academic Advising
- Statement of Core Values
- Council for the Advancement of Standards in Higher Education Standards sand Guidelines for Academic Advising

These sets of guiding principles affirm the role of academic advising in higher education, thereby supporting institutional missions, while at the same time anticipating the needs of twenty-first-century students, academic advisors, and institutions.

They can be used for a variety of purposes, including the professional development of academic advisors and program assessment. They also can be used when implementing a new advising program or revising a current one.

Academic advising is carried out by a vast array of individuals, including faculty and staff members. These guiding principles are intended for use by all who advise.

These documents support all categories of institutions with every type of advising delivery system. Intentionally, they do not address every detail and nuance of academic advising. Rather they should be used as starting points and references for a discussion of academic advising, providing the framework for a coherent approach to implementing a well-functioning academic advising program that would meet any specified institutional goals.

CONCEPT OF ACADEMIC ADVISING

Academic advising is integral to fulfilling the teaching and learning mission of higher education. Through academic advising, students learn to become members of their higher education community, to think critically about their roles and responsibilities as students, and to prepare to be educated citizens of a democratic society and a global community. Academic advising engages students beyond their own worldviews, while acknowledging their individual characteristics, values, and motivations as they enter, move through, and exit the institution. Regardless of the diversity of our institutions, our students, our advisors, and our organizational structures, academic advising has three components: curriculum (what advising deals with), pedagogy (how advising does what it does), and student learning outcomes (the result of academic advising).

The Curriculum of Academic Advising

Academic advising draws primarily from theories in the social sciences, humanities, and education. The curriculum of academic advising ranges from the ideals of higher education to the pragmatics of enrollment. This curriculum includes, but is not limited to, the institution's mission, culture, and expectations; the meaning, value, and interrelationship of the institution's curriculum and cocurriculum; modes of thinking, learning, and decision-making; the selection of academic programs and courses; the development of life and career goals; campus and community resources, policies, and procedures; and the transferability of skills and knowledge.

The Pedagogy of Academic Advising

Academic advising, as a teaching and learning process, requires a pedagogy that incorporates the preparation, facilitation, documentation, and assessment of advising interactions. Although the specific methods, strategies, and techniques may vary, the relationship between advisors and students is fundamental and is characterized by mutual respect, trust, and ethical behavior.

Student Learning Outcomes of Academic Advising

The student learning outcomes of academic advising are guided by an institution's mission, goals, curriculum, and cocurriculum. These outcomes, defined in an advising curriculum, articulate what students will demonstrate, know, value, and do as a result of participating in academic advising. Each institution must develop its own set of student learning outcomes and the methods to assess them. The following is a representative sample. Students will:

- craft a coherent educational plan based on assessment of abilities, aspirations, interests, and values
- use complex information from various sources to set goals, reach decisions, and achieve those goals
- assume responsibility for meeting academic program requirements
- articulate the meaning of higher education and the intent of the institution's curriculum
- cultivate the intellectual habits that lead to a lifetime of learning
- behave as citizens who engage in the wider world around them

CONCLUSION

Academic advising, based in the teaching and learning mission of higher education, is a series of intentional interactions with a curriculum, a pedagogy, and a set of student learning outcomes. Academic advising synthesizes and contextualizes students' educational experiences within the frameworks of their aspirations, abilities, and lives to extend learning beyond campus boundaries and timeframes.

APPENDIX B

THE STATEMENT OF CORE VALUES OF ACADEMIC ADVISING

The National Academic Advising Association (NACADA) is comprised of professional and faculty advisors, administrators, students, and others with a primary interest in the practice of academic advising. With diverse backgrounds, perspectives, and experiences, NACADA members advise in a variety of settings and work to promote quality academic advising within their institutions.

NACADA recognizes and celebrates the contributions of professional, faculty, paraprofessional, and peer advisors to the advising profession. NACADA acknowledges the complex nature of higher education institutions and the role academic advising plays within them, the wide variety of settings and responsibilities of academic advisors, and advisors' diverse backgrounds and experiences. NACADA provides a Statement of Core Values to affirm the importance of advising within the academy and acknowledge the impact that advising interactions can have on individuals, institutions, and society.

The Statement of Core Values consists of three parts: (1) Introduction, (2) Declaration, and (3) Exposition, a descriptive section expanding on each of the Core Values. While each part stands alone, the document's richness and fullness of meaning lies in its totality.

The Statement of Core Values provides a framework to guide professional practice and reminds advisors of their responsibilities to students, colleagues, institutions, society, and themselves. Those charged with advising responsibilities are expected to reflect the values of the advising profession in their daily interactions at their institutions.

The Statement of Core Values does not attempt to dictate the manner in or process through which academic advising takes place, nor does it advocate one particular advising philosophy or model over another. Instead, these Core Values are the reference points advisors use to consider their individual philosophies, strengths, and opportunities for professional growth. Furthermore, the Core Values do not carry equal weight. Advisors will find some Core Values more applicable or valuable to their situations than others. Advisors should consider each Core Value with regard to their own values and those of their institutions.

Advising constituents, and especially students, deserve dependable, accurate, timely, respectful, and honest responses. Through this Statement of Core Values, NACADA communicates the expectations that others should hold for advisors in their advising roles. Advisors' responsibilities to their many constituents form the foundation upon which the Core Values rest.

NATIONAL ACADEMIC ADVISING ASSOCIATION

The Statement of Core Values of Academic Advising

Declaration

1) Advisors are responsible to the individuals they advise.

Academic advisors work to strengthen the importance, dignity, potential, and unique nature of each individual within the academic setting. Advisors' work is guided by their beliefs that students:

- have diverse backgrounds that can include different ethnic, racial, domestic, and international communities; sexual orientations; ages; gender and gender identities; physical, emotional, and psychological abilities; political, religious, and educational beliefs
- hold their own beliefs and opinions
- are responsible for their own behaviors and the outcomes of those behaviors
- can be successful based upon their individual goals and efforts
- have a desire to learn
- have learning needs that vary based upon individual skills, goals, responsibilities, and experiences
- use a variety of techniques and technologies to navigate their world.

In support of these beliefs, the cooperative efforts of all who advise include, but are not limited to, providing accurate and timely information, communicating in useful and efficient ways, maintaining regular office hours, and offering varied contact modes.

Advising, as part of the educational process, involves helping students develop a realistic self-perception and successfully transition to the postsecondary institution. Advisors encourage, respect, and assist students in establishing their goals and objectives.

Advisors seek to gain the trust of their students and strive to honor students' expectations of academic advising and its importance in their lives.

2) Advisors are responsible for involving others, when appropriate, in the advising process.

Effective advising requires a holistic approach. At many institutions, a network of people and resources is available to students. Advisors serve as mediators and facilitators who effectively use their specialized knowledge and experience for student benefit. Advisors recognize their limitations and make referrals to qualified persons when appropriate. To connect academic advising to students' lives, advisors actively seek resources and inform students of specialists who can further assess student needs and provide access to appropriate programs and services. Advisors help students integrate information so they can make well-informed academic decisions.

3) Advisors are responsible to their institutions.

Advisors nurture collegial relationships. They uphold the specific policies, procedures, and values of their departments and institutions. Advisors maintain clear lines of communication with those not directly involved in the advising process but who have responsibility and authority for decisions regarding academic advising at the institution. Advisors recognize their individual roles in the success of their institutions.

4) Advisors are responsible to higher education.

Academic advisors honor academic freedom. They realize that academic advising is not limited to any one theoretical perspective and that practice is informed by a variety of theories from the fields of social sciences, the humanities, and education. They are free to base their work with students on the most relevant theories and on optimal models for the delivery of academic advising programs. Advisors advocate for student educational achievement to the highest attainable standard, support student goals, and uphold the educational mission of the institution.

5) Advisors are responsible to their educational community.

Academic advisors interpret their institution's mission as well as its goals and values. They convey institutional information and characteristics of student success to the local, state, regional, national, and global communities that support the student body. Advisors are sensitive to the values and mores of the surrounding community. They are familiar with community programs and services that may provide students with additional educational opportunities and resources. Advisors may become models for students by participating in community activities.

6) Advisors are responsible for their professional practices and for themselves personally.

Advisors participate in professional-development opportunities, establish appropriate relationships and boundaries with advisees, and create environments that promote physical, emotional, and spiritual health. Advisors maintain a healthy balance in their lives and articulate personal and professional needs when appropriate. They consider continued professional growth and development to be the responsibility of both themselves and their institutions.

NATIONAL ACADEMIC ADVISING ASSOCIATION

The Statement of Core Values of Academic Advising

Exposition

Core Value 1: Advisors are responsible to the individuals they advise.

- Academic advising is an integral part of the educational process and affects students in numerous ways. As advisors enhance student learning and development, advisees have the opportunity to become participants in and contributors to their own education. In one of the most important potential outcomes of this process, academic advising fosters individual potential.

- Regular student contact through in-person appointments, mail, telephone, e-mail, or other computer-mediated systems helps advisors gain meaningful insights into students' diverse academic, social, and personal experiences and needs. Advisors use these insights to assist students as they transition to new academic and social communities, develop sound academic and career goals, and ultimately, become successful learners.

- Advisors recognize and respect that students' diverse backgrounds are comprised of their ethnic and racial heritage, age, gender, sexual orientation, and religion, as well as their physical, learning, and psychological abilities. Advisors help students develop and reinforce realistic self-perceptions and help them use this information in mapping out their futures.

- Advisors introduce and assist students with their transitions to the academic world by helping them see value in the learning process, gain perspective on the college experience, become more responsible and accountable, set priorities and evaluate their progress, and uphold honesty with themselves and others about their successes and limitations.

- Advisors encourage self-reliance and support students as they strive to make informed and responsible decisions, set realistic goals, and develop lifelong learning and self-management skills.

- Advisors respect students' rights to their individual beliefs and opinions.

- Advisors guide and teach students to understand and apply classroom concepts to everyday life.

- Advisors help students establish realistic goals and objectives and encourage them to be responsible for their own progress and success.

- Advisors seek to understand and modify barriers to student progress, identify ineffective and inefficient policies and procedures, and work to affect change. When the needs of students and the institution are in conflict, advisors seek a resolution that is in the best interest of both parties. In cases in which the student finds the resolution unsatisfactory, they inform students regarding appropriate grievance procedures.

- Advisors recognize the changing nature of the college and university environment and diversity within the student body. They acknowledge the changing communication technologies used by students and the resulting new learning environments. They are sensitive to the responsibilities and pressures placed on students to balance courseloads, financial and family issues, and interpersonal demands.

- Advisors are knowledgeable and sensitive regarding national, regional, local, and institutional policies and procedures, particularly those governing matters that address harassment, use of technology, personal relationships with students, privacy of student information, and equal opportunity.

- Advisors are encouraged to investigate all available avenues to help students explore academic opportunities.

- Advisors respect student confidentiality rights regarding personal information. Advisors practice with an understanding of the institution's interpretation of applicable laws such as the Federal Educational Rights and Privacy Act (FERPA).

- Advisors seek access to and use student information only when the information is relevant to the advising process. Advisors enter or change information on students' records only with appropriate institutional authorization to do so.

- Advisors document advising contacts adequately to meet institutional disclosure guidelines and aid in subsequent advising interactions.

Core Value 2: Advisors are responsible for involving others, when appropriate, in the advising process.

- Academic advisors must develop relationships with personnel critical to student success, including those in such diverse areas as admissions, orientation, instruction, financial aid, housing, health services, athletics, academic departments, and the registrar's office. They also must establish relationships with those who can attend to specific physical and educational needs of students, such as personnel in disability services, tutoring, psychological counseling, international study, and career development. Advisors must also direct students, as needed, to experts who specialize in credit transfers, cocurricular programs, and graduation clearance.

- Because of the nature of academic advising, advisors often develop a broad understanding of an institution and a detailed understanding of student needs and the resources available to help students meet those needs. Based upon this understanding:
  - Advisors can have an interpretative role with students regarding their interactions with faculty, staff, administrators, and fellow students, and
  - Advisors can help the institution's administrators gain a greater understanding of students' needs.
- Students involved in the advising process (such as peer advisors or graduate assistants) must be adequately trained and supervised for adherence to the same policies and practices required of the professional and faculty advisors and other specially trained staff advising in the unit or institution.

Core Value 3: Advisors are responsible to their institutions.

- Advisors work in many types of higher education institutions and abide by the specific policies, procedures, and values of the department and institution in which they work. When circumstances interfere with students' learning and development, advisors advocate for change on the advisees' behalf with the institution's administration, faculty, and staff.
- Advisors keep those not directly involved in the advising process informed and aware of the importance of academic advising in students' lives. They articulate the need for administrative support of advising and related activities.
- Advisors increase their collective professional strength by constructively and respectfully sharing their advising philosophies and techniques with colleagues.
- Advisors respect the opinions of their colleagues; remain neutral when students make comments or express opinions about other faculty or staff; are nonjudgmental about academic programs; and do not impose their personal agendas on students.
- Advisors encourage the use of models for the optimal delivery of academic advising programs within their institutions.
- Advisors recognize their individual roles in the success of their institutions and accept and participate in institutional commitments that can include, but are not limited to, administrative and committee service, teaching, research, and writing.

Core Value 4: Advisors are responsible to higher education in general.

- Advisors accept that one goal of education is to introduce students to the world of ideas in an environment of academic freedom. Advisors demonstrate appreciation for academic freedom.
- Advisors base their work with students on the most relevant theoretical perspectives and practices drawn from the fields of social sciences, the humanities, and education.

- One goal of advising is to establish, between students and advisors, a partnership that will guide students through their academic programs. Advisors help students understand that learning can be used in day-to-day application through exploration, trial and error, challenge, and decision making.

- Advisors advocate for student educational achievement to the highest attainable standards and support student goals as they uphold the educational mission of the institution.

- Advisors advocate for the creation, enhancement, and strengthening of programs and services that recognize and meet student academic needs.

Core Value 5: Advisors are responsible to their educational community.

- Many institutions recognize the importance of integrating classroom learning with community experience, study abroad, and programs that bridge the gap between the academic and off-campus environments. Where such programs exist, advisors help students understand the relationship between the institution and local, regional, national, and international communities.

- Advisors advocate for students who desire to include study abroad or community service learning in their cocurricular college experience, and they make appropriate referrals to enable students to achieve these goals.

- Advisors understand the intricacies of transfer between institutions and make appropriate referrals to enable students to achieve their goals.

Core Value 6: Advisors are responsible for their professional practices and for themselves personally.

- Advisors use the Statement of Core Values to guide their professional actions.

- Advisors seek opportunities to grow professionally. They identify appropriate workshops, classes, literature, research publications, and groups, both inside and outside the institution, that can keep their interest high, hone professional skills, and advance expertise within specific areas of interest.

- Advisors seek cross-cultural opportunities to interact with and learn more about ethnic communities, racial groups, religions, sexual preferences, genders, and age levels, as well as physical, learning, and psychological abilities and disabilities found among the general student population.

- Advisors recognize that research topics are embedded in academic advising practice and theory. Advisors engage in research and publication related to advising as well as in areas allied with their training and disciplinary backgrounds. Advisors' research agendas safeguard privacy and provide for the humane treatment of subjects.

- Advisors are alert to the demands surrounding their work with students and the necessity of taking care of themselves physically, emotionally, and spiritually to best respond to high-level demands. They learn how to maintain a "listening ear" and provide sensitive, timely responses that teach students to accept their responsibilities. Advisors establish and maintain appropriate boundaries, nurture others when necessary, and seek support for themselves both within and outside the institution.The Statement of Core Values of Academic Advising

Council for the Advancement of Standards in Higher Education Standards and Guidelines for Academic Advising

PART 1. MISSION

The primary purpose of the Academic Advising Program (AAP) is to assist students in the development of meaningful educational plans.

AAP must incorporate student learning and student development in its mission. AAP must enhance overall educational experiences. AAP must develop, record, disseminate, implement, and regularly review its mission and goals. Its mission statement must be consistent with the mission and goals of the institution and with the standards in this document. AAP must operate as an integral part of the institution's overall mission.

The institution must have a clearly written mission statement pertaining to academic advising that must include program goals and expectations of advisors and advisees.

PART 2. PROGRAM

The formal education of students is purposeful and holistic, and consists of the curriculum and the cocurriculum. The AAP must identify relevant and desirable student learning and development outcomes and provide programs and services that encourage the achievement of those outcomes.

Relevant and desirable outcomes include: intellectual growth, effective communication, realistic self-appraisal, enhanced self-esteem, clarified values, career choices, leadership development, healthy behaviors, meaningful interpersonal relations, independence, collaboration, social responsibility, satisfying and productive lifestyles, appreciation of diversity, spiritual awareness, and achievement of personal and educational goals.

AAP must provide evidence of its impact on the achievement of student learning and development outcomes.

The table below offers examples of achievement of student learning and development outcomes.

Desirable Student Learning and Development Outcomes	Examples of Achievement
Intellectual growth	Examines information about academic majors and minors. Understands the requirements of an academic degree plan, as well as institutional policies and procedures. Uses critical thinking in problem-solving on selection of major and course selection. Uses complex information from a variety of sources, including personal experience and observation to form a decision or opinion. Declares a major. Achieves educational goals. Applies previously understood information and concepts to a new situation or setting. Demonstrates understanding of a general education and expresses appreciation for literature, the fine arts, mathematics, sciences, and social sciences.
Personal and educational goals	Sets, articulates, and pursues individual goals. Articulates personal and educational goals and objectives. Uses personal and educational goals to guide decisions. Produces a schedule of classes in consultation with advisors. Understands the effect of one's personal and education goals on others.
Enhanced self-esteem	Shows self-respect and respect for others. Initiates actions toward achievement of goals. Evaluates reasonable risks with regard to academic course selection and courseload when conferring with advisors.
Realistic self-appraisal	Evaluates personal and academic skills, abilities, and interests and uses this appraisal to establish appropriate educational plans. Makes decisions and acts in congruence with personal values and other personal and life demands. Focuses on areas of academic ability and interest and mitigates academic weaknesses. Uses information on degree program requirements, courseload, and course availability to construct a course schedule. Seeks opportunities for involvement in cocurricular activities. Seeks feedback from advisors. Learns from past experiences. Seeks services for personal needs (e.g., writing labs and counseling).

Desirable Student Learning and Development Outcomes	Examples of Achievement
Clarified values	Demonstrates ability to evaluate personal values and beliefs regarding academic integrity and other ethical issues. Articulates personal values. Acts in congruence with personal values. Identifies personal, work, and lifestyle values and explains how they influence decision-making in regard to course selection, courseload, and major and minor selections.
Career choices	Describes career choice and choices of academic major and minor based on interests, values, skills, and abilities. Documents knowledge, skills, and accomplishments resulting from formal education, work experience, community service, and volunteer experiences. Makes the connections between classroom and out-of-classroom learning. Identifies the purpose and role of career services in the development and attainment of academic and career goals.
Independence	Operates autonomously by attending advising sessions or programs or by seeking the advice of advisors in a timely fashion. Correctly interprets and applies degree audit information. Selects, schedules, and registers for courses in consultation with advisors.
Effective communication	Communicates personal and academic strengths and weaknesses that affect academic plans. Demonstrates ability to use campus technology resources. Composes appropriate questions when inquiring about particular requirements, departments, and resources.
Leadership development	Articulates leadership philosophy or style. Serves in a leadership position in student, community, or professional organizations. Comprehends the dynamics of a group. Exhibits democratic principles as a leader. Exhibits ability to visualize a group purpose and desired outcomes.
Healthy behavior	Exhibits personal behaviors that promote a healthy lifestyle. Articulates the relationship between health and wellness and accomplishing life long goals. Exhibits behaviors that advance a healthy campus and community.
Meaningful interpersonal relationships	Develops relationships with academic advisors, faculty members, students, and other institution staff to be engaged with the institution in meaningful ways. Listens to and considers others' points of view. Treats others with respect.

(Continued)

Desirable Student Learning and Development Outcomes	Examples of Achievement
Collaboration	Works cooperatively with others. Seeks the involvement of others. Seeks feedback from others. Contributes to achievement of group goals. Exhibits effective listening skills.
Social responsibility	Understands the requirements of the codes of conduct. Understands and practices principles of academic integrity. Understands and participates in relevant governance systems. Understands, abides by, and participates in the development, maintenance, and orderly change of community, social, and legal standards or norms. Appropriately challenges the unfair, unjust, or uncivil behavior of other individuals or groups. Participates in service and volunteer activities.
Satisfying and productive lifestyles	Achieves balance among academic courseload requirements, work, and leisure time. Develops plans to satisfy academic requirements, work expectations, and leisure pursuits. Identifies and works to overcome obstacles that hamper goal achievement. Functions on the basis of personal identity, ethical, spiritual, and moral values. Articulates long-term goals and objectives.
Appreciating diversity	Selects course offerings that will increase understanding of one's own and others' identity and cultures. Seeks involvement with people different from oneself. Demonstrates an appreciation for diversity and the impact it has on society.
Spiritual awareness	Identifies campus and community spiritual and religious resources, including course offerings. Develops and articulates personal belief system. Understands roles of spirituality in personal and group values and behaviors.

Students and advisors must assume shared responsibility in the advising process. AAP must assist students to make the best academic decisions possible by encouraging identification and assessment of alternatives and consideration of the consequences of their decisions.

The ultimate responsibility for making decisions about educational plans and life goals should rest with the individual student.

AAP must be guided by a set of written goals and objectives that are directly related to its stated mission. AAP must:

- Promote student growth and development.
- Assist students in assessing their interests and abilities, examining their educational goals, making decisions, and developing short-term and long-term plans to meet their objectives.

- Discuss and clarify educational, career, and life goals.
- Provide accurate and timely information and interpret institutional, general education, and major requirements.
- Assist students to understand the educational context within which they are enrolled.
- Advise on the selection of appropriate courses and other educational experiences.
- Clarify institutional policies and procedures.
- Evaluate and monitor student academic progress and the impact on achievement of goals.
- Reinforce student self-direction and self-sufficiency.
- Direct students with educational, career, or personal concerns, or skill or learning deficiencies to other resources and programs on the campus when necessary.
- Make students aware of and refer to educational, institutional, and community resources and services (e.g., internship, study abroad, honors, service- learning, research opportunities).
- Collect and distribute relevant data about student needs, preferences, and performance for use in institutional decisions and policy.

AAP should provide information about student experiences and concerns regarding their academic program to appropriate decision-makers.

AAP must be: (a) intentional, (b) coherent, (c) based on theories and knowledge of teaching, learning, and human development, (d) reflective of developmental and demographic profiles of the student population, and (e) responsive to the needs of individuals, special populations, and communities.

AAP should make available to academic advisors all pertinent research (e.g., about students, the academic advising program, and perceptions of the institution).

The academic advisor must review and use available data about students' academic and educational needs, performance, and aspirations.

AAP must identify environmental conditions that may positively or negatively influence student academic achievement and propose interventions that may neutralize negative conditions.

AAP must provide current and accurate advising information to students and academic advisors.

AAP should use the latest technologies for delivery of advising information.

Academic advising conferences must be available to students each academic term.

Academic advisors should offer conferences in a format that is convenient to the student—that is, in person, by telephone, or online. Advising conferences may be carried out individually or in groups.

Academic advising caseloads must be consistent with the time required for the effective performance of this activity.

The academic status of the student being advised should be taken into consideration when determining caseloads. For example, first year, undecided, underprepared, and honors students may require more advising time than upper division students who have declared their majors.

Academic advisors should allow an appropriate amount of time for students to discuss plans, programs, courses, academic progress, and other subjects related to their educational programs.

When determining workloads it should be recognized that advisors may work with students not officially assigned to them and that contacts regarding advising may extend beyond direct contact with the student.

PART 3. LEADERSHIP

Effective and ethical leadership is essential to the success of all organizations. Institutions must appoint, position, and empower Academic Advising Program (AAP) leaders within the administrative structure to accomplish stated missions. Leaders at various levels must be selected on the basis of formal education and training, relevant work experience as an advisor, personal skills and competencies, knowledge of the literature of academic advising, relevant professional credentials, as well as potential for promoting learning and development in students, applying effective practices to educational processes, and enhancing institutional effectiveness. Institutions must determine expectations of accountability for AAP leaders and fairly assess their performance.

AAP leaders must exercise authority over resources for which they are responsible to achieve their respective missions.

AAP leaders must:

- articulate a vision for their organization
- set goals and objectives based on the needs and capabilities of the population served
- promote student learning and development
- prescribe and practice ethical behavior
- recruit, select, supervise, and develop others in the organization
- manage financial resources
- coordinate human resources
- plan, budget for, and evaluate personnel and programs
- apply effective practices to educational and administrative processes
- communicate effectively
- initiate collaborative interactions between individuals and agencies that possess legitimate concerns and interests in academic advising

AAP leaders must identify and find means to address individual, organizational, or environmental conditions that inhibit goal achievement.

AAP leaders must promote campus environments that result in multiple opportunities for student learning and development.

AAP leaders must continuously improve programs and services in response to changing needs of students and other constituents and evolving institutional priorities.

PART 4. ORGANIZATION AND MANAGEMENT

Guided by an overarching intent to ensure student learning and development, Academic Advising Programs (AAP) must be structured purposefully and managed effectively to achieve stated goals. Evidence of appropriate structure must include current and accessible policies and procedures, written performance expectations for all employees, functional workflow graphics or organizational charts, and clearly stated service delivery expectations.

Evidence of effective management practices must include use of comprehensive and accurate information for decisions, clear sources and channels of authority, effective communication practices, decision-making and conflict-resolution procedures, responsiveness to changing conditions, accountability and evaluation systems, and recognition and reward processes. AAP must provide channels within the organization for regular review of administrative policies and procedures.

The design of AAP must be compatible with the institution's organizational structure and its students' needs. Specific advisor responsibilities must be clearly delineated, published, and disseminated to both advisors and advisees.

Students, faculty advisors, and professional staff must be informed of their respective advising responsibilities.

AAP may be a centralized or decentralized function within an institution, with a variety of people throughout the institution assuming responsibilities.

AAP must provide the same services to distance learners as it does to students on campus. The distance education advising must provide for appropriate real-time or delayed interaction between advisors and students.

PART 5. HUMAN RESOURCES

The Academic Advising Program (AAP) must be staffed adequately by individuals qualified to accomplish its mission and goals. Within established guidelines of the institution, AAP must establish procedures for staff selection, training, and evaluation; set expectations for supervision; and provide appropriate professional-development opportunities. AAP must strive to improve the professional competence and skills of all personnel it employs.

Academic advising personnel may be full-time or part-time professionals who have advising as their primary function or may be faculty whose responsibilities include academic advising. Paraprofessionals (e.g., graduate students, interns, or assistants) or peer advisors may also assist advisors.

An academic advisor must hold an earned graduate degree in a field relevant to the position held or must possess an appropriate combination of educational credentials and related work experience.

Academic advisors should have an understanding of student development, student learning, career development, and other relevant theories in education, social sciences, and humanities.

Academic advisors should have a comprehensive knowledge of the institution's programs, academic requirements, policies and procedures, majors, minors, and support services.

Academic advisors should demonstrate an interest and effectiveness in working with and assisting students and a willingness to participate in professional activities.

Sufficient personnel must be available to address students' advising needs without unreasonable delay.

Degree- or credential-seeking interns must be qualified by enrollment in an appropriate field of study and by relevant experience. These individuals must be trained and supervised adequately by professional staff members holding educational credentials and related work experience appropriate for supervision.

Student employees and volunteers must be carefully selected, trained, supervised, and evaluated. They must be trained on how and when to refer those in need of assistance to qualified staff members and have access to a supervisor for assistance in making these judgments. Student employees and volunteers must be provided clear and precise job descriptions, preservice training based on assessed needs, and continuing staff development.

AAP must have technical and support staff members adequate to accomplish its mission. Staff members must be technologically proficient and qualified to perform their job functions, be knowledgeable of ethical and legal uses of technology, and have access to training. The level of staffing and workloads must be adequate and appropriate for program and service demands.

Support personnel should maintain student records, organize resource materials, receive students, make appointments, and handle correspondence and other operational needs. Technical staff may be used in research, data collection, systems development, and special projects.

Technical and support personnel must be carefully selected and adequately trained, supervised, and evaluated.

AAP staff must recognize the limitations of their positions and be familiar with institutional resources to make appropriate referrals.

Salary levels and fringe benefits for all AAP staff members must be commensurate with those for comparable positions within the institution, in similar institutions, and in the relevant geographic area.

AAP must institute hiring and promotion practices that are fair, inclusive, and nondiscriminatory. AAP must employ a diverse staff to provide readily identifiable role models for students and to enrich the campus community.

AAP must create and maintain position descriptions for all staff members and provide regular performance planning and appraisals.

AAP must have a system for regular staff evaluation and must provide access to continuing education and professional-development opportunities, including in-service training programs and participation in professional conferences and workshops.

AAP must strive to improve the professional competence and skills of all personnel it employs.

Continued professional development should include areas such as the following and how they relate to academic advising:

- theories of student development, student learning, career development, and other relevant theories in education, social sciences, and humanities
- academic policies and procedures, including institutional transfer policies and curricular changes
- legal issues, including the U.S. Family Education and Records Privacy Act (FERPA) and the Canadian Freedom Of Information and Protection of Privacy (FOIPP) and other privacy laws and policies
- technology and software training (e.g., degree audit, Web registration)
- institutional resources (e.g., research opportunities, career services, internship opportunities, counseling and health services, tutorial services)
- Americans with Disabilities Act (ADA) compliance issues

PART 6. FINANCIAL RESOURCES

The Academic Advising Program (AAP) must have adequate funding to accomplish its mission and goals. Funding priorities must be determined within the context of the stated mission, goals, objectives, and comprehensive analysis of the needs and capabilities of students and the availability of internal and external resources.

AAP must demonstrate fiscal responsibility and cost-effectiveness consistent with institutional protocols.

Special consideration should be given to providing funding for the professional development of advisors.

Financial resources should be sufficient to provide high-quality print and Web-based information for students and training materials for advisors. Sufficient financial resources should be provided to promote the academic advising program.

PART 7. FACILITIES, TECHNOLOGY, AND EQUIPMENT

The Academic Advising Program (AAP) must have adequate, suitably located facilities, adequate technology, and equipment to support its mission and goals efficiently and effectively. Facilities, technology, and equipment must be evaluated regularly and be in compliance with relevant federal, state, provincial, and local requirements to provide for access, health, safety, and security.

AAP must ensure that online and technology-assisted advising includes appropriate mechanisms for obtaining approvals, consultations, and referrals.

Data about students maintained on individual workstations and departmental or institutional servers must be secure and must comply with institutional policies on data stewardship.

Academic advisors must have access to computing equipment, local networks, student databases, and the Internet.

Privacy and freedom from visual and auditory distractions must be considered in designing appropriate facilities.

PART 8. LEGAL RESPONSIBILITIES

The Academic Advising Program (AAP) staff members must be knowledgeable about and responsive to laws and regulations that relate to their respective responsibilities. Staff members must inform users of programs and services and officials, as appropriate, of legal obligations and limitations, including constitutional, statutory, regulatory, and case law; mandatory laws and orders emanating from federal, state, provincial, and local governments; and the institution's policies.

Academic advisors must use reasonable and informed practices to limit the liability exposure of the institution, its officers, employees, and agents. Academic advisors must be informed about institutional policies regarding personal liability and related insurance-coverage options.

The institution must provide access to legal advice for academic advisors as needed to carry out assigned responsibilities.

The institution must inform academic advisors and students, in a timely and systematic fashion, about extraordinary or changing legal obligations and potential liabilities.

PART 9. EQUITY AND ACCESS

The Academic Advising Program (AAP) staff members must ensure that services and programs are provided on a fair and equitable basis. Facilities, programs, and services must be accessible. Hours of operation and delivery of and access to programs and services must be responsive to the needs of all students and other constituents. AAP must adhere to the spirit and intent of equal opportunity laws.

AAP must be open and readily accessible to all students and must not discriminate except where sanctioned by law and institutional policy. Discrimination must especially be avoided on the basis of age; color; creed; cultural heritage; disability; ethnicity; gender identity; nationality; political affiliation; religious affiliation; sex; sexual orientation; or social, economic, marital, or veteran status.

Consistent with the mission and goals, AAP must take affirmative action to remedy significant imbalances in student participation and staffing patterns.

As the demographic profiles of campuses change and new instructional delivery methods are introduced, institutions must recognize the needs of students who participate in distance learning for access to programs and services offered on campus. Institutions must provide appropriate services in ways that are accessible to distance learners and assist them in identifying and gaining access to other appropriate services in their geographic region.

PART 10. CAMPUS AND EXTERNAL RELATIONS

The Academic Advising Program (AAP) must establish, maintain, and promote effective relations with relevant campus offices and external agencies.

Academic advising is integral to the educational process and depends upon close working relationships with other institutional agencies and the administration. AAP should be fully integrated into other processes of the institution. Academic advisors should be consulted when there are modifications to or closures of academic programs.

For referral purposes, AAP should provide academic advisors a comprehensive list of relevant external agencies, campus offices, and opportunities.

PART 11. DIVERSITY

Within the context of the institution's unique mission, diversity enriches the community and enhances the collegiate experience for all; therefore the Academic Advising Program (AAP) must nurture environments in which similarities and differences among people are recognized and honored.

AAP must promote educational experiences that are characterized by open and continuous communication that deepen understanding of one's own identity, culture, and heritage and that of others. AAP must educate and promote respect about commonalties and differences in historical and cultural contexts.

AAP must address the characteristics and needs of a diverse population when establishing and implementing policies and procedures.

PART 12. ETHICS

All persons involved in the delivery of the Academic Advising Program (AAP) must adhere to the highest of principles of ethical behavior. AAP must develop or adopt and implement appropriate statements of ethical practice. AAP must publish these statements and ensure their periodic review by relevant constituencies.

Advisors must uphold policies, procedures, and values of their departments and institutions.

Advisors should consider ethical standards or other statements from relevant professional associations.

AAP staff members must ensure that privacy and confidentiality are maintained with respect to all communications and records to the extent that such records are protected under the law and appropriate statements of ethical practice. Information contained in students' education records must not be disclosed without written consent except as allowed by relevant laws and institutional polices. AAP staff members must disclose to appropriate authorities information judged to be of an emergency nature, especially when the safety of the individual or others is involved, or when otherwise required by institutional policy or relevant law.

When emergency disclosure is required, AAP should inform the student that it has taken place, to whom, and why.

All AAP staff members must be aware of and comply with the provisions contained in the institution's human subjects research policy and in other relevant institutional policies addressing ethical practices and confidentiality of research data concerning individuals.

All AAP staff members must recognize and avoid personal conflict of interest or appearance thereof in their transactions with students and others.

All AAP staff members must strive to ensure the fair, objective, and impartial treatment of all persons with whom they deal. AAP staff members must not participate in nor condone any form of harassment that demeans persons or creates intimidating, hostile, or offensive campus environment.

When handling institutional funds, all AAP staff members must ensure that such funds are managed in accordance with established and responsible accounting procedures and the fiscal policies or processes of the institution.

AAP staff members must perform their duties within the limits of their training, expertise, and competence. When these limits are exceeded, individuals in need of further assistance must be referred to persons possessing appropriate qualifications.

AAP staff members must use suitable means to confront and otherwise hold accountable other staff members who exhibit unethical behavior.

AAP staff members must be knowledgeable about and practice ethical behavior in the use of technology.

PART 13. ASSESSMENT AND EVALUATION

The Academic Advising Program (AAP) must conduct regular assessment and evaluations. AAP must use effective qualitative and quantitative methods as appropriate, to determine whether and to what degree the stated mission, goals, and student learning and development outcomes are being met. The process must use sufficient and sound assessment measures to ensure comprehensiveness. Data collected must include responses from students and other affected constituencies.

AAP must evaluate periodically how well they complement and enhance the institution's stated mission and educational effectiveness.

Results of these evaluations must be used in revising and improving programs and services and in recognizing staff performance and the performance of academic advisors.

The NATIONAL ACADEMIC ADVISING ASSOCIATION (NACADA), promotes and supports quality academic advising in institutions of higher education to enhance the educational development of students. NACADA provides a forum for discussion, debate, and the exchange of ideas pertaining to academic advising through numerous activities and publications.

The National Academic Advising Association evolved from the first National Conference on Academic Advising in 1977 and has over 10,000 members representing all 50 states, Puerto Rico, Canada and several other international countries. Members represent higher education institutions across the spectrum of Carnegie classifications and include professional advisors/counselors, faculty, administrators and students whose responsibilities include academic advising.

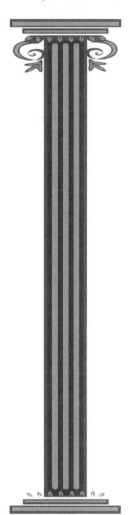

- **Conferences and Institutes** offered at reduced member rates to enhance professional development.
- **Webinars** – professional development presented over the Internet
- **Graduate Certificate and Masters Degree in Advising** – Kansas State University, in partnership with NACADA, offers a 15 semester-hour certificate and Masters Degree via the Internet.
- **Career Member Services** features a free list of position openings by geographic area.
- **Academic Advising Consultants and Speakers Service** provides experts to help institutions enhance their campus services.
- *Clearinghouse of Academic Advising Resources* up-to-the-minute resources for issues crucial to advising presented via the Web.
- **Publications** include the *NACADA Journal*, quarterly e-publication, monthly highlights, special publications, videos, CDs, monographs and books.
- **Email Lists** available for global discussion of academic advising issues.
- **Awards** recognize exemplary work in the fields of individual and institutional advising, research, and electronic publications.
- **Scholarships** provide financial support to members pursuing graduate education or professional development.
- **Research Grants** support individual research contributing to the field of academic advising.

Check out the opportunities on the NACADA web site

www.nacada.ksu.edu

NAME INDEX

SUBJECT INDEX

ABC assessment mnemonic, 370–371
Academic Advising: A Comprehensive Handbook, 168
Academic advising; administrators' perceptions of, 415–435; career, 104–113; as developmental process, 142–143; educative, 30; first era (1636–1870) of, 3–5; involving students in process of, 345; "learning-centered paradigm" of, 29–30; primary source of, 71*fig*; role of technology in delivering, 292–305; role of theory in, 18–31; satisfaction by year in school and gender, 72*fig*; satisfaction by year in school and race/ethnicity, 73*fig*; second era (1870–1970) of, 5–7; "Statement of Core Values" of, 47–48; "strengths-based," 21, 23; third era (1970s to present) of, 7–8; *See also* Academic advising services; Academic advisors; Advising awards
Academic Advising and Career Development Centers (CDC), 502
Academic advising models; centralized, 245, 447; decentralized models, 244–245*fig*, 447; Dual model, 7, 246, 247*fig*, 248; Faculty-Only model, 7–8, 10–11, 244*fig*, 248, 268, 451; Satellite model, 8, 11, 244–245*fig*, 248; Self-Contained model, 8, 10–13, 245, 246*fig*, 248; shared, 245–248, 447; Split model, 7, 10–11, 245–246, 247*fig*, 268; Supplementary model, 7, 245, 246*fig*; Total

intake model, 7, 246–248; Transactional Model, 346–349
Academic advising principles; 1: advising is ground in talent-development philosophy, 75–76; 2: advising is a tag team activity, 77–78; 3: students are expected to map out path to success, 78–79; 4: every advising contact as meaningful interaction, 79–81; 5: recognize advising as cultural/culture-bound activity, 81;
Academic advising program objectives; approaches to designing, 236–238*fig*; process model for developing, 238*fig*–240; relationship of vision, mission, goals, and, 231–234*fig*
Academic advising programs; administrative duties for leading, 440–443; assessment required to improve, 386–387; building credibility for the, 439–440; creating an assessment plan at level of, 390–393; critical elements of, 387–390; objectives of, 231–240; *See also* Exemplary advising programs
Academic advising services; assessment of, 369–383; campus role of, 249–251; factors influencing organization of, 243; by faculty, 253–264; key components of effective, 248–249; in nonadvising offices, 276–278; one-on-one, 288–289, 342–354; organizational models of, 244*fig*–248; support staff of, 275–276; technology